# 2018
# RUGBY
## ALMANACK

# 2018
# RUGBY
# ALMANACK

Edited by Clive Akers, Geoff Miller &
Adrian Hill

A catalogue record for this book is available from the National Library of New Zealand.

**A Mower Book**
Published in 2018 by Upstart Press Ltd
Level 4, 15 Huron Street, Takapuna 0622
Auckland, New Zealand

ISBN 978-1-988516-13-4
© 2018 Text C.A. Akers, G.D. Miller and A.D. Hill
The moral rights of the authors have been asserted.
© 2018 Upstart Press Ltd

Typesetting and design by CVD Limited (www.cvdgraphics.nz)
Printed by Printlink Ltd, Wellington

The editors welcome notification of any errors or omissions.

*Please correspond directly with the editors.*

Clive Akers
Opiki
RD4
Palmerston North 4474
Phone: 06 329 1822
email: akers@xtra.co.nz

Geoff Miller
8 Whalers Rise
Whalers Gate
New Plymouth 4310
email: rugbystat@xtra.co.nz

Adrian Hill
1/212 Grove Road
Hastings 4122
email: adhill@xtra.co.nz

## ACKNOWLEDGEMENTS

The publishers and editors acknowledge the assistance of the New Zealand Rugby Union and appreciate their co-operation and the co-operation of the 26 rugby unions in compiling the *2018 Rugby Almanack*.

## KEY

*In team record charts*

| | |
|---|---|
| RS | Ranfurly Shield |
| LC | Sir Brian Lochore Cup |
| MC | Sir Colin Meads Cup |
| P | Mitre 10 Cup Premiership |
| C | Mitre 10 Cup Championship |
| P/C | Mitre 10 Cup crossover match |
| H | Mitre 10 Heartland Championship |

*In individual appearance charts*

| | |
|---|---|
| 15 | fullback |
| 14 | right wing |
| 13 | centre |
| 12 | second five-eighth |
| 11 | left wing |
| 10 | first five-eighth |
| 9 | halfback |
| 8 | number eight |
| 7 | open-side flanker |
| 6 | blind-side flanker |
| 5 | right lock |
| 4 | left lock |
| 3 | right (tighthead) prop |
| 2 | hooker |
| 1 | left (loosehead) prop |
| * | retired injured or substituted |
| s | substitute |
| t | includes penalty try |

# CONTENTS

# EDITORIAL

The All Blacks retained their number one ranking in world rugby for the eighth straight year, but it was the 2017 World Cup-winning Black Ferns who received the major awards of the year and deservedly so. New Zealand won the World Under 20 Championship held in Georgia with a massive 64–17 win over England in the final. The Black Ferns Sevens won their World Series with five cup titles from six tournaments, while the All Blacks Sevens finished fourth in their series.

The eagerly awaited visit by the British and Irish Lions was, as expected, the season's highlight, and a tremendous boost to the economy. Although the games were confined to the major centres, tourists infiltrated the provinces to see as much of New Zealand as time allowed. There would be few, if any, hotels or taverns that did not receive a visit by Lions supporters. Many travelled about the provinces before the Lions even arrived and many remained after the tour to explore and experience heartland New Zealand. They were a happy army of travellers, here to enjoy themselves and mingle with locals. As had occurred during the last visit, in 2005, Lions fans were a reminder to New Zealanders that rugby is a game to enjoy and make lasting friendships.

It had been expected that the All Blacks would comfortably win the three-test DHL New Zealand Lions series but, as so often happens in close games, there were controversies that sparked debate. It is now history that in four hours of rugby the Lions were ahead on the scoreboard for only four minutes — the final four minutes of the second test during which the All Blacks had to play with only 14 players for much of the test. That the Lions managed to draw the series was an achievement for the Warren Gatland-coached team. For many New Zealanders, the departure of the Lions will leave treasured memories of their socialising with the cheerful travelling fans. Thousands will remember the tour not for what happened on the field, but for the army of supporters.

The All Blacks won the Investec Rugby Championship, retained the Bledisloe Cup and were unbeaten on the Vista Northern Tour at the end of the year. The best performance by the All Blacks was the astonishing 57–0 win over the Springboks at Albany. The loss to the Wallabies in the third Bledisloe Cup fixture, at Brisbane, was a reminder that any slight complacency can cost a team dearly.

The World Rugby rankings still have the All Blacks at number one, followed by England. The two teams haven't met since 2014 and with England's success in recent years it could be debated as to which is the better team. The rankings are merely a guide, based on results. Perhaps the time will come, sometime in the future, when consideration will be given for a merger of the northern hemisphere's Six Nations Championship and the southern hemisphere's four-nations Investec Rugby Championship. Each of the 10 nations play each other during the year, no final being played, with the nation compiling the most championship points after the round-robin being declared winner.

The Black Ferns were outplayed by a very experienced and efficient England team at Rotorua during the June series. Northern hemisphere nations have the advantage of the annual Six Nations Championship, enabling them to develop combinations that the Black Ferns at present cannot achieve because of the limited schedule of games arranged annually. Yet at the World Cup in Ireland, during August, the Black Ferns played superbly, especially in the semi-final against a strong USA team when the team produced an almost faultless display. This was followed by a similar performance during the second half of the final when the Black Ferns destroyed England. Women's rugby has not previously attracted much public attention, but things are certainly changing. Those fans who watched the World Cup games could only admire the outstanding play and skills of the team.

The numbers participating in women's rugby are steadily increasing, but for many participants rugby remains a part-time sport and some of the players also took part in the 2017 Women's Rugby League World Cup. More games annually for the Black Ferns would attract more to the code, which would strengthen the Black Ferns. Stars are emerging with names becoming familiar to rugby followers. Names like Kendra Cocksedge, Kelly Brazier, Fiao'o Fa'amausili, Sarah Goss, Selica Winiata and Portia Woodman are leading the way in women's rugby, their success and commitment being an inspiration to budding schoolgirl players.

The format of the Investec Super Rugby competition remains a concern with the conference system not pleasing for all fans. No Australian team was able to defeat a New Zealand team, which is a concern for trans-Tasman rivalry. From 18 teams it was a significant achievement that three of the four semi-finalists were New Zealand teams and the Crusaders emerged winners. While there will be three fewer teams in 2018, the competition will again span 25 weeks and test the appetite of fans.

There were 143 yellow cards issued during the 141 games of Super Rugby, a significant increase from the previous year. This was largely due to more infringements being brought within the card category. Rugby is a great contest when played between two full strength sides, but it can suffer from a fan perspective when a card is issued. The opposition gains an advantage that it does its best to exploit. Red cards are rare but when issued the contest is defused. Two classic examples have occurred in internationals in recent years. At the 2011 World Cup, Welsh captain Sam Warburton was sent off in the 18th minute of Wales' semi-final clash with France. It was heart-breaking for the Welsh fans who had paid big money to be at Eden Park that day. In the second test against the 2017 Lions the All Blacks played with 14 players for 56 minutes following the sending off of Sonny Bill Williams. The All Blacks struggled throughout the 65 minutes. Would the Lions have won the test, and consequently drawn the series, had the test been 15-a-side throughout? We doubt it. We would prefer to see even contests and players placed on report for post-match examination, rather than time wasted while officials study television replays before making their decisions. There are instances when a player completely loses control and deserves to be sent to the sideline, but couldn't they be replaced to continue the contest the public have paid to witness?

One competition that has not altered for over 100 years and retains its special interest is the Ranfurly Shield. Canterbury, regarded in recent years as being the strongest and most successful provincial union, looked set to retain the shield through the season. That was until the Taranaki challenge. After 32 minutes Canterbury held a commanding 31–7 lead before the challengers made one of the most remarkable fightbacks in shield history to draw level 38–38 in the 58th minute and eventually win 55–43. The Ranfurly Shield continues to produce the occasional surprise that reflects provincial pride.

However, Canterbury's stronghold on domestic rugby was maintained with the winning of the Mitre 10 Premiership Cup and the women winning the Farah Palmer Premiership Cup.

In the Heartland Championship Horowhenua Kapiti, who finished ninth in 2016, produced their best ever result in national championship rugby by hosting the Meads Cup final. Despite losing to regular champions Wanganui, the final attracted the largest crowd seen at Levin for many years.

Perhaps the biggest disappointment of 2017 was to see the loss of a number of sports reporters from regional newspapers. While this has little impact in the major cities, it will severely cut the communication between sports and the followers of local sports. Several provincial unions will be hit hard. Some unions do run an efficient and up-to-date website, but many followers of rugby do not use computers.

The success of local sportspersons and sports teams at national competitions, whether at primary school, secondary school, or senior level, feeds pride within the region. The coming months will be interesting to see how the affected provinces cope with no regular and knowledgeable reporter providing stories of local club and schools rugby and to what extent it impacts on spectator support at games. Newspapers have been a way of life to readers ever since the invention of the printing press. Sadly, in many regions, sports enthusiasts have lost their connection with local sports.

The biggest loss to rugby in 2017 was the passing of Sir Colin Meads, a hard-working farmer from the hills of the King Country who played rugby for enjoyment and satisfaction but whose attitude and determination saw him become one of the greatest players of all time in international rugby. Also lost were former All Blacks Head Coach Peter Burke whose contribution as a coach and administrator spans decades, and Sir John Graham who, as a secondary school headmaster, had a strong influence on the development of sporting careers of pupils as well as assisting coaches who later became outstanding All Blacks coaches.

The Editors wish to acknowledge the generous assistance of many who provided information towards this publication. In addition to New Zealand Rugby, provincial unions and team managers that provide official records we appreciate the contributions by Campbell Burnes (NZ Barbarians), Chris Jansen (Referees), Adam Julian (Schools), John Lea (Overseas Players), Kevin Pivac (Deaf Rugby) and Melodie Robinson (Women's Rugby). Lindsay Knight kindly wrote obituaries of some of the former All Blacks who died during the year. There was also assistance from Brent Drabble, Ross Everiss, Ron Palenski and Kelvin Plummer. In August we lost Len King (see Obituaries) who for many years was a very reliable and efficient contact in South Canterbury providing yearly reviews of his union's season as well as notifying us of deaths of former representative players. We welcome being notified of the deaths of former provincial first-class players and referees.

Support from overseas colleagues John Griffiths and Stuart Farmer (England), Eddie Grieb (South Africa), Gilles Etienne (France) and John Blanch (Australia) are also appreciated.

*Clive Akers, Geoff Miller, Adrian Hill*
*January 2018*

# UNION DIRECTORY

**New Zealand Rugby Union**
*Auckland office:*
 4A, 125 The Strand, Parnell, Auckland
 *Postal:* PO Box 2453, Shortland Street,
  Auckland 1140
 *Telephone:* 09 300 4995
*Wellington office:*
 New Zealand Rugby House, Level 4,
 100 Molesworth Street, Wellington
 *Postal:* PO Box 2172, Wellington 6140
 *Telephone:* 04 499 4995
 *Fax:* 04 499 4224
 *email:* info@nzrugby.co.nz
 *Websites:* www.allblacks.com
  www.nzrugby.co.nz

**Auckland RFU**
*Office:* Eden Park, Walters Rd, Auckland
*Postal:* PO Box 56-152, Dominion Rd,
 Auckland 1446
*Telephone:* 09 815 4850
*Fax:* 09 849 5300
*email:* info@aucklandrugby.co.nz
*Website:* www.aucklandrugby.co.nz

**Bay of Plenty RFU**
*Office:* Bay Park,
 81 Truman Rd, Mt Maunganui
*Postal:* PO Box 4058, Mt Maunganui South 3149
*Telephone:* 07 574 2037
*Fax:* 07 574 2046
*email:* info@boprugby.co.nz
*Website:* www.boprugby.co.nz

**Buller RFU**
*Office:* 83 Domett St, Westport
*Postal:* PO Box 361, Westport 7866
*Telephone:* 03 789 8330
*Fax:* 03 789 8330
*email:* ceo@bullerrugby.co.nz
*Website:* www.bullerrugby.co.nz

**Canterbury RFU**
*Office:* Level One, 5 Durham St, Christchurch
*Postal:* PO Box 755, Christchurch 8140
*Telephone:* 03 379 8300
*Fax:* 03 365 3565
*email:* info@crfu.co.nz
*Website:* www.crfu.co.nz

**Counties Manukau RFU**
*Office:* Franklin Rd, Pukekohe
*Postal:* PO Box 175, Pukekohe 2340
*Telephone:* 09 237 0033
*Fax:* 09 237 1172
*email:* admin@steelers.co.nz
*Website:* www.steelers.co.nz

**Hawke's Bay RFU**
*Office:* McLean Park, Napier
*Postal:* PO Box 201, Napier 4140
*Telephone:* 06 835 7617
*Fax:* 06 835 4630
*email:* admin@hbrugby.co.nz
*Website:* www.hbmagpies.co.nz

**Horowhenua Kapiti RFU**
*Office:* cnr Bristol & Stanley St, Levin
*Postal:* PO Box 503, Levin 5540
*Telephone:* 06 367 8059
*Fax:* 06 367 8062
*email:* office@hkrfu.co.nz
*Website:* www.hkrfu.co.nz

**King Country RFU**
*Office:* Cotter St, Te Kuiti
*Postal:* PO Box 394, Te Kuiti 3941
*Telephone:* 07 878 7545
*Fax:* 07 878 7540
*email:* generalmanager@kingcountryrugby.co.nz

**Manawatu RFU**
*Office:* Central Energy Trust Arena, Palmerston Nth
*Postal:* PO Box 1729, Palmerston North 4440
*Telephone:* 06 357 2633
*Fax:* 06 354 1670
*email:* info@manawaturugby.co.nz
*Website:* www.manawaturugby.co.nz

**Mid Canterbury RFU**
*Office:* A&P Showgrounds, Ashburton
*Postal:* PO Box 98, Ashburton 7740
*Telephone:* 03 308 8718
*Fax:* 03 308 0103
*email:* joanne.burrows@midcanterburyrugby.co.nz
*Website:* www.midcanterburyrugby.co.nz

**Ngati Porou East Coast RFU**
*Office:* 187 Waiomatatini Rd, Ruatoria
*Postal:* PO Box 106, Ruatoria 4032
*Telephone:* 06 864 8812
*Fax:* 06 864 8813
*email:* admin@npec.co.nz
*Website:* www.npec.co.nz

**North Harbour RFU**
*Office:* North Harbour Stadium, Albany
*Postal:* PO Box 300 492, North Shore City 0752
*Telephone:* 09 447 2100
*Fax:* 09 447 2101
*email:* harbour@harbourrugby.co.nz
*Website:* www.harbourrugby.co.nz

**North Otago RFU**
*Office:* Shop 6a, Thames Arcade, Oamaru
*Postal:* PO Box 102, Oamaru 9444
*Telephone:* 03 434 2053
*Fax:* 03 434 2054
*email:* admin@northotagorugby.co.nz
*Website:* www.northotagorugby.co.nz

**Northland RFU**
*Office:* 50 Kioreroa Rd, Port Whangarei
*Postal:* PO Box 584, Whangarei 0140
*Telephone:* 09 438 4743
*Fax:* 09 438 9185
*email:* reception@northlandrugby.co.nz
*Website:* www.taniwha.co.nz

**Otago RFU**
*Office:* Stadium, Anzac Avenue, Dunedin
*Postal:* PO Box 691, Dunedin 9054
*Telephone:* 03 477 0928
*email:* orfu@orfu.co.nz
*Website:* www.orfu.co.nz

**Poverty Bay RFU**
*Office:* River Oak Mews
74 Grey St, Gisborne
*Postal:* PO Box 520, Gisborne 4040
*Telephone:* 06 868 9968
*Fax:* 06 868 9954
*email:* karen@povertybayrugby.co.nz
*Website:* www.povertybayrugby.co.nz

**Rugby Southland**
*Office:* Rugby Park Stadium, Invercargill
*Postal:* PO Box 291, Invercargill 9840
*Telephone:* 03 216 8694
*Fax:* 03 216 8695
*email:* rugby@rugbysouthland.co.nz
*Website:* www.rugbysouthland.co.nz

**South Canterbury RFU**
*Office:* 328 Church St, Timaru
*Postal:* PO Box 787, Timaru 7940
*Telephone:* 03 688 8653
*Fax:* 03 688 6179
*email:* tracey@scrfu.co.nz
*Website:* www.scrfu.co.nz

**Taranaki RFU**
*Office:* Yarrow Stadium, New Plymouth
*Postal:* PO Box 5004, New Plymouth 4343
*Telephone:* 06 759 0167
*Fax:* 06 757 3859
*email:* trfu@trfu.co.nz
*Website:* www.trfu.co.nz

**Tasman RFU**
*Office:* Hathaway Terrace, Nelson
*Postal:* PO Box 7157, Nelson 7042
*Telephone:* 03 548 7030
*Fax:* 03 548 8282
*email:* enquiries@tasmanrugby.co.nz
*Website:* www.makos.co.nz

**Thames Valley RFU**
*Office:* 140a Normanby Rd, Paeroa
*Postal:* PO Box 245, Paeroa 3640
*Telephone:* 07 862 6352
*Fax:* 07 862 7677
*email:* swampfoxes@xtra.co.nz
*Website:* www.thamesvalleyswampfoxes.co.nz

**Waikato RFU**
*Office:* FMG Stadium,
128 Seddon Road, Hamilton
*Postal:* PO Box 9507, Hamilton 3240
*Telephone:* 07 839 5675
*Fax:* 07 838 9911
*email:* admin@mooloo.co.nz
*Website:* www.mooloo.co.nz

**Wairarapa Bush RFU**
*Office:* 149 Dixon St, Masterton
*Postal:* PO Box 372, Masterton 5840
*Telephone:* 06 378 8369
*Fax:* 06 378 0012
*email:* info@waibush.co.nz
*Website:* www.waibush.co.nz

**Wanganui RFU**
*Office:* 40 Maria Place Extn, Wanganui
*Postal:* PO Box 4213, Wanganui 4541
*Telephone:* 06 349 2313
*Fax:* 06 347 8006
*email:* info@wanganuirugby.co.nz
*Website:* www.wanganuirugby.co.nz

**Wellington RFU**
*Office:* 113 Adelaide Rd, Wellington
*Postal:* PO Box 7201, Wellington South 6242
*Telephone:* 04 389 0020
*Fax:* 04 389 0889
*email:* mail@wrfu.co.nz
*Website:* www.wrfu.co.nz

**West Coast RFU**
*Office:* 123 Main South Rd, Greymouth
*Postal:* PO Box 31, Greymouth 7840
*Telephone:* 03 768 7822
*Fax:* 03 768 6361
*email:* wcrugby@netaccess.co.nz
*Website:* www.westcoastrfu.co.nz

**New Zealand Rugby Museum**
326 Main St, Palmerston North
*Postal:* PO Box 36, Palmerston North 4440
*Telephone:* 06 358 6947
*Fax:* 06 358 6947
*email:* info@rugbymuseum.co.nz
*Website:* www.rugbymuseum.co.nz

# NEW ZEALAND RUGBY UNION

## OFFICE BEARERS
2017-2018

### Patron
Sir Brian Lochore ONZ, KNZM, OBE

### President
M.W. Trapp (*Auckland*)

### Vice-president
W.M. Osborne (*Tauranga*)

### Chairman
B.G. Impey

### Board

| | |
|---|---|
| *Elected members:* | A.J. Golightly (*Northland*), J.S. Mitchell (*Canterbury*), S.T. Morris (*Manawatu*) M.P. Robinson (*Taranaki*), G.K. Wahlstrom (*Auckland*). |
| *Appointed members:* | R.P. Dellabarca (*Auckland*), B.G. Impey (*Auckland*), P.N. Kean (*Auckland*). |
| *Maori representative:* | Dr F.R. Palmer ONZM (*Manawatu*). |

### Chief Executive Officer
S.J. Tew

### Life Members
R.A. Guy ONZM; E.J. Tonks CBE; R.A. Fisher ONZM;
J.A Sturgeon ONZM, MBE; Sir Brian Lochore ONZ, KNZM, OBE;
A.R. Leslie MNZM; Sir Graham Henry KNZM

### NZRU Team Coaches, Selectors

| | |
|---|---|
| *New Zealand:* | S.W. Hansen (*coach*), I.D. Foster (*assistant*), G.J. Fox (*selector*). |
| *New Zealand Under 20:* | C.A. Philpott (*coach*), C.N. Brown (*assistant*), W.T.C. Rickards (*assistant*). |
| *New Zealand Maori:* | C.G. Cooper (*coach*) to July; C.R. McMillan from September. |
| *New Zealand Heartland:* | B.A. Matthews (*coach, South Canterbury*), C.M. Scanlon (*assistant, Buller*), E.W. Kirton (*selector*). |
| *New Zealand Sevens:* | S.L. Waldron; C. Clark from June. |
| *New Zealand Secondary Schools:* | J.J. Holland (*coach*), T. Cairns (*assistant*). |
| *New Zealand Women:* | G.M. Moore (*coach*), W. Clarke (*assistant*), G. Keenan (*assistant*). |
| *New Zealand Women's Sevens:* | A.M. Bunting (*coach*). |

# 2017 HONOURS
## THE ALMANACK NEW ZEALAND XV

Ben Smith
*Highlanders*

Waisake Naholo          Ryan Crotty          Rieko Ioane
*Highlanders*            *Crusaders*           *Blues*

Sonny Bill Williams
*Chiefs*

Beauden Barrett
*Hurricanes*

Aaron Smith
*Highlanderss*

Kieran Read (capt)
*Crusaders*

Sam Cane          Samuel Whitelock          Brodie Retallick          Liam Squire
*Chiefs*             *Crusaders*               *Chiefs*                 *Highlanders*

Owen Franks          Codie Taylor          Joe Moody
*Crusaders*           *Crusaders*           *Crusaders*

**Reserves –**

Dane Coles (*Hurricanes*), Kane Hames (*Chiefs*), Nepo Laulala (*Chiefs*), Scott Barrett (*Crusaders*), Matthew Todd (*Crusaders*), TJ Perenara (*Hurricanes*), Damian McKenzie (*Chiefs*), Anton Lienert-Brown (*Chiefs*).

## COMMENTS

The All Blacks had a record of 11 wins, one draw and two defeats in the 14 tests this year. The defeat and draw to the British and Irish Lions in the second and third tests were both there for the winning — but not taken. With 14 men for the last 56 minutes in the second test the All Blacks could not quite hold out at the end, while in the third test the All Blacks missed try chances in a dominant first half and ought to have been more than 12–6 ahead at halftime. Our following comment on players is mainly on those who appeared in Super Rugby, as All Black selection for the June home test series and the Rugby Championship was made on performance in Super Rugby.

**Fullbacks:** Even though he only appeared in four tests this year — due to injury against the British and Irish Lions and a sabbatical after the second Australian test — Ben Smith remains the premier fullback in the country. His experience and accurate decision-making makes him our choice.

Jordie Barrett, who appeared twice in tests before succumbing to a season-ending shoulder injury in the Hurricanes semi-final match, seems destined to take over. His debut season for the Hurricanes was a superb one and he will only get even better. Damian McKenzie played the most tests at fullback in 2017. For the Chiefs his counter-attacking play was, many times, sublime but the opportunities for this were far fewer at test level. With Aaron Cruden's departure for France, McKenzie does seem to be next in line at first five-eighth at the Chiefs, which will make it interesting to see in which position he might appear for the All Blacks in 2018 should he do so.

David Havili's All Black debut was the beneficiary of injury to two players. When Israel Dagg required knee surgery, Havili revelled in the chance to get regular starts and had a breakout season at the Crusaders. Then with Jordie Barrett's injury he was called into the All Blacks, but behind Damian McKenzie.

Shaun Stevenson had an encouraging debut season with the Chiefs and continued the good form with North Harbour. In the Mitre 10 Cup there were standout performances from George

Bridge (although played on the wing for the Crusaders) and exciting newcomer Will Jordan. Solomon Alaimalo lit up the Northland attack from the back.

**Wing three-quarters**: The pair of Waisake Naholo and Rieko Ioane were in scintillating form in Super Rugby and for the All Blacks.

Nehe Milner-Skudder (fullback or wing) and Israel Dagg had injury-plagued seasons, and it looks for Dagg as if he is seen more as a wing than fullback these days by the Crusaders and All Blacks, which could make future selection in the All Blacks tenuous. Another whose future All Black selection must be tenuous is Julian Savea. He had another indifferent season and after the third test against the British and Irish Lions, in which poor handling prevented a certain try, he was discarded. This is hard to understand for someone who has scored 46 tries in 54 tests, but equally, when the Rugby Championship squad was announced, and Savea was omitted, there was not an outcry against the decision. Also, having been first choice for the Hurricanes all season he was then on the bench for the semi-final.

Matt Duffie was probably the most consistent performer in the Blues backline, even allowing for Rieko Ioane's exploits, and seamlessly continued the form for North Harbour with his positional play on defence and finishing ability on attack. He is yet another with the ability to play wing or fullback, which seems to fit in with the All Black selectors' preference of back three types. Having previously been a midfielder, Seta Tamanivalu was put onto the wing by the Crusaders as a replacement for the departed Nemani Nadolo. This turned out to be a good move for both Tamanivalu and the club as the player delivered several strong performances for the Crusaders.

James Lowe was the best of the wings that did not play for New Zealand in 2017, and left for Irish club Leinster at the end of the year in probably the form of his career with the Chiefs and Tasman.

At Mitre 10 Cup level there were excellent debuts from the Canterbury pairing Braydon Ennor and Josh McKay, along with Otago's Jona Nareki. Of the experienced players North Harbour's Tevita Li was a high-class finisher even with a little bit of space, and the Bay of Plenty pair Monty Ioane and Joe Webber finished the season impressively. Vince Aso was easily the best in a below-par Auckland backline.

**Centre three-quarter:** Ryan Crotty and Anton Lienert-Brown were the two players who occupied the centre position for the All Blacks. Even though Crotty played the whole season for the Crusaders at second five-eighth, he was the first choice of the All Blacks selectors at centre and is our choice. He appeals as a backline coordinator and very reliable defender under pressure and did not let the team down in any match. Lienert-Brown was something of a revelation last year, but his form for the Chiefs was variable in 2017. The strategy seemed to be for him to come off the bench for the All Blacks in the second half of matches to add some attacking punch.

Vince Aso played his Mitre 10 Cup rugby on the wing, but at centre for the Hurricanes he formed a brilliant midfield combination with Ngani Laumape, both of them passing Tana Umaga's season try-scoring record. Jack Goodhue got better and better as the season progressed for the Crusaders, and for the Highlanders Malakai Fekitoa regained some of the attacking spark that was missing last year but then departed for French club Toulon. George Moala only gave glimpses of the form he produced last year for the Blues.

Playing at wing or centre for Taranaki, Seta Tamanivalu played so well that he earned an All Black recall on the back of his form on the wing for the Crusaders. Other good performers at Mitre 10 Cup level were the experienced players Tim Bateman and Rene Ranger while of the younger players Matthew Vaega at North Harbour caught the eye.

**Second five-eighth:** Sonny Bill Williams was the All Black selectors' clear preference in this position even though others produced better Super Rugby form. We debated before eventually choosing him as our selection based on the fact he started in 13 of the 14 tests with no one else to compare against at that highest level. His defence was strong and introduced the grubber kick to his repertoire, but the offloads and running were not prominent. Unfortunately, his season will probably be remembered for his red card in the second British and Irish Lions test.

In Super Rugby Ngani Laumape was the standout in this position, his 16 tries being a new Hurricanes season record. His defence let him down on occasion, which may have been a factor (coupled with lack of experience) in the All Black selectors' preferring Williams. But Laumape can only improve. Ryan Crotty was again great value to the Crusaders, and would have been a valid pick in the All Blacks in this position. Rob Thompson is a consistent, and probably underrated, performer for the Highlanders.

The clear standout in the Mitre 10 Cup in this position was Jack Goodhue, following his season at centre for Crusaders. He displayed a fine all-round game on attack and defence. An honourable mention goes to Canterbury's Rob Thompson while newcomer Thomas Umaga-Jensen had a fine first season at Wellington as did Matthew Johnson at Southland.

**First five-eighth:** Winning World Rugby's international player of the year award for the second year running is enough for us to re-select Beauden Barrett. His year was not as superlative as last year with opposition teams at Super and test level clearly having devoted homework to counteracting what he produced in 2016.

Lima Sopoaga missed a fair bit of game time with the Highlanders due to injury and, because of it, was not the force of last year. Marty Banks was a very capable player for the Highlanders in his place. Aaron Cruden departed for French club Montpellier after having given very good service to the Chiefs over the last six years.

Richie Mo'unga again controlled things superbly for the Super Rugby champions the Crusaders, his running game and goal-kicking being first-class. Then he just simply carried the form over into the Mitre 10 Cup champions Canterbury. His All Black selection was thoroughly deserved.

Jackson Garden-Bachop was a completely different player for Wellington than in previous years, having arrived back from a stint in Super Rugby with the Melbourne Rebels. His running game gave a whole new dimension to his play. Stephen Perofeta and Mitchell Hunt performed well for their respective Taranaki and Tasman teams. James Lash was the kingpin for Buller and set the standard in the Heartland Championship.

**Halfback:** Carrying on from where he left off last year TJ Perenara was the form halfback in Super Rugby, edging out fellow All Blacks Aaron Smith and Tawera Kerr-Barlow. There was not a lot of difference between them. For the All Blacks Smith displayed his best form, speed to the breakdown, crisp clearing of the ball, and added a bit more kicking and running.

There was a good battle at the Crusaders between Bryn Hall and Mitchell Drummond, with Hall getting the starts in the playoffs, and Augustine Pulu's shift to the Blues worked out well for both parties, getting regular starts to utilise his strong running game.

Drummond and Hall also featured prominently in the Mitre 10 Cup for Canterbury and North Harbour respectively and Drummond's swift pass and sniping runs earned him a call-up into the All Blacks' end-of-year tour. Others worthy of mention were Taranaki's Te Toiroa Tahuriorangi and Sam Nock of Northland.

**Number eight:** Injury restricted Kieran Read to appearing in less than half the Crusaders matches and yet his performance, and captaincy, in the first British and Irish Lions test was one of his best ever, which demonstrated his ability to rise to the occasion. There were other comparable performances against Australia at Dunedin and South Africa at Albany, but he ended the season requiring surgery and will miss a significant part of the 2018 Crusaders campaign, which must be a concern to the All Blacks selectors.

In Super Rugby the two outstanding players in this position were Brad Shields and Luke Whitelock, with Shields playing the first half of the season at blindside flanker and the second half at number eight. Both displayed strong all-round games in the tight and on attack with Shields also prominent in the lineout. They continued this wonderful form into the Mitre 10 Cup with their respective title-winning provinces. When Jerome Kaino was invalided out of the All Blacks' end-of-year tour, Brad Shields declined the call-up as replacement and the opportunity passed to Whitelock.

Jordan Taufua was another to show good form throughout the year for the Crusaders and Tasman, while Akira Ioane seemed to lose a bit of confidence playing for the Blues but recaptured it again for Auckland in the Mitre 10 Cup.

Appearing for Taranaki in the Mitre 10 Cup, Toa Halafihi was almost unstoppable, turning in a number of high-class performances with his efforts in the lineout, strong tackling, and breaking the advantage line. Despite his outstanding form he was not re-signed by the Hurricanes and departed for French club Lyon.

**Flankers:** As with halfback, the openside flanker position has a triumvirate that is clear of the rest. Ardie Savea and Matt Todd might have edged Sam Cane during Super Rugby, but as the All Blacks' incumbent Sam Cane did not give either rival a chance to take his place with his consistent displays in the tests, and is one of our players of the year for 2017.

Blake Gibson made the biggest stride towards challenging the leading three with his best ever season for the Blues, always seeming to be in the action with his carrying, tackling or breakdown work. Dillon Hunt was a relative unknown at the beginning of the year when called into the Highlanders as temporary cover for injuries, but after 12 matches and then a full Mitre 10 Cup season with Otago was selected for the All Blacks' end-of-year tour to complete a whirlwind season.

Jerome Kaino's form at blindside flanker for the Blues and in the three tests against the British and Irish Lions was well down on last year and there is a real sense that his All Blacks career is at an end. Liam Squire definitely advanced with his increased exposure at the highest level, and Vaea Fifita announced himself to test rugby with a sensational try on debut against Argentina. Both men looked very energetic in the open and very physical in the tight exchanges.

Liam Messam returned to the Chiefs after concentrating on sevens last year and fitted straight back in showing his versatility among the loose forward roles, while Elliot Dixon's form for the Highlanders regressed but he redeemed himself with a very good Mitre 10 Cup effort with Southland in a losing cause. Tom Sanders hardly got any game time with the Chiefs but was at his best with Canterbury, and the same could be said for Murphy Taramai with the Blues and for North Harbour.

Non-Super Rugby players who created favourable impressions in the Mitre 10 Cup were Billy Harmon for Canterbury, newcomer Du Plessis Kirifi for Wellington, and Pita Sowakula of Taranaki.

**Locks:** Brodie Retallick and Sam Whitelock remain our premier lock forwards, both world class, and a big gap still remains back to the pack.

Scott Barrett, Luke Romano and Patrick Tuipulotu all appeared in tests, but none of them established themselves ahead of the other two. Scott Barrett does appear more likely to have the versatility to play at blindside flanker if required during a match.

After his efforts for the Highlanders and Bay of Plenty Tom Franklin was unlucky not to gain selection on the All Blacks' end-of-year tour, the All Blacks selectors choosing to recall Dominic Bird of the Crusaders and Canterbury. There can't have been much between their respective merits. Sam Lousi with the Hurricanes and Scott Scrafton with the Blues both had promising debut seasons and no doubt their 2018 seasons will be watched with interest.

Manawatu's Jackson Hemopo, North Harbour's Jarrad Hoeata, Canterbury's Mitchell Dunshea, Otago's Josh Furno, and Jimmy Tupou of Counties Manukau all showed out well in the Mitre 10 Cup.

**Props:** This is a position which is building depth nicely even with the departure of Charlie Faumuina overseas after the British and Irish Lions series. Joe Moody and Owen Franks deserve to head the queue at loosehead and tighthead prop respectively, and it was a shame both suffered season-ending injuries during the Rugby Championship. Kane Hames and Nepo Laulala were the beneficiaries and took the ample opportunity presented to show their abilities. Barring injury or serious loss of form, even from this far out these look the four with which to go to the 2019 World Cup.

Wyatt Crockett and Ofa Tu'ungafasi fulfilled their substitution roles well for the end-of-year tour, while loosehead Tim Perry was a surprise call-up and Jeff To'omaga-Allen earned a recall. Atu Moli was called into the All Blacks environment during the Rugby Championship in an apprentice role and played one match on the end-of-year tour.

Blues and Counties Manukau loosehead Pauliasi Manu received a World Cup winners medal just two years ago, but it would seem any further chance of All Blacks call-up has now passed him by.

Twenty-year-old Alex Fidow made a big impression in the Mitre 10 Cup. The Wellington tighthead was very hard to stop with ball in hand and his scrummaging ability improved significantly on last year. Other good performances in the competition came from the Taranaki pairing of Mitchell Graham and Angus Ta'avao, Canterbury's Alex Hodgman, Tasman's Tim Perry, Northland's Ross Wright and Otago's Craig Millar. Newcomer Mike Tamoaieta at North Harbour had a promising debut season.

**Hooker:** Codie Taylor was the leading hooker throughout the year, staying fit and in form in a full season for the Crusaders and the All Blacks. Concussion issues meant Dane Coles only played six times for the Hurricanes and missed the entire British and Irish Lions series. Then on the end-of-year tour he suffered a knee injury against France that will see him miss a lot of the 2018 Super Rugby campaign.

Liam Coltman was the form hooker, along with Taylor, in Super Rugby, but it was Nathan Harris the All Black selectors chose as third hooker. Coltman also had the misfortune to miss the entire Mitre 10 Cup for Otago with injury. Ricky Riccitelli got more game time at the Hurricanes than he would have anticipated and enhanced his reputation considerably, being very physical in the tight and threw with excellent accuracy into the lineout. His form was good for Taranaki in the Mitre 10 Cup, too.

Asafo Aumua gave a hint of his ability in last year's Mitre 10 Cup. In this year's competition it was there for all to see — his seven tries, strong carrying, pace in the open, and improvement in his lineout and scrummaging on last year. And all this was just a continuation of the form he displayed for New Zealand at the Under 20 World Cup. His selection on the All Blacks' end-of-year tour was as expected. Others to impress in the Mitre 10 Cup were North Harbour's James Parsons, Hawke's Bay's Ash Dixon, Northland's Matt Moulds and Canterbury's Ben Funnell.

# FIVE PLAYERS OF THE YEAR

**Samuel Jordan Cane** *(Chiefs)* retained the All Blacks number seven jersey throughout 2017. With New Zealand rugby showing a lot of depth at openside flanker, Cane had to withstand continued challenges from Ardie Savea and Matt Todd. All the stats of tackles made, carries, passes and turnovers made by the three in Super Rugby were healthy, but the All Black selectors started with Cane, the incumbent.

His form was irresistible, appearing in 13 (12 starts) of the All Blacks' 14 tests, culminating in a standout defensive performance in the final test of the year against Wales. With the All Blacks only having 35 per cent possession, Cane made an astonishing 21 tackles. After the match Steve Hansen endorsed Cane's form for the year as being 'a model of consistency'. In October he re-signed with NZR, Chiefs and Bay of Plenty through to the end of the 2021 season in a deal NZR labelled as 'a major coup'.

Sam Cane was previously a Promising Player in 2011.

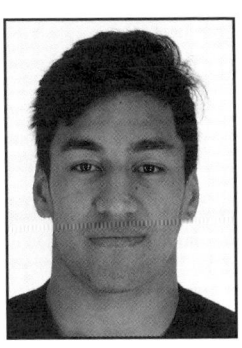

In his first match of 2017 **Rieko Ioane** *(Blues)* scored three tries for the Blues against the Rebels, and in his last match of the year he scored two tries and assisted in two others, as the All Blacks defeated Wales. They were both outstanding performances by the 20-year-old, and many of the matches in between were quite good too.

He played the first eight Blues matches at centre (four tries), but with the return of Sonny Bill Williams to the side in midfield Ioane was shifted to the wing. His try rate rocketed with seven tries in seven appearances, and he ended the Super Rugby season with 11 tries for the Blues. The next best was five. Selected on the wing for the All Blacks, he scored 10 tries in his 11 tests, those tries being second only to the 12 scored by Australia's Israel Folau for test rugby in 2017. At the annual World Rugby Awards Ioane received the Breakthrough Player of the Year award and was also one of the shortlisted five finalists for International Player of the Year award that was won by teammate Beauden Barrett.

All up in 2017, he was equal top try-scorer in New Zealand first-class rugby with 21 tries and at the NZ Rugby Awards he received the Tom French Memorial Cup as Maori Player of the Year to complete a wonderful season.

Rieko was born on 18 March 1997 at Auckland and educated at Auckland Grammar, spending his last two years there (2013–14) in the first XV. In his final year he captained the NZ Secondary Schools team and was signed by the Blues.

After impressing for Auckland at the 2015 national sevens in January, he was picked in the NZ Sevens team for the remaining six tournaments in the 2014/15 World Series Sevens schedule. In July he made his first-class debut when appearing for NZ Maori on the wing against Fiji and marked it with a try. His debut for Auckland followed with six appearances in the ITM Cup and he represented Auckland A at the Jock Hobbs Memorial Under 19 tournament.

With sevens making its debut at the Olympic Games in 2016, he played for Auckland again at the national sevens and spent the next seven months appearing for the NZ Sevens team and making his debut for the Blues with five appearances. He gained selection, along with brother Akira, for the Olympic Games in Rio de Janeiro where the NZ team finished fifth. Upon his return it was straight into the Auckland team for the Mitre 10 Cup. Appearing at centre, his 10 tries made him the top try-scorer in the competition. With such form his selection for the All Blacks end-of-year tour was something of a formality and he made his test debut as a substitute against Italy and scored a try. He made one more test appearance on the tour as a substitute against France. At the NZ Rugby Awards he received the NZ Sevens Player of the Year award.

His father Eddie represented Samoa at the 1991 World Cup at lock, and elder brother Akira has also played for Auckland, the Blues, NZ Maori, NZ Sevens and this year made his All Blacks' debut.

**Waisake Ratunideuba Naholo** *(Highlanders)* continued the outstanding form, and high try-scoring rate, that has characterised his rugby since 2014. This year he was equal top try-scorer in NZ first-class rugby with 21 tries in 22 matches, and in the last four seasons he has scored 59 tries in 75 first-class matches.

Ten tries in 12 games for the Highlanders and five tries in three games for Taranaki was almost obligatory. As impressive as those figures are, it was for the All Blacks on their end-of-year tour that he probably produced his best football of the year. With no Israel Dagg, Ben Smith, Julian Savea and Nehe Milner-Skudder, he was the senior player in the back three. Against the Barbarians he provided the last pass for tries scored by TJ Perenara and Vaea Fifita and produced an outstanding save to deny speedy South African flanker Kwagga Smith a try. Then in the following tests he scored twice against both France and Wales.

Born at Sigatoka, Fiji, on 8 May 1991, he attended Cuvu College for three years before arriving in New Zealand at the start of 2009 at the invitation of his uncle Meli Nauga to stay with him in Wanganui, to which his parents agreed. Meli had played three games for Wanganui in 1995–96.

Enrolling at Wanganui City College as Waisake Ratunideuba, in April he participated in the North Island Secondary Schools Track and Field championship at Newtown, finishing second in the 100 metres with a time of 11.02 seconds and third in the 200 metres at 22.59 seconds. Just three months later he made his first-class debut for Wanganui in the Ranfurly Shield challenge against Wellington, and finished the season having appeared in all 11 of Wanganui's matches, scoring six tries as the province went on win the Heartland Championship. His form attracted the attention of Taranaki who promptly signed him to their Academy before the year was out.

Working as a roofer, he joined the Inglewood club for 2010 and preferred to use the name Waisake Naholo. The following year he switched clubs to Spotswood United and made the New Zealand Under 20 squad that won the IRB World Championship in Italy, then played his first five games for Taranaki.

He started the 2012 year in the NZ Sevens team that went on to win the IRB World Series Sevens title, and five tries in eight matches for Taranaki saw him picked up by the Blues for 2013. Two appearances was his lot for the Blues and he was not re-signed for 2014; however, an excellent 2014 season for Taranaki, with nine tries in 12 matches helping the province take out the ITM Cup title, gained a signature with the Highlanders for 2015.

Before the 2015 Super Rugby tournament started Naholo signed a two-year contract with French club Clermont Auvergne to leave after the ITM Cup. Such was his form for the Highlanders that the phrases 'Waisake Naholo' and 'World Cup squad' became intertwined, and in June it was announced that Naholo was staying with suggestions from Clermont Auvergne of NZR involvement. The Highlanders went on to take their maiden Super Rugby title in July and Naholo's 13 tries made him the top try-scorer in the tournament.

Just 13 days after the Highlanders' triumph he made his All Blacks debut against Argentina at Christchurch on 17 July, leaving the field after 51 minutes with what was diagnosed as a stress fracture of the right fibula. The verdict was out for three months and missing the World Cup. But when the squad was announced on 30 August Naholo was in, having made a remarkable recovery. In England he made just the two appearances in pool matches but still came home with a winners' medal as the All Blacks retained the world title.

The next season, 2016, was injury plagued, with another stress fracture of the right leg during the Highlanders campaign and a hamstring injury for the All Blacks, yet he still finished the year with 13 tries in 18 first-class matches.

**Codie Joshua Dane Taylor** *(Crusaders)* confirmed himself as next in line for the All Blacks hooking position with a number of very capable performances in 2017 for both New Zealand and the Crusaders. He executed the core roles of the position very consistently and was mobile around the field as he proved by chasing down Beauden Barrett in the Crusaders-Hurricanes match at Christchurch. In the absence of the established Dane Coles for half the international season due to concussion, Taylor appeared in all 14 tests, starting all seven for which Coles was not available. He had also been an integral part of Crusader's first Super Rugby title success since 2008. During the year he re-signed with NZR, Crusaders and Canterbury to the end of 2021.

He was born at Levin on 31 March 1991 and shifted to Brisbane with his parents when he was six months old. His sport of choice there became rugby league, but at the age of 11 the family returned to Levin. Educated at Horowhenua College, he captained the first XV in 2008, and represented Horowhenua Kapiti at the Hurricanes under 18 tournament. The following year he attended Feilding High School as a boarder and was selected in the NZ Secondary Schools team that defeated Australia in their annual encounter.

Taylor shifted to Christchurch in 2010 to join the Canterbury Academy and made his first-class debut in 2011 with the NZ Under-20 team that triumphed at the World Championship in Italy. The Crusaders picked him as one of their eight wider training squad members for 2012, and his Canterbury ITM Cup debut followed, playing in the 2012 final as a substitute in the win over Auckland. The Crusaders selected him on a full contract for 2013, making his debut with three appearances, but he did not appear in the ITM Cup due to injury. In 2014 it was just two more appearances for the Crusaders and another full season for Canterbury in claiming the ITM Cup, finishing the year with selection in the NZ Maori team for their two matches in Japan against the national side.

In 2015 significant strides were made. He played in 15 of the Crusaders' 16 matches, ending the campaign as the starting hooker. In this World Cup year, the All Blacks' third hooker position was up for grabs and Taylor made his test debut during the abbreviated Rugby Championship, and made the squad to England where he played one pool match as the All Blacks retained the World Cup. Last year was another full campaign for the Crusaders and 11 more tests for the All Blacks.

Taylor is a great-great-grandson of 1893 All Black Walter Pringle.

**Portia Louise Woodman** *(Counties Manukau)* richly deserved the numerous awards presented to her in 2017. Her performances at the Rugby World Cup were reminiscent of Jonah Lomu at the 1995 Rugby World Cup — both played on the left wing and both scored four tries in a crucial semi-final. Woodman's first try in the semi-final, against a powerful USA team, was a stunning 45-metre run during which she fended off three tacklers and evaded two more before scoring under the posts. The game had been even with the Black Ferns holding a narrow 8–7 lead until Woodman's try in the 25th minute. Shortly after halftime she scored again, with the score advancing to 20–7, and the confidence of the Americans was broken. Two more tries by the wing and the Black Ferns won 45–12. Woodman's brilliant individual try won the voting by Sky fans as the best try of the year.

Woodman scored 16 tries in her eight tests of 2017, eight tries being against Hong Kong during the cup pool rounds. She was also a huge contributor towards the success of the Black Ferns Sevens in winning the World Series, scoring 35 tries in the five tournaments she attended. She was World Rugby's Player of the Year. Another honour came from the *Planet Rugby* website, which chose its team of the year with Woodman being the sole female in a team which included five All Blacks.

Born at Kawakawa on 12 July 1991, Portia Woodman moved with her family from Kaikohe to Auckland's North Shore in 1997 and attended Birkdale Primary School, Kowhai Intermediate, and Mt Albert Grammar. She played netball until being attracted to sevens rugby in 2012 and was a member of the NZ Sevens team in both of its tournaments that year. At the 2013 World Cup Sevens, at Moscow, won by New Zealand, Woodman scored 12 tries and two weeks later made her debut for the Black Ferns, appearing in all three tests against England. However, she did not appear again for the Black Ferns until 2016 as she focused on sevens. She was World Rugby's Sevens Player of the Year in 2015 and has now scored 182 tries in 28 tournaments.

Woodman is a star for the national teams yet, surprisingly, has appeared in only four provincial games, once for Auckland in 2013 and three games for Counties Manukau in 2016.

Portia Woodman is a daughter of 1984 All Black Kawhena Woodman.

# PROMISING PLAYERS
# OF THE YEAR

In a season where the performance of the Southland team was one of the worst in the union's history, second five-eighth **Matthew Johnson Jr** *(Southland)* stood out as a reliable tackler coupled with an ability to challenge the opposition in attack, scoring a try in each of his first two games. At 1.91 m and 100 kg he was one of the bigger second five-eighths in the Mitre 10 Cup, and the only member of the Southland squad to start in all 10 games.

Born on 20 April 1994 at Auckland, Matthew was educated at Roscommon Primary School and did both his intermediate and secondary schooling at St Peter's College in 2006–07 and 2008–12 respectively. He was in the first XV for his last three years of 2010–12. He had attracted the interest of the Melbourne Storm rugby league club and spent the next year with their under-20 team. Returning to New Zealand, and rugby, late in the 2013 season, he represented the Waikato Under-20 team.

In 2014 he joined the Suburbs club, and enrolled at the University of Auckland for a Bachelor of Sport and Exercise programme. In the 2014–15 New Zealand summer he left for England and played a season for the Moortown rugby club in Leeds.

Back in the country, he shifted to Southland and the Midlands club for the 2015 season in an attempt to break into provincial rugby, following the path of past Suburbs club players, also transferring his studies to Southern Institute of Technology. When the Midlands club did not field a team in the premier division in 2016 he transferred to the Marist club and made the Southland B team for the second year.

To complete a memorable 2017, he was picked in the Blues squad for 2018 and graduated with his Bachelor of Sport and Exercise.

**William Thomas Jordan** *(Tasman)* had a most successful debut season in first-class rugby, scoring 14 tries in 17 games, which saw him rank as one of the country's top try-scorers. The 1.89 m 93 kg fullback revealed pace, strength and ability to beat a man, and willingness to counter-attack from anywhere on the field. His nine tries for New Zealand Under-20 and five tries for Tasman made him the top try-scorer for both teams as the New Zealand team won the Under-20 World Championship and Tasman finished runner-up in the Mitre 10 Cup.

At the Under-20 World Championship he made the five finalists for the player of the tournament award (along with fellow teammate Tiaan Falcon), which was won by South African Juarno Augustus. Will's tournament statistics were 418 metres made, 11 clean breaks and 12 defenders beaten. In the Mitre 10 Cup for Tasman his statistics were 977 metres made (second highest in the competition), 30 clean breaks (seventh highest) and 41 defenders beaten (second highest). He concluded the year being named in the Crusaders squad for 2018.

Born at Christchurch on 24 February 1998, he started his rugby career at the age of five by joining the High School Old Boys club and playing in midfield. He was educated at Fendalton Primary School and Cobham Intermediate, then enrolled at Christchurch Boys' High School 2011–15. Initially playing as a halfback, in his final two years he was at fullback playing for the first XV. In his last year Christchurch Boys High School won the Crusaders Schools championship with Will scoring 19 tries in 11 games, and he also represented the Canterbury Metropolitan Under 18 team at the South Island tournament.

Will also played for the cricket first XI at the 2014 and 2015 national Gillette Cup 50-over tournaments. The title was won in 2014 and at the 2015 tournament, against Palmerston North Boys' High School, he scored 102 not out off 83 balls batting at number three.

Upon leaving school in 2016 he started a double degree of Bachelor of Commerce and Law at the University of Canterbury and joined the Christchurch rugby club. He appeared for Canterbury at the Jock Hobbs Memorial Under-19 tournament and signed for Tasman the following month. Canterbury and former New Zealand Under-20 rep Hamish Dalzell is a cousin.

**Du Plessis Ariu Kirifi** *(Wellington)* was a very noticeable part of the Wellington loose forward combination as Wellington steamrolled their way through the Mitre 10 Championship and back into the Premiership for 2018. At 20 years of age, the youngest of the Wellington loose forwards, the openside flanker at 1.82 m and 98 kg was no less effective than his more experienced and older confrères in the loose, appearing in 10 of the 12 games.

Named by his father in honour of Springbok captain and number eight Morne du Plessis, Du Plessis was born at New Plymouth on 3 March 1997. He was educated at Moturoa Primary School and then Francis Douglas Memorial College in 2008–14 for both his intermediate and high school years. In his two years in the first XV he was voted best debutant (2013) and then the MVP award in 2014.

While at Francis Douglas Memorial College he represented the Taranaki Under 14s 2010–11 (captain 2011), and the Taranaki Under 16s 2012–13 (captain 2013), then in his final year he captained the Taranaki Under 18 team.

In his first year out of school he joined the Tukapa club and represented Taranaki at the Jock Hobbs Memorial Under 19 tournament and the Taranaki sevens team. In 2016 he moved to Hamilton to play for Fraser Tech and played at the Jock Hobbs Memorial Under 19 tournament again, this time for Waikato who won the title. This year, now captaining Fraser Tech, he played for the Chiefs Under-20 and Development teams before signing with Wellington in August, where he enrolled at Victoria University to undertake a Bachelor of Commerce.

His father, Poluaiu'amea (Jack) Kirifi, played two first-class matches for Auckland B 1985–86 as a flanker, and played over a hundred games for the Ponsonby club senior team.

**Vilimoni Tukutukulevu Koroi** *(Otago)* burst onto the sevens circuit, earning high praise from international commentators. Six of the eight tournaments he attended were before his nineteenth birthday. During the year Koroi exhibited rare skills with the ability to create openings when opportunities seemingly did not exist. While there is still much for him to learn about in sevens, he has the potential to become a long-serving playmaker similar to former stars Amasio Valence and Tomasi Cama. World Rugby nominated the teenager as a finalist for sevens rookie of the year.

Born at Wanganui on 17 April 1998, Koroi attracted attention on the rugby field from an early age. At Wanganui High School he was a star at sevens and fifteens before he moved to board at Feilding High School during 2014–16. In March 2014, when aged 16, he was one of three promising young players invited to attend the wider All Blacks Sevens training squad at a camp at Mount Maunganui. Manawatu sevens coach Tomasi Cama included the schoolboy in his team at the national sevens in January 2016. In October he was selected for the NZ Secondary Schools squad for internationals against Fiji and Australia but was injured during training and had to withdraw.

The Manawatu union had hopes of signing for the 2017 season Koroi and fellow former Feilding High School pupil Jona Nareki, also a Fijian, but the pair chose to sign with Otago. Koroi appeared in nine games for Otago, four at fullback, one on the right wing and four as a substitute.

When the 2017 North Harbour squad for the Mitre 10 Cup was named **Mike Tamoaieta** *(North Harbour)* was the only one of the six props that had not appeared at first-class level previously. In 2016 the resurgence in fortune of the province saw North Harbour win promotion to the premiership on the back of a good forward pack, which produced one of the best scrums in the Mitre 10 Cup. By the end of the 2017 competition the 1.75 m 122 kg tighthead prop had appeared in all 11 games, and not only displaced the incumbent but also deservedly earned himself a Blues contract for 2018 after an impressive season.

Born at Auckland on 6 July 1995, Mike's initial schooling was at St Pius X Catholic and St Joseph Orakei primary schools followed by attending Sacred Heart College in Auckland 2009–13. Always a tighthead prop, he played for the first XV 2011–13, and in his final year was selected in the New Zealand Secondary Schoolboys team.

The following year he took up employment as a builder and linked up with the Grammar TEC club, gaining selection in the Blues Under 20 team and the Auckland Under-19 A team at the Jock Hobbs Memorial National tournament. In 2015 Mike represented Auckland Colts and was selected by Samoa for the Under-20 World Championship. He was Grammar TEC player of the year for 2016 and 2017.

# NEW ZEALAND
# REPRESENTATIVES 2017

There were 13 new faces among the 55 who played for the All Blacks this year. Of these 13, the four chosen midyear played in test matches and the nine chosen for the end of year tour have yet to feature in a test match.

Details of the 13 new All Blacks are:

**AUMUA, Asafo Junior** *born Lower Hutt, May 5, 1997*
**All Blacks #1163**
New Zealand Under 20 2016 (7), 2017 (7); Wellington 2016 (10), 2017 (10); New Zealand 2017 (2).

**BARRETT, Jordie Matthew** *born New Plymouth, February 17, 1997*
**All Blacks #1158**
New Zealand Under 20 2016 (7); Canterbury 2016 (12); Hurricanes 2017 (18); New Zealand 2017 (2).

**DRUMMOND, Mitchell David** *born Nelson, February 15, 1994*
**All Blacks #1169**
Canterbury 2013 (1), 2014 (11), 2015 (12), 2016 (3), 2017 (10); Crusaders 2014 (1), 2015 (15), 2016 (3), 2017 (17); New Zealand Under 20 2014 (4); UK Barbarians 2017 (1); New Zealand 2017 (1).

**DUFFIE, Matthew David** *born Auckland, August 16, 1990*
**All Blacks #1164**
Blues 2016 (11), 2017 (14); North Harbour 2016 (11), 2017 (10); New Zealand 2017 (2).

**FIFITA, Vaea Tangitau Lapota** *born Neiafu, Tonga, June 17, 1992*
**All Blacks #1159**
Wellington 2013 (1), 2014 (9), 2015 (10), 2016 (8), 2017 (2); Hurricanes 2015 (2), 2016 (18), 2017 (13); New Zealand 2017 (6).

**GOODHUE, Elais Jack** *born Whangarei, June 13, 1995*
**All Blacks #1165**
Canterbury 2014 (5), 2015 (2), 2016 (11); New Zealand Under 20 2015 (7); Crusaders 2017 (15); Northland 2017 (9); New Zealand 2017 (1).

**HAVILI, David Keatau** *born Nelson, December 23, 1994*
**All Blacks #1161**
New Zealand Under 20 2014 (1); Tasman 2014 (10), 2015 (11), 2016 (10), 2017 (1); Crusaders 2015 (11), 2016 (14), 2017 (18); New Zealand 2017 (5).

**HUNT Dillon** *born Auckland, February 23, 1995*
**All Blacks #1170**
Otago 2016 (5), 2017 (8); Highlanders 2017 (12); UK Barbarians 2017 (1), New Zealand 2017 (1).

**IOANE Akira Latrell**　　　　　　　　　　*born Auckland, June 16, 1995*
**All Blacks #1166**
Blues 2015 (9), 2016 (8), 2017 (16); New Zealand Under 20 2015 (5); Auckland 2015 (11), 2016 (10), 2017 (6); Maori All Blacks 2015 (2), 2016 (3), 2017 (3); New Zealand 2017 (1).

**LAUMAPE Koinonia Halafungani (Ngani)**　　　*born Palmerston North, April 22, 1993*
**All Blacks #1160**
Hurricanes 2016 (10), 2017 (18); Manawatu 2016 (10), 2017 (2); New Zealand 2017 (6).

**MOLI Atunaisa**　　　　　　　　　　*born Gisborne, June 12, 1995*
**All Blacks #1168**
New Zealand Under 20 2014 (5), 2015 (7); Waikato 2015 (6), 2016 (7), 2017 (5); Chiefs 2016 (11), 2017 (17); UK Barbarians 2017 (1); New Zealand 2017 (1).

**MO'UNGA Richard**　　　　　　　　*born Christchurch, May 25, 1994*
**All Blacks #1167**
Canterbury 2013 (8), 2014 (10),2015 (10), 2016 (11), 2017 (10); New Zealand Under 20 2014 (5); Crusaders 2016 (16), 2017 (14); UK Barbarians 2016 (2); 2017 (1); New Zealand 2017 (1).

# ALL BLACKS MANAGEMENT 2017

| | |
|---|---|
| *Head Coach:* | Steve Hansen |
| *Assistant Coach (Selector):* | Ian Foster |
| *Assistant Coach (Forwards):* | Mike Cron |
| *Assistant Coach (Defence):* | Wayne Smith (until October) |
| *Assistant Coach (Defence):* | Scott McLeod |
| *Selector:* | Grant Fox |
| *Manager (Business):* | Darren Shand |
| *Manager (Leadership):* | Gilbert Enoka |
| *Coach (Strength and Conditioning):* | Dr Nic Gill |
| *Player Development Manager:* | Mike Anthony |
| *Performance Analysis Manager:* | Jason Healy |
| *Performance Analyst:* | Jamie Hamilton |
| *Doctor:* | Dr Tony Page |
| *Physiotherapist:* | Peter Gallagher |
| *Manual Therapist:* | George Duncan |
| *Nutritionist:* | Katrina Darry |
| *Team Services Manager:* | Bianca Thiel |
| *Media Manager:* | Joe Locke |
| *Logistics Manager:* | James Iversen |

# TEST MATCH RECORDS OF 2017
# NEW ZEALAND REPRESENTATIVES
## ALL BLACK CAREER RECORDS TO JANUARY 1, 2018

| | Debut | Tests | Starts | Wins | Winning % | Tries | Conversions | Penalty Goals | Dropped Goals | Points |
|---|---|---|---|---|---|---|---|---|---|---|
| Beauden Barrett | 2012 | 62 | 32 | 56 | 90.3 | 24 | 111 | 41 | - | 465 |
| Jordie Barrett | 2017 | 2 | 1 | 1 | 50 | 1 | - | - | - | 5 |
| Scott Barrett | 2016 | 16 | 4 | 12 | 75 | 2 | - | - | - | 10 |
| Sam Cane | 2012 | 53 | 34 | 47 | 88.7 | 13 | - | - | - | 65 |
| Dane Coles | 2012 | 56 | 42 | 50 | 89.3 | 10 | - | - | - | 50 |
| Wyatt Crockett | 2009 | 71 | 25 | 66 | 93 | 2 | - | - | - | 10 |
| Ryan Crotty | 2013 | 35 | 24 | 31 | 88.6 | 9 | - | - | - | 45 |
| Aaron Cruden | 2010 | 50 | 26 | 44 | 88 | 5 | 63 | 56 | 1 | 322 |
| Israel Dagg | 2010 | 66 | 63 | 60 | 90.9 | 26 | 1 | 2 | - | 138 |
| Charlie Faumuina | 2012 | 50 | 12 | 44 | 88 | 4 | - | - | - | 20 |
| Malakai Fekitoa | 2014 | 24 | 15 | 19 | 79.2 | 8 | - | - | - | 40 |
| Vaea Fifita | 2017 | 5 | 4 | 5 | 100 | 2 | - | - | - | 10 |
| Owen Franks | 2009 | 95 | 85 | 82 | 86.3 | - | - | - | - | - |
| Kane Hames | 2016 | 9 | 7 | 8 | 88.9 | - | - | - | - | - |
| Nathan Harris | 2014 | 11 | 1 | 9 | 81.8 | - | - | - | - | - |
| David Havili | 2017 | 3 | - | 2 | 66.7 | 1 | - | - | - | 5 |
| Rieko Ioane | 2016 | 13 | 11 | 11 | 84.6 | 11 | - | - | - | 55 |
| Jerome Kaino | 2004 | 81 | 74 | 68 | 83.9 | 12 | - | - | - | 60 |
| Tawera Kerr-Barlow | 2012 | 27 | 2 | 26 | 96.3 | 2 | - | - | - | 10 |
| Nepo Laulala | 2015 | 13 | 9 | 11 | 84.6 | - | - | - | - | - |
| Ngani Laumape | 2017 | 4 | 1 | 2 | 50 | 1 | - | - | - | 5 |
| Anton Lienert-Brown | 2016 | 22 | 12 | 19 | 86.4 | 5 | - | - | - | 25 |
| Damian McKenzie | 2016 | 12 | 11 | 11 | 91.7 | 5 | - | - | - | 25 |
| Nehe Milner-Skudder | 2015 | 11 | 11 | 10 | 90.9 | 11 | - | - | - | 55 |
| Joe Moody | 2014 | 31 | 24 | 26 | 83.9 | 1 | - | - | - | 5 |
| Waisake Naholo | 2015 | 18 | 16 | 15 | 83.3 | 12 | - | - | - | 60 |
| TJ Perenara | 2014 | 42 | 9 | 37 | 88.1 | 8 | - | - | - | 40 |
| Kieran Read | 2008 | 109 | 102 | 94 | 86.2 | 23 | - | - | - | 115 |
| Brodie Retallick | 2012 | 68 | 56 | 62 | 91.2 | 3 | - | - | - | 15 |
| Luke Romano | 2012 | 31 | 24 | 28 | 90.3 | 2 | - | - | - | 10 |
| Ardie Savea | 2016 | 22 | 4 | 18 | 81.8 | 4 | - | - | - | 20 |
| Julian Savea | 2012 | 54 | 51 | 48 | 88.9 | 46 | - | - | - | 230 |
| Aaron Smith | 2012 | 71 | 67 | 62 | 87.3 | 13 | 1 | - | - | 67 |
| Ban Smith | 2009 | 64 | 54 | 58 | 90.6 | 29 | - | - | - | 145 |
| Lima Sopoaga | 2015 | 16 | 2 | 15 | 93.8 | 1 | 16 | 6 | - | 55 |
| Liam Squire | 2016 | 15 | 10 | 13 | 86.7 | 2 | - | - | - | 10 |
| Seta Tamanivalu | 2016 | 3 | - | 3 | 100 | - | - | - | - | - |
| Codie Taylor | 2015 | 29 | 10 | 24 | 82.8 | 7 | - | - | - | 35 |
| Matt Todd | 201 | 13 | 4 | 13 | 100 | - | - | - | - | - |
| Patrick Tuipulotu | 2014 | 16 | 5 | 14 | 87.5 | 2 | - | - | - | 10 |
| Ofa Tu'ungafasi | 2016 | 14 | - | 12 | 85.7 | 1 | - | - | - | 5 |
| Luke Whitelock | 2013 | 2 | 1 | 2 | 100 | - | - | - | - | - |
| Samuel Whitelock | 2010 | 96 | 78 | 85 | 88.5 | 5 | - | - | - | 25 |
| Sonny Bill Williams | 2010 | 46 | 33 | 42 | 91.3 | 11 | - | - | - | 55 |

# NON-TEST MATCHES
# BY CURRENT ALL BLACKS

| | Debut | Games | Starts | Wins | Tries | Conversions | Penalty goals | Dropped Goals | Points |
|---|---|---|---|---|---|---|---|---|---|
| Asafo Aumua | 2017 | 2 | - | 2 | - | - | - | - | - |
| Beauden Barrett | 2017 | 1 | 1 | 1 | - | 3 | - | - | 6 |
| Scott Barrett | 2017 | 2 | 1 | 2 | - | - | - | - | - |
| Dominic Bird | 2017 | 1 | 1 | 1 | - | - | - | - | - |
| Sam Cane | 2017 | 1 | - | 1 | 1 | - | - | - | 5 |
| Wyatt Crockett | 2009 | 1 | 1 | - | - | - | - | - | - |
| Mitchell Drummond | 2017 | 1 | - | 1 | - | - | - | - | - |
| Matt Duffie | 2017 | 2 | 1 | 2 | 1 | - | - | - | 5 |
| Vaea Fifita | 2017 | 1 | 1 | 1 | 1 | - | - | - | 5 |
| Jack Goodhue | 2017 | 1 | 1 | 1 | - | - | - | - | - |
| Kane Hames | 2017 | 1 | 1 | 1 | - | - | - | - | - |
| Nathan Harris | 2017 | 2 | 2 | 2 | 1 | - | - | - | 5 |
| David Havili | 2017 | 2 | 2 | 2 | - | - | - | - | - |
| Dillon Hunt | 2017 | 1 | - | 1 | - | - | - | - | - |
| Akira Ioane | 2017 | 1 | - | 1 | - | - | - | - | - |
| Jerome Kaino | 2004 | 2 | 2 | 2 | 1 | - | - | - | 5 |
| Tawera Kerr-Barlow | 2017 | 2 | 1 | 2 | - | - | - | - | - |
| Ngani Laumape | 2017 | 2 | 2 | 2 | 2 | - | - | - | 10 |
| Anton Lienert-Brown | 2017 | 1 | 1 | 1 | - | - | - | - | - |
| Atu Moli | 2017 | 1 | - | 1 | - | - | - | - | - |
| Richie Mo'unga | 2017 | 1 | - | 1 | - | 1 | - | - | 2 |
| Waisake Naholo | 2017 | 1 | 1 | 1 | - | - | - | - | - |
| TJ Perenara | 2017 | 1 | 1 | 1 | 1 | - | - | - | 5 |
| Tim Perry | 2017 | 2 | 1 | 2 | - | - | - | - | - |
| Kieran Read | 2008 | 1 | - | 1 | - | - | - | - | - |
| Luke Romano | 2017 | 1 | 1 | 1 | - | - | - | - | - |
| Ardie Savea | 2017 | 2 | 2 | 2 | - | - | - | - | - |
| Ben Smith | 2009 | 1 | 1 | - | 1 | - | - | - | 5 |
| Lima Sopoaga | 2017 | 2 | 1 | 2 | - | 3 | - | - | 6 |
| Liam Squire | 2017 | 1 | 1 | 1 | 1 | - | - | - | 5 |
| Seta Tamanivalu | 2017 | 2 | 2 | 2 | - | - | - | - | - |
| Jeffrey To'omaga-Allen | 2017 | 2 | 1 | 2 | - | - | - | - | - |
| Patrick Tuipulotu | 2017 | 2 | 1 | 2 | 1 | - | - | - | 5 |
| Ofa Tu'ungafasi | 2017 | 2 | 1 | 2 | - | - | - | - | - |
| Luke Whitelock | 2017 | 1 | 1 | 1 | - | - | - | - | - |

# SAMOA, BRITISH AND IRISH LIONS IN NEW ZEALAND, INVESTEC RUGBY CHAMPIONSHIP AND BLEDISLOE CUP

| | Franchise | Date of Birth | Height | Weight | Tests at 1/1/17 |
|---|---|---|---|---|---|
| B.J. (Beauden) Barrett | Hurricanes | 27/5/91 | 1.87 | 91 | 49 |
| J.M. (Jordie) Barrett | Hurricanes | 15/2/97 | 1.95 | 96 | – |
| S.K. (Scott) Barrett | Crusaders | 20/11/93 | 1.97 | 112 | 4 |
| S.J. (Sam) Cane | Chiefs | 13/1/92 | 1.89 | 109 | 40 |
| D.S. (Dane) Coles | Hurricanes | 10/12/86 | 1.84 | 112 | 49 |
| W.W.V. (Wyatt) Crockett | Crusaders | 24/1/83 | 1.93 | 116 | 58 |
| R.S. (Ryan) Crotty | Crusaders | 23/9/88 | 1.81 | 94 | 26 |
| A.W. (Aaron) Cruden | Chiefs | 8/1/89 | 1.78 | 80 | 47 |
| I.J.A. (Israel) Dagg | Crusaders | 6/6/88 | 1.86 | 98 | 61 |
| C.C. (Charlie) Faumuina | Blues | 24/12/86 | 1.84 | 131 | 46 |
| M.F. (Malakai) Fekitoa | Highlanders | 10/5/92 | 1.87 | 99 | 23 |
| V.T.L. (Vaea) Fifita | Hurricanes | 17/6/92 | 1.84 | 113 | – |
| O.T. (Owen) Franks | Crusaders | 23/12/87 | 1.85 | 120 | 90 |
| K.S. (Kane) Hames | Chiefs | 28/8/88 | 1.80 | 113 | 1 |
| N.P. (Nathan) Harris | Chiefs | 8/3/92 | 1.86 | 110 | 4 |
| D.K. (David) Havili | Crusaders | 23/12/94 | 1.84 | 88 | – |
| R.E. (Rieko) Ioane | Blues | 18/3/97 | 1.89 | 102 | 2 |
| J. (Jerome) Kaino | Blues | 6/4/83 | 1.96 | 109 | 77 |
| T.N.J. (Tawera) Kerr-Barlow | Chiefs | 15/8/90 | 1.87 | 89 | 25 |
| N.E. (Nepo) Laulala | Chiefs | 6/11/91 | 1.84 | 116 | 4 |
| K.H. (Ngani) Laumape | Hurricanes | 24/4/93 | 1.69 | 107 | – |
| A.R. (Anton) Lienert-Brown | Chiefs | 15/4/95 | 1.87 | 103 | 9 |
| D.S. (Damian) McKenzie | Chiefs | 20/4/95 | 1.75 | 82 | 2 |
| N.R. (Nehe) Milner-Skudder | Hurricanes | 15/12/90 | 1.82 | 90 | 8 |
| J.P.T. (Joe) Moody | Crusaders | 18/9/89 | 1.88 | 120 | 24 |
| W.R. (Waisake) Naholo | Highlanders | 8/5/91 | 1.86 | 105 | 12 |
| T.T.R. (TJ) Perenara | Hurricanes | 23/1/92 | 1.84 | 90 | 29 |
| K.J. (Kieran) Read (capt) | Crusaders | 26/10/85 | 1.93 | 109 | 97 |
| B.A. (Brodie) Retallick | Chiefs | 31/5/91 | 2.04 | 123 | 60 |
| L. (Luke) Romano | Crusaders | 16/2/86 | 1.99 | 116 | 26 |
| A.S. (Ardie) Savea | Hurricanes | 14/10/93 | 1.88 | 103 | 12 |
| S.J. (Julian) Savea | Hurricanes | 7/8/90 | 1.92 | 108 | 52 |
| A.S. (Aaron) Smith | Highlanders | 21/11/88 | 1.71 | 83 | 58 |
| B.R. (Ben) Smith | Highlanders | 1/6/88 | 1.86 | 94 | 60 |
| L.Z. (Lima) Sopoaga | Highlanders | 3/2/91 | 1.75 | 92 | 6 |
| L.I.J. (Liam) Squire | Highlanders | 20/3/91 | 1.96 | 109 | 8 |
| C.J. (Codie) Taylor | Crusaders | 31/3/91 | 1.83 | 108 | 15 |
| M.B. (Matt) Todd | Crusaders | 14/4/88 | 1.85 | 104 | 8 |
| P.T. (Patrick) Tuipulotu | Blues | 23/1/93 | 1.98 | 125 | 12 |
| A.O.H.M. (Ofa) Tu'ungafasi | Blues | 19/4/92 | 1.95 | 122 | 4 |
| S.L. (Samuel) Whitelock | Crusaders | 12/10/88 | 2.02 | 122 | 84 |
| S. (Sonny Bill) Williams | Blues | 3/8/85 | 1.91 | 108 | 33 |

## SAMOA, BRITISH AND IRISH LIONS IN NEW ZEALAND, INVESTEC RUGBY CHAMPIONSHIP AND BLEDISLOE CUP 2017

### ALL BLACKS 2017

| | Samoa | B.I Lions 1 | B.I Lions 2 | B.I Lions 3 | Australia 1 | Australia 2 | Argentina 1 | South Africa 1 | Argentina 2 | South Africa 2 | Australia 3 | TOTALS |
|---|---|---|---|---|---|---|---|---|---|---|---|---|
| B. Smith | 15 | 15* | – | – | 14 | 14 | – | – | – | – | – | 4 |
| J. Barrett | s | – | – | 15 | – | – | – | – | – | – | – | 2 |
| McKenzie | – | – | – | – | 15* | 15 | 15 | 15 | 15 | 15 | 15 | 7 |
| Havili | – | – | – | – | – | – | – | – | s | s | s | 3 |
| Dagg | 14* | 14 | 15 | 14 | – | – | 14* | – | – | – | – | 5 |
| Naholo | – | – | 14* | – | – | – | – | – | 14 | – | 14 | 3 |
| J. Savea | 11 | – | – | 11* | – | – | – | – | – | – | – | 2 |
| Ioane | – | 11 | 11 | – | 11 | 11 | – | 11 | 11* | 11 | 11 | 8 |
| Milner-Skudder | – | – | – | – | – | – | 11 | 14* | – | 14* | – | 3 |
| Fekitoa | – | – | – | s | – | – | – | – | – | – | – | 1 |
| Lienert-Brown | 13 | s | 13 | 13 | s | s | 13 | s | 13 | – | s | 10 |
| Crotty | – | 13* | – | – | 13* | 13* | – | 13 | – | 13 | 13* | 6 |
| Williams | 12 | 12 | 12* | – | 12 | 12* | 12* | 12* | 12* | 12 | 12 | 10 |
| Laumape | – | – | s | 12* | – | – | s | – | s | – | – | 4 |
| B. Barrett | 10* | 10 | 10 | 10 | 10 | 10 | 10 | 10 | 10 | 10* | – | 10 |
| Cruden | – | s | s | s | – | – | – | – | – | – | – | 3 |
| Sopoaga | s | – | – | – | s | s | s | s | – | s | 10* | 7 |
| A. Smith | 9* | 9* | 9* | 9* | 9* | 9* | – | 9* | 9* | 9* | 9* | 10 |
| Perenara | s | s | s | s | s | s | 9* | s | s | – | s | 10 |
| Kerr-Barlow | – | – | – | – | – | – | s | – | – | s | – | 2 |
| Read | – | 8* | 8 | 8 | 8 | 8 | 8 | 8 | 8 | 8 | 8 | 10 |
| Cane | 7 | 7 | 7* | 7* | 7 | 7* | s | 7* | – | 7* | 7 | 10 |
| A. Savea | 8 | s | s | s | s | s | 7* | s | s | – | s | 10 |
| Todd | – | – | – | – | – | . | – | – | 7* | s | – | 2 |
| Kaino | 6* | 6* | 6* | 6* | – | – | – | – | – | – | – | 4 |
| Squire | – | – | – | – | 6* | 6 | – | 6* | – | 6 | 6* | 5 |
| Fifita | s | – | – | – | – | – | 6 | – | 6* | – | – | 3 |
| Whitelock | 5 | 5 | 5* | 5* | 5* | 5 | – | 5 | – | 4 | 4 | 9 |
| Retallick | 4* | 4 | 4 | 4 | 4 | 4 | 5 | 4 | – | – | – | 8 |
| S. Barrett | s | s | s | s | – | s | s | s | 5 | 5* | 5* | 10 |
| Romano | – | – | – | s | – | 4* | – | 4 | – | – | – | 3 |
| Tuipulotu | – | – | – | – | – | – | – | – | s | s | s | 3 |
| Hanks | 3* | 3* | 3* | 3* | 3* | – | – | – | – | – | – | 5 |
| Laulala | – | – | – | – | – | 3* | 3* | 3* | 3* | 3* | 3* | 6 |
| Faumuina | s | s | s | s | – | – | – | – | – | – | – | 4 |
| Tu'ungafasi | – | – | – | – | s | s | s | s | s | s | s | 7 |
| Moody | 1* | 1* | 1* | 1* | 1* | 1* | 1* | – | – | – | – | 7 |
| Hames | – | – | – | – | – | s | – | 1* | 1* | 1* | 1* | 5 |
| Crockett | s | s | s | s | s | – | s | s | s | s | s | 10 |
| Taylor | 2* | 2* | 2* | 2* | 2* | s | s | s | s | s | s | 11 |
| Harris | s | s | s | s | – | – | – | – | – | – | – | 5 |
| Coles | – | – | – | – | – | 2* | 2* | 2* | 2* | 2* | 2* | 6 |

## INDIVIDUAL SCORING

| | Tries | Con | PG | DG | Points | | Tries | Con | PG | DG | Points |
|---|---|---|---|---|---|---|---|---|---|---|---|
| B. Barrett | 5 | 34 | 14 | – | 135 | J. Barrett | 1 | – | – | – | 5 |
| Ioane | 8 | – | – | – | 40 | S. Barrett | 1 | – | – | – | 5 |
| Sopoaga | 1 | 8 | 4 | – | 33 | Cane | 1 | – | – | – | 5 |
| McKenzie | 4 | – | – | – | 20 | Havili | 1 | – | – | – | 5 |
| Crotty | 3 | – | – | – | 15 | Laumape | 1 | – | – | – | 5 |
| Milner-Skudder | 3 | – | – | – | 15 | Perenara | 1 | – | – | – | 5 |
| Taylor | 3 | – | – | – | 15 | Retallick | 1 | – | – | – | 5 |
| Dagg | 2 | – | – | – | 10 | J. Savea | 1 | – | – | – | 5 |
| Fifita | 2 | – | – | – | 10 | A.Smith | 1 | – | – | – | 5 |
| Lienert-Brown | 2 | – | – | – | 10 | Squire | 1 | – | – | – | 5 |
| Naholo | 2 | – | – | – | 10 | Tu'ungafasi | 1 | – | – | – | 5 |
| Read | 2 | – | – | – | 10 | | | | | | |
| A. Savea | 2 | – | – | – | 10 | **Totals** | **54** | **42** | **18** | **0** | **408** |
| B. Smith | 2 | – | – | – | 10 | | | | | | |
| Williams | 2 | – | – | – | 10 | *Opposition scored* | *21* | *14* | *20* | *1* | *196* |

**SAMOA, BRITISH AND IRISH LIONS IN NEW ZEALAND, INVESTEC RUGBY CHAMPIONSHIP AND BLEDISLOE CUP SCORING RECORD 2017**

| Date | Opponent | Location | Played 11 | Won 8 | Drawn 1 | Lost 2 | Points for 408 | | Points against 196 |
|---|---|---|---|---|---|---|---|---|---|
| | | | Score | Tries | | Con | PG | DG | Referee |
| June 16 | Samoa | Auckland | 78–0 | B. Barrett (2), A. Savea (2), Lienert-Brown, Williams, Dagg, J. Savea, Taylor, Fifita, Perenara, Cane | | B. Barrett (7), Sopoaga(2) | | | M. Rayral *France* |
| June 24 | B & I Lions | Auckland | 30–15 | Ioane (2), Taylor | | B. Barrett(3) | B. Barrett(3) | | J. Peype *South Africa* |
| July 1 | B & I Lions | Wellington | 21–24 | | | | B. Barrett (7) | | J. Garces *France* |
| July 8 | B & I Lions | Auckland | 15–15 | Laumape, J. Barrett | | B. Barrett | B. Barrett | | R. Poite *France* |
| August 19 | Australia | Sydney | 54–34 | Ioane (2), Crotty (2), Squire, Williams, McKenzie, B. Smith | | B. Barrett(7) | | | W. Barnes *England* |
| August 26 | Australia | Dunedin | 35–29 | B. Barrett (2), Ioane, A. Smith, B. Smith | | B. Barrett(5) | | | N. Owens *Wales* |
| September 9 | Argentina | New Plymouth | 39–22 | Milner-Skudder, Lienert-Brown, Dagg, Fifita, McKenzie, B. Barrett | | Sopoaga(3) | Sopoaga | | A. Gardner *Australia* |
| September 16 | South Africa | Albany | 57–0 | Milner-Skudder (2), Ioane, S. Barrett, Retallick, Tu'ungafasi, Sopoaga, Taylor | | B. Barrett(7) | B. Barrett | | N. Owens *Wales* |
| September 30 | Argentina | Buenos Aires | 36–10 | Read (2), McKenzie, Naholo, Havili | | B. Barrett(4) | B. Barrett | | J. Peyper *South Africa* |
| October 7 | South Africa | Cape Town | 25–24 | Crotty, Ioane, McKenzie | | Sopoaga(2) | B. Barrett, Sopoaga | | J. Garces *France* |
| October 21 | Australia | Brisbane | 18–23 | Naholo, Ioane | | Sopoaga | Sopoaga(2) | | W. Barnes *England* |

# NEW ZEALAND v SAMOA

| Test # 553 | Eden Park, Auckland | June 16, 2017 |
|---|---|---|

## Won by New Zealand 78–0

### NEW ZEALAND

Ben Smith(capt)

| Israel Dagg | Anton Lienert-Brown | Julian Savea |
|---|---|---|

Sonny Bill Williams

Beauden Barrett

Aaron Smith

Ardie Savea

| Sam Cane | Samuel Whitelock | Brodie Retallick | Jerome Kaino |
|---|---|---|---|
| Owen Franks | | Codie Taylor | Joe Moody |

| Viliamu Afatia | Manu Leiataua | Census Johnston |
|---|---|---|
| Falemiga Selesele | Fa'atiga Lemalu | Chris Vui | Piula Fa'asalele |

Faifili Levave

Kahn Fotuali'i(capt)

Tusi Pisi

Alapati Leiua

| Tim Nanai-Williams | Kieron Fonotia | Albert Nikoro |
|---|---|---|

Ah See Tuala

### SAMOA

**Reserves: New Zealand —** Scott Barrett (sub Whitelock 50m), Wyatt Crockett (sub Moody 50m), Charlie Faumuina (sub Franks 50m), TJ Perenara (sub A. Smith 56m), Vaea Fifita (sub Kaino 56m), Lima Sopoaga (sub B. Barrett 60m), Jordie Barrett (sub B. Smith 62m), Nathan Harris (sub Taylor 62m).

**Samoa —** Paul Alo Emile (sub Johnston 50m), Ken Pisi (sub Nikoro 56m), Alafoti Faosiliva (sub Fa'aselele 56m), Seilala Lam (sub Leiataua 59m), Taiasina Tuifua (sub Vui 59m), D'Angelo Leuila (sub T. Pisi 63m), Nephi Leatigaga (sub Afatia 68m), Dwayne Polataivao (sub Fotuali'i 73m).

**Referee:** Mathieu Raynal (*France*)  **Kick-off:** 8pm
**Assistant Referees:** Rohan Hoffmann (*Australia*)  **Attendance:** 26,129
Jordan Way (*Australia*)  **Conditions:** No wind, surface greasy
**TMO:** Ian Smith (*Australia*)

**Scorers:** *New Zealand:*  *Samoa:*
*Tries:* B. Barrett (2), A. Savea (2),
Lienert-Brown, Williams, Dagg,
J. Savea, Taylor, Fifita, Perenara, Cane
*Conversions:* B. Barrett (7), Sopoaga (2)

**Scoring:**
First half: 11m Lienert-Brown try, B. Barrett conversion 7–0, 29m B. Barrett try, B. Barrett conversion 14–0, 33m A. Savea try, B. Barrett conversion 21–0, 39m Williams try, B. Barrett conversion 28–0.

Second half: 44m Dagg try, B. Barrett conversion 35–0, 51m J. Savea try 40–0, 55m Taylor try, B. Barrett conversion 47–0, 58m B. Barrett try, B. Barrett conversion 54–0, 61m Fifita try, Sopoaga conversion 61–0, 71m Perenara try 66–0, 75m A. Savea try, Sopoaga conversion 73–0, 78m Cane try 78–0.

Vaea Fifita and Jordie Barrett made their debuts for the All Blacks.

Beauden, Scott and Jordie Barrett became the fourth trio of All Black brothers to play for the All Blacks. The Barretts were the first three brothers to all play in the same test match.

# NEW ZEALAND v BRITISH AND IRISH LIONS

Test # 554                    Eden Park, Auckland                    June 24, 2017

## Won by New Zealand 30–15

### *NEW ZEALAND*

Ben Smith

Israel Dagg                    Ryan Crotty                    Rieko Ioane

Sonny Bill Williams

Beauden Barrett

Aaron Smith

Kieran Read (capt)

Sam Cane          Samuel Whitelock    Brodie Retallick          Jerome Kaino

Owen Franks                    Codie Taylor                    Joe Moody

Mako Vunipola                    Jamie George                    Tadhg Furlong

Sean O'Brien          Alun Wyn Jones          George Kruis    Peter O'Mahony (capt)

Taulupe Faletau

Conor Murray

Owen Farrell

Ben Te'o

Elliot Daly                    Jonathan Davies                    Anthony Watson

Liam Williams

### *LIONS*

*Reserves: New Zealand —* Aaron Cruden (sub B. Smith 26m), Anton Lienert-Brown (sub Crotty 32m), Ardie Savea (sub Kaino 46m), Wyatt Crockett (sub Moody 53m), Charlie Faumuina(sub Franks 53m), TJ Perenara (sub A. Smith 56m), Nathan Harris (sub Taylor 66m), Scott Barrett (sub Read 76m, Savea to #8).

*Lions —* Maro Itoje (sub Wyn Jones 47m), Jack McGrath (sub Vunipola 51m), Sam Warburton (sub O'Brien 53m), Jonathan Sexton (sub Te'o 57m, Farrell to #12), Kyle Sinckler (sub Furlong 58m), Ken Owens (sub George 67m), Rhys Webb (sub Murray 67m), Leigh Halfpenny (sub Williams 70m).

*Referee:* Jaco Peyper (*South Africa*)                    *Kick-off:* 7.35pm
*Assistant Referees:* Romain Poite (*France*)          *Attendance:* 48,181
          Jerome Garces (*France*)          *Conditions:* Surface soft, some rain
*TMO:* George Ayoub (*Australia*)

Scorers:    New Zealand:                    Lions:
          *Tries:* Ioane (2), Taylor          *Tries:* O'Brien, Webb
          *Conversions:* B. Barrett (3),          *Conversion:* Farrell
          *Penalties:* B. Barrett (3),          *Penalty:* Farrell

*Scoring:* First half: 13m B. Barrett penalty goal 3–0, 17m Taylor try, B. Barrett conversion 10–0, 30m Farrell penalty goal 10–3, 33m B. Barrett penalty goal 13–3, 35m O'Brien try, 13–8.

Second half: 54m Ioane try, B. Barrett conversion 20–8, 62m B. Barrett penalty goal 23–8, 69m Ioane try, B. Barrett conversion 30–8, 82m Webb try, Farrell conversion 30–15.

# NEW ZEALAND v BRITISH AND IRISH LIONS

Test # 555          Westpac Stadium, Wellington          July 1, 2017

### Won by British and Irish Lions 24–21

## NEW ZEALAND

Israel Dagg

Waisake Naholo          Anton Lienert-Brown          Rieko Ioane

Sonny Bill Williams

Beauden Barrett

Aaron Smith

Kieran Read (capt)

Sam Cane          Samuel Whitelock     Brodie Retallick          Jerome Kaino

Owen Franks          Codie Taylor          Joe Moody

Mako Vunipola          Jamie George          Tadhg Furlong

Sean O'Brien          Alun Wyn Jones     Maro Itoje          Sam Warburton (capt)

Taulupe Faletau

Conor Murray

Jonathan Sexton

Owen Farrell

Elliot Daly          Jonathan Davies          Anthony Watson

Liam Williams

## LIONS

*Reserves: New Zealand* — Ngani Laumape (sub Kaino 25m), Wyatt Crockett (sub Moody 52m), Charlie Faumuina (sub Franks 52m), Aaron Cruden (sub Naholo 58m, Barrett to #15, Dagg to #14), Ardie Savea (sub Cane 63m), TJ Perenara (sub Smith 65m), Scott Barrett (sub Whitelock 72m), Nathan Harris (sub Taylor 78m).

*Lions* — Jack Nowell (temp sub Watson 25–30m), Courtney Lawes (sub Wyn Jones 58m), Kyle Sinckler (sub Furlong 62m), Jack McGrath (temp sub O'Brien 63–65m), Ken Owens, CJ Stander, Rhys Webb, Ben Te'o.

*Referee:* Jerome Garces (*France*)
*Assistant Referees:* Romain Poite (*France*)
               Jaco Peyper (*South Africa*)
*TMO:* George Ayoub (*Australia*)

*Kick-off:* 7.35pm
*Attendance:* 38,000
*Conditions:* Rain, no significant wind

*Scorers:*   New Zealand:
           Penalties: B. Barrett (7)

Lions:
*Tries:* Faletau, Murray
*Conversion:* Farrell
*Penalties:* Farrell (4)

*Scoring:* First half: 19m B. Barrett penalty goal 3–0, 23m Farrell penalty goal 3–3, 31m B. Barrett penalty goal 6–3, 33m Farrell penalty goal 6–6, 36m B. Barrett penalty goal 9–6, 41m Farrell penalty goal 9–9.

Second half: 47m B. Barrett penalty goal 12–9, 53m B. Barrett penalty goal 15–9, 57m B. Barrett penalty goal 18–9, 59m Faletau try 18–14, 66m B. Barrett penalty goal 21–14, 68m Murray try, Farrell conversion 21–21, 76m Farrell penalty goal 21–24.

Beauden Barrett is the first player to kick seven penalty goals against the Lions.
*Red card* — Sonny Bill Williams at 24m. Suspended for four weeks.
*Yellow card* — Mako Vunipola at 55m.
*Citing* — Sean O'Brien.

# NEW ZEALAND v BRITISH AND IRISH LIONS

Test # 556          Eden Park, Auckland          July 8, 2017

Match drawn 15–15

## NEW ZEALAND

Jordie Barrett

Israel Dagg          Anton Lienert-Brown          Julian Savea

Ngani Laumape

Beauden Barrett

Aaron Smith

Kieran Read (capt)

Sam Cane          Samuel Whitelock     Brodie Retallick          Jerome Kaino

Owen Franks          Codie Taylor          Joe Moody

Mako Vunipola          Jamie George          Tadhg Furlong

Sean O'Brien     Alun Wyn Jones     Maro Itoje     Sam Warburton (capt)

Taulupe Faletau

Conor Murray

Jonathan Sexton

Owen Farrell

Elliot Daly          Jonathan Davies          Anthony Watson

Liam Williams

## LIONS

*Reserves: New Zealand* — Wyatt Crockett (sub Moody 57m), Charlie Faumuina (sub Franks 57m), Ardie Savea (sub Cane 60m), Malakai Fekitoa (sub Laumape 66m), Nathan Harris (sub Taylor 72m), Aaron Cruden (sub J. Savea 72m, J. Barrett to wing, B. Barrett to Fullback), TJ Perenara (sub Smith 73m), Scott Barrett (sub Whitelock 77m).

*Lions* — CJ Stander (sub O'Brien 40m), Ben Te'o (temp sub Sexton 47–53m, sub Sexton 73m), Courtney Lawes (sub Wyn Jones 49m), Jack McGrath (sub Vunipola 61m), Kyle Sinckler (sub Furlong 60m), Rhys Webb (sub Murray 68m), Ken Owens (sub George 69m), Jack Nowell (sub Watson 69m).

*Referee:* Romain Poite (*France*)
*Assistant Referees:* Jerome Garces (*France*)
          Jaco Peyper (*South Africa*)
*TMO:* George Ayoub (*Australia*)

*Kick-off:* 7.35pm
*Attendance:* 36,000
*Conditions:* Clear following earlier heavy rain. Ground firm

*Scorers:*     New Zealand:
          *Tries:* Laumape, J. Barrett
          *Conversion:* B. Barrett
          *Penalty:* B. Barrett

Lions:
*Penalties:* Farrell (4), Daly

*Scoring:* First half: 14m Laumape try, B. Barrett conversion 7–0, 20m Farrell penalty goal 7–3, 32m Farrell penalty goal 7–6, 35m J. Barrett try 12–6.

Second half: 41m Daly penalty goal 12–9, 60m Farrell penalty goal 12–12, 67m B. Barrett penalty goal 15–12, 77m Farrell penalty goal 15–15.

This was the first test match that the All Blacks had three brothers on the field at the same time.
*Yellow card* — Jerome Kaino at 49m.

# INVESTEC RUGBY CHAMPIONSHIP
## NEW ZEALAND v AUSTRALIA
### *Bledisloe Cup*

Test # 557 Bledisloe Cup     ANZ Stadium, Sydney     August 19, 2017

#### Won by New Zealand 54–34

### *NEW ZEALAND*

Damian McKenzie

Ben Smith        Ryan Crotty        Rieko Ioane

Sonny Bill Williams

Beauden Barrett

Aaron Smith

Kieran Read (capt)

| Sam Cane | Samuel Whitelock   Brodie Retallick | Liam Squire |
|---|---|---|
| Owen Franks | Codie Taylor | Joe Moody |

| Scott Sio | Stephen Moore | Allan Ala'alatoa |
|---|---|---|
| Michael Hooper (capt) | Rory Arnold    Adam Coleman | Ned Hanigan |

Sean McMahon

Will Genia

Bernard Foley

Kurtley Beale

Curtis Rona        Samu Kerevi        Henry Speight

Israel Folau

### *AUSTRALIA*

*Reserves: New Zealand* — Ofa Tu'ungafasi (sub Franks 43m), Anton Lienert-Brown (sub Crotty 49m), Wyatt Crockett (sub Moody 50m), TJ Perenara (sub A. Smith 52m), Luke Romano (sub Whitelock 60m), Ardie Savea (sub Squire 62m), Moody (sub Crockett 64m), Lima Sopoaga (sub McKenzie 66m, Nathan Harris sub Taylor 66m).

*Australia* — Tevita Kuridrani (sub Kerevi 40m), Tatafu Polota-Nau (sub Moore 40m), Rob Simmons (sub Arnold 48m), Nick Phipps (sub Genia 49m), Sekope Kepu (sub Ala'alatoa 49m), Tom Robertson (sub Sio 60m), Lopeti Timani (sub McMahon 63m), Reece Hodge (sub Rona 67m).

*Referee:* Wayne Barnes (*England*)     *Kick-off:* 8pm
*Assistant Referees:* Nigel Owens (*Wales*)     *Attendance:* 54,836
      Andrew Brace (*Ireland*)     *Conditions:* Warm and windy, ground firm
*TMO:* Rowan Kitt (*England*)

*Scorers:*   **New Zealand:**                   **Australia:**
         *Tries:* Crotty (2), Ioane (2), Squire     *Tries:* Rona, Kuridrani,
         Williams, McKenzie, B. Smith        Beale, Folau
         *Conversions:* B. Barrett (7)         *Conversions:* Foley (4)
                                       *Penalties:* Foley (2)

*Scoring:* First half: 4m Foley penalty goal 0–3, 9m Squire try, Barrett conversion 7–3, 15m Foley penalty goal 7–6, 17m Ioane try 12–6, 20m Ioane try, Barrett conversion 19–6, 24m Crotty try, Barrett conversion 26–6, 33m Williams try, Barrett conversion 33–6, 40m Crotty try, Barrett conversion 40–6.

Second half: 42m McKenzie try, Barrett conversion 47–6, 47m Ben Smith try, Barrett conversion 54–6, 51m Rona try, Foley conversion 54–13, 54m Kuridrani try, Foley conversion 54–20, 61m Beale try, Foley conversion 54–27, 68m Folau try, Foley conversion 54–34.

This is the highest score the All Blacks have recorded against Australia.

# NEW ZEALAND v AUSTRALIA
*Bledisloe Cup*

Test # 558 · Forsyth Barr Stadium, Dunedin · August 26, 2017

Won by New Zealand 35–29

## *NEW ZEALAND*

Damian McKenzie

Ben Smith · Ryan Crotty · Rieko Ioane

Sonny Bill Williams

Beauden Barrett

Aaron Smith

Kieran Read (capt)

Sam Cane · Samuel Whitelock · Brodie Retallick · Liam Squire

Nepo Laulala · Dane Coles · Joe Moody

Scott Sio · Stephen Moore · Allan Ala'alatoa

Michael Hooper (capt) · Rory Arnold · Rob Simmons · Ned Hanigan

Sean McMahon

Will Genia

Bernard Foley

Kurtley Beale

Dane Haylett-Petty · Tevita Kuridrani · Henry Speight

Israel Folau

## *AUSTRALIA*

*Reserves: New Zealand* — Ardie Savea (sub Cane 11m), Anton Lienert-Brown (temp sub Crotty 27-39m, sub Williams 62m), Lima Sopoaga (temp sub B. Barrett 45-54m), Ofa Tu'ungafasi (sub Laulala 62m), Williams (sub Crotty 66m), TJ Perenara (sub A. Smith 66m), Codie Taylor (sub Coles 67m), Kane Hames (sub Moody 67m), Lima Sopoaga (sub Williams 73m), Scott Barrett (sub Squire 76m).

*Australia* — Tatafu Polota-Nau (sub Moore 38m), Sekope Kepu (sub Ala'alatoa 40m), Lopeti Timani (sub Hanigan 60m), Reece Hodge (sub Haylett-Petty 62m), Tom Robertson (sub Sio 63m), Izack Rodda (sub Simmons 63m), Nick Phipps, Curtis Rona.

*Referee:* Nigel Owens (*Wales*)  ·  *Kick-off:* 7.48pm
*Assistant Referees:* Wayne Barnes (*England*)  ·  *Attendance:* 27,085
Andrew Brace (*Ireland*)  ·  *Conditions:* Under cover, ground firm
*TMO:* Rowan Kitt (*England*)

*Scorers:*

**New Zealand:**
*Tries:* B. Barrett (2), Ioane, A. Smith, B. Smith
*Conversions:* B. Barrett (5)

**Australia:**
*Tries:* Folau Hooper, Foley, Genia, Beale
*Conversions:* Foley (2)

*Scoring:* First half: 24secs Folau try 0–5, 10m Hooper try, Foley conversion 0–12, 14m Foley try 0–17, 21m Ioane try, B. Barrett conversion 7–17, 40m A. Smith try, B. Barrett conversion 14–17.

*Second half:* 60m B. Barrett try, B. Barrett conversion 21–17, 66m Genia try 21–22, 70m B. Smith try, B. Barrett conversion 28–22, 75m Beale try, Foley conversion 28–29, 77m B. Barrett try, B. Barrett conversion 35–29.

# NEW ZEALAND v ARGENTINA

| Test # 559 | Yarrow Stadium, New Plymouth | September 9, 2017 |
|---|---|---|

### Won by New Zealand 39–22

## *NEW ZEALAND*

Damian McKenzie

| Israel Dagg | Anton Lienert-Brown | Nehe Milner-Skudder |
|---|---|---|

Sonny Bill Williams

Beauden Barrett

TJ Perenara

Kieran Read (capt)

| Ardie Savea | Brodie Retallick | Luke Romano | Vaea Fifita |
|---|---|---|---|
| Nepo Laulala | | Dane Coles | Joe Moody |

| Lucas Noguera | Agustin Creevy (capt) | Nahuel Chaparro |
|---|---|---|
| Javier Desio | Guido Petti    Matias Alemanno | Pablo Matera |

Benjamin Macome

Tomas Cubelli

Nicolas Sanchez

Jeronimo de la Fuente

| Emiliano Boffelli | Matias Moroni | Santiago Cordero |
|---|---|---|

Joaquin Tuculet

## *ARGENTINA*

**Reserves: New Zealand —** Sam Cane (sub Savea 42m), Lima Sopoaga (sub Dagg 49m), Scott Barrett (sub Romano 52m), Wyatt Crockett (sub Moody 64m), Tawera Kerr-Barlow (sub Perenara 64m), Ofa Tu'ungafasi (sub Laulala 67m), Codie Taylor (sub Coles 67m), Ngani Laumape (sub Williams 75m).

**Argentina —** Matias Orlando (temp sub Moroni 38m–40m), sub Cordero 67m), Marcos Kremer (sub Alemanno 60m), Tomas Lezana (sub Macome 60m), Julian Montoya (sub Creevy 62m), Enrique Pieretto (sub Chaparro 64m), Martin Landajo (sub Cubelli 64m), Santiago Iglesias (sub de la Fuente 69m), Garcia Botta (sub Noguera 69m).

| | |
|---|---|
| **Referee:** Angus Gardner (*Australia*) | **Kick-off:** 7.35pm |
| **Assistant Referees:** Nigel Owens (*Wales*) | **Attendance:** 22,118 |
| Matthew Carley (*England*) | **Conditions:** cold, ground soft, some rain |
| **TMO:** George Ayoub (*Australia*) | |

**Scorers:**

| New Zealand: | Australia: |
|---|---|
| *Tries:* Milner-Skudder, Lienert-Brown | *Try:* Sanchez |
| Dagg, Fifita, McKenzie, B. Barrett | *Penalties:* Sanchez (2), |
| *Conversions:* Sopoaga (3) | Boffelli (2) |
| *Penalty:* Sopoaga | *Conversion:* Sanchez |
| | *Dropped goal:* Sanchez |

**Scoring:** First half: 7m Milner-Skudder try 5–0, 13m Sanchez penalty goal 5–3, 17m Lienert-Brown try 10–3, 24m Boffelli penalty goal 10–6, 27m Sanchez dropped goal 10–9, 36m Dagg try 15–9, 40m Sanchez try, Sanchez conversion 15–16.

Second half: 42m Boffelli penalty goal 15–19, 49m Sanchez penalty goal 15–22, 50m Fifita try, Sopoaga conversion 22–22, 62m McKenzie try, Sopoaga conversion 29–22, 69m Sopoaga penalty goal 32–22, 77m B. Barrett try, Sopoaga conversion 39–22.

*Yellow card* — B. Barrett 43m.

All Blacks debut for Vaea Fifita.

The try scored by Damian McKenzie brought up 1000 points for the All Blacks scored against Argentina.

# NEW ZEALAND v SOUTH AFRICA

Test # 560      QBE Stadium, Albany      September 16, 2017

### Won by New Zealand 57–0

### *NEW ZEALAND*

Damian McKenzie

Nehe Milner-Skudder      Ryan Crotty      Rieko Ioane

Sonny Bill Williams

Beauden Barrett

Aaron Smith

Kieran Read (capt)

Sam Cane    Samuel Whitelock    Brodie Retallick    Liam Squire

Nepo Laulala      Dane Coles      Kane Hames

Tendai Mtawarira      Malcom Marx      Ruan Dreyer

Siya Kolisi    Eben Etzebeth (capt)    Franco Mostert    Jean-Luc du Preez

Uzair Cassiem

Francois Hougaard

Elton Jantjies

Jan Serfontein

Courtnall Skosan      Jesse Kriel      Raymond Rhule

Andries Coetzee

### *SOUTH AFRICA*

**Reserves: New Zealand —** Scott Barrett (sub Squire 27m), Wyatt Crockett (sub Hames 42m), Ofa Tu'ungafasi (sub Laulala 52m), Lima Sopoaga (sub Williams 53m), Anton Lienert-Brown (sub Milner Skudder 53m), TJ Perenara (sub Smith 57m), Sam Cane (sub Savea 57m), Codie Taylor (sub Coles 57m).

**South Africa —** Lood de Jager (sub Mostert 44m), Steven Kitshoff (sub Mtawarira 44m), Pieter-Steph du Toit (sub du Preez 44m), Trevor Nyakane (sub Dreyer 54m), Bongi Mbonambi (sub Marx 57m), Handre Pollard (sub Jantjies 57m), Rudy Paige (sub Hougaard 58m), Damian de Allende (sub Serfontein 69m).

**Referee:** Nigel Owens (*Wales*)      **Kick-off:** 7.35pm
**Assistant Referees:** Angus Gardner (*Australia*)      **Attendance:** 30,021
       Matthew Carley (*England*)      **Conditions:** Fine, cool
**TMO:** George Ayoub (*Australia*)

**Scorers:**    New Zealand:                        South Africa:
           *Tries:* Milner-Skudder (2), Ioane
           S. Barrett, Retallick, Tu'ungafasi,
           Sopoaga, Taylor
           *Conversions:* B. Barrett (7)
           *Penalty:* B. Barrett

**Scoring:** First half: 13m B. Barrett penalty goal 3–0, 16m Ioane try, B. Barrett conversion 10–0, 20m Milner-Skudder try, B. Barrett conversion 17–0, 33m S. Barrett try, B. Barrett conversion 24–0, 36m Retallick try, B. Barrett conversion 31–0.

Second half: 52m Milner-Skudder try 36–0, 63m Tu'ungafasi try, B. Barrett conversion 43–0, 73m Sopoaga try, Barrett conversion 50–0, 80m Taylor try, Barrett conversion 57–0.

This was the heaviest defeat ever for South Africa.
The seven conversions kicked by Beauden Barrett are the most by any player against South Africa.

# NEW ZEALAND v ARGENTINA

**Test # 561**     Estadio Velez Sarsfield, Buenos Aires     September 30, 2017

## Won by New Zealand 36–10

### NEW ZEALAND

Damian McKenzie

Waisake Naholo          Anton Lienert-Brown          Rieko Ioane

Sonny Bill Williams

Beauden Barrett

Aaron Smith

Kieran Read (capt)

Matt Todd          Scott Barrett     Luke Romano          Vaea Fifita

Nepo Laulala          Dane Coles          Kane Hames

Lucas Noguera          Agustin Creevy (capt)          Nahuel Chaparro

Tomas Lezana          Guido Petti     Tomas Lavanini          Pablo Matera

Juan Leguizamon

Tomas Cubelli

Nicolas Sanchez

Jeronimo de la Fuente

Emiliano Boffelli          Matias Orlando          Matias Moroni

Joaquin Tuculet

### ARGENTINA

**Reserves: New Zealand** — TJ Perenara (sub Smith 50m), Ofa Tu'ungafasi (sub Laulala 50m), Wyatt Crockett (sub Hames 54m), Codie Taylor (sub Coles 54m), Ngani Laumape (sub Williams 62m), Patrick Tuipulotu (sub Fifita 62m, S. Barrett to #6), Ardie Savea (sub Todd 67m), David Havili (sub Ioane 69m, McKenzie to #11).

**Argentina** — Martin Landajo (sub Cubelli 32m), Ramiro Herrera (sub Chaparro 43m), Javier Desio (sub Lezana 51m), Garcia Botta (sub Noguera 52m), Juan Hernandez (sub Sanchez 54m), Santiago Cordero (sub Orlando 57m), Julian Montoya (sub Creevy 59m), Marcos Kremer (sub Lavanini 60m).

**Referee:** Jaco Peyper (*South Africa*)
**Assistant Referees:** Mathieu Raynal (*France*)
Marius van der Westhuizen
(*South Africa*)
**TMO:** Marius Jonker (*South Africa*)

**Kick-off:** 7.45pm
**Attendance:** 30,140
**Conditions:** Surface good,
some cold rain

**Scorers:    New Zealand:**
*Tries:* Read (2), McKenzie,
Naholo, Havili
*Conversions:* B. Barrett (4)
*Penalty:* B. Barrett

**Argentina:**
*Try:* Leguizamon
*Conversion:* Sanchez
*Penalty:* Sanchez

**Scoring:** First half: 3m B. Barrett penalty goal 3–0, 4m Sanchez penalty goal 3–3, 6m Read try 8–3, 15m McKenzie try, B. Barrett conversion 15–3, 19m Naholo try, B. Barrett conversion 22–3, 26m Read try, B. Barrett conversion 29–3.

Second half: 53m Leguizamon try, Sanchez conversion 29–10, 79m Havili try, B. Barrett conversion 36–10.

*Yellow cards* — Todd 36m, Lavanini 21m, Read 50m, Herrera 67m.

All Black debut for David Havili.

# NEW ZEALAND v SOUTH AFRICA

Test # 562        Newlands, Cape Town        October 7, 2017

## Won by New Zealand 25–24

### NEW ZEALAND

Damian McKenzie

Nehe Milner-Skudder      Ryan Crotty      Rieko Ioane

Sonny Bill Williams

Beauden Barrett

Aaron Smith

Kieran Read (capt)

Sam Cane      Scott Barrett      Samuel Whitelock      Liam Squire

Nepo Laulala      Dane Coles      Kane Hames

Steven Kitshoff      Malcolm Marx      Ruan Dreyer

Siya Kolisi      Eben Etzebeth (capt)      Lood de Jager      Pieter-Steph du Toit

Francois Louw

Ross Cronje

Elton Jantjies

Jan Serfontein

Courtnall Skosan      Jesse Kriel      Dillyn Leyds

Andries Coetzee

### SOUTH AFRICA

*Reserves: New Zealand* — Lima Sopoaga (sub B. Barrett 33m), David Havili (sub Milner-Skudder 47m, McKenzie to #14), Codie Taylor (sub Coles 45m), Wyatt Crockett (sub Hames 45m), Ofa Tu'ungafasi (sub Laulala 45m), Matt Todd (sub Cane 47m), Tawera Kerr-Barlow (sub Smith 60m), Patrick Tuipulotu (sub S. Barrett 66m).

*South Africa* — Wilco Louw (sub Dreyer 47m), Handre Pollard (sub Jantjies 47m), Jean-Luc du Preez (sub F. Louw 47m), Francois Mostert (sub de Jager 47m), Damian de Allende (sub Serfontein 51m), Trevor Nyakane (sub Kitshoff 76m), Chiliboy Ralepelle, Rudy Paige.

*Referee:* Jerome Garces (*France*)      *Kick-off:* 5.05pm
*Assistant Referees:* Romain Poite (*France*)      *Attendance:* 47,342
                Shuhei Kubo (*Japan*)      *Conditions:* Good
*TMO:* Rowan Kitt (*England*)

*Scorers:*    *New Zealand:*                      *South Africa:*
          *Tries:* Crotty, Ioane, McKenzie          *Tries:* Cronje, du Preez, Marx
          *Conversions:* Sopoaga (2)              *Conversions:* Jantjies (2), Pollard
          *Penalties:* B. Barrett, Sopoaga            *Penalty:* Jantjies

*Scoring:* First half: 9m Jantjies penalty goal 0–3, 11m B. Barrett penalty goal 3–3, 32m Crotty try 8–3.

Second half: 44m Cronje try, Jantjies conversion 8–10, 59m Ioane try, Sopoaga conversion 15–10, 65m du Preez try, Pollard conversion 15–17, 69m McKenzie try, Sopoaga conversion 22–17, 76m Sopoaga penalty goal 25–17, 78m Marx try, Jantjies conversion 25–24.

*Red card* — de Allende 75m, reduced off field to a yellow card.
Because the ball was not kicked dead for ten minutes after normal halftime, the first half was played for 50 minutes.

# NEW ZEALAND v AUSTRALIA
## *Bledisloe Cup (Non Rugby Championship)*

**Test # 563**  Suncorp Stadium, Brisbane  October 21, 2017
### Won by Australia 23–18

### *NEW ZEALAND*

Damian McKenzie

| | | |
|---|---|---|
| Waisake Naholo | Ryan Crotty | Rieko Ioane |

Sonny Bill Williams

Lima Sopoaga

Aaron Smith

Kieran Read (capt)

| | | | |
|---|---|---|---|
| Sam Cane | Scott Barrett | Samuel Whitelock | Liam Squire |
| Nepo Laulala | Dane Coles | | Kane Hames |
| Scott Sio | Tatafu Polota-Nau | | Sekope Kepu |
| Michael Hooper (capt) | Adam Coleman | Rob Simmons | Jack Dempsey |

Sean McMahon

Will Genia

Bernard Foley

Kurtley Beale

| | | |
|---|---|---|
| Reece Hodge | Tevita Kuridrani | Marika Koroibete |

Israel Folau

### *AUSTRALIA*

***Reserves: New Zealand*** — David Havili (temp sub Ioane 22–30m, sub Sopoaga 60m, McKenzie to #10), Wyatt Crockett (sub Hames 37m), Ofa Tu'ungafasi (sub Laulala 50m), Codie Taylor (sub Coles 60m), TJ Perenara (sub Smith 64m), Patrick Tuipulotu (sub Barrett 64m), Anton Lienert-Brown (sub Crotty 69m), Ardie Savea (sub Squire 74m).

***Australia*** — Lukhan Tui (sub Simmons 42m), Allan Ala'alatoa (sub Kepu 60m), Stephen Moore (sub Polota-Nau 60m), Ned Hanigan (temp sub Hooper 60–65m, sub Dempsey 70m), Tom Robertson (sub Sio 64m), Samu Kerevi (sub Beale 69m), Nick Phipps (sub Genia 74m), Henry Speight.

***Referee:*** Wayne Barnes (*England*)
***Assistant Referees:*** Marius van der Westhuizen (*South Africa*)
Egon Seconds (*South Africa*)
***TMO:*** Marius Jonker (*South Africa*)

***Kick-off:*** 8pm
***Attendance:*** 45,107
***Conditions:*** Rain, ground very soft in places

***Scorers:*** **New Zealand:**
*Tries:* Naholo, Ioane,
*Conversion:* Sopoaga
*Penalties:* Sopoaga (2)

**Australia:**
*Tries:* Hodge, Folau, Koroibete
*Conversion:* Foley
*Penalties:* Hodge 2

***Scoring:*** First half: 7m Hodge try, Foley conversion 0–7, 13m Naholo try, Sopoaga conversion 7–7, 25m Sopoaga penalty goal 10–7, 30m Sopoaga penalty goal 13–7, 39m Folau try 13–12.

Second half: 56m Koroibete try 13–17, 64m Hodge penalty goal 13–20, 70m Ioane try 18–20, 78m Hodge penalty goal 18–23.

New Zealand retained the Bledisloe Cup 2–1.

# SOUTH AFRICA v ARGENTINA

Nelson Mandela Stadium, Port Elizabeth                    August 19, 2017
#### Won by South Africa 37–15

### SOUTH AFRICA

Andries Coetzee

Raymond Rhule          Jesse Kriel              Courtnall Skosan

Jan Serfontein

Elton Jantjies

Ross Cronje

Uzair Cassiem

Jaco Kriel      Eben Etzebeth (capt)    Franco Mostert          Siya Kolisi

Tendai Mtawarira              Malcolm Marx              Coenie Oosthuizen

Nahuel Chaparro          Agustin Creevy (capt)         Enrique Pieretto

Tomas Lezana        Guido Petti      Tomas Lavanini        Pablo Matera

Leonardo Senatore

Martin Landajo

Nicolas Sanchez

Jeronimo de la Fuente

Emiliano Boffelli              Matias Orlando              Ramiro Moyano

Joaquin Tuculet

### ARGENTINA

**Reserves: South Africa** — Steven Kitshoff (sub Mtawarira 56m), Pieter-Steph du Toit (sub Mostert 60m), Jean-Luc du Preez (sub Jaco Kriel 60m), Francois Hougaard (sub Cronje 63m), Bongi Mbonambi (sub Marx 73m), Trevor Nyakane (sub Oosthuizen 73m), Damian de Allende (sub Serfontein 73m), Curwin Bosch (sub Jantjies 76m).

**Argentina** — Javier Desio (sub Senatore 14m), Ramiro Herrera (sub Pieretto 54m), Tomas Cubelli (sub Landajo 57m), Juan Hernandez (sub Sanchez 54m), Matias Moroni (sub Orlando 56m), Julian Montoya (sub Creevy 64m), Lucas Noguera (sub Chaparro 67m), Marcos Kremer (sub Lavanini 69m).

**Referee:** Romain Poite (*France*)                    **Kick-off:** 5.05pm
**Assistant Referees:** Pascal Gauzere (*France*)       **Attendance:** 42,513
                        Nic Berry (*Australia*)          **Conditions:** Fine
**TMO:** Glenn Newman (*New Zealand*)

**Scorers:**  **South Africa:**                          **Argentina:**
         *Tries:* Skosan, Rhule, Kolisi, du Toit       *Tries:* Landajo, Boffelli
         *Conversions:* Jantjies (4)                    *Conversion:* Hernandez
         *Penalties:* Jantjies (3)                      *Penalty:* Sanchez

**Scoring:** First half: 12m Jantjies penalty goal 3–0, 20m Jantjies penalty goal 6–0, 32m Landajo try 6–5, 37m Skosan try, Jantjies conversion 13–5.

Second half: 46m Sanchez penalty goal 13–8, 48m Jantjies penalty goal 16–8, 52m Rhule try, Jantjies conversion 23–8, 59m Boffelli try, Hernandez conversion 23–15, 66m Kolisi try, Jantjies conversion 30–15, 72m du Toit try, Jantjies conversion 37–15.

# SOUTH AFRICA v ARGENTINA

**Ernesto Maltearena, Salta**                                    **August 26, 2017**

### Won by South Africa 41–23

### *SOUTH AFRICA*

Andries Coetzee

Raymond Rhule          Jesse Kriel                    Courtnall Skosan

Jan Serfontein

Elton Jantjies

Francois Hougaard

Uzair Cassiem

| Jaco Kriel | Eben Etzebeth (capt) | Franco Mostert | Siya Kolisi |
|---|---|---|---|
| Tendai Mtawarira | Malcolm Marx | | Coenie Oosthuizen |

| Lucas Noguera | Agustin Creevy (capt) | | Ramiro Herrera |
|---|---|---|---|
| Tomas Lezana | Matias Alemanno | Tomas Lavanini | Pablo Matera |

Juan Leguizamon

Tomas Cubelli

Juan Hernandez

Jeronimo de la Fuente

Emiliano Boffelli          Matias Orlando                Ramiro Moyano

Joaquin Tuculet

### *ARGENTINA*

**Reserves: South Africa** — Steven Kitshoff (sub Mtawarira 51m), Pieter-Steph du Toit (sub Mostert 51m), Jean-Luc du Preez (sub Cassiem 51m), Trevor Nyakane (sub Oosthuizen 54m), Rudy Paige (sub Hougaard 58m), Damian de Allende (sub Serfontein 72m), Bongi Mbonambi (sub Marx 77m), Curwin Bosch.

**Argentina** — Enrique Pieretto (sub Herrera 50m), Javier Desio (sub Lezana 50m), Julian Montoya (sub Creevy 57m), Nicolas Sanchez (sub Hernandez 57m), Marcos Kremer (sub Matera 58m), Martin Landajo (sub Cubelli 58m), Matias Moroni (sub Moyano 58m), Santiago Botta.

**Referee:** Pascal Gauzere *(France)*          **Kick-off:** 4.30pm
**Assistant Referees:** Romain Poite *(France)*          **Attendance:** 17,435
               Nic Berry *(Australia)*          **Conditions:** Fine
**TMO:** Glenn Newman *(New Zealand)*

**Scorers:**      *South Africa:*                              *Argentina*
          Tries: Kolisi (2), Jantjies, penalty try          Tries: Moyano, Moroni
          du Preez                                    Conversions: Hernandez,
          Conversions: Jantjies (4)                    Sanchez
          Penalties: Jantjies (2)                      Penalties: Boffelli (2), Hernandez

**Scoring:** First half: 3m Boffelli penalty goal 0–3, 20m Kolisi try, Jantjies conversion 7–3, 27m Jantjies penalty goal 10–3, 28m Moyano try, Hernandez conversion 10–10, 39m Jantjies try, Jantjies conversion 17–10.

Second half: 44m Hernandez penalty goal 17–13, 49m Kolisi try, Jantjies conversion 24–13, 57m penalty try 31–13, 59m Moroni try, Sanchez conversion 31–20, 61m Boffelli penalty goal 31–23, 72m Jantjies penalty goal 34–23, 78m du Preez try, Jantjies conversion 41–23.

*Red card* — Lavanini 57m.

*Yellow cards* — Lavanini 9m, Leguizamon 48m, Coetzee 59m.

# AUSTRALIA v SOUTH AFRICA

nib Stadium, Perth                                    September 9, 2017

## Match drawn 23–23

### *AUSTRALIA*

Israel Folau

Henry Speight          Tevita Kuridrani          Reece Hodge

Kurtley Beale

Bernard Foley

Will Genia

Sean McMahon

Michael Hooper (capt)     Adam Coleman     Rory Arnold     Ned Hanigan

Sekope Kepu          Tatafu Polota-Nau          Scott Sio

Tendai Mtawarira          Malcom Marx          Coenie Oosthuizen

Siya Kolisi     Eben Etzebeth (capt)     Pieter-Steph du Toit     Jaco Kriel

Uzair Cassiem

Ross Cronje

Elton Jantjies

Jan Serfontein

Courtnall Skosan          Jesse Kriel          Raymond Rhule

Andries Coetzee

### *SOUTH AFRICA*

*Reserves: Australia* — Jordan Uelese (temp sub Polota-Nau 17m–26m, sub 69m), Rob Simmons (sub Arnold 57m), Allan Ala'alatoa (sub Kepu 61m), Jack Dempsey (sub McMahon 61m), Tom Robertson (sub Sio 67m), Curtis Rona (sub Speight 67m), Nick Phipps (sub Genia 70m), Samu Kerevi (sub Kuridrani 75m).

*South Africa* — Steven Kitshoff (sub Mtawarira 54m), Lood de Jager (sub du Toit 65m), Francois Hougaard (sub Cronje 65m), Trevor Nyakane (temp sub Oosthuizen 69m–75m), Bongi Mbonambi, Jean-Luc du Preez, Handre Pollard, Damian de Allende.

*Referee:* Glen Jackson (*New Zealand*))          *Kick-off:* 6pm
*Assistant Referees:* John Lacey (*Ireland*)          *Attendance:* 17,528
          Paul Williams (*New Zealand*)     *Conditions:* Fine
*TMO:* Ben Skeen (*New Zealand*)

*Scorers:*     *Australia:*                         *South Africa:*
          *Tries:* Beale, Polota-Nau          *Tries:* Jesse Kriel, Marx
          *Conversions:* Foley (2)          *Conversions:* Jantjies (2)
          *Penalties:* Foley (3)               *Penalties:* Jantjies (3)

*Scoring:* First half: 3m Jantjies penalty goal 0–3, 7m Foley penalty goal 3–3, 24m Jesse Kriel try, Jantjies conversion 3–10, 26m Beale try, Foley conversion 10–10, 40m Foley penalty goal 13–10.

Second half: 46m Polota-Nau try, Foley conversion 20–10, 53m Jantjies penalty goal 20–13, 58m Marx try, Jantjies conversion 20–20, 67m Jantjies penalty goal 20–23, 69m Foley penalty goal 23–23.

# AUSTRALIA v ARGENTINA

GIO Stadium, Canberra                                         September 16, 2017

## Won by Australia 45–20

### *AUSTRALIA*

Israel Folau

Henry Speight            Tevita Kuridrani            Reece Hodge

Kurtley Beale

Bernard Foley

Will Genia

Sean McMahon

Michael Hooper (capt)    Adam Coleman      Rory Arnold      Ned Hanigan

Sekope Kepu              Tatafu Polota-Nau                  Scott Sio

Lucas Noguera            Agustin Creevy (capt)        Nahuel Chaparro

Javier Desio      Guido Petti      Matias Alemanno      Pablo Matera

Tomas Lezana

Martin Landajo

Nicolas Sanchez

Jeronimo de la Fuente

Ramiro Moyano            Matias Orlando            Matias Moroni

Emiliano Boffelli

### *ARGENTINA*

**Reserves:Australia —** Jordan Uelese (temp sub Polota-Nau 48–61m, sub 71m), Marika Koroibete (sub Speight 49m), Izack Rodda (sub Simmons 54m), Jack Dempsey (sub Hanigan 59m), Allan Ala'alatoa (sub Kepu 64m), Samu Kerevi (sub Kuridrani 64m), Tom Robertson (sub Sio 67m), Nick Phipps (sub Genia 71m).

**Argentina —** Manuel Montera (sub Moyano 40m), Tomas Cubelli (sub Landajo 61m), Julian Montoya (sub Creevy 61m), Juan Leguizamon (sub Matera 64m), Enrique Pieretto (sub Chaparro 64m), Marcos Kremer (sub Petti 69m), Chaparro (sub Desio 71m), Garcia Botta (sub Noguera 71m), Santiago Iglesias (sub de la Fuente 73m).

**Referee:** John Lacey (*Ireland*))                **Kick-off:** 8pm
**Assistant Referees:** Glen Jackson (*New Zealand*)    **Attendance:** 14,229
             Paul Williams (*New Zealand*)    **Conditions:** Fine, cold
**TMO:** Ben Skeen (*New Zealand*)

**Scorers:**   **Australia:**                          **Argentina:**
         *Tries:* Folau (2), Kepu, Genia,           *Tries:* Landajo, Moroni
         Phipps, Uelese
         *Conversions:* Foley (6)                   *Conversions:* Sanchez (2)
         *Penalties:* Foley                         *Penalties:* Sanchez (2)

**Scoring:** First half: 5m Foley penalty goal 3–0, 14m Sanchez penalty goal 3–3, 22m Landajo try, Sanchez conversion 3–10, 28m Folau try, Foley conversion 10–10, 35m Sanchez penalty goal 10–13.

Second half: 48m Kepu try, Foley conversion 17–13, 52m Folau try, Foley conversion 24–13, 71m Genia try, Foley conversion 31–13, 73m Phipps try, Foley conversion 38–13, 77m Moroni try, Sanchez conversion 38–20, 80m Uelese try, Foley conversion 45–20.

*Yellow Card* — Pieretto 69m.

# SOUTH AFRICA v AUSTRALIA

Toyota Stadium, Bloemfontein                                September 30, 2017

## Drawn 27–27

## *SOUTH AFRICA*

Andries Coetzee

Dillyn Leyds          Jesse Kriel          Courtnall Skosan

Jan Serfontein

Elton Jantjies

Ross Cronje

Uzair Cassiem

Francois Louw    Eben Etzebeth (capt)    Franco Mostert          Siya Kolisi

Tendai Mtawarira          Malcolm Marx          Ruan Dreyer

Scott Sio          Tatafu Polota-Nau          Sekope Kepu

Michael Hooper (capt)    Izack Rodda    Adam Coleman          Jack Dempsey

Sean McMahon

Will Genia

Bernard Foley

Kurtley Beale

Reece Hodge          Tevita Kuridrani          Marika Koroibete

Israel Folau

## *AUSTRALIA*

*Reserves: South Africa* — Jean-Luc du Preez (sub Cassiem 18m), Steven Kitsoff (sub Mtawarira 58m), Trevor Nyakane (sub Dreyer 58m), Pieter-Steph du Toit (sub Louw 65m), Damian de Allende (sub Serfontein 70m), Rudy Paige (sub Cronje 74m), Chiliboy Ralepelle, Handre Pollard.

*Australia* — Rob Simmons (sub Rodda 47m), Ned Hanigan (sub Dempsey 52m), Stephen Moore (sub Polota-Nau 61m), Allan Ala'alatoa (sub Kepu 61m), Lukhan Tui (sub Coleman 61m), Tom Robertson (sub Sio 61m), Samu Kerevi (sub Beale 74m), Nick Phipps (sub Genia 75m).

*Referee:* Ben O'Keeffe (*New Zealand*)          *Kick-off:* 5pm
*Assistant Referees:* Jerome Garces (*France*)          *Attendance:* 33,805
          Shuhei Kubo (*Japan*)          *Conditions:* Perfect
*TMO:* Rowan Kitt (*England*)

*Scorers:*      *South Africa:*                          *Australia:*
          *Tries:* Dreyer, Serfontein, Skosan          *Tries:* Koroibete (2), Folau
          *Conversions:* Jantjies (3)                *Conversions:* Foley (3)
          *Penalties:* Jantjies (2)                *Penalties:* Foley (2)

*Scoring:* First half: 10m Folau try, Foley conversion 0–7, 17m Dreyer try, Jantjies conversion 7–7, 21m Foley penalty goal 7–10, 25m Jantjies penalty goal 10–10, 34m Foley penalty goal 10–13.

Second half: 42m Serfontein try, Jantjies conversion 17–13, 45m Koroibete try, Foley conversion 17–20, 48m Skosan try, Jantjies conversion 24–20, 56m Koroibete try, Foley conversion 24–27, 69m Jantjies penalty goal 27–27.

# AUSTRALIA v ARGENTINA

Estadio Malvinas Argentinas, Mendoza      October 7, 2017

## Won by Australia 37–20

### *AUSTRALIA*

Israel Folau

Marika Koroibete      Tevita Kuridrani      Reece Hodge

Kurtley Beale

Bernard Foley

Will Genia

Sean McMahon

Michael Hooper (capt)   Adam Coleman   Izack Rodda   Jack Dempsey

Sekope Kepu      Tatafu Polota-Nau      Scott Sio

Lucas Noguera      Agustin Creevy (capt)      Nahuel Chaparro

Javier Desio      Marcos Kremer   Matias Alemanno   Pablo Matera

Tomas Lezana

Martin Landajo

Nicolas Sanchez

Santiago Iglesias

Emiliano Boffelli      Matias Orlando      Matias Moroni

Joaquin Tuculet

### *ARGENTINA*

**Reserves:** ***Australia*** — Allan Ala'alatoa (sub Kepu 53m), Rob Simmons (sub Rodda 54m), Lukhan Tui (sub McMahon 64m), Stephen Moore (sub Polota-Nau 64m), Tetera Faulkner (sub Sio 64m), Samu Kerevi (sub Beale 67m), Nick Phipps (sub Genia 73m), Henry Speight (sub Koroibete 73m).

***Argentina*** — Enrique Pieretto (sub Chaparro 40m), Leonardo Senatore (sub Desio 54m), Benjamin Macome (sub Lezana 58m), Santiago Cordero (sub Tuculet 59m), Garcia Botta (sub Noguera 63m), Julian Montoya (sub Botta 67m), Juan Hernandez (sub Sanchez 69m), Gonzalo Bertranou (sub Landajo 73m).

*Referee:* Mathieu Raynal (*France*)      *Kick-off:* 7.30pm
*Assistant Referees:* Jaco Peyper (*South Africa*)      *Attendance:* 30,256
      Marius van der Westhiuzen      *Conditions:* Fine
      (*South Africa*)
*TMO:* Marius Jonker (*South Africa*)

*Scorers:*   **Australia:**      **Argentina:**
      *Tries:* Hodge(2), Koroibete, Foley   *Tries:* Alemanno, Iglesias
      Genia      *Conversions:* Sanchez (2)
      *Conversions:* Foley (3)      *Penalties:* Sanchez (2)
      *Penalties:* Foley (2)

**Scoring:** First half: 15m Foley penalty goal 3–0, 19m Koroibete try 8–0, 24m Alemanno try, Sanchez conversion 8–7, 29m Sanchez penalty goal 8–10, 33m Hodge try 13–10, 37m Sanchez penalty goal 13–13.

Second half: 51m Foley try, Foley conversion 20–13, 57m Iglesias try, Sanchez conversion 20–20, 60m Genia try, Foley conversion 27–20, 70m Foley penalty goal 30–20, 76m Hodge try, Foley conversion 37–20.

*Yellow Card* — Kremer 69m.

# INVESTEC RUGBY CHAMPIONSHIP

## Results

| | | | | | | |
|---|---|---|---|---|---|---|
| August 19 | New Zealand | 54 | Australia | 34 | at Sydney |
| August 19 | South Africa | 37 | Argentina | 15 | at Port Elizabeth |
| August 26 | New Zealand | 35 | Australia | 29 | at Dunedin |
| August 26 | South Africa | 41 | Argentina | 23 | at Salta |
| September 9 | New Zealand | 39 | Argentina | 22 | at New Plymouth |
| September 9 | Australia | 23 | South Africa | 23 | at Perth |
| September 16 | New Zealand | 57 | South Africa | 0 | at Albany |
| September 16 | Australia | 45 | Argentina | 20 | at Canberra |
| September 30 | South Africa | 27 | Australia | 27 | at Bloemfontein |
| September 30 | New Zealand | 36 | Argentina | 10 | at Buenos Aires |
| October 7 | New Zealand | 25 | South Africa | 24 | at Cape Town |
| October 7 | Australia | 37 | Argentina | 20 | at Mendoza |

## Final Standings

| Team | P | W | D | L | For | Against | Bonus | Total |
|---|---|---|---|---|---|---|---|---|
| New Zealand | 6 | 6 | – | – | 246 | 119 | 4 | 28 |
| Australia | 6 | 2 | 2 | 2 | 195 | 179 | 3 | 15 |
| South Africa | 6 | 2 | 2 | 2 | 152 | 170 | 2 | 14 |
| Argentina | 6 | – | – | 6 | 110 | 235 | – | 0 |

## Scoring Distribution

| Team | FOR | | | | | AGAINST | | | | |
|---|---|---|---|---|---|---|---|---|---|---|
| | T | C | PG | DG | Pts | T | C | PG | DG | Pts |
| New Zealand | 35 | 28 | 5 | – | 246 | 14 | 11 | 8 | 1 | 119 |
| Australia | 25 | 20 | 10 | – | 195 | 22 | 21 | 9 | – | 179 |
| South Africa | 17[t] | 16 | 11 | – | 152 | 20 | 17 | 12 | – | 170 |
| Argentina | 10 | 9 | 13 | 1 | 110 | 31[t] | 24 | 10 | – | 235 |
| **TOTALS** | **87** | **73** | **39** | **1** | **703** | **87** | **73** | **39** | **1** | **703** |

[t] *denotes penalty try*

# BRITISH AND IRISH LIONS IN NEW ZEALAND 2017

| Player | Country | Date of Birth | Height | Weight |
|---|---|---|---|---|
| R.D. (Rory) Best | Ireland | 15/8/82 | 1.80 | 106 |
| D.R. (Dan) Biggar | Wales | 16/10/89 | 1.85 | 93 |
| D.R. (Dan) Cole | England | 9/5/87 | 1.89 | 120 |
| K.D.V. (Kristian) Dacey | Wales | 25/7/89 | 1.88 | 119 |
| E.F. (Elliot) Daly | England | 8/10/92 | 1.82 | 97 |
| D.G. (Gareth) Davies | Wales | 18/8/90 | 1.78 | 85 |
| J.J.V. (Jonathan)Davies | Wales | 5/4/88 | 1.86 | 103 |
| A.M.E. (Allan) Dell | Scotland | 16/3/92 | 1.86 | 106 |
| T.T. (Taulupe) Faletau | Wales | 12/11/90 | 1.92 | 109 |
| O.A. (Owen) Farrell | England | 24/9/91 | 1.86 | 93 |
| T.W. (Tomas) Francis | Wales | 27/4/92 | 1.86 | 129 |
| T. (Tadhg) Furlong | Ireland | 14/11/92 | 1.85 | 123 |
| J.E. (Jamie) George | England | 22/10/90 | 1.83 | 110 |
| S.L. (Leigh) Halfpenny | Wales | 22/12/88 | 1.78 | 87 |
| J.A.W. (James) Haskell | England | 2/4/85 | 1.93 | 120 |
| W.I. (Iain) Henderson | Ireland | 21/2/92 | 2.00 | 118 |
| R. (Robbie) Henshaw | Ireland | 12/6/93 | 1.90 | 102 |
| C.L. (Cory) Hill | Wales | 10/2/92 | 1.93 | 114 |
| S.W. (Stuart) Hogg | Scotland | 24/6/92 | 1.80 | 100 |
| O.M. (Maro) Itoje | England | 28/10/94 | 1.95 | 117 |
| A.W. (Alun) Wyn Jones | Wales | 19/9/85 | 1.98 | 118 |
| J.B.A. (Jonathan) Joseph | England | 21/5/91 | 1.83 | 95 |
| G.E.J. (George) Kruis | England | 22/2/90 | 1.98 | 117 |
| G.D. (Greig) Laidlaw | Scotland | 12/10/85 | 1.75 | 80 |
| C.L. (Courtney) Lawes | England | 23/2/89 | 2.01 | 115 |
| J.W.G. (Joe) Marler | England | 7/7/90 | 1.83 | 114 |
| J.C. (Jack) McGrath | Ireland | 11/10/89 | 1.82 | 120 |
| C.R. (Ross) Moriarty | Wales | 18/4/94 | 1.90 | 106 |
| G.C. (Conor) Murray | Ireland | 20/4/89 | 1.88 | 94 |
| G.P. (George) North | Wales | 13/4/92 | 1.93 | 108 |
| J.T. (Jack) Nowell | England | 11/4/93 | 1.80 | 98 |
| S.K. (Sean) O'Brien | Ireland | 14/2/87 | 1.87 | 108 |
| P.J. (Peter) O'Mahony | Ireland | 17/9/89 | 1.91 | 108 |
| K.J. (Ken) Owens | Wales | 3/1/87 | 1.84 | 108 |
| J.B. (Jared) Payne | Ireland | 13/10/85 | 1.83 | 98 |
| F.A. (Finn) Russell | Scotland | 23/9/92 | 1.83 | 91 |
| J.J. (Jonathan) Sexton | Ireland | 11/7/85 | 1.88 | 93 |
| T.S.P. (Tommy) Seymour | Scotland | 1/7/88 | 1.83 | 94 |
| B.J. (Ben) Te'o | England | 27/1/87 | 1.88 | 106 |
| K.N.J.S. (Kyle) Sinckler | England | 30/3/93 | 1.80 | 122 |
| C.J. (Christiaan) Stander | Ireland | 5/4/90 | 1.89 | 115 |
| J.C. (Justin) Tipuric | Wales | 6/8/89 | 1.88 | 101 |
| M.W.W.N.A. (Mako) Vunipola | England | 13/1/91 | 1.83 | 121 |
| S.K. (Sam) Warburton (capt) | Wales | 5/10/88 | 1.90 | 103 |

| A.K.C. (Anthony) Watson | England | 26/2/94 | 1.84 | 94 |
| R. (Rhys) Webb | Wales | 9/12/88 | 1.83 | 92 |
| L.B. (Liam) Williams | Wales | 9/4/91 | 1.88 | 86 |

*Head Coach:* Warren Gatland (Wales)

*Coaches:* Steve Borthwick (England), Andy Farrell (England), Rob Howley (England), Neil Jenkins (Wales), Graham Rowntree (England)

*Manager:* John Spencer (England)

| BRITISH AND IRISH LIONS 2017 | Barbarians | Blues | Crusaders | Highlanders | Maori All Blacks | Chiefs | New Zealand | Hurricanes | New Zealand | New Zealand | TOTALS |
|---|---|---|---|---|---|---|---|---|---|---|---|
| Leigh Halfpenny | – | 15 | – | – | 15 | – | s | s | – | – | 4 |
| Stuart Hogg | 15 | – | 15 | – | – | – | – | – | – | – | 2 |
| Jack Nowell | – | 14 | – | 14 | – | 14 | – | 15 | s | s | 6 |
| Anthony Watson | 14 | – | s | – | 14 | – | 14 | – | 14 | 14 | 6 |
| Liam Williams | – | s | 11 | – | – | 15 | 15 | – | 15 | 15 | 6 |
| George North | – | – | 14 | – | 11 | – | – | 11 | – | – | 3 |
| Tommy Seymour | 11 | – | – | 11 | – | s | – | 14 | – | – | 4 |
| Elliot Daly | – | 11 | – | s | s | 11 | 11 | – | 11 | 11 | 7 |
| Jared Payne | – | 13 | – | 15 | – | 13 | – | – | – | – | 3 |
| Jonathan Davies | – | – | 13 | – | 13 | – | 13 | – | 13 | 13 | 5 |
| Jonathan Joseph | 13 | – | – | 13 | – | – | – | 13 | – | – | 3 |
| Robbie Henshaw | – | 12 | – | 12 | – | 12 | – | 12 | – | – | 4 |
| Ben Te'o | 12 | – | 12 | – | 12 | – | 12 | – | – | s | 5 |
| Dan Biggar | – | 10 | – | 10 | s | 10 | – | 10 | – | – | 5 |
| Owen Farrell | s | – | 10 | s | – | – | 10 | – | 12 | 12 | 6 |
| Jonathan Sexton | 10 | s | s | – | 10 | – | s | – | 10 | 10 | 7 |
| Greig Laidlaw | 9 | s | – | s | s | 9 | – | 9 | – | – | 6 |
| Conor Murray | – | – | 9 | – | 9 | – | 9 | – | 9 | 9 | 5 |
| Rhys Webb | s | 9 | – | 9 | – | – | s | – | – | s | 5 |
| Finn Russell | – | – | – | – | – | – | – | s | – | – | 1 |
| Taulupe Faletau | 8 | – | 8 | – | 8 | – | 8 | – | 8 | 8 | 6 |
| CJ Stander | – | 8 | s | 8 | – | 8 | – | 8 | – | s | 6 |
| James Haskell | – | 6 | – | 6 | – | 6 | – | 6 | – | – | 4 |
| Sam Warburton | 7 | – | – | 7 | s | – | s | – | 6 | 6 | 6 |
| Sean O'Brien | – | – | 7 | – | 7 | – | 7 | – | 7 | 7 | 5 |
| Peter O'Mahony | – | s | – | – | 6 | – | 6 | – | – | – | 3 |
| Ross Moriarty | 6 | – | 6 | – | – | – | – | – | – | – | 2 |
| Justin Tipuric | s | 7 | – | s | – | 7 | – | 7 | – | – | 5 |
| Maro Itoje | – | 4 | s | – | 4 | – | s | – | 4 | 4 | 6 |
| Iain Henderson | 5 | s | – | 5 | s | 4 | – | 4 | – | – | 6 |
| Alun Wyn Jones | 4 | – | 4 | s | – | s | 4 | – | 5 | 5 | 7 |
| George Kruis | s | – | 5 | s | – | 5 | s | – | – | – | 5 |
| Courtney Lawes | – | 5 | – | 4 | – | 5 | – | 5 | s | s | 6 |
| Dan Cole | – | 3 | s | s | – | 3 | – | 3 | – | – | 5 |
| Tadhg Furlong | s | – | 3 | – | 3 | – | 3 | – | 3 | 3 | 6 |
| Jack McGrath | – | 1 | s | s | s | – | s | – | s | s | 6 |
| Joe Marler | 1 | s | – | 1 | – | 1 | – | 1 | – | – | 5 |
| Kyle Sinckler | 3 | s | – | 3 | s | – | s | – | s | s | 7 |
| Mako Vunipola | s | – | 1 | – | 1 | – | 1 | – | 1 | 1 | 6 |
| Rory Best | 2 | s | – | 2 | – | 2 | – | 2 | – | – | 5 |
| Jamie George | s | – | 2 | – | 2 | – | 2 | – | 2 | 2 | 6 |
| Ken Owens | – | 2 | s | s | s | – | s | – | – | s | 6 |
| Allan Dell | – | – | – | – | – | s | – | – | – | – | 1 |

## INDIVIDUAL SCORING

| | Tries | Con | PG | DG | Points |
|---|---|---|---|---|---|
| Farrell | – | 3 | 13 | – | 45 |
| Biggar | – | 7 | 7 | – | 35 |
| Halfpenny | – | 2 | 9 | – | 31 |
| Seymour | 3 | – | – | – | 15 |
| penalty tries | 2 | – | – | – | 14 |
| Nowell | 2 | – | – | – | 10 |
| Watson | 1 | – | – | – | 5 |
| North | 1 | – | – | – | 5 |
| Payne | 1 | – | – | – | 5 |
| Joseph | 1 | – | – | – | 5 |
| Murray | 1 | – | – | – | 5 |
| Webb | 1 | – | – | – | 5 |

| | Tries | Con | PG | DG | Points |
|---|---|---|---|---|---|
| Faletau | 1 | – | – | – | 5 |
| Stander | 1 | – | – | – | 5 |
| Warburton | 1 | – | – | – | 5 |
| O'Brien | 1 | – | – | – | 5 |
| Itoje | 1 | – | – | – | 5 |
| Daly | – | – | 1 | – | 3 |
| Laidlaw | – | – | 1 | – | 3 |
| Sexton | – | – | 1 | – | 3 |
| **Totals** | **18** | **12** | **32** | **0** | **214** |
| Opposition scored | 16 | 14 | 20 | 0 | 168 |

## BRITISH AND IRISH LIONS TEAM RECORD 2017

**Played 10 · Won 5 · Drawn 2 · Lost 3 · Points for 214 · Points against 168**

| Date | Opponent | Location | Score | Tries | Con | PG | DG | Referee |
|------|----------|----------|-------|-------|-----|----|----|---------|
| June 3 | Provincial Barbarians | Whangarei | 13–7 | Watson | Farrell | Sexton Laidlaw | | A. Gardner *Australia* |
| June 7 | Blues | Auckland | 16–22 | Stander | Halfpenny | Halfpenny (3) | | P. Gauzare *France* |
| June 10 | Crusaders | Christchurch | 12–3 | | | Farrell (4) | | M. Raynal *France* |
| June 13 | Highlanders | Dunedin | 22–23 | Joseph, Seymour, Warburton | Biggar (2) | Biggar | | A. Gardner *Australia* |
| June 17 | Maori All Blacks | Rotorua | 32–10 | penalty try Itoje | Halfpenny | Halfpenny (6) | | J. Peyer *South Africa* |
| June 20 | Chiefs | Hamilton | 34–6 | penalty try Nowell (2), Payne | Biggar (3) | Biggar (2) | | J. Garces *France* |
| June 24 | New Zealand | Auckland | 15–30 | O'Brien, Webb | Farrell | Farrell | | J. Peyer *South Africa* |
| June 27 | Hurricanes | Wellington | 31–31 | Seymour (2), North | Biggar (2) | Biggar (4) | | R. Poite *France* |
| July 1 | New Zealand | Wellington | 24–21 | Faletau, Murray | Farrell | Farrell (4) | | J. Garces *France* |
| July 8 | New Zealand | Auckland | 15–15 | | | Farrell (4) Daly | | R. Poite *France* |

# BRITISH AND IRISH LIONS
# v NEW ZEALAND PROVINCIAL BARBARIANS

**Toll Stadium, Whangarei**                                    **June 3, 2017**

## Won by Lions 13–7

### *LIONS*

Stuart Hogg

Anthony Watson     Jonathan Joseph     Tommy Seymour

Ben Te'o

Jonathan Sexton

Greig Laidlaw

Taulupe Faletau

Sam Warburton (capt)    Iain Henderson    Alun Wyn Jones    Ross Moriarty

Kyle Sinckler     Rory Best     Joe Marler

Oliver Jager     Sam Anderson-Heather (capt)     Aidan Ross

Lachlan Boshier    Keepa Mewett    Josh Goodhue    James Tucker

Mitchell Dunshea

Jack Stratton

Bryn Gatland

Dwayne Sweeney

Sevu Reece     Inga Finau     Sam Vaka

Luteru Laulala

### *BARBARIANS*

*Reserves: Lions* — Owen Farrell (sub Sexton 48m), Jamie George (sub Best 49m), Mako Vunipola (sub Marler 49m), Tadhg Furlong (sub Sinckler 49m), George Kruis (sub Moriarty 49m), Rhys Webb (sub Laidlaw 57m), Justin Tipuric (sub Warburton 65m), Elliot Daly.

*Barbarians* — Jonah Lowe (sub Finau 18m), Andrew Makalio (sub Anderson-Heather 40m), Matt Matich (sub Boshier 45m), Tolu Fahamokioa (sub Ross 49m), Richard Judd (sub Stratton 52m), Joe Webber (sub Gatland 57m), Marcel Renata (sub Jager 60m), Peter Rowe (sub Mewett 60m).

*Referee:* Angus Gardner (*Australia*)
*Assistant Referees:* Mike Fraser (*New Zealand*)
Brendon Pickerill
(*New Zealand*)
*TMO:* Aaron Paterson (*New Zealand*)

*Kick-off:* 7.35pm
*Attendance:* 19,951
*Conditions:* good considering
preceded by heavy rain

*Scorers:* **Lions:**
*Try:* Watson
*Conversion:* Farrell
*Penalties:* Sexton, Laidlaw

**Barbarians:**
*Try:* Anderson-Heather
*Conversion:* Gatland

*Scoring:* First half: 16m Sexton penalty goal 3–0, 22m Anderson Heather try, Gatland conversion 3–7.

Second half: 42m Laidlaw penalty goal 6–7, 51m Watson try, Farrell conversion 13–7.

The Barbarians were essentially a national section of provincial players with minimal Super Rugby experience.

# BRITISH AND IRISH LIONS v BLUES

**Eden Park, Auckland**                                        **June 7, 2017**

## Won by Blues 22–16

### LIONS

Leigh Halfpenny

Jack Nowell          Jared Payne          Elliot Daly

Robbie Henshaw

Dan Biggar

Rhys Webb

CJ Stander

Justin Tipuric     Courtney Lawes     Maro Itoje     James Haskell

Dan Cole        Ken Owens (capt)       Jack McGrath

Ofa Tu'ungafasi      James Parsons (capt)      Charlie Faumuina

Blake Gibson     Scott Scrafton     Gerard Cowley-Tuioti     Akira Ioane

Steven Luatua

Augustine Pulu

Stephen Perofeta

Sonny Bill Williams

Rieko Ioane         George Moala        Matt Duffie

Michael Collins

### BLUES

**Reserves: Lions** — Jonathan Sexton (sub Biggar 35m), Liam Williams (sub Payne 47m), Peter O'Mahony (sub Haskell 53m), Joe Marler (sub McGrath 53m), Kyle Sinckler (sub Cole 54m), Rory Best (sub Owens 68m), Iain Henderson (sub Lawes 74m), Greig Laidlaw (sub Webb 74m).

**Blues** — TJ Faiane (temp sub Duffie 41m – 40m\*, sub Moala 66m), Ihaia West (sub Perofeta 50m), Alex Hodgman (sub Tu'ungafasi 57m), Sione Mafileo (sub Faumuina 57m), Jimmy Tupou (sub Cowley-Tuioti 57m), Kara Pryor (sub Gibson 66m), Hame Faiva (sub Parsons 72m), Sam Nock (sub Pulu 72m).

**Referee:** Pascal Gauzere (*France*)      **Kick-off:** 7.35pm
**Assistant Referees:** Mathieu Raynal (*France*)      **Attendance:** 40,639
               Angus Gardner (*Australia*)      **Conditions:** Light rain, excellent
**TMO:** Marius Jonker (*South Africa*)      ground conditions

**Scorers:**    **Lions:**                         **Blues:**
            *Try:* Stander                  *Tries:* R. Ioane, Williams, West
            *Conversion:* Halfpenny        *Conversions:* Perofeta, West
            *Penalties:* Halfpenny (3)        *Penalty:* West

**Scoring:** First half: 6m R. Ioane try 0–5, 17m Stander try, Halfpenny conversion 7–5, 24m Halfpenny penalty goal 10–5, 42m Williams try, Perofeta conversion 10–12.

Second half: 52m West penalty goal 10–15, 65m Halfpenny penalty goal 13–15, 70m Halfpenny penalty goal 16–15, 73m West try, West conversion 16–22.

*Yellow card* — L. Williams 56m.

\*Duffie was replaced in the 41st minute of the first half and returned at the start of the second half.

# BRITISH AND IRISH LIONS v CRUSADERS

AMI Stadium, Christchurch                                      June 10, 2017

## Won by Lions 12–3

### *LIONS*

Stuart Hogg

George North              Jonathan Davies              Liam Williams

Ben Te'o

Owen Farrell

Conor Murray

Taulupe Faletau

Sean O'Brien        George Kruis        Alun Wyn-Jones (capt)        Peter O'Mahony

Tadhg Furlong              Jamie George              Mako Vunipola

Joe Moody              Codie Taylor              Owen Franks

Matt Todd        Samuel Whitelock (capt)        Luke Romano        Heiden Bedwell-Curtis

Jordan Taufua

Bryn Hall

Richie Mo'unga

David Havili

George Bridge              Jack Goodhue              Seta Tamanivalu

Israel Dagg

### *CRUSADERS*

*Reserves: Lions* — Anthony Watson (sub Hogg 19m), Jonathan Sexton (sub Davies 27m), CJ Stander (sub O'Brien 55m), Jack McGrath (sub Vunipola 61m), Maro Itoje (sub Kruis 61m), Ken Owens (sub George 65m), Dan Cole (sub Furlong 65m).

*Crusaders* — Wyatt Crockett (sub Moody 50m), Ben Funnell (sub Taylor 50m), Michael Ala'alatoa (sub Franks 50m), Quinten Strange (sub Romano 55m), Mitchell Drummond (sub Hall 61m), Jed Brown (sub Bedwell-Curtis 61m), Tim Bateman (sub Bridge 65m), Mitchell Hunt (sub Mo'unga 74m).

*Referee:* Mathieu Raynal (*France*)               *Kick-off:* 7.35pm
*Assistant Referees:* Pascal Gauzere (*France*)               *Attendance:* 20,500
               Angus Gardner (*Australia*)               *Conditions:* surface greasy
*TMO:* Marius Jonker (*South Africa*)

*Scorers:* **Lions:**                                            **Crusaders:**
               Penalties: Farrell (4)                              Penalty: Mo'unga

*Scoring:* First half: 12m Farrell penalty goal 3–0, 15m Farrell penalty goal 6–0, 24m Mo'unga penalty goal 6–3, 30m Farrell penalty goal 9–3.

Second half: 70m Farrell penalty goal 12–3.

# BRITISH AND IRISH LIONS v HIGHLANDERS
Forsyth Barr Stadium, Dunedin        June 13, 2017
## Won by Highlanders 23–22
### *LIONS*

Jared Payne

Jack Nowell      Jonathan Joseph      Tommy Seymour

Robbie Henshaw

Dan Biggar

Rhys Webb

CJ Stander

Sam Warburton (capt)     Iain Henderson     Courtney Lawes     James Haskell

Kyle Sinckler       Rory Best       Joe Marler

Daniel Lienert-Brown      Liam Coltman      Siate Tokolahi

Dillon Hunt     Jackson Hemopo     Alex Ainley     Gareth Evans

Luke Whitelock (capt)

Kayne Hammington

Lima Sopoaga

Tei Walden

Tevita Li      Malakai Fekitoa      Waisake Naholo

Richard Buckman

### *HIGHLANDERS*

*Reserves: Lions* — Ken Owens (temp sub Best 20–28m, sub Best 58m), Alun Wyn Jones (sub Lawes 26m), Greig Laidlaw (sub Webb 47m), Dan Cole (sub Sinckler 48m), Jack McGrath (sub Marler 54m), Eliot Daly (sub Payne 62m), Owen Farrell (sub Biggar 67m), Justin Tipuric (sub Warburton 67m).

*Highlanders* — Marty Banks (temp sub Fekitoa 10–16m, sub Sopoaga 54m), Josh Dickson (sub Ainley 54m), James Lentjes (sub Hunt 58m), Aki Seiuli (sub Lienert-Brown 58m), Siosiua Halanukonuka (sub Tokolahi 67m), Patrick Osborne (sub Li 67m), Greg Pleasants-Tate (sub Coltman 67m).

*Referee:* Angus Gardner (*Australia*)      *Kick-off:* 7.35pm
*Assistant Referees:* Pascal Gauzere (*France*)      *Attendance:* 26,920
          Mathieu Raynal (*France*)      *Conditions:* Excellent
*TMO:* Marius Jonker (*South Africa*)

*Scorers:*   **Lions:**                        **Highlanders:**
         *Tries:* Joseph, Seymour, Warburton      *Tries:* Naholo, Coltman
         *Conversions:* Biggar (2)               *Conversions:* Sopoaga, Banks
         *Penalty:* Biggar                   *Penalties:* Sopoaga (2), Banks

*Scoring:* First half: 4m Sopoaga penalty goal 3–0, 16m Biggar penalty goal 3–3, 25m Naholo try, Sopoaga conversion 10–3, 29m Joseph try, Biggar conversion 10–10.

Second half: 42m Seymour try 10–15, 49m Sopoaga penalty 13–15, 53m Warburton try, Biggar conversion 13–22, 59m Coltman try, Banks conversion 20–22, 73m Banks penalty goal 23–22.

# BRITISH AND IRISH LIONS v MAORI ALL BLACKS
**International Stadium, Rotorua**                                    **June 17, 2017**

## Won by Lions 32–10

### *LIONS*

Leigh Halfpenny

Anthony Watson      Jonathan Davies      George North

Ben Te'o

Jonathan Sexton

Conor Murray

Taulupe Faletau

Sean O'Brien      George Kruis      Maro Itoje      Peter O'Mahony (capt)

Tadhg Furlong      Jamie George      Mako Vunipola

Kane Hames      Ash Dixon (capt)      Ben May

Elliot Dixon      Joe Wheeler      Tom Franklin      Akira Ioane

Liam Messam

Tawera Kerr-Barlow

Damian McKenzie

Charlie Ngatai

Rieko Ioane      Matt Proctor      Nehe Milner-Skudder

James Lowe

### *MAORI ALL BLACKS*

**Reserves: Lions —** Iain Henderson (sub Kruis 58m), Jack McGrath (sub Vunipola 58m), Elliot Daly (sub North 62m), Sam Warburton (sub O'Mahony 62m), Ken Owens (sub George 64m), Kyle Sinckler (sub Furlong 64m), Greig Laidlaw (sub Murray 66m), Dan Biggar (sub Sexton 66m).

**Maori All Blacks —** Rob Thompson (sub Proctor 52m), Chris Eves (sub Hames 58m), Ihaia West (sub McKenzie 66m), Hika Elliot (sub A. Dixon 72m), Marcel Renata (sub May 72m), Kara Pryor (sub E. Dixon 72m), Leighton Price (sub Wheeler 72m), Bryn Hall (sub Kerr-Barlow 74m).

**Referee:** Jaco Peyper (*South Africa*)          **Kick-off:** 7.35pm
**Assistant Referees:** Jerome Garces (*France*)          **Attendance:** 28,177
          Romain Poite (*France*)          **Conditions:** Light rain, no wind surface greasy
**TMO:** Ian Smith (*Australia*)

**Scorers Lions:**                                        **Maori All Blacks:**
*Tries:* penalty try, Itoje                              *Try:* Messam
*Conversion:* Halfpenny                                  *Conversion:* McKenzie
*Penalties:* Halfpenny (6)                               *Penalty:* McKenzie

**Scoring:** First half: 4m Halfpenny penalty goal 3–0, 9m Halfpenny penalty goal 6–0, 11m Messam try, McKenzie conversion 6–7, 19m Halfpenny penalty goal 9–7, 21m McKenzie penalty goal 9–10, 32m Halfpenny penalty goal 12–10.

Second half: 43m Halfpenny penalty goal 15–10, 50m penalty try 22–10, 53m Itoje try, Halfpenny conversion 29–10, 68m Halfpenny penalty goal 32–10.

*Yellow card* — Kerr-Barlow 46m.

# BRITISH AND IRISH LIONS v CHIEFS

FMG Stadium, Hamilton                                                June 20, 2017

## Won by Lions 34–6

### *LIONS*

Liam Williams

Jack Nowell             Jared Payne             Elliot Daly

Robbie Henshaw

Dan Biggar

Greig Laidlaw

CJ Stander

Justin Tipuric      Iain Henderson      Courtney Lawes      James Haskell

Dan Cole             Rory Best (capt)             Joe Marler

Siegfried Fisi'ihoi             Liam Polwart             Nepo Laulala

Lachlan Boshier      Michael Allardice      Dominic Bird      Mitchell Brown

Tom Sanders

Finlay Christie

Stephen Donald (capt)

Johnny Fa'auli

Solomon Alaimalo      Tim Nanai-Williams             Toni Pulu

Shaun Stevenson

### *CHIEFS*

*Reserves: Lions* — Allan Dell (temp sub Haskell 13–23m), Alun Wyn Jones (sub Lawes 51m), Tommy Seymour (sub Daly 59m), Daly (sub Payne 76m), Kristian Dacey, Tomas Francis, Cory Hill, Gareth Davies, Finn Russell.

*Chiefs* — Chase Tiatia (sub Pulu 11m), Liam Messam (sub Sanders 55m), Jonathan Taumateine (sub Christie 57m), Hika Elliot (sub Polwart 60m), Mitch Karpik (sub Bird 64m), Aidan Ross (sub Fisi'ihoi 64m), Atu Moli (sub N. Laulala 64m), Luteru Laulala (sub Alaimalo 65m).

*Referee:* Jerome Garces (*France*)              *Kick-off:* 7.35pm
*Assistant Referees:* Jaco Peyper (*South Africa*)      *Attendance:* 29,974
                    Romain Poite (*France*)         *Conditions:* Good
*TMO:* Ian Smith (*Australia*)

*Scorers:*      *Lions:*                                    *Chiefs:*
            *Tries:* Nowell (2), Payne, penalty try      *Penalties:* Donald (2)
            *Conversions:* Biggar (3)
            *Penalties:* Biggar (2)

*Scoring:* First half: 9m Biggar penalty goal 3–0, 17m Biggar penalty goal 6–0, 20m Donald penalty goal 6–3, 24m Nowell try, Biggar conversion 13–3, 40m Donald penalty goal 13–6.

Second half: 53m penalty try 20–6, 58m Nowell try, Biggar conversion 27–6, 63m Payne try, Biggar conversion 34–6.

*Yellow cards* — Marler 11m, Brown 53m.

# BRITISH AND IRISH LIONS v HURRICANES

Westpac Stadium, Wellington                                        June 27, 2017

## Match drawn 31–31

### *LIONS*

Jack Nowell

Tommy Seymour          Jonathan Joseph                      George North

Robbie Henshaw

Dan Biggar

Greig Laidlaw

CJ Stander

Justin Tipuric          Iain Henderson      Courtney Lawes          James Haskell

Dan Cole                Rory Best (capt)                    Joe Marler

Ben May                 Ricky Riccitelli        Jeffery To'omaga-Allen

Callum Gibbins          Mark Abbott      Sam Lousi              Vaea Fifita

Brad Shields (capt)

Te Toiroa Tahuriorangi

Otere Black

Ngani Laumape

Julian Savea                Vince Aso                  Nehe Milner-Skudder

Jordie Barrett

### *HURRICANES*

*Reserves: Lions* — Leigh Halfpenny (sub Robbie Henshaw 20m), Finn Russell ( temp sub Biggar 43–47m), George Kruis (sub Lawes 53m), Kristian Dacey, Allan Dell, Tomas Francis, Cory Hill, Gareth Davies.

*Hurricanes* — Reed Prinsep (sub Shields 55m), Chris Eves (sub May 55m), Leni Apisai(sub Riccitelli 61m), Wes Goosen (sub Black 61m), Cory Jane (sub Savea 67m), Kemara Hauiti-Parapara (sub Tahuriorangi 67m), James Blackwell, Mike Kainga.

*Referee:* Romain Poite (*France*)
*Assistant Referees:* Jaco Peyper (*South Africa*)
               Jerome Garces (*France*)
*TMO:* George Ayoub (*Australia*)

*Kick-off:* 7.35pm
*Attendance:* 29,974
*Conditions:* Fine, cool, excellent surface

*Scorers:*   *Lions:*
        *Tries:* Seymour (2), North
        *Conversions:* Biggar (2)
        *Penalties:* Biggar (4)

  *Hurricanes:*
        *Tries:* Gibbins, Laumape, Goosen, Fifita
        *Conversions:* J. Barrett (4)
        *Penalty:* J. Barrett

*Scoring:* First half: 9m Biggar penalty goal 3–0, 17m Seymour try, Biggar conversion 10–0, 23m Biggar penalty goal 13–0, 27m Gibbins try, J. Barrett conversion 13–7, 31m Biggar penalty goal 16–7, 36m North try, Biggar conversion 23–7.

Second half: 41m Laumape try, J. Barrett conversion 23–14, 49m J. Barrett penalty goal 23–17, 51m Biggar penalty goal 26–17, 54m Seymour try 31–17, 66m Goosen try, J. Barrett conversion 31–24, 70m Fifita try, J. Barrett conversion 31–31.

*Yellow cards* — Tahuriorangi 51m, Henderson 65m.

Photo by Bruce Jarvis Photographic Services Ltd

## ALL BLACKS — 2017 AMERICAN EXPRESS PASIFIKA CHALLENGE (V SAMOA) AND DHL NEW ZEALAND LIONS SERIES

**BACK ROW:** S. Williams, J. Barrett, B. Retallick, L. Romano, S. Barrett, L. Squire, O. Tu'ungafasi, M. Cron (*Assistant Coach*). **FOURTH ROW:** P. Iversen (*Logistics Manager*), J. Hamilton (*Performance Analyst*), G. Duncan (*Muscle Therapist*), L. Coltman, J. Savea, V. Fifita, M. Todd, C. Taylor, J. Locke (*Media Manager*), J. Healy (*Performance Analysis Manager*), N. Gill (*S&C Coach*). **THIRD ROW:** G. Enoka (*Manager — Leadership*), A. Page (*Doctor*), J. Malcolm (*Assistant Media Manager*), A. Lienert-Brown, C. Faumuina, A. Savea, S. Cane, J. Moody, N. Harris, K. Darry (*Nutritionist*), P. Gallagher (*Physio*), D. Shand (*Manager — Business & Operations*). **SECOND ROW:** I. Foster (*Assistant Head Coach*), B. Thiel (*Team Services Manager*), L. Sopoaga, N. Laumape, T. Perenara, B. Barrett, J. Goodhue, W. Nabolo, R. Crotty, G. Fox (*Selector*), W. Smith (*Assistant Coach*). **FRONT ROW:** A. Cruden, O. Franks, J. Kaino, S. Whitelock, K. Read (*Captain*), S. Hansen (*Head Coach*), B. Smith, I. Dagg, W. Crockett, A. Smith. **INSETS:** D. Coles, T. Kerr-Barlow, A. Ioane, R. Ioane.

Photo by Bruce Jarvis Photographic Services Ltd

## ALL BLACKS

*Winners of the 2017 Investec Rugby Championship and Holders of the Bledisloe Cup*

**BACK ROW**: G. Enoka (*Manager — Leadership*), V. Fifita, S. Williams, L. Romano, S. Barrett, L. Squire, O. Tu'ungafasi, M. Cron (*Asst Coach*), J. Locke (*Media Manager*). **FOURTH ROW**: G. Duncan (*Muscle Therapist*), J. Hamilton (*Performance Analyst*), P. Iversen (*Logistics Manager*), D. Havili, D. Coles, R. Ioane, N. Laulala, J. Moody, C. Taylor, J. Healy (*Performance Analysis Manager*), N. Gill (*S&C Coach*). **THIRD ROW**: M. Anthony (*S&C Coach*), A. Page (*Doctor*), A. Lienert-Brown, T. Kerr-Barlow, A. Savea, S. Cane, N. Harris, N. Milner-Skudder, A. Moli (*Apprentice*), K. Darry (*Nutritionist*), D. Shand (*Manager — Business & Operations*). **SECOND ROW**: I. Foster (*Asst Head Coach*), B. Thiel (*Team Services Manager*), L. Sopoaga, N. Laumape, T. Perenara, B. Barrett, D. McKenzie, W. Naholo, R. Crotty, W. Smith (*Asst Coach*), P. Gallagher (*Physio*). **FRONT ROW**: I. Dagg, O. Franks, J. Kaino, S. Whitelock, K. Read (*Captain*), S. Hansen (*Head Coach*), B. Smith, B. Retallick, W. Crockett, A. Smith. **INSETS**: R. Riccitelli, J. To'omaga-Allen, P. Tuipulotu, G. Fox (*Selector*), K. Hames, M. Todd, A. Ioane

## ALL BLACKS — 2017 VISTA NORTHERN TOUR

*BACK ROW:* P. Iversen (*Logistics Manager*), G. Enoka (*Manager — Leadership*), V. Fifita, P. Tuipulotu, D. Bird, S. Barrett, M. Duffie, O. Tu'ungafasi, M. Cron (*Asst Coach*). *FOURTH ROW:* M. Anthony (*S&C Coach*), S. McLeod (*Assistant Coach*), J. To'omaga-Allen, R. Ioane, A. Savea, S. Tamanivalu, J. Goodhue, M. Todd, D. Hunt, T. Perry, N. Gill (*S&C Coach*). *THIRD ROW:* J. Hamilton (*Performance Analyst*), G. Duncan (*Muscle Therapist*), A. Moli, N. Laulala, N. Laumape, A. Lienert-Brown, D. Havili, C. Taylor, M. Drummond, D. Shand (*Manager — Business & Operations*), J. Locke (*Media Manager*). *SECOND ROW:* B. Thiel (*Team Services Manager*), I. Foster (*Asst Head Coach*), L. Sopoaga, A. Aumua, T. Perenara, D. McKenzie, T. Kerr-Barlow, K. Hames, W. Naholo, R. Mo'unga, K. Darry (*Nutritionist*), J. Healy (*Performance Analysis Manager*), P. Gallagher (*Physio*). *FRONT ROW:* L. Romano, S. Cane, S. Williams, J. Kaino, S. Whitelock, K. Read (*Captain*), S. Hansen (*Head Coach*), B. Barrett, D. Coles, W. Crockett, A. Smith, R. Crotty. *INSETS:* G. Fox (*Selector*), A. Page (*Doctor*), L. Squire, N. Harris, R. Ioane, L. Whitelock.

**BLACK FERNS — 2017 WOMEN'S RUGBY WORLD CUP CHAMPIONS**

*BACK ROW:* G. Keenan (*Asst Coach*), C. Gubb, C. McMenamin, R. Wood, C. Smith, A. Mata'u, A. Nelson, V. Subritzky-Nafatali, S. Goss, J. Tout (*S&C Coach*). *THIRD ROW:* D. Robinson (*Doctor*), H. Porter (*Campaign Manager*), A. Itunu, K. Brazier, C. Alley, P. Woodman, L-A. Ketu, I. Freeman (*Physio*), W. Clarke (*Asst Coach*). *SECOND ROW:* M. Keys (*Media Manager*), S. Talawadua, K. Sue, S. Waaka, Te K. Ngata-Aerengamate, T. Fitzpatrick, H. Tubic, T. Natua, L. Cournane (*Manager*), M. Ray (*Analyst*). *FRONT ROW:* E. Blackwell, R. Wickliffe, K. Cocksedge, G. Moore (*Head Coach*), F. Fa'amausili (*Captain*), S. Winiata, L. Irunu, C. Hohepa, A. Savage.

## KING COUNTRY RAMS

**BACK ROW:** M. Horrocks, A. Dunster, A. Wise. **THIRD ROW:** P. Olsen (*Asst Coach*), R. Alabaster, C. Carmichael, O. Kay, N. Neustroski, J. Williams, A. Thrupp. **SECOND ROW:** D. Alofa (*Head Coach*), C. Hancock (*Physio*), N. Smith, S. Turner, A. Morris, B. Brown, S. Burr, P. Ratima (*Trainer*), N. Clarke (*Manager*). **FRONT ROW:** T. Tufala, A. Mathewson, K. Rollinson, J. Dais (*Co-captain*), R. Sherson (*Co-captain*), R. Macdonald, D. Church, S. Wanden. **ABSENT:** B. Taylor, S. McCarthy, S. Vosaki.

## TARANAKI BULLS
*2017 Ranfurly Shield Holders*

**BACK ROW:** M. Wills (*President*), S. Perofeta, M. Mataele, T. Florence, S. Wainui, L. Boshier, C. Matoe, A. Hay (*S&C Coach*), O. Curran (*Asst S&C Coach*). **FOURTH ROW:** J. Hooper (*Scrum Coach*), L. Thompson (*Chairman*), D. Maka, M. Kainga, J. Proffit, A. Sorovaki, T. Halafihi, A. Wyrill, D. Neilson (*Analyst*), S. Smith (*Doctor*). **THIRD ROW:** P. Riley (*Doctor*), P. Tito (*Asst Coach*), P-G. Sowakula, B. Tucker, K. Thompson, F. Hoeata, J. Barrett, D. O'Donnell, D. Lilley (*Skills Coach*), M. Collins (*CEO*). **SECOND ROW:** D. Spicer (*Manager*), A. Walsh (*Physio*), L. Holland (*PDM*), J. Fa'auli, Te T. Tahuriorangi, R. Riccitelli, R. O'Neill, L. Crowley, B. Waaka, A. Larkin (*Physio*), R. Vaughan (*Sports Psychologist*), J. Hamilton (*Asst Analyst*). **FRONT ROW:** C. Cooper (*Coach*), K. O'Donnell, S. Lea, M. McKenzie, A. Ta'avao (*Co-captain*), C. Ngatai (*Co-captain*), L. Price (*Co-captain*), S. Tamanivalu, M. Graham, L. Power, W. Rickards (*Asst Coach*). **ABSENT:** L. Vaeno, B. Barrett, S. Barrett, W. Naholo, J. Ormond, M. Torrance-Read, D. Waite, B. Slater, W. Lahmert, A. Lewis.

## BAY OF PLENTY VOLCANIX

*Winners of the Farah Palmer Cup Championship*

**BACK ROW:** A. Ness (*Asst Physio*), T. Thompson, N. Stone, C. Mayes, A. Aldridge, M. Daysh, C. Corbett, J. Buescher, L. Connor, M. Houltham (*Asst Manager*), B. Walker, O. Williams. **SECOND ROW:** M. Lewis (*Asst Coach*), K. Roberts (*Trainer*), T-R. Raharuhi, L. Florence, E. Williams, S. Te Aonui, Z. Scott, A-R. Stephens-Daly, J. Lewis, B. Jacob, S. Kay, F. Gutschalg (*Physio*). **FRONT ROW:** Z. Winslade (*Asst Coach*), L. Elder, J. Tuilaepa, K. Reynolds, C. Yule (*Co-captain*), K. James (*Co-captain*), S. Whareaorere, S. Tapsell, A. Clarke, A. Thompson (*Manager*), B. Webby (*Coach*). **ABSENT:** B. Cameron, D. Thompson, K. Henwood, P. Playle.

## POVERTY BAY

**BACK ROW:** M. Counsell, I. Vuki, W. Grogan, J. Holmes, K. Love, T. Jones. **THIRD ROW:** L. Hills, T. Apatu-Nepe (*Trainer*), M-P. Brown, J. Allen, J. Cook, A. Tauatevalu, B. Lam, S. Smith (*Manager*). **SECOND ROW:** G. Brown (*Chairman*), K. Smith, T. Hill, S. Akana, F. White, M. McGuire, K. MacPherson, R. Daurua, M. Evans (*Physio*). **FRONT ROW:** A. Karauria, W. Tamatea, S. Moala, D. Russell (*Asst Coach*), J. Grogan (*Captain*), M. 'Otai (*Head Coach*), E. Reeves, S. Ngatu, E. Reid. **ABSENT:** I. Leach, J. Fleming, T. Stewart, A. Leatio'o, G. Halley.

## WAIKATO FPC

**BACK ROW:** T. Natua, H. Harding, D. Fermanis, L. Tomu, T. Te Aho, K. Grason (*Manager*), T. Kalounivale, C. Alley, L. Kloppers, C. Wihone, H. Brough, K. Faneva, M. Tainui-Mclean, K. Turvey (*Physio*). **FRONT ROW:** A. Bayler, M. Riki-Te Kanawa, M. Montague, S. Hyde-Richards, E. Heta, N. Delamere, R. Hayes, G. Houpapa-Barrett, K. Anderson, R. Paraone, J. Semple (*Asst coach*). **INSET:** W. Maxwell (*Head coach*).

## BAY OF PLENTY STEAMERS

**BACK ROW:** B. Mayo (*Head S&C Trainer*), L. Campbell, K. Trask, J.M. Lay, M. Karpik, L. Polwart, J. O'Reilly, S. Siataga, R. Judd, M. Roberts (*Analyst*). **THIRD ROW:** T. Stebbing (*Asst S&C Trainer*), S. Sherwood (*Asst Analyst*), L. Steel, J. Davey, A. Mua, T. Hepetema, J. Webber, E. Nicholas, J.A. Lay, J. Johnston, S. Funaki, B. Johnson (*Operations Manager*), E. Solomon (*Doctor*). **SECOND ROW:** C. Newland (*Physio*), D. Somerset (*PDM*), M. Garland, M. Axtens, L. Masirewa, B. Wardlaw, T. Franklin, J. Parete, H. Stowers, T. Mafileo, T. Ardron, S. Ropati, W. Brill (*Campaign Manager*), D. Hill (*Asst Coach*), B. Drabble (*Statistician*). **FRONT ROW:** R. Gibbs (*Asst Coach*), K. Haimona, A. Ross, S. Sakalia, T. Callander, J. Thwaites, C. Retallick, K. Mewett (*Captain*), M. Delany, L. Foketi, C. Tiatia, H. Blake, M. Ioane, N. Harris, C. McMillan (*Head Coach*). **INSETS:** S. Cane, B. Simonsson, I. Te Aute.

## THAMES VALLEY

**BACK ROW:** L. Easton, G. Lelenoa, A. Bradley, T. Erceg, H. Riwhi, K. Lewis, M. Rolston, A. Carroll, B. Ranga, H. Laufituanai, R. Moloney, S. Topou. **SECOND ROW:** L. Spring (*Asst Physio*), J. Murray (*Asst Coach*), J. van Doorn (*Physio*), E. Roycroft, R. Voyocaki, C. McVerry, C. Mart, J. Goodall, S. McCahon, J. Wood, D. Harrison (*Asst Coach*), L. McIver (*Manager*), C. Bishop (*Asst Manager*). **FRONT ROW:** M. Bartleet (*Coach*), J. Law, T. Keith, C. Doak, S. Hill (*Co-captain*), H. Wisnewski (*Co-captain*), B. Bonnar, L. Matai-Povey, B. Hamilton, E. McLean, E. Leahy (*CEO*). **ABSENT:** E. Lavery, J. Bayliss, H. Anderson, R. Cairns, T. Tiumafifi, T. Scott.

## WAIKATO

**BACK ROW:** D. Byrne (*Asst Trainer*), S. Caird, J. Christy (*Analyst*), L. McWhannell, C. Argus (*Head Trainer*). **FOURTH ROW:** E. Pene (*Asst Physio*), S. Kautai, L. Jacobson, J. Iosefa-Scott, L. Fifita, J. Manihera, A. Moli, T. Te Tamaki (*Physio*). **THIRD ROW:** P. Kennedy (*Doctor*), Z. Guildford, A. Johnstone, S. Lopeti, J. Brown, B. Sullivan, I. Ratuva Tavuyara, M. Lansdown, B. Foote (*CEO*). **SECOND ROW:** K. Abbott (*Nutritionist*), Z. Khouri (*Doctor*), T. Taufui, H. Levien, T. Campbell, P. Ahki, S. Taukei'aho, S. Reece, P. Cowley, R. Takarangi, M. Crawford (*Manager*). **FRONT ROW:** C. Hoeft (*Asst Coach*), S. Christie, H. Faiva, J. Tucker (*Co-captain*), A. Burn (*Co-captain*), D. Sweeney (*Captain*), J. Skeen (*Co-captain*), L. Talakai, L. Uhila, M. Jacobson, S. Botherway (*Head Coach*). **ABSENT:** R. Randle (*Asst Coach*), T. Kerr-Barlow, A. Lienert-Brown, D. McKenzie, D. Nginingini, D. Collier, A. Mikaele-Tu'u, T. Barker (*Asst Trainer*), R. Stephenson (*PDM*).

## COUNTIES MANUKAU HEAT

**BACK ROW:** I. Ozorio, E. Kitson, T. Leaf, S. Brown, G. Gogo, Y. Ono. **THIRD ROW:** H. Lemon (*Physio*), A. Te Iringa, U. Atonio, G. Lidgard, C. Aitken (*Analyst*), C. Wong, B. Robertson, H. Pomare. **SECOND ROW:** J. Clark (*Asst Coach*), G. Hastings (*Manager*), H. Brough, A. Matau, H. Te Iringa, L. Perese, J. Levi (*Asst Coach*), D. White (*Head Coach*). **FRONT ROW:** L.L.E. Silva, J. Lavea, V. Subritzky-Nafatali, H. Tubic, A. Marino (*Captain*), Te K. Ngata-Aerengamate, L. Steed, J. Karena, S. Murray-Wihongi. **ABSENT:** J. Wong, A. Heta, V. Meki, L. Veainu.

## COUNTIES MANUKAU STEELERS

**BACK ROW:** S. Tupou, J. Adams, K. Hala, L. Laulala, J. Royal, L. Daniela, G. Su'a, V. Tagicakibau. **THIRD ROW:** J. Souchon (*Analyst*), J. Knox (*Trainer*), O. Leger, T. Pulu, A. Nikoro, S. Furniss, C. Te Whata-Colley, K. Tuiloma, S. Henwood, F. Lokotui, G. Fisiiahi, T. Burgess (*Trainer*), B. Tarapa (*Masseur*). **SECOND ROW:** B. Hoggard (*CEO*), K. Maihi (*President*), S. Baker (*Doctor*), T. Nabura), N. Ah Wong, M. Vaai, M. Martin, D. Leasuasu, V. Taulani, J. Kawau, S. Tukania, C. Carter (*Chairman*), M. Leilua (*Manager*), T. Ralph (*Physio*). **FRONT ROW:** S. Sititi (*Asst Coach*), S. Bagshaw, S. Taufalele, P. Manu, S. Donald, J. Tupou (*Co-captain*), D. Suasua (*Coach*), A. Pulu (*Co-captain*), T. Nanai-Williams, R. Raaymakers, B. Kerr, V. Rarasea, G. Henson (*Asst Coach*). **ABSENT:** J. Taumateine, K. Read, S. Williams, N. Laulala, S. Fifita, L. Jack.

## AUCKLAND

***BACK ROW:*** B. Nee-Nee, S. Slade, A. Ioane, S. Scrafton, M. Fatialofa, T. Seu. ***FOURTH ROW***: J. Moore (*PDM*), L. Fosita, D. Papali'i, H. Sotutu, O. Mausia, S. Ulufonua, J. Fa'anana-Schultz, I. Tu'ungafasi, J. Yarnton (*Analyst*). ***FOURTH ROW:*** L. Fukofuka, B. Gibson, S. Kaifa, M. Nanai, J. Ravouvou, D. Fa'amoana, M. Renata, J. Trainor, M. McCartney (*Hydrologist*). ***THIRD ROW:*** W. Groarke (*Doctor*), L. Milo-Harris, T. Elkington-MacDonald, P. Collier, S. Havili, H. Plummer, C. Clarke, E. Tamura-Paki, T. McHugh, P. Downes (*S&C Coach*). ***SECOND ROW:*** M. Plummer (*Physio*), M. Donovan (*Chairman*), N. Costa, T. Manu, J. Sauni, G. Pleasants-Tate, W. Faiane, D. Bowden, J. Bear (*CEO*), J. Dalton (*Massage Therapist*). ***FRONT ROW:*** B. Cadwallader (*Coach*), K. Eklund, L. McClintock (*Manager*), M. Fekitoa, S. Prattley, T.J. Faiane (*Captain*), P. Tuipulotu (*Captain*), G. Moala, N. White (*Head Coach*), J. Hickey, G. Moon (*Coach*). ***ABSENT:*** S. Dominikovich-Murray, L. Dunshea, M. Fepuleai, R. Ioane, J. Kaino, J. Lane, O. Tu'ungafasi.

## AUCKLAND STORM

***BACK ROW:*** C. Gubb, M. Huni, R. Burch, J. Fanene, A.P. Nelson, E. Blackwell, C. Varea. ***THIRD ROW:*** B. Reeves, L. Itunu, R. Demant, C. McMenamin, A. Wright (*Manager*), M. Fineaso-Levi, E. Leiataua, L. Thompson, F. Fa'amausili. ***SECOND ROW:*** A. Itunu, E. Jensen, O. Leiataua, C. Nanai, T. Ngawati, U. Sao Taliu, F. Sao Taliu, V. Henry. ***FRONT ROW:*** G. Milne (*Physio*), A. Warbrooke, R. Lemanu, K. Stowers (*Co-captain*), JP. Fa'amausili (*Coach*), M. Hufanga (*Co-captain*), H. Watene, L. Mafi, K. Cribb (*Trainer*). ***ABSENT:*** C. Tautiaga (*Coach*), W. Sotutu (*Coach*), J. Aiono, K. Cuthers, C. Fukuda, H. Leiataua, M. Saena, M. Tova.

## NORTH HARBOUR HIBISCUS

**BACK ROW:** P. Tapsell, S. Fisher, B. Mitchinson (*Manager*), O. Ward-Duin, R. Wood. **THIRD ROW:** B. Wigglesworth (*Coach*), C. Tofa, K. Williams, M. Penman, C. Wikaira, E. Harbour (*Trainer*). **SECOND ROW:** S. McIlroy, B. Lamont (*Manager*), N. Ngarongo-Porima, Te H-N. Tuterangiwhiu, R. Dunn, L. Duggan (*Physio*), B. Morton (*Analyst*). **FRONT ROW:** B-J. Jones, J. Vizirgianakis, A. Robertshaw (*Captain*), C. Erasmus, T. To'o, C. Cox. **ABSENT:** J. Letham (*Coach*), C. Smith, C. McMeekin, N. Dallow, A. Fraser, E. Iverson, L. Jones, K. Longopoa, B. McNamara, J. Palmer, C. Luafaleauo, M. Ilalu, L. Halaleva.

## NORTH HARBOUR

**BACK ROW:** P. White (*Manager*), B. Volavola, J. Tyrell, S. Neville, J. Hoeata, G. Preston, T. Doolan, D. Gibson (*General Manager*). **FOURTH ROW:** D. Allnutt (*Kit Manager*), I. Stewart (*Doctor*), C. Eves, S. Stevenson, H. Moala-Liava'a, M. Telea, D. Hilton-Jones, A. King (*S&C Coach*), R. Hilton-Jones (*Director of Rugby*). **THIRD ROW:** R. Kidd (*President*), M. Wenham (*Physio*), S. Tucker, M. Taramai, H. Groundwater, K. Tuinukuafe, C. Collett, A. Smith, S. Nixon (*Chairman*), S. Mulholland-Goad (*Analyst*). **SECOND ROW:** F. Brading (*PDM*), T. Coventry (*Coach*), L. Gjaltema, S. Misa, B. Gatland, M. Tamoaieta, M. Royal, D. Halangahu (*Asst Coach*), C. Kelly (*Asst Manager*). **FRONT ROW:** N. Mayhew, G. Cowley-Tuioti, B. Nansen, B. Hall, J. Parsons (*Co-captain*), M. Duffie (*Co-captain*), C. Smylie, T. Li, M. Vaega, S. Mafileo. **ABSENT:** S. Treeby, B. Afeaki (*Scrum Coach*), L. Coleman (*Doctor*).

## NEW ZEALAND HEARTLAND XV

**BACK ROW:** P. Masoe (*Physio*), P. McHugh (*Doctor*) T. Reekie, J. Percival, C. Clare, N. Strachan, L. Masoe, G. Miller (*Trainer*), T. Harrison (*Manager*). **SECOND ROW:** B. Matthews (*Head Coach*), S. Koroitamana, N. Kendrick, B. Hudson, E. Reid, E. Duff, S. Moala, A. Ellis, S. Cameron, C. Scanlon (*Assistant Coach*). **FRONT ROW:** E. Reeves, W. Paia'aua, E. Pollock, M. Kolinisau, K. Coll, A. Stephens (*Captain*), M. Fetu, R. Darling, C. Crowley, W. Wright.

## NORTHLAND

**BACK ROW:** B. Parkes (*Asst S&C Coach*), A. McGinn (*CEO*), A. Balasingham (*Chairman*), T. Dow (*PDM*), D. Subritzky-Clark, M. Marwick, R. Rinakama, B. Hohaia, P-J. Atkins, J. Matiu, T. Blundell, M. MacLeod, B. Te Haara (*Manager*), J. Smethurst (*Physio*), T. Hurst (*Head S&C Coach*), H. Slobbe (*Asst S&C Coach*). **SECOND ROW:** C. Locke (*Doctor*), B. Woodward (*Technical Advisor*), D. Witcombe (*Head Coach*), P. Breen, M. Matich, T. Robinson, T. Bond, M. Douglas, J. Larsen, T. Tua, S. Gregory, E. Pittman, D. MacLeod (*Asst Coach*), F. Deformes (*Scrum Coach*), M. Carpinter (*Analyst*). **FRONT ROW:** S. Alaimalo, J. Ram, K. Pryor, J. Hyland, J. Goodhue, D. Hawkins, M. Moulds (*Captain*), R. Ranger, M. Wright, S. Nock, J. Olsen, N. Waa, H. Sililoto. **INSETS:** R. Wright, M. Faleafa, T. Gilbert, P. Kite, C. Apoua, J. Goodhue, J. Macilai, D. Pryor, G. Subritzky (*Asst Manager*).

## MAORI ALL BLACKS — 2017 NORTHERN TOUR TO CANADA & FRANCE

*BACK ROW:* M. Renata, S. Wainui, A. Curtis, A. Ioane, J. Hemopo, Te K. Mewett, J. Manihera, T. Lomax, S. Stevenson, D. Pryor. *THIRD ROW:* S. Thomas (*S&C Coach*), R. Durie (*Doctor*), T. Umaga (*Assistant Coach*), J. Garden-Bachop, J. Ruru, S. Henwood, R. Wright, C. Hoeft (*Set Piece Coach*), A. Draper (*Physio*). *SECOND ROW:* J. Ross (*Analyst*), P. Minehan (*Baggagaman/masseur*), Te T. Tahuriorangi, L. Polwart, T. Walden, R. Thompson, S. Paranihi, B. Weber, T. Ward (*Team Manager*), M. Sexton (*Campaign Manager*). *FRONT ROW:* T. Franklin, C. Eves, J. Hoeata, L. Crawford (*Kaumatua*), A. Dixon (*Captain*), C. McMillan (*Head Coach*), T. Bateman, I. West, C. Ngatai.

## BLACK FERNS SEVENS — 2017 KITAKYUSHU TOURNAMENT

*BACK ROW:* C. Sweeney (*Asst Coach*), S. Ross (*Asst Coach/Analyst*), B. Anderson (*S&C Coach*), C. Robins-Reti, M. Blyde, K. Whata-Simpkins, R. Cordero-Tufuga, T. Fitzpatrick, T. Willison, P. Woodman, A. Bunting (*Head Coach*), J. Strickland (*Manager*), N. Armstrong (*Physio*). *FRONT ROW:* N. Williams, R. Tui, T. Nathan-Wong, S. Goss (*Captain*), K. Brazier, A. Saili, L. Faleafaga.

## ALL BLACKS SEVENS — 2017 LAS VEGAS & VANCOUVER TOURNAMENTS

*BACK ROW:* T. Cama (*Asst Coach*), A. Chang (*S&C Coach*), V. Koroi, A. Knewstubb, T. Joass, I. Iopu-Aso, T. Ng Shiu, B. Waaka, I. Te Tamaki, T. Martin (*Analyst*), K. Rottier (*Physio*). *FRONT ROW:* S. Waldrom (*Coach*), S. Molia, S. Stowers, T. Mikkelson, S. Curry, D. Forbes, A. Curtis, D. Collier, R. Everiss (*Manager*).

## NEW ZEALAND UNDER 20 — 2017 JUNIOR WORLD CHAMPIONS

**BACK ROW:** J. McKay, A. Fidow, T. Umaga-Jensen, C. Clarke, W. Jordan, A. Choat, T. Fainga'anuku. **THIRD ROW:** N. Whitehead (*Doctor*), J. Nareki, K. Hauiti-Parapara, T. Christie, J. Sauni, B. Ennor, T. Falcon, P. Rakete-Stones, R. Coxon, S. Pinfold (*S&C Coach*). **SECOND ROW:** D. Neilson (*Analyst*), M. Anthony (*Campaign Manager*), T. Tua, M. Mikaele-Tu'u, I. Walker-Leaware, S. Caird, J. Pierce, S. Slade, T. Farrell, E. Lindenmuth, D. Banks (*Physio*), M. Vercoe (*Manager*). **FRONT ROW:** C. Brown (*Asst Coach*), O. Leger, A. Aumua, W. Rickards (*Asst Coach*), L. Jacobson (*Captain*), C. Philpott (*Head Coach*), E. Enari, D. Papali'i, D. Hewett (*Set Piece Coach*). **INSETS:** S. Perofeta, H. Allan, A. Mitchell.

## NEW ZEALAND SCHOOLS

**BACK ROW:** T. Funaki, S. Cooper, A. Pole, C. Grace, D. Flanders, L. Fainga'anuku, G. Dyer, E. Nanai, D. Toala, J. Mua, L. McClutchie. **SECOND ROW:** P. Bowden (*Analyst*), Q. Tapsell, R. Reihana, N. Ah Kuoi, T. Vaa'i, T. Williams, C. Alaimalo, T. Kapea, I. Punivai, N. Reid (*Manager*). **FRONT ROW:** E. Brumwell (*S&C Coach*), S. Klein, K. Nasolo, F. Paea, T. Cairns (*Coach*), Q. Tupaea (*Captain*), J. Holland (*Coach*), J. Tavita-Metcalfe, H. Sheild, J. Southall, K. Harrington (*Physio*).

**Photo by Farrelly Photos**

**BLUES**

**BACK ROW:** D. O'Donnell, J. Tupou, B. Nansen, L. Price, S. Scrafton, R. Ioane, A. Ioane, G. Cowley-Tuioti, P. Tuipulotu, J. Goodhue, B. Guyton. **FOURTH ROW:** J. Ryan (*Asst S&C Coach*), K. Pryor, M. Moulds, M. Nanai, A. Hodgman, S. Williams, M. Duffie, S. Prattley, M. Taramai, D. Ellis (*Skills Coach*). **THIRD ROW:** A. Storey (*Sports Science Coach*), S. Perofeta, A. Pulu, M. Collins, B. Gibson, J. Trainor, P. Francis, J. Royal, P. Manu, K. Wilson (*Mental Skills Coach*), S. Jackson (*Asst Coach*). **SECOND ROW:** J. Yarnton (*Asst Analyst*), T. Webber (*Analyst*), M. Plummer (*Physio*), S. Nock, M. Vaega, S. Mafileo, H. Faiva, T.J. Faiane, B. Gatland, J. Price (*Head S&C Coach*), A. Draper (*Physio*), S. Kara (*Doctor*). **FRONT ROW:** R. Fry (*Manager*), O. Tu'ungafasi, S. Luatua, C. Faumuina, J. Parsons (*Co-captain*), T. Umaga (*Head Coach*), J. Kaino (*Co-captain*), R. Ranger, G. Moala, I. West, A. Rogers (*Asst Coach*).

*Photo by Richard Spranger Photography*

## CHIEFS

*BACK ROW:* T. Nanai-Williams, T. Pulu, S. Taukeiaho, K. Hames, L. Laulala, C. Tiatia, B. Mitchell, S. Siataga, L. Polwart, F. Christie, J. Taumateine, J. Fa'auli, B. Weber. *THIRD ROW:* M. Karpik, S. McNicol, N. Laulala, A. Lienert-Brown, S. Kautai, S. Stevenson, T. Sanders, N. Harris, A. Moli, A. Ross, M. Gra1-am, A. Nankivell, G. Fisiahi, S. Fisiihoi. *SECOND ROW:* K. McQuoid *(Physio)*, R. Hall *(Analyst)*, P. Healey *(S&C Coach)*, L. Boshier, M. Brown, J. Tucker, T. Seu, D. Bird, M. Allardice, S. Alaimalo, M. Leitch, B. Mills *(Asst S&C Coach)*, Z. Khouri *(Doctor)*, D. Shergold *(Asst Manager)*, T. Ito *(Physio)*. *FRONT ROW:* S. Williams *(Manager)*, C. Hoeft *(Asst Coach)*, K. Keane *(Asst Coach)*, C. Ngatai, J. Lowe, S. Donald, L. Messam, A. Cruden *(Co-captain)*, S. Cane *(Co-captain)*, H. Elliot, B. Retallick, T. Kerr-Barlow, D. McKenzie, A. Strawbridge *(Asst Coach)*, N. Barnes *(Asst Coach)*, D. Rennie *(Head Coach)*.

## HURRICANES

***BACK ROW:*** D. Larsen (*Recruitment & Development Manager*), N. Milner-Skudder, K. Hauiti-Parapara, M. Tuitama, L. Uhila, J. Lowe, N. Laumape, V. Aso, W. Goosen, Te T. Tahuriorangi, TJ. Va'a, J. O'Reilly, P. Ahki. ***THIRD ROW:*** R. Runciman (*Asst analyst*), J. Ross (*Analyst*), P. Minehan (*Baggageman/Masseur*), K. O'Donnell, R. Riccitelli, J. Barrett, H. Renton, J. Blackwell, M. Proctor, P. Umaga-Jensen, M. Kainga, R. Prinsep, T. Halafihi, V. Fifita, A. Kirikiri, R. Lagdarde (*S&C Intern*), D. Cron (*Scrum Coach*), J. Buckley (*S&C Coach*). ***SECOND ROW:*** S. Symonds (*PDM*), D. Wildash (*S&C Coach*), J. Dickie (*S&C Coach*), B. Jones (*Nutritionist*), G. Cridge, S. Lousi, M. Fatialofa, M. Abbott, C. Gibbins, O. Black, L. Apisai, B. Lam, C. Shaw (*Head Physio*), D. Gray (*Head S&C Coach*), L. Santos (*Physio*), C. Stirling (*GM High Performance*), S. Tafua (*Asst Analyst*). ***FRONT ROW:*** T. Ward (*Manager*), C. Jane, C. Eves, J. Holland (*Asst Coach*), B. Shields, B. Barrett, C. Boyd (*Head Coach*), T. Perenara (*Vice-captain*), D. Coles (*Captain*), J. Plumtree (*Coach*), J. To'omaga-Allen, R. Goodes, B. May, J. Savea, A. Savea, R. Watt (*Asst Coach*). ***ABSENT:*** T. Dorfling (*Doctor*), N. Hogg (*Mental Skills Coach*).

Photo by Ken Baker Photography

## CRUSADERS

*2017 Investec Super Rugby Champions*

**BACK ROW:** O. Jager, Q. Strange, S. Barrett, M. Dunshea, S. Wainui. **FOURTH ROW:** J. Roche (*Physio*), D. Havili, J. Taufua, S. Fifita, H. Bedwell-Curtis, S. Tamanivalu, M. Ala'alatoa, J. Goodhue, T. Perry, P. Samu, G. Bridge, S. Thomas (*Head S&C Coach*). **THIRD ROW:** J. Martin (*Asst Analyst*), J. Gardner (*Analyst*), L. Fukofuka, D. Ioane, M. Mataele, C. Taylor, B. Hall, J. Macalai, J. Brown, N. Tucker (*Asst Physio*), M. Swan (*Doctor*). **SECOND ROW:** S. Fletcher (*Manager*), J. Miles (*Logistics*), J. Ryan (*Coach*), R. Mo'unga, M. McKenzie, A. Makalio, M. Drummond, E. Enari, M. Hunt, G. Duder (*Asst S&C Coach*), J. Maddock (*Asst Coach*), L. MacDonald (*Coach*). **FRONT ROW:** I. Dagg, L. Romano, K. Read, R. Crotty (*Vice-captain*), S. Robertson (*Head Coach*), S. Whitelock (*Captain*), M. Todd (*Vice-captain*), T. Bateman, O. Franks, B. Funnell, J. Moody. **INSETS:** W. Crockett, V. Fredericks, W. Douglas, B. Mooar (*Coach*).

*Photo by McRobie Studios, Dunedin*

## HIGHLANDERS

***BACK ROW:*** G. Evans, L. Whitelock, A. Ainley, T. Franklin, J. Wheeler, J. Dickson, L. Squire, J. Hempo, D. Hunt. ***FOURTH ROW:*** J. Montgomery *(Asst Physio)*, S. Christie, M. Faddes, J. Lenties, M. Banks, D. Pyror, R. Buckman, W. Naholo, C. Millar, A. Letts *(Physio)*. ***FOURTH ROW:*** N. Ives *(Baggage Master)*, F. Simpson *(Dietician)*, A. Seiuli, D. Lienert-Brown, R. Thompson, G. Millar, T. Li, M. Ranby *(PDM)*, P. McLaughlan *(Manager)*. ***THIRD ROW:*** H. Chapman *(Asst Analyst)*, A. Watts *(Analyst)*, J. Ioane, P. Tomkinson, G. Pleasants-Tate, M. Fekitoa, S. Halanukonuka, T. Walden, R. Clark *(CEO)*, G. O'Brien *(General Manager, Rugby)*. ***SECOND ROW:*** I. Blake *(Asst S&C Coach)*, G. Macleod *(Doctor)*, J. Emery, S. Tokolahi, F. Smith, J. Renton, K. Hammington, A. Beardmore *(S&C Coach)*, J. Preston *(Skills Coach)*. ***FRONT ROW:*** T. Brown *(Head Coach)*, S. McLeod *(Asst Coach)*, L. Sopoaga, E. Dixon, A. Dixon *(Co-captain)*, B. Smith *(Co-captain)*, A. Smith, L. Coltman, M. Hammett *(Asst Coach)*, C. Dermody *(Scrum Coach)*. ***ABSENT:*** B. Edmonds, H. Parker, S. Pole, P. Osborne, A. Smith, T. Sopoaga.

## WANGANUI

*Winners of the Meads Cup*

**BACK ROW:** K. Stembridge (*Physio*), A. Middleton K. Latu, T. Gilbert, E. Robinson, D. Whale, C. Hemi, S. Dibben, H. Mellow, C. Clare, C. Crowley, H. Fitzgerald (*Physio*). **SECOND ROW:** C. Back (*Manager*), T. Seruwalu, B. Hudson, J. Sawailau, J. Lane, T. Ratu, S. Kalou, S Madams, C. Hart, N. Harding, C. Robinson, S. Kubunavanua, K. Soutar (*Video Analyst*). **FRONT ROW:** R. Williams (*Defence Coach*), M. McGrath (*Selector*). G. Hakaraia, K. Dabenaise, L. Horrocks, J. Hamlin (*Co-coach*), C. Baldwin (*Co-captain*), R. Tutauha (*Co-captain*), J. Caskey (*Co-coach*), J. Hughes, T. Stewart, V. Tofa, D. Hoskin (*President*).

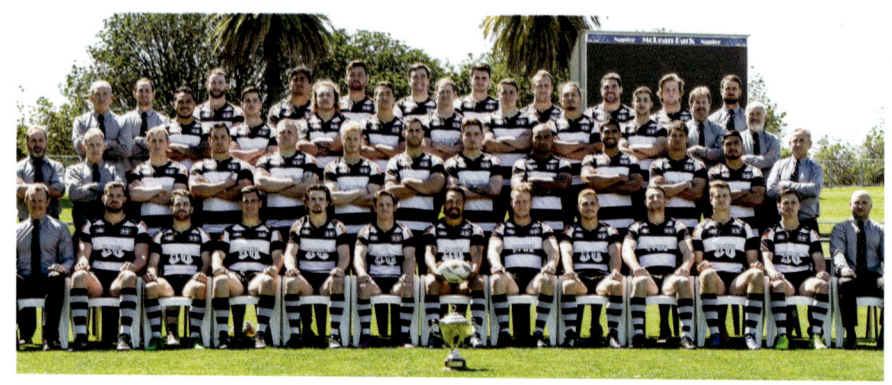

## HAWKE'S BAY MAGPIES

**BACK ROW:** A. Horrell (*Asst Coach*), M. Gardner, M. Mikaele-Tu'u, J. Eden-Whaitiri, N. Palmer, B. Parsons, H. Renton, B. May, T. Farrell, L. Stephenson (*Trainer*). **THIRD ROW:** M. Nicol (*Physio*), P. Dunn, H. Hann, M. Kean, T. Falcon, D. Snee, J. Devery, P. Rakete-Stones, Z. Donaldson, P. O'Shaughnessy (*Analyst*), B. Jenkinson (*Asst Manager*). **SECOND ROW:** I. Taylor (*Doctor*), J. Syms (*Asst Coach*), B. Hamelink, J. Aoake, M. Braidwood, S. McNicol, L. Goodin, R. Hayes, F. Selesele, C. Vaega, J. Lowe, T. Vaega, T. Gittings (*Manager*). **FRONT ROW:** C. Philpott (*Head Coach*), G. Cridge, M. Emerson, J. Long, R. Buckman, B. Weber (*Vice-captain*), A. Dixon (*Captain*), G. Evans (*Vice-captain*), I. West, T. Lamborn, M. Allardice, E. Wilson, M. Ozich (*Asst Coach*). **ABSENT:** I. Dagg, B. Retallick, C. Eaton, J. Tangaere.

## HAWKE'S BAY TUIS

**BACK ROW:** K. Bray (*Manager*), Y. Whaitiri, C. Lauvao, R. Hurae, K. Kirkpatrick, N. Jefferson, N. Greville, S. Rohe (*Physio*), T. Maeva (*Head Coach*). **SECOND ROW:** D. Bunce (*S&C Coach*), R. Holmes, L. Eden, J. Bennett, F. Burkin, N. Cotton, D. Pomare-Mackay, G. Woods, H. Hakopa, A. Ene (*Coach*). **FRONT ROW:** J. Ferguson-Ngawaka, J. Taukamo-Apiata, S. Tipiwai, A. Williams (*Captain*), A. Tangen-Wainohu, F. Powdrell, L. Blake. **ABSENT:** C. Hoggard, T. Edwards, T. Ferguson.

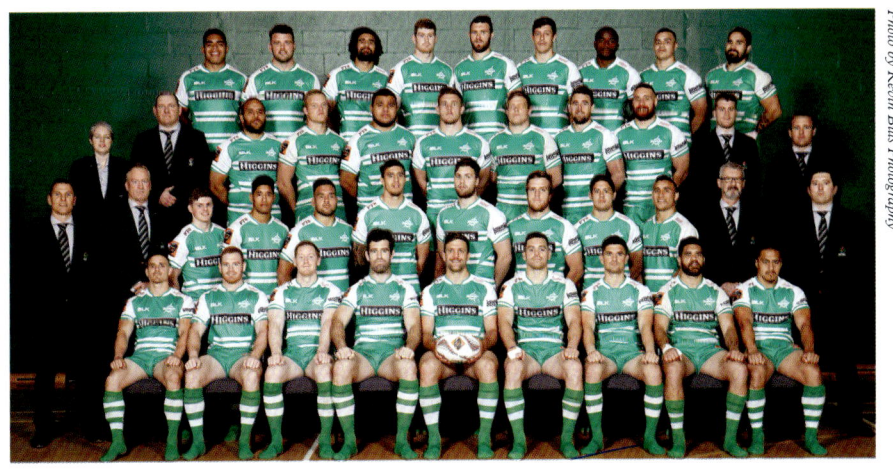

## MANAWATU TURBOS

***BACK ROW:*** M. Ala'alatoa, F. Armstrong, J. Hemopo, L. Hallam-Eames, T. Parsons, L. Mitchell, W. Ambakak, B. Iose, T. Raimona. ***THIRD ROW:*** N. Bolger (*Physio*), G. Fleming (*Scrum Coach*), N. Tudreu, C. Reid, S. Asi, T. Crozier, H. Prescott, K. Baker, B. Henderson, J. Lowl (*Asst Trainer*), S. Pinfold (*Trainer*). ***SECOND ROW:*** A. Good (*Asst Coach*), J. Cotter (*Head Coach*), S. Malcolm, Te R. Waitokia, S. Paranihi, A. Curtis, H. Brewer, T. Cadwallader, J. Te Rure, N. Tudreu, V. Wilson (*Manager*), T. Martin (*Analyst*). ***FRONT ROW:*** K. Hammington, J. Booth, H. Northcott, N. Crosswell, H. Bedwell-Curtis (*Captain*), A. Kiri Kiri, O. Black, L. Marshall, J. Emery. ***ABSENT:*** A. Smith, N. Milner-Skudder, N. Laumape, S. Lombard (*Doctor*).

## MANAWATU CYCLONES

***BACK ROW:*** A. Liumaihetua Darling, J. Ngaia, S. Hemingway, J. Fagan-Pease, M. Canterbury, G. Ponsonby, M. Polson. ***THIRD ROW:*** R. Malanicagi, S. Littleworth, W. Leota, S. Loye, A. Knight, F. Veikoso, S. Tipene. ***SECOND ROW:*** F. Feaunati (*Head Coach*), W. Stent (*Manager*), L. Nimarota, K. Tipene, C. Windle, A. Nuku, L. Balsillie, B. Walker (*Trainer*), S. Lewis (*Asst Coach*). ***FRONT ROW:*** K. Templeman, H. Wainohu, N. Dickins (*Vice-captain*), S. Winiata (*Captain*), E. Goulden, J. Nuku, J. Vaughan. ***ABSENT:*** K. Belcher (*Physio*), P. Walker, R. Ferris, K. Sue, S. McIntosh, R-L. Rawleigh, R. Finau.

## WAIRARAPA BUSH

**BACK ROW:** D. Tafatu (*Trainer*), E. Rayaqayaqa, N. Hohepa, B. Kete, J. Goodger, L. McFadzean, A. McLean, R. Pope, N. Ewe, P. Weepu, S. Malatai, J. Schweizer (*Physio*). **SECOND ROW:** B. Hansen (*Strapper*), G. Hodder (*Manager*), J. Pakoti, J. Mason, S. Tufui, S. Monaghan, C. McFadzean, T. Isaac, M. Kawana, P. Tafa, J. Bruce (*Asst Coach*), T. Nathan (*Chairman*). **FRONT ROW:** R. Dahlberg (*President*), W. Reiri (*Strapper*), R. Anderson, C. Baker, C. Raymond, B. Campbell (*Co-captain*), E. Cranston (*Co-captain*), T. Priest, I. Katia, T. Haira, J. Harwood (*Coach*), S. O'Gorman (*Asst Manager*). **ABSENT:** J. Hull. G. Faitotoi, A. Sanders, H. Vella, M. McCrae, N. Olson, C. Matthews, S. Gammie, D. Pickering.

## HOROWHENUA KAPITI

**BACK ROW:** T. Barnsley (*Physio*), E. Wade, W. Paia'aua, S. Bishop, A. McDougall, K. Tamou, L. McMahon, D. Jackson (*Strapper*). **SECOND ROW:** K. Takeuchi (*Asst Coach*), C. Wilton (*Coach*), N. Kendrick, T. Reti, T. Maki, L. Tovo, H. Taiapa, E. Pollock, N. Taylor (*Asst Manager*), N. Picchi (*Manager*). **FRONT ROW:** D. McErlean, A. Lahmert, W. Lander, R. Shelford (*Captain*), S. Cameron, R. Millar, R. Praat, C. Kennett (*CEO*). **ABSENT:** K. Kelemete, J. So'oialo, S. Jackson, D. Taylor, T. Paringatai, I. Eksteen.

Photo by Dave Lintott/lintottphoto.co.nz

## WELLINGTON LIONS

*Winners of the Mitre 10 Championship*

**BACK ROW:** A. Aumua, V. Sakaria, T. Umaga-Jensen, M. Tuitama, P. Umaga-Jensen, R. Verney, D. Kirifi, L. Filipo, K. Hauiti-Parapara, A. Wells, J. Tuiatua. **THIRD ROW:** B. Jones (*Nutritionist*), N. Hogg (*Mental Skills*), A. Fidow, T. Ben-Nicholas, B. Lam, B. Proctor, L. Harmon, M. Kafatolu, S. Paongo, C. Price, T. Renata, H. Ahio, B. Sigmund (*PDM*), R. Runciman (*Asst Analyst*). **SECOND ROW:** S. Rogers (*CEO*), M. Poutoa (*Manager*), J. Ross (*Head Analyst*), G. Stanbridge (*Logistics*), J. Apikotoa, I. Walker-Leawere, S. Lousi, W. Mangos, A. Dalzell, L. Santos (*Head Physio*), J. Dickie (*Head S&C Coach*), J. Marshall (*Asst S&C Coach*), M. Higgins (*S&C Intern*), A. Narayan (*Doctor*), M. Doonan (*Asst Physio*). **FRONT ROW:** S. Rangihuna, D. Kirkpatrick, M. Proctor, W. Goosen, J. Garden-Bachop, A. Bell (*Asst Coach*), C. Gibbes (*Head Coach*), J. Blackwell, B. Shields (*Captain*), B. Gardner (*President*), J. Savea, G. Taufale, R. So'oialo (*Asst Coach*), A. Muir (*Scrum Coach*), L. Apisai, R. Goodes, V. Fifita, T. Fahamokioa, G. Foe. **ABSENT:** J. To'omaga-Allen, C. Middleton, T. Va'a, S. Tafua (*Asst Analyst*), D. Coles, A. Savea, T. Perenara.

Photo by In Photography

## WELLINGTON PRIDE

**BACK ROW:** M. Tagoai, A. Print, R. Lolo, L. Leti, T. Svanborg, A. Uila, B. Tauaneai, G. Williamson. **THIRD ROW:** H. McDonald, L. Mapu, J. Ngan-Woo, P. Kriklanova, T. Taumoli, K. Mei, D. Faleafaga. **SECOND ROW:** J. Bryce, C. Marshall (*Physio*), R. Bond (*Coach*), M. Conley (*Manager*), M. Poutoa (*Asst Coach*), J. Clabburn (*Skills Coach*), D. Jensen (*Trainer*), R. Stirling. **FRONT ROW:** C. Copeland, K. Lopa, S. To'oala-Ryder, A. Te Iwimate, J. Patea-Fereti (*Captain*), R. Uluinayau, V. Marsters, P. Kalolo-Apolinario, T. Hamlin. **ABSENT:** G. Hilsdon (*Asst Coach*), A. Leti-l'iga, S. Ualesi, S. Levave.

## TASMAN MAKO

**BACK ROW:** S. Christie, B. Thornalley (*Asst Manager*), B. Asomua-Goodman, M. Hunt, F. Christie, W. Jordan, T. Hill. A. Makalio, A. Nankivell, T. Paulo, B. Stewart, J. Hawkey, V. Lolohea, C. Donovan (*Physio*), V. Ekysma (*Physio*). **THIRD ROW:** J. Hoden (*S&C Coach*), N. Price (*Analyst*), A. Goodman (*Asst Coach*), L. Aumua, T. Lomax, E. Blackadder, Q. Strange, S. Frizell, P.P. Parkinson, Te A. Cirikidaveta, T. Fainga'anuku, T. O'Malley, T. Ng Shiu, T. Joass, G. Somerville (*Set Piece Coach*), N. Marquet (*Asst Trainer*). **SECOND ROW:** M. Vercoe (*Manager*), L. MacDonald (*Head Coach*), J. Taufua, S. Halanukonuka, B. Guyton, T. Perry (*Vice-captain*), A. Ainley (*Captain*), V. Fredericks, J. Lowe, P. Samu, D. Havili, L. Crowley (*Asst Coach*). **FRONT ROW:** R. Coxon, W. Scott, I. Salmon, R. Parkinson, S. Moli.

## TASMAN MAKO FPC

**BACK ROW:** L. Adams (*Trainer*), P. Andrews, S. Tuitupou, S. Wilkins, H. Gillespie, K. Couper, S. Mitchell, M. Curry, A. Nathan, L. Siaki, I. Koevoet (*Physio*). **SECOND ROW:** G. Alsop (*Manager*), M. O'Cain (*Coach*), M. Kelly (*Coach*), S. Davis, R. Buchanan-Brown, C. Clarke, T. Silcock, A. Kwaid, L. Fotumoala, L. Sekai, N. Buchanan-Brown (*Manager*). **FRONT ROW:** K. Stanford, J. Drummond, R. Pouri-Lane, N. Scott, F. Hoskin, J. Foster (*Captain*), N. Tiumalu, S. Kohe, W. Greig, D. Wilson, S. Barry. **ABSENT:** R. Olsen, H. Leota.

## BULLER

**BACK ROW:** K. Parata, I. Hogarth, S. Marris, B. McIlroy, S. Crackett, S. Neighbours, I. Ravudra, J. Tuidriva, J. Lash. **SECOND ROW:** C. Adams (*Statistics*), A. Ellis, P. Saukuru, Z. Walsh, J. Lepa, J. Hedley, R. Bonisch, D. Egelstaff, A. Tailua, P. Bonisch (*Manager*). **FRONT ROW:** R. Abbey (*Physio*), C. Scanlon (*Coach*), L. Brownlee, A. Stephens (*Captain*), L. Mundy, G. Duncan, C. Neill (*Coach*), J. Duncan (*Chairman*). **ABSENT:** M. Lealava'a, J. Mackay, P. Beveridge, C. Jenkins, A. Paterson, L. Watson, E. Tau.

## WEST COAST

**BACK ROW:** M. Mudu, G. Fahey, D. Davis, S. McClure, P. Te Rakau, R. Thomson, R. Stanton, B. Tauwhare, J. Tomlinson, C. Flynn, D. Crouchley. **SECOND ROW:** J. Costello (*Stats/Video Analysis*), V. Turpin (*Masseur*), T. Struthers, T. Reekie, A. Tukana, K. Rasmussen, I. Lewaqai, D. Ford J. MacRae, S. Cameron, S. Soper, B. Watt (*Asst Manager/Trainer*). **FRONT ROW:** L. McNeish (*Manager*), S. Cuttance (*Coach*), N. Hamilton, J. Ferguson (*Vice-captain*), J. Manning (*Captain*), T. Tauwhare, N. Cumming, N. Makea (*Asst Coach*), K. Koch (*Physio*). **ABSENT:** J. Pitman-Joass, L. Babe, R. O'Gorman.

## CANTERBURY

*Winners of the Mitre 10 Cup*

*BACK ROW*: R. Prinsep, M. Dunshea, J. Osborne, H. Dalzell, J. Manning, B. Morris, O. Jager, P. Waqanibau. *FOURTH ROW*: D. Nel, C. Gawler, T. Sanders, N. Werahiko, A. Hodgman, J. Straker, J. Stratton, G. Bridge, B. Ennor. *THIRD ROW*: G. Duder (*Trainer*), N. Tucker (*Physio*), C. Makene, N. Vella, B. Harmon, M. Suckling, M. Swan (*Doctor*), J. Martin (*Analyst*). *SECOND ROW*: N. Mauger (*Coach*), J. Miles (*Logistics*), J. Hintz, I. Finau, J. McKay, S. Tokolahi, B. Cameron, T. Williamson (*Manager*), M. Brown (*Coach*). *FRONT ROW*: R. Thompson, B. Funnell, J. Maddock (*Coach*), T. Bateman, L. Whitelock (*Captain*), G. Delaney (*Head Coach*), D. Bird, M. Drummond. *ABSENT*: J. Brown, D. Lienert-Brown, R. Mo'unga, E. Enari, M. Todd, S. Alfeld, S. Goodwin, N. Gibb, F. Kaitu'u, M. Maitland, M. Green, N. Punivai, A. Nicole, F. Strawbridge, T. Christie.

*Photo by Ken Baker Photography*

## CANTERBURY FPC

*Winners of the Farah Palmer Cup Premiership*

**BACK ROW**: C. Engler, L. Anderson, N. Poletti, C. Bremner, A. Bremner, C. Poko, C. Siataga. **THIRD ROW**: M. Vanner (*Trainer*). R. Todd, J. Hansen, G. Brooker, O. McGoverne, K. Tavendale, P. Love, K. Kite (*Coach*). **SECOND ROW**: N. Wong (*Manager*), C. Greenslade, E. Uren, S. Curtis, T. Curtis, C. Thompson, L. Jenkins, M. Williams (*Physio*), A. Tiplady (*Doctor*). **FRONT ROW**: M. Ruscoe (*Asst Coach*), K. Ebrahim, B. Davidson, S. Te Ohaere-Fox (*Captain*), S. Pauaraisa, N. Purdom, M. Puckett, W. Love (*Coach*). **INSETS**: L. Armitage (*Analyst*), K. Cocksedge, L. Pera, C. Poko, C. Whiley.

Photo by Hazel Redmond, The Photo Shop, Ashburton

## MID CANTERBURY

*Winners of the Lochore Cup*

***BACK ROW:*** R. Deuchrass (*Trainer*), P. Mills, K. Polson, W. McGoon, P. Watson, M. King, A. Lindsay, J. Percival, N. Caucau, G. Rushton (*Chairman*), R. Wightman (*Physio*). ***SECOND ROW:*** T. Harrison (*Manager*), G. Frew (*Technical Advisor*), S. Koroitamana, H. Mackenzie, T. Hanham-Carter, S. Finau, M. Bentley, C. Vainerere, T. Heywood, M. Sau, J. Jowsey (*Co-coach*), C. Dunlea (*Co-coach*). ***FRONT ROW:*** C. Toomalatai, A. Williamson, I. Masiwini, W. Mackenzie, E. Duff, J. Donlan (*Captain*), R. Elworthy, A. Stewart, T. Blackburn, D. Visesio, D. Fransen. ***ABSENT:*** M. Andrew, T. Nabakeke, G. Lambrechts, I. Dawai.

## SOUTH CANTERBURY

**BACK ROW:** G. Thompson (*Physio*), K. Hellier, K. Darby, B. Hemopo, H. Bryce, B. Oliver, J-P. Keon. **SECOND ROW:** K. Leatigaga, G. Miller (*Trainer*), G. Sturgess, J. Gilmore, W. Joines, P. Henderson, K. Moore, L. Brice, J. Simpson (*Technical Advisor*), M. Beckham. **FRONT ROW:** C. Coll (*Manager*), W. Wright, M. Medlicott, M. Fetu, G. McFarlane, (*Asst Coach*), K. Coll (*Captain*), B. Matthews (*Coach*), B. Hewitson, J. Trevathan, M. Roberts (*President*). **ABSENT:** N. Strachan, G. Folau, J. Kingsford, S. Anderson, L. Toumohuni, S. Sauqaqa, T. Davidson, V. Tora.

## OTAGO SPIRIT

**BACK ROW:** J. Kendall, J. Gorinski, A. van Vliet, G. Muir, E. Doyle, K. Smith, M. Henderson, S. Umaga-Jensen. **THIRD ROW:** J. Tarbotton (*Asst Physio*), C. Cunningham, L. Tye, L. Harrison, S. Norris, S. Hollows, S. Kaufanga, G. Millar, K. Wereta, J. Tuhega (*Manager*). **SECOND ROW:** R. Bennett, G. Mason, L. van Vugt, O. Waldron, C. Antunes, I. Pringle, N. Kennedy, T. Hollows, A. Wilson (*Physio*). **FRONT ROW:** J. Al-Attar (*Trainer*), W. Kearney (*Coach*), M. Day, Z. Whatarau, S. Hume, A. Sisifa, M. Walker, K. Moata'ane, K. Jury (*Coach*), C. Charles (*Manager*). **ABSENT:** S. Crabbe.

## OTAGO

**BACK ROW:** J. Koroi, T. Rowe, J. Dickson, J. Furno, B. Tweed. **FOURTH ROW:** G. Stark, H. Sasagi, A. Knight, P. Sio, S. Teu, L. van Dam, J. Lentjes, D. Hunt. **FOURTH ROW:** A. Stiven (*Physio*), R. Jackson, J. Timu, G. Bower, M. Faddes, J. Aoina, S. McDowall, J. Ruru, L. Allan (*Defence Coach*). **THIRD ROW:** S. Mapusua (*Skills Coach*), M. Scott, J. Ioane, P. Tomkinson, L. Vaeno, S. Pole, F. Smith. H. Croft (*Analyst*), K. Bloxham (*S&C Coach*), J. Parker (*Massage Therapist*). **SECOND ROW:** J. Bishop (*Doctor*), K. Cooper (*Chairman*), R. Kinley (*General Manager*), J. Renton, V. Koroi, K. Hammer, J. Nareki, G. Hubbard (*Manager*), S. Wallace (*Asst Manager*). **FRONT ROW:** D. Smith (*President*), C. Brown (*Head Coach*), D. Brighouse, H. Parker, A. Seiuli, S. Anderson-Heather (*Captain*), T. Walden, M. Collins, C. Millar, T. Donnelly (*Asst Coach*). **ABSENT:** B. Colling (*PDM*), L. Coltman, M. Mafi, K. Meeuws (*Scrum Coach*), B. Smith.

## SOUTHLAND STAGS

**BACK ROW:** J. McKenzie (*PDM*), T. Tuimavave, S. Stewart, G. Dyer, J. Renton, F. Thomas, N. Fomai, L. Howley, R. Tongia, J. Wallace, H. Chapman (*Analyst*), C. Dermody (*Asst Coach*). **THIRD ROW:** R. Smith (*Manager*), H. Cheetham (*Head Trainer*), T. Huia (*Asst Trainer*), S. Stodart, W. Talataina-Mu, P. Halder, T. Sopoaga, A. Morris, J. Garrad (*Asst Trainer*), K. McDonald (*Physio*), J. Franklin (*Chairman*). **SECOND ROW:** A. Tanabe (*Asst Coach*), B. Fotheringham, L. Ormond, M. Selby-Rickit, M. McKee, J. Capil, T. Thomas, M. Johnson, J. Walsh, G. Morrison (*Asst Manager*). **FRONT ROW:** J. Kawau (*Asst Coach*), J. Ngaluafe, M. Mitchell, G. Millar, B. Mitchell (*Captain*), T. Boys, S. Eade, B. Fukofuka, J. Schrader, M. Molloy, H. Macdonald (*Head Coach*). **INSETS:** A. Moreton (*General Manager*), C. Stewart (*Doctor*), E. Dixon, L. Sopoaga.

'Rugby is a game for gentlemen in all classes but for no bad sportsman in any class.'
*Reverend W J Casey, 1894*

# NZ BARBARIAN RUGBY CLUB
## BY CAMPBELL BURNES

The 2017 season was one of the biggest in the 80-year existence of the New Zealand Barbarian Rugby Club. The June 3 fixture for the NZ Barbarians Provincial XV against the touring British and Irish Lions was the highest profile first-class fixture in its history, and was the centrepiece of a busy year full of the activities by which the club is renowned.

Along with its sponsorship of the NZ Barbarians Schools, a team which has seen its first All Black – Damian McKenzie from the class of 2012 – the Barbarians were heavily involved with the national, co-ed and girls' schools Top 4 tournament in Palmerston North, where the Barbarians Cup and Trophy were up for grabs, and the annual programme for the NZ Barbarians Area Schools.

The 28th annual Barbarians Fun Day was held on June 25 at the usual venue of Ngataringa Bay on Auckland's North Shore, and continues to be a highlight of a packed calendar.

The hope is that the Barbarians team, which plays in the iconic scarlet jerseys featuring the gambolling lamb over the left chest, will be able to undertake a tour in the near future, after successful outings against the Lions and the Maori All Blacks (2010 and 2015), and in the wake of well-received flag-waving tours of the UK in 1987, 1996 and 2003.

The club was formed in 1937, driven by All Blacks Hugh McLean and Ron Bush, and has the aim of promoting and furthering the ethos of rugby. As a non-profit organisation, the Barbarians aim to use any money gained to nurture or improve the game and in recent years have become a major sponsor of primary school, secondary school and middleweight (weight restricted) rugby at both the Auckland and national level.

In the early 1970s the club purchased a property at 17 Cricket Ave which served the Barbarians well for 40 years. That area of the property was required for the redevelopment of Eden Park for Rugby World Cup 2011, so a new facility was built. Then patron Bob Sorenson opened the new premises on level 6 of the ASB Stand at Eden Park on June 24, 2010. This club base is dripping with memorabilia and has grown to be a popular meeting place for members and guests on match-days.

Membership sits at well over 400 and is by invitation. Outgoing president, former All Blacks prop Ron Williams, is to be replaced by former Auckland captain Neil Cullimore for 2018.

# VISTA ALL BLACKS 2017
# NORTHERN TOUR OF ENGLAND, FRANCE, SCOTLAND, WALES

| | Franchise | Date of Birth | Height | Weight | Tests at 31/10/17 |
|---|---|---|---|---|---|
| A.J. (Asafo) Aumua | Hurricanes | 5/5/97 | 1.77 | 108 | – |
| B.J. (Beauden) Barrett | Hurricanes | 27/5/91 | 1.87 | 91 | 59 |
| S.K. (Scott) Barrett | Crusaders | 20/11/93 | 1.97 | 112 | 14 |
| D.J. (Dominic) Bird | Chiefs | 9/4/91 | 2.06 | 112 | 2 |
| S.J. (Sam) Cane | Chiefs | 13/1/92 | 1.89 | 109 | 50 |
| D.S. (Dane) Coles | Hurricanes | 10/12/86 | 1.84 | 112 | 55 |
| W.W.V. (Wyatt) Crockett | Crusaders | 24/1/83 | 1.93 | 116 | 68 |
| R.S. (Ryan) Crotty | Crusaders | 23/9/88 | 1.81 | 94 | 32 |
| M.D. (Mitch) Drummond | Crusaders | 15/2/94 | 1.80 | 86 | – |
| M.D. (Matt) Duffie | Blues | 16/8/90 | 1.92 | 95 | – |
| V.T.L. (Vaea) Fifita | Hurricanes | 17/6/92 | 1.84 | 113 | 3 |
| E.J. (Jack) Goodhue | Crusaders | 13/6/95 | 1.87 | 98 | – |
| K.S. (Kane) Hames | Chiefs | 28/8/88 | 1.80 | 113 | 6 |
| N.P. (Nathan) Harris | Chiefs | 8/3/92 | 1.86 | 110 | 9 |
| D.K. (David) Havili | Crusaders | 23/12/94 | 1.84 | 88 | 3 |
| D. (Dillon) Hunt | Highlanders | 23/2/95 | 1.89 | 103 | – |
| A. L. (Akira) .Ioane | Blues | 16/6/95 | 1.94 | 113 | – |
| R.E. (Rieko) Ioane | Blues | 18/3/97 | 1.89 | 102 | 10 |
| J. (Jerome) Kaino | Blues | 6/4/83 | 1.96 | 109 | 81 |
| T.N.J. (Tawera) Kerr-Barlow | Chiefs | 15/8/90 | 1.87 | 89 | 27 |
| N.E. (Nepo) Laulala | Chiefs | 6/11/91 | 1.84 | 116 | 10 |
| K.H. (Ngani) Laumape | Hurricanes | 24/4/93 | 1.69 | 107 | 4 |
| A.R. (Anton) Lienert-Brown | Chiefs | 15/4/95 | 1.87 | 103 | 19 |
| D.S. (Damian) McKenzie | Chiefs | 20/4/95 | 1.75 | 82 | 9 |
| A. (Atu) Moli | Chiefs | 12/6/95 | 1.89 | 127 | – |
| R. (Richie) Mo'unga | Crusaders | 25/5/94 | 1.76 | 86 | – |
| W.R. (Waisake) Naholo | Highlanders | 8/5/91 | 1.86 | 105 | 15 |
| T.T.R. (TJ) Perenara | Hurricanes | 23/1/92 | 1.84 | 90 | 39 |
| T.G. (Tim) Perry | Crusaders | 1/8/88 | 1.88 | 122 | – |
| K.J. (Kieran) Read (capt) | Crusaders | 26/10/85 | 1.93 | 109 | 107 |
| L. (Luke) Romano | Crusaders | 16/2/86 | 1.99 | 116 | 29 |
| A.S. (Ardie) Savea | Hurricanes | 14/10/93 | 1.88 | 103 | 22 |
| A.L. (Aaron) Smith | Highlanders | 21/11/88 | 1.71 | 83 | 68 |
| L.Z. (Lima) Sopoaga | Highlanders | 3/2/91 | 1.75 | 92 | 13 |
| L.I.J. (Liam) Squire | Highlanders | 20/3/91 | 1.96 | 109 | 13 |
| S. (Seta) Tamanivalu | Crusaders | 23/1/92 | 1.89 | 104 | 3 |
| C.J. (Codie) Taylor | Crusaders | 31/3/91 | 1.83 | 108 | 26 |
| M.B. (Matt) Todd | Crusaders | 14/4/88 | 1.85 | 104 | 10 |
| J.L. (Jeffery) To'omaga-Allen | Hurricanes | 19/11/90 | 1.92 | 125 | 1 |
| P.T. (Patrick) Tuipulotu | Blues | 23/1/93 | 1.98 | 125 | 15 |
| A.O.H.M. (Ofa) Tu'ungafasi | Blues | 19/4/92 | 1.95 | 122 | 11 |
| L.C. (Luke) Whitelock | Highlanders | 29/1/91 | 1.93 | 112 | 1 |
| S.L. (Samuel) Whitelock | Crusaders | 12/10/88 | 2.02 | 122 | 93 |
| S. (Sonny Bill) Williams | Blues | 3/8/85 | 1.91 | 108 | 43 |

## VISTA ALL BLACKS 2017 NORTHERN TOUR — ENGLAND, FRANCE, SCOTLAND AND WALES

### ALL BLACKS 2017

| | UK Barbarians | France | French XV | Scotland | Wales | TOTALS |
|---|---|---|---|---|---|---|
| McKenzie | – | 15 | – | 15 | 15 | 3 |
| Havili | 15 | – | 15 | – | – | 2 |
| Naholo | 14 | 14 | – | 14 | 14 | 4 |
| Duffie | s | – | 14 | – | – | 2 |
| R. Ioane | – | 11 | – | 11 | 11 | 3 |
| Tamanivalu | 11 | – | 11 | – | – | 2 |
| Mo'unga | – | – | s | – | – | 1 |
| Lienert-Brown | 13 | s | – | s | s | 4 |
| Crotty | – | 13 | – | 13 | 13 | 3 |
| Laumape | 12 | – | 12 | – | – | 2 |
| Goodhue | – | – | 13 | – | – | 1 |
| Williams | – | 12 | – | 12 | 12 | 3 |
| B. Barrett | 10 | 10 | – | 10 | 10 | 4 |
| Sopoaga | s | s | 10 | s | s | 5 |
| Smith | – | 9 | – | 9 | 9 | 3 |
| Perenara | 9 | s | – | s | s | 4 |
| Kerr-Barlow | s | – | 9 | – | – | 2 |
| Drummond | – | – | s | – | – | 1 |
| Read | – | 8 | – | 8 | – | 2 |
| Kaino | 8 | – | – | – | – | 1 |
| L. Whitelock | – | – | 8 | – | 8 | 2 |
| Cane | s | 7 | – | 7 | 7 | 4 |
| Savea | 7 | – | 7 | – | – | 2 |
| Todd | – | s | – | s | s | 3 |
| Squire | – | – | 6 | s | 6 | 3 |
| Fifita | 6 | 6 | – | 6 | – | 3 |
| A. Ioane | – | – | s | – | – | 1 |
| Hunt | – | – | s | – | – | 1 |
| S. Whitelock | – | 5 | – | 5 | 5 | 3 |
| Bird | – | – | 5 | – | – | 1 |
| S. Barrett | 5 | s | s | – | s | 4 |
| Romano | 4 | 4 | – | 4 | – | 3 |
| Tuipulotu | s | – | 4 | – | 4 | 3 |
| Laulala | – | 3 | – | 3 | 3 | 3 |
| Tu'ungafasi | 3 | s | s | s | s | 5 |
| To'omaga-Allen | s | – | 3 | – | – | 2 |
| Hames | 1 | 1 | – | 1 | 1 | 4 |
| Crockett | – | s | – | s | s | 3 |
| Perry | s | – | 1 | – | – | 2 |
| Moli | – | – | s | – | – | 1 |
| Coles | – | 2 | – | – | – | 1 |
| Taylor | – | s | – | 2 | 2 | 3 |
| Harris | 2 | – | 2 | s | s | 4 |
| Aumua | s | – | s | – | – | 2 |

### INDIVIDUAL SCORING

| | Tries | Con | PG | DG | Points |
|---|---|---|---|---|---|
| B. Barrett | 1 | 14 | 2 | – | 39 |
| Naholo | 4 | – | – | – | 20 |
| Cane | 2 | – | – | – | 10 |
| R. Ioane | 2 | – | – | – | 10 |
| Laumape | 2 | – | – | – | 10 |
| Sopoaga | – | 3 | – | – | 6 |
| Crotty | 1 | – | – | – | 5 |
| Duffie | 1 | – | – | – | 5 |
| Fifita | 1 | – | – | – | 5 |
| Coles | 1 | – | – | – | 5 |
| Harris | 1 | – | – | – | 5 |
| Lienert-Brown | 1 | – | – | – | 5 |
| Perenara | 1 | – | – | – | 5 |
| Squire | 1 | – | – | – | 5 |
| Taylor | 1 | – | – | – | 5 |
| McKenzie | 1 | – | – | – | 5 |
| Tuipulotu | 1 | – | – | – | 5 |
| Mo'unga | – | 1 | – | – | 2 |
| **Totals** | **22** | **18** | **2** | **0** | **152** |
| Opposition scored | 13 | 6 | 7 | 0 | 98 |

## NEW ZEALAND IN ENGLAND, FRANCE, SCOTLAND & WALES 2017  Played 5  Won 5  Points for 152  Points against 98

| Date | Opponent | Location | Score | Tries | Con | PG | DG | Referee |
|---|---|---|---|---|---|---|---|---|
| November 4 | UK Barbarians | Twickenham | 31–22 | Perenara, Fifita, Laumape, Cane, Harris | Barrett(3) | | | N. Owens *Wales* |
| November 11 | France | St Denis | 38–18 | Naholo (2), Coles, Crotty, Cane | Barrett(5) | Barrett | | A. Gardner *Australia* |
| November 14 | French XV | Lyon | 28–23 | Squire, Duffie, Tuipulotu, Laumape | Sopoaga(3) Mo'unga | | | L. Pearce *England* |
| November 18 | Scotland | Edinburgh | 22–17 | Taylor, McKenzie, Barrett | Barrett(2) | Barrett | | M. Carley *England* |
| November 25 | Wales | Cardiff | 33–18 | Naholo (2), R. Ioane (2), Lienert-Brown | Barrett(4) | | | W. Barnes *England* |

# NEW ZEALAND v UK BARBARIANS

Twickenham, London                    November 4, 2017

## Won by New Zealand 31–22

### NEW ZEALAND

David Havili

Waisake Naholo          Anton Lienert-Brown          Seta Tamanivalu

Ngani Laumape

Beauden Barrett (capt)

TJ Perenara

Jerome Kaino

Ardie Savea          Scott Barrett          Luke Romano          Vaea Fifita

Ofa Tu'ungafasi          Nathan Harris          Kane Hames

Jacques van Rooyen          Adriaan Strauss          Atu Moli

Kwagga Smith          Dominic Bird          Sam Carter          Steven Luatua

Luke Whitelock

Andy Ellis (capt)

Richie Mo'unga

Harold Vorster

Vince Aso          Richard Buckman          Julian Savea

George Bridge

### UK BARBARIANS

*Reserves: New Zealand* — Lima Sopoaga (temp sub B. Barrett 14–21m, sub Havili 47m), Sam Cane (sub Kaino 47m), Tawera Kerr-Barlow (sub Perenara 47m), Tim Perry (sub Hames 53m), Patrick Tuipulotu (sub S. Barrett 57m), S. Barrett (temp sub Romano 63–67m), Jeffery To'omaga-Allen (sub Tu'ungafasi 67m), Matt Duffie (sub Naholo 67m), Asafo Aumua (sub Harris 67m).

*UK Barbarians* — Ben Franks (sub van Rooyen 47m), Ruan Smith (sub Moli 47m), Willie Britz (sub Bird 49m), Mitch Drummond (sub Ellis 51m), Ruan Ackermann (sub Carter 52m), Acker van der Merwe (sub Strauss 61m), Dillon Hunt (sub Luatua 62m), Robert du Preez (sub Buckman 70m).

*Referee:* Nigel Owens (*Wales*)
*Assistant Referees:* Nic Berry (*Australia*)
          Ben Whitehouse (*Wales*)
*TMO:* Rowan Kitt (*England*)

*Kick-off:* 7.01pm
*Attendance:* 62,500
*Conditions:* rain

*Scorers:*     **New Zealand:**
          *Tries:* Perenara, Fifita, Laumape
          Cane, Harris

          **UK Barbarians:**
          *Tries:* Bridge (2), Mo'unga, Carter

*Conversions:* B. Barrett (3)

          *Conversion:* Mo'unga

*Scoring:* First half: 8m Mo'unga try 0–5, 15m Bridge try 0–10, 17m Perenara try 5–10, 29m Carter try, Mo'unga conversion 5–17, 34m Fifita try 10–17.

Second half: 53m laumape try, B. Barrett conversion 17–17, 55m Cane try, B. Barrett conversion 24–17, 59m Harris try, B. Barrett conversion 31–17, 80m Bridge try 31–22.

Asafo Aumua and Tim Perry made their All Blacks debut.

The All Blacks won the Killick Cup.

# NEW ZEALAND v FRANCE

| Test #564 | Stade de France, Saint Denis | November 11, 2017 |
|---|---|---|

### Won by New Zealand 38–18

## NEW ZEALAND

Damian McKenzie

| Waisake Naholo | Ryan Crotty | Rieko Ioane |
|---|---|---|

Sonny Bill Williams

Beauden Barrett

Aaron Smith

Kieran Read (capt)

| Sam Cane | Samuel Whitelock | Luke Romano | Vaea Fifita |
|---|---|---|---|
| Nepo Laulala | | Dane Coles | Kane Hames |

| Jefferson Poirot | Guilhem Guirado (capt) | Rabah Slimani |
|---|---|---|

| Kevin Gourdon | Paul Gabrillagues | Sebastien Vahaamahina | Judicael Concoriet |
|---|---|---|---|

Louis Picamoles

Antoine Dupont

Anthony Belleau

Mathieu Basteraud

| Yoann Huget | Geoffrey Doumayrou | Teddy Thomas |
|---|---|---|

Nans Ducuing

## FRANCE

**Reserves: New Zealand** — Codie Taylor (sub Coles 23m), S. Barrett (temp sub Romano29–38m, sub Romano 65m), Matt Todd (sub Read 47m, Cane to #8), Wyatt Crockett (sub Hames 47m), Ofa Tu'ungafasi (sub Laulala 60m), Anton Lienert-Brown (sub Crotty 65m), Lima Sopoaga (sub Havili 66m, B. Barrett to #15), TJ Perenara (sub Smith 68m).

**France** — Raphael Chaume (sub Poirot 35m), Daniel Kotze (sub Slimani 60m), Paul Jedrasick (sub Gabrillagues 60m), Damian Penaud (sub Doumayrou 60m), Anthony Jellonch (sub Picamoles 60m), Clement Maynadier (sub Guirado 70m), Baptiste Serin (sub Dupont 72m), Francois Trinh-Duc (sub Belleau 75m).

**Referee:** Angus Gardner (*Australia*)
**Assistant Referees:** Matthew Carley (*England*)
Tim Foley (*England*)
**TMO:** Rowan Kitt (*England*)

**Kick-off:** 7.45pm
**Attendance:** 81,500
**Conditions:** rain, ground soft

| **Scorers:** | **New Zealand:** | **France:** |
|---|---|---|
| | *Tries:* Naholo (2), Coles, Crotty, Cane | *Tries:* Thomas, penalty try |
| | *Conversions:* B. Barrett (5) | *Penalties:* Belleau (2) |
| | *Penalty:* B. Barrett | |

**Scoring:** First half: 8m Coles try, B. Barrett conversion 7–0, 16 m B. Barrett penalty goal 10–0, 22m Naholo try, B. Barrett conversion 17–0, 26m Thomas try 17–5, 31m Crotty try, B. Barrett conversion 24–5, 39m Cane try, B. Barrett conversion 31–5.

Second half: 42m Belleau penalty goal 31–8, 47m penalty try 31–15, 51m Belleau penalty goal 31–18, 80m Naholo try, B. Barrett conversion 38–18..

Yellow cards to Slimani (France 35m, Williams (*NZ*) 46m.

The All Blacks wore white jerseys with black across the shoulders, and a Flanders poppy on the left sleeve.

# NEW ZEALAND v FRENCH XV
**Groupama Stadium, Lyon,**        **November 14, 2017**
## Won by New Zealand 28–23
### NEW ZEALAND
David Havili

Matt Duffie      Jack Goodhue      Seta Tamanivalu

Ngani Laumape

Lima Sopoaga

Tawera Kerr-Barlow

Luke Whitelock (capt)

Ardie Savea      Dominic Bird    Patrick Tuipulotu      Liam Squire

Jeffery Toʻomaga-Allen      Nathan Harris      Tim Perry

Dany Priso      Camile Chat      Malik Hamadacke

Sekou Macalou    Yoann Maestri (capt)   Romain Taofifenua      Wenceslas Lauret

Marco Tauleigne

Yann Lesgourgues

Francois Trinh Duc

Jonathan Danty

Hugo Bonneval      Henry Chavancy      Gabriel Lacroix

Scott Spedding
### FRENCH XV

**Reserves: New Zealand —** Akira Ioane (sub Squire 52m), Richie Moʻunga (sub Sopoaga 52m), Atu Moli (sub Perry 56m), Scott Barrett (sub Tuipulotu 65m), Asafo Aumua (sub Harris 70m), Ofa Tuʻungafasi (sub Toʻomaga-Allen 66m), Dillon Hunt (sub Savea 70m), Mitchell Drummond (sub Kerr-Barlow 70m).

**French XV —** Fabien Sarconnie (sub Tauleigne 14m), Vincent Rattez (temp sub Danty 26–36m, sub 56m), Julian Le Devedec (sub Taofifenua 53m), Lucas Pointud (sub Priso 53m), Cedate Gomes Sa (sub Hamadache 58m), Christopher Tolofua (sub Chat 58m), Francois Trinh-Duc (sub Plisson 59m), Chat (temp sub Sanconnie 65–70m), Maxime Machenaud (sub Lacroix 67m).

**Referee:** Luke Pearce (*England*)      **Kick-off:** 6.55pm
**Assistant Referees:** Andrew Brace      **Attendance:** 58,607
           David Wilkinson      **Conditions:** Cold, soft surface
**TMO:** Sean Davey

**Scorers:**    **New Zealand:**            **French XV:**
         *Tries:* Squire, Duffie, Tuipulotu,      *Tries:* Lacroix (2), Chavancy
         Laumape                       *Conversion:* Trinh Duc
         *Conversions:* Sopoaga (3), Moʻunga    *Penalties:* Trinh Duc, Plisson

**Scoring:** First half: 10m Squire try, Sopoaga conversion 7–0, 14m Lacroix try, Trin Duc conversion 7–7, 23m Duffie try, Sopoaga conversion 14–7, 27m Lacroix try 14–12, 15m Trinh Duc penalty goal 14–15.

Second half:51m Tuipulotu try, Sopoaga conversion 21–15, 55m Laumape try, Moʻunga conversion 28–15, 60m Plisson penalty goal 28–18, 72m Chavancy try 28–23.

Yellow card Jack Goodhue 66m

Jack Goodhue, Akira Ioane, Richie Moʻunga, Atu Moli, Mitchell Drummond and Dillon Hunt made their All Blacks debut.

# NEW ZEALAND v SCOTLAND

Test #565              Murrayfield, Edinburgh              November 18, 2017

Won by New Zealand 22–17

### NEW ZEALAND

Damian McKenzie

Waisake Naholo          Ryan Crotty          Rieko Ioane

Sonny Bill Williams

Beauden Barrett

Aaron Smith

Kieran Read (capt)

Sam Cane          Samuel Whitelock     Luke Romano          Vaea Fifita

Nepo Laulala               Codie Taylor               Kane Hames

Darryl Marfo               Stuart McInally          Zander Fagerson

Hamish Watson       Jonny Gray          Ben Toolis     John Barclay (capt)

Cornell du Preez

Ali Price

Finn Russell

Alex Dunbar

Lee Jones          Huw Jones          Tommy Seymour

Stuart Hogg

### SCOTLAND

**Reserves: New Zealand** — Liam Squire (sub Romano 44m, Fifita to #4), Wyatt Crockett (sub Hames 51m, Ofa Tu'ungafasi (sub Laulala 59m), TJ Perenara (sub Smith 64m), Anton Lienert-Brown (sub Crotty 64m), Hames (sub Fifita 70m, Read to #4), Nathan Harris (sub Taylor 70m), Matt Todd (sub Cane 70m), Lima Sopoaga (sub Naholo 70m).

**Scotland** — Luke Hamilton (sub Watson 26m), Simon Berghan (sub Fagerson 40m), Peter Horne (sub Dunbar 44m), George Turner (sub Hamilton 49m, McInally to #7), Jamie Bhatti (sub Marfo 51m), Grant Gilchrist (sub Toolis 51m), Byron McGuigan (sub L. Jones 64m), Henry Pyrgos.

**Referee:** Matthew Carley (*England*)
**Assistant Referees:** Romain Poite (*France*)
     Ian Davies (*Wales*)
**TMO:** Graham Hughes (*England*)

**Kick-off** 6.15pm
**Attendance:** 65,000
**Conditions:** cold, otherwise excellent

**Scorers: New Zealand:**
  *Tries:* Taylor, McKenzie, Barrett
  *Conversions:* B. Barrett (2)
  *Penalty:* B. Barrett

**Scotland:**
  *Tries:* Gray, H. Jones
  *Conversions:* Russell (2)
  *Penalty:* Russell

**Scoring:** First half: 6m Russell penalty goal 0–3, 38m Barrett penalty goal 3–3.

Second half: 44m Taylor try 8–3, 51m McKenzie try , Barrett conversion 15–3, 61m Gray try, Russell conversion 15–10, 66m Barrett try, Barrett conversion 22–10, 76m H. Jones try, Russell conversion 22–17.

Yellow cards to Cane 61m, Crockett 70m

# NEW ZEALAND v WALES

**Test #566**　　　　**Principality Stadium, Cardiff**　　　　**November 25, 2017**

**Won by New Zealand 33–18**

### NEW ZEALAND

Damian McKenzie

Waisake Naholo　　　　Ryan Crotty　　　　Rieko Ioane

Sonny Bill Williams

Beauden Barrett

Aaron Smith

Luke Whitelock

| Sam Cane | Samuel Whitelock (capt) | Patrick Tuipulotu | Liam Squire |

Nepo Laulala　　　　Codie Taylor　　　　Kane Hames

Rob Evans　　　　Ken Owens　　　　Tomas Francis

Josh Navidi　　　　Jake Ball　　　　Alun Wyn Jones (capt)　　　　Aaron Shingler

Taulupe Faletau

Rhys Webb

Dan Biggar

Owen Williams

Steff Evans　　　　Scott Williams　　　　Hallam Amos

Leigh Halfpenny

### WALES

**Reserves: New Zealand —** Anton Lienert-Brown (sub Crotty 18m), Ofa Tu'ungafasi (sub Laulala 40m), Matt Todd (sub L. Whitelock 45m), Scott Barrett (sub Tuipulotu 45m), Wyatt Crockett (sub Hames 59m), TJ Perenara (sub Smith 63m), Nathan Harris (sub Taylor 71m), Lima Sopoaga (sub Naholo 71m).

**Wales —** Gareth Davies (sub Webb 8m), Cory Hill (sub Ball 18m), Jamie Roberts (sub S. Williams 57m), Wyn Jones (sub R. Evans 57m), Rhys Priestland (sub Biggar 63m), Justin Tipuric (sub Shingler 72m), Kristian Dacey (sub Owens 75m), Leon Brown (sub Francis 75m).

**Referee:** Wayne Barnes (*England*)　　　　**Kick-off** 5.15pm
**Assistant Referees:** Jerome Garces (*France*)　　　　**Attendance:** 74,169
　　　　Frank Murphy (*Ireland*)　　　　**Conditions:** Roof closed, warm, ground soft
**TMO:** Rowan Kitt (*England*)

**Scorers:**　　**New Zealand:**　　　　　　　　　　**Wales:**
　　　　*Tries:* Naholo (2), Ioane (2),　　　　　*Tries:* S. Williams, Davies
　　　　Lienert-Brown　　　　　　　　　　　*Conversion:* Halfpenny
　　　　*Conversions:* B. Barrett (4)　　　　　*Penalties:* Halfpenny (2)

**Scoring:** First half: 9m Halfpenny penalty goal 0–3, 14m Naholo try, Barrett conversion 7–3, 34m Halfpenny penalty goal 7–6, 38m Naholo try 12–6, 40m S. Williams try 12–11.

Second half: 56m Lienert-Brown try, Barrett conversion 19–11, 61m Ioane try, Barrett conversion 26–11, 69m Davies try, Halfpenny conversion 26–18, 74m Ioane try, Barrett conversion 33–18.

Yellow card to S. Whitelock 67m

# NEW ZEALAND UNDER 20
## WORLD RUGBY U20 CHAMPIONSHIPS

New Zealand won the World Rugby Under 20 tournament, held in Georgia, for the sixth time in 10 attempts. Along the way they scored a record 41 tries and 282 points. The climax came in the grand final when New Zealand scored a record 64 points, including 10 tries, against England. Four New Zealand players scored hat-tricks of tries in a match during the tournament. Will Jordan and the tournament's top point's scorer, Tiaan Falcon, were nominees for Player of the Tournament.

**Pool A**

| May 31 | England | 74 | Samoa | 17 | Tbilsi |
|---|---|---|---|---|---|
|  | Australia | 24 | Wales | 17 | Tbilsi |
| June 4 | Australia | 33 | Samoa | 26 | Tbilsi |
|  | England | 34 | Wales | 22 | Tbilsi |
| June 8 | Wales | 54 | Samoa | 20 | Tbilsi |
|  | England | 20 | Australia | 19 | Tbilsi |

**Pool B**

| May 31 | New Zealand | 42 | Scotland | 20 | Kutaisi |
|---|---|---|---|---|---|
|  | Italy | 22 | Ireland | 21 | Kutaisi |
| June 4 | Ireland | 38 | Scotland | 32 | Kutaisi |
|  | New Zealand | 68 | Italy | 26 | Kutaisi |
| June 8 | Scotland | 17 | Italy | 16 | Kutaisi |
|  | New Zealand | 69 | Ireland | 3 | Kutaisi |

**Pool C**

| May 31 | South Africa | 23 | France | 23 | Tbilsi |
|---|---|---|---|---|---|
|  | Argentina | 37 | Georgia | 26 | Tbilsi |
| June 4 | France | 26 | Argentina | 25 | Tbilsi |
|  | South Africa | 38 | Georgia | 14 | Tbilsi |
| June 8 | South Africa | 72 | Argentina | 14 | Tbilsi |
|  | France | 54 | Georgia | 0 | Tbilsi |

**9th place semi-final**

| June 13 | Ireland | 52 | Samoa | 20 | Tbilsi |
|---|---|---|---|---|---|
|  | Georgia | 26 | Argentina | 25 | Tbilsi |

**5th place semi-final**

| June 13 | Australia | 42 | Italy | 19 | Tbilsi |
|---|---|---|---|---|---|
|  | Scotland | 29 | Wales | 20 | Tbilsi |

**Semi-finals**

| June 13 | England | 24 | South Africa | 22 | Tbilsi |
|---|---|---|---|---|---|
|  | New Zealand | 39 | France | 20 | Tbilsi |

**11th place playoff**

| June 18 | Argentina | 53 | Samoa | 22 | Tbilsi |
|---|---|---|---|---|---|

**9th place playoff**

| June 18 | Ireland | 24 | Georgia | 18 | Tbilsi |
|---|---|---|---|---|---|

**7th place playoff**

| June 18 | Scotland | 24 | Australia | 17 | Tbilsi |
|---|---|---|---|---|---|

**5th place playoff**

| June 18 | Wales | 25 | Italy | 24 | Tbilsi |
|---|---|---|---|---|---|

| 3rd place playoff | | | | | |
|---|---|---|---|---|---|
| June 18 | South Africa | 37 | France | 15 | Tbilsi |
| **Final** | | | | | |
| June 18 | New Zealand | 64 | England | 17 | Tbilsi |

## NEW ZEALAND UNDER 20, 2017

| Player | Union | Date of birth | Height | Weight | Oceania | World Cup |
|---|---|---|---|---|---|---|
| H.M. (Harrison) Allen | Canterbury | 7/5/97 | 1.83 | 107 | P | P |
| A.J. (Asafo) Aumua | Wellington | 5/5/97 | 1.77 | 108 | P | P |
| S.W. (Sam) Caird | Waikato | 18/3/97 | 2.02 | 116 | P | P |
| A.J. (Adrian) Choat | Auckland | 20/11/97 | 1.90 | 100 | P | P |
| T.M. (Thomas) Christie | Canterbury | 4/3/98 | 1.86 | 103 | P | P |
| C.D. (Caleb) Clarke | Auckland | 29/3/99 | 1.86 | 105 | P | P |
| R.C. (Ryan) Coxon | Waikato | 30/9/97 | 1.83 | 118 | P | P |
| E.C.S. (Ereatara) Enari | Canterbury | 30/5/97 | 1.78 | 83 | P | P |
| B.M. (Brayden) Ennor | Canterbury | 16/7/97 | 1.86 | 92 | P | P |
| L.T. (Tima) Fainga'anuku | Tasman | 26/4/97 | 1.88 | 103 | P | P |
| T.J. (Tiaan) Falcon | Hawke's Bay | 19/6/97 | 1.81 | 88 | P | P |
| T.J. (Tim) Farrell | Hawke's Bay | 23/6/98 | 1.91 | 115 | P | P |
| A.F. (Alex) Fidow | Wellington | 19/8/97 | 1.87 | 128 | P | P |
| K.M. (Kemara) Hauiti-Parapara | Wellington | 5/3/97 | 1.74 | 81 | P | P |
| L.B. (Luke) Jacobson (capt) | Waikato | 20/4/97 | 1.90 | 106 | P | P |
| W.T. (Will) Jordan | Tasman | 24/2/98 | 1.88 | 91 | P | P |
| O.N.T. (Orbyn) Leger | Counties Manukau | 13/3/97 | 1.84 | 90 | P | P |
| E. (Ezekiel) Lindenmuth | Auckland | 14/7/97 | 1.87 | 116 | P | P |
| J.A. (Josh) McKay | Canterbury | 10/10/97 | 1.81 | 88 | P | P |
| C.R. (Ciarahn) Matoe | Taranaki | 16/11/98 | 1.81 | 89 | P | – |
| M.E.R. (Marino) Mikaele-Tu'u | Hawke's Bay | 6/11/97 | 1.93 | 114 | P | P |
| A.J. (Alex) Mitchell* | Taranaki | 12/3/97 | 1.85 | 114 | – | – |
| J.N. (Jona) Nareki | Otago | 27/12/97 | 1.77 | 80 | P | P |
| D.R. (Dalton) Papali'i | Auckland | 11/10/97 | 1.90 | 104 | P | P |
| S. (Stephen) Perofeta | Taranaki | 12/3/97 | 1.81 | 85 | – | P |
| J.W.L. (Jacob) Pierce | Auckland | 10/9/97 | 2.01 | 106 | P | P |
| C.T. (Carlos) Price | Wellington | 30/9/98 | 1.78 | 80 | P | – |
| P.G. (Pouri) Rakete-Stones | Hawke's Bay | 17/6/97 | 1.81 | 113 | P | P |
| J.P. (John) Sauni | Auckland | 7/7/97 | 1.80 | 113 | P | P |
| S.W. (Samuel) Slade | Auckland | 28/8/97 | 1.94 | 111 | P | P |
| T.R. (Tamati) Tua | Northland | 26/11/97 | 1.91 | 98 | P | P |
| T.C. (Thomas) Umaga-Jensen | Wellington | 31/12/97 | 1.87 | 107 | P | P |
| I.E.T. (Isaia) Walker-Leawere | Wellington | 16/4/97 | 1.98 | 118 | P | P |

*Manager:* Martyn Vercoe          *Head coach:* Craig Philpott
*Assistant coaches:* Cory Brown, David Hewett, Willie Rickards

## NEW ZEALAND UNDER 20 APPEARANCES AT WORLD RUGBY CHAMPIONSHIP 2017

| | Scotland | Italy | Ireland | France | England | Totals |
|---|---|---|---|---|---|---|
| Jordan | 15 | 15 | 15 | 15 | 15 | 5 |
| McKay | 14 | – | s | s | s | 4 |
| Nareki | – | 14 | – | – | – | 1 |
| Fainga'anuku | 11 | s | 14 | 14 | 14 | 5 |
| Clarke | s | 11 | 11 | 11 | 11 | 5 |
| Tua | 13 | s | – | – | s | 3 |
| Ennor | – | 13 | 13 | 13 | 13 | 4 |
| Leger | 12 | 12 | 12 | 12 | 12 | 5 |
| Umaga-Jensen | s | – | s | – | – | 2 |
| Falcon | 10 | 10 | 10 | 10 | – | 4 |
| Perofeta | – | – | – | – | 10 | 1 |
| Enari | 9 | s | 9 | 9 | 9 | 5 |
| Hauiti-Parapara | s | 9 | s | s | s | 5 |
| Jacobson | 8 | 6 | 8 | 6 | 6 | 5 |
| Mikaele-Tu'u | s | 8 | s | 8 | 8 | 5 |
| Christie | 7 | s | 7 | s | s | 5 |
| Papali'i | 6 | – | – | 7 | 7 | 3 |
| Choat | – | 7 | s | – | – | 2 |
| Slade | 5 | – | 6 | 5 | 5 | 4 |
| Caird | – | 5 | 5 | s | s | 4 |
| Pierce | s | s | – | – | – | 2 |
| Walker-Leawere | 4 | 4 | 4 | 4 | 4 | 5 |
| Coxon | 3 | s | – | – | – | 2 |
| Fidow | s | s | 3 | s | s | 5 |
| Rakete-Stones | – | 3 | s | 3 | 3 | 4 |
| Lindenmuth | 1 | 1 | 1 | 1 | 1 | 5 |
| Farrell | s | – | – | – | – | 1 |
| Allen | – | s | s | s | s | 4 |
| Aumua | 2 | – | 2 | 2 | 2 | 4 |
| Sauini | s | 2 | s | s | s | 5 |

## INDIVIDUAL SCORING AT RUGBY WORLD CHAMPIONSHIP

| | Tries | Con | PG | DG | Points |
|---|---|---|---|---|---|
| Falcon | 2 | 19 | 7 | – | 69 |
| Clarke | 6 | – | – | – | 30 |
| Aumua | 5 | – | – | – | 25 |
| Jordan | 5 | – | – | – | 25 |
| Fainga'anuku | 3 | – | – | – | 15 |
| Papali'i | 3 | – | – | – | 15 |
| Leger | 2 | 2 | – | – | 14 |
| Perofeta | – | 7 | – | – | 14 |
| Choat | 2 | – | – | – | 10 |
| Ennor | 2 | – | – | – | 10 |
| Jacobson | 2 | – | – | – | 10 |

| | Tries | Con | PG | DG | Points |
|---|---|---|---|---|---|
| McKay | 2 | – | – | – | 10 |
| Rakete-Stones | 2 | – | – | – | 10 |
| Christie | 1 | – | – | – | 5 |
| Enari | 1 | – | – | – | 5 |
| Nareki | 1 | – | – | – | 5 |
| Tua | 1 | – | – | – | 5 |
| Walker-Leawere | 1 | – | – | – | 5 |
| **Totals** | **41** | **28** | **7** | **0** | **282** |
| *Opposition scored* | *14* | *8* | *2* | *0* | *92* |

## NEW ZEALAND UNDER 20 APPEARANCES AT OCEANIA TOURNAMENT 2017

| | Fiji | Samoa | Australia | TOTALS |
|---|---|---|---|---|
| Jordan | 15 | – | 15 | 2 |
| McKay | – | 15 | 14 | 2 |
| Nareki | 11 | 14 | – | 2 |
| Fainga'anuku | 14 | – | 11 | 2 |
| Clarke | s | 11 | s | 3 |
| Tua | 13 | – | 13 | 2 |
| Ennor | – | 13 | – | 1 |
| Leger | 12 | s | 12 | 3 |
| Umaga-Jensen | – | 12 | s | 2 |
| Falcon | 10 | s | 10 | 3 |
| Matoe | s | 10 | – | 2 |
| Enari | – | – | 9 | 1 |
| Hauiti-Parapara | 9 | s | s | 3 |
| Price | s | 9 | – | 2 |
| Jacobson | 8 | 6 | 8 | 3 |
| Mikaele-Tu'u | – | 8 | – | 1 |
| Christie | 7 | – | 7 | 2 |
| Papali'i | 6 | s | 6 | 3 |
| Choat | s | 7 | s | 3 |
| Slade | 5 | 4 | – | 2 |
| Caird | – | 5 | 5 | 2 |
| Pierce | 4 | s | s | 3 |
| Walker-Leawere | s | – | 4 | 2 |
| Coxon | 3 | 3 | – | 2 |
| Fidow | – | – | s | 1 |
| Rakete-Stones | s | s | 3 | 3 |
| Lindenmuth | – | s | 1 | 2 |
| Farrell | s | 1 | – | 2 |
| Allen | 1 | – | s | 2 |
| Aumua | s | 2 | 2 | 3 |
| Sauini | 2 | s | s | 3 |

## INDIVIDUAL SCORING AT OCEANIA TOURNAMENT 2017

| | Tries | Con | PG | DG | Points |
|---|---|---|---|---|---|
| Falcon | – | 14 | 4 | – | 40 |
| Jordan | 4 | – | – | – | 20 |
| Matoe | – | 8 | – | – | 16 |
| Christie | 3 | – | – | – | 15 |
| Jacobson | 3 | – | – | – | 15 |
| Coxon | 2 | – | – | – | 10 |
| Ennor | 2 | – | – | – | 10 |
| Papali'i | 2 | – | – | – | 10 |
| Aumua | 1 | – | – | – | 5 |
| Clarke | 1 | – | – | – | 5 |
| Leger | 1 | – | – | – | 5 |

| | Tries | Con | PG | DG | Points |
|---|---|---|---|---|---|
| Lindenmuth | 1 | – | – | – | 5 |
| Nareki | 1 | – | – | – | 5 |
| Price | 1 | – | – | – | 5 |
| Slade | 1 | – | – | – | 5 |
| Tua | 1 | – | – | – | 5 |
| Umaga-Jensen | 1 | – | – | – | 5 |
| Walker-Leawere | 1 | – | – | – | 5 |
| | | | | | |
| Totals | 26 | 22 | 4 | 0 | 186 |
| Opposition scored | 2 | 2 | 6 | 0 | 32 |

## NEW ZEALAND UNDER 20 TEAM RECORD AT OCEANIA TOURNAMENT AND WORLD RUGBY CHAMPIONSHIP 2017

| | | | | Played 8 | Won 8 | Points for 468 | | Points against 124 |
|---|---|---|---|---|---|---|---|---|
| Date | Opponent | Location | Score | Tries | Con | PG | | Referee |
| April 28 | Fiji Oceania | Gold Coast | 63–3 | Jordan (3), Christie (2), Coxon, Leger, Papali'i | Falcon (5) Matoe (2) | Falcon (3) | | E. Martin Australia |
| May 2 | Samoa Oceania | Gold Coast | 80–23 | Ennor (2), Nareki, Clarke, Price, Umaga-Jensen, Jacobson, Papali'i, Slade, Coxon, Aumua, Lindenmuth | Matoe (6) Falcon (4) | | | T. Rokoverini Fiji |
| May 6 | Australia Oceania | Gold Coast | 43–6 | Jacobson (2), Jordan, Tua, Walker-Leawere, Christie | Falcon (5) | Falcon | | J. Way Australia |
| May 21 | Scotland WRC | Kutaisi | 42–20 | Fainga'anuku (3), Aumua, Papali'i, Leger | Falcon (3) | Falcon (2) | | T. Foley England |
| June 4 | Italy WRC | Kutaisi | 68–26 | Clarke (2), Jordan, Leger, Nareki, Rakete-Stones, Ennor, Tua, Choat | Falcon (5) Leger (2) | Falcon (3) | | P. de Luca Argentina |
| June 8 | Ireland WRC | Kutaisi | 69–3 | Clarke (3), Jordan (3), Ennor, Christie, Enari, McKay, Falcon | Falcon (7) | | | J. van Heerden South Africa |
| June 13 | France WRC (semi-final) | Tbilisi | 39–26 | Jordan, Falcon, Papali'i, Clarke, Aumua | Falcon (4) | Falcon (2) | | M. Adamson Scotland |
| June 18 | England WRC (final) | Tbilisi | 64–17 | Aumua (3), Jacobson (2), Papali'i, Rakete-Stones, Walker-Leawere, McKay, Christie | Perofeta (7) | | | N. Berry Australia |

# MAORI ALL BLACKS 2017

| | Province | Date of Birth | Height | Weight | Games to 1/1/18 |
|---|---|---|---|---|---|
| T.E.S. (Tim) Bateman | Canterbury | 3/6/87 | 1.82 | 91 | 14 |
| A.A.D. (Ambrose) Curtis | Manawatu | 17/4/92 | 1.91 | 101 | 1 |
| A.L. (Ash) Dixon (capt) | Hawke's Bay | 1/9/88 | 1.82 | 102 | 11 |
| E.C. (Elliot) Dixon | Southland | 9/4/89 | 1.93 | 111 | 10 |
| H.T.P (Hika) Elliot | – | 22/12/86 | 1.86 | 115 | 10 |
| C.I. (Chris) Eves | North Harbour | 11/12/87 | 1.87 | 117 | 10 |
| T.S.G. (Tom) Franklin | Bay of Plenty | 11/8/90 | 2.00 | 110 | 7 |
| J.K. (Jackson) Garden-Bachop | Wellington | 3/10/94 | 1.83 | 99 | 2 |
| B.D. (Bryn) Hall | North Harbour | 3/2/92 | 1.83 | 93 | 1 |
| K.S. (Kane) Hames | Tasman | 28/8/88 | 1.84 | 120 | 6 |
| J.K. (Jackson) Hemopo | Manawatu | 14/11/93 | 1.94 | 113 | 2 |
| S.T. (Sam) Henwood | Counties Manukau | 28/3/91 | 1.86 | 109 | 2 |
| J.M.R.A. (Jarrad) Hoeata | North Harbour | 12/12/83 | 1.98 | 115 | 10 |
| A.L. (Akira) Ioane | Auckland | 16/6/95 | 1.94 | 113 | 8 |
| R.E. (Rieko) Ioane | Auckland | 18/3/97 | 1.88 | 103 | 4 |
| T.N.J. (Tawera) Kerr-Barlow | Waikato | 15/8/90 | 1.87 | 89 | 4 |
| T. (Tyrell) Lomax | Tasman | 1/6/96 | 1.92 | 127 | 2 |
| J.F.R. (James) Lowe | Tasman | 8/7/92 | 1.87 | 104 | 6 |
| D.S. (Damian) McKenzie | Waikato | 20/4/95 | 1.75 | 81 | 4 |
| J.M. (Jordan) Manihera | Waikato | 8/5/93 | 1.96 | 114 | 2 |
| B. (Ben) May | Hawke's Bay | 13/10/82 | 1.94 | 119 | 13 |
| L.J. (Liam) Messam | Waikato | 25/3/84 | 1.90 | 109 | 13 |
| T.K.H. (Keepa) Mewett | Bay of Plenty | 10/5/87 | 1.98 | 115 | 1 |
| N.R. (Nehe) Milner-Skudder | Manawatu | 15/13/19 | 1.80 | 90 | 3 |
| C.J. (Charlie) Ngatai | Taranaki | 17/8/90 | 1.86 | 100 | 12 |
| L.J. (Liam) Polwart | Bay of Plenty | 2/4/95 | 1.85 | 107 | 2 |
| L.T. (Leighton) Price | Taranaki | 24/3/89 | 1.98 | 112 | 4 |
| M.P. (Matt) Proctor | Wellington | 26/10/92 | 1.80 | 90 | 10 |
| D.J. (Dan) Pryor | Northland | 14/4/88 | 1.90 | 104 | 5 |
| M.T. (Marcel) Renata | Auckland | 24/2/94 | 1.89 | 118 | 7 |
| J. (Jono) Ruru | Otago | 2/2/93 | 1.83 | 94 | 1 |
| S.T. (Shaun) Stevenson | North Harbour | 14/11/96 | 1.93 | 95 | 2 |
| T.T.H. (Te Toiroa) Tahuriorangi | Taranaki | 31/3/95 | 1.73 | 84 | 1 |
| R. (Rob) Thompson | Canterbury | 2/8/91 | 1.84 | 103 | 3 |
| S.T. (Sean) Wainui | Taranaki | 23/10/95 | 1.92 | 104 | 5 |
| T.T. (Tei) Walden | Otago | 25/5/93 | 1.82 | 94 | 1 |
| B.M. (Brad) Weber | Hawke's Bay | 17/1/91 | 1.75 | 75 | 7 |
| I.T. (Ihaia) West | Hawke's Bay | 16/1/92 | 1.75 | 84 | 10 |
| J.T. (Joe) Wheeler | – | 20/10/87 | 2.00 | 111 | 4 |
| R.G. (Ross) Wright | Northland | 25/8/86 | 1.80 | 113 | 2 |

*Coach:* Colin Cooper for the Lions game. Clayton McMillan for the End of Year Tour.
*Assistant coach:* Tana Umaga

## INDIVIDUAL SCORING

| | Tries | Con | PG | DG | Points |
|---|---|---|---|---|---|
| West | – | 4 | 2 | – | 14 |
| Garden-Bachop | 1 | 1 | 1 | – | 10 |
| Wainui | 2 | – | – | – | 10 |
| penalty try | 1 | – | – | – | 7 |
| Curtis | 1 | – | – | – | 5 |
| Franklin | 1 | – | – | – | 5 |
| A.Ioane | 1 | – | – | – | 5 |
| Messam | 1 | – | – | – | 5 |
| Ngatai | 1 | – | – | – | 5 |
| Stevenson | 1 | – | – | – | 5 |
| McKenzie | – | 1 | 1 | – | 5 |
| **Totals** | **10t** | **6** | **4** | **0** | **76** |
| *Opposition scored* | *4t* | *1* | *12* | *0* | *60* |

## TEAM 2017

| | B I Lions | Canada | French Barbarians | TOTALS |
|---|---|---|---|---|
| Lowe | 15 | – | – | 1 |
| Ngatai | 12 | 15 | 15 | 3 |
| Wainui | – | 14 | 14 | 2 |
| Milner-Skudder | 14 | – | – | 1 |
| R. Ioane | 11 | – | – | 1 |
| Curtis | – | 11 | – | 1 |
| Stevenson | – | s | 11 | 2 |
| Proctor | 13 | – | – | 1 |
| Bateman | – | 13 | 13 | 2 |
| Thompson | s | 12 | 12 | 3 |
| Walden | – | – | s | 1 |
| McKenzie | 10 | – | – | 1 |
| West | s | 10 | s | 3 |
| Garden-Bachop | – | s | 10 | 2 |
| Kerr-Barlow | 9 | – | – | 1 |
| Hall | s | – | – | 1 |
| Weber | – | 9 | 9 | 2 |
| Tahuriorangi | – | s | – | 1 |
| Ruru | – | – | s | 1 |
| Messam | 8 | – | – | 1 |
| A.Ioane | 6 | 8 | 8 | 3 |
| Manihera | – | s | s | 2 |
| E. Dixon | 7 | – | – | 1 |
| Pryor | s | 7 | s | 3 |
| Henwood | – | s | 7 | 2 |
| Franklin | 5 | 6 | 6 | 3 |
| Hoeata | – | 5 | – | 1 |
| Mewett | – | – | 5 | 1 |
| Wheeler | 4 | – | – | 1 |
| Price | s | – | – | 1 |
| Hemopo | – | 4 | 4 | 2 |
| May | 3 | – | – | 1 |
| Renata | s | 3 | 3 | 3 |
| Lomax | – | s | s | 2 |
| Hames | 1 | – | – | 1 |
| Eves | s | 1 | 1 | 3 |
| Wright | – | s | s | 2 |
| A.Dixon | 2 | 2 | 2 | 3 |
| Elliot | s | – | – | 1 |
| Polwart | – | s | s | 2 |

## MAORI ALL BLACKS TEAM RECORD, 2017

Played 3    Won 1    Lost 2    Points for 76    Points against 60

| Date | Opponent | Location | Score | Tries | Con | PG | DG | Referee |
|------|----------|----------|-------|-------|-----|-----|-----|---------|
| June 17 | B I Lions | Rotorua | 10–32 | Messam | McKenzie | McKenzie | | J. Peyper *South Africa* |
| November 3 | Canada | Vancouver | 51–9 | Curtis, A.Ioane, Franklin, Ngatai, Stevenson, Garden-Bachop, Wainui | West (4) Garden-Bachop | West (2) | | K. Weaver *USA* |
| November 10 | French Barbarians | Bordeaux | 15–19 | Wainui, penalty try | | Garden-Bachop | | S. Kubo *Japan* |

# NEW ZEALAND UNIVERSITIES

New Zealand Universities had a two-match programme in 2017, for which just 23 players were selected. Results were: April 25, v Wasps, Blake Park, Mount Maunganui, lost 21–38 (not first-class); April 29, v Kanto, Hamilton, won 17–14

The match against Kanto was the curtain-raiser to the Chiefs v Sunwolves Super Rugby match. It was 14–14 at halftime, the only score in the second half being a penalty goal to Tyrone Elkington-MacDonald.

## v KANTO

**FMG Waikato Stadium, Hamilton**                     **April 29, 2017**

### Won 17–14

Sam Healy
*Massey*

Te Wihi Wright          Harrison Groundwater          Tyler Campbell
*OB Univ*                      *Lincoln*                          *Waikato*

Hamish Northcott
*Massey*

Jason Robertson
*Waikato*

Jack Stratton (capt.)
*Lincoln*

Kirk Tufuga
*Massey*

Damien Scott     Jonathan Osbourne     Jack Sherratt          Sam Godwin
*Auckland*              *Lincoln*                *Otago*               *Canterbury*

Angus Williams                Nick Grogan               Finnbarr Kerr-Newell
*Otago*                        *Massey*                        *OB Univ*

---

*Reserves:* Tyrone Elkington-MacDonald *Auckland* (for Robertson, 50 min); Chris Gawler *Lincoln* (for Williams, 58); Valentine Tauamiti *Auckland* (for Sherratt, 74); Tom Hardy *Otago* (for Grogan, 74); Nigel Gibbs *Canterbury* (for Groundwater, 76); Marius Tonu'u *Auckland* (for Stratton, 79); Morgyn Cowan *Canterbury* (for Tufuga, 79). Not used: Reed Wilson *Waikato*

*Scorers:*
*Tries:* Groundwater, Robertson
*Conversions:* Robertson (2)
*Penalty Goal:* Elkington-MacDonald

*Referee:* Michael Lash

Before the team assembled original selections Sinclair Dominkovich-Murray (*Auckland*) and Will Mangos (*Old Boys University*) withdrew and were replaced by Morgyn Cowan and Valentine Tauamati respectively.

After the match versus Wasps, Caleb Makene (*Lincoln*), Sam Malcolm (*Massey*) and Marcel Renata (*Auckland*) withdrew due to injury and were replaced by Tyler Campbell, Tyrone Elkington-MacDonald and Reed Wilson respectively.

*Manager:* P.R. (Peter) Magson (*Lincoln*)
*Coach:* B.P. (Brendon) Timmins (*Otago*)
*Assistant Coach:* S.J. (Simon) Forrest (*Otago*)
*Doctor:* S.J. (Stephen) Williams (*Otago*)
*Physio:* J.D. (Jonathon) Moyle (*Auckland*)

# KANTO RUGBY UNION

Kanto Rugby Union from Japan made a three-match tour in April. The results were:
April 23 v Auckland University-Marist RFC, at Colin Maiden Park, Auckland. Won 123–0 (not first-class).
April 26 v Counties Manukau Cavaliers, at Massey Park, Papakura. Won 14–12 (not first-class).
April 29 v New Zealand Universities, at FMG Waikato Stadium, Hamilton. Lost 14–17.

## v NEW ZEALAND UNIVERSITIES

**FMG Waikato Stadium, Hamilton**                    **April 29, 2017**

**Lost 14–17**

Naoki Moriya

Hideto Kondo          Kwon Yuin          Tokio Harada

Daisuke Hamano

Tetsu Uehara

Toshiki Amano (capt)

Ben Gunter

Ryota Suginaga     Yuki Aoki     Ryota Hasegawa     Daisuke Kurihara

Shohei Hirano          Ryo Miura          Suguru Igarashi

*Reserves:* Daigo Hashimoto (for Miura), Ryutaro Ueda (for Igarashi), Sotaro Okawa (for Hirano), Takumi Mikami (for Aoki), Yuta Nakano (for Gunter), Ippei Okada (for Nishhibahi), Kodai Kameyama (for Uehara), Hayoto Nishhibahi (for Amano)

*Scorers:*
*Tries:* Hasegawa, Igarashi
*Conversions:* Uehara (2)

*Referee:* Michael Lash

*Kanto Chairman:* Toshio Unuma
*Kanto General Manager:* Akira Aita
*Head Coach:* Fumitaki Katukura
*Assistant Coach:* Yoshitake Mizumo
*Referee:* Tasuku Kawahara
*Doctor:* Yoshiki Shiota
*Trainers:* Nobuyuki Suzuki, Shinya Takeba
*Interpreter:* Hisamon Araro

## KANTO TOUR SQUAD, 2017

| | Club/University | Born | Height | Weight |
|---|---|---|---|---|
| Tatsuhide Akabori | Ricoh Black Rams/Meiji | 02/10/1988 | 1.87 | 96 |
| Toshiki Amano | Canon Eagles/Teikyo | 27/10/1990 | 1.70 | 83 |
| Yuki Aoki | Kubota Spears/Nippon Sports Science | 23/02/1992 | 1.88 | 105 |
| Ben Gunter | Panasonic Wild Knights/ Brisbane BHS | 24/10/1997 | 1.95 | 118 |
| Daisuke Hamano | Ricoh Black Rams/Teikyo | 06/01/1994 | 1.72 | 85 |
| Tokiro Harada | Canon Eagles/Waseda | 09/07/1990 | 1.64 | 74 |
| Ryota Hasegawa | Panasonic Wild Knights/Daito Bunko | 12/05/1993 | 1.88 | 100 |
| Daigo Hashimoto | Toshiba Brave Lupus/Tsukuba | 28/01/1994 | 1.74 | 106 |
| Shohei Hirano | Panasonic Wild Knights/Tokai | 03/08/1993 | 1.78 | 125 |
| Suguru Igarashi | Canon Eagles/Tokai | 22/11/1993 | 1.71 | 101 |
| Kodai Kameyama | NEC Green Rockets/Tsukuba | 24/03/1993 | 1.74 | 83 |
| Hideto Kondo | Kubota Spears/Tokai | 16/04/1993 | 1.78 | 94 |
| Daisuke Kurihara | NTT Shining Arcs/Keio | 17/03/1990 | 1.82 | 102 |
| Hikaru Kuzure | Hino Red Dolphins/Tokai | 09/09/1991 | 1.80 | 113 |
| Koichi Matsura | NEC Green Rockets/Meiji Gakuin | 03/08/1993 | 1.78 | 125 |
| Takumi Mikami | Panasonic Wild Knights/Tokai | 15/05/1990 | 1.92 | 103 |
| Ryo Miura | NTT Shining Arcs/Seikei | 17/11/1990 | 1.78 | 100 |
| Naoki Moriya | Canon Eagles/Hosei | 07/04/1991 | 1.81 | 88 |
| Yuta Nakano | Kamaishi Seawaves/Waseda | 16/11/1989 | 1.80 | 100 |
| Hayato Nishhibahi | NTT Shining Arcs/Waseda | 12/10/1990 | 1.70 | 78 |
| Koki Noda | Tokyo Gas/Teikyo | 08/04/1991 | 1.76 | 80 |
| Ippei Okada | Kubota Spears/Waseda | 16/02/1994 | 1.66 | 80 |
| Sotaro Okawa | Ricoh Black Rams/Tsukuba | 25/10/1991 | 1.81 | 107 |
| Satoshi Saita | Kubota Spears/Doshisha | 07/06/1993 | 1.81 | 125 |
| Shuri Sakamoto | Tokyo Gas/Tokai | 16/02/1992 | 1.85 | 112 |
| Ryota Suginaga | Canon Eagles/Teikyo | 29/06/1992 | 1.84 | 100 |
| Shohei Toyoshima | Toshiba Brave Lupus/Tokai | 09/01/1989 | 1.75 | 87 |
| Ryutaro Ueda | NTT Shining Arcs/Waseda | 27/06/1990 | 1.82 | 107 |
| Tetsu Uehara | Canon Eagles/Meiji Gakuin | 05/02/1994 | 1.77 | 86 |
| Kwon Yuin | Panasonic Wild Knights/Teikyo | 09/04/1992 | 1.83 | 90 |

# NEW ZEALAND HEARTLAND

The sole engagement for the NZ Heartland team in 2017 was the annual MacRae Cup match against NZ Marist. Only a squad of 23 players was selected. NZ Heartland came from 14–36 down after 44 minutes to win 41–39.

## v NEW ZEALAND MARIST

**Alpine Energy Stadium, Timaru**                    **4 November, 2017**

### Won 41–39

Ethine Reeves
*Poverty Bay*

Cameron Crowley              Craig Clare              Willie Paia'aua
*Wanganui*                   *Wanganui*              *Horowhenua Kapiti*

Ethan Pollock
*Horowhenua Kapiti*

Jarred Percival
*Mid Canterbury*

Andrew Stephens (capt)
*Buller*

Siosiua Moala
*Poverty Bay*

Seta Koroitamana      Kieran Coll       Eric Duff        Bryn Hudson
*Mid Canterbury*   *South Canterbury*  *Mid Canterbury*   *Wanganui*

Scott Cameron              Anthony Ellis              Ralph Darling
*Horowhenua Kapiti*           *Buller*                *North Otago*

*Reserves:* Willie McGoon *Mid Canterbury* (sub Paia'aua 52 min), Nick Strachan *South Canterbury* (sub Moala 55 min), Everard Reid *Poverty Bay* (sub Coll 55 min), Nathan Kendrick *Horowhenua Kapiti* (sub Ellis 55 min), Willie Wright *South Canterbury* (sub Stephens 55 min), Meli Kolinisau *North Otago* (sub Cameron 59 min), Tom Reekie *West Coast* (sub Pollock 62 min), Matthew Fetu *South Canterbury* (sub Darling 64 min).

*Scorers:*
*Tries:* Clare (2), Cameron (2), Percival, Wright
*Conversions:* Percival (4)
*Penalty Goal:* Percival

*Referee:* Jamie Nutbrown

Original selections Sam Madams (*Wanganui*), Lemi Masoe (*North Otago*) and Maleli Sau (*Mid Canterbury*) withdrew after selection and replaced by Everard Reid, Willie McGoon, and Cameron Crowley respectively.

*Coach:* Barry Matthews (*South Canterbury*)
*Assistant Coach:* Craig Scanlon (*Buller*)
*Manager:* Tony Harrison (*Mid Canterbury*)
*Physio:* Philippa Masoe (*North Otago*)
*Trainer:* Gavin Miller (*South Canterbury*)
*Doctor:* Patrick McHugh (*Poverty Bay*)

# NEW ZEALAND MARIST

Each affiliated club nominates three players for consideration, but the side can only be selected after the NZ Heartland team is named, as the NZ Heartland team takes priority on eligible players, including on those that may also have been nominated for the NZ Marist team.

## v NEW ZEALAND HEARTLAND

Alpine Energy Stadium, Timaru                                              4 November, 2017

### Lost 39–41

Ben Werthmuller
*OB Marist, Palm Nth*

Christian Vainerere           Kameli Kuruyabaki           Dylan Lolohea
*Celtic, Ashburton*           *OB Marist, Palm Nth*       *Marist Albion, Chch*

James Hawkey
*Marist, Nelson*

Peter Breen
*OB Marist, Whangarei*

Zac Donaldson
*OB Marist, Napier*

Brad Tucker (capt)
*Marist, Hamilton*

Dyllon Pedersen
*Marist St Michaels,*        Viliame Rarasea            Josh Manning            Sam Vea
*Rotorua*                    *Marist, Ardmore*          *Marist Albion, Chch*   *Marist, Hamilton*

Sesimani Tupou               Jacob Devery               Viki Tofa
*Marist, Ardmore*            *Hastings RS*              *Marist, Wanganui*

*Reserves:* Cameron Flavell *Marist, Ardmore* (sub Pedersen 55 min), Scott Mellow *Tukapa, New Plymouth* (sub Tofa 61 min), Regan Sword *Marist St Pats, Wgtn* (sub Donaldson 64 min), Angus Lindsay *Celtic, Ashburton* (sub Rarasea 66 min), Simon Dibben *Marist, Wanganui* (sub Vainerere 70 min), Anthony Guerin *OB Marist, Palm Nth* (sub Tupou 70 min), Antini Brown *Athletic Marist, Oamaru* (sub Werthmuller 72 min), Jarred Gilmore *Celtic, Timaru* (sub Devery 76 min).

*Scorers:*
*Tries:* Vainerere (2), Kuruyabaki, Werthmuller, Tupou
*Conversions:* Breen (4)
*Penalty Goals:* Breen (2)

*Referee:* Jamie Nutbrown

Original selections James Tucker (*Marist, Hamilton*), Cameron Crowley (*Marist, Wanganui*) and Renata Te Nana (*OB Marist, Whangarei*) withdrew after selection and replaced by Jarred Gilmore, Simon Dibben, and Peter Breen respectively.

*Co-Coaches:* Shaun Breen, Nigel Walsh (both *Celtic, Timaru*)
*Manager:* Chris Back (*Marist, Wanganui*)
*Physios:* Mike Prenderville (*Celtic, Timaru*), Geoff Thompson (*South Canterbury*)

# OVERSEAS INVITATION MATCHES

## U.K. BARBARIANS

Thirteen players registered first-class appearances when playing for the Barbarians club. Former Australian coach Alan Jones coached the team against Australia and Robbie Deans coached the team against New Zealand and Tonga.

The match against New Zealand was in celebration of the New Zealand Rugby Union's 125th jubilee this year.

### U.K. BARBARIANS 2017

| | | Australia | New Zealand | Tonga | TOTALS |
|---|---|---|---|---|---|
| T.T. (Tim) Nanai-Williams | Counties Manukau | 15 | – | – | 1 |
| George Moala | Auckland | 12 | – | – | 1 |
| A.W. (Augustine) Pulu | Counties Manukau | 9 | – | – | 1 |
| G.C. (George) Bridge | Canterbury | – | 15 | 15 | 2 |
| S.J. (Julian) Savea | Wellington | – | 14 | – | 1 |
| R.J. (Richard) Buckman | Hawke's Bay | – | 13 | 13 | 2 |
| Vince Aso | Auckland | – | 11 | 11 | 2 |
| Richie Mo'unga | Canterbury | – | 10 | – | 1 |
| L.C. (Luke) Whitelock | Canterbury | – | 8 | – | 1 |
| D.J. (Dominic) Bird | Canterbury | – | 5 | – | 1 |
| Atunaisa Moli | Waikato | – | 3 | – | 1 |
| M.D. (Mitchell) Drummond | Canterbury | – | s | – | 1 |
| Dillon Hunt | Otago | – | s | – | 1 |

After appearing for the Barbarians against New Zealand, Bird, Drummond, Hunt, Mo'unga, Moli and Whitelock then joined the All Blacks to principally participate in the midweek match in Lyon. The first five players were named when the All Blacks' touring squad was announced, while Whitelock was added as a replacement for Jerome Kaino who injured himself playing against the Barbarians and returned home.

Vince Aso, Richard Buckman, Corey Flynn and Greg Pleasants-Tate played for a World XV v Japan at Fukuoka on 28 October. Both teams used more than 23 players so no first-class appearances are credited.

| Date | Opponent | Location | Score | Tries | Con | PG | DG | Referee |
|---|---|---|---|---|---|---|---|---|
| October 28 | Australia | Allianz Stadium, Sydney | 28–31 | | | | | B.E. Pickerill (New Zealand) |
| November 4 | New Zealand | Twickenham, London | 22–31 | Bridge (2), Mo'unga | Mo'unga | | | N. Owens (Wales) |
| November 10 | Tonga | Thomond Park, Limerick | 27–24 | Bridge | | | | F. Murphy (Ireland) |

# INVESTEC SUPER RUGBY 2017

Taking out teams ranked 11, 12 and 13 from an 18-team competition is likely to emphasise the extremes of the competition. The current placing of the Waratahs is surely an aberration, but to cut the Force, currently sitting second in the Australian conference, and retain the distant last Rebels is difficult to rationalise.

That the Lions led the competition without playing teams ranked second, third, fourth, fifth and sixth irked the New Zealand teams and demonstrated a weakness in the seeding of the competition.

Having each of the three foundation countries host a quarter-final seemed reasonable, but no one predicted that the top Australian team would be placed ninth on the points table, yet qualify for a home quarter-final. There will be embarrassment when the Jaguares finish in the top three and don't qualify for a home quarter-final. Having the Jaguares move up to mid-table was an encouraging sign.

Each New Zealand team defeated every Australian team for a run of 26 victories.

## BLUES

The season began with 56 points scored against the Rebels in Melbourne, the highest score by the Blues in seven years. The Blues scored the sixth equal most tries in the round robin, which is a marked improvement on the previous year's position of 12th most tries. In just three previous years, including 1996 and 1997, have they scored more tries than this year's 55.

Moving from 11th-ranked team to eighth-ranked put the Blues into the top half of the competition, but the competition structure did not allow them into the playoffs. It might have still been possible had they taken five points from the last match against the lowly ranked Sunwolves. Instead the Blues suffered a humiliating record defeat. On the credit side, they were the first Super Rugby team to defeat the British and Irish Lions.

The promise of Rieko Ioane blossomed with his 11 tries being the most by a Blues player since Doug Howlett with 12 in 2003. A unique feature was the selection of Piers Francis for England's midyear tour of Argentina. The introduction of Augustine Pulu – to relieve the Chiefs of one of their three All Blacks halfbacks – added greatly to the Blues' performance this year.

Playing the Reds in Apia was an interesting experiment. Will it be repeated?

## CHIEFS

Defeating South Africa's second-placed Stormers in the semi-final at Cape Town for the second consecutive year was a remarkable achievement because few teams win a playoff match after crossing the Indian Ocean. Making the semi-finals was creditable, but one felt there was more in this team than they actually delivered. In 13 wins, 16 points was their second biggest winning margin.

Losing two frontline players, Mitch Graham and Brad Weber, to broken legs seconds apart at an early season 'Tens' tournament (which the Chiefs won) in Australia was a major blow to the Chiefs and players concerned, both of whom had highly promising careers interrupted. The 57 tries scored was the second most in a season for the Chiefs.

Not always first-choice goal kicker, Damian McKenzie finished among the top point scorers in the tournament. His footwork continues to entertain. James Lowe had a personal best 11 tries in his final season for the Chiefs. His strong running and strong kicking will be missed. Veteran Stephen Donald returned after several years' absence to bring up his 100 games for the Chiefs.

An under-strength Chiefs team was drubbed by the British and Irish Lions.

# HURRICANES

Beginning the season with 24 tries and 154 points in their first two games – albeit against bottom of the table teams – was a pace hard to keep up, as their loss in the third game to the Chiefs was to prove.

They say you can't improve on first place. Maybe, but even though they did not make first place this year, the Hurricanes still managed some outstanding achievements. Scoring 97 tries in the Super Rugby competition set a new record. The top two try scorers in Super Rugby were the midfield backs Ngani Laumape (15) and Vince Aso (14), a most unusual situation as frequently with midfield backs one makes the breaks and the other scores the tries.

An eagerly awaited arrival was Jordie Barrett, the younger brother of World Rugby Player of the Year Beauden Barrett. Jordie may well have exceeded the high expectations.

A high-scoring come-from-behind drawn match with the British and Irish Lions was well earned.

# CRUSADERS

It was only eight years since they last held the Super Rugby trophy, but it felt a lifetime for the Crusaders supporters. There were also times during the season when that lifetime seemed extended.

The matches against the Highlanders, the Reds and the Blues had the Crusaders trailing embarrassingly mid-match, yet managing to conjure up victories: trailing 6–27 against the Highlanders then finishing with a 30–27 victory; trailing 7–20 against the Reds then finishing with a 22–20 victory; trailing 5–24 against the Blues then finishing with a 33–24 victory. There was also the last-minute dropped goal against the Highlanders that turned a draw into a win.

Six consecutive scores in excess of 40 points mid-season suggested that normal order had been returned – and so it turned out.

Nine-point losses to the Hurricanes and the British and Irish Lions within a week quickly slipped into history as the Super Rugby title was brought home following a crossing of the Indian Ocean.

It had been observed that visiting players lift their game when playing for the Crusaders. We had never seen Whetu Douglas, Seta Tamanivalu, Jack Goodhue and Mitch Hunt play as well as they did this year. Richie Mo'unga relieved the fear that 'they will never replace Daniel Carter'.

# HIGHLANDERS

Losing their first two matches suggested it would be an uphill battle, but better was to come. Just two further matches were lost and the fourth most championship points attained. In another world this might have meant a home semi-final.

Not an original selection, Marty Banks made a strong return. His tactical acumen was among the best in the competition. Waisake Naholo demonstrated his quality with 10 tries that included four pairs. It was great to see Richard Buckman get more rugby this year. He is an understated talent. Luke Whitelock had his best season yet, leading the team well from number eight.

The British and Irish Lions suffered a fifth 'provincial' defeat in Dunedin.

## ALMANACK NEW ZEALAND RUGBY SUPER XV

As the publication of the *Rugby Almanack* comes 12 months after the previous Super Rugby season, memories can become dimmed or confused as the current season occupies the mind. It was thought that a publication of a Super Rugby form XV would fix in place those players who provided widespread enjoyment with their form in the previous season. Note that selection for this XV was based on Super Rugby form. It is not a potential All Blacks team.

### ALMANACK NEW ZEALAND SUPER RUGBY XV

Damian McKenzie
*Chiefs*

Waisake Naholo
*Highlanders*

Vince Aso
*Hurricanes*

Rieko Ioane
*Blues*

Ngani Laumape
*Hurricanes*

Beauden Barrett
*Hurricanes*

TJ Perenara
*Hurricanes*

Luke Whitelock
*Highlanders*

Matt Todd
*Crusaders*

Brodie Retallick
*Chiefs*

Samuel Whitelock
*Crusaders*

Brad Shields
*Hurricanes*

Charlie Faumuina
*Blues*

Codie Taylor
*Crusaders*

Wyatt Crockett
*Crusaders*

Reserves: Liam Coltman (*Highlanders*), Joe Moody (*Crusaders*), Owen Franks (*Crusaders*), Vaea Fifita (*Hurricanes*), Ardie Savea (*Hurricanes*), Aaron Smith (*Highlanders*), Richie Mo'unga (*Crusaders*), Jordie Barrett (*Hurricanes*).

# SUPER RUGBY STANDINGS

Final standings after round robin:

| | P | W | D | L | B³ | B⁷ | Pts | FOR | | | | | AGAINST | | | | |
|---|---|---|---|---|---|---|---|---|---|---|---|---|---|---|---|---|---|
| | | | | | | | | T | C | PG | DG | Pts | T | C | PG | DG | Pts |
| Lions | 15 | 14 | – | 1 | 9 | – | 65 | 81² | 59 | 19 | 2 | 590 | 27 | 23 | 28 | 1 | 268 |
| Crusaders | 15 | 14 | – | 1 | 7 | – | 63 | 77¹ | 50 | 18 | 1 | 544 | 37 | 32 | 18 | – | 303 |
| Stormers | 15 | 10 | – | 5 | 3 | – | 43 | 64¹ | 48 | 24 | – | 490 | 61 | 43 | 15 | – | 436 |
| Brumbies | 15 | 6 | – | 9 | 3 | 7 | 34 | 41¹ | 27 | 18 | – | 315 | 32¹ | 21 | 25 | – | 279 |
| Hurricanes | 15 | 12 | – | 3 | 9 | 1 | 58 | 89 | 62 | 9 | – | 596 | 31 | 24 | 23 | – | 272 |
| Chiefs | 15 | 12 | 1 | 2 | 6 | 1 | 57 | 55 | 37 | 28 | – | 433 | 30 | 23 | 32 | – | 292 |
| Highlanders | 15 | 11 | – | 4 | 5 | 2 | 51 | 62¹ | 49 | 26 | – | 488 | 40¹ | 26 | 17 | 1 | 308 |
| Sharks | 15 | 9 | 1 | 5 | 1 | 3 | 42 | 38 | 29 | 47 | 1 | 392 | 37 | 24 | 28 | 2 | 323 |
| Blues | 15 | 7 | 1 | 7 | 4 | 3 | 37 | 55 | 39 | 24 | – | 425 | 50¹ | 35 | 23 | – | 391 |
| Jaguares | 15 | 7 | – | 8 | 1 | 4 | 33 | 49² | 31 | 31 | – | 404 | 45¹ | 33 | 31 | – | 386 |
| Kings | 15 | 6 | – | 9 | 1 | 3 | 28 | 49² | 35 | 22 | 2 | 391 | 60¹ | 42 | 28 | – | 470 |
| Force | 15 | 6 | – | 9 | 1 | 1 | 26 | 36² | 24 | 27 | – | 313 | 55 | 36 | 19 | – | 404 |
| Cheetahs | 15 | 4 | – | 11 | 1 | 4 | 21 | 46 | 39 | 29 | – | 395 | 75² | 56 | 20 | – | 551 |
| Reds | 15 | 4 | – | 11 | 1 | 4 | 21 | 46 | 29 | 11 | – | 321 | 61³ | 39 | 30 | – | 479 |
| Bulls | 15 | 4 | – | 11 | – | 4 | 20 | 39 | 33 | 26 | – | 339 | 59 | 40 | 27 | 1 | 459 |
| Waratahs | 15 | 4 | – | 11 | 1 | 2 | 19 | 52 | 41 | 18 | – | 396 | 68¹ | 48 | 27 | 1 | 522 |
| Sunwolves | 15 | 2 | – | 13 | 1 | 3 | 12 | 41¹ | 27 | 18 | – | 315 | 96¹ | 72 | 15 | – | 671 |
| Rebels | 15 | 1 | 1 | 13 | – | 3 | 9 | 23 | 14 | 31 | – | 236 | 79¹ | 56 | 20 | – | 569 |
| **Totals** | | | | | | | | 943 | 673 | 426 | 6 | 7383 | 943 | 673 | 426 | 6 | 7383 |

*Points: 4 points for a win*
*2 points for a draw*
*B³ =bonus points for three tries or more than opponent*
*B⁷ =bonus points for a seven point or less loss*
*Superscript indicates number of penalty tries that count for seven points*

## PREVIOUS WINNERS

| | | | |
|---|---|---|---|
| 1996 | Auckland Blues | 2007 | Bulls |
| 1997 | Auckland Blues | 2008 | Crusaders |
| 1998 | Crusaders | 2009 | Bulls |
| 1999 | Crusaders | 2010 | Bulls |
| 2000 | Crusaders | 2011 | Reds |
| 2001 | Brumbies | 2012 | Chiefs |
| 2002 | Crusaders | 2013 | Chiefs |
| 2003 | Blues | 2014 | Waratahs |
| 2004 | Brumbies | 2015 | Highlanders |
| 2005 | Crusaders | 2016 | Hurricanes |
| 2006 | Crusaders | | |

# SUPER RUGBY RECORDS

*(S12 and S14 records have been rolled forward)*

## BY THE TEAMS

| | BEST IN 2017 | RECORD |
|---|---|---|

*Season totals*

| | | |
|---|---|---|
| Points | 660 Hurricanes | 660 Hurricanes *2017* |
| Tries | 97 Hurricanes | 97 Hurricanes *2017* |
| Conversions | 68 Hurricanes | 68 Hurricanes *2017* |
| Penalty goals | 49 Sharks | 76 Sharks *2014* |
| Dropped goals | 2 Highlanders | 11 Bulls *2009* |

*Match totals*

| | | |
|---|---|---|
| Points | 94 by Lions v Sunwolves | 96 by Crusaders v Waratahs *2002* |
| Tries | 14 by Lions v Sunwolves | 14 by Crusaders v Waratahs *2002* |
| | | by Cheetahs v Sunwolves *2016* |
| | | by Lions v Sunwolves *2017* |
| Conversions | 12 by Lions v Sunwolves | 13 by Crusaders v Waratahs *2002* |
| Penalty goals | 6 by Cheetahs v Lions | 9 by Hurricanes v Blues *2010* |
| Dropped goals | 1 on six occasions | 4 by Bulls v Crusaders *2009* |

## BY THE PLAYERS

| | BEST IN 2017 | RECORD |
|---|---|---|

*Season totals*

| | | |
|---|---|---|
| Points | 197 E.T. Jantjies (Lions) | 263 M. Steyn (Bulls) *2010* |
| Tries | 15 K.H. Laumape (Hurricanes) | 15 J.W.C. Roff (Brumbies) *1997* |
| | | 15 R.L. Gear (Crusaders) *2005* |
| | | 15 K.H. Laumape (Hurricanes) *2017* |

*Match totals*

| | | |
|---|---|---|
| Points | 27 C.D. Bosch (Sharks v Waratahs) | 50 G.E. Lawless (Natal v Highlanders) *1997* |
| Tries | 4 C.D. Skosan (Lions v Reds) | 4 J.W.C. Roff (Brumbies v Natal) *1996* |
| | | 4 G.E. Lawless (Natal v Highlanders) *1997* |
| | | 4 S. Terblanche (Sharks v Chiefs) *1998* |
| | | 4 J. Vidiri (Blues v Bulls) *2000* |
| | | 4 D.C. Howlett (Blues v Hurricanes) *2002* |
| | | 4 J.M. Muliaina (Blues v Bulls) *2002* |
| | | 4 C.S. Ralph (Crusaders v Waratahs) *2002* |
| | | 4 S.W. Sivivatu (Chiefs v Blues) *2009* |
| | | 4 D.A. Mitchell (Waratahs v Lions) *2010* |
| | | 4 S.D. Maitland (Crusaders v Brumbies) *2011* |
| | | 4 A.T. Tikoirotuma (Chiefs v Blues) *2012* |
| | | 4 C.J. Ngatai (Chiefs v Force) *2016* |
| | | 4 H.R.F. Jones (Stormers v Kings) *2016* |
| | | 4 C.D. Skosan (Lions v Reds) *2017* |
| Conversions | 9 O.W. Black (Hurricanes v Sunwolves) | 13 A.P. Mehrtens (Crusaders v Waratahs) *2002* |
| Penalty goals | 6 F. Zeilinga (Cheetahs v Lions) | 9 E.T. Jantjies (Lions v Cheetahs) *2012* |
| Dropped goals | 1 on six occasions | 4 M. Steyn (Bulls v Crusaders) *2009* |

## MOST GAMES

| Games | Player | Teams |
|---|---|---|
| 187 | W.W.V. Crockett | Crusaders |
| 177 | S.T. Moore | Reds / Brumbies |
| 175 | K.F. Mealamu | Blues / Chiefs |
| 162 | N.C. Sharpe | Reds / Force |
| 161 | L.J. Messam | Chiefs |
| 160 | M.A. Nonu | Hurricanes / Highlanders / Blues |
| 157 | G.B. Smith | Brumbies / Reds |
| 155 | S.U.T. Polota-Nau | Force / Waratahs |
| 153 | A.M. Ellis | Crusaders |
| 150 | C.R. Flynn | Crusaders |

## MOST POINTS

| Points | Player | Team | Games | Tries | Conv | PG | DG |
|---|---|---|---|---|---|---|---|
| 1708 | D.W. Carter | Crusaders | 141 | 36 | 287 | 307 | 11 |
| 1449 | M. Steyn | Bulls | 123 | 13 | 242 | 275 | 25 |
| 1037 | S.A. Mortlock | Brumbies | 138 | 55 | 162 | 146 | - |
| 998 | B.J. Barrett | Hurricanes | 97 | 25 | 180 | 170 | 1 |
| 990 | A.P. Mehrtens | Crusaders | 87 | 13 | 134 | 202 | 17 |

## MOST TRIES

| Tries | Player | Teams |
|---|---|---|
| 59 | D.C. Howlett | Blues / Highlanders / Hurricanes |
| 58 | C.S. Ralph | Chiefs / Crusaders |
| 57 | J.W.C. Roff | Brumbies |
| 56 | C.M. Cullen | Hurricanes |
| 56 | B.G. Habana | Bulls / Stormers |
| 55 | S.A. Mortlock | Brumbies |
| 53 | M.A. Nonu | Hurricanes / Blues / Highlanders |

# BLUES

**Postal address:** Box 77 012 Mt Albert,
Auckland 1350
**Telephone:** (09) 846 5425
**Email:** info@theblues.co.nz
**Home venues:** Eden Park, Auckland; North Harbour Stadium, Albany
**Colours:** Royal and navy blue with white trim.

Played 296, Won 157, Lost 133, Drew 6

|  | Tries | Conv | Pen | DG | Points |
|---|---|---|---|---|---|
| For | 946 | 643 | 628 | 11 | 7,933 |
| Against | 793 | 546 | 688 | 26 | 7,201 |

## RECORDS — TEAM

| | | |
|---|---|---|
| **Most points in a game** | 74 | *v Stormers, 1998* |
| **Most points in a season** | 513 | *1997* |
| **Biggest winning margin** | 53 | *60–7 v Hurricanes, 2002* |
| **Most tries in a game** | 11 | *v Stormers, 1998* |
| **Most tries in a season** | 70 | *1996* |

## RECORDS — INDIVIDUAL

| | | |
|---|---|---|
| **Most points in a game** | 29 | *G.W. Anscombe, v Bulls, 2012* |
| **Most points in a season** | 180 | *A.R. Cashmore, 1998* |
| **Most points in a career** | 619 | *A.R. Cashmore* |
| **Most tries in a game** | 4 | *J. Vidiri, v Bulls, 2000;* |
| | | *D.C. Howlett, v Hurricanes 2002;* |
| | | *J.M. Muliaina, v Bulls, 2002* |
| **Most tries in a season** | 12 | *D.C. Howlett, 2003* |
| **Most tries in a career** | 55 | *D.C. Howlett* |
| **Most conversions in a game** | 7 | *A.R. Cashmore, v Stormers, 1998;* |
| | | *A.R. Cashmore, v Bulls, 2000;* |
| | | *C.J. Spencer, v Bulls, 2002* |
| **Most conversions in a season** | 34 | *A.R. Cashmore, 1998* |
| **Most conversions in a career** | 120 | *C.J. Spencer* |
| **Most penalty goals in a game** | 6 | *A.R. Cashmore, v Chiefs, 1998;* |
| | | *A.R. Cashmore, v Hurricanes, 1999;* |
| | | *J.A. Arlidge, v Bulls, 2001;* |
| | | *S.A. Brett, v Bulls, 2010;* |
| | | *C.M. Noakes, v Stormers, 2013* |
| **Most penalty goals in a season** | 34 | *A.R. Cashmore, 1999* |
| **Most penalty goals in a career** | 114 | *A.R. Cashmore* |
| **Most dropped goals in a game** | 1 | *on 11 occasions* |
| **Most dropped goals in a season** | 2 | *O. Ai'i, 2000* |
| **Most dropped goals in a career** | 3 | *C.J. Spencer* |
| **Most games** | 164 | *K.F. Mealamu* |

| Player | Union | Date of birth | Height | Weight | Blues Games | Blues Points |
|--------|-------|---------------|--------|--------|-------------|--------------|
| M.W.V. (Michael) Collins | Otago | 3/6/93 | 1.86 | 99 | 14 | 10 |
| G. (Gerrard) Cowley-Tuioti | North Harbour | 16/6/92 | 1.96 | 110 | 17 | 15 |
| M.D. (Matt) Duffie | North Harbour | 16/8/90 | 1.92 | 90 | 21 | 35 |
| T.J. Faiane | Auckland | 24/8/95 | 1.84 | 92 | 8 | – |
| E.H. (Hame) Faiva | Waikato | 9/5/94 | 1.81 | 108 | 7 | – |
| C.C. (Charlie) Faumuina | Auckland | 24/12/86 | 1.86 | 125 | 99 | 35 |
| P.G. (Piers) Francis | Counties Manukau | 20/6/90 | 1.88 | 92 | 24 | 112 |
| B.E.C. (Bryn) Gatland | North Harbour | 5/10/95 | 1.78 | 88 | 4 | 11 |
| B.T. (Blake) Gibson | Auckland | 19/4/95 | 1.86 | 102 | 27 | 10 |
| J.K. (Josh) Goodhue | Northland | 13/6/95 | 1.99 | 115 | 2 | – |
| B-J.A. (Billy) Guyton | Tasman | 17/3/90 | 1.87 | 91 | 24 | 10 |
| A.T.O.A. (Alex) Hodgman | Canterbury | 16/7/93 | 1.90 | 122 | 5 | – |
| A.L. (Akira) Ioane | Auckland | 16/6/95 | 1.94 | 113 | 33 | 25 |
| R.E. (Reiko) Ioane | Auckland | 18/3/97 | 1.88 | 103 | 20 | 65 |
| J. (Jerome) Kaino | Auckland | 6/4/83 | 1.96 | 105 | 127 | 70 |
| D.S. (Steven) Luatua | Auckland | 29/4/91 | 1.94 | 109 | 75 | 40 |
| S. (Sione) Mafileo | North Harbour | 14/4/93 | 1.78 | 128 | 24 | – |
| P. (Pauliasi) Manu | Counties Manukau | 23/12/87 | 1/84 | 115 | 17 | 5 |
| G. (George) Moala | Auckland | 5/11/90 | 1.88 | 99 | 69 | 105 |
| M.G. (Matt) Moulds | Northland | 15/5/91 | 1.88 | 106 | 14 | 5 |
| M. (Melani) Nanai | Auckland | 3/8/93 | 1.92 | 92 | 38 | 65 |
| S.J. (Sam) Nock | Northland | 18/6/96 | 1.78 | 85 | 8 | – |
| D.P.T.K. (Declan) O'Donnell | Taranaki | 28/11/90 | 1.88 | 94 | 2 | – |
| J.N. (James) Parsons | North Harbour | 27/11/86 | 1.85 | 106 | 79 | 35 |
| S. (Stephen) Perofeta | Taranaki | 12/3/97 | 1.81 | 85 | 3 | 11 |
| S.M.J. (Sam) Prattley | Auckland | 16/1/90 | 1.96 | 116 | 40 | 5 |
| L.T. (Leighton) Price | Taranaki | 24/3/89 | 1.98 | 114 | 2 | – |
| K. (Kara) Pryor | Northland | 2/4/91 | 1.89 | 104 | 18 | 15 |
| A.W. (Augustine) Pulu | Counties Manukau | 4/1/90 | 1.80 | 90 | 15 | 25 |
| R.M.N. (Rene) Ranger | Northland | 30/9/86 | 1.82 | 96 | 76 | 140 |
| S.N. (Scott) Scrafton | Auckland | 18/4/93 | 2.00 | 114 | 12 | 15 |
| M.V.U. (Murphy) Taramai | North Harbour | 17/8/92 | 1.86 | 100 | 8 | – |
| J.V. (Jordan) Trainor | Waikato | 31/1/96 | 1.88 | 86 | 1 | – |
| P.T. (Patrick) Tuipulotu | Auckland | 23/1/93 | 1.98 | 120 | 43 | 35 |
| S.J. (Jimmy) Tupou | Counties Manukau | – | – | 109 | 9 | – |
| A.O.H.M. (Ofa) Tu'ungafasi | Auckland | 19/4/92 | 1.95 | 129 | 57 | – |
| I.T. (Ihaia) West | Hawke's Bay | 16/1/92 | 1.75 | 85 | 45 | 357 |
| S. (Sonny Bill) Williams | Counties Manukau | 3/8/85 | 1.91 | 108 | 7 | 5 |

Cowley-Tuioti was previously known as Tuioti Mariner Nanai was previously known as Nanai-Vai.

**Manager:** Richard Fry          **Coach:** Tana Umaga
**Assistant coaches:** Steven Jackson, Alistair Rogers

## BLUES 2017

| | Rebels | Chiefs | Highlanders | Crusaders | Bulls | Force | Highlanders | Hurricanes | Brumbies | Waratahs | Cheetahs | Stormers | Chiefs | Reds | B I Lions | Sunwolves | TOTALS |
|---|---|---|---|---|---|---|---|---|---|---|---|---|---|---|---|---|---|
| Collins | 15 | 15 | 15 | 15 | 15 | 15 | 15 | 15 | 15 | 15 | – | s | 15 | – | 15 | 15 | 14 |
| Trainor | – | – | – | – | – | – | – | – | – | – | – | – | – | s | – | – | 1 |
| Duffie | 14 | 14 | 14 | 14 | 14 | 14 | 14 | 14 | 14 | 14 | – | 14 | 14 | – | 14 | 14 | 14 |
| O'Donnell | – | – | – | – | – | – | – | – | – | – | 14 | – | – | 11 | – | – | 2 |
| Nanai | 11 | 11 | s | 11 | 11 | 11 | 11 | 11 | s | s | 15 | 15 | – | 15 | – | 11 | 14 |
| Ranger | s | s | 11 | – | – | – | – | – | – | – | – | – | – | 13 | – | s | 5 |
| R. Ioane | 13 | 13 | 13 | 13 | 13 | s | 13 | 13 | 11 | 11 | 11 | 11 | 11 | 14 | 11 | – | 15 |
| Moala | s | s | 12 | 12 | 12 | 13 | 12 | s | 13 | 13 | 13 | 13 | 13 | – | 13 | 13 | 15 |
| Faiane | – | – | – | s | s | 12 | – | – | – | – | 12 | – | s | 12 | s | 12 | 8 |
| Williams | – | – | – | – | – | – | s | 12 | 12 | 12 | – | 12 | 12 | – | 12 | – | 7 |
| Francis | 12 | 12 | s | 10 | 10 | 10 | 10 | 10 | – | 10 | 10 | 10 | 10 | 10 | – | – | 13 |
| West | 10 | 10 | 10 | – | s | s | – | – | – | – | – | s | – | – | s | 10 | 8 |
| Gatland | – | – | – | – | – | – | – | – | s | 10 | s | – | s | – | – | – | 4 |
| Perofeta | – | – | – | – | – | – | – | – | – | – | – | – | – | s | 10 | s | 3 |
| Pulu | 9 | 9 | 9 | 9 | 9 | 9 | 9 | 9 | 9 | 9 | 9 | 9 | 9 | – | 9 | 9 | 15 |
| Nock | s | – | – | – | – | – | – | – | – | – | s | s | s | 9 | s | s | 7 |
| Guyton | – | s | s | s | s | s | s | s | s | s | s | s | – | – | s | – | 10 |
| A.Ioane | 8 | 8 | s | s | s | s | s | s | 8 | 8 | 8 | 8 | 8 | s | 6 | 6 | 16 |
| Taramai | s | – | 8 | s | s | 7 | – | – | s | s | – | – | – | s | – | – | 8 |
| Gibson | 7 | 7 | 7 | 7 | 7 | – | 7 | 7 | 7 | 7 | 7 | 7 | 7 | – | 7 | 7 | 14 |
| Pryor | – | – | – | – | – | – | – | – | – | – | s | s | s | 7 | s | – | 5 |
| Luatua | 6 | 6 | – | – | – | – | 8 | 8 | 6 | 6 | 6 | 6 | 6 | 8 | 8 | 8 | 12 |
| Kaino | – | s | 6 | 8 | 8 | 8 | 6 | 6 | – | – | – | – | – | – | – | s | 8 |
| Scrafton | s | – | – | – | – | s | 5 | 5 | 5 | 5 | 5 | 5 | 5 | – | 5 | 5 | 11 |
| Tuipulotu | – | s | 5 | 5 | 5 | 5 | – | – | – | – | 4 | s | 4 | 4 | – | – | 9 |
| Tupou | 4 | 4 | 4 | 6 | 6 | 6 | s | – | – | – | – | – | – | 6 | s | – | 9 |
| Cowley-Tuioti | 5 | 5 | s | 4 | 4 | 4 | 4 | 4 | 4 | 4 | s | 4 | s | 5 | 4 | 4 | 16 |
| Goodhue | – | – | – | – | – | – | s | – | – | – | – | – | – | – | – | s | 2 |
| Price | – | – | – | – | – | – | – | – | s | s | – | – | – | – | – | – | 2 |
| Mafileo | 3 | 3 | s | s | s | s | – | s | s | s | s | s | s | 3 | s | s | 15 |
| Faumuina | s | s | – | – | 3 | 3 | 3 | 3 | 3 | 3 | 3 | 3 | 3 | – | 3 | 3 | 13 |
| Manu | 1 | 1 | 1 | 1 | 1 | 1 | 1 | 1 | 1 | 1 | 1 | – | – | – | – | s | 12 |
| Prattley | s | – | s | s | s | – | s | s | – | – | – | – | – | s | – | – | 6 |
| Tu'ungafasi | – | s | 3 | 3 | s | – | s | s | s | s | – | 1 | 1 | s | 1 | 1 | 13 |
| Hodgman | – | – | – | – | – | – | – | – | – | – | s | s | s | 1 | s | – | 5 |
| Moulds | 2 | 2 | s | s | s | s | s | s | s | s | – | – | – | – | – | – | 10 |
| Parsons | – | – | 2 | 2 | 2 | 2 | 2 | 2 | 2 | 2 | 2 | 2 | 2 | 2 | 2 | 2 | 14 |
| Faiva | s | s | – | – | – | – | – | – | – | – | s | s | – | s | s | s | 7 |

## BLUES INDIVIDUAL SCORING

| | Tries | Con | PG | DG | Points | | Tries | Con | PG | DG | Points |
|---|---|---|---|---|---|---|---|---|---|---|---|
| Francis | – | 20 | 13 | – | 79 | Faumuina | 2 | – | – | – | 10 |
| West | 2 | 17 | 9 | – | 71 | Parsons | 2 | – | – | – | 10 |
| R. Ioane | 11 | – | – | – | 55 | Ranger | 2 | – | – | – | 10 |
| Duffie | 5 | – | – | – | 25 | Tuipulotu | 2 | – | – | – | 10 |
| Nanai | 5 | – | – | – | 25 | Gibson | 1 | – | – | – | 5 |
| Pulu | 5 | – | – | – | 25 | Luatua | 1 | – | – | – | 5 |
| A.Ioane | 4 | – | – | – | 20 | Manu | 1 | – | – | – | 5 |
| Cowley-Tuioti | 3 | – | – | – | 15 | Moulds | 1 | – | – | – | 5 |
| Moala | 3 | – | – | – | 15 | Pryor | 1 | – | – | – | 5 |
| Scrafton | 3 | – | – | – | 15 | Williams | 1 | – | – | – | 5 |
| Perofeta | 1 | 3 | – | – | 11 | | | | | | |
| Gatland | – | 1 | 3 | – | 11 | **Totals** | **58** | **41** | **25** | **0** | **447** |
| Collins | 2 | – | – | – | 10 | | | | | | |
| | | | | | | Opposition scored | 51 | 36 | 26 | 0 | 407 |

# BLUES TEAM RECORD 2017

**Played 16 Won 8 Drew 1 Lost 7 Points for 447 Points against 407**

| Date | Opponent | Location | Score | Tries | Con | PG | DG | Referee |
|------|----------|----------|-------|-------|-----|-----|-----|---------|
| February 23 | Rebels | Melbourne | 56–18 | R. Ioane (3), Manu, Duffie, Pulu, Nanai | West (6) | West (2), Francis | | A. Gardner *Australia* |
| March 3 | Chiefs | Hamilton | 26–41 | Tuipulotu, Faumuina, Ranger | West | West (3) | | B. O'Keeffe |
| March 11 | Highlanders | Auckland | 12–16 | | | West (3), Francis | | G. Jackson |
| March 17 | Crusaders | Christchurch | 24–33 | Moala (2), Pulu | Francis (3) | Francis | | B. Pickerill |
| March 25 | Bulls | Albany | 38–14 | Duffie (2), Pulu, West, Moala Nanai | Francis (2), West (2) | | | N. Berry *Australia* |
| April 1 | Force | Auckland | 24–15 | A. Ioane, Duffie, R. Ioane, Collins | Francis West | | | S. Kubo *Japan* |
| April 8 | Highlanders | Dunedin | 20–26 | Faumuina, Cowley-Tuioti | Francis (2) | Francis (2) | | J. Nutbrown |
| April 15 | Hurricanes | Auckland | 24–28 | Pulu, Nanai, Scrafton | Francis (2) Gatland | Gatlanc | | M. Fraser |
| April 30 | Brumbies | Canberra | 18–12 | Duffie, A. Ioane, Nanai | | Gatland | | N. Briant |
| May 6 | Waratahs | Sydney | 40–33 | R. Ioane (2), Scrafton, A. Ioane | Francis (4) | Francis (4) | | A. Gardner *Australia* |
| May 12 | Cheetahs | Auckland | 50–32 | R. Ioane (2), Scrafton, A. Ioane, Tuipulotu, Luatua, Pulu, Nanai | West (3) Francis (2) | | | B. Pickerill |
| May 19 | Stormers | Cape Town | 22–30 | Moala, Parsons, Gibson | Francis (2) | Gatland | | J. van Heerden *South Africa* |
| May 26 | Chiefs | Auckland | 16–16 | R. Ioane | Francis | Francis (3) | | N. Briant |
| June 2 | Reds | Apia (Samoa) | 34–29 | Ranger, R. Ioane, Pryor, Cowley-Tuioti, Perofeta | Perofeta (2) Francis | Francis | | B. O'Keeffe |
| June 7 | British and Irish Lions | Auckland | 22–16 | R. Ioane, Williams, West | Perofeta West | West | | P. Gauzere *France* |
| July 15 | Sunwolves | Tokyo | 21–48 | Parsons, Cowley-Tuioti, Collins | West (3) | | | R. Rasivhenge *South Africa* |

# CHIEFS

**Postal address:** Box 4292, Hamilton East 3247
**Telephone:** (07) 853 0231
**Email:** admin@chiefs.co.nz
**Home venues:** Waikato Stadium, Hamilton; Yarrow Stadium,
New Plymouth; International Stadium, Rotorua
**Colours:** Black base with yellow and red panels down the sides.
Black shorts with yellow panel and red trim.

Played 298, Won 160, Lost 130, Drew 8

|  | Tries | Conv | Pen | DG | Points |
|---|---|---|---|---|---|
| For | 881 | 636 | 679 | 8 | 7,738 |
| Against | 798 | 570 | 711 | 23 | 7,332 |

## RECORDS — TEAM

| | | |
|---|---|---|
| Most points in a game | 72 | v Lions, 2010 |
| Most points in a season | 560 | 2016 |
| Biggest winning margin | 45 | 50–5 v Reds, 2016 |
| Most tries in a game | 9 | v Force, 2007 |
| | 9 | v Blues, 2009 |
| | 9 | v Lions, 2010 |
| | 9 | v Force 2016 |
| Most tries in a season | 76 | 2016 |

## RECORDS — INDIVIDUAL

| | | |
|---|---|---|
| Most points in a game | 32 | S.R. Donald, v Lions, 2010 |
| Most points in a season | 251 | A.W. Cruden, 2012 |
| Most points in a career | 875 | S.R. Donald |
| Most tries in a game | 4 | S.W. Sivivatu, v Blues, 2009 |
| | 4 | A.T. Tikoirotuma, v Blues 2012 |
| | 4 | C.J. Ngatai v Force 2016 |
| Most tries in a season | 12 | R.Q. Randle, 2002 |
| Most tries in a career | 42 | S.W. Sivivatu |
| Most conversions in a game | 9 | S.R. Donald, v Lions, 2010 |
| Most conversions in a season | 43 | A.W. Cruden, 2012 |
| | 43 | D.S. McKenzie 2016 |
| Most conversions in a career | 151 | S.R. Donald |
| Most penalty goals in a game | 6 | G.W. Jackson, v Reds, 2001 |
| | 6 | S.R. Donald, v Crusaders, 2007 |
| Most penalty goals in a season | 50 | A.W. Cruden, 2012 |
| Most penalty goals in a career | 153 | S.R. Donald |
| Most dropped goals in a game | 1 | on eight occasions |
| Most dropped goals in a season | 2 | I.D. Foster, 1996 |
| Most dropped goals in a career | 2 | I.D. Foster |
| | 2 | G.W. Jackson |
| Most games | 161 | L.J. Messam |

| Player | Union | Date of birth | Height | Weight | Chiefs Games[1] | Chiefs Points |
|---|---|---|---|---|---|---|
| S. (Solomona) Alaimalo | Northland | 27/12/95 | 1.95 | 97 | 9 | 10 |
| M.G. (Michael) Allardice | Hawke's Bay | 19/10/91 | 2.00 | 115 | 22 | – |
| D.J. (Dominic) Bird | Canterbury | 9/4/91 | 2.06 | 119 | 17 | 10 |
| L.S. (Lachlan) Boshier | Taranaki | 16/11/94 | 1.90 | 102 | 19 | 15 |
| M. (Mitchell) Brown | Taranaki | 15/8/93 | 1.93 | 110 | 18 | 5 |
| S.J. (Sam) Cane | Bay of Plenty | 13/1/92 | 1.89 | 105 | 95 | 60 |
| F.T. (Finlay) Christie | Tasman | 19/9/95 | 1.77 | 84 | 9 | – |
| A.W. (Aaron) Cruden | Manawatu | 8/1/89 | 1.78 | 85 | 89 | 682 |
| S.R. (Stephen) Donald | Waikato | 3/12/83 | 1.90 | 98 | 104 | 883 |
| H.T.P. (Hika) Elliot | Taranaki | 22/12/86 | 1.86 | 115 | 117 | 45 |
| J.F. (Johnny) Fa'auli | Taranaki | 13/9/95 | 1.80 | 100 | 6 | 5 |
| S. (Sigfried) Fisi'ihoi | Bay of Plenty | 8/6/89 | 1.85 | 122 | 26 | – |
| K.S. (Kane) Hames | Tasman | 28/8/88 | 1.84 | 120 | 25 | 10 |
| N.P. (Nathan) Harris | Bay of Plenty | 8/3/92 | 1.86 | 110 | 31 | 15 |
| M.R. (Mitch) Karpik | Bay of Plenty | 2/6/95 | 1.86 | 103 | 7 | – |
| S.S.V. (Sosefo) Kautai | Waikato | 16/8/96 | 1.89 | 135 | 4 | – |
| T.N.J. (Tawera) Kerr-Barlow | Waikato | 15/8/90 | 1.87 | 89 | 83 | 50 |
| L.E. (Luteru) Laulala | Counties Manukau | 30/5/95 | 1.86 | 94 | 1 | – |
| N.E. (Nepo) Laulala | Counties Manukau | 6/11/91 | 1.84 | 116 | 15 | – |
| M. (Michael) Leitch | – | 7/10/88 | 1.86 | 105 | 34 | 35 |
| A.R. (Anton) Lienert-Brown | Waikato | 15/4/95 | 1.85 | 94 | 39 | 5 |
| J.F.R. (James) Lowe | Tasman | 8/7/92 | 1.87 | 103 | 53 | 132 |
| D.S. (Damian) McKenzie | Waikato | 20/4/95 | 1.75 | 80 | 50 | 362 |
| S.J. (Sam) McNicol | Wellington | 6/10/95 | 1.85 | 94 | 18 | 15 |
| L.J. (Liam) Messam | Waikato | 25/3/84 | 1.90 | 109 | 162 | 160 |
| B.T. (Brayden) Mitchell | Southland | 24/1/89 | 1.80 | 103 | 5 | – |
| A.(Atu) Moli | Waikato | 12/6/95 | 1.89 | 125 | 28 | 10 |
| T.T. (Tim) Nanai-Williams | – | – | – | – | – | – |
|  | Counties Manukau | 12/6/89 | 1.82 | 87 | 85 | 141 |
| A.P. (Alex) Nankivell | Tasman | 25/10/96 | 1.88 | 98 | 4 | – |
| C.J. (Charlie) Ngatai | Taranaki | 17/8/90 | 1.81 | 97 | 44 | 85 |
| L.J. (Liam) Polwart | Bay of Plenty | 2/4/95 | 1.85 | 107 | 6 | – |
| T.N. (Toni) Pulu | Counties Manukau | 28/11/89 | 1.85 | 95 | 21 | 50 |
| B.A. (Brodie) Retallick | Hawke's Bay | 31/5/91 | 2.04 | 121 | 85 | 40 |
| A.(Aiden) Ross | Bay of Plenty | 25/10/95 | 1.87 | 112 | 7 | – |
| T.B. (Tom) Sanders | Canterbury | 5/2/94 | 1.91 | 109 | 20 | 20 |
| T.J.A. (Taleni) Seu | Auckland | 26/12/93 | 1.98 | 110 | 29 | 10 |
| S.P. (Sebastian) Siataga | Bay of Plenty | 27/1/93 | 1.81 | 107 | 2 | – |
| S.T. (Shaun) Stevenson | Waikato | 14/11/96 | 1.94 | 88 | 24 | 30 |
| S.F. (Samisoni) Taukei'aho | Waikato | 8/8/97 | 1.83 | 115 | 2 | – |
| J.A. (Jonathan) Taumateine | Counties Manukau | 28/9/96 | 1.77 | 82 | 7 | – |
| C.J. (Chase) Tiatia | Bay of Plenty | 14/10/95 | 1.81 | 93 | 1 | – |
| J.F. (James) Tucker | Waikato | 5/8/94 | 1.97 | 112 | 5 | – |

Sam Cane and Aaron Cruden shared the captaincy duties.

*Manager:* Stu Williams  **Coach:** Dave Rennie
*Assistant coaches:* Andrew Strawbridge, Neil Barnes, Kieran Keane

## CHIEFS 2017

| | Highlanders | Blues | Hurricanes | Rebels | Bulls | Stormers | Cheetahs | Force | Sunwolves | Reds | Crusaders | Blues | Waratahs | Hurricanes | B I Lions | Brumbies | Stormers | Crusaders | TOTALS |
|---|---|---|---|---|---|---|---|---|---|---|---|---|---|---|---|---|---|---|---|
| McKenzie | 15 | 15 | 15 | 10 | 15 | 15 | 15 | 15 | 15 | 15 | 15 | 15 | 15 | 15 | – | 15 | 15 | 15 | **17** |
| Stevenson | s | s | s | 15 | 14 | s | s | 14 | s | s | s | s | s | s | 15 | s | s | s | **18** |
| L. Laulala | – | – | – | – | – | – | – | – | – | – | – | – | – | – | s | – | – | – | **1** |
| Pulu | 14 | s | 14 | 14 | – | 14 | 14 | – | – | 14 | – | – | 14 | – | 14 | – | – | – | **9** |
| Nanai-Williams | s | 14 | 13 | – | – | – | – | – | – | – | 14 | 14 | – | – | 13 | – | s | 14 | **8** |
| Lowe | 11 | 11 | 11 | – | 11 | 11 | 11 | 11 | s | 11 | 11 | 11 | 11 | 11 | – | 11 | 11 | 11 | **16** |
| Alaimalo | – | – | – | 11 | s | – | – | s | 14 | – | – | – | s | 14 | 11 | 14 | 14 | – | **9** |
| Tiatia | – | – | – | – | – | – | – | – | – | – | – | – | – | – | s | – | – | – | **1** |
| Lienert-Brown | 13 | 13 | 12 | 13 | 13 | 13 | 12 | 12 | 13 | 13 | 12 | 13 | 13 | 13 | – | – | 13 | 13 | **16** |
| McNicol | – | – | – | – | – | s | 13 | 13 | 11 | s | 13 | – | – | – | – | – | – | – | **6** |
| Fa'auli | 12 | 12 | – | s | 12 | – | – | – | – | – | – | 12 | – | – | 12 | – | – | – | **6** |
| Nankivell | – | – | – | – | – | s | s | – | – | – | – | – | – | s | – | 13 | – | – | **4** |
| Ngatai | – | – | – | – | – | – | – | – | 12 | – | – | – | 12 | – | 12 | – | – | 12 | **4** |
| Cruden | 10 | 10 | 10 | s | 10 | 10 | 10 | 10 | 10 | – | 10 | 10 | 10 | 10 | – | 10 | 10 | 10 | **16** |
| Donald | – | – | s | 12 | s | 12 | – | s | 12 | 10 | s | – | 12 | – | 10 | s | 12 | s | **13** |
| Kerr-Barlow | 9 | 9 | 9 | 9 | 9 | 9 | 9 | 9 | – | 9 | 9 | 9 | 9 | 9 | – | 9 | 9 | 9 | **16** |
| Taumateine | s | s | – | – | – | – | – | – | 9 | s | – | s | s | – | s | – | – | – | **7** |
| Christie | – | – | s | s | s | s | – | s | s | – | – | – | – | – | s | 9 | s | – | **9** |
| Messam | 8 | 6 | – | 8 | 6 | 6 | s | 6 | s | s | s | 8 | 8 | 8 | s | – | 6 | 6 | **16** |
| Leitch | – | 8 | 8 | – | 8 | 8 | 8 | 8 | – | 8 | 8 | – | – | – | – | 8 | 8 | 8 | **11** |
| Karpik | 7 | – | – | s | s | – | – | – | 7 | – | – | – | s | – | s | 7 | – | – | **7** |
| Boshier | s | 7 | s | – | – | 7 | – | s | – | – | – | s | – | s | 7 | 6 | s | s | **11** |
| Cane | – | – | 7 | 7 | 7 | – | 7 | 7 | 8 | 7 | 7 | 7 | 7 | 7 | – | – | 7 | 7 | **13** |
| Seu | 6 | s | s | s | s | 4 | s | 5 | 5 | s | s | s | – | – | – | – | – | – | **11** |
| Brown | s | – | 6 | s | – | s | 6 | – | s | 6 | 6 | 6 | 6 | 6 | 6 | 5 | 4 | 4 | **15** |
| Sanders | – | s | – | 6 | – | – | – | – | 6 | – | – | – | – | s | 8 | s | – | – | **6** |
| Retallick | 5 | 5 | 5 | 5 | 5 | 5 | 5 | 5 | – | 5 | 5 | 5 | 5 | – | – | – | 5 | 5 | **14** |
| Allardice | – | – | – | – | – | – | – | – | – | – | – | – | s | 5 | 5 | 4 | – | – | **4** |
| Bird | 4 | 4 | 4 | 4 | 4 | 4 | s | 4 | 4 | 4 | 4 | 4 | 4 | 4 | – | s | s | s | **17** |
| Tucker | – | – | – | – | – | – | – | – | – | – | – | – | – | – | – | s | – | – | **1** |
| N. Laulala | 3 | 3 | 3 | 3 | 3 | – | – | – | 3 | 3 | 3 | 3 | 3 | 3 | 3 | 3 | 3 | 3 | **15** |
| Moli | s | s | s | s | s | 3 | 3 | 3 | – | s | s | s | s | s | s | s | s | s | **17** |
| Hames | 1 | 1 | 1 | 1 | s | 1 | 1 | – | 1 | 1 | 1 | 1 | 1 | 1 | – | 1 | 1 | 1 | **16** |
| Fisi'ihoi | s | s | s | s | 1 | s | s | 1 | – | s | s | s | s | s | 1 | – | – | – | **14** |
| Kautai | – | – | – | – | – | s | s | s | s | – | – | – | – | – | – | – | – | – | **4** |
| Ross | – | – | – | – | – | – | s | s | – | – | – | – | – | – | s | s | s | s | **6** |
| Elliot | 2 | 2 | 2 | s | 2 | 2 | s | s | 2 | 2 | s | s | – | – | s | – | – | – | **13** |
| Taukei'aho | s | s | – | – | – | – | – | – | – | – | – | – | – | – | – | – | – | – | **2** |
| Siataga | – | – | s | 2 | – | – | – | – | – | – | – | – | – | – | – | – | – | – | **2** |
| Mitchell | – | – | – | – | s | s | 2 | 2 | s | – | – | – | – | – | – | – | – | – | **5** |
| Harris | – | – | – | – | – | – | – | – | – | s | 2 | 2 | 2 | 2 | – | 2 | 2 | 2 | **8** |
| Polwart | – | – | – | – | – | – | – | – | – | – | – | – | s | s | 2 | s | s | s | **6** |

## CHIEFS INDIVIDUAL SCORING

| | Tries | Con | PG | DG | Points | | Tries | Con | PG | DG | Points |
|---|---|---|---|---|---|---|---|---|---|---|---|
| McKenzie | 6 | 22 | 22 | – | 140 | Boshier | 1 | – | – | – | 5 |
| Cruden | 2 | 16 | 12 | – | 78 | Brown | 1 | – | – | – | 5 |
| Lowe | 11 | – | – | – | 55 | Cane | 1 | – | – | – | 5 |
| Pulu | 5 | – | – | – | 25 | Fa'auli | 1 | – | – | – | 5 |
| Elliot | 4 | – | – | – | 20 | Leitch | 1 | – | – | – | 5 |
| Stevenson | 4 | – | – | – | 20 | Lienert-Brown | 1 | – | – | – | 5 |
| Donald | 2 | – | 2 | – | 16 | Moli | 1 | – | – | – | 5 |
| Kerr-Barlow | 3 | – | – | – | 15 | Nanai-Williams | 1 | – | – | – | 5 |
| Retallick | 3 | – | – | – | 15 | Ngatai | 1 | – | – | – | 5 |
| Alaimalo | 2 | – | – | – | 10 | | | | | | |
| Bird | 2 | – | – | – | 10 | **Totals** | **57** | **38** | **36** | **0** | **469** |
| Hames | 2 | – | – | – | 10 | | | | | | |
| Messam | 2 | – | – | – | 10 | *Opposition scored* | *39ᵗ* | *28* | *37* | *0* | *364* |

## CHIEFS TEAM RECORD 2017

**Played 18   Won 13   Drew 1   Lost 4   Points for 469   Points against 364**

| Date | Opponent | Location | Score | Tries | Con | PG | DG | Referee |
|---|---|---|---|---|---|---|---|---|
| February 24 | Highlanders | Dunedin | 24–15 | Lowe (2), Elliot | Cruden (3) | Cruden | | M. Fraser |
| March 3 | Blues | Hamilton | 41–26 | Messam, McKenzie, Elliot, Boshier, Lowe, Lienert-Brown | Cruden (4) | Cruden | | B. O'Keeffe |
| March 10 | Hurricanes | Hamilton | 26–18 | Retallick, Pulu | McKenzie (2) | McKenzie (4) | | B. Pickerill |
| March 17 | Rebels | Melbourne | 27–13 | Bird, Retallick, Cane, Stevenson | McKenzie (2) | McKenzie | | F. Anselmi *Argentina* |
| April 1 | Bulls | Hamilton | 28–12 | Stevenson, McKenzie, Moli | Cruden (2) | Cruden (3) | | N. Briant |
| April 8 | Stormers | Cape Town | 26–34 | Pulu (2), Lowe | Cruden | Cruden (2) McKenzie | | J. Peyper *South Africa* |
| April 15 | Cheetahs | Bloemfontein | 41–27 | Pulu (2), Kerr-Barlow, Lowe, Stevenson, Elliot | Cruden (4) | Cruden | | J. van Heerden *South Africa* |
| April 22 | Force | Perth | 16–7 | Messam | Cruden | Cruden (3) | | N. Berry *Australia* |
| April 29 | Sunwolves | Hamilton | 27–20 | McKenzie (2), Elliot, Alaimalo | McKenzie (2) | McKenzie | | W. Houston *Australia* |
| May 6 | Reds | New Plymouth | 46–17 | Donald (2), Hames, Ngatai, Bird, Lowe | McKenzie (5) | McKenzie (2) | | J. Nutbrown |
| May 19 | Crusaders | Suva, Fiji | 24–31 | Nanai-Williams, Lowe, Hames, Cruden | Cruden McKenzie | | | M. Fraser |
| May 26 | Blues | Auckland | 16–16 | McKenzie, Fa'auli | | McKenzie Cruden | | N. Briant |
| June 3 | Waratahs | Hamilton | 46–31 | Lowe (3), Kerr-Barlow (2), Brown | McKenzie (5) | McKenzie (2) | | P. Williams |
| June 9 | Hurricanes | Wellington | 17–14 | Cruden, Lowe | McKenzie (2) | McKenzie | | N. Briant |
| June 20 | British and Irish Lions | Hamilton | 6–34 | | | Donald (2) | | J. Garces *France* |
| July 15 | Brumbies | Hamilton | 28–10 | McKenzie, Alaimalo, Leitch | McKenzie (2) | McKenzie (3) | | B. O'Keeffe |
| July 22 | Stormers (quarter-final) | Cape Town | 17–11 | Stevenson | | McKenzie (4) | | J. Peyper *South Africa* |
| July 29 | Crusaders (semi-final) | Christchurch | 13–27 | Retallick | McKenzie | McKenzie (2) | | G. Jackson |

# HURRICANES
**Postal address:** Box 7201, Wellington
**Telephone:** (04) 389 0020
**Email:** mail@wrfu.co.nz
**Home venues:** Westpac Stadium Wellington; McLean Park,
Napier; FMG Stadium, Palmerston North
**Colours:** Yellow and black.

Played 298, Won 165, Lost 128, Drew 5

|  | Tries | Conv | Pen | DG | Points |
|---|---|---|---|---|---|
| For | 951 | 667 | 638 | 5 | 8,018 |
| Against | 786 | 540 | 705 | 24 | 7,197 |

## RECORDS — TEAM
| | | |
|---|---|---|
| Most points in a game | 83 | *v Sunwolves 2017* |
| Most points in a season | 691 | *2017* |
| Biggest winning margin | 66 | *83-17 v Sunwolves 2017* |
| Most tries in a game | 13 | *v Sunwolves 2017* |
| Most tries in a season | 101 | *2017* |

## RECORDS — INDIVIDUAL
| | | |
|---|---|---|
| Most points in a game | 30 | *D.E. Holwell v Highlanders, 2001* |
| Most points in a season | 223 | *B.J. Barrett, 2016* |
| Most points in a career | 998 | *B.J. Barrett* |
| Most tries in a game | 3 | *on 15 occasions* |
| Most tries in a season | 16 | *K.H. Laumape, 2017* |
| Most tries in a career | 56 | *C.M. Cullen* |
| Most conversions in a game | 9 | *B.J. Barrett v Rebels, 2012* |
| | | *O.W. Black v Sunwolves, 2017* |
| Most conversions in a season | 50 | *B.J. Barrett, 2016* |
| Most conversions in a career | 180 | *B.J. Barrett* |
| Most penalty goals in a game | 7 | *J.B. Cameron v Blues, 1996* |
| | 7 | *D.E. Holwell v Highlanders, 2001* |
| Most penalty goals in a season | 40 | *B.J. Barrett, 2014* |
| Most penalty goals in a career | 170 | *B. J. Barrett* |
| Most dropped goals in a game | 1 | *by five players* |
| Most dropped goals in a season | 1 | *by five players* |
| Most dropped goals in a career | 1 | *by five players* |
| Most games | 126 | *M.A. Nonu* |
| | 126 | *C.G. Smith* |

| Player | Union | Date of birth | Height | Weight | Hurricanes Games | Hurricanes Points |
|---|---|---|---|---|---|---|
| M.H. (Mark) Abbott | Hawke's Bay | 20/2/90 | 1.98 | 112 | 46 | 30 |
| P.J. (Pita) Ah Ki | North Harbour | 24/9/92 | 1.80 | 95 | 1 | - |
| L.C.A. (Loni) Apisai | Wellington | 8/3/96 | 1.81 | 108 | 16 | 15 |
| V.T. (Vince) Aso | Auckland | 5/1/95 | 1.86 | 98 | 32 | 80 |
| B.J. (Beauden) Barrett | Taranaki | 27/5/91 | 1.86 | 91 | 97 | 998 |
| J.M. (Jordie) Barrett | Canterbury | 15/2/92 | 1.95 | 96 | 18 | 144 |
| O.W. (Otere) Black | Manawatu | 4/5/95 | 1.85 | 86 | 22 | 54 |
| J. (James) Blackwell | Wellington | 1/4/95 | 1.90 | 106 | 6 | - |
| D.S. (Dane) Coles (capt) | Wellington | 10/12/86 | 1.84 | 110 | 100 | 70 |
| C.I. (Chris) Eves | Manawatu | 11/12/87 | 1.87 | 123 | 63 | 5 |
| M.J. (Michael) Fatialofa | Auckland | 14/9/92 | 1.98 | 113 | 22 | 10 |
| V.T.L. (Vaea) Fifita | Wellington | 17/6/92 | 1.96 | 112 | 33 | 35 |
| C.J. (Callum) Gibbins | Manawatu | 14/9/88 | 1.86 | 102 | 42 | 30 |
| W.T. (Wes) Goosen | Wellington | 20/10/95 | 1.79 | 92 | 14 | 50 |
| S.T. (Toa) Halafihi | Taranaki | 27/11/93 | 1.84 | 102 | 2 | - |
| K.M. (Kemara) Hauiti-Parapara | Wellington | 5/3/97 | 1.74 | 82 | 1 | - |
| C.S. (Cory) Jane | Wellington | 8/2/83 | 1.83 | 89 | 121 | 160 |
| M.Z.H. (Mike) Kainga | Bay of Plenty | 28/1/91 | 1.87 | 117 | 12 | - |
| M.B. (Ben) Iam | Auckland | 9/6/91 | 1.94 | 106 | 5 | 5 |
| K.H. (Ngani) Laumape | Manawatu | 24/4/93 | 1.69 | 107 | 29 | 100 |
| S.T. (Sam) Lousi | Wellington | 20/7/91 | 1.97 | 122 | 11 | - |
| B. (Ben) May | Wellington | 31/10/82 | 1.94 | 119 | 63 | 5 |
| N.R. (Nehe) Milner-Skudder | Manawatu | 15/12/90 | 1.82 | 90 | 25 | 35 |
| J.P. (James) O'Reilly | Bay of Plenty | 19/11/94 | 1.82 | 103 | 1 | - |
| T.T.R. (TJ) Perenara | Wellington | 23/1/92 | 1.84 | 94 | 96 | 220 |
| R.J. (Reed) Prinsep | Canterbury | 17/2/93 | 1.92 | 108 | 16 | 5 |
| M.P. (Matt) Proctor | Wellington | 26/10/92 | 1.80 | 90 | 43 | 40 |
| H.T. (Hugh) Renton | Hawke's Bay | 12/5/96 | 1.89 | 104 | 1 | - |
| J.R. (Ricky) Riccitelli | Hawke's Bay | 3/2/95 | 1.75 | 110 | 27 | 5 |
| A.S. (Ardie) Savea | Wellington | 14/10/93 | .88 | 99 | 65 | 80 |
| S.J. (Julian) Savea | Wellington | 7/8/90 | 1/90 | 100 | 104 | 230 |
| B.D.F. (Brad) Shields | Wellington | 2/4/91 | 1.93 | 111 | 87 | 45 |
| C.B. (Chris) Smylie | Taranaki | 22/3/82 | 1.80 | 91 | 42 | 10 |
| H.J.T. (Hohepa) Tahuriorangi | Taranaki | 31/3/95 | 1.73 | 82 | 11 | - |
| B.N. (Blade) Thomson | Taranaki | 4/12/90 | 1.98 | 107 | 39 | 40 |
| J.L. (Jeff) To'omaga-Allen | Wellington | 19/11/90 | 1.92 | 122 | 87 | 20 |
| L. (Loni) Uhila | Waikato | 7/4/89 | 1.81 | 125 | 24 | 10 |

Perenara captained in the absence of Coles.

**Manager:** Tony Ward          **Coach:** Chris Boyd
**Assistant coach:** John Plumtree, Jason Holland

## HURRICANES 2017

| | Sunwolves | Rebels | Chiefs | Highlanders | Reds | Waratahs | Blues | Brumbies | Stormers | Crusaders | Cheetahs | Bulls | Force | Chiefs | B.I.Lions | Crusaders | Brumbies | Lions | TOTALS |
|---|---|---|---|---|---|---|---|---|---|---|---|---|---|---|---|---|---|---|---|
| J. Barrett | 15 | s | s | 15 | 15 | 15 | 15 | 15 | 15 | 15 | s | 15 | 15 | 15 | 15 | 13 | 13 | 15 | 18 |
| Milner-Skudder | – | 15 | 15 | – | – | – | – | – | – | – | – | – | s | 14 | 14 | 15 | 15 | 14 | 8 |
| Jane | – | – | – | – | – | 14 | s | 14 | 14 | 14 | – | s | 14 | – | s | s | s | – | 10 |
| Goosen | s | – | – | s | – | 11 | 14 | – | – | s | 14 | 14 | – | s | s | 14 | 14 | 11 | 12 |
| J. Savea | 11 | 11 | 11 | 11 | 11 | – | 11 | 11 | 11 | 11 | 11 | 11 | 11 | – | 11 | 11 | 11 | s | 16 |
| Lam | – | – | – | – | – | – | – | s | s | – | s | s | 11 | – | – | – | – | – | 5 |
| Aso | 14 | 14 | 14 | 14 | 14 | s | 13 | 13 | 13 | 13 | 13 | 13 | 13 | 13 | 13 | – | – | 13 | 16 |
| Proctor | 13 | 13 | 13 | 13 | 13 | 13 | – | – | – | – | – | – | – | s | – | – | – | – | 7 |
| Laumape | 12 | 12 | 12 | 12 | 12 | 12 | 12 | 12 | 12 | 12 | 12 | 12 | 12 | 12 | 12 | 12 | 12 | 12 | 18 |
| Ah Ki | – | – | – | – | s | – | – | – | – | – | – | – | – | – | – | – | – | – | 1 |
| B. Barrett | s | 10 | 10 | 10 | 10 | 10 | 10 | 10 | 10 | 10 | 15 | – | 10 | 10 | – | – | 10 | 10 | 15 |
| Black | 10 | s | s | s | s | s | s | s | – | – | 10 | 10 | s | – | 10 | 10 | s | s | 15 |
| Perenara | 9 | 9 | 9 | 9 | 9 | 9 | 9 | s | 9 | 9 | 9 | 9 | 9 | 9 | – | 9 | 9 | 9 | 17 |
| Smyllie | s | s | – | – | – | – | – | – | – | – | – | – | – | – | – | – | – | – | 2 |
| Tahuriorangi | – | – | – | s | s | – | – | 9 | s | – | s | s | s | – | 9 | – | s | s | 10 |
| Hauiti-Parapara | – | – | – | – | – | – | – | – | – | – | – | – | – | – | – | s | – | – | 1 |
| Thomson | 8 | – | – | – | – | – | – | 8 | – | – | – | – | – | – | – | – | – | – | 2 |
| Prinsep | s | 8 | 8 | s | s | 8 | s | – | s | 6 | 6 | s | 6 | s | s | – | s | s | 16 |
| A.Savea | 7 | 7 | 7 | 8 | 8 | – | 8 | 7 | 8 | 7 | 7 | 7 | s | 8 | – | 7 | 7 | 7 | 16 |
| Gibbins | s | s | s | 7 | 7 | 7 | 7 | s | 7 | – | – | s | 7 | 7 | 7 | s | s | s | 16 |
| Shields | 6 | 6 | 6 | 6 | 6 | 6 | 6 | 6 | 6 | 8 | 8 | 8 | 8 | 6 | 8 | 8 | 8 | 8 | 18 |
| Halafihi | – | – | – | – | s | – | – | – | – | s | – | – | – | – | – | – | – | – | 2 |
| Renton | – | – | – | – | – | – | – | – | – | – | s | – | – | – | – | – | – | – | 1 |
| Fatialofa | 5 | 5 | 5 | 5 | 5 | 5 | 5 | – | – | – | – | – | – | – | – | – | – | – | 7 |
| Lousi | – | – | – | s | s | – | – | – | – | s | 4 | 5 | 4 | 4 | 5 | 5 | 5 | 5 | 11 |
| Fifita | – | – | – | – | – | s | s | 5 | 5 | 5 | 5 | 6 | 5 | 5 | 6 | 6 | 6 | 6 | 13 |
| Blackwell | 4 | 4 | s | – | – | – | s | s | – | – | – | s | – | – | – | – | – | – | 6 |
| Abbott | – | s | 4 | 4 | 4 | 4 | 4 | 4 | 4 | 4 | s | 4 | – | – | 4 | 4 | 4 | 4 | 15 |
| To'omaga–Allen | 3 | 3 | 3 | 3 | 3 | 3 | 3 | 3 | 3 | 3 | 3 | 3 | s | 3 | 3 | 3 | 3 | 3 | 18 |
| Kainga | s | s | – | s | s | s | s | s | – | – | – | – | s | – | – | – | – | – | 9 |
| Eves | 1 | 1 | 1 | 1 | 1 | s | s | s | s | 1 | s | s | s | 1 | s | s | s | s | 18 |
| May | s | s | s | s | s | 1 | 1 | 1 | 1 | s | 1 | s | 3 | – | 1 | 1 | 1 | 1 | 17 |
| Uhila | – | – | 1 | – | – | – | – | – | – | s | s | 1 | 1 | s | – | s | s | s | 9 |
| Riccitelli | 2 | s | s | s | 2 | 2 | 2 | 2 | 2 | 2 | 2 | 2 | s | 2 | 2 | 2 | s | | 18 |
| Coles | s | 2 | 2 | 2 | – | – | – | – | – | – | – | – | – | – | – | – | s | 2 | 6 |
| Apisai | – | – | – | – | s | s | s | s | s | s | s | s | s | 2 | s | – | – | – | 11 |
| O'Reilly | – | – | – | – | – | – | – | – | – | – | – | – | – | – | – | – | s | – | 1 |

## HURRICANES INDIVIDUAL SCORING

| | Tries | Con | PG | DG | Points | | Tries | Con | PG | DG | Points |
|---|---|---|---|---|---|---|---|---|---|---|---|
| J. Barrett | 7 | 38 | 11 | – | 144 | Fatialofa | 2 | – | – | – | 10 |
| Lumape | 16 | – | – | – | 80 | Jane | 2 | – | – | – | 10 |
| Aso | 14 | – | – | – | 70 | Proctor | 2 | – | – | – | 10 |
| B. Barrett | 4 | 17 | 2 | – | 60 | Lam | 1 | – | – | – | 5 |
| Goosen | 9 | – | – | – | 45 | Prinsep | 1 | – | – | – | 5 |
| Black | – | 17 | 1 | – | 37 | Riccitelli | 1 | – | – | – | 5 |
| Perenara | 7 | – | – | – | 35 | Shields | 1 | – | – | – | 5 |
| J. Savea | 7 | – | – | – | 35 | Thomson | 1 | – | – | – | 5 |
| A.Savea | 6 | – | – | – | 30 | To'omaga-Allen | 1 | – | – | – | 5 |
| Abbott | 5 | – | – | – | 25 | Uhila | 1 | – | – | – | 5 |
| Fifita | 4 | – | – | – | 20 | | | | | | |
| Apisai | 3 | – | – | – | 15 | **Totals** | **101** | **72** | **14** | **0** | **691** |
| Gibbins | 3 | – | – | – | 15 | Opposition scored | 43 | 32 | 28 | 0 | 363 |
| Milner-Skudder | 3 | – | – | – | 15 | | | | | | |

# HURRICANES TEAM RECORD 2017

**Played 18  Won 13  Drew 1  Lost 4**

**Points for 691  Points against 363**

| Date | Opponent | Location | Score | Tries | Con | PG | DG | Referee |
|---|---|---|---|---|---|---|---|---|
| February 25 | Sunwolves | Tokyo | 83–17 | A. Savea (2), Fatialofa (2), Aso (2), Riccitelli, Perenara, J. Savea, Laumape, Thomson, Shields, Goosen | Black (9) | | | E. Seconds *South Africa* |
| March 4 | Rebels | Wellington | 71–6 | Milner-Skudder (3), Aso (2), Laumape (2), Proctor, A. Savea, Prinsep, J. Savea | B. Barrett (6) Black (2) | | | N. Berry *South Africa* |
| March 10 | Chiefs | Hamilton | 18–26 | Perenara, J. Savea | B. Barrett | B. Barrett (2) | | B. Pickerill |
| March 18 | Highlanders | Wellington | 41–15 | Laumape (2), Aso (2), A. Savea, Proctor, J. Savea | B. Barrett (2) J. Barrett | | | A.Gardner *Australia* |
| April 1 | Reds | Melbourne | 34–15 | J. Savea, Perenara, Aso, J. Barrett, B. Barrett | J. Barrett (3) | J. Barrett | | A.Gardner *Australia* |
| April 7 | Waratahs | Wellington | 38–28 | Laumape (2), B. Barrett, J. Barrett, Goosen, Abbott | J. Barrett (4) | | | M. van der Westhuizen *South Africa* |
| April 15 | Blues | Auckland | 28–24 | Abbott (2), Laumape, B. Barrett | J. Barrett (4) | | | M. Fraser |
| April 21 | Brumbies | Napier | 56–21 | Aso (3), Gibbins (2), Jane, Abbott, Laumape | J. Barrett (7) Black | | | B. Pickerill |
| May 5 | Stormers | Wellington | 41–22 | J. Barrett (2), Laumape (2), Jane, A. Savea, B. Barrett | J. Barrett (3) | | | G. Jackson |
| May 13 | Crusaders | Christchurch | 12–20 | | | J. Barrett (4) | | J. Peyper *South Africa* |
| May 20 | Cheetahs | Wellington | 61–7 | Aso (3), Fifita, A. Savea, Perenara, To'omaga-Allen, Lam, Apisai | B. Barrett (5) Black (3) | | | N. Berry *Australia* |
| May 27 | Bulls | Pretoria | 34–20 | J. Barrett, Laumape, Goosen, Abbott, Apisai | Black (2) J. Barrett | Black | | E. Seconds *South Africa* |
| June 3 | Force | Perth | 34–12 | Laumape (2), Uhila, Apisai, Aso, Perenara | B. Barrett (2) | | | R. Hoffman *Australia* |
| June 9 | Chiefs | Wellington | 14–17 | Fifita, Goosen | J. Barrett (2) | | | N. Briant |
| June 27 | B.I. Lions | Wellington | 31–31 | Gibbins, Laumape, Goosen, Fifita | J. Barrett (4) | J.Barrett | | R. Poite *France* |
| July 15 | Crusaders | Wellington | 31–22 | J. Barrett, J. Savea, Goosen, Fifita | J. Barrett (4) | J. Barrett | | G. Jackson |
| July 21 | Brumbies (quarter-final) | Canberra | 35–16 | Goosen (2), J. Barrett, Perenara | J. Barrett (3) | J. Barrett (3) | | G. Jackson |
| July 29 | Lions (semi-final) | Johannesburg | 29–44 | Goosen, Laumape, Perenara, A. Savea | J. Barrett (2) B. Barrett | J. Barrett | | J. Peyper *South Africa* |

# CRUSADERS

**Postal address:** Box 755, Christchurch
**Telephone:** (03) 379 8300
**Email:** juliet.calder@crfu.co.nz
**Home venue:** AMI Stadium, Addington, Christchurch
**Colours:** Red and black.

Played 318, Won 217, Lost 95, Drew 6

|  | Tries | Conv | Pen | DG | Points |
|---|---|---|---|---|---|
| For | 1,072 | 744 | 846 | 46 | 9,526 |
| Against | 745 | 531 | 669 | 28 | 6,878 |

## RECORDS — TEAM

| | | |
|---|---|---|
| Most points in a game | 96 | *v Waratahs, 2002* |
| Most points in a season | 616 | *2017* |
| Biggest winning margin | 77 | *96–19 v Waratahs, 2002* |
| Most tries in a game | 14 | *v Waratahs, 2002* |
| Most tries in a season | 86 | *2017* |

## RECORDS — INDIVIDUAL

| | | |
|---|---|---|
| Most points in a game | 31 | *T.J. Taylor, v Stormers, 2012* |
| Most points in a season | 221 | *D.W. Carter, 2006* |
| Most points in a career | 1708 | *D.W. Carter* |
| Most tries in a game | 4 | *C.S. Ralph, v Waratahs, 2002* |
| | 4 | *S.D. Maitland, v Brumbies, 2011* |
| Most tries in a season | 15 | *R.L. Gear, 2005* |
| Most tries in a career | 52 | *C.S. Ralph* |
| Most conversions in a game | 13 | *A.P. Mehrtens, v Waratahs, 2002* |
| Most conversions in a season | 38 | *D.W. Carter, 2006* |
| Most conversions in a career | 287 | *D.W. Carter* |
| Most penalty goals in a game | 8 | *T.J. Taylor, v Stormers, 2012* |
| Most penalty goals in a season | 46 | *C.R. Slade, 2014* |
| Most penalty goals in a career | 307 | *D.W. Carter* |
| Most dropped goals in a game | 3 | *A.P. Mehrtens, v Highlanders, 1998* |
| Most dropped goals in a season | 4 | *A.P. Mehrtens, 1998, 1999, 2002* |
| Most dropped goals in a career | 17 | *A.P. Mehrtens* |
| Most games | 187 | *W.W.V. Crockett* |

| Player | Union | Date of birth | Height | Weight | Crusaders Games | Crusaders Points |
|---|---|---|---|---|---|---|
| M.S. (Michael) Ala'alatoa | Manawatu | 28/8/91 | 1.89 | 135 | 34 | 5 |
| S.K. (Scott) Barrett | Canterbury | 20/11/93 | 1.97 | 111 | 36 | 25 |
| T.E.S. (Tim) Bateman | | 3/6/87 | 1.82 | 91 | 42 | 35 |
| H.K. (Heiden) Bedwell-Curtis | Manawatu | 25/6/91 | 1.88 | 108 | 7 | 10 |
| G.C. (George) Bridge | Canterbury | 1/4/95 | 1.85 | 96 | 19 | 40 |
| J.C. (Jed) Brown | Canterbury | 12/3/91 | 1.86 | 102 | 6 | 10 |
| W.W.V. (Wyatt) Crockett | Canterbury | 24/1/83 | 1.93 | 118 | 188 | 50 |
| R.S. (Ryan) Crotty | Canterbury | 23/9/88 | 1.81 | 98 | 122 | 100 |
| I.J.A. (Israel) Dagg | Hawke's Bay | 6/6/88 | 1.86 | 96 | 84 | 135 |
| W.H. (Whetu) Douglas | Waikato | 18/4/94 | 1.90 | 109 | 6 | 15 |
| M.D. (Mitchell) Drummond | Canterbury | 15/2/94 | 1.80 | 86 | 46 | 55 |
| M.T.W. (Mitch) Dunshea | Canterbury | 18/1195 | 1.96 | 107 | 1 | – |
| E.C. (Ereatara) Enari | Canterbury | 30/5/97 | 1.78 | 84 | 1 | – |
| O.T. (Owen) Franks | Canterbury | 23/12/87 | 1.83 | 118 | 138 | 10 |
| V.J. (Vern) Fredericks | Tasman | 7/7/90 | 1.84 | 106 | 1 | – |
| L. (Leon) Fukofuka | Auckland | 8/8/94 | 1.85 | 91 | 5 | – |
| B.C.J. (Ben) Funnell | Canterbury | 6/6/90 | 1.81 | 108 | 75 | 35 |
| E.J. (Jack) Goodhue | Canterbury | 13/6/95 | 1.86 | 98 | 15 | 15 |
| B.D. (Bryn) Hall | North Harbour | 3/2/92 | 1.83 | 89 | 18 | 20 |
| D.K. (David) Havili | Tasman | 23/12/94 | 1.84 | 88 | 43 | 60 |
| M.J. (Mitchell) Hunt | Auckland | 19/6/95 | 1.74 | 80 | 15 | 68 |
| D.A.N. (Digby) Ioane | | 14/7/95 | 1.79 | 94 | 3 | 5 |
| O.G.J.T. (Oliver) Jager | Canterbury | 5/7/95 | 1.92 | 120 | 5 | – |
| M.R. (Marty) McKenzie | Taranaki | 14/8/92 | 1.83 | 87 | 9 | 19 |
| A.(Andrew) Makalio | Tasman | 22/1/92 | 1.82 | 122 | 5 | 5 |
| M.M.B.T. (Manasa) Mataele | Taranaki | 27/11/96 | 1.85 | 100 | 8 | 30 |
| J.P.T. (Joe) Moody | Canterbury | 18/9/88 | 1.88 | 117 | 62 | 5 |
| R. (Richie) Mo'unga | Canterbury | 25/5/94 | 1.79 | 86 | 30 | 315 |
| T.G. (Tim) Perry | Tasman | 1/8/88 | 1.88 | 116 | 13 | 5 |
| K.J. (Kieran) Read | Canterbury | 26/10/85 | 1.93 | 110 | 140 | 135 |
| L. (Luke) Romano | Canterbury | 16/2/86 | 1.99 | 118 | 99 | 35 |
| P. (Pete) Samu | Tasman | 17/12/91 | 1.85 | 101 | 19 | 35 |
| Q.J. (Quinten) Strange | Tasman | 21/8/96 | 1.99 | 112 | 7 | – |
| S. (Seta) Tamanivalu | Taranaki | 28/1/92 | 1.89 | 108 | 16 | 50 |
| J. (Jordan) Taufua | Counties Manukau | 29/1/92 | 1.82 | 100 | 68 | 45 |
| C.J. (Codie) Taylor | Canterbury | 31/3/91 | 1.83 | 107 | 51 | 40 |
| M.B. (Matt) Todd | Canterbury | 24/3/88 | 1.85 | 105 | 108 | 105 |
| S.T. (Sean) Wainui | Taranaki | 23/10/95 | 1.91 | 102 | 9 | – |
| S.L. (Samuel) Whitelock (capt) | Canterbury | 12/10/88 | 2.02 | 116 | 118 | 25 |

**Manager:** Angus Gardiner    **Coach:** Scott Robertson
**Assistant coaches:** Leon MacDonald, David Hewett

| CRUSADERS 2017 | Brumbies | Highlanders | Reds | Blues | Force | Waratahs | Sunwolves | Stormers | Cheetahs | Bulls | Hurricanes | Chiefs | Rebels | Highlanders | B I Lions | Hurricanes | Highlanders | Chiefs | Lions | TOTALS |
|---|---|---|---|---|---|---|---|---|---|---|---|---|---|---|---|---|---|---|---|---|
| Dagg | 15 | 14 | 15 | – | – | – | – | – | – | – | – | 14 | s | 15 | 15 | 14 | 14 | 14 | 14 | 10 |
| Havili | s | 15 | – | 15 | 15 | 15 | 15 | 15 | 15 | 15 | 15 | 15 | 15 | 15 | 12 | 12 | 15 | 15 | 15 | 18 |
| Tamanivalu | 14 | 11 | 14 | – | – | – | 14 | 14 | 14 | 14 | 14 | 14 | 13 | 14 | 14 | 14 | 11 | 11 | 11 | 16 |
| Ioane | – | – | 11 | – | 14 | 14 | – | – | – | – | – | – | – | – | – | – | – | – | – | 3 |
| Mataele | – | – | – | 14 | s | s | 11 | s | s | – | – | s | 11 | – | – | – | – | – | – | 8 |
| Bridge | 11 | s | s | 11 | 11 | 11 | s | 11 | 11 | 11 | 11 | 11 | s | 11 | 11 | 11 | s | s | s | 19 |
| Goodhue | 13 | 13 | 13 | – | – | – | 13 | 13 | 13 | 13 | 13 | 13 | – | 13 | 13 | 13 | 13 | 13 | 13 | 15 |
| Bateman | – | – | s | 13 | 13 | 12 | – | – | 12 | – | – | 12 | – | s | – | – | – | – | – | 7 |
| Wainui | – | – | – | 13 | – | – | – | – | – | – | – | – | – | – | – | s | – | – | – | 2 |
| Crotty | 12 | 12 | 12 | 12 | 12 | 12 | – | 12 | 12 | s | 12 | 12 | – | 12 | – | – | 12 | 12 | 12 | 15 |
| Mo'unga | 10 | – | – | – | – | – | 10 | 10 | 10 | 10 | 10 | 10 | 10 | 10 | 10 | 10 | 10 | 10 | 10 | 14 |
| Hunt | – | 10 | 10 | 10 | 10 | 10 | – | s | s | s | – | – | s | s | s | – | s | s | – | 13 |
| McKenzie | – | s | s | – | s | s | s | – | – | – | – | – | – | – | – | – | – | – | – | 5 |
| Fukofuka | – | – | – | – | – | – | s | – | – | – | – | – | – | – | – | – | – | – | – | 1 |
| Hall | 9 | 9 | s | 9 | s | s | – | s | 9 | s | s | 9 | 9 | s | 9 | 9 | 9 | 9 | 9 | 18 |
| Drummond | – | s | 9 | s | 9 | 9 | 9 | 9 | s | 9 | 9 | s | s | 9 | s | s | – | s | s | 17 |
| Enari | s | – | – | – | – | – | – | – | – | – | – | – | – | – | – | – | – | – | – | 1 |
| Douglas | 8 | 8 | 8 | 8 | – | 8 | s | – | – | – | – | – | – | – | – | – | – | – | – | 6 |
| Read | – | – | – | – | – | – | 8 | 8 | 8 | – | – | – | – | – | – | 8 | 8 | 8 | 8 | 7 |
| Samu | 7 | – | 6 | s | s | s | 6 | s | s | 6 | 6 | 7 | 7 | – | – | – | s | s | s | 15 |
| Todd | – | 7 | – | – | 7 | 7 | 7 | 7 | 7 | 7 | 7 | – | – | 7 | 7 | 7 | 7 | 7 | 7 | 14 |
| Brown | s | s | – | 7 | – | – | – | – | – | – | – | – | s | s | s | – | – | – | – | 6 |
| Bedwell-Curtis | – | – | 7 | – | – | – | – | – | – | – | s | s | 6 | 6 | 6 | 6 | – | – | – | 7 |
| Taufua | 6 | 6 | s | 6 | 8 | 6 | – | 6 | 6 | 8 | 8 | 8 | 8 | 8 | 8 | 6 | 6 | 6 | 6 | 18 |
| Fredericks | – | – | – | – | – | – | – | – | – | – | – | s | – | – | – | – | – | – | – | 1 |
| Whitelock | 5 | 5 | 5 | 5 | 5 | 5 | 5 | 5 | 5 | – | – | 5 | 5 | 5 | 5 | s | 5 | 5 | 5 | 17 |
| Barrett | 4 | 4 | 4 | 4 | 6 | 4 | – | 4 | 4 | 5 | 5 | – | – | – | 5 | 4 | 4 | 4 | – | 14 |
| Romano | s | s | s | s | 4 | s | 4 | s | s | 4 | 4 | 4 | s | 4 | 4 | 4 | s | s | s | 19 |
| Dunshea | – | – | – | – | s | – | – | – | – | – | – | – | – | – | – | – | – | – | – | 1 |
| Strange | – | – | – | – | – | – | s | s | – | s | s | s | 4 | s | – | – | – | – | – | 7 |
| Franks | 3 | 3 | – | 3 | 3 | 3 | – | 3 | 3 | 3 | 3 | 3 | – | 3 | 3 | – | 3 | 3 | 3 | 15 |
| Ala'alatoa | s | s | 3 | s | s | s | 3 | s | s | s | s | s | 3 | s | s | 3 | s | s | s | 19 |
| Moody | 1 | 1 | 1 | 1 | – | 1 | s | 1 | 1 | s | 1 | 1 | s | – | 1 | – | 1 | 1 | 1 | 16 |
| Crockett | s | s | – | s | 1 | s | 1 | s | s | 1 | s | s | 1 | s | s | 1 | s | s | s | 18 |
| Jager | – | – | s | – | – | – | s | – | – | – | – | – | – | s | 1 | – | s | – | – | 5 |
| Perry | – | – | s | – | s | – | – | – | – | – | – | – | – | – | – | s | – | – | – | 3 |
| Taylor | s | 2 | 2 | 2 | 2 | 2 | – | 2 | 2 | 2 | 2 | 2 | – | 2 | 2 | – | 2 | 2 | 2 | 16 |
| Funnell | 2 | s | s | s | s | s | 2 | s | – | – | s | s | 2 | s | s | 2 | s | s | s | 17 |
| Makalio | – | – | – | – | – | – | s | – | s | s | – | – | – | s | – | s | – | – | – | 5 |

## CRUSADERS INDIVIDUAL SCORING

| | Tries | Con | PG | DG | Points | | Tries | Con | PG | DG | Points |
|---|---|---|---|---|---|---|---|---|---|---|---|
| Mo'unga | 2 | 36 | 18 | – | 136 | Brown | 2 | – | – | – | 10 |
| Hunt | 2 | 15 | 5 | 1 | 58 | Bedwell-Curtis | 2 | – | – | – | 10 |
| Tamanivalu | 10 | – | – | – | 50 | Dagg | 2 | – | – | – | 10 |
| Bridge | 8 | – | – | – | 40 | Taylor | 2 | – | – | – | 10 |
| Havili | 8 | – | – | – | 40 | McKenzie | – | 5 | – | – | 10 |
| Mataele | 6 | – | – | – | 30 | Todd | 2 | – | – | – | 10 |
| Drummond | 5 | – | – | – | 25 | Ala'alatoa | 1 | – | – | – | 5 |
| Funnell | 5 | – | – | – | 25 | Ioane | 1 | – | – | – | 5 |
| Samu | 5 | – | – | – | 25 | Makalio | 1 | – | – | – | 5 |
| Hall | 4 | – | – | – | 20 | Moody | 1 | – | – | – | 5 |
| Read | 4 | – | – | – | 20 | Romano | 1 | – | – | – | 5 |
| Bateman | 3 | – | – | – | 15 | penalty try | 1 | – | – | – | 7 |
| Douglas | 3 | – | – | – | 15 | | | | | | |
| Goodhue | 3 | – | – | – | 15 | **Totals** | **86ᵗ** | **56** | **23** | **1** | **616** |
| Barrett | 2 | – | – | – | 10 | | | | | | |
| | | | | | | Opposition scored | 44 | 39 | 26 | 0 | 376 |

## CRUSADERS TEAM RECORD 2017

**Played 19  Won 17  Lost 2  Points for 616  Points against 376**

| Date | Opponent | Location | Score | Tries | Con | PG | DG | Referee |
|---|---|---|---|---|---|---|---|---|
| February 25 | Brumbies | Christchurch | 17–13 | Tamanivalu, Douglas, Samu | Mo'unga | | | G. Jackson |
| March 4 | Highlanders | Dunedin | 30–27 | penalty try, Havili, Douglas, Tamanivalu | McKenzie | Hunt (2) | | P. Williams |
| March 11 | Reds | Brisbane | 22–20 | Hall (2), Drummond | Hunt (2) | Hunt | | W. Houston *Australia* |
| March 17 | Blues | Christchurch | 33–24 | Mataele, Samu, Funnell, Hunt, Drummond | Hunt (4) | | | B. Pickerill |
| March 24 | Force | Christchurch | 45–17 | Ioane, Todd, Barrett, Romano, Taylor, Havili, Funnell | Hunt (4) McKenzie | | | R. Hoffmann *Australia* |
| April 2 | Waratahs | Sydney | 41–22 | Bateman (2), Bridge, Havili, Hall, Funnell | Hunt (3) McKenzie | Hunt | | M. van der Westhuizen *South Africa* |
| April 14 | Sunwolves | Christchurch | 50–3 | Mataele (3), Read, Funnell, Samu, Bridge, Douglas | Mo'unga (3) McKenzie (2) | | | N. Berry *Australia* |
| April 22 | Stormers | Christchurch | 57–24 | Bridge (3), Read (2), Ala'alatoa, Samu, Mataele | Mo'unga (6) Hunt | Mo'unga | | P. Williams |
| April 29 | Cheetahs | Bloemfontein | 48–21 | Bridge (3), Havili (2), Mo'unga, Drummond | Mo'unga (5) | Mo'unga | | F. Anselmi *Argentina* |
| May 6 | Bulls | Pretoria | 62–24 | Goodhue (2), Samu, Bateman, Barrett, Tamanivalu, Havili, Mo'unga, Makalio, Hunt | Mo'unga (5) Hunt | | | N. Berry *Australia* |
| May 13 | Hurricanes | Christchurch | 20–12 | Todd | | Mo'unga (5) | | J. Peyper *South Africa* |
| May 19 | Chiefs | Suva, Fiji | 31–24 | Bedwell-Curtis, Havili, Funnell | Mo'unga (2) | Mo'unga (4) | | M. Fraser |
| May 27 | Rebels | Melbourne | 41–19 | Brown (2), Mataele, Tamanivalu, Havili, Drummond | Mo'unga (4) | Mo'unga | | G. Jackson |
| June 3 | Highlanders | Christchurch | 25–22 | Drummond, Tamanivalu, Bedwell-Curtis | Mo'unga (2) | Hunt | Hunt | G. Jackson |
| June 10 | British and Irish Lions | Christchurch | 3–12 | | | Mo'unga | | M. Raynal *France* |
| July 15 | Hurricanes | Wellington | 22–31 | Tamanivalu (2), Dagg | Mo'unga (2) | Mo'unga | | G. Jackson |
| July 22 | Highlanders (quarter-final) | Christchurch | 17–0 | Moody, Taylor | Mo'unga (2) | Mo'unga | | A. Gardner *Australia* |
| July 29 | Chiefs (semi-final) | Christchurch | 27–13 | Tamanivalu (2), Dagg, Hall | Mo'unga (2) | Mo'unga | | G. Jackson |
| August 5 | Lions (final) | Johannesburg | 25–17 | Read, Goodhue, Tamanivalu | Mo'unga (2) | Mo'unga (2) | | J. Peyper *South Africa* |

# HIGHLANDERS

**Postal address:** Box 6070, Dunedin 9059
**Telephone:** (03) 479 9280
**Email:** contactus@highlanders.net.nz
**Home venues:** Forsyth Barr Stadium, Dunedin;
Rugby Park Stadium, Invercargill
**Colours:** Blue with gold and maroon.

Played 297, Won 147, Lost 148, Drew 2

|         | Tries | Conv | Pen | DG | Points |
|---------|-------|------|-----|----|--------|
| For     | 802   | 554  | 708 | 27 | 7,325  |
| Against | 837   | 596  | 634 | 15 | 7,326  |

## RECORDS — TEAM

| | | |
|---|---|---|
| **Most points in a game** | 65 | *v Bulls, 1999* |
| **Most points in a season** | 530 | *2015* |
| **Biggest winning margin** | 49 | *55-6 v Force 2017* |
| **Most tries in a game** | 9 | *v Bulls, 1999* |
| **Most tries in a season** | 64 | *2017* |

## RECORDS — INDIVIDUAL

| | | |
|---|---|---|
| **Most points in a game** | 28 | *B.A. Blair, v Sharks, 2005* |
| **Most points in a season** | 191 | *L.Z. Sopoaga, 2015* |
| **Most points in a career** | 857 | *T.E. Brown* |
| **Most tries in a game** | 3 | *T.M. Vaega, v Western Province, 1996* |
| | 3 | *D.C. Howlett, v Chiefs, 1997* |
| | 3 | *J.W. Wilson, v Stormers, 1998* |
| | 3 | *J.C. Stanley, v Stormers, 1998* |
| | 3 | *T.R. Nicholas, v Bulls, 2002* |
| | 3 | *B.A. Blair, v Sharks, 2005* |
| | 3 | *I.J.A. Dagg, v Bulls, 2010* |
| | 3 | *A.J. Thomson, v Rebels, 2012* |
| | 3 | *K.I. Poki, v Cheetahs, 2013* |
| | 3 | *M.A. Faddes v Kings 2016* |
| **Most tries in a season** | 13 | *W.R. Naholo, 2015* |
| **Most tries in a career** | 35 | *J.W. Wilson* |
| **Most conversions in a game** | 7 | *T.E. Brown, v Bulls, 1999* |
| **Most conversions in a season** | 38 | *L.Z. Sopoaga 2015* |
| **Most conversions in a career** | 137 | *T.E. Brown* |
| **Most penalty goals in a game** | 8 | *W.C. Walker, v Chiefs, 2003* |
| **Most penalty goals in a season** | 34 | *T.E. Brown, 2000* |
| **Most penalty goals in a career** | 180 | *T.E. Brown* |
| **Most dropped goals in a game** | 1 | *on twenty seven occasions* |
| **Most dropped goals in a season** | 3 | *L.Z. Sopoaga, 2015* |
| **Most dropped goals in a career** | 6 | *T.E. Brown* |
| **Most games** | 129 | *B.R. Smith* |

| Player | Union | Date of birth | Height | Weight | Highlanders Games | Highlanders Points |
|---|---|---|---|---|---|---|
| A.N. (Alex) Ainley | Tasman | 16/7/81 | 1.97 | 109 | 32 | - |
| M. (Marty) Banks | Tasman | 19/9/89 | 1.90 | 90 | 32 | 165 |
| R. J.(Richard) Buckman | Hawke's Bay | 27/5/89 | 1.84 | 95 | 42 | 55 |
| L.J. (Liam) Coltman | Otago | 25/1/90 | 1.85 | 110 | 72 | 10 |
| J.M. (Josh) Dickson | Otago | 2/11/94 | 2.00 | 109 | 1 | - |
| A.L. (Ash) Dixon | Hawke's Bay | 1/9/88 | 1.82 | 105 | 46 | 5 |
| E.C. (Elliot) Dixon | Southland | 4/9/89 | 1.93 | 110 | 78 | 50 |
| G.O. (Gareth) Evans | Hawke's Bay | 5/8/91 | 1.90 | 107 | 35 | 35 |
| M.A. (Matt) Faddes | Otago | 6/11/91 | 1.85 | 95 | 27 | 80 |
| M. (Malakai) Fekitoa | Auckland | 10/5/82 | 1.87 | 99 | 66 | 100 |
| T.S.G. (Tom) Franklin | Otago | 11/8/90 | 2.00 | 113 | 54 | 5 |
| S. (Sio) Halanukonuka | Tasman | 9/8/86 | 1.81 | 117 | 28 | - |
| K.W. (Kayne) Hammington | Manawatu | 24/9/90 | 1.70 | 75 | 13 | 5 |
| J.N. (Jackson) Hemopo | Manawatu | 14/11/93 | 1.94 | 113 | 10 | - |
| D. (Dillon) Hunt | Otago | 23/2/95 | 1.89 | 103 | 12 | 10 |
| J.A.R. (James) Lentjes | Otago | 16/1/91 | 1.87 | 103 | 16 | 5 |
| T. (Tevita) Li | North Harbour | 23/3/95 | 1.82 | 94 | 12 | 20 |
| D.P. (Daniel) Lienert-Brown | Canterbury | 9/2/93 | 1.84 | 113 | 44 | 15 |
| C.W. (Craig) Millar | Otago | 29/10/90 | 1.85 | 110 | 10 | - |
| G.P. (Guy) Millar | Southland | 23/4/92 | 1.86 | 117 | 4 | - |
| W.R. (Waisake) Naholo | Taranaki | 8/5/91 | 1.86 | 96 | 38 | 155 |
| P.J.J. (Patrick) Osborne | Canterbury | 14/6/87 | 1.89 | 105 | 54 | 100 |
| G.W. (Greg) Pleasants-Tate | Auckland | 12/5/91 | 1.82 | 110 | 13 | 10 |
| S.J. (Sekonia) Pole | Otago | 2/4/95 | 1.80 | 112 | 3 | - |
| D.J. (Dan) Pryor | Northland | 14/4/88 | 1.90 | 103 | 33 | 30 |
| J.D. (Josh) Renton | Otago | 25/5/94 | 1.75 | 81 | 5 | - |
| A.J. (Aki) Seiuli | Otago | 22/12/92 | 1.84 | 116 | 22 | 20 |
| A.A.V. (Adrian) Smith | North Harbour | 27/4/87 | 1.85 | 112 | 2 | - |
| A.L. (Aaron) Smith | Manawatu | 21/11/88 | 1.71 | 83 | 109 | 100 |
| B.R. (Ben) Smith | Otago | 1/6/86 | 1.86 | 93 | 129 | 168 |
| F.H. (Fletcher) Smith | Otago | 1/3/95 | 1.80 | 88 | 10 | 14 |
| L.Z. (Lima) Sopoaga | Southland | 3/2/91 | 1.77 | 91 | 74 | 721 |
| T. (Tupou) Sopoaga | | 6/5/92 | 1.85 | 104 | 1 | - |
| L.I.J. (Liam) Squire | Tasman | 20/3/91 | 1.95 | 113 | 22 | 25 |
| R. (Robert) Thompson | Canterbury | 29/8/91 | 1.84 | 103 | 20 | 35 |
| S.F. (Siate) Tokolahi | Canterbury | 16/3/92 | 1.84 | 116 | 17 | - |
| P.F. (Sio) Tompkinson | Otago | 27/5/96 | 1.82 | 93 | 3 | 5 |
| T.T. (Tei) Walden | Otago | 25/5/93 | 1.82 | 94 | 10 | 5 |
| J.T. (Joe) Wheeler | Tasman | 20/10/87 | 2.00 | 111 | 61 | 5 |
| L.C. (Luke) Whitelock | Canterbury | 29/1/91 | 1.94 | 108 | 24 | 5 |

Ben Smith and Shane Christie shared the captaincy duties.

*Manager:* Paul McLaughlan     *Coach:* Jamie Joseph
*Assistant coaches:* Tony Brown, Scott McLeod

## HIGHLANDERS 2017

| | Chiefs | Crusaders | Blues | Hurricanes | Brumbies | Rebels | Blues | Sunwolves | Sharks | Cheetahs | Bulls | Force | Waratahs | Crusaders | B I Lions | Reds | Crusaders | TOTALS |
|---|---|---|---|---|---|---|---|---|---|---|---|---|---|---|---|---|---|---|
| B. Smith | 15 | – | – | 15 | 15 | – | 15 | 15 | 15 | – | – | – | 15 | 15 | – | – | 15 | 9 |
| Faddes | s | – | – | s | s | 15 | s | 13 | s | 15 | 15 | 15 | – | s | – | – | – | 11 |
| Buckman | – | 15 | 15 | 14 | 12 | 12 | 12 | – | – | – | 12 | 12 | 12 | 11 | 15 | 15 | 11 | 13 |
| Naholo | 14 | 14 | 14 | – | – | – | – | 14 | 14 | 14 | 14 | – | 14 | 14 | 14 | 14 | 14 | 12 |
| Tompkinson | – | – | – | – | 14 | – | – | s | – | – | – | – | – | – | – | s | – | 3 |
| Li | 11 | 11 | 11 | 11 | – | 14 | 14 | 11 | – | s | – | 11 | 11 | – | 11 | 11 | – | 12 |
| Osborne | – | s | – | – | 11 | 11 | 11 | – | 11 | 11 | 11 | 14 | – | – | s | – | – | 9 |
| Fekitoa | 13 | 13 | 13 | 13 | 13 | 13 | 13 | 12 | 13 | 13 | 13 | 13 | 13 | 13 | 13 | 13 | 13 | 17 |
| Thompson | 12 | 12 | 12 | 12 | – | – | – | – | 12 | 12 | – | s | s | 12 | – | 12 | 12 | 11 |
| Walden | – | – | – | – | – | s | – | s | – | – | s | – | – | – | 12 | – | – | 4 |
| L. Sopoaga | 10 | 10 | 10 | – | – | – | – | – | – | – | – | – | s | s | s | 10 | 10 | 10 | 9 |
| Banks | – | – | s | s | s | 10 | 10 | 10 | 10 | 10 | 10 | 10 | 10 | 10 | s | s | s | 15 |
| F. Smith | s | s | – | 10 | 10 | s | – | – | s | s | s | – | – | – | – | – | – | 8 |
| A.L. Smith | 9 | 9 | 9 | 9 | 9 | 9 | 9 | 9 | 9 | 9 | 9 | 9 | s | 9 | 9 | – | 9 | 15 |
| Hammington | s | s | s | s | – | s | s | – | s | s | – | 9 | s | – | 9 | 9 | s | 13 |
| Renton | – | – | – | – | – | – | – | s | – | – | – | – | – | – | – | s | – | 2 |
| Squire | 8 | 8 | – | – | – | – | s | 6 | 8 | 6 | – | – | – | – | – | 6 | 6 | 8 |
| Whitelock | – | – | 8 | 8 | 8 | 8 | 8 | 8 | – | 8 | – | – | 8 | 8 | 8 | 8 | 8 | 12 |
| Lentjes | 7 | 7 | – | – | – | – | – | – | – | – | – | – | – | 7 | s | 7 | 7 | 6 |
| Hunt | – | – | s | 7 | 7 | 7 | 7 | 7 | 7 | 7 | 7 | 7 | 7 | – | 7 | – | – | 12 |
| E. Dixon | s | 6 | 7 | 6 | 6 | s | 6 | – | – | s | 6 | 8 | 6 | s | – | – | s | 13 |
| Evans | 6 | s | 6 | s | – | 6 | – | s | 6 | s | 8 | 6 | s | 6 | 6 | s | s | 15 |
| T. Sopoaga | – | – | – | – | – | – | s | – | – | – | – | – | – | – | – | – | – | 1 |
| Pryor | – | – | – | – | – | – | – | – | – | – | – | – | – | – | – | s | – | 1 |
| Franklin | 5 | 5 | 5 | 5 | 5 | 5 | 5 | s | 5 | 5 | 5 | 5 | 5 | 5 | – | 5 | 5 | 16 |
| Hemopo | s | – | s | s | – | – | – | – | s | – | s | s | – | – | 5 | 4 | 4 | 9 |
| Ainley | 4 | 4 | 4 | – | 4 | – | 4 | 4 | 4 | – | 4 | 4 | 4 | 4 | 4 | – | s | 13 |
| Wheeler | – | s | s | 4 | s | 4 | s | 5 | s | 4 | s | s | s | s | – | – | – | 13 |
| Dickson | – | – | – | – | – | – | – | – | – | – | – | – | – | – | – | s | – | 1 |
| Tokolahi | 3 | s | s | 3 | 3 | 3 | s | 3 | s | s | s | 3 | 3 | 3 | 3 | 3 | 3 | 17 |
| G. Millar | s | – | – | s | – | – | – | – | – | – | – | s | – | – | – | s | – | 4 |
| Halanukonuka | – | 3 | 3 | – | s | s | 3 | s | 3 | 3 | 3 | s | s | s | s | – | s | 14 |
| Lienert-Brown | 1 | 1 | 1 | 1 | 1 | s | 1 | 1 | 1 | 1 | s | – | s | 1 | 1 | 1 | 1 | 16 |
| C. Millar | s | s | – | – | – | – | – | – | – | – | – | – | – | – | – | – | – | 2 |
| Seiuli | – | – | s | s | s | 1 | s | s | s | s | 1 | 1 | 1 | s | s | s | s | 15 |
| Coltman | 2 | 2 | 2 | 2 | 2 | 2 | 2 | 2 | 2 | 2 | – | 2 | 2 | 2 | 2 | 2 | 2 | 16 |
| A.A.V. Smith | s | – | – | – | – | – | – | – | – | – | – | s | – | – | – | – | – | 2 |
| Pole | – | s | s | s | – | – | – | – | – | – | – | – | – | – | – | – | – | 3 |
| Pleasants-Tate | – | – | – | – | – | s | s | s | s | – | s | – | – | – | s | – | – | 6 |
| A.Dixon | – | – | – | – | – | – | – | – | – | s | 2 | – | s | s | – | s | s | 6 |

## HIGHLANDERS INDIVIDUAL SCORING

| | Tries | Con | PG | DG | Points | | Tries | Con | PG | DG | Points |
|---|---|---|---|---|---|---|---|---|---|---|---|
| Banks | 1 | 36 | 16 | – | 125 | B. Smith | 2 | – | – | – | 10 |
| Sopoaga | 1 | 12 | 11 | – | 62 | Squire | 2 | – | – | – | 10 |
| Naholo | 10 | – | – | – | 50 | penalty try | 1 | – | – | – | 7 |
| Faddes | 6 | – | – | – | 30 | A. Dixon | 1 | – | – | – | 5 |
| Fekitoa | 6 | – | – | – | 30 | E. Dixon | 1 | – | – | – | 5 |
| Thompson | 5 | – | – | – | 25 | Hammington | 1 | – | – | – | 5 |
| Buckman | 4 | – | – | – | 20 | Lentjes | 1 | – | – | – | 5 |
| Li | 4 | – | – | – | 20 | Lienert-Brown | 1 | – | – | – | 5 |
| Osborne | 3 | – | – | – | 15 | A.L. Smith | 1 | – | – | – | 5 |
| Seiuli | 3 | – | – | – | 15 | Tomkinson | 1 | – | – | – | 5 |
| F. Smith | – | 3 | 2 | – | 12 | Whitelock | 1 | – | – | – | 5 |
| Coltman | 2 | – | – | – | 10 | | | | | | |
| Evans | 2 | – | – | – | 10 | **Totals** | **64** | **51** | **29** | **0** | **511** |
| Hunt | 2 | – | – | – | 10 | | | | | | |
| Pleasants-Tate | 2 | – | – | – | 10 | *Opposition scored* | *45* | *30* | *19* | *1* | *347* |

## HIGHLANDERS TEAM RECORD 2017

**Played 17    Won 12    Lost 5    Points for 511    Points against 387**

| Date | Opponent | Location | Score | Tries | Con | PG | DG | Referee |
|---|---|---|---|---|---|---|---|---|
| February 24 | Chiefs | Dunedin | 15–24 | | | L. Sopoaga (5) | | M. Fraser |
| March 4 | Crusaders | Dunedin | 27–30 | Naholo (2), Evans | L. Sopoaga (3) | L. Sopoaga (2) | | P. Williams |
| March 11 | Blues | Auckland | 16–12 | Fekitoa | L. Sopoaga | L. Sopoaga (2) Banks | | G. Jackson |
| March 18 | Hurricanes | Wellington | 15–41 | Faddes, E. Dixon | Banks | F. Smith | | A. Gardner *Australia* |
| March 25 | Brumbies | Canberra | 18–13 | Tompkinson, Seiuli | Banks | Banks (2) | | M. van der Westhuizen *South Africa* |
| March 31 | Rebels | Dunedin | 51–12 | Fekitoa (2), Whitelock, Buckman, Evans, Pleasants-Tate | Banks (5) F. Smith | Banks (3) | | G. Jackson |
| April 8 | Blues | Dunedin | 26–29 | B. Smith, Fekitoa | Banks (2) | Banks (4) | | J. Nutbrown |
| April 22 | Sunwolves | Dunedin | 40–15 | Faddes (2), Fekitoa, Squire, A.L. Smith, B. Smith | Banks (5) | | | J. Nutbrown |
| April 28 | Stormers | Dunedin | 57–14 | Osborne (2), Naholo (2), Squire, Thompson, Hunt, Pleasants-Tate, Faddes | Banks (5) F. Smith | | | G. Jackson |
| May 5 | Cheetahs | Bloemfontein | 45–41 | Naholo (2), Banks, Thompson, Li, Faddes | Banks (6) | Banks | | M. van der Westhuizen *South Africa* |
| May 13 | Bulls | Pretoria | 17–10 | Faddes, Fekitoa | F. Smith Banks | F. Smith | | J. van Heerden *South Africa* |
| May 20 | Force | Perth | 55–6 | Seiuli (2), Thompson (2), Li, Osborne, Hunt, Buckman | Banks (6) | Banks | | S. Kubo *Japan* |
| May 27 | Waratahs | Dunedin | 44–28 | Buckman, Coltman, Li, Thompson, Lienert-Brown, L. Sopoaga | L. Sopoaga (3) Banks | Banks (2) | | B. O'Keeffe |
| June 3 | Crusaders | Christchurch | 22–25 | Naholo (2), Buckman | Banks (2) | Banks | | G. Jackson |
| June 13 | British and Irish Lions | Dunedin | 23–22 | Naholo, Coltman | Sopoaga Banks | Sopoaga (2) Banks | | A. Gardner *Australia* |
| July 14 | Reds | Dunedin | 40–17 | Naholo, Lentjes, Hammington, Li, penalty try, A. Dixon | Sopoaga (4) | | | M. Fraser |
| July 22 | Crusaders (quarter final) | Christchurch | 0–17 | | | | | A. Gardner *Australia* |

# SUPER RUGBY 2017 SCORING

*At Melbourne February 23*
**Blues 56** R. Ioane 3, Manu, Duffie, Pulu, Nanai tries; West 6 conversions; West 2, Francis penalties **defeated Rebels 18** Stirzaker, Garden-Bachop tries; Garden-Bachop conversion; Hodge 2 penalties. *Referee:* A. Gardner *(Australia)*

*At Dunedin February 24*
**Chiefs 24** Lowe 2, Elliot tries; Cruden 3 conversions; Cruden penalty **defeated Highlanders 15** Sopoaga 5 penalties. *Referee:* M. Fraser *(New Zealand)*

*At Brisbane February 24*
**Reds 28** Kerevi 2, Higginbotham, Tuttle tries; Cooper conversion; Cooper 2 penalties **defeated Sharks 26** J-L du Plessis, Mtembu tries; Lambie 2 conversions; Lambie 4 penalties. *Referee:* N. Briant *(New Zealand)*

*At Tokyo February 25*
**Hurricanes 83** A. Savea (2), Fatialofa (2), Aso (2), Riccitelli, Perenara, J. Savea, Laumape, Thomson, Shields, Goosen tries; Black 9 conversions **defeated Sunwolves 17** Viljoen, Kim, Britz tries; Lafaele conversion. *Referee:* E. Seconds *(South Africa)*

*At Christchurch February 25*
**Crusaders 17** Tamanivalu, Douglas, Samu tries; Mo'unga conversion **defeated Brumbies 13** Arnold try; Hawera conversion; Hawera 2 penalties. *Referee:* G. Jackson *(New Zealand)*

*At Sydney February 25*
**Waratahs 19** Skelton try; Robinson conversion; Robinson 4 penalties **defeated Force 13** Lance try; Lance conversion; Lance 2 penalties. *Referee:* B. O'Keeffe *(New Zealand)*

*At Bloemfontein February 25*
**Lions 28** penalty try, Janse van Rensburg 2 tries; Jantjies conversion; Jantjies 3 penalties **defeated Cheetahs 25** Rhule try; Zeilinga conversion; Zeilinga 6 penalties. *Referee;* Q. Immelman *(South Africa)*

*At Port Elizabeth February 25*
**Jagurares 39** Bertranou, Senatore, Tuculet tries; Iglesias 2, Bonilla conversions; Iglesias 3, Bonilla 3 penalties **defeated Kings 26** Mapimpi, Vulindlu tries; Cronje 2 conversions; Cronje 4 penalties. *Referee* J. Peyper *(South Africa)*

*At Cape Town February 25*
**Stormers 37** Marais, Kolbe, Carr, Kolisi, Leyds tries; J-L du Plessis 3 conversions; J-L du Plessis 2 penalties **defeated Bulls 24** Liebenberg 2, P. Schoeman, P. van Zyl tries; Pollard, T. Schoeman conversions. *Referee:* J. van Heerden *(South Africa)*

*At Perth March 2*
**Force 26** Peni, Phillip, Rona tries; Lance conversion; Prior 3 penalties **defeated Reds 19** Nabuli 3 tries; Cooper 2 conversions. *Referee:* F. Anselmi *(Argentina)*

*At Hamilton March 3*
**Chiefs 41** Messam, McKenzie, Elliot, Boshier, Lowe, Lienert-Brown tries; Cruden 4 conversions; Cruden penalty **defeated Blues 26** Tuipulotu, Faumuina, Ranger tries; West conversion; West 3 penalties. *Referee:* B. O'Keeffe *(New Zealand)*

*At Wellington March 4*
**Hurricanes 71** Milner-Skudder 3, Aso 2, Laumape 2, Proctor, A. Savea, Prinsep, J. Savea tries; B. Barrett 6, Black 2 conversions **defeated Rebels 6** Hodge 2 penalties. *Referee:* N. Berry *(South Africa)*

*At Dunedin March 4*
**Crusaders 30** penalty try, Havili, Douglas, Tamanivalu tries; McKenzie conversion; Hunt 2 penalties **defeated Highlanders 27** Naholo 2, Evans tries; Sopoaga 3 conversions; Sopoaga 2 penalties. *Referee:* P. Williams *(New Zealand)*

*At Canberra March 4*
**Sharks 27** Mtawarira, Am tries; Lambie conversion; Lambie 5 penalties **defeated Brumbies 22** Speight, Mann-Rea, Kuridrani tries; Hawera 2 conversions; Hawera penalty. *Referee:* A Gardner *(Australia)*

*At Singapore March 4*
**Kings 37** van Rooyen, Cloete, Lerm, Jaer tries; Cronje 4 conversions; Cronje 3 penalties **defeated Sunwolves 23** Lafaele, Fukuoka, Nakazaru tries; Cripps conversion; Cripps 2 penalties. *Referee* M. van der Westhuizen *(South Africa)*

*At Johannesburg March 4*
**Lions 55** Janse van Rensburg 2, Whiteley, Ackermann, A. Coetzee, Cronje, Mahuza, Marx tries; Jantjies 6 conversions; Jantjies dropped goal **defeated Waratahs 36** Horne, Hooper, Hegarty, McDuling, Folau tries; Robinson 3, Hegarty conversions; Robinson penalty. *Referee;* J. van Heerden *(South Africa)*

*At Cape Town March 4*
**Stormers 32** penalty try, Viljoen, Vermaak, Marais tries; J-L du Plessis 2 conversions; J-L du Plessis 2 penalties **defeated Jaguares 25** Cordero 2, Creevy tries; Sanchez, Iglesias conversions; Sanchez 2 penalties. *Referee:* J. Peyper *(South Africa)*

*At Bloemfontein March 4*
**Cheetahs 34** Mohoje 2, Swart, Basson tries; Zeilinga 4 conversions; Zeilinga 2 penalties **defeated Bulls 28** Jordaan, P. van Zyl, Ulengo tries; T. Schoeman 2 conversions; Pollard 3 penalties. *Referee;* S. Kubo *(Japan)*

*At Hamilton March 10*
**Chiefs 26** Retallick, Pulu tries; McKenzie 2 conversions; McKenzie 4 penalties **defeated Hurricanes 18** Perenara, J. Savea tries; B. Barrett conversion; B. Barrett 2 penalties. *Referee:* B. Pickerill *(New Zealand)*

*At Canberra March 10*
**Brumbies 25** Speight, Hawera, Godwin, Abel tries; Hawera conversion; Hawera penalty **defeated Force 17** Tessman, Peni tries; Lance 2 conversions; Lance penalty. *Referee; R.* Hoffmann *(Australia)*

*At Auckland March 11*
**Highlanders 16** Fekitoa try; Sopaga conversion; Sopaga 2, Banks penalties **defeated Blues 12** West 3, Francis penalties. *Referee:* G. Jackson *(New Zealand)*

*At Brisbane March 11*
**Crusaders 22** Hall 2, Drummond tries; Hunt 2 conversions; Hunt penalty **defeated Reds 20** Kerevi, Nabuli tries; Cooper 2; Cooper 2 penalties. *Referee:* W. Houston *(Australia)*

*At Port Elizabeth March 11*
**Stormers 41** Leyds, Basson, du Preez, Elstadt, Phillips, Viljoen tries; du Preez 2, Coleman 2 conversions; du Preez penalty **defeated Kings 10** Mapimpi try; Cronje conversion; Cronje penalty. *Referee: S. Kubo (Japan)*

*At Bloemfontein March 11*
**Cheetahs 38** Benjamin, Mohoje, Swart, van Jaarsveld tries; Zeilinga 3 conversions; Zeilinga 4 penalties **defeated Sunwolves 31** Fukuoka 2, Cripps, Emi tries; Cripps 2, Taulagi 2 conversions; Cripps penalty. *Referee: R. Rasivhenge (South Africa)*

*At Durban March 11*
**Sharks 37** Mtembu, Bosch, van Wyk tries; Bosch 2 conversions; Bosch 6 penalties **defeated Waratahs 14** Folau 2 tries; Robinson 2 converions. *Referee: M. van der Westhuizen (South Africa)*

*At Buenos Aires March 11*
**Jaguares 36** Tuculet, Moyano, de la Fuente, Sanchez tries; Sanchez 2 conversions; Sanchez 4 penalties **defeated Lions 24** Whiteley 2, van Rooyen, Marx tries; Reynolds, van der Walt conversions. *Referee: N. Briant (New Zealand)*

*At Christchurch March 17*
**Crusaders 33** Mataele, Samu, Funnell, Hunt, Drummond tries; Hunt 4 conversions **defeated Blues 24** Moala 2, Pulu tries; Francis 3 conversions; Francis penalty. *Referee: B. Pickerill (New Zealand)*

*At Melbourne March 17*
**Chiefs 27** Bird, Retallick, Cane, Stevenson tries; McKenzie 2 conversions; McKenzie penalty **defeated Rebels 14** Koroibete try; Garden-Bachop 3 penalties. *Referee: F. Anselmi (Argentina)*

*At Pretoria March 17*
**Bulls 34** Serfontein 2, P. Schoeman, Jenkins tries; Pollard 3, T. Schoeman conversions; Pollard, T. Schoeman penalties **defeated Sunwolves 21** Fukuoka, Quirk tries; Ogura conversion, Cripps 3 penalties. *Referee: J. Nutbrown (New Zealand)*

*At Wellington March 18*
**Hurricanes 41** Laumape 2, Aso 2, A. Savea, Proctor, J. Savea tries; B. Barrett 2, J. Barrett conversions **defeated Highlanders 15** Faddes, E. Dixon tries; Banks conversion; F. Smith penalty. *Referee: A. Gardner (Australia)*

*At Sydney March 18*
**Brumbies 28** Speight 2, Kuridrani, Abel tries; Hawera 4 conversions **defeated Waratahs 12** Robertson, Gordon tries; Robinson conversion.
*Referee G. Jackson (New Zealand)*

*At Johannesburg March 18*
**Lions 44** Skosan 4, Kriel, Janse van Rensburg, Marx tries; Jantjies 2, Coetzee conversions; Jantjies penalty **defeated Reds 14** Perese, Tupou tries; McIntyre 2 conversions. *Referee: M. Fraser (New Zealand)*

*At Durban March 18*
**Sharks 19** Adriaanse, van Wyk tries; Bosch 3 penalties **defeated Kings 17** Lerm, Mapimpi tries; Cronje 2 conversions; Cronje penalty. *Referee: E. Seconds (South Africa)*

*At Buenos Aires March 18*
**Jaguares 41** penalty try, Moyano 3, Alemanno tries; Hernandez 4 conversions; Hernandez 2 penalties **defeated Cheetahs 14** van der Spuy, Dweba tries; Marais 2 conversions. *Referee: P. Williams (New Zealand)*

*At Christchurch March 24*
**Crusaders 45** Ioane, Todd, Barrett, Romano, Taylor, Havili, Funnell tries; Hunt 4, McKenzie conversions **defeated Force 17** Newsome, Peni tries; Lance 2 conversions; Lance penalty. *Referee:* R. Hoffmann *(Australia)*

*At Melbourne March 24*
**Waratahs 32** Hanigan, Robinson, Wells, Horwitz tries; Foley 3 conversions; Folely 2 penalties **defeated Rebels 25** Hodge 2, English tries; Hodge 2 conversions; Hodge 2 penalties. *Referee:* B. Pickerill *(New Zealand)*

*At Albany March 25*
**Blues 38** Duffie 2, Pulu, West, Moala, Nanai tries; Francis 2, West 2 conversions **defeated Bulls 14** Gqoboka, Paige tries; Pollard, T. Schoeman conversions. *Referee:* N. Berry *(Australia)*

*At Canberra March 25*
**Highlanders 18** Tompkinson, Seiuli tries; Banks conversion; Banks 2 penalties **defeated Brumbies 13** Alcock try; Hawera conversion; Hawera 2 penalties. *Referee:* M. van der Westhuizen *(South Africa)*

*At Singapore March 25*
**Stormers 44** Viljoen, Elstadt, Louw, Duvenage, Mbonambi, Basson tries; du Preez 4 conversions; du Preez 2 penalties **defeated Sunwolves 31** Carpenter 2, Emi, Moli tries; Ogura 4 conversions; Ogura penalty. *Referee:* F. Anselmi *(Argentina)*

*At Port Elizabeth March 25*
**Lions 42** Tambwe 2, Marx, Jantjies, Kriel, Vorster tries; Jantjies 5, Coetzee conversions **defeated Kings 19** Ntsila, Penxe, Jaer tries; Cronje 2 conversions. *Referee:* Q. Immelman *(South Africa)*

*At Bloemfontein March 25*
**Sharks 38** van Wyk 2, Mvovo, D. du Preez tries; Bosch 3 conversions; Bosch 4 penalties **defeated Cheetahs 30** F. Venter, Jonker, Rhule tries; Zeilinga 3 conversions; Zeilinga 3 penalties. *Referee:* J. Peyper *(South Africa)*

*At Buenos Aires March 25*
**Jaguares 22** de la Fuente 2, Moyano tries; Hernandez 2 conversions; Hernandez penalty **defeated Reds 8** Higginbotham try; McIntyre penalty. *Referee:* M. Fraser *(New Zealand)*

*At Dunedin March31*
**Highlanders 51** Fekitoa 2, Whitelock, Buckman, Evans, Pleasants-Tate tries; Banks 5, F. Smith conversions; Banks 3 penalties **defeated Rebels 12** English, Hodge tries; Hodge conversion. *Referee:* G. Jackson *(New Zealand)*

At Auckland April 1
**Blues 24** A. Ioane, Duffie, R. Ioane, Collins tries; Francis, West conversions **defeated Force 15** Arnold, D. Haylett-Petty tries; Prior conversion; Lance penalty goal. *Referee:* S. Kubo *(Japan)*

*At Hamilton April 1*
**Chiefs 28** Stevenson, McKenzie, Moli tries; Cruden 2 conversions; Cruden 3 penalties **defeated Bulls 12** Pollard 4 penalties. *Referee:* N. Briant *(New Zealand)*

*At Brisbane April 1*
**Hurricanes 34** J. Savea, Perenara, Aso, J. Barrett, B. Barrett tries; J. Barrett 3 conversions; J. Barrett penalty **defeated Reds 15** Kuridrani, Higginbotham tries; McIntyre conversion; McIntyre penalty. *Referee:* A. Gardner *(Australia)*

*At Cape Town April 1*
**Stormers 53** Notshe 3, Leyds 2, du Plessis, du Preez, Kolisi tries; du Preez 4, Coleman conversions; du Preez penalty **defeated Cheetahs 10** Schoeman try; Zeilinga conversion; Zeilinga penalty. *Referee:* R. Rasivhenge *(South Africa)*

*At Johannesburg April 1*
**Lions 34** Marx, Skosan, Kriel tries; Jantjies 2 conversions; Jantjies 4 penalties, Coetzee dropped goal **defeated Sharks 29** C. Oosthuizen, van Wyk tries; Bosch 2 conversions; Bosch 4 penalties; Bosch dropped goal. *Referee:* J. van Heerden *(South Africa)*

*At Sydney April 2*
**Crusaders 41** Bateman 2, Bridge, Havili, Hall, Funnell tries; Hunt 3, McKenzie conversions; Hunt penalty **defeated Waratahs 22** Hooper, Gordon, Naiyaravoro tries; Robinson 2 conversions; Robinson penalty. *Referee:* M. van der Westhuizen *(South Africa)*

*At Wellington April 7*
**Hurricanes 38** Laumape 2, B. Barrett, J. Barrett, Goosen, Abbott tries; J. Barrett 4 conversions **defeated Waratahs 28** Hanigan, Hegarty, Gordon, Kellaway tries; Foley 4 conversions. *Referee:* M. van der Westhuizen *(South Africa)*

*At Tokyo April 8*
**Sunwolves 21** Warren-Vosayaco, Nakazuru tries; Y. Tamura conversion; Cripps 2, Y. Tamura penalties **defeated Bulls 20** Odendaal, Ismaeil tries; T. Schoeman 2 conversions; T. Schoeman 2 penalties. *Referee:* W. Houston *(Australia)*

*At Dunedin April 8*
**Highlanders 26** B. Smith, Fekitoa tries; Banks 2 conversions; Banks 4 penalties **defeated Blues 20** Faumuina, Cowley-Tuioti tries; Francis 2 conversions; Francis 2 penalties. *Referee:* J. Nutbrown *(New Zealand)*

*At Canberra April 8*
**Brumbies 43** T. Kuridrani, Abel, Toua, Butler, Dargaville, Alcock tries; Hawera 5 conversions; Hawera penalty **defeated Reds 10** C. Kuridrani try; Tuttle conversion; Tuttle penalty. *Referee:* N. Briant *(New Zealand)*

*At Durban April 8*
**Sharks 18** Reinach, Esterhuizen tries; Bosch conversion; Bosch 2 penalties **defeated Jaguares 13** Creevy try; B. Ezcurra conversion; Sanchez 2 penalties. *Referee:* A. Gardner *(Australia)*

*At Cape Town April 8*
**Stormers 34** Notshe, Kolisi, du Preez, Marais tries; du Preez 4 conversions; Marais 2 penalties **defeated Chiefs 26** Pulu 2, Lowe reies; Cruden conversion; Cruden 2 , McKenzie penalties. *Referee:* J. Peyper *(South Africa)*

*At Perth April 9*
**Force 46** penalty try, Newsome2, Lance, D. Haylett-Petty, McCalman tries; Lance 2, Prior 2 conversions; Lance 2 penalties **defeated Kings 41** Jaer 3, Forwood, Penxe, Mapimpi tries; Cronje 4 conversions; Cronje penalty. *Referee*: R. Rasivhenge *(South Africa)*

*At Christchurch April 14*
**Crusaders 50** Mataele 3, Read, Funnell, Samu, Bridge, Douglas tries; Mo'unga 3, McKenzie 2 conversions **defeated Sunwolves 3** Tamura penalty. *Referee:* N. Berry *(Australia)*

*At Brisbane April 15*
**Reds 47** Nabuli 2, Hunt 2, Perese 2, Smith tries; Cooper 6 conversions **defeated Kings 34** Mapimpi 2, Cloete, Schreuder, Banda tries; Cronje 2, de Wet conversions; Cronje penalty. *Referee:* Q. Immelman *(South Africa)*

*At Auckland April 15*
**Hurricanes 28** Abbott 2, Laumape, B. Barrett tries; J. Barrett 4 conversions **defeated Blues 24** Pulu, Nanai, Scrafton tries; Francis 2, Gatland conversions; Gatland penalty. *Referee:* M. Fraser *(New Zealand)*

*At Melbourne April 15*
**Rebels 19** Naivalu try; Hodge conversion; Hodge 4 penalties **defeated Brumbies 17** Speight 2, Butler tries; Hawera conversion. *Referee:* G. Jackson *(New Zealand)*

*At Bloemfontein April 15*
**Chiefs 41** Pulu 2, Kerr-Barlow, Lowe, Stevenson, Elliot tries; Cruden 4 conversions; Cruden penalty **defeated Cheetahs 27** Rhule, van Jaarsveld, F. Venter tries; Marais 3 conversions; Marais 2 penalties. *Referee:* J. van Heerden *(South Africa)*

*At Cape Town April 15*
**Lions 29** Marx, Vorster, Kriel, Mahuza tries; Jantjies 3 conversions; Jantjies penalty **defeated Stormers 16** Leyds try; R. du Preez conversion; Marais 2, R. du Preez penalties. *Referee:* J. Peyper *(South Africa)*

*At Pretoria April 15*
**Bulls 26** Ismaiel, L. de Jager tries; Pollard 2 conversions; Pollard 4 penalties **defeated Jaguares 13** Bertranou try; Iglesias conversion; Iglesias 2 penalties. *Referee:* B. O'Keeffe *(New Zealand)*

*At Johannesburg April 20*
**Lions 24** Vorster, Mapoe, Ackermann tries; Jantjies 3 conversions; Jantjies penalty **defeated Jaguares 21** Orlando, Baez, Petti tries; Sanchez 3 conversions. *Referee:* A. Gardner *(Australia)*

*At Napier April 21*
**Hurricanes 56** Aso 3, Gibbins 2, Jane, Abbott, Laumape tries; J. Barrett 7, Black conversions **defeated Brumbies 21** Kuridrani, Carter, Powell tries; Hawera 3 conversions. *Referee:* B. Pickerill *(New Zealand)*

*At Sydney April 21*
**Kings 26** penalty try, Forwood, Banda, Willemse tries; Cronje 2 conversions **defeated Waratahs 24** Naiyaravoro 2, Horne, Clark tries; Foley 2 conversions. *Referee:* R. Hoffmann *(Australia)*

*At Invercargill April 22*
**Highlanders 40**
Faddes 2, Fekitoa, Squire, A.L. Smith, B. Smith tries; Banks 5 conversions **defeated Sunwolves 15** Britz, Warren-Vosayaco tries; Y. Tamura conversion; Y. Tamura penalty. *Referee:* J. Nutbrown *(New Zealand)*

*At Christchurch April 22*
**Crusaders 57** Bridge 3, Read 2, Ala'alatoa, Samu, Mataele tries; Mo'unga 6 , Hunt conversions, Mo'unga penalty **defeated Stormers 24** Kolbe, Basson, Malherbe tries; du Preez 3 conversions; du Preez penalty. *Referee:* P. Williams *(New Zealand)*

*At Perth April 22*
**Chiefs 16** Messam try; Cruden conversion; Cruden 3 penalties **defeated Force 7** Hodgson try; Prior conversion. *Referee:* N. Berry *(Australia)*

*At Pretoria April 22*
**Bulls 20** Potgieter, Kriel tries; T. Schoeman 2 conversions; T. Schoeman 2 penalties **defeated Cheetahs 14** Schoeman try; Marais 3 penalties. *Referee:* B. O'Keeffe *(New Zealand)*

*At Durban April 22*
**Sharks 9** Bosch 3 penalties **drew with Rebels 9** Hodge 3 penalties. *Referee:* M. van der Westhuizen *(South Africa)*

*At Dunedin April 28*
**Highlanders 57** Osborne 2, Naholo 2, Squire, Thompson, Hunt, Pleasants-Tate, Faddes tries; Banks 5, F. Smith conversions **defeated Stormers 14** Carr, Duvenage tries; du Preez 2 conversions. *Referee:* G. Jackson *(New Zealand)*

*At Hamilton April 29*
**Chiefs 27** McKenzie 2, Elliot, Alaimalo tries; McKenzie 2 conversions; McKenzie penalty **defeated Sunwolves 20** Tanaka, Carpenter tries; Taulagi 2 conversions; Cripps, Taulagi penalties. *Referee:* W. Houston (Australia)

*At Brisbane April 29*
**Waratahs 29** Phipps, Hooper tries; Foley 2 conversions; Foley 5 penalties **defeated Reds 26** Hunt, L. Tui, Pereze, Moore tries; Cooper 3 conversions. *Referee:* P. Williams *(New Zealand)*

*At Perth April 29*
**Lions 24** Mapoe, Skosan, Jantjies tries; Jantjies 3 conversions; Jantjies penalty **defeated Force 15** Prior 5 penalties. *Referee:* A. Gardner *(Australia)*

*At Bloemfontein April 29*
**Crusaders 48** Bridge 3, Havili 2, Mo'unga, Drummond tries; Mo'unga 5 conversions; Mo'unga penalty **defeated Cheetahs 21** Rhule, Nche, Petersen tries; Marais 3 conversions. *Referee:* F. Anselmi *(Argentina)*

*At Port Elizabeth April 29*
**Kings 44** Mjekevu, Bezuidenhout, Paul, de Wet, Maipimpi, Banda tries; de Wet 3, Cronje conversions; Cronje 2 penalties **defeated Rebels 3** Hodge penalty. *Referee:* M. van der Westhuizen *(South Africa)*

*At Buenos Aires April 29*
**Sharks 33** van der Walt, E. Oosthuizen, du Toit tries; Bosch 3 conversions; Bosch 4 penalties **defeated Jaguares 25** Tuculet, Orlando, B. Ezcurra tries; Sanchez 2 conversions; Sanchez 2 penalties. *Referee:* J. Peyper *(South Africa)*

*At Canberra April 30*
**Blues 18** Duffie, A. Ioane, Nanai tries; Gatland penalty **defeated Brumbies 12** Hawera 4 penalties. *Referee:* N. Briant *(New Zealand)*

*At Wellington May 5*
**Hurricanes 41** J. Barrett 2, Laumape 2, Jane, A. Savea, B. Barrett tries; J. Barrett 3 conversions **defeated Stormers 22** Samuels try; R. du Preez conversion; Marais 4, R. du Preez penalties. *Referee:* G. Jackson *(New Zealand)*

*At Bloemfontein May 5*
**Highlanders 45** Naholo 2, Banks, Thompson, Li, Faddes tries; Banks 6 conversions; Banks penalty **defeated Cheetahs 41** Meyer 2, Petersen, van Jaarsveld, Mohoje, Nche tries; Zeilinga 4 conversions; Zeilinga penalty. Referee: M. van der Westhuizen *(South Africa)*

*At Melbourne May 6*
**Lions 47** penalty try, Smith, Cronje, Skosan, Mahuza, Volmink, Whiteley tries; Jantjies 5 conversions **defeated Rebels 10** English try; Hodge conversion; Hodge penalty goal. *Referee:* S. Kubo *(Japan)*

*At New Plymouth May 6*
**Chiefs 46** Donald 2, Hames, Ngatai, Bird, Lowe tries; McKenzie 5 conversions; McKenzie 2 penalties **defeated Reds 17** Moore, Nabuli, Magnay tries; Cooper conversion. *Referee:* J. Nutbrown *(New Zealand)*

*At Sydney May 6*
**Blues 40** R. Ioane 2, Scrafton, A. Ioane tries; Francis 4 conversions; Francis 4 penalties **defeated Waratahs 33** Folau 2, Latu, Foley, Ryan tries; Foley 4 conversions. *Referee:* A. Gardner *(Australia)*

*At Durban May 6*
**Sharks 37** Ward, J-L du Preez, Bosch, Am tries; Bosch 3, Lambie conversions; Bosch 3 penalties **defeated Force 12** Verity-Amm, Brache tries; Prior conversion. *Referee:* R. Rasivhenge *(South Africa)*

*At Pretoria May 6*
**Crusaders 62** Goodhue 2, Samu, Bateman, Barrett, Tamanivalu, Havili, Mo'unga, Makalio, Hunt tries; Mo'unga 5, Hunt conversions **defeated Bulls 24** Kriel, Ulengo, Serfontein tries; Brummer 3 conversions; T. Schoeman penalty. *Referee:* N. Berry *(Australia)*

*At Buenos Aires May 6*
**Jaguares 46** penatly try, Creevy 2, Senatore, Bofelli, Alemanno, Moroni tries; Hernandez 2, Bonilla conversions; Hernandez penalty **defeated Sunwolves 39** Y. Tamura 2, Tupou, Emi, Wykes tries; Y. Tamura 4 conversions; Y. Tamura 2 penalties. *Referee:* J. van Heerden *(South Africa)*

*At Auckland May 12*
**Blues 50** R. Ioane 2, Scrafton, A. Ioane, Tuipulotu, Luatua, Pulu, Nanai tries; West 3, Francis 2 conversions **defeated Cheetahs 32** Huggett 2, F. Venter, van Jaarsveld tries; Zeilinga 3 conversions; Zeilinga 2 penalties. *Referee:* B. Pickerill *(New Zealand)*

*At Canberra May 12*
**Lions 13** Smith try; Jantjies conversion; Jantjies, A. Coetzee penalties **defeated Brumbies 6** Hawera 2 penalties. *Referee:* P. Williams *(New Zealand)*

*At Christchurch May 13*
**Crusaders 20** Todd try; Mo'unga 5 penalties **defeated Hurricanes 12** J. Barrett 4 penalties. *Referee:* J. Peyper *(South Africa)*

*At Melbourne May 13*
**Reds 29** Kerevi 2, Nabuli, Moore, Higginbotham tries; Cooper 2 conversion **defeated Rebels 24** Miller, Koroibete tries; Hodge conversion; Hodge 4 penalties. *Referee:* M. van der Westhuizen *(South Africa)*

*At Pretoria May 13*
**Highlanders 17** Faddes, Fekitoa tries; F. Smith, Banks conversions; F. Smith penalty **defeated Bulls 10** Gelant try; T. Schoeman conversion; T. Schoeman penalty. *Referee:* J. van Heerden *(South Africa)*

*At Port Elizabeth May 13*
**Kings 35** Bock 2, Cronje, de Wet tries; Cronje 3 conversions; Cronje 2 penalties; Cronje dropped goal **defeated Sharks 32** D. du Preez, Mvovo tries; Lambie, April conversions; April 4, Lambie 2 penalties. *Referee:* F. Anselmi *(Argentina)*

*At Buenos Aires May 13*
**Force 16** Newsome, Naisarara tries; Prior 2 penalties **defeated Jaguares 6** Hernandez 2 penalties. *Referee:* B. O'Keeffe *(New Zealand)*

*At Suva, Fiji May 19*
**Crusaders 31** Bedwell-Curtis, Havili, Funnell tries; Mo'unga 2 conversions; Mo'unga 4 penalties **defeated Chiefs 24** Nanai-Williams, Lowe, Hames, Cruden tries; Cruden, McKenzie conversions. *Referee:* M. Fraser *(New Zealand)*

*At Cape Town May 19*
**Stormers 30** Kolisi, Leyds, Notshe tries; Marais 3 conversions; Marais 3 penalties, **defeated Blues 22** Moala, Parsons, Gibson tries; Francis 2 conversions; Gatland penalty. *Referee:* J. van Heerden *(South Africa)*

*At Wellington May 20*
**Hurricanes 61** Aso 3, Fifita, A. Savea, Perenara, To'omaga-Allen, Lam, Apisai tries; B. Barrett 5, Black 3 conversions **defeated Cheetahs 7** Zeilinga try; Zeilinga conversion. *Referee:* N. Berry *(Australia)*

*At Perth May 20*
**Highlanders 55** Seiuli 2, Thompson 2, Li, Osborne, Hunt, Buckman tries; Banks 6 conversions; Banks penalty **defeated Force 6** Prior 2 penalties. *Referee:* S. Kubo *(Japan)*

*At Singapore May 20*
**Sharks 38** Mvovo 3, Nikosi 2, Botha tries; April 3, Janse van Rensburg conversions **defeated Sunwolves 17** Hino, Matsusashi tries; Tamura 2 conversions; Oguru penalty. *Referee:* R. Hoffmann *(Australia)*

*At Johannesburg May 20*
**Lions 51** Combrink 2, Smith, Dreyer, Whiteley, Mostert, Mapoe tries; Jantjies 5 conversions; Jantjies 2 penalties **defeated Bulls 14** Serfontein, Kriel tries; Brummer 2 conversions. *Referee:* Q. Immelmann *(South Africa)*

*At Port Elizabeth May 20*
**Brumbies 19** Mann- Rea, Toua, Banks tries; Hawera 2 conversions **defeated Kings 10** penalty try; Cronje penalty. *Referee:* J. Peyper *(South Africa)*

At Sydney May 21
**Waratahs 50** Folau 2, Phipps, Mumm, Hanigan, Hooper, Fitzpatrick, Hegarty tries; Foley 5 conversions **defeated Rebels 23** Placid 2, Mafi tries; Volavola conversion; Volavola 2 penalties. *Referee*: A. Gardner *(Australia)*

*At Auckland May 26*
**Blues 16** R. Ioane try; Francis conversion; Francis 3 penalties **drew with Chiefs 16** McKenzie, Fa'auli tries; McKenzie, Cruden penalties. *Referee:* N. Briant *(New Zealand)*

*At Brisbane May 26*
**Force 40** penalty try, R. Haylett-Petty, Brache, Polota -Nau tries; Grant 3 conversions; Grant 4 penalties **defeated Reds 26** Moore 2, Paia'aua, L. Tui tries; Cooper 3 conversions. *Referee:* B. Pickerill *(New Zealand)*

*At Tokyo May 27*
**Cheetahs 47** Cassiem 2, Jordaan, Marais, van Jaarsveld, Meyer, Petersen tries; Marais 5, Uys conversions **defeated Sunwolves 7** Wykes try, Tamura conversion. *Referee:* W. Houston *(Australia)*

*At Dunedin May 27*
**Highlanders 44** Buckman, Coltman, Li, Thompson, Lienert-Brown, Sopoaga tries; Sopoaga 3, Banks conversions; Banks 2 penalties **defeated Waratahs 28** Gordon 2, Folau, Naiyaravoro tries; Foley 4 conversions. *Referee:* B. O'Keeffe *(New Zealand)*

*At Melbourne May 27*
**Crusaders 41** Brown 2, Mataele, Tamanivalu, Havili, Drummond tries; Mo'unga 4 conversions; Mo'unga penalty **defeated Rebels 19** Koroibete 2, T. Smith tries; Volavola, Hodge conversions. *Referee:* G. Jackson *(New Zealand)*

*At Pretoria May 27*
**Hurricanes 34** J. Barrett, Laumape, Goosen, Abbott, Apisai tries; Black 2, J. Barrett conversions; Black penalty **defeated Bulls 20** Matthews, N. de Jager tries; T. Schoeman, T. Jantjies conversions; T. Schoeman 2 penalties. *Referee:* E. Seconds *(South Africa)*

*At Durban May 27*
**Sharks 22** Deysel, Lewies, Nkosi tries; April 2 conversions; April penalty **defeated Stormers 10** Marais try; Marais conversion; Marais penalty. *Referee:* M. van der Westhuizen *(South Africa)*

*At Buenos Aires May 27*
**Brumbies 39** Banks 2, Muirhead 2, Carter, Speight tries; Hawera 3 conversions; Hawera penalty **defeated Jaguares 15** Lavanini, Petti tries; Iglesias conversion; Sanchez penalty. *Referee:* M. Fraser *(New Zealand)*

*At Johannesburg May 28*
**Lions 54** Smith 2, Ferreira, Skosan, Marx, van Rooyen, de Klerk, A. Coetzee tries; Jantjies 5, A. Coetzee 2 conversions **defeated Kings 10** Vulindlu try; de Wet conversion; de Wet penalty. *Referee:* J. Peyper *(South Africa)*

*At Apia, Samoa June 2*
**Blues 34** Ranger, R. Ioane, Pryor, Cowley-Tuitoti, Perofeta tries; Perofeta 2, Francis conversions; Francis penalty goal **defeated Reds 29** Tupou 2, Ready, Korczyk tries; Cooper 3 conversions; Cooper penalty. *Referee:* B. O'Keeffe *(New Zealand)*

*At Christchurch June 3*
**Crusaders 25** Drummond, Tamanivalu, Bedwell-Curtis tries; Mo'unga 2 conversions; Hunt penalty, Hunt dropped goal **defeated Highlanders 22** Naholo 2, Buckman tries; Banks 2 conversions; Banks penalty. *Referee:* G. Jackson *(New Zealand)*

*At Hamilton June 3*
**Chiefs 46** Lowe 3, Kerr-Barlow 2, Brown tries; McKenzie 5 conversions; McKenzie 2 penalties **defeated Waratahs 31** Horne, Skelton, Clark, Kepu tries; Foley 4 conversions; Foley penalty. *Referee:* P. Williams *(New Zealand)*

*At Canberra June 3*
**Brumbies 32** Smiler, Kuridrani, Hawera, Ah Wong tries; Hawera 3 conversions; Hawera 2 penalties **defeated Rebels 3** Hodge penalty. *Referee:* N. Briant *(New Zealand)*

*At Perth June 3*
**Hurricanes 34** Laumape 2, Uhila, Apisai, Aso, Perenara tries; B. Barrett 2 conversions **defeated Force 12** D. Haylett-Petty, Hardwick tries; Grant conversion. *Referee:* R. Hoffmann *(Australia)*

*At Wellington June 9*
**Chiefs 17** Cruden, Lowe tries; McKenzie 2 conversions; McKenzie penalty **defeated Hurricanes 14** Fifita, Goosen tries; J. Barrett 2 conversions. *Referee:* N. Briant *(New Zealand)*

*At Durban June 30*
**Bulls 30** Gelant 3, N. de Jager tries; T. Schoeman 2 conversions; T. Schoeman 2 penalty goals **defeated Sharks 17** du Toit, Bosch tries; Bosch 2 conversions; Bosch penalty goal. *Referee:* A. Gardner *(Australia)*

*At Buenos Aires June 30*
**Kings 31** Mapimpi 2, Vulindlu, Mjkevu tries; Cronje 4 conversions; Cronje penalty goal **defeated Jaguares 30** Tuculet 2, Leguizamon, Bottelli, Sanchez tries, Sanchez conversion; Sanchez penalty goal. *Referee:* J. Nutbrown *(New Zealand)*

*At Bloemfontein July 1*
**Stormers 40** Kolbe 3, Willemse, Notshe, Senatla tries; Kolbi 4, S. Marais conversions **defeated Cheetahs 34** Hugo, Huggett, Rhule, Swart tries; D. Marais 4 conversions; D. Marais 2 penalty goals. *Referee:* J. van Heerden *(South Africa)*

*At Johannesburg July 1*
**Lions 94** Combrink 3, Smith 2, Kriel 2, Cronje, Jantjies, van der Merwe, Skosan, de Klerk, Mahuza, Ackermann tries; Jantjies 6, Combrink 5, de Klerk conversions **defeated Sunwolves 7** Helu try; Ogura conversion. *Referee:* E. Seconds *(South Africa)*

*At Brisbane July 7*
**Reds 16** Stewart try; Cooper conversion; Cooper 3 penalty goals **defeated Brumbies 15** penalty try, Godwin tries; Hawera penalty goal. *Referee:* B. Pickerill *(New Zealand)*

*At Perth July 7*
**Force 31** Meakes, Coleman, Hardwick, Peni tries; Grant 4 conversions; Grant penalty goal **defeated Rebels 22** Koroibete 2, Fainga'a tries; Hodge 2 conversions; Hodge penalty goal. *Referee:* W. Houston *(Australia)*

*At Sydney July 8*
**Jaguares 40** Matera, Orlando, Macome, Creevy, Moroni tries; Sanchez 3 conversions; Sanchez 3 penalty goals **defeated Waratahs 27** Foley 2, Folau tries; Foley 3 conversions; Foley 2 penalty goals. *Referee:* B. O'Keeffe *(New Zealand)*

*At Pretoria July 8*
**Kings 31** Mapimpi, Cronje, Jaer tries; Cronje 2 conversions; Cronje 3 penalty goals; Cronje dropped goal **defeated Bulls 30** Jenkins, Matthews, Visagie tries; T. Schoeman 3 conversions; T. Schoeman 3 penalty goals. *Referee:* F. Anselmi *(Argentina)*

*At Cape Town July 8*
**Stormers 52** Kolbe 3, Leyds 2, Viljoen, Senatla, Willemse tries; Willemse 4, Kolbe 2 conversions **defeated Sunwolves 15** Goto, Hino tries; Tamura conversion; Tamura penalty goal. *Referee:* Q. Immelman *(South Africa)*

*At Dunedin July 14*
**Highlanders 40**
Naholo, Lentjes, Hammington, Li, penalty try, A. Dixon tries; Sopoaga 4 conversions **defeated Reds 17** Rodda, Mafi, Timu tries; Cooper conversion. *Referee:* M. Fraser *(New Zealand)*

*At Melbourne July 14*
**Jaguares 32** Cordero 2, Petti, Bertranou tries; Sanchez 2, Hernandez conversions; Sanchez 2 penalty goals **defeated Rebels 29** Hodge, Cummins tries; Hodge, Meehan conversions; Hodge 5 penalty goals. *Referee:* A. Gardner *(Australia)*

*At Port Elizabeth July 14*
**Cheetahs 21** Rhule, Swart tries; Marais conversion; Zeilinga 2, Marais penalty goals **defeated Kings 20** Mapimpi, Mjkevu, Mtyanda tries; Cronje conversion, Cronje penalty goal. *Referee:* E. Seconds *(South Africa)*

*At Tokyo July 15*
**Sunwolves 48** Lafaele 3, Uchida, Yamanaka, penalty try, Shigeno, Tokunaga tries; Tamura 2, Ogura conversions **defeated Blues 21** Parsons, Cowley-Tuioti, Collins tries; West 3 conversions. *Referee:* R. Rasivhenge *(South Africa)*

*At Hamilton July 15*
**Chiefs 28** McKenzie, Alaimalo, Leitch tries; McKenzie 2 conversions; McKenzie 3 penalty goals **defeated Brumbies 10** Ah Wong try; Hawera conversion; Hawera penalty goal. *Referee:* B. O'Keeffe *(New Zealand)*

*At Wellington July 15*
**Hurricanes 31** J. Barrett, J. Savea, Goosen, Fifita tries; J. Barrett 4 conversions; J. Barrett penalty goal **defeated Crusaders 22** Tamanivalu 2, Dagg tries; Mo'unga 2 conversions; Mo'unga penalty goal. *Referee:* G. Jackson *(New Zealand)*

*At Perth July 15*
**Force 40** Newsome, Polota-Nau, Brache, Lance, Hodgson tries; Grant 3 conversions; Lance 2, Hodgson penalty goals **defeated Waratahs 11** Roach try; Foley 2 penalty goals. *Referee:* N. Berry *(Australia)*

*At Durban July 15*
**Lions 27** Marx, Coetzee, Kriel tries; Jantjies 4 penalty goals **defeated Sharks 10** van Wyk try; April conversion; April penalty goal. *Referee:* M van der Westhuizen *(South Africa)*

*At Pretoria July 15*
**Stormers 41** Kolbe; Kolisi, Leyds, Notshe, Senatla, Willemse tries; Willemse 3, Kolbe conversions; Willemse penalty goal **defeated Bulls 33** Kriel 2, Jenkins, Matthews, P. van Zyl tries; T. Schoeman 3, Jantjies conversions. *Referee:* S. Kubo *(Japan)*

## QUARTER FINALS

*At Canberra July 21*
**Hurricanes 35** Goosen 2, J. Barrett, Perenara tries; J. Barrett 3 conversions; J. Barrett 3 penalty goals **defeated Brumbies 16** Dargaville, Mann-Rea tries; Hawera 2 penalty goals. *Referee:* G. Jackson *(New Zealand)*

*At Christchurch July 22*
**Crusaders 17** Moody, Taylor tries; Mo'unga 2 conversions; Mo'unga penalty goal **defeated Highlanders 0** *Referee:* A. Gardner *(Australia)*

*At Cape Town July 22*
**Chiefs 17** Stevenson try; McKenzie 4 penalty goals **defeated Stormers 11** Kolisi try; Marais 2 penalty goals. *Referee:* J. Peyper *(South Africa)*

*At Johannesburg July 22*
**Lions 23** Mostert, Kriel, Mapoe tries; Jantjies conversion; Jantjies, Combrink penalty goals; **defeated Sharks 21** van Wyk, D. du Preez tries; Bosch conversion; Bosch 2 penalty goals; Bosch dropped goal. *Referee:* M. van der Westhuizen *(South Africa)*

## SEMI-FINALS

*At Christchurch July 29*
**Crusaders 27** Tamanivalu 2, Dagg, Hall tries; Mo'unga 2 conversions; Mo'unga penalty goal **defeated Chiefs 13** Retallick try; McKenzie conversion; McKenzie 2 penalty goals. *Referee:* G. Jackson *(New Zealand)*

*At Johannesburg July 29*
**Lions 44** Marx, van Rooyen, Smith, Cronje, Vorster, Jantjies tries; Jantjies 4 conversions; Jantjies 2 penalty goals **defeated Hurricanes 29** Goosen, Laumape, Perenara, A. Savea tries; J. Barrett 2, B. Barrett conversions; J. Barrett penalty goal. *Referee:* J. Peyper *(South Africa)*

## FINAL

*At Johannesburg August 5*
**Crusaders 25** Read, Goodhue, Tamanivalu tries: Mo'unga 2 conversions; Mo'unga 2 penalty goals **defeated Lions 17** Marx, Fourie tries; Jantjies 2 conversions; Jantjies penalty goal. *Referee:* J. Peyper (South Africa)

# RESULTS FROM 2017 FIRST-CLASS SEASON

| Key: | RC | SANZAAR Rugby Championship |
|---|---|---|
| | W20 | World Rugby Under 20 Championship |
| | OJC | Oceania Rugby Junior Championship |
| | S15 | SANZAAR Super 15 |
| | RS | Ranfurly Shield |
| | P | ITM Cup Premiership |
| | C | ITM Cup Championship |
| | P/C | Crossover match between teams from ITM Cup Premiership and Championship divisions. |
| | H | Heartland Championship |
| | MC | Meads Cup |
| | LC | Lochore Cup |
| | qf | Quarter-final |
| | sf | Semi-final |
| | f | Final |
| | * | not first-class |

Winning team listed first

### January

| Sat-Sun | 14-15 | * | National Sevens | | | | Rotorua |
|---|---|---|---|---|---|---|---|
| Sat-Sun | 28-29 | * | Round Three World Rugby Sevens | | | | Wellington |

### February

| Sat-Sun | 4-5 | * | Round Four World Rugby Sevens | | | | Sydney |
|---|---|---|---|---|---|---|---|
| Thurs | 23 | S18 | Blues | 56 | Rebels | 18 | Melbourne |
| Fri | 24 | S18 | Chiefs | 24 | Highlanders | 15 | Dunedin |
| Sat | 25 | S18 | Hurricanes | 83 | Sunwolves | 17 | Tokyo |
| | 25 | S18 | Crusaders | 17 | Brumbies | 13 | Christchurch |

### March

| Fri | 3 | S18 | Chiefs | 41 | Blues | 26 | Hamilton |
|---|---|---|---|---|---|---|---|
| Fri-Sun | 3-5 | * | Round Five World Rugby Sevens | | | | Las Vegas |
| Sat | 4 | S18 | Hurricanes | 71 | Rebels | 6 | Wellington |
| | 4 | S18 | Crusaders | 30 | Highlanders | 27 | Dunedin |
| Fri | 10 | S18 | Chiefs | 26 | Hurricanes | 18 | Hamilton |
| Sat | 11 | S18 | Highlanders | 16 | Blues | 12 | Auckland |
| | 11 | S18 | Crusaders | 22 | Reds | 20 | Brisbane |
| Sat-Sun | 11-12 | * | Round Six World Rugby Sevens | | | | Vancouver |
| Fri | 17 | S18 | Crusaders | 33 | Blues | 24 | Christchurch |
| | 17 | S18 | Chiefs | 27 | Rebels | 14 | Melbourne |
| Sat | 18 | S18 | Hurricanes | 41 | Highlanders | 15 | Wellington |
| Fri | 24 | S18 | Crusaders | 45 | Force | 17 | Christchurch |
| Sat | 25 | S18 | Blues | 38 | Bulls | 14 | Albany |
| | 25 | S18 | Highlanders | 18 | Brumbies | 13 | Canberra |
| Fri | 31 | S18 | Highlanders | 51 | Rebels | 12 | Dunedin |

130

## April

| | | | | | | | | |
|---|---|---|---|---|---|---|---|---|
| Sat | 1 | S18 | Blues | 24 | Force | 15 | Auckland |
| | 1 | S18 | Chiefs | 28 | Bulls | 12 | Hamilton |
| | 1 | S18 | Hurricanes | 34 | Reds | 15 | Brisbane |
| Sun | 2 | S18 | Crusaders | 41 | Waratahs | 22 | Sydney |
| Fri-Sun | 7-9 | * | Round Seven World Rugby Sevens | | | | Hong Kong |
| Fri | 7 | S18 | Hurricanes | 38 | Waratahs | 28 | Wellington |
| Sat | 8 | S18 | Highlanders | 26 | Blues | 20 | Dunedin |
| | 8 | S18 | Stormers | 34 | Chiefs | 26 | Cape Town |
| Fri | 14 | S18 | Crusaders | 50 | Sunwolves | 3 | Christchurch |
| Sat | 15 | S18 | Hurricanes | 28 | Blues | 24 | Auckland |
| | 15 | S18 | Chiefs | 41 | Cheetahs | 27 | Bloemfontein |
| Sat-Sun | 15-16 | * | Round Eight World Rugby Sevens | | | | Singapore |
| Fri | 21 | S18 | Hurricanes | 56 | Brumbies | 21 | Napier |
| Sat | 22 | S18 | Highlanders | 40 | Sunwolves | 15 | Invercargill |
| | 22 | S18 | Crusaders | 57 | Stormers | 24 | Christchurch |
| | 22 | S18 | Chiefs | 16 | Force | 7 | Perth |
| Fri | 28 | O20 | NZ Under 20 | 63 | Fiji Under 20 | 3 | Gold Coast |
| | 28 | S18 | Highlanders | 57 | Stormers | 14 | Dunedin |
| Sat | 29 | | NZ Universities | 17 | Kanto | 14 | Hamilton |
| | 29 | S18 | Chiefs | 27 | Sunwolves | 20 | Hamilton |
| | 29 | S18 | Crusaders | 48 | Cheetahs | 21 | Bloemfontein |
| Sun | 30 | S18 | Blues | 18 | Brumbies | 12 | Canberra |

## May

| | | | | | | | | |
|---|---|---|---|---|---|---|---|---|
| Tues | 2 | O20 | NZ Under 20 | 80 | Samoa Under 20 | 23 | Gold Coast |
| Fri | 5 | S18 | Hurricanes | 41 | Stormers | 22 | Wellington |
| | 5 | S18 | Highlanders | 45 | Cheetahs | 41 | Bloemfontein |
| Sat | 6 | O20 | NZ Under 20 | 43 | Australia Under 20 | 6 | Gold Coast |
| | 6 | S18 | Chiefs | 46 | Reds | 17 | New Plymouth |
| | 6 | S18 | Blues | 44 | Waratahs | 30 | Sydney |
| | 6 | S18 | Crusaders | 62 | Bulls | 24 | Pretoria |
| Fri | 12 | S18 | Blues | 50 | Cheetahs | 32 | Auckland |
| Sat | 13 | S18 | Crusaders | 20 | Hurricanes | 12 | Christchurch |
| | 13 | S18 | Highlanders | 17 | Bulls | 10 | Pretoria |
| Sat-Sun | 13-14 | * | Round Nine World Rugby Sevens | | | | Paris |
| Fri | 19 | S18 | Crusaders | 31 | Chiefs | 24 | Suva |
| | 19 | S18 | Stormers | 30 | Blues | 22 | Cape Town |
| Sat | 20 | S18 | Hurricanes | 61 | Cheetahs | 7 | Wellington |
| | 20 | S18 | Highlanders | 55 | Force | 6 | Perth |
| Sat-Sun | 20-21 | * | Round Ten World Rugby Sevens | | | | London |
| Fri | 26 | S18 | Blues | 16 | Chiefs | 16 | Auckland |
| Sat | 27 | S18 | Highlanders | 44 | Waratahs | 28 | Dunedin |
| | 27 | S18 | Crusaders | 41 | Rebels | 19 | Melbourne |
| | 27 | S18 | Hurricanes | 34 | Bulls | 20 | Pretoria |
| Wed | 31 | W20 | NZ Under 20 | 42 | Scotland Under 20 | 20 | Kutaisi |

## June

| Day | Date | Comp | Team 1 | Score | Team 2 | Score | Venue |
|---|---|---|---|---|---|---|---|
| Fri | 2 | S18 | Blues | 34 | Reds | 29 | Apia |
| Sat | 3 | S18 | Crusaders | 25 | Highlanders | 22 | Christchurch |
| | 3 | | Poverty Bay | 38 | East Coast | 23 | Gisborne |
| | 3 | S18 | Chiefs | 46 | Waratahs | 31 | Hamilton |
| | 3 | | British & Irish Lions | 13 | NZ Provincial Barbarians | 7 | Whangarei |
| | 3 | S18 | Hurricanes | 34 | Force | 12 | Perth |
| Sun | 4 | W20 | NZ Under 20 | 68 | Italy Under 20 | 26 | Kutaisi |
| Wed | 7 | | Blues | 22 | British & Irish Lions | 16 | Auckland |
| Thurs | 8 | W20 | NZ Under 20 | 69 | Ireland Under 20 | 3 | Kutaisi |
| Sat | 10 | | British & Irish Lions | 12 | Crusaders | 3 | Christchurch |
| Tues | 13 | | Highlanders | 23 | British and Irish Lions | 22 | Dunedin |
| | 13 | W20 sf | NZ Under 20 | 39 | France Under 20 | 26 | Tbilisi |
| Sat | 17 | | British & Irish Lions | 32 | New Zealand Maori | 10 | Rotorua |
| Sun | 18 | W20 f | NZ Under 20 | 64 | England Under 20 | 17 | Tbilisi |
| Tues | 20 | | British & Irish Lions | 34 | Chiefs | 6 | Hamilton |
| Wed | 21 | RS | Canterbury | 71 | Wanganui | 5 | Christchurch |
| Sat | 24 | | New Zealand | 30 | British & Irish Lions | 15 | Auckland |
| Tues | 27 | | British & Irish Lions | 31 | Hurricanes | 31 | Wellington |

## July

| Day | Date | Comp | Team 1 | Score | Team 2 | Score | Venue |
|---|---|---|---|---|---|---|---|
| Sat | 1 | | British & Irish Lions | 24 | New Zealand | 21 | Wellington |
| Sat | 8 | | New Zealand | 15 | British & Irish Lions | 15 | Auckland |
| Fri | 14 | S18 | Highlanders | 40 | Reds | 17 | Dunedin |
| Sat | 15 | S18 | Sunwolves | 48 | Blues | 21 | Tokyo |
| | 15 | S18 | Chiefs | 28 | Brumbies | 10 | Hamilton |
| | 15 | S18 | Hurricanes | 31 | Crusaders | 22 | Wellington |
| Fri | 21 | S18 qf | Hurricanes | 35 | Brumbies | 16 | Canberra |
| Sat | 22 | S18 qf | Crusaders | 17 | Highlanders | 0 | Christchurch |
| | 22 | S18 qf | Chiefs | 17 | Stormers | 11 | Cape Town |
| Sat | 29 | S18 sf | Crusaders | 27 | Chiefs | 13 | Christchurch |
| | 29 | S18 sf | Lions | 44 | Hurricanes | 29 | Johannesburg |

## August

| Day | Date | Comp | Team 1 | Score | Team 2 | Score | Venue |
|---|---|---|---|---|---|---|---|
| Fri | 4 | RS | Canterbury | 69 | Mid Canterbury | 7 | Ashburton |
| Sat | 5 | S18 f | Crusaders | 25 | Lions | 17 | Johannesburg |
| Sat | 12 | | Poverty Bay | 31 | Wairarapa Bush | 6 | Gisborne |
| Thurs | 17 | P/C | North Harbour | 19 | Otago | 17 | Albany |
| Fri | 18 | P | Canterbury | 39 | Tasman | 0 | Nelson |
| Sat | 19 | C | Hawke's Bay | 24 | Southland | 16 | Napier |
| | 19 | P | Taranaki | 34 | Waikato | 29 | New Plymouth |
| | 19 | P | Counties Manukau | 16 | Auckland | 14 | Pukekohe |
| | 19 | RC | New Zealand | 54 | Australia | 34 | Sydney |
| Sun | 20 | C | Northland | 28 | Bay of Plenty | 23 | Whangarei |
| | 20 | C | Wellington | 41 | Manawatu | 29 | Palmerston North |
| Thurs | 24 | P/C | North Harbour | 45 | Southland | 20 | Invercargill |
| Fri | 25 | C | Bay of Plenty | 46 | Hawke's Bay | 17 | Rotorua |
| | 25 | P | Waikato | 33 | Counties Manukau | 21 | Hamilton |
| Sat | 26 | H | Buller | 27 | South Canterbury | 24 | Westport |
| | 26 | H | Thames Valley | 42 | East Coast | 13 | Ruatoria |
| | 26 | H | Horowhenua Kapiti | 22 | North Otago | 19 | Levin |
| | 26 | H | West Coast | 17 | King Country | 6 | Taupo |

|       | 26 | H       | Mid Canterbury      | 34 | Poverty Bay      | 5  | Ashburton          |
|-------|----|---------|---------------------|----|------------------|----|--------------------|
|       | 26 | H       | Wanganui            | 79 | Wairarapa Bush   | 7  | Wanganui           |
|       | 26 | P/C     | Wellington          | 42 | Taranaki         | 26 | Wellington         |
|       | 26 | P/C     | Auckland            | 10 | Northland        | 8  | Auckland           |
|       | 26 | RC      | New Zealand         | 35 | Australia        | 29 | Dunedin            |
| Sun   | 27 | P/C     | Manawatu            | 35 | Tasman           | 20 | Palmerston North   |
|       | 27 | P/C RS  | Canterbury          | 30 | Otago            | 24 | Christchurch       |
| Wed   | 30 | P       | Waikato             | 35 | Auckland         | 27 | Auckland           |
| Thurs | 31 | C       | Wellington          | 31 | Bay of Plenty    | 10 | Rotorua            |
| **September** |
| Fri   | 1  | P/C     | Canterbury          | 53 | Hawke's Bay      | 10 | Napier             |
| Sat   | 2  | H       | North Otago         | 31 | Mid Canterbury   | 25 | Oamaru             |
|       | 2  | H       | Wanganui            | 21 | Thames Valley    | 19 | Paeroa             |
|       | 2  | H       | Horowhenua Kapiti   | 39 | Poverty Bay      | 5  | Gisborne           |
|       | 2  | H       | South Canterbury    | 42 | King Country     | 36 | Timaru             |
|       | 2  | H       | Wairarapa Bush      | 36 | East Coast       | 10 | Masterton          |
|       | 2  | H       | Buller              | 34 | West Coast       | 19 | Greymouth          |
|       | 2  | C       | Otago               | 40 | Manawatu         | 30 | Dunedin            |
|       | 2  | C       | Northland           | 44 | Southland        | 13 | Invercargill       |
|       | 2  | P       | Taranaki            | 30 | Counties Manukau | 27 | New Plymouth       |
| Sun   | 3  | P       | Tasman              | 31 | Waikato          | 29 | Hamilton           |
|       | 3  | P       | North Harbour       | 57 | Auckland         | 10 | Auckland           |
| Wed   | 6  | C       | Wellington          | 40 | Hawke's Bay      | 27 | Wellington         |
| Thurs | 7  | P       | North Harbour       | 27 | Counties Manukau | 18 | Pukekohe           |
| Fri   | 8  | P/C RS  | Canterbury          | 78 | Southland        | 20 | Christchurch       |
|       | 8  | C       | Bay of Plenty       | 20 | Manawatu         | 17 | Palmerston North   |
| Sat   | 9  | H       | West Coast          | 32 | East Coast       | 19 | Ruatoria           |
|       | 9  | H       | Buller              | 33 | North Otago      | 31 | Westport           |
|       | 9  | H       | Horowhenua Kapiti   | 13 | Thames Valley    | 10 | Levin              |
|       | 9  | H       | King Country        | 32 | Wairarapa Bush   | 25 | Te Kuiti           |
|       | 9  | H       | South Canterbury    | 31 | Mid Canterbury   | 16 | Ashburton          |
|       | 9  | H       | Wanganui            | 25 | Poverty Bay      | 14 | Wanganui           |
|       | 9  | P       | Taranaki            | 49 | Auckland         | 38 | Auckland           |
|       | 9  | P/C     | Northland           | 37 | Waikato          | 7  | Whangarei          |
|       | 9  | RC      | New Zealand         | 39 | Argentina        | 22 | New Plymouth       |
| Sun   | 10 | P/C     | Tasman              | 37 | Wellington       | 35 | Blenheim           |
|       | 10 | C       | Otago               | 64 | Hawke's Bay      | 21 | Napier             |
| Wed   | 13 | P RS    | Canterbury          | 78 | Counties Manukau | 5  | Christchurch       |
| Thurs | 14 | P/C     | North Harbour       | 31 | Northland        | 22 | Whangarei          |
| Fri   | 15 | P/C     | Auckland            | 27 | Southland        | 17 | Invercargill       |
|       | 15 | P/C     | Taranaki            | 29 | Bay of Plenty    | 7  | New Plymouth       |
| Sat   | 16 | H       | Thames Valley       | 26 | Buller           | 7  | Paeroa             |
|       | 16 | H       | North Otago         | 28 | King Country     | 26 | Oamaru             |
|       | 16 | H       | Poverty Bay         | 35 | East Coast       | 15 | Gisborne           |
|       | 16 | H       | South Canterbury    | 21 | Wanganui         | 17 | Timaru             |
|       | 16 | H       | Mid Canterbury      | 60 | Wairarapa Bush   | 24 | Masterton          |
|       | 16 | P/C     | Manawatu            | 23 | Waikato          | 10 | Hamilton           |
|       | 16 | H       | West Coast          | 24 | Horowhenua Kapiti| 18 | Greymouth          |
|       | 16 | P/C     | Tasman              | 29 | Otago            | 27 | Dunedin            |
|       | 16 | RC      | New Zealand         | 57 | South Africa     | 0  | Albany             |

| Sun | 17 | P/C | Counties Manukau | 33 | Hawke's Bay | 14 | Pukekohe |
|---|---|---|---|---|---|---|---|
| | 17 | P/C | Wellington | 60 | Canterbury | 14 | Wellington |
| Wed | 20 | C | Bay of Plenty | 57 | Southland | 0 | Rotorua |
| Thurs | 21 | P/C | Otago | 34 | Auckland | 26 | Dunedin |
| Fri | 22 | C | Manawatu | 39 | Northland | 25 | Palmerston North |
| Sat | 23 | H | Buller | 29 | Wairarapa Bush | 24 | Westport |
| | 23 | H | Horowhenua Kapiti | 52 | East Coast | 3 | Otaki |
| | 23 | H | Thames Valley | 45 | King Country | 36 | Te Kuiti |
| | 23 | H | Mid Canterbury | 40 | Wanganui | 39 | Ashburton |
| | 23 | H | Poverty Bay | 36 | West Coast | 19 | Gisborne |
| | 23 | H | South Canterbury | 36 | North Otago | 29 | Timaru |
| | 23 | P | Canterbury | 41 | North Harbour | 28 | Albany |
| | 23 | P/C | Wellington | 34 | Waikato | 10 | Hamilton |
| | 23 | P/C | Taranaki | 48 | Hawke's Bay | 17 | Napier |
| Sun | 24 | P/C | Bay of Plenty | 31 | Counties Manukau | 31 | Tauranga |
| | 24 | P/C | Tasman | 50 | Southland | 17 | Nelson |
| Wed | 27 | C | Northland | 32 | Otago | 30 | Whangarei |
| Thurs | 28 | P | Taranaki | 40 | Tasman | 26 | New Plymouth |
| Fri | 29 | P/C | North Harbour | 33 | Hawke's Bay | 30 | Albany |
| Sat | 30 | H | South Canterbury | 45 | West Coast | 38 | Greymouth |
| | 30 | H | North Otago | 34 | Poverty Bay | 12 | Oamaru |
| | 30 | H | Mid Canterbury | 25 | Thames Valley | 16 | Paeroa |
| | 30 | H | Buller | 54 | East Coast | 17 | Ruatoria |
| | 30 | H | Wanganui | 80 | King Country | 3 | Wanganui |
| | 30 | C | Manawatu | 25 | Southland | 20 | Invercargill |
| | 30 | P/C | Auckland | 38 | Bay of Plenty | 19 | Auckland |
| | 30 | P RS | Canterbury | 37 | Waikato | 17 | Christchurch |
| | 30 | RC | New Zealand | 36 | Argentina | 10 | Buenos Aires |

**October**

| Sun | 1 | H | Horowhenua Kapiti | 38 | Wairarapa Bush | 12 | Wellington |
|---|---|---|---|---|---|---|---|
| | 1 | C | Wellington | 27 | Otago | 24 | Wellington |
| | 1 | P/C | Counties Manukau | 25 | Northland | 16 | Pukekohe |
| Wed | 4 | P | Tasman | 21 | North Harbour | 14 | Blenheim |
| Thurs | 5 | P/C | Counties Manukau | 29 | Manawatu | 24 | Palmerston North |
| Fri | 6 | P RS | Taranaki | 55 | Canterbury | 43 | Christchurch |
| Sat | 7 | H | North Otago | 57 | East Coast | 14 | Oamaru |
| | 7 | H | Horowhenua Kapiti | 15 | Wanganui | 8 | Levin |
| | 7 | H | Buller | 40 | Mid Canterbury | 32 | Ashburton |
| | 7 | H | Poverty Bay | 43 | King Country | 29 | Gisborne |
| | 7 | H | South Canterbury | 29 | Wairarapa Bush | 20 | Timaru |
| | 7 | H | West Coast | 24 | Thames Valley | 17 | Greymouth |
| | 7 | C | Bay of Plenty | 36 | Otago | 28 | Dunedin |
| | 7 | C | Northland | 34 | Hawke's Bay | 7 | Whangarei |
| | 7 | C | Wellington | 61 | Southland | 12 | Invercargill |
| | 7 | RC | New Zealand | 25 | South Africa | 24 | Cape Town |
| Sun | 8 | P | Tasman | 31 | Auckland | 18 | Nelson |
| | 8 | P | North Harbour | 13 | Waikato | 11 | Hamilton |
| Wed | 11 | P/C RS | Taranaki | 46 | Manawatu | 25 | New Plymouth |
| Thurs | 12 | C | Wellington | 36 | Northland | 18 | Wellington |
| Fri | 13 | P | Canterbury | 32 | Auckland | 27 | Auckland |

| | | | | | | | |
|---|---|---|---|---|---|---|---|
| Sat | 14 | H | Poverty Bay | 35 | Thames Valley | 34 | Te Aroha |
| | 14 | H | Horowhenua Kapiti | 30 | Buller | 26 | Westport |
| | 14 | H | South Canterbury | 45 | East Coast | 7 | Ruatoria |
| | 14 | H | Wanganui | 10 | North Otago | 6 | Wanganui |
| | 14 | P/C | Bay of Plenty | 36 | Waikato | 32 | Tauranga |
| | 14 | H | Mid Canterbury | 43 | King Country | 38 | Taupo |
| | 14 | C | Otago | 43 | Southland | 19 | Dunedin |
| | 14 | H | West Coast | 36 | Wairarapa Bush | 26 | Masterton |
| | 14 | P | Counties Manukau | 52 | Tasman | 30 | Pukekohe |
| Sun | 15 | P | North Harbour | 64 | Taranaki | 33 | Albany |
| | 15 | C | Hawke's Bay | 36 | Manawatu | 31 | Napier |
| Fri | 20 | C sf | Wellington | 49 | Northland | 21 | Wellington |
| Sat | 21 | MC sf | Horowhenua Kapiti | 18 | Buller | 17 | Levin |
| | 21 | MC sf | Wanganui | 29 | South Canterbury | 24 | Timaru |
| | 21 | LC sf | West Coast | 24 | North Otago | 14 | Greymouth |
| | 21 | LC sf | Mid Canterbury | 56 | Poverty Bay | 22 | Ashburton |
| | 21 | C sf | Bay of Plenty | 48 | Otago | 32 | Tauranga |
| | 21 | P sf | Canterbury | 35 | North Harbour | 24 | Christchurch |
| | 21 | P sf | Tasman | 30 | Taranaki | 29 | New Plymouth |
| | 21 | | Australia | 23 | New Zealand | 18 | Brisbane |
| Fri | 27 | C f | Wellington | 59 aet | Bay of Plenty | 45 aet | Wellington |
| Sat | 28 | MC f | Wanganui | 30 | Horowhenua Kapiti | 14 | Levin |
| | 28 | | Australia | 31 | UK Barbarians | 28 | Sydney |
| | 28 | P f | Canterbury | 35 | Tasman | 13 | Christchurch |
| Sun | 29 | LC f | Mid Canterbury | 47 | West Coast | 15 | Methven |
| **November** | | | | | | | |
| Fri | 3 | | NZ Maori | 51 | Canada | 9 | Vancouver |
| Sat | 4 | | NZ Heartland | 41 | NZ Marist | 39 | Timaru |
| | 4 | | New Zealand | 31 | UK Barbarians | 22 | London |
| Fri | 10 | | France Barbarians | 19 | NZ Maori | 15 | Bordeaux |
| | 10 | | UK Barbarians | 27 | Tonga | 24 | Limerick |
| Sat | 11 | | New Zealand | 38 | France | 18 | Paris |
| Tues | 14 | | New Zealand | 28 | France XV | 23 | Lyon |
| Sat | 18 | | New Zealand | 22 | Scotland | 17 | Edinburgh |
| Sat | 25 | | New Zealand | 33 | Wales | 18 | Cardiff |
| **December** | | | | | | | |
| Fri-Sat | 1-2 | * | Round One World Rugby Sevens | | | | Dubai |
| Sat-Sun | 9-10 | * | Round Two World Rugby Sevens | | | | Cape Town |

235 first-class matches

# NATIONAL PROVINCIAL CHAMPIONSHIP WINNERS

| | First Division | Second Division (North) | Second Division (South) |
|---|---|---|---|
| 1976 | Bay of Plenty | Taranaki | South Canterbury |
| 1977 | Canterbury | North Auckland | South Canterbury |
| 1978 | Wellington | Bay of Plenty | Marlborough |
| 1979 | Counties | Hawke's Bay | Marlborough |
| 1980 | Manawatu | Waikato | Mid Canterbury |
| 1981 | Wellington | Wairarapa Bush | South Canterbury |
| 1982 | Auckland | Taranaki | Southland |
| 1983 | Canterbury | Taranaki | Mid Canterbury |
| 1984 | Auckland | Taranaki | Southland |

| | First Division | Second Division | Third Division |
|---|---|---|---|
| 1985 | Auckland | Taranaki | North Harbour |
| 1986 | Wellington | Waikato | South Canterbury |
| 1987 | Auckland | North Harbour | Poverty Bay |
| 1988 | Auckland | Hawke's Bay | Thames Valley |
| 1989 | Auckland | Southland | Wanganui |
| 1990 | Auckland | Hawke's Bay | Thames Valley |
| 1991 | Otago | King Country | South Canterbury |
| 1992 | Waikato | Taranaki | Nelson Bays |
| 1993 | Auckland | Counties | Horowhenua |
| 1994 | Auckland | Southland | Mid Canterbury |
| 1995 | Auckland | Taranaki | Thames Valley |
| 1996 | Auckland | Southland | Wanganui |
| 1997 | Canterbury | Northland | Marlborough |
| 1998 | Otago | Central Vikings | Mid Canterbury |
| 1999 | Auckland | Nelson Bays | East Coast |
| 2000 | Wellington | Bay of Plenty | East Coast |
| 2001 | Canterbury | Hawke's Bay | South Canterbury |
| 2002 | Auckland | Hawke's Bay | North Otago |
| 2003 | Auckland | Hawke's Bay | Wanganui |
| 2004 | Canterbury | Nelson Bays | Poverty Bay |
| 2005 | Auckland | Hawke's Bay | Wairarapa Bush |

| | Air New Zealand Cup | Meads Cup | Lochore Cup |
|---|---|---|---|
| 2006 | Waikato | Wairarapa Bush | Poverty Bay |
| 2007 | Auckland | North Otago | Poverty Bay |
| 2008 | Canterbury | Wanganui | Poverty Bay |
| 2009 | Canterbury | Wanganui | North Otago |

| | ITM Cup | | |
|---|---|---|---|
| 2010 | Canterbury | North Otago | Wairarapa Bush |

| | ITM Premiership | ITM Championship | Meads Cup | Lochore Cup |
|---|---|---|---|---|
| 2011 | Canterbury | Hawke's Bay | Wanganui | Poverty Bay |
| 2012 | Canterbury | Counties Manukau | East Coast | Buller |
| 2013 | Canterbury | Tasman | Mid Canterbury | South Canterbury |
| 2014 | Taranaki | Manawatu | Mid Canterbury | Wanganui |
| 2015 | Canterbury | Hawke's Bay | Wanganui | King Country |

| | MITRE 10 CUP | | MITRE 10 HEARTLAND CHAMPIONSHIP | |
|---|---|---|---|---|
| | Premiership | Championship | Meads Cup | Lochore Cup |
| 2016 | Canterbury | North Harbour | Wanganui | North Otago |
| 2017 | Canterbury | Wellington | Wanganui | Mid-Canterbury |

# MITRE 10 CUP

Canterbury continued their extraordinary dominance of the national championship, winning it for the ninth time in the last ten years, while Tasman finished runner-up for the third time in the last four years.

Waikato suffered relegation from the Premiership to the Championship for 2018, and were replaced in next year's Premiership by Wellington who defeated Bay of Plenty in extra time to win the Championship final.

Wellington's 74 tries erased from the record books the long-standing record of 70 tries scored by Auckland in 1984. Only one dropped goal was kicked in the Mitre 10 Cup, equalling the record low of the one scored in the 2005 first division.

## ROUND ROBIN

Each team played all six other teams in their division plus crossover matches against four teams in the other division for a total of ten matches.

| | P | W | D | L | B⁴ | B⁷ | Pts | T | C | PG | DG | Total | T | C | PG | DG | Total |
|---|---|---|---|---|---|---|---|---|---|---|---|---|---|---|---|---|---|
| | | | | | | | | | FOR | | | | | AGAINST | | | |
| **PREMIERSHIP DIVISION** | | | | | | | | | | | | | | | | | |
| Taranaki | 10 | 8 | 0 | 2 | 10 | 0 | **42** | 56 | 39 | 9 | 1 | 390 | 44 | 31 | 12 | 0 | 318 |
| Canterbury | 10 | 8 | 0 | 2 | 9 | 0 | **41** | 59 | 51 | 16 | 0 | 445 | 33 | 27 | 8 | 1 | 246 |
| North Harbour | 10 | 8 | 0 | 2 | 4 | 1 | **37** | 39 | 28 | 26 | 0 | 331 | 25 | 21 | 18 | 0 | 223 |
| Tasman | 10 | 6 | 0 | 4 | 7 | 0 | **31** | 38 | 27 | 9 | 0 | 275 | 43 | 31 | 9 | 0 | 306 |
| Counties Manukau | 10 | 5 | 1 | 4 | 4 | 1 | **27** | 35 | 25 | 10 | 0 | 257 | 38 | 31 | 15 | 0 | 297 |
| Auckland | 10 | 3 | 0 | 7 | 4 | 2 | **18** | 29 | 20 | 16 | 0 | 235 | 38 | 26 | 18 | 0 | 298 |
| Waikato | 10 | 2 | 0 | 8 | 5 | 4 | **17** | 31 | 16 | 8 | 0 | 213 | 38 | 29 | 15 | 0 | 293 |
| | | | | | | | | | | | | | | | | | |
| **CHAMPIONSHIP DIVISION** | | | | | | | | | | | | | | | | | |
| Wellington | 10 | 9 | 0 | 1 | 10 | 1 | **47** | 59 | 44 | 8 | 0 | 407 | 27 | 18 | 12 | 0 | 207 |
| Bay of Plenty | 10 | 5 | 1 | 4 | 5 | 1 | **28** | 38 | 26 | 13 | 0 | 285 | 34 | 24 | 11 | 0 | 251 |
| Otago | 10 | 4 | 0 | 6 | 5 | 5 | **26** | 43 | 31 | 18 | 0 | 331 | 33 | 20 | 20 | 0 | 269 |
| Northland | 10 | 5 | 0 | 5 | 4 | 1 | **25** | 29 | 22 | 25 | 0 | 264 | 25 | 18 | 20 | 0 | 221 |
| Manawatu | 10 | 4 | 0 | 6 | 5 | 3 | **24** | 34 | 24 | 20 | 0 | 278 | 40 | 23 | 13 | 0 | 287 |
| Hawke's Bay | 10 | 2 | 0 | 8 | 2 | 1 | **11** | 28 | 21 | 7 | 0 | 203 | 52 | 43 | 16 | 0 | 398 |
| Southland | 10 | 0 | 0 | 10 | 0 | 1 | **1** | 18 | 14 | 12 | 0 | 154 | 66 | 46 | 10 | 0 | 454 |
| **TOTALS** | | | | | | | | 536 | 388 | 197 | 1 | 4068 | 536 | 388 | 197 | 1 | 4068 |

B⁴ *bonus points for four or more tries in a match.*     B⁷ *bonus points for loss by seven or fewer points.*

# PLAYOFF SUMMARY

In the semi-finals, the top qualifier was home to the fourth-placed qualifier and the second-placed qualifier was home to the third-place qualifier. In the final, the highest qualifier of the two participants played at home.

## PREMIERSHIP

**Semi-finals:** Canterbury 35 v North Harbour 24, Christchurch
Tasman 30 v Taranaki 29, New Plymouth

**Final:** Canterbury 35 v Tasman 13, Christchurch

## CHAMPIONSHIP

**Semi-finals:** Wellington 49 v Northland 21, Wellington
Bay of Plenty 48 v Otago 32, Tauranga

**Final:** Wellington 59 aet v Bay of Plenty 45 aet, Wellington

# ALMANACK NEW ZEALAND MITRE 10 CUP XV

George Bridge
*Canterbury*

Matt Duffie          Seta Tamanivalu          Tevita Li
*North Harbour*          *Taranaki*          *North Harbour*

Jack Goodhue
*Northland*

Richie Mo'unga
*Canterbury*

Mitchell Drummond
*Canterbury*

Luke Whitelock
*Canterbury*

Lachlan Boshier          Dominic Bird          Mitchell Dunshea          Tom Sanders
*Taranaki*          *Canterbury*          *Canterbury*          *Canterbury*

Alex Fidow          Asafo Aumua          Ross Wright
*Wellington*          *Wellington*          *Northland*

**Reserves:** Ricky Riccitelli (*Taranaki*), Craig Millar (*Otago*), Atu Moli (*Waikato*), Jimmy Tupou (*Counties Manukau*), Toa Halafihi (*Taranaki*), Bryn Hall (*North Harbour*), Jackson Garden-Bachop (*Wellington*), Will Jordan (*Tasman*).

# RECORDS

## BY THE TEAMS

### BEST PERFORMANCES 2017

### In a Season

| | BEST PERFORMANCES 2017 | | RECORD 1976–2017 |
|---|---|---|---|
| Most points | 515 | Canterbury<br>Wellington | 521 Otago, 1998 |
| Most tries | 74 | Wellington | 74 Wellington, 2017 |
| Most conversions | 57 | Canterbury | 57 Canterbury, 2017 |
| Most penalty goals | 27 | North Harbour | 45 Otago, 2012 |
| Most dropped goals | 1 | Taranaki | 12 Bay of Plenty, 1985 |

### In a Match

| | BEST PERFORMANCES 2017 | | RECORD 1976–2017 |
|---|---|---|---|
| Highest Score | 78 | Canterbury v Southland<br>Canterbury v Counties Manukau | 97 Auckland v King Country, 1993 |
| Biggest winning margin | 73 | Canterbury v Counties Manukau (78–5) | 94 Auckland v King Country, 1993 (97–3) |
| Most tries | 11 | Canterbury v Southland<br>Canterbury v Counties Manukau | 15 Auckland v King Country, 1993 |
| Most conversions | 10 | Canterbury v Southland<br>Canterbury v Counties Manukau | 12 Canterbury v Southland, 2012 |
| Most penalty goals | 6 | Northland v Otago<br>Tasman v Taranaki, sf | 9 Taranaki v Bay of Plenty, 2011 |
| Most dropped goals | 1 | Taranaki v Canterbury | 4 Bay of Plenty v Waikato, 1985 |

# BY THE PLAYERS

## BEST PERFORMANCES 2017

### In a Season

| | | |
|---|---|---|
| Most points | 160 R. Mo'unga (*Canterbury*) | 196 T.E. Brown (*Otago*), 1998 |
| Most tries | 11 T. Li (*North Harbour*) | 15 T.J. Wright (*Auckland*), 1984 |
| | | B.J. Laney (*Otago*), 1998 |

### In a Match

| | | |
|---|---|---|
| Most points | 34 F. Smith (*Otago*) v Hawke's Bay | 37 B.A. Blair (*Canterbury*) v Counties Manukau, 1999 |
| Most tries | 5 T. Li (*North Harbour*) v Taranaki | 5 T.J. Wright (*Auckland*) v Manawatu, 1984 |
| | | W.R. Gordon (*Waikato*) v Southland, 1990 |
| | | C.J. Spencer (*Auckland*) v Otago, 1996 |
| | | M.P. Robinson (*Taranaki*) v Southland, 1997 |
| | | J. Maddock (*Canterbury*) v North Harbour, 2002 |
| | | S.W. Sivivatu (*Waikato*) v Auckland, 2004 |
| | | T. Li (*North Harbour*) v Taranaki, 2017 |
| Most conversions | 10 R.Mo'unga (*Canterbury*) v Counties Manukau | 12 T.J. Taylor (*Canterbury*) v Southland, 2012 |
| Most penalty goals | 6 P.J.L. Breen (*Northland*) v Otago | 9 B.J. Barrett (*Taranaki*) v Bay of Plenty, 2011 |
| | M.J. Hunt (*Tasman*) v Taranaki, sf | |
| Most dropped goals | 1 S. Perofeta (*Taranaki*) v Canterbury | 4 R.J. Preston (*Bay of Plenty*) v Waikato, 1985 |

**Leading point-scorers in the Mitre 10 Cup:**

| | | |
|---|---|---|
| R. Mo'unga | *Canterbury* | 160 |
| J.K. Garden-Bachop | *Wellington* | 142 |
| F.H. Smith | *Otago* | 116 |
| M.R. McKenzie | *Taranaki* | 100 |
| B.E.C. Gatland | *North Harbour* | 96 |

**Leading Try scorers in the Mitre 10 Cup:**

| | | |
|---|---|---|
| T. Li | *North Harbour* | 11 |
| B.M. Ennor | *Canterbury* | 10 |
| J.M. Nareki | *Otago* | 9 |
| T.E.S. Bateman | *Canterbury* | 9 |
| L.L.A. Foketi | *Bay of Plenty* | 8 |
| T.J. Webber | *Bay of Plenty* | 8 |
| A.F. Fidow | *Wellington* | 8 |

# MITRE 10 HEARTLAND CHAMPIONSHIP

Wanganui were Heartland champions for the sixth time in the history of the 12-year competition, achieving their third successive Meads Cup title.

Mid Canterbury won the Lochore Cup for the first time and join North Otago, Wairarapa Bush and Wanganui in having won both the Meads Cup and Lochore Cup.

An interesting feature of this year's competition were the appearances of four former All Blacks in Corey Flynn (West Coast), Regan King (Mid Canterbury), Alby Mathewson (King Country) and Piri Weepu (Wairarapa Bush). Their involvement was good to see and certainly enhanced the profile of the competition.

James Lash's 147 points for Buller was a new individual points-scoring record in a season for the Heartland Championship.

# ROUND ROBIN SUMMARY

| | P | W | D | L | B⁴ | B⁸ | Pts | FOR | | | | | AGAINST | | | | |
|---|---|---|---|---|---|---|---|---|---|---|---|---|---|---|---|---|---|
| | | | | | | | | T | C | PG | DG | Total | T | C | PG | DG | Total |
| South Canterbury | 8 | 7 | 0 | 1 | 7 | 1 | **36** | 42 | 30 | 1 | 0 | 273 | 23 | 18 | 13 | 0 | 190 |
| Horowhenua Kapiti | 8 | 7 | 0 | 1 | 3 | 1 | **32** | 26 | 20 | 19 | 0 | 227 | 12 | 7 | 11 | 0 | 107 |
| Buller | 8 | 6 | 0 | 2 | 3 | 1 | **28** | 28 | 25 | 18 | 2 | 250 | 29 | 20 | 6 | 0 | 203 |
| Wanganui | 8 | 5 | 0 | 3 | 3 | 3 | **26** | 37 | 23 | 16 | 0 | 279 | 13 | 12 | 12 | 0 | 125 |
| Mid Canterbury | 8 | 5 | 0 | 3 | 5 | 1 | **26** | 36 | 25 | 15 | 0 | 275 | 31 | 21 | 9 | 0 | 224 |
| West Coast | 8 | 5 | 0 | 3 | 5 | 1 | **26** | 32 | 19 | 2 | 1 | 209 | 25 | 19 | 11 | 1 | 201 |
| North Otago | 8 | 4 | 0 | 4 | 5 | 4 | **25** | 29 | 24 | 14 | 0 | 235 | 22 | 16 | 11 | 1 | 178 |
| Poverty Bay | 8 | 4 | 0 | 4 | 4 | 0 | **20** | 27 | 18 | 4 | 0 | 185 | 31 | 22 | 10 | 0 | 229 |
| Thames Valley | 8 | 3 | 0 | 5 | 4 | 4 | **20** | 27 | 18 | 12 | 0 | 209 | 22 | 17 | 10 | 0 | 174 |
| King Country | 8 | 1 | 0 | 7 | 5 | 3 | **12** | 26 | 19 | 12 | 0 | 206 | 45 | 29 | 12 | 0 | 323 |
| Wairarapa Bush | 8 | 1 | 0 | 7 | 4 | 2 | **10** | 25 | 17 | 5 | 0 | 174 | 43 | 30 | 12 | 0 | 313 |
| East Coast | 8 | 0 | 0 | 8 | 0 | 0 | **0** | 13 | 9 | 5 | 0 | 98 | 52 | 36 | 6 | 1 | 353 |
| **TOTALS** | | | | | | | | 348 | 247 | 123 | 3 | 2620 | 348 | 247 | 123 | 3 | 2620 |

B⁴ *bonus point for scoring four or more tries in a match.*          B⁸ *bonus point for a loss by seven points or less.*

*Wanganui, Mid Canterbury and West Coast all finished on 26 points. The first tiebreak rule used when three or more teams finish on the same number of points is ranking by points differential which was Wanganui (+154), Mid Canterbury (+51) and West Coast (+8). Poverty Bay and Thames Valley both finished on 20 points. Poverty Bay had the higher ranking due to winning their individual match.*

# PLAYOFF SUMMARY

The top four teams played off for the Meads Cup, and the teams finishing fifth to eighth played off for the Lochore Cup.

## MEADS CUP (1st–4th)

**Semi-finals:**     Horowhenua Kapiti 18 v Buller 17, Levin
Wanganui 29 v South Canterbury 24, Timaru

**Final:**     Wanganui 30 v Horowhenua Kapiti 14, Levin

## LOCHORE CUP (5th–8th)

**Semi-finals:**     West Coast 24 v North Otago 14, Greymouth
Mid Canterbury 56 v Poverty Bay 22, Ashburton

**Final:**     Mid Canterbury 47 v West Coast 15, Methven

# HEARTLAND CHAMPIONSHIP RECORDS

## BY THE TEAMS

| | BEST PERFORMANCE 2017 | RECORD (2006–2017) |
|---|---|---|
| **In a Season** | | |
| Most points | 378 Mid Canterbury | 440 Wanganui, 2016 |
| Most tries | 50 Mid Canterbury | 63 Wanganui, 2008 |
| Most conversions | 34 Mid Canterbury | 45 Wanganui, 2008 |
| Most penalty goals | 28 Horowhenua Kapiti | 30 Wairarapa Bush, 2012 |
| Most dropped goals | 2 Buller | 2 on ten occasions (eight teams) |
| | | |
| **In a Match** | | |
| Most points | 80 Wanganui v King Country | 116 North Otago v East Coast, 2010 |
| Biggest winning margin | 77 Wanganui v King Country (80–3) | 113 North Otago v East Coast, 2010 (116–3) |
| Most tries | 13 Wanganui v King Country | 17 North Otago v East Coast, 2010 |
| Most conversions | 10 Wanganui v Wairarapa Bush | 14 North Otago v East Coast, 2010 |
| Most penalty goals | 6 Horowhenua Kapiti v Buller, MC sf | 7 Thames Valley v Mid Canterbury, 2009<br>Thames Valley v East Coast, 2011<br>Poverty Bay v Buller, 2013 |
| Most dropped goals | 1 5 occasions | 1 54 occasions |

# BY THE PLAYERS

## BEST PERFORMANCE 2017

### In a Season

| | | |
|---|---|---|
| Most points | 147 | J.J. Lash (Buller) |
| Most tries | 12 | M.L. Sau (Mid Canterbury) |

### In a Match

| | | |
|---|---|---|
| Most points | 30 | W.A. Wright (South Canterbury) v West Coast |
| Most tries | 3 | Seven occasions (seven players) |
| Most conversions | 7 | J.J. Lash (Buller) v East Coast |
| Most penalty goals | 6 | J.S. So'oialo (Horowhenua Kapiti) v Buller, MC sf |
| Most dropped goals | 1 | Five occasions (four players) |

## RECORD (2006–2017)

| | | |
|---|---|---|
| | 147 | J.J. Lash (Buller), 2017 |
| | 14 | P. Fetuai (Wanganui), 2006 |

| | | |
|---|---|---|
| | 35 | S.C. Leighton (Poverty Bay) v Thames Valley, 2007 |
| | 5 | L.M. Herden (North Otago) v East Coast, 2010 |
| | 9 | R.F. Aloe (Horowhenua Kapiti) v East Coast, 2008 |
| | | B. Patston (North Otago) v East Coast, 2010 |
| | 7 | D.P. Harrison (Thames Valley) v Mid Canterbury, 2009; |
| | | J.R. Reynolds (Thames Valley) v East Coast, 2011 |
| | | S.P. Parkes (Poverty Bay) v Buller, 2013 |
| | 1 | on 54 occasions (38 players) |

### Leading Points-scorers in the Championship:

| | | |
|---|---|---|
| J.J. Lash | Buller | 147 |
| J.R. Percival | Mid Canterbury | 140 |
| J.S. So'oialo | Horowhenua Kapiti | 130 |
| W.A. Wright | South Canterbury | 101 |
| C.D. Clare | Wanganui | 95 |

### Leading Try scorers in the Championship:

| | | |
|---|---|---|
| M.L. Sau | Mid Canterbury | 12 |
| W.B. McGoon | Mid Canterbury | 9 |
| T.S. Seruwalu | Wanganui | 8 |
| W.A. Wright | South Canterbury | 7 |
| V.T. Tora | South Canterbury | 7 |
| K.V. Leatigaga | South Canterbury | 7 |

# AUCKLAND

2017 **Status:** Mitre 10 Cup Premiership
**Founded 1883.** Original member
**President:** B.M. (Bruce) Gemmell
**Chairman:** M.J. (Mike) Donovan
**Chief executive officer:** J.M. (Jarrod) Bear
**Coach:** N.C. (Nick) White
**Assistant coaches:** B.J. (Bevan) Cadwallader,
        G.E. (Geoff) Moon
**Main ground:** Eden Park, Auckland
**Capacity:** 47,000
**Colours:** Blue and white

## RECORDS

| | | |
|---|---|---|
| Most appearances | 196 | *Snow White, 1949–63* |
| Most points | 2746 | *Grant Fox, 1982–93* |
| Most tries | 112 | *Terry Wright, 1984–93* |
| Most points in a season | 322 | *Grant Fox, 1990* |
| Most tries in a season | 19 | *Terry Wright, 1984* |
| Most conversions in a season | 77 | *Grant Fox, 1990* |
| Most penalty goals in a season | 48 | *Grant Fox, 1989, 1990* |
| Most dropped goals in a season | 8 | *Grant Fox, 1990* |
| Most points in a match | 43 | *Adrian Cashmore v Mid Canterbury, 1995* |
| Most tries in a match | 8 | *John Kirwan v North Otago, 1993* |
| Most conversions in a match | 12 | *Grant Fox v Marlborough, 1984* |
| | | *Brett Craies v Horowhenua, 1986* |
| | | *Grant Fox v Nelson Bays, 1991* |
| | | *Lachie Munro v North Otago, 2008* |
| Most penalty goals in a match | 7 | *Grant Fox v Canterbury, 1990* |
| | | *Grant Fox v Waikato, 1992* |
| Highest team score | 139 | *v North Otago, 1993* |
| Record victory (points ahead) | 134 | *139–5 v North Otago, 1993* |
| Highest score conceded | 59 | *v Waikato, 2004* |
| Record defeat (points behind) | 48 | *11–59 v Waikato, 2004* |

Auckland's three wins in the Mitre 10 Cup was its worst ever performance in the history of the national provincial championship. Their three wins were all against Championship sides, with losses to all Premiership teams including a thrashing at the hands of neighbour North Harbour. In the final round it was either Auckland or Waikato that would be relegated to the Championship. Auckland, not unexpectedly, lost to Canterbury while the following day Waikato's loss to Championship side Bay of Plenty meant Auckland retained Premiership status for 2018.

With a large number of Super Rugby players, and a low turnover from last year, the team struggled to maximise the individual array of talent possessed. The forward pack battled away well, but the backline just did not click collectively. Injury was a big factor in the first half of the season with an extraordinary 39 players appearing in the first five matches. The two best performances of the season came in the final three matches — against Bay of Plenty and Canterbury — which suggests the team was starting to improve and gain consistency.

Missing from last year were Simon Hickey, Joe Edwards, Steven Luatua, Liaki Moli (all overseas), Michael Fatialofa and Tom McHugh (both injured). Players arriving in were Jordan

Trainor from Waikato and Dan Bowden back from overseas to don the Auckland jersey for the first time since 2009.

At fullback new signing Jordan Trainor looked good on counter-attack but lost his position for the final three matches to Melani Nanai who had missed the first half of the season due to injury. Vince Aso, one of only two players to start every match, appeared mostly on the right wing and had a successful season to be top try-scorer with seven tries. He was the best of the backline. NZ Sevens rep Joseva Ravouvou played the last three matches on the left wing, and looked unstoppable in scoring three good tries.

The midfield of All Blacks Malakai Fekitoa and George Moala did not provide the class expected and at times looked ordinary, with Fekitoa missing the last three matches due to injury before departing overseas. At first five-eighth Dan Bowden only appeared three times, suffering concussion in the big loss to North Harbour, while Jono Hickey was a sound, all-round halfback and an accurate goalkicker.

Loose forward Blake Gibson was a standout and received a call-up into the All Blacks' squad as injury cover for the Argentine test at New Plymouth while Akira Ioane was also in good form and missed matches through being in the All Blacks' environment. Jerome Kaino played three matches, showing up well against Southland, representing his province for the first time since 2010.

After a below par Super Rugby season with the Blues, Patrick Tuipulotu was given the Auckland captaincy and responded superbly to earn a recall into the All Blacks. Locking partner Scott Scrafton started the season well but an injured shoulder against Northland put him out for the remainder of the season, his replacement being Ben Nee Nee who can be pleased with his first full season in the team. In the front row Marcel Renata started every match, while fellow prop Sam Prattley and hooker Greg Pleasants-Tate missed just one match each.

## AUCKLAND REPRESENTATIVES 2017

| | Club | Games for Union | Points for Union | | Club | Games for Union | Points for Union |
|---|---|---|---|---|---|---|---|
| Vince Aso | Ponsonby | 38 | 75 | Jamie Lane | Ponsonby | 2 | 0 |
| Daniel Bowden | Ponsonby | 10 | 60 | Tumua Manu | College Rifles | 4 | 0 |
| Caleb Clarke | Suburbs | 3 | 0 | Otumaka Mausia | College Rifles | 3 | 0 |
| Pryor Collier | Ponsonby | 12 | 15 | Lisati Milo-Harris | Grammar TEC | 6 | 0 |
| Nico Costa | Eden | 3 | 0 | George Moala | Grammar TEC | 53 | 150 |
| Sinclair Dominkovich-Murray | University | 8 | 0 | Melani Nanai | Manukau Rovers | 24 | 35 |
| Lyndon Dunshea | University | 1 | 0 | Ben Nee-Nee | Pakuranga | 15 | 5 |
| Kurt Eklund | University | 32 | 20 | Dalton Papali'i | Pakuranga | 4 | 0 |
| Tyrone Elkington-MacDonald | University | 9 | 2 | Greg Pleasants-Tate | Ponsonby | 25 | 30 |
| Dexter Fa'amoana | College Rifles | 5 | 0 | Harry Plummer | Grammar TEC | 3 | 4 |
| Jamason Fa'anana-Shultz | Suburbs | 1 | 0 | Sam Prattley | Pakuranga | 43 | 5 |
| Tinoai "TJ" Faiane | Pakuranga | 17 | 5 | Joseva Ravouvou | College Rifles | 8 | 20 |
| Wiseguy Faiane | Pakuranga | 1 | 0 | Marcel Renata | University | 21 | 10 |
| Malakai Fekitoa | Pakuranga | 29 | 30 | John "JP" Sauni | College Rifles | 1 | 0 |
| Marco Fepuleai | Ponsonby | 1 | 0 | Scott Scrafton | Grammar TEC | 24 | 5 |
| Latiume Fosita | Mt Wellington | 13 | 5 | Taleni Seu | Grammar TEC | 21 | 35 |
| Leon Fukofuka | Marist | 19 | 0 | Samuel Slade | Ponsonby | 6 | 0 |
| Blake Gibson | Ponsonby | 21 | 10 | Emersen Tamura-Paki | College Rifles | 7 | 0 |
| Sione Havili-Talitui | College Rifles | 2 | 5 | Jordan Trainor | Ponsonby | 8 | 12 |
| Jono Hickey | Grammar TEC | 32 | 129 | Isileli Tu'ungafasi | Suburbs | 19 | 0 |
| Akira Ioane | Ponsonby | 27 | 25 | Patrick Tuipulotu | Ponsonby | 21 | 25 |
| Josh Kaifa | Manukau Rovers | 7 | 0 | Sam Ulufonua | Ponsonby | 2 | 0 |
| Jerome Kaino | University | 57 | 50 | | | | |

| AUCKLAND 2017 | Counties Manukau | Northland | Waikato | North Harbour | Taranaki | Southland | Otago | Bay of Plenty | Tasman | Canterbury | TOTALS |
|---|---|---|---|---|---|---|---|---|---|---|---|
| J.V. Trainor | 15 | 15 | 15 | – | 15 | 15 | 15 | s | – | s | 8 |
| M.H. Nanai | – | – | – | – | – | 11 | 11 | 15 | 15 | 15 | 5 |
| V. Aso | 14 | 14 | 14 | 14 | 14 | 14 | 14 | 13 | 13 | 14 | 10 |
| C.D. Clarke | 11 | 11 | – | 11 | – | – | – | – | – | – | 3 |
| T. Manu | – | – | 11 | – | s | – | – | 14 | 14 | – | 4 |
| P.G. Collier | – | – | s | 15 | 11 | – | – | – | – | – | 3 |
| J. Ravouvou | – | – | – | – | – | – | – | 11 | 11 | 11 | 3 |
| M.F. Fekitoa | 13 | 13 | – | 13 | 13 | s | 13 | – | – | – | 6 |
| G. Moala | 12 | 12 | 13 | 12 | – | 13 | 12 | – | s | 13 | 8 |
| T. Faiane | s | s | 12 | s | 12 | 12 | s | 12 | 12 | 12 | 10 |
| D.R. Bowden | 10 | 10 | – | 10 | – | – | – | – | – | – | 3 |
| O. Mausia | – | s | s | s | – | – | – | – | – | – | 3 |
| W.S. Faiane | – | – | 10 | – | – | – | – | – | – | – | 1 |
| T.D. Elkington-MacDonald | – | – | – | – | 10 | 10 | 10 | 10 | 10 | – | 5 |
| L. Fosita | – | – | – | – | s | s | s | – | – | – | 3 |
| H.R.J. Plummer | – | – | – | – | – | – | – | s | s | 10 | 3 |
| J.D. Hickey | 9 | 9 | s | 9 | 9 | 9 | 9 | 9 | 9 | 9 | 10 |
| L.M. Milo-Harris | s | – | 9 | s | s | s | s | – | – | – | 6 |
| L.P.C. Fukofuka | – | s | – | – | – | – | – | – | – | – | 1 |
| N.Costa | – | – | – | – | – | – | – | s | s | s | 3 |
| A.L. Ioane | 8 | – | 8 | – | – | – | 6 | 8 | 8 | 8 | 6 |
| I. Kaino | – | – | – | – | 8 | 8 | 8 | – | – | – | 3 |
| B.T. Gibson | 7 | 8 | – | 8 | 7 | 7 | 7 | 7 | 7 | 7 | 9 |
| S.C. Dominkovich-Murray | – | 7 | – | – | s | s | s | s | s | – | 6 |
| S.A. Kaifa | – | s | 7 | – | – | – | – | – | – | – | 2 |
| S. Havili-Talitui | – | – | s | 7 | – | – | – | – | – | – | 2 |
| S.V. Slade | 6 | 6 | 6 | 6 | – | – | – | – | 4 | 4 | 6 |
| J.T.T.T. Fa'anana-Shultz | s | – | – | – | – | – | – | – | – | – | 1 |
| T.J.A. Seu | – | – | – | s | 6 | 6 | – | 6 | 6 | 6 | 6 |
| D.R. Papali'i | – | – | – | – | – | s | – | s | s | s | 4 |
| S.N. Scrafton | 5 | 5 | – | – | – | – | – | – | – | – | 2 |
| B.P. Nee-Nee | s | s | 5 | 5 | 5 | 5 | 5 | 5 | 5 | 5 | 10 |
| P.T. Tuipulotu (capt) | 4 | 4 | 4 | 4 | 4 | 4 | 4 | – | – | – | 7 |
| S.F.M.H Ulufonua | – | – | s | s | – | – | – | – | – | – | 2 |
| L.J. Dunshea | – | – | – | – | s | – | – | – | – | – | 1 |
| J.H. Lane | – | – | – | – | – | – | s | 4 | – | – | 2 |
| M.T. Renata | 3 | 3 | 3 | 3 | 3 | 3 | 3 | 3 | 3 | 3 | 10 |
| D.F. Fa'amoana | s | s | – | – | – | – | – | s | s | s | 5 |
| M.L. Fepuleai | – | – | – | – | s | – | – | – | – | – | 1 |
| S.M.J. Prattley | 1 | 1 | 1 | 1 | – | 1 | 1 | 1 | 1 | 1 | 9 |
| I. Tu'ungafasi | s | – | s | s | 1 | s | s | – | s | – | 7 |
| E.R. Tamura-Paki | – | s | s | s | s | s | s | – | – | – | 7 |
| G.W. Pleasants-Tate | 2 | 2 | – | 2 | 2 | 2 | 2 | s | s | 2 | 9 |
| K.A.N. Eklund | s | s | 2 | s | s | s | s | 2 | 2 | s | 10 |
| J.P. Sauni | – | – | s | – | – | – | – | – | – | – | 1 |

T. Faiane captained in the final three matches.

## INDIVIDUAL SCORING

| | Tries | Con | PG | DG | Points | | Tries | Con | PG | DG | Points |
|---|---|---|---|---|---|---|---|---|---|---|---|
| Hickey | 1 | 14 | 14 | – | 75 | Kaino | 1 | – | – | – | 5 |
| Aso | 7 | – | – | – | 35 | Pleasants-Tate | 1 | – | – | – | 5 |
| Moala | 3 | – | – | – | 15 | Nanai | 1 | – | – | – | 5 |
| Seu | 3 | – | – | – | 15 | Nee-Nee | 1 | – | – | – | 5 |
| Ravouvou | 3 | – | – | – | 15 | TJ Faiane | 1 | – | – | – | 5 |
| Trainor | – | 3 | 2 | – | 12 | Plummer | – | 2 | – | – | 4 |
| Renata | 2 | – | – | – | 10 | Elkington-MacDonald | – | 1 | – | – | 2 |
| Penalty Try | 1 | – | – | – | 7 | | | | | | |
| Fekitoa | 1 | – | – | – | 5 | **Totals** | **29** | **20** | **16** | **0** | **235** |
| Eklund | 1 | – | – | – | 5 | | | | | | |
| Tuipulotu | 1 | – | – | – | 5 | *Opposition scored* | *38* | *26* | *18* | *0* | *298* |
| Havili-Talitui | 1 | – | – | – | 5 | | | | | | |

Higher honours went to:

| | |
|---|---|
| ***New Zealand:*** | C. Faumuina, M. Fekitoa, A. Ioane, R. Ioane, J. Kaino, P. Tuipulotu, O. Tu'ungafasi |
| ***New Zealand Maori:*** | A. Ioane, R. Ioane, M. Renata |
| ***New Zealand Under 20:*** | A. Choat, C. Clarke, E. Lindenmuth, D. Papali'i, J. Pierce, J. Sauni, S. Slade |
| ***New Zealand Sevens:*** | R. Khan, J. Ravouvou |

## AUCKLAND TEAM RECORD, 2017

**Played 10  Won 3  Lost 7  Points for 235  Points against 298**

| Date | Opponent | Location | Score | Tries | Con | PG | DG | Referee |
|---|---|---|---|---|---|---|---|---|
| August 19 | Counties Manukau (P) | Pukekohe | 14–16 | Hickey, Fekitoa | Hickey (2) | | | C.J. Sione |
| August 26 | Northland (P/C) | Auckland | 10–8 | Eklund | Hickey | Hickey | | S. Kubo *Japan* |
| August 30 | Waikato (P) | Auckland | 27–35 | Tuipulotu, Renata, Havili-Talitui | Trainor (3) | Trainor (2) | | R.P. Kelly |
| September 3 | North Harbour (P) | Albany | 10–57 | Moala | Hickey | Hickey | | G.W. Jackson |
| September 9 | Taranaki (P) | Auckland | 38–49 | Aso (3), Renata, Seu | Hickey, Elkington-MacDonald | Hickey (3) | | M.I. Fraser |
| September 15 | Southland (P/C) | Invercargill | 27–17 | Kaino, Aso, Pleasants-Tate, Seu | Hickey (2) | Hickey | | J.D. Murro |
| September 21 | Otago (P/C) | Dunedin | 26–34 | Moala (2), Aso, Penalty Try | Hickey (2) | Hickey | | G.W. Jackson |
| September 30 | Bay of Plenty (P/C) | Auckland | 38–19 | Ravouvou (2), Aso, Nanai | Hickey (3) | Hickey (4) | | C.J. Stone |
| October 8 | Tasman (P) | Nelson | 18–31 | Seu, Nee Nee | Plummer | Hickey (2) | | B.E. Pickerill |
| October 13 | Canterbury (P) | Auckland | 27–32 | Aso, Ravouvou, T. Faiane | Hickey (2), Plummer | Hickey (2) | | B.E. Pickerill |

# BAY OF PLENTY

**2017 Status:** Mitre 10 Cup Championship
**Founded 1911.** Affiliated 1911
**President:** P.J. (Phil) Barnett
**Chairman:** P.L. (Paul) Owen
**Chief executive officer:** M.W. (Mike) Rogers
**Coach:** C.R. (Clayton) McMillan
**Assistant coaches:** R.P. (Rodney) Gibbs, D.W. (David) Hill
**Main ground:** Bay Park Stadium, Mt Maunganui
**Capacity:** 18,000
**Colours:** Blue and gold.

## RECORDS

| | | |
|---|---|---|
| Most appearances | 161 | *Greg Rowlands, 1969–82* |
| Most points | 1008 | *Greg Rowlands, 1969–82* |
| Most tries | 62 | *Graeme Moore, 1967–80* |
| Most points in a season | 245 | *Andrew Miller, 1996* |
| Most tries in a season | 14 | *Damon Kaui, 1995* |
| Most conversions in a season | 53 | *Andrew Miller, 1996* |
| Most penalty goals in a season | 48 | *Eion Crossan, 1991* |
| Most dropped goals in a season | 13 | *Ron Preston, 1985* |
| Most points in a match | 36 | *Adrian Cashmore v Thames Valley, 1993* |
| Most tries in a match | 5 | *Ian Backhouse v North Otago, 1965* |
| | | *Damon Kaui v Thames Valley, 1995* |
| Most conversions in a match | 9 | *Eion Crossan v Poverty Bay, 1991* |
| Most penalty goals in a match | 6 | *Ron Preston v Poverty Bay, 1982* |
| | | *Eion Crossan v North Harbour, 1990* |
| | | *Eion Crossan v Fiji President's XV, 1991* |
| | | *Eion Crossan v Western Samoa, 1991* |
| | | *Erin Cossey v Hawke's Bay, 1994* |
| | | *Andrew Miller v Counties, 1995* |
| | | *Andrew Miller v King Country, 1996* |
| | | *Glen Jackson v Northland, 2001* |
| | | *Glen Jackson v Otago, 2004* |
| | | *Mike Delany v Waikato, 2009* |
| Highest team score | 88 | *v East Coast, 1972* |
| Record victory (points ahead) | 79 | *88–9 v East Coast, 1972* |
| | | *82–3 v Thames Valley, 1995* |
| Highest score conceded | 93 | *v New Zealand XV, 1993* |
| Record defeat (points behind) | 88 | *5–93 v New Zealand XV, 1993* |

Bay of Plenty produced a strong finish in 2017 to record their best season since 2004 and end ninth in the provincial rankings.

After an up and down season of three wins and a draw in the first eight games, Bay of Plenty produced a superb effort against Otago, winning in Dunedin for the first time since 1980, followed by a hard-earned victory against premiership side Waikato to finish second in the Championship round robin. The semi-final, again against Otago, was a high-scoring victory, which meant a visit to rampant Wellington for the final. Against their more fancied opponents, the Bay fought point for point to finish 40 points all at fulltime, sending the contest into extra time before ultimately losing after having contributed magnificently to a 100-minute final.

At fullback Chase Tiatia was superb in the final four games when his experience shone through. Isaac Te Aute was not in the form of the previous year with injuries finally ending his year. Of the wings, Joe Webber finally made his Bay debut after being sidelined with injury in 2016. He showed some clever footwork and speed and scored some scintillating tries, none more so than in the final. Monty Ioane was in great form in broken play with plenty of space where the opposition found him hard to contain. Elijah Nicholas was an able back-up when his chances arose.

Lalakai Foketi at centre was again a leading figure in the midfield with sound defence and eight tries while Liam Steel had his season cut short when he broke his jaw against Taranaki. Second-five Terrence Hepetema was a steady influence with a knack of also finding the tryline.

At first-five, the remarkable Mike Delany made a return after last appearing in 2010. His experience set the backline in good stead and also his goal-kicking was accurate, which was a huge plus from the previous year. Kelly Haimona was only used twice when Delany was temporarily injured. Of the halfbacks, Richard Judd was the preferred starter and gave some solid displays, getting good ball out well and was very sound in defence. Luke Campbell was a smooth operator and played a great game in the final after Judd had been invalided out with injury.

Number eight Jesse Parete was a strong customer with the ball in hand and very handy at lineout time while Tyler Ardron performed well when he got his opportunities. Of the flankers, Hugh Blake featured in every game, giving good service, and Mitchell Karpik finally debuted, after missing 2016 through injury, making a big difference, particularly in the last three games. Henry Stowers was a robust and sound loose forward with his general all-round play.

Lock Tom Franklin was outstanding, figuring in everything that was going. A giant in the lineout, he was tremendous running with ball in hand and his tackle count was at the top end of the scale. When injuries hit the loose forwards, he was moved to the flank, which proved to be a masterstroke by the coach. He was the BOPRU player of the year for 2017.

Captain Keepa Mewett led from the front, and was rewarded with selection in the NZ Maori team. The old workhorse Culum Retallick returned from the Melbourne Rebels and again contributed well, although injury cut short his season. Troy Callander got more game time this year, which should set him in good stead for next season.

The union was well served at prop. Siegfried Fisi'ihoi played the first four games until taking up a playing contract in France. Aidan Ross and Jeff Thwaites started most games putting in good all-round performances and set a good platform at scrum time. The Lay brothers, Jordan and James, appeared mostly off the bench, being a solid duo who gave plenty in their time on the field. Both gained selection in the Samoa test team at the end of the season. Injury curtailed Solomona Sakalia's season.

Liam Polwart and James O'Reilly were the most used hookers, neither disappointing and gave good solid performances. Nathan Harris made three appearances in his comeback from injury to give him game time before rejoining the All Blacks.

Of the 2016 squad Joe Tupe (Japan) Shahn Eru, Dan Hollinshead (both France) and Te Rangi Fraser (Western Australia) had departed overseas while Regan Ware and Teddy Stanaway linked with the NZ Sevens team. New players in for 2017 were Mathew Garland (Hawke's Bay), Liam Steel and James Lay (both Auckland), Tom Franklin (Otago), Mike Delany (returned from England) and Canadian international Tyler Ardron.

Higher honours went to:
*New Zealand:* S. Cane, N. Harris
*New Zealand Maori:* T. Franklin, K. Mewett, L. Polwart
*New Zealand Sevens:* S. Curry, B. Simonsson, T. Stanaway, R. Ware, J. Webber

## BAY OF PLENTY REPRESENTATIVES 2017

| | Club | Games for Union | Points for Union | | Club | Games for Union | Points for Union |
|---|---|---|---|---|---|---|---|
| Tyler Ardron | Papamoa | 7 | 5 | Jordan Lay | Whakarewarewa | 9 | 0 |
| Matt Axtens | Mt Maunganui | 7 | 0 | Keepa Mewett | Tauranga Sports | 35 | 5 |
| Hugh Blake | Te Puke Sports | 20 | 15 | Elijah Nicholas | Te Puna | 17 | 10 |
| Troy Callendar | Greerton Marist | 22 | 0 | James O'Reilly | Hutt OB Marist [1] | 17 | 5 |
| Luke Campbell | Te Puke Sports | 16 | 31 | Jesse Parete | Rangataua | 20 | 50 |
| Mike Delany | Mt Maunganui | 72 | 583 | Liam Polwart | Greerton Marist | 14 | 0 |
| Siegfried Fisi'ihoi | Rotoiti | 32 | 20 | Culum Retallick | Tauranga Sports | 110 | 45 |
| Lalakai Foketi | Rangataua | 30 | 75 | Aidan Ross | Te Puke Sports | 24 | 10 |
| Tom Franklin | Opotiki | 11 | 10 | Solomona Sakalia | Mt Maunganui | 33 | 10 |
| Mathew Garland | Whakarewarewa | 3 | 0 | Sebastian Siataga | Mt Maunganui | 13 | 0 |
| Kelly Haimona | Whakarewarewa | 27 | 55 | Liam Steel | Mt Maunganui | 4 | 0 |
| Nathan Harris | Te Puke Sports | 29 | 5 | Henry Stowers | Arataki | 17 | 20 |
| Terrence Hepetama | Te Puna | 19 | 50 | Isaac Te Aute | Mt Maunganui | 17 | 5 |
| Monty Ioane | Greerton Marist | 22 | 30 | Jeff Thwaites | Te Puna | 21 | 0 |
| Richard Judd | Mt Maunganui | 10 | 5 | Chase Tiatia | Rangataua | 26 | 30 |
| Mitchell Karpik | Rangataua | 6 | 5 | Te Aihe Toma | Te Puna | 36 | 30 |
| Aileone "AJ" Lafaele-Mua | Tauranga Sports | 1 | 0 | Baden Wardlaw | Rotoiti | 1 | 0 |
| James Lay | Whakarewarewa | 10 | 0 | Joe Webber | Te Puke Sports | 11 | 40 |

[1] Wellington RU

## INDIVIDUAL SCORING

| | Tries | Con | PG | DG | Points | | Tries | Con | PG | DG | Points |
|---|---|---|---|---|---|---|---|---|---|---|---|
| Delany | – | 29 | 12 | – | 94 | Haimona | – | 1 | 2 | – | 8 |
| Foketi | 8 | – | – | – | 40 | Fisi'ihoi | 1 | – | – | – | 5 |
| Webber | 8 | – | – | – | 40 | Nicholas | 1 | – | – | – | 5 |
| Hepetama | 7 | – | – | – | 35 | Judd | 1 | – | – | – | 5 |
| Parete | 6 | – | – | – | 30 | Sakalia | 1 | – | – | – | 5 |
| Campbell | 3 | 5 | – | – | 25 | Ardron | 1 | – | – | – | 5 |
| Penalty Try | 3 | – | – | – | 21 | Karpik | 1 | – | – | – | 5 |
| Ioane | 3 | – | – | – | 15 | | | | | | |
| Franklin | 2 | – | – | – | 10 | **Totals** | **52** | **35** | **14** | **0** | **378** |
| Blake | 2 | – | – | – | 10 | | | | | | |
| Stowers | 2 | – | – | – | 10 | Opposition scored | 47 | 31 | 15 | 0 | 342 |
| Tiatia | 2 | – | – | – | 10 | | | | | | |

| BAY OF PLENTY 2017 | Northland | Hawke's Bay | Wellington | Manawatu | Taranaki | Southland | Counties Manukau | Auckland | Otago | Waikato | Otago | Wellington | TOTALS |
|---|---|---|---|---|---|---|---|---|---|---|---|---|---|
| C.J. Tiatia | 15 | 15 | 15 | 15 | 11 | 15 | 15 | 15 | 15 | 15 | 15 | 15 | 12 |
| I.N. Te Aute | s | – | – | s | 15 | s | s | s | – | – | – | – | 6 |
| M.W. Ioane | 14 | 14 | 14 | 14 | 14 | 14 | – | 14 | 14 | 14 | 14 | 14 | 11 |
| T.J. Webber | 11 | 11 | 11 | 11 | – | 11 | 11 | 11 | 11 | 11 | 11 | 11 | 11 |
| E.W. Nicholas | s | s | – | – | s | s | 14 | s | s | s | s | s | 10 |
| L.L.A. Foketi | 13 | 13 | 13 | 13 | 12 | 13 | 13 | 13 | 13 | 13 | 13 | 13 | 12 |
| T.R.T. Hepetama | 12 | 12 | 12 | 12 | s | 12 | 12 | 12 | 12 | 12 | 12 | 12 | 12 |
| L.T. Steel | – | s | s | s | 13 | – | – | – | – | – | – | – | 4 |
| M.D. Garland | – | – | – | – | – | – | s | – | – | – | s | s | 3 |
| M.P. Delany | 10 | 10 | 10 | – | s | 10 | 10 | 10 | 10 | 10 | 10 | 10 | 11 |
| K.J. Haimona | – | – | – | 10 | 10 | – | – | – | – | – | – | – | 2 |
| R.P. Judd | 9 | 9 | 9 | 9 | – | 9 | 9 | 9 | 9 | 9 | 9 | – | 10 |
| L.A. Campbell | s | s | s | s | 9 | s | s | s | s | s | s | 9 | 12 |
| T.A.T.M.L.A. Toma | – | – | – | – | – | – | – | – | – | – | – | s | 1 |
| T.J. Ardron | 8 | 8 | – | 8 | 8 | – | – | – | – | s | s | 8 | 7 |
| J.W.Z. Parete | – | s | 8 | – | 6 | 8 | 8 | 8 | 8 | 8 | 8 | s | 10 |
| A. Lafaele-Mua | – | – | – | – | – | – | – | – | s | – | – | – | 1 |
| M.R. Karpik | 7 | 7 | 7 | – | – | – | – | – | – | s | 6 | 6 | 6 |
| H.P. Blake | 6 | 6 | 6 | 7 | s | 7 | 7 | 7 | 7 | 7 | 7 | 7 | 12 |
| H.J. Stowers | s | – | s | s | 7 | s | – | s | – | – | s | – | 7 |
| M.S. Axtens | – | – | – | – | – | – | s | – | s | – | – | – | 2 |
| T.K.H. Mewett (capt) | 5 | 5 | 5 | 5 | – | 5 | 5 | 5 | 4 | 4 | 4 | 4 | 11 |
| T.S.G. Franklin | 4 | 4 | 4 | 6 | s | 6 | 6 | 6 | 6 | 6 | – | 5 | 11 |
| T.H. Callender | s | – | s | 4 | 4 | s | s | 4 | 5 | – | 5 | s | 10 |
| C.J. Retallick | – | s | s | s | 5 | 4 | 4 | – | – | 5 | – | – | 7 |
| B.M. Wardlaw | – | – | – | – | – | – | – | s | – | – | – | – | 1 |
| S. Fisi'ihoi | 3 | 3 | s | s | – | – | – | – | – | – | – | – | 4 |
| J.R. Thwaites | s | – | – | 3 | 3 | 3 | 3 | 3 | 3 | 3 | 3 | 3 | 10 |
| James M. Lay | – | s | 3 | – | s | s | s | s | s | s | s | s | 10 |
| A. Ross | 1 | 1 | – | s | 1 | – | s | 1 | 1 | 1 | 1 | 1 | 10 |
| Jordan A. Lay | s | – | 1 | – | s | s | – | s | s | s | s | s | 9 |
| S.L. Sakalia | – | s | s | 1 | – | 1 | 1 | – | – | – | – | – | 5 |
| J.P. O'Reilly | 2 | 2 | – | s | s | – | s | 2 | – | – | s | s | 8 |
| S.P. Siataga | – | s | – | – | 2 | – | – | s | s | – | – | – | 4 |
| N.P. Harris | – | – | 2 | – | – | s | – | – | – | s | – | – | 3 |
| L.J. Polwart | – | – | s | 2 | – | 2 | 2 | – | 2 | 2 | 2 | 2 | 8 |

C.J. Retallick captained v Taranaki.

## BAY OF PLENTY TEAM RECORD, 2017

Played 12　Won 6　Drew 1　Lost 5　Points for 378　Points against 342

| Date | Opponent | Location | Score | Tries | Con | PG | DG | Referee |
|---|---|---|---|---|---|---|---|---|
| August 20 | Northland (C) | Whangarei | 23–28 | Franklin, Ioane | Delany (2) | Delany (3) | | B.E.Pickerill |
| August 25 | Hawke's Bay (C) | Rotorua | 46–17 | Webber (2), Parete (2), Fisi'ihoi, Foketi | Delaney (4), Campbell | Delany (2) | | J.J. Doleman |
| August 31 | Wellington (C) | Rotorua | 10–31 | Hepetama | Delany | Delany | | M.C.J. Winter |
| September 8 | Manawatu (C) | Palmerston North | 20–17 | Webber, Penalty Try | Haimona | Haimona (2) | | B.D. O'Keeffe |
| September 15 | Taranaki (P/C) | New Plymouth | 7–29 | Nicholas | Delany | | | J.R. Nutbrown |
| September 20 | Southland (C) | Rotorua | 57–0 | Ioane (2), Foketi (2), Penalty Try, Blake, Judd, Hepetama, Parete | Delany (3), Campbell (2) | | | P.M. Williams |
| September 24 | Counties Manukau (P/C) | Tauranga | 31–31 | Sakalia, Hepetama, Foketi, Parete | Delany (4) | Delany | | M.G. Lash |
| September 30 | Auckland (P/C) | Auckland | 19–38 | Stowers, Franklin, Parete | Campbell (2) | | | C.J. Stone |
| October 7 | Otago (C) | Dunedin | 36–28 | Blake, Hepetama, Webber, Tiatia, Campbell | Delany | Delany (3) | | B.D. O'Keeffe |
| October 14 | Waikato (P/C) | Tauranga | 36–32 | Foketi (2), Tiatia, Hepetama, Campbell | Delany (4) | Delany | | J.J. Doleman |
| October 21 | Otago (C semi-final) | Tauranga | 48–32 | Foketi (2), Webber (2), Stowers, Hepetama, Penalty Try | Delany (4) | Delany | | B.E. Pickerill |
| October 27 | Wellington (C final) | Wellington | 45–59 a.e.t. | Webber (2), Campbell, Ardron, Parete, Hepetama, Karpik | Delany (5) | | | P.M. Williams |

a.e.t. *after extra time*

# BULLER

**2017 Status:** Heartland
**Founded 1894,** Affiliated 1894
**Chairman:** E.J. (Jane) Duncan
**Chief executive officer:** B.A. (Brian) Ahern
**Co-coaches:** C.W. (Craig)Neill and
C.M. (Craig) Scanlon
**Main ground:** Victoria Square, Westport
**Capacity:** 5000
**Colours:** Cardinal and blue

## RECORDS

| | | |
|---|---|---|
| **Highest attendance** | 5000 | *West Coast-Buller v South Africa, 1956* |
| **Most appearances** | 167 | *L.G. Brownlee, 1999-2017* |
| **Most points** | 575 | *D.J. Baird, 1981–91* |
| **Most tries** | 44 | *T.J. Stuart, 1984–99* |
| **Most points in a season** | 147 | *J.J. Lash, 2017* |
| **Most tries in a season** | 11 | *I. Ravudra, 2014* |
| **Most conversions in a season** | 32 | *J.J. Lash, 2016* |
| **Most penalty goals in a season** | 27 | *D.J. Baird, 1985* |
| **Most dropped goals in a season** | 7 | *D.J. Baird, 1984* |
| **Most points in a match** | 25 | *J.J. Lash, v Mid Canterbury, 2017* |
| **Most tries in a match** | 4 | *J. Easton v Wellington Colts, 1935* |
| | | *T.J. Stuart v West Coast, 1992* |
| | | *M. Taylor v East Coast, 2007* |
| | | *I. Ravudra v Wairarapa Bush, 2014* |
| | | *S.T. Sauqaqa v Thames Valley, 2015* |
| **Most conversions in a match** | 7 | *J.J. Lash v Wairarapa Bush, 2014* |
| | | *J.J. Lash v East Coast, 2017* |
| **Most penalty goals in a match** | 6 | *D.J. Baird v East Coast, 1987* |
| | | *C.J. Hart v East Coast, 1999* |
| | | *S.N. Jack, v Wairarapa Bush, 2002* |
| | | *A.P. Stephens v Horowhenua Kapiti, 2010* |
| **Highest team score** | 67 | *v East Coast, 2014* |
| **Record victory (points ahead)** | 61 | *67–6 v East Coast, 2014* |
| **Highest score conceded** | 81 | *v Wanganui, 1994* |
| **Record defeat (points behind)** | 73 | *0–73 v Horowhenua Kapiti, 1999* |

Buller had another good season, once again making the Heartland Championship top four to qualify for the Meads Cup playoffs with an identical round robin record of six wins and two losses as last year. In a dramatic semi-final at Levin, Buller went down 17–18 to Horowhenua Kapiti when conceding a last-minute penalty goal.

The union was able to field an experienced team with the luxury of having 10 players start every match. Last year's local regulars who did not reappear in 2017 were Ciaran Neilsen, Matthew Bonisch (both injured), Simon Abel (overseas), Setefano Sauqaqa (South Canterbury) and Daniel Hytongue (Tasman), although Hytongue did make one appearance on loan. Two players to return were Iliesa Ravudra (Tasman) and Michael Lealava'a (Wellington) after an absence of one and two years respectively.

In the forward pack, number eight David Egelstaff, flanker Blair McIlroy, Samoan international

Jeff Lepa at lock, and prop Anthony Ellis were the leading performers. They were supported by loosehead prop Stephen Crackett who played in every game. Luke Watson showed a lot of improvement at flanker in his second season.

When injuries hit the squad just before the Heartland Championship Phil Beveridge made himself available again, while flanker Luke Brownlee had slowed down a little but was still a tireless worker in adding six more appearances to his record total. Both men have now appeared for the union 19 seasons each, a truly remarkable record.

Andrew Stephens and James Lash were the best halfback/first five-eighth pairing in the Heartland Championship. Stephens was in wonderful form and Lash turned in some brilliant performances, combining well in both attack and defence. Lash set a new season points-scoring record for both Buller and the Heartland Championship competition with 147.

Iliesa Ravudra was an excellent finisher on the wing and topped the try-scoring with six. Anthony Tailua was sound at fullback but not as dangerous as last year. Scott Neighbours and Isaac Hogarth both suffered injury against North Otago to cause a reshuffle in the backline for the remainder of the season.

Higher honours went to:
**New Zealand Heartland:**   A. Ellis, A. Stephens

## BULLER REPRESENTATIVES 2017

| | Club | Games for Union | Points for Union | | Club | Games for Union | Points for Union |
|---|---|---|---|---|---|---|---|
| Phil Beveridge | White Star | 154 | 56 | Sam Marris | White Star | 60 | 30 |
| Robert Bonisch | White Star | 9 | 0 | Blair McIlroy | Darfield [2] | 57 | 26 |
| Luke Brownlee | White Star | 167 | 15 | Jareth McKay | Westport | 13 | 0 |
| Stephen Crackett | Westport | 45 | 0 | Logan Mundy | White Star | 96 | 10 |
| Glen Duncan | Westport | 45 | 0 | Scott Neighbours | Westport | 46 | 36 |
| David Egelstaff | Ngakawau-Karamea | 19 | 11 | Kahu Parata | Westport | 6 | 5 |
| Anthony Ellis | Ngakawau-Karamea | 23 | 10 | Alex Paterson | White Star | 1 | 0 |
| Joshua Hedley | Westport | 6 | 0 | Iliesa Ravudra | White Star | 35 | 115 |
| Isaac Hogarth | White Star | 7 | 5 | Petaia Saukuru | Westport | 17 | 0 |
| Daniel Hytongue | Waimea OB [1] | 11 | 18 | Andrew Stephens | Ngakawau-Karamea | 94 | 261 |
| Corey Jenkins | Westport | 2 | 0 | Anthony Tailua | White Star | 19 | 58 |
| James Lash | Waimea OB [1] | 30 | 413 | Erenimo Tau | Waimea OB [1] | 1 | 5 |
| Michael Lealava'a | Ngakawau-Karamea | 27 | 37 | Joshua Tuidriva | White Star | 19 | 28 |
| Jeff Lepa | Waimea OB [1] | 9 | 5 | Luke Watson | White Star | 15 | 0 |

[1] *Tasman RU*      [2] *Canterbury RU*

In the 2015 and 2016 seasons, players recorded as playing for Ngakawau club should be recorded as playing for Ngakawau-Karamea club.

## INDIVIDUAL SCORING

| | Tries | Con | PG | DG | Points | | Tries | Con | PG | DG | Points |
|---|---|---|---|---|---|---|---|---|---|---|---|
| Lash | 6 | 27 | 19 | 2 | 147 | Lepa | 1 | – | – | – | 5 |
| Ravudra | 6 | – | – | – | 30 | Tau | 1 | – | – | – | 5 |
| Stephens | 3 | – | – | – | 15 | Parata | 1 | – | – | – | 5 |
| Tuidriva | 2 | – | – | – | 10 | Egelstaff | 1 | – | – | – | 5 |
| Ellis | 2 | – | – | – | 10 | Hogarth | 1 | – | – | – | 5 |
| Tailua | 2 | – | – | – | 10 | | | | | | |
| Lealava'a | 2 | – | – | – | 10 | **Totals** | **30** | **27** | **19** | **2** | **267** |
| McIlroy | 1 | – | – | – | 5 | | | | | | |
| Neighbours | 1 | – | – | – | 5 | Opposition scored | 29 | 20 | 12 | 0 | 221 |

| **BULLER 2017** | South Canterbury | West Coast | North Otago | Thames Valley | Wairarapa Bush | East Coast | Mid Canterbury | Horowhenua Kapiti | Horowhenua Kapiti | TOTALS |
|---|---|---|---|---|---|---|---|---|---|---|
| A. Tailua | 15 | 15 | 15 | 15 | 15 | 15 | 15 | 15 | 15 | 9 |
| S.W. Neighbours | 14 | 14 | 14 | – | – | – | – | – | – | 3 |
| I. Ravudra | 11 | 11 | 13 | 13 | 11 | 11 | 11 | 11 | 11 | 9 |
| J.T. Tuidriva | 13 | 13 | 11 | 11 | 14 | 14 | 14 | 14 | 14 | 9 |
| S.A. Marris | – | – | – | s | s | s | – | – | – | 3 |
| E. Tau | – | – | – | – | 13 | – | – | – | – | 1 |
| I.C. Hogarth | 12 | – | 12 | – | – | – | – | – | s | 3 |
| M.S. Lealava'a | s | 12 | – | 12 | 12 | 13 | 13 | 13 | 13 | 8 |
| A.M.J. Paterson | – | – | – | – | – | s | – | – | – | 1 |
| P.T. Saukuru | s | – | s | 14 | s | 12 | 12 | 12 | 12 | 8 |
| J.J. Lash | 10 | 10 | 10 | 10 | 10 | 10 | 10 | 10 | 10 | 9 |
| A.P. Stephens (capt) | 9 | 9 | 9 | 9 | 9 | 9 | 9 | 9 | 9 | 9 |
| C.W. Jenkins | – | – | – | s | – | s | – | – | – | 2 |
| D.L. Egelstaff | 8 | 8 | 8 | 8 | 8 | 8 | 8 | 8 | 8 | 9 |
| B.S. McIlroy | 7 | 7 | 6 | – | – | 6 | 7 | 6 | 6 | 7 |
| L.G. Brownlee | – | s | 7 | – | 7 | 7 | – | 7 | 7 | 6 |
| D.W.L. Hytongue | – | – | – | 7 | – | – | – | – | – | 1 |
| L.W. Watson | 6 | 6 | – | 6 | 6 | – | 6 | – | s | 6 |
| K.G. Parata | – | – | – | s | – | s | s | s | s | 5 |
| P.J. Lepa | 5 | 5 | 5 | 5 | 5 | 5 | 5 | 5 | 5 | 9 |
| R. Bonisch | 4 | 4 | 4 | 4 | 4 | 4 | 4 | 4 | 4 | 9 |
| J.M. Hedley | s | – | s | s | s | s | – | s | – | 6 |
| A.W. Ellis | 3 | 3 | 3 | 3 | 3 | 3 | 3 | 2 | 2 | 9 |
| S.R. Crackett | 1 | 1 | 1 | 1 | 1 | 1 | 1 | 1 | 1 | 9 |
| P.J. Beveridge | s | s | s | s | s | – | – | 3 | 3 | 7 |
| L.M. Mundy | – | – | – | – | – | s | s | s | s | 4 |
| J.J.J.I. McKay | 2 | 2 | 2 | 2 | 2 | – | s | – | – | 6 |
| G.A. Duncan | s | s | s | s | s | 2 | 2 | s | s | 9 |

## BULLER TEAM RECORD, 2017

Played 9   Won 6   Lost 3   Points for 267   Points against 221

| Date | Opponent | Location | Score | Tries | Con | PG | DG | Referee |
|---|---|---|---|---|---|---|---|---|
| August 26 | South Canterbury (H) | Westport | 27–24 | McIlroy, Neighbours, Lash | Lash (3) | Lash (2) |  | V.F. Ringrose |
| September 2 | West Coast (H) | Greymouth | 34–19 | Lepa, Tuidriva, Stephens | Lash (2) | Lash (4) | Lash | H.G. Reed |
| September 9 | North Otago (H) | Westport | 33–31 | Ravudra, Ellis, Lash– | Lash (3) | Lash (3) | Lash | T.M.T. Cottrell |
| September 16 | Thames Valley (H) | Paeroa | 7–26 | Tailua | Lash |  |  | R.J.M. Gordon |
| September 23 | Wairarapa Bush (H) | Westport | 29–24 | Lash (2), Tuidriva, Tau | Lash (3) | Lash |  | N.E.R. Hogan |
| September 30 | East Coast (H) | Ruatoria | 54–17 | Lealava'a (2), Stephens (2), Ravudra (2), Lash, Parata | Lash (7) |  |  | B.J. Jurlina |
| October 7 | Mid Canterbury (H) | Ashburton | 40–32 | Ravudra (2), Lash, Egelstaff | Lash (4) | Lash (4) |  | B.J. Jurlina |
| October 14 | Horowhenua Kapiti (H) | Westport | 26–30 | Ravudra, Ellis | Lash (2) | Lash (4) |  | J.D. Munro |
| October 21 | Horowhenua Kapiti (MC semi-final) | Levin | 17–18 | Hogarth, Tailua | Lash (2) | Lash |  | M.C.J. Winter |

# CANTERBURY

**2017 Status:** Mitre 10 Cup Premiership
**Founded 1879.** Affiliated 1894
**President:** V.E.T. (Vance) Stewart
**Chairman:** T.J. (Trevor) McIntyre (to August)
P.A. (Peter) Winchester (interim)
**Chief executive officer:** Nathan Godfrey (from January)
**Coach:** G.N. (Glenn) Delaney
**Assistant coaches:** J.S. (Joe) Maddock,
N.K. (Nathan) Mauger
**Main ground:** AMI Stadium, Addington
**Capacity:** 20,000
**Colours:** Red and black

## RECORDS

| | | |
|---|---|---|
| Most appearances | 222 | *Fergi McCormick, 1958–75* |
| Most points | 1625 | *Robbie Deans, 1979–90* |
| Most tries | 94 | *Paula Bale, 1989–96* |
| Most points in a season | 279 | *Robbie Deans, 1989* |
| Most tries in a season | 24 | *Paula Bale, 1989* |
| Most conversions in a season | 52 | *Greg Coffey, 1991* |
| | | *Ben Blair, 2001* |
| Most penalty goals in a season | 50 | *Robbie Deans, 1989* |
| Most dropped goals in a season | 10 | *Andrew Mehrtens, 1994* |
| Most points in a match | 44 | *Jon Preston v West Coast, 1992* |
| Most tries in a match | 7 | *Bruce McPhail v Combined Services, 1959* |
| Most conversions in a match | 20 | *Jon Preston v West Coast, 1992* |
| Most penalty goals in a match | 7 | *Robbie Deans v Counties, 1984* |
| | | *Andrew Mehrtens v Fiji, 2003* |
| | | *Cameron McIntyre v Wellington, 2003* |
| Highest team score | 128 | *v West Coast, 1992* |
| Record victory (points ahead) | 128 | *128–0 v West Coast, 1992* |
| Highest score conceded | 60 | *v Wellington, 2017* |
| Record defeat (points behind) | 46 | *14–60 v Wellington, 2017* |

Canterbury were once again national champions with their third consecutive title — and ninth in the last ten years — to continue their phenomenal dominance of the provincial scene. Their performances at the beginning of the season indicated the team was firmly on course for retention of both the National Championship and Ranfurly Shield with resounding victories in all opening seven games, apart from the Otago match where they had to come from behind to win.

Then came the match against Wellington where Canterbury received the worst defeat in their history in what was the shock scoreline of the season. Three games later Taranaki arrived at Christchurch and won the Ranfurly Shield in an enthralling match, these two matches being Canterbury's only losses of the season. In both the semi-final and final Canterbury overcame early 0–10 deficits to defeat a resilient North Harbour then dominate Tasman in the second half to take the title.

Regulars missing from last year were Jordie and Scott Barrett (both to Taranaki), Johnny McNicholl (to Welsh club Scarlets), Jack Goodhue (Northland), Nathan Earle (returned to English club Saracens), David McDuling (returned to Australia) and Ben Volavola (North Harbour).

With one of the best forward packs in the country, the brilliant backs were given plenty of possession, and all the backline featured prominently on the try-scoring table. The outstanding player in the backline was first five-eighth Richie Mo'unga. He was the top points-scorer in the Mitre 10 Cup, showing composure, good decision making, good goal-kicking, and an eye for the gap, producing another sublime display in the final as he had done in last year's final. He deservedly earned an All Blacks call-up. Newcomer Brett Cameron got a lot of game time as Mo'unga's understudy, having a particularly good game against Hawke's Bay. They were both well served by halfback Mitchell Drummond, who has one of the best passes going and scored four tries against Counties Manukau. His All Black selection for the end-of-year tour was well earned.

Tim Bateman had returned from Japan last year but played no rugby except for the NZ Maori end-of-year tour. This year, available for everything, he represented the red and blacks for the first time since 2009 and had a successful season at centre, scoring nine tries. At second five-eighth Rob Thompson formed a very good partnership with Bateman on both attack and defence.

After impressing on the wing last year, George Bridge played most ably at his preferred fullback position, being very quick to counter-attack and scored seven tries. Two members of the victorious NZ Under 20 team debuted on the wings, the exciting pairing of Braydon Ennor and Josh McKay scored 10 and seven tries respectively and appear to have bright futures.

The experienced Canterbury pack had great strength in the loose forward department where captain Luke Whitelock, Jed Brown, Billy Harmon, Reed Prinsep, Tom Sanders and Matt Todd all did sterling work. Injury followed by a recall into the All Blacks limited Matt Todd to just one game, while Jed Brown's season ended with injury against Waikato.

In the tight five the locking partnership of Mitchell Dunshea and Dominic Bird played significant roles and Hamish Dalzell was an efficient deputy. Alex Hodgman and Siate Tokolahi, together with Ben Funnell, were a formidable front row, while Oli Jager was a good backup at tighthead. Daniel Lienert-Brown's season ended with injury in the opening national championship match.

Higher honours went to:

*New Zealand*:          D. Bird, W. Crockett, R. Crotty, M. Drummond, O. Franks, J. Moody, R. Mo'unga, L. Romano, C. Taylor, M. Todd, L. Whitelock, S. Whitelock

*New Zealand Maori:*    T. Bateman, R. Thompson

*New Zealand Under 20:*    H. Allen, T. Christie, E. Enari, B. Ennor, J. McKay

*New Zealand Sevens:*    S. Dickson, J. Houston

## CANTERBURY REPRESENTATIVES 2017

| | Club | Games for Union | Points for Union | | Club | Games for Union | Points for Union |
|---|---|---|---|---|---|---|---|
| Steve Alfeld | Christchurch | 12 | 5 | Daniel Lienert-Brown | Chch HSOB | 21 | 10 |
| Tim Bateman | Christchurch | 49 | 115 | Mark Maitland | Waihora | 2 | 5 |
| Dominic Bird | Lincoln University | 53 | 25 | Caleb Makene | Lincoln University | 4 | 10 |
| George Bridge | Chch HSOB | 18 | 60 | Joshua Manning | Marist Albion | 12 | 0 |
| Jed Brown | Burnside | 37 | 10 | Josh McKay | Lincoln University | 12 | 41 |
| Brett Cameron | Lincoln University | 11 | 80 | Richie Mo'unga | Linwood | 49 | 336 |
| Tom Christie | Christchurch | 1 | 0 | Ben Morris | Lincoln University | 1 | 0 |
| Hamish Dalzell | Lincoln University | 11 | 5 | Dylan Nel | Sumner | 4 | 5 |
| Mitchell Drummond | Chch HSOB | 37 | 47 | Amanaki Nicole | Sydenham | 1 | 0 |
| Mitchell Dunshea | Lincoln University | 23 | 15 | Jonathan Osborne | Lincoln University | 2 | 0 |
| Ereatara Enari | Lincoln University | 17 | 0 | Reed Prinsep | Chch HSOB | 35 | 10 |
| Braydon Ennor | Canterbury University | 10 | 50 | Ngane Punivai | Lincoln University | 1 | 0 |
| Kaveinga Finau | Christchurch | 14 | 10 | Tom Sanders | Lincoln University | 35 | 40 |
| Ben Funnell | Hurunui | 77 | 65 | Jack Straker | Sydenham | 3 | 0 |
| Chris Gawler | Lincoln University | 14 | 0 | Jack Stratton | Lincoln University | 24 | 35 |
| Nigel Gibb | Canterbury University | 1 | 5 | Marshall Suckling | Sumner | 21 | 55 |
| Sam Godwin | Canterbury University | 1 | 0 | Robert Thompson | Linwood | 49 | 120 |
| Michael Green | Sydenham | 4 | 0 | Matt Todd | Christchurch | 72 | 80 |
| Billy Harmon | New Brighton | 20 | 15 | Siate Tokolahi | Sydenham | 43 | 0 |
| Finn Hart-Strawbridge | Lincoln University | 1 | 4 | Nathan Vella | New Brighton | 22 | 30 |
| Joel Hintz | Lincoln University | 2 | 0 | Poasa Waqanibau | Sumner | 8 | 15 |
| Alex Hodgman | Linwood | 45 | 5 | Nicholas Werahiko | Lincoln University | 6 | 10 |
| Oliver Jager | New Brighton | 20 | 0 | Luke Whitelock | Canterbury University | 63 | 45 |
| Alifeleti Kaitu'u | New Brighton | 1 | 0 | | | | |

## INDIVIDUAL SCORING

| | Tries | Con | PG | DG | Points | | Tries | Con | PG | DG | Points |
|---|---|---|---|---|---|---|---|---|---|---|---|
| Mo'unga | 5 | 42 | 17 | – | 160 | Vella | 2 | – | – | – | 10 |
| Cameron | 2 | 26 | 6 | – | 80 | Maitland | 1 | – | – | – | 5 |
| Ennor | 10 | – | – | – | 50 | Nel | 1 | – | – | – | 5 |
| Bateman | 9 | – | – | – | 45 | Alfeld | 1 | – | – | – | 5 |
| McKay | 7 | 3 | – | – | 41 | Gibb | 1 | – | – | – | 5 |
| Bridge | 7 | – | – | – | 35 | Dalzell | 1 | – | – | – | 5 |
| Drummond | 7 | – | – | – | 35 | Bird | 1 | – | – | – | 5 |
| Suckling | 5 | – | – | – | 25 | Whitelock | 1 | – | – | – | 5 |
| Thompson | 5 | – | – | – | 25 | Funnell | 1 | – | – | – | 5 |
| Stratton | 4 | – | – | – | 20 | Finau | 1 | – | – | – | 5 |
| Dunshea | 3 | – | – | – | 15 | Harmon | 1 | – | – | – | 5 |
| Waqanibau | 3 | – | – | – | 15 | Finn-Strawbridge | – | 2 | – | – | 4 |
| Sanders | 3 | – | – | – | 15 | | | | | | |
| Werahiko | 2 | – | – | – | 10 | **Totals** | **88** | **73** | **23** | **0** | **655** |
| Makene | 2 | – | – | – | 10 | | | | | | |
| Brown | 2 | – | – | – | 10 | *Opposition scored* | *39* | *32* | *11* | *1* | *295* |

## CANTERBURY 2017

| | Wanganui | Mid Canterbury | Tasman | Otago | Hawke's Bay | Southland | Counties Manukau | Wellington | North Harbour | Waikato | Taranaki | Auckland | North Harbour | Tasman | TOTALS |
|---|---|---|---|---|---|---|---|---|---|---|---|---|---|---|---|
| M.D. Maitland | 15 | 15 | – | – | – | – | – | – | – | – | – | – | – | – | 2 |
| C.L. Makene | s | – | s | 15 | – | – | – | – | – | – | – | 15 | – | – | 4 |
| G.C. Bridge | – | – | 15 | – | 15 | 15 | 15 | 15 | 15 | 15 | 15 | – | 15 | 15 | 10 |
| N.G.J. Punivai | 14 | – | – | – | – | – | – | – | – | – | – | – | – | – | 1 |
| P.M. Waqanibau | 13 | 13 | 14 | 14 | – | – | 14 | 14 | – | – | – | – | – | – | 6 |
| M.R.G. Suckling | 11 | 11 | – | – | 14 | 14 | – | s | s | s | – | s | s | – | 9 |
| J.A. McKay | – | 14 | 11 | – | s | s | s | 11 | 14 | 14 | 14 | 14 | 14 | 14 | 12 |
| N.E. Gibb | – | s | – | – | – | – | – | – | – | – | – | – | – | – | 1 |
| B.M. Ennor | – | – | – | 11 | 11 | 11 | 11 | – | 11 | 11 | 11 | 11 | 11 | 11 | 10 |
| T.E.S. Bateman | – | – | 13 | 13 | 13 | 13 | 13 | – | 13 | 13 | 13 | 13 | 13 | 13 | 11 |
| M.D. Green | 12 | 12 | – | – | – | – | – | – | – | – | – | – | – | – | 2 |
| R. Thompson | – | – | 12 | 12 | 12 | – | 12 | 12 | 12 | 12 | 12 | – | 12 | 12 | 10 |
| K.F. Finau | – | – | – | s | s | 12 | – | 13 | – | – | – | 12 | s | s | 7 |
| B.D. Cameron | 10 | 10 | s | – | 10 | s | s | 10 | – | s | – | s | 10 | s | 11 |
| F.C. Hart-Strawbridge | s | – | – | – | – | – | – | – | – | – | – | – | – | – | 1 |
| A.P. Nicole | – | s | – | – | – | – | – | – | – | – | – | – | – | – | 1 |
| R. Mo'unga | – | – | 10 | 10 | – | 10 | 10 | s | 10 | 10 | 10 | 10 | – | 10 | 10 |
| J.B. Stratton | 9 | 9 | s | – | 9 | – | – | – | – | s | – | s | s | s | 8 |
| S.K. Alfeld | s | – | – | – | – | – | – | – | – | – | – | – | – | – | 1 |
| E.C.S. Enari | – | s | – | s | s | s | s | 9 | s | – | – | 9 | – | – | 8 |
| M.D. Drummond | – | – | 9 | 9 | – | 9 | 9 | s | 9 | 9 | 9 | – | 9 | 9 | 10 |
| D.M. Nel | 8 | s | – | – | s | – | – | – | – | – | – | – | – | – | 3 |
| L.C. Whitelock (capt) | – | – | 8 | 8 | 8 | 8 | 8 | – | – | – | – | 8 | 8 | 8 | 8 |
| R.J. Prinsep | – | – | s | – | 6 | 6 | s | 8 | 8 | 8 | 8 | s | s | s | 11 |
| W.K. Harmon | 7 | 6 | s | – | s | s | 7 | s | s | s | 7 | 7 | 7 | 7 | 13 |
| J.C. Brown | – | 7 | 7 | s | 7 | 7 | s | 7 | 7 | 7 | – | – | – | – | 9 |
| M.B. Todd | – | – | – | 7 | – | – | – | – | – | – | – | – | – | – | 1 |
| S.R. Godwin | 6 | – | – | – | – | – | – | – | – | – | – | – | – | – | 1 |
| J.T.A. Osborne | s | 4 | – | – | – | – | – | – | – | – | – | – | – | – | 2 |
| T.B. Sanders | – | 8 | 6 | 6 | – | – | 6 | 6 | 6 | 6 | 6 | 6 | 6 | 6 | 11 |
| T.M. Christie | – | – | – | – | – | – | – | – | – | – | – | – | s | – | 1 |
| H.A. Dalzell | 5 | 5 | – | – | 5 | s | – | 4 | – | s | s | 4 | s | 4 | 10 |
| M.T.W. Dunshea | 4 | – | 4 | 4 | 4 | 4 | 4 | s | 4 | 4 | 4 | s | 4 | – | 12 |
| J.J. Manning | s | – | – | – | – | – | – | – | – | – | – | – | – | – | 1 |
| B.J. Morris | – | s | – | – | – | – | – | – | – | – | – | – | – | – | 1 |
| D.J. Bird | – | – | 5 | 5 | – | 5 | 5 | 5 | 5 | 5 | 5 | 5 | 5 | 5 | 11 |
| O.G.J.T. Jager | 3 | – | s | s | 3 | s | 3 | – | s | s | s | 3 | s | s | 12 |
| J.J. Straker | s | 3 | – | – | – | – | s | – | – | – | – | – | – | – | 3 |
| S.F. Tokolahi | – | – | 3 | 3 | s | 3 | s | 3 | 3 | 3 | 3 | s | 3 | 3 | 12 |
| C.M. Gawler | 1 | s | – | – | s | s | s | s | s | – | 1 | s | s | s | 11 |
| J.N. Hintz | s | s | – | – | – | – | – | – | – | – | – | – | – | – | 2 |
| A.T.O.A. Hodgman | – | 1 | s | 1 | 1 | 1 | 1 | 1 | 1 | 1 | 1 | s | 1 | 1 | 13 |
| D.P. Lienert-Brown | – | – | 1 | – | – | – | – | – | – | – | – | – | – | – | 1 |
| N.W.K. Werahiko | 2 | s | – | – | s | s | s | – | – | – | – | – | – | – | 5 |
| A.T. Kaitu'u | s | – | – | – | – | – | – | – | – | – | – | – | – | – | 1 |
| N.B. Vella | – | 2 | s | s | 2 | 2 | 2 | s | s | s | s | 2 | s | s | 13 |
| B.C.J. Funnell | – | – | 2 | 2 | – | – | – | 2 | 2 | 2 | 2 | s | 2 | 2 | 9 |

J.B. Stratton captained the first two matches; D.J. Bird v Wellington; T.E.S. Bateman v North Harbour (1st), Waikato and Taranaki.

## CANTERBURY TEAM RECORD, 2017

Played 14   Won 12   Lost 2   Points for 655   Points against 295

| Date | Opponent | Location | Score | Tries | Con | PG | DG | Referee |
|---|---|---|---|---|---|---|---|---|
| June 21 | Wanganui (RS) | Christchurch | 71–5 | Werahiko (2), Stratton, Maitland, Nel, Suckling, Dunshea, Waqanibau, Alfeld, Makene | Cameron (7), Hart-Strawbridge (2) | Cameron | | R.P. Kelly |
| August 4 | Mid Canterbury (RS) | Ashburton | 69–7 | Suckling (2), Vella (2), Brown, Sanders, Cameron, McKay, Gibb, Waqanibau, Dalzell | Cameron (4), McKay (3) | | | J.J. Dcleman |
| August 18 | Tasman (P) | Nelson | 39–0 | Bridge, Bird, Whitelock, Thompson, Dunshea | Mo'unga (3), Cameron | Mo'unga (2) | | B.D. O'Keeffe |
| August 27 | Otago (P/C) (RS) | Christchurch | 30–24 | Funnell, Dunshea, Bateman, Brown | Mo'unga (2) | Mo'unga (2) | | P.M. Williams |
| September 1 | Hawke's Bay (P/C) | Napier | 53–10 | Suckling (2), Ennor (2), Cameron, McKay, Finau | Cameron (6) | Cameron (2) | | C.J. Stone |
| September 8 | Southland (P/C) (RS) | Christchurch | 78–20 | Ennor (4), Bridge (3), Mo'unga (2), McKay, Bateman | Mo'unga (5), Cameron (5) | Mo'unga | | N.P. Briant |
| September 13 | Counties Manukau (P) (RS) | Christchurch | 78–5 | Drummond (4), Bateman (3), Ennor, Thompson, Waqanibau, McKay | Mo'unga (10) | Mo'unga | | B.E. Pickerill |
| September 17 | Wellington (P/C) | Wellington | 14–60 | McKay, Bridge | Mo'unga (2) | | | R.P. Kelly |
| September 23 | North Harbour (P) | Albany | 41–28 | Drummond (2), Mo'unga, Bateman, McKay | Mo'unga (5) | Mo'unga (2) | | A.W.B. Mabey |
| September 30 | Waikato (P) (RS) | Christchurch | 37–17 | Ennor, Thompson, McKay, Sanders | Mo'unga (4) | Mo'unga (3) | | G.W. Jackson |
| October 6 | Taranaki (P) (RS) | Christchurch | 43–55 | Thompson (2), Sanders, Bateman, Bridge, Ennor | Mo'unga (5) | Mo'unga | | M.I. Fraser |
| October 13 | Auckland (P) | Auckland | 32–27 | Stratton (2), Ennor, Makene | Mo'unga (3) | Mo'unga (2) | | B.E. Pickerill |
| October 21 | North Harbour (P semi-final) | Christchurch | 35–24 | Drummond, Bridge, Harmon, Bateman | Cameron (3) | Cameron (3) | | B.D. O'Keeffe |
| October 28 | Tasman (P final) | Christchurch | 35–13 | Mo'unga (2), Bateman, Stratton | Mo'unga (3) | Mo'unga (3) | | M.I. Fraser |

RS *Ranfurly Shield*

# COUNTIES MANUKAU

**2017 Status:** Mitre 10 Cup Premiership
**Founded 1926** as South Auckland and affiliated to Auckland.
Granted full union status as South Auckland Counties in 1955.
Name changed to Counties 1956, to Counties Manukau 1996.
**President:** K.D. (Kere) Maihi
**Chairman:** C.W. (Craig) Carter
**Chief executive officer:** A.R. (Andrew) Maddock (to April)
                     B.A. (Barton) Hoggard (from May)
**Coach:** D.B. (Darryl) Suasua
**Assistant coaches:** G.W. (Grant) Henson, Semo Sititi
**Main ground:** ECOLight Stadium, Pukekohe
**Capacity:** 18,000
**Colours:** Red, white and black

## RECORDS

| | | |
|---|---|---|
| **Most appearances** | 201 | *Alan Dawson, 1976–89* |
| **Most points** | 698 | *Danny Love, 1993–96* |
| **Most tries** | 59 | *Alan Dawson, 1976–89* |
| **Most points in a season** | 208 | *Danny Love, 1995* |
| **Most tries in a season** | 22 | *Luke Erenavula, 1993* |
| **Most conversions in a season** | 52 | *Danny Love, 1993* |
| **Most penalty goals in a season** | 47 | *Stu Hollier, 1989* |
| **Most dropped goals in a season** | 4 | *Bob Lendrum, 1976* |
| | | *Joe Harvey, 1983* |
| **Most points in a match** | 37 | *Jim Graham v East Coast, 1972* |
| **Most tries in a match** | 5 | *K.Koiatu v King Country, 2004* |
| **Most conversions in a match** | 14 | *Jim Graham v East Coast, 1972* |
| **Most penalty goals in a match** | 6 | *Stu Hollier v France, 1989* |
| | | *Stu Hollier v Thames Valley, 1989* |
| | | *Danny Love v Manawatu, 1994* |
| | | *James Semple v Manawatu, 2011* |
| | | *Baden Kerr v Auckland 2012* |
| **Highest team score** | 108 | *v Horowhenua, 1994* |
| **Record victory (points ahead)** | 103 | *103–0 v Poverty Bay, 1993* |
| **Highest score conceded** | 100 | *v Auckland, 2004* |
| **Record defeat (points behind)** | 85 | *15–100 v Auckland, 2004* |

The Steelers had an indifferent season and slipped slightly from 2016, not making the semi-finals of the Premiership as they had done last year. After an opening win over Auckland, Counties Manukau then suffered four consecutive defeats, including a drubbing in the Ranfurly Shield match, to be bottom of the Premiership at the halfway point. A win over Taranaki had slipped through their grasp when conceding a last-minute try after having led by 13 points.

The next four matches were all crossover matches against Championship sides, resulting in three wins and a draw, and the last match was a resounding defeat of Tasman, for an unbeaten second half of the season to comfortably retain Premiership status for 2018.

Last year's regulars that did not appear in 2017 were Sherwin Stowers (retired), Sione Fifita, Toni Pulu (both injured), Cardiff Vaega (Hawke's Bay), Richard Judd (Bay of Plenty), Jordan Taufua (Tasman), while Sam Vaka, Piers Francis, So'otala Fa'aso'o, Sione Faletau and Hika Elliot were all playing overseas.

Baden Kerr and Tim Nanai-Williams returned from overseas, both last appearing in 2014, while Ronald Raaymakers reappeared after the serious shoulder injury sustained in his last appearance in 2014 had threatened to end his career. All Black captain Kieran Read signed for the province of his birth and schooling and, inevitably, did not appear, but one All Black who did appear was Stephen Donald, a late signing who had last turned out for the union in 2003. Joe Royal (Bay of Plenty) and Albert Nikoro (Tasman/Waikato) arrived with previous provincial experience, while Nigel Ah Wong had represented the Brumbies in Super Rugby the last three years and Tevita Nabura had Fiji sevens experience.

The big forward pack gained ample possession for the backs, and had a very good scrum. In the front row Pauliasi Manu was full value at loosehead with his scrummaging and tight work, while Joe Royal and debutant Coree Te Whata-Colley took over from Gafatasi Su'a and Kalolo Tuiloma in their respective hooker and tighthead positions after the Canterbury match. Matiaha Martin built nicely on last year's debut and fellow lock, and co-captain, Jimmy Tupou led from the front being skilful in the lineout and uncompromising in the tight, while Viliame Rarasea was another to lose his position after the Canterbury match.

Number eight Sam Henwood was dynamic in the loose and his was an outstanding contribution to the team's efforts. Fotu Lokotui was also a prominent part of the loose forward effort, having particularly good games against Northland and Tasman, while Ronald Raaymakers made a good comeback after his long-term injury.

Halfback and co-captain Augustine Pulu was again in good form with his running and passing game but first five-eighth Baden Kerr played below his best form. Stephen Donald was better placed at his normal first five-eighth position than at second five-eighth, particularly as NZ Under 20 rep Orbyn Leger was showing much promise in his debut season in the 12 jersey.

Nigel Ah Wong performed well, starting on the wing before moving into centre, and was equal top try-scorer on five with Tim Nanai-Williams. Nanai-Williams appeared at left wing and centre before spending the second half of the season in his best position at fullback, from where he produced brilliant form with his running and was reliable defensively.

Higher honours went to:

| | |
|---|---|
| *New Zealand:* | N. Laulala, K. Read, S. Williams |
| *New Zealand Maori:* | S. Henwood |
| *New Zealand Under 20:* | O. Leger |
| *New Zealand Sevens:* | D.J. Forbes, S. Molia, S. Stowers |

## COUNTIES MANUKAU REPRESENTATIVES 2017

| | Club | Games for Union | Points for Union | | Club | Games for Union | Points for Union |
|---|---|---|---|---|---|---|---|
| Jarred Adams | Pukekohe | 4 | 0 | Matiaha Martin | Bombay | 18 | 0 |
| Nigel Ah Wong | Patumahoe | 10 | 25 | Tevita Nabura | Waiuku | 8 | 5 |
| Sean Bagshaw | Onewhero | 41 | 0 | Tim Nanai-Williams | Manurewa | 65 | 287 |
| Liam Daniela | Bombay | 3 | 5 | Albert Nikoro | Pukekohe | 6 | 10 |
| Stephen Donald | Waiuku | 31 | 203 | Augustine Pulu | Karaka | 73 | 80 |
| Sam Furniss | Patumahoe | 5 | 0 | Ronald Raaymakers | Waiuku | 61 | 15 |
| Kalione Hala | Karaka | 2 | 0 | Viliame Rarasea | Ardmore Marist | 33 | 15 |
| Sam Henwood | Pukekohe | 22 | 20 | Joe Royal | Patumahoe | 10 | 10 |
| Leroy Jack | Onewhero | 5 | 0 | Gafatasi Su'a | Pukekohe | 30 | 10 |
| Jonathan Kawau | Bombay | 13 | 5 | Viliami Taulani | Manurewa | 8 | 0 |
| Baden Kerr | Karaka | 39 | 376 | Jonathan Taumateine | Ardmore Marist | 10 | 10 |
| Luteru Laulala | Ardmore Marist | 21 | 49 | Coree Te Whata-Colley | Bombay | 10 | 0 |
| Orbyn Leger | Karaka | 10 | 10 | Kalalo Tuiloma | Bombay | 20 | 25 |
| Fotu Lokotui | Patumahoe | 10 | 15 | Sione "Jimmy" Tupou | Patumahoe | 57 | 27 |
| Pauliasi Manu | Karaka | 34 | 15 | Sesimani Tupou | Ardmore Marist | 1 | 0 |

## INDIVIDUAL SCORING

| | Tries | Con | PG | DG | Points |
|---|---|---|---|---|---|
| Kerr | 1 | 13 | 6 | – | 49 |
| Donald | 3 | 5 | 1 | – | 28 |
| Laulala | 1 | 6 | 3 | – | 26 |
| Nanai-Williams | 5 | – | – | – | 25 |
| Ah Wong | 5 | – | – | – | 25 |
| Lokotui | 3 | – | – | – | 15 |
| Pulu | 2 | – | – | – | 10 |
| Taumateine | 2 | – | – | – | 10 |
| Royal | 2 | – | – | – | 10 |
| Nikoro | 2 | – | – | – | 10 |
| Leger | 2 | – | – | – | 10 |
| Penalty Try | 1 | – | – | – | 7 |

| | Tries | Con | PG | DG | Points |
|---|---|---|---|---|---|
| Nabura | 1 | – | – | – | 5 |
| Kawau | 1 | – | – | – | 5 |
| Tuiloma | 1 | – | – | – | 5 |
| Daniela | 1 | – | – | – | 5 |
| Raaymakers | 1 | – | – | – | 5 |
| Henwood | 1 | – | – | – | 5 |
| J. Tupou | – | 1 | – | – | 2 |
| **Totals** | **35** | **25** | **10** | **0** | **257** |
| *Opposition scored* | 38 | 31 | 15 | 0 | 297 |

## COUNTIES MANUKAU 2017

| | Auckland | Waikato | Taranaki | North Harbour | Canterbury | Hawke's Bay | Bay of Plenty | Northland | Manawatu | Tasman | TOTALS |
|---|---|---|---|---|---|---|---|---|---|---|---|
| L.E. Laulala | 15 | 15 | 15 | 15 | 15 | s | s | s | 14 | 11 | 10 |
| T.T. Nanai-Williams | 11 | 11 | s | 13 | 13 | 15 | 15 | 15 | 15 | 15 | 10 |
| N.F. Ah Wong | 14 | 14 | 14 | 14 | 14 | 14 | 13 | 13 | 13 | 13 | 10 |
| K.H.K. Hala | s | – | – | – | – | – | – | – | – | – | 1 |
| T. Nabura | – | s | 11 | 11 | – | 11 | 11 | 11 | 11 | s | 8 |
| A.N.T. Nikoro | – | – | – | s | 11 | s | 14 | 14 | – | 14 | 6 |
| S.C. Furniss | 13 | 13 | 13 | – | s | 13 | – | – | – | – | 5 |
| S.R. Donald | 12 | 12 | s | 10 | 12 | – | s | s | 10 | 10 | 9 |
| O.N.T. Leger | s | s | 12 | 12 | s | 12 | 12 | 12 | 12 | 12 | 10 |
| B.H. Kerr | 10 | 10 | 10 | s | 10 | 10 | 10 | 10 | s | s | 10 |
| A.W. Pulu (co-capt) | 9 | 9 | – | – | 9 | 9 | 9 | 9 | 9 | – | 7 |
| J.A. Taumateine | s | s | 9 | 9 | s | s | – | – | – | – | 6 |
| L.T. Daniela | – | – | – | s | – | – | s | – | – | 9 | 3 |
| S.T. Henwood | 8 | 8 | 7 | 8 | 8 | 8 | 8 | 8 | 8 | 8 | 10 |
| F.S. Lokotui | 7 | 7 | – | 7 | s | 7 | 7 | 7 | 7 | 7 | 9 |
| R.J. Raaymakers | 6 | 6 | 6 | 6 | 6 | 4 | 4 | 6 | 6 | 6 | 10 |
| V.T.H. Taulani | s | s | – | – | – | – | s | – | – | – | 3 |
| J.D. Kawau | – | – | s | s | 7 | 6 | 6 | s | s | s | 7 |
| M. Martin | 5 | 5 | 5 | 5 | – | – | – | 5 | 5 | 5 | 7 |
| V.L. Rarasea | 4 | – | 4 | 4 | 4 | s | s | s | s | s | 9 |
| Sione S. Tupou (co-capt) | – | 4 | 8 | – | 5 | 5 | 5 | 4 | 4 | 4 | 8 |
| L.J. Jack | – | s | s | s | s | s | – | – | – | – | 5 |
| K.E. Tuiloma | 3 | 3 | 3 | 3 | 3 | s | s | s | s | – | 9 |
| C.J.W. Te Whata-Colley | s | s | s | s | s | 3 | 3 | 3 | 3 | 3 | 10 |
| Sesimani Tupou | – | – | – | – | – | – | – | – | – | s | 1 |
| P.P. Manu | 1 | 1 | 1 | 1 | 1 | 1 | 1 | 1 | 1 | – | 9 |
| S. Bagshaw | s | s | s | s | s | s | s | – | s | 1 | 9 |
| J.F. Adams | – | – | – | – | – | – | – | – | – | s | 1 |
| G.W. Su'a | 2 | 2 | 2 | s | 2 | s | s | – | s | s | 9 |
| J.W. Royal | s | s | s | 2 | s | 2 | 2 | 2 | 2 | 2 | 10 |

S.R. Donald captained v North Harbour.

## COUNTIES MANUKAU TEAM RECORD, 2017

| Date | Opponent | Location | Score | Tries | Con | PG | DG | Referee |
|---|---|---|---|---|---|---|---|---|
| | | | | **Played 10** | **Won 5** | **Drew 1** | **Lost 4** | **Points for 257** / **Points against 297** |
| August 19 | Auckland (P) | Pukekohe | 16–14 | Lokotui | Kerr | Kerr (3) | | C.J. Stone |
| August 25 | Waikato (P) | Hamilton | 21–33 | Donald, Pulu, Taumateine | Kerr (3) | | | M.I. Fraser |
| September 2 | Taranaki (P) | New Plymouth | 27–30 | Nabura, Taumateine, Royal | Kerr (3) | Kerr (2) | | A.W.B. Mabey |
| September 7 | North Harbour (P) | Pukekohe | 18–27 | Laulala, Nanai-Williams | Laulala | Laulala (2) | | J.J. Doleman |
| September 13 | Canterbury (P) (RS) | Christchurch | 5–78 | Ah Wong | | | | B.E. Pickerill |
| September 17 | Hawke's Bay (P/C) | Pukekohe | 33–14 | Nanai-Williams (2), Lokotui, Kawau, Tuiloma | Kerr (3), Laulala | | | M.G. Lash |
| September 24 | Bay of Plenty (P/C) | Tauranga | 31–31 | Lokotui, Pulu, Nikoro, Ah Wong, Daniela | Kerr (2), Laulala | | | M.G. Lash |
| October 1 | Northland (P/C) | Pukekohe | 25–16 | Nikoro, Nanai-Williams, Donald | Kerr, Laulala | Kerr, Laulala | | M.I. Fraser |
| October 5 | Manawatu (P/C) | Palmerston North | 29–24 | Raaymakers, Donald, Leger, Ah Wong | Donald (3) | Donald | | G.W. Jackson |
| October 14 | Tasman (P) | Pukekohe | 52–30 | Ah Wong (2), Royal, Leger, Penalty Try, Nanai-Williams, Henwood, Kerr | Donald (2), Laulala (2), J. Tupou | | | P.M. Williams |

RS *Ranfurly Shield*

# EAST COAST

**2017 Status:** Heartland
**Founded 1921** as East Coast and affiliated 1921.
Name changed to Ngati Porou East Coast 2017
**President:** G.N. (Graeme) Summersby
**Chairman:** C.W. (Campbell) Dewes
**Chief executive officer:** Cushla Tangaere-Manuel
**Co-coaches:** W.L. (Wayne) Ensor and T.D. (Troy) Para
**Main ground:** Whakarua Park, Ruatoria
**Capacity:** 3000
**Colours:** Sky blue and white

## RECORDS

| | | |
|---|---|---|
| Highest attendance | 4000 | *v Poverty Bay (Div 3 final), 1999* |
| Most appearances | 115 | *E.M. Waitoa, 1979–2006* |
| Most points | 406 | *E.J. Manuel, 1985–98* |
| Most tries | 24 | *J.R. Kururangi, 1979–96* |
| Most points in a season | 145 | *M.R. Flutey, 2000* |
| Most tries in a season | 9 | *S. Vorenasu, 2011* |
| Most conversions in a season | 20 | *M.R. Flutey, 2001* |
| | | *J.R. Semple, 2012* |
| Most penalty goals in a season | 30 | *M.R. Flutey, 2000* |
| Most dropped goals in a season | 3 | *M.R. Flutey, 2000* |
| Most points in a match | 22 | *V.P. Taingahue v Buller, 1999* |
| Most tries in a match | 3 | *W. Peachy v Bush, 1954* |
| | | *T.M. Reedy v Horowhenua, 1958* |
| | | *J.R. Kururangi v West Coast, 1992* |
| | | *J. Higgins v Poverty Bay, 1993* |
| | | *M. Vere v Buller, 1999* |
| | | *T.W. Delamere v Horowhenua Kapiti, 2000* |
| | | *H.F.Haerewa v Poverty Bay, 2012* |
| | | *S.P. Destounis, v Poverty Bay, 2016* |
| Most conversions in a match | 8 | *V.P. Taingahue v Buller, 1999* |
| Most penalty goals in a match | 7 | *M.R. Flutey v Nelson Bays, 2001* |
| Highest team score | 74 | *v Buller, 1999* |
| Record victory (points ahead) | 69 | *72–3 v West Coast, 1992* |
| Highest score conceded | 116 | *v North Otago, 2010* |
| Record defeat (points behind) | 113 | *3–116 v North Otago, 2010* |

East Coast endured another winless season in the Heartland Championship, losing all eight games and only scoring 13 tries. The two best performances were against West Coast when they closed to within three points midway through the second half and against Poverty Bay when they led midway through the second half, but were unable to score again either time.

The coaches called upon 40 players for the season, of whom only 10 had played more than 10 matches for the union and 19 were debuting. Of the debutants Te Peehi Fairlie and Patrick Allen had previously represented Poverty Bay and Te Wehi Wright had played for NZ Universities. A big loss was last year's halfback and captain Sam Parkes to Tasman.

The general fitness of the players was better than usual, but there was the perennial problem of the size of the forward pack usually conceding height and weight to their opponents. In spite of this, Parekura Lalaga, Hone Haerewa and Patrick Allen were a tireless loose forward trio who always gave their best, as did hooker Kareti Palmer. Lock Manaia Nyman showed some promise in his debut season, and Pera Bishop did a lot of good work at prop but missed matches with injury.

At first five-eighth Verdon Bartlett was the best of the backs, his experience proving a great asset. Loan player Sailosi Vatubua was a powerful runner in midfield but did have a tendency to ignore his outsides. When injuries affected the halfbacks, Charlie Harrison earned a recall to take his tally of appearances to 113, just two short of the East Coast record.

No player was called upon for higher honours.

## EAST COAST REPRESENTATIVES 2017

| | Club | Games for Union | Points for Union | | Club | Games for Union | Points for Union |
|---|---|---|---|---|---|---|---|
| Tevita Ahoafi | Tihirau Victory Club | 7 | 6 | Jayden Milner | Ruatoria City | 18 | 6 |
| Patrick Allen | Ruatoria City | 8 | 0 | Jordan Murray-Birch | Uawa | 1 | 0 |
| Tim Barbarich | Ruatoria City | 14 | 0 | Reg Namana | Uawa | 2 | 0 |
| Verdon Bartlett | Tihirau Victory Club | 60 | 36 | Moana Nuku | Uawa | 5 | 0 |
| Pera Bishop | Ruatoria City | 32 | 5 | Manaia Nyman | Tihirau Victory Club | 8 | 0 |
| Lorne Boyce-Goldsmith | Ruatoria City | 1 | 0 | Kareti Palmer | Hikurangi | 32 | 21 |
| Ryan Buchanan | Hicks Bay | 3 | 0 | Kris Palmer | Hikurangi | 38 | 134 |
| Michael Chambers | Tokomaru United | 17 | 0 | Hayden Pardoe | Uawa | 1 | 0 |
| Laman Davies | Uawa | 12 | 0 | Harley Phillips | Uawa | 14 | 0 |
| Te Peehi Fairlie | Tokomaru United | 8 | 10 | Keelan Poi | Waiapu | 3 | 0 |
| Richard Green | Waiapu | 6 | 0 | Morgan Poi | OB University [2] | 3 | 0 |
| Hone Haerewa [1] | Wellington [2] | 24 | 17 | Trent Proffit | Hikurangi | 3 | 0 |
| Charlie Harrison | Hikurangi | 113 | 40 | Neihana Ratahi-Brown | Ruatoria City | 7 | 5 |
| Fabyan Kahaki | Hikurangi | 6 | 0 | Tari Ao Stevenson-Tuhura | Waiapu | 1 | 10 |
| Daniel Knubley | Uawa | 9 | 0 | Slade Tiopira | Waiapu | 4 | 8 |
| Parekura Lalaga | Northern United [2] | 15 | 10 | Sailosi Vatubua | Suburbs [4] | 7 | 20 |
| Pati Lemapu | Uawa | 1 | 0 | Rhys Walker | Hikurangi | 17 | 0 |
| Epeli Lotawa | United Matamata Sports [3] | 4 | 5 | Kahu Ward | Hikurangi | 23 | 6 |
| Perrin Manuel | Waiapu | 17 | 11 | Callan Whaitiri-White | Ruatoria City | 2 | 0 |
| Ngatu Mauheni | Waiapu | 8 | 0 | Te Wehi Wright | OB University [2] | 4 | 0 |

[1] *Player of Origin*  [2] *Wellington RU*  [3] *Waikato RU*  [4] *Auckland RU*

## EAST COAST 2017

| | Poverty Bay | Thames Valley | Wairarapa Bush | West Coast | Poverty Bay | Horowhenua Kapiti | Buller | North Otago | South Canterbury | TOTALS |
|---|---|---|---|---|---|---|---|---|---|---|
| Kris Palmer | – | 15 | 15 | 15 | 15 | 15 | 15 | 15 | 15 | 8 |
| J.S. Murray-Birch | 14 | – | – | – | – | – | – | – | – | 1 |
| T. Stevenson-Tahura | 11 | – | – | – | – | – | – | – | – | 1 |
| J.P. Milner | 15 | 11 | 11 | 11 | 11 | 11 | 14 | 14 | 14 | 9 |
| T.W.O.M. Wright | – | 13 | 14 | 14 | 14 | – | – | – | – | 4 |
| E. Lotawa | – | – | – | – | – | 14 | 11 | 11 | 11 | 4 |
| T.P. H.H. Fairlie | 13 | 14 | s | 13 | 13 | 13 | – | 13 | 13 | 8 |
| N.T.B. Mauheni | 12 | – | – | – | – | – | – | – | – | 1 |
| P. Lemapu | s | – | – | – | – | – | – | – | – | 1 |
| S. Vatubua | – | – | 13 | 12 | 12 | 12 | 13 | 12 | 12 | 7 |
| K. Ward | – | 12 | 12 | – | s | s | 10 | s | s | 7 |
| S.T.W. Tiopira | 10 | s | s | s | – | – | – | – | – | 4 |
| K.T.R. Poi | – | 10 | 10 | – | – | – | s | – | – | 3 |
| V.R.M. Bartlett | – | s | s | 10 | 10 | 10 | 12 | 10 | 10 | 8 |
| T. Ahoafi | 9 | – | – | – | – | – | – | – | – | 1 |
| F. Kahaki | s | s | – | – | – | s | s | s | 9 | 6 |
| N. Ratahi-Brown | – | 9 | – | s | – | – | 9 | 9 | s | 5 |
| R. Buchanan | – | – | 9 | 9 | 9 | – | – | – | – | 3 |
| C.F. Harrison | – | – | – | – | s | 9 | s | s | s | 5 |
| M.P. Poi | 8 | 5 | – | – | 1 | – | – | – | – | 3 |
| P. Lalaga | – | 8 | 8 | 8 | – | 8 | 8 | 8 | 8 | 7 |
| P. Allen | 5 | 7 | 7 | 7 | 8 | 7 | 7 | – | 7 | 8 |
| H. Haerewa | 6 | 4 | 4 | 6 | 6 | 6 | 6 | – | 6 | 8 |
| R. Green | s | – | – | – | – | s | s | 6 | s | 5 |
| T.C. Proffit | – | 6 | 6 | – | 7 | – | – | – | – | 3 |
| L. Boyce-Goldsmith | – | – | – | – | – | – | – | s | – | 1 |
| H.W. Pardoe | 4 | – | – | – | – | – | – | – | – | 1 |
| H.N. Phillips | s | – | – | – | – | – | – | – | – | 1 |
| M.H. Nyman | s | s | s | 4 | 4 | 4 | 4 | – | 4 | 8 |
| R.T.T.K. Walker | – | s | 5 | 5 | s | 5 | 5 | 5 | 5 | 8 |
| T.J. Barbarich | – | – | s | s | – | s | s | 4 | s | 6 |
| C. Whaitiri-White | – | – | – | s | 5 | – | – | – | – | 2 |
| R. Namana | – | – | – | – | – | – | – | s | – | 1 |
| M.R. Chambers | 3 | 1 | 1 | 1 | – | 1 | – | 3 | – | 6 |
| L.L.A. Davies | 1 | 3 | 3 | – | s | – | – | 1 | s | 6 |
| D.W. Knubley | s | s | – | s | – | s | s | s | – | 6 |
| P.P. Bishop | s | – | – | 3 | 3 | 3 | 3 | – | 3 | 6 |
| Kareti Palmer | 7 | s | s | 2 | 2 | 2 | 2 | 7 | 2 | 9 |
| P.J. Manuel (capt) | 2 | 2 | 2 | – | – | – | 1 | 2 | 1 | 6 |
| M. Nuku | – | – | – | s | – | s | s | s | s | 5 |

P. Allen captained v West Coast, Poverty Bay (2nd) and Horowhenua Kapiti.

## INDIVIDUAL SCORING

| | Tries | Con | PG | DG | Points | | Tries | Con | PG | DG | Points |
|---|---|---|---|---|---|---|---|---|---|---|---|
| Kris Palmer | 1 | 9 | 5 | – | 38 | Ratahi-Brown | 1 | – | – | – | 5 |
| Vatubua | 4 | – | – | – | 20 | Lotawa | 1 | – | – | – | 5 |
| Stevenson-Tahura | 2 | – | – | – | 10 | Haerewa | 1 | – | – | – | 5 |
| Lalaga | 2 | – | – | – | 10 | | | | | | |
| Fairlie | 2 | – | – | – | 10 | **Totals** | **16** | **10** | **7** | **0** | **121** |
| Tiopira | – | 1 | 2 | – | 8 | | | | | | |
| Manuel | 1 | – | – | – | 5 | Opposition scored | 58 | 40 | 6 | 1 | 391 |
| Bishop | 1 | – | – | – | 5 | | | | | | |

## EAST COAST TEAM RECORD, 2017

**Played 9   Won 0   Lost 9   Points for 121   Points against 391**

| Date | Opponent | Location | Score | Tries | Con | PG | DG | Referee |
|---|---|---|---|---|---|---|---|---|
| June 3 | Poverty Bay | Gisborne | 23–38 | Stevenson (2), Manuel | Tiopira | Tiopira (2) | | R.J.M. Gordon |
| August 26 | Thames Valley (H) | Ruatoria | 13–42 | Lalaga | Kris Palmer | Kris Palmer (2) | | M.C.J. Winter |
| September 2 | Wairarapa Bush (H) | Masterton | 10–36 | Lalaga | Kris Palmer | Kris Palmer | | T. Kajiwara *Japan* |
| September 9 | West Coast (H) | Ruatoria | 19–32 | Vatubua (2), Bishop | Kris Palmer (2) | | | V.F. Rincrose |
| September 16 | Poverty Bay (H) | Gisborne | 15–35 | Vatubua, Fairlie | Kris Palmer | Kris Palmer | | N.E.R. Hogan |
| September 23 | Horowhenua Kapiti (H) | Otaki | 3–52 | | | Kris Palmer | | T.N. Griffiths |
| September 30 | Buller (H) | Ruatoria | 17–54 | Ratahi-Brown, Kris Palmer, Vatubua | Kris Palmer | | | B.J. Jurlina |
| October 7 | North Otago (H) | Oamaru | 14–57 | Lotawa, Fairlie | Kris Palmer | Kris Palmer (2) | | T.N. Griffiths |
| October 14 | South Canterbury (H) | Ruatoria | 7–45 | Haerewa | Kris Palmer | | | M.C.J. Winter |

# HAWKE'S BAY

**2017 Status:** Mitre 10 Cup Championship
**Founded 1884.** Original member
**President:** P.G. (Paul) Daniel
**Chairman:** B.J. (Brendon) Mahony
**Chief executive officer:** M.J. (Mike) Bishop
**Coach:** C.A. (Craig) Philpott
**Assistant coach:** M.D. (Mark) Ozich
**Main ground:** McLean Park, Napier
**Capacity:** 16,500
**Colours:** Black and white

## RECORDS

| | | |
|---|---|---|
| Most appearances | 158 | *N.W. Thimbleby, 1959–71* |
| Most points | 998 | *J.B. Cunningham, 1990–98* |
| Most tries | 73 | *B.A. Grenside, 1919–31* |
| Most points in a season | 237 | *J.B. Cunningham, 1994* |
| Most tries in a season | 18 | *B.A. Grenside, 1926* |
| | | *P.J. Cooke, 1986* |
| Most conversions in a season | 47 | *J.B. Cunningham, 1995* |
| Most penalty goals in a season | 37 | *M.W. Berquist, 2009* |
| Most dropped goals in a season | 7 | *B.D.M. Furlong, 1968* |
| | | *M.K. Sisam, 1979* |
| Most points in a match | 36 | *M.K. Sisam v East Coast, 1979* |
| Most tries in a match | 6 | *R.P. Hunter v East Coast, 1979* |
| Most conversions in a match | 13 | *J.B. Cunningham v Cook Islands, 1995* |
| Most penalty goals in a match | 7 | *J.B. Cunningham v Manawatu, 1993* |
| | | *J.B. Cunningham v King Country, 1994* |
| | | *R.G.E. Lewis v North Harbour, 2001* |
| Highest team score | 99 | *v Cook Islands, 1995* |
| | | *v Mid Canterbury, 2003* |
| Record victory (points ahead) | 99 | *99–0 v Cook Islands, 1995* |
| Highest score conceded | 86 | *v Waikato, 1999* |
| Record defeat (points behind) | 86 | *0–86 v Waikato, 1999* |

The Magpies had a poor season with just two wins — coming in their first and last games — with eight consecutive defeats in between. They had such a horror run with injuries that for the opening match against Southland there were six unavailable, before the second-round match against Bay of Plenty it was 10, after the fourth-round match against Wellington it was up to 13, while for the final match of the season against Manawatu it was down to seven players unavailable. But as with last season tackling was poor through missed tackles and not enough aggression at the tackle and breakdown.

There were a number of changes from the Hawke's Bay team of 2016 with Mark Abbott, Robbie Fruean, Billy Ropiha (all overseas), Tolu Fahamokioa (Wellington), Ricky Riccitelli (Taranaki), Matthew Garland (Bay of Plenty), Lewis Marshall (Manawatu), Ross Filipo (retired) and Trent Boswell-Wakefield (unavailable) all absent. Arrivals were the return of Richard Buckman, Cardiff Vaega (Counties Manukau), and Pasqualle Dunn (Auckland) and Nick Palmer (Sydney club Norths). Cardiff Vaega's younger brother To'o (TJ) also arrived, having represented Auckland Under 19 last year.

Injury necessitated a young inexperienced tight five taking the field in a lot of matches, and not surprisingly failed to dominate. This had an adverse effect on the loose forwards and backs. The loss of prop Ben May for the whole season to injury was a serious one, while Super Rugby players Gareth Evans and Michael Allardice appeared only twice and five times respectively due to injury.

Ash Dixon, an expert hooker and tireless worker, led by example as captain and tried hard to lift the performances of his team. He was ably supported by Jason Long at loosehead prop while two of this year's NZ Under 20 props Pouri Rakete-Stones and Tim Farrell made their debuts. Locks Geoff Cridge and Michael Allardice were a good pairing, particularly with their skill in the lineout, but both missed matches with injury and only played together half the season.

The loose forwards did not have many opportunities to shine on attack, spending more time in close supporting roles to the tight forwards, nevertheless Tony Lamborn, Hugh Renton, and another of this year's NZ Under 20 team Marino Mikaele-Tu'u were a relatively settled trio and performed creditably in the circumstances. Gareth Evans gave an outstanding performance against Manawatu to show what the side missed with his injury.

The lack of a regular fullback caused difficulties with the position being shared by Tiaan Falcon, Richard Buckman and Ihaia West who were all better suited elsewhere. Sam McNicol finally made his Magpies' debut after missing all of last year and initially played on the wing, but his sole appearance at fullback against Manawatu in the final match looked the right fit. Mason Emerson was a busy wing but received few chances, while Cardiff Vaega was eventually shifted to the right wing after his tackling was found wanting in midfield. Richard Buckman and Jonah Lowe shored up the midfield in the second half of the season and did provide an attacking threat.

After his serious injury earlier in the year on Chiefs duty, Brad Weber was getting back to his best at season's end, while outside him Ihaia West had a mixed season but remained a competent goal-kicker.

Higher honours went to:

| | |
|---|---|
| *New Zealand:* | I. Dagg, B. Retallick |
| *New Zealand Maori:* | A. Dixon, B. May, B. Weber, I. West |
| *New Zealand Under 20:* | T. Falcon, T. Farrell, M. Mikaele-Tu'u, P. Rakete-Stones |
| *New Zealand Sevens:* | T. Samuels |

## HAWKE'S BAY REPRESENTATIVES 2017

| | Club | Games for Union | Points for Union | | Club | Games for Union | Points for Union |
|---|---|---|---|---|---|---|---|
| Michael Allardice | Pirates | 41 | 20 | Mason Kean | Tamatea | 6 | 0 |
| Jarvy Aoake | Napier OB Marist | 22 | 10 | Tony Lamborn | Havelock North | 46 | 45 |
| Mark Braidwood | Tech OB | 16 | 5 | Jason Long | Hastings RS | 30 | 20 |
| Richard Buckman | Tech OB | 73 | 121 | Jonah Lowe | Clive | 24 | 52 |
| Geoff Cridge | Hastings RS | 18 | 10 | Sam McNicol | Napier OB Marist | 5 | 5 |
| Jacob Devery | Hastings RS | 7 | 0 | Marino Mikaele-Tu'u | Hastings RS | 11 | 15 |
| Ash Dixon | Tech OB | 82 | 35 | Nick Palmer | Taradale | 8 | 0 |
| Zac Donaldson | Napier OB Marist | 1 | 0 | Ben Parsons | Hastings RS | 3 | 0 |
| Pasqualle Dunn | Havelock North | 6 | 5 | Pouri Rakete-Stones | Pirates | 10 | 0 |
| Chris Eaton | Taradale | 113 | 45 | Hugh Renton | Hastings RS | 13 | 5 |
| Josh Eden-Whaitiri | Clive | 11 | 0 | Fa'alemiga Seselele | MAC | 18 | 5 |
| Mason Emerson | Hastings RS | 22 | 30 | Dan Snee | Havelock North | 3 | 8 |
| Gareth Evans | Havelock North | 9 | 10 | Jorian Tangaere | Clive | 19 | 5 |
| Tiaan Falcon | Clive | 19 | 14 | Cardiff Vaega | Pirates | 10 | 20 |
| Tim Farrell | Tech OB | 5 | 0 | To'o "TJ" Vaega | Pirates | 7 | 5 |
| Lucas Goodin | Clive | 3 | 0 | Brad Weber | Napier OB Marist | 17 | 15 |
| Ben Hamelink | Hastings RS | 8 | 0 | Ihaia West | Havelock North | 62 | 628 |
| Hayden Hann | Pirates | 6 | 0 | Ellery Wilson | Napier OB Marist | 29 | 10 |
| Ricky Hayes | Napier OB Marist | 1 | 0 | | | | |

## INDIVIDUAL SCORING

| | Tries | Con | PG | DG | Points | | Tries | Con | PG | DG | Points |
|---|---|---|---|---|---|---|---|---|---|---|---|
| West | 2 | 15 | 6 | – | 58 | Tangaere | 1 | – | – | – | 5 |
| C. Vaega | 4 | – | – | – | 20 | Wilson | 1 | – | – | – | 5 |
| Mikaele-Tu'u | 3 | – | – | – | 15 | Dunn | 1 | – | – | – | 5 |
| Falcon | 1 | 2 | 1 | – | 12 | Aoake | 1 | – | – | – | 5 |
| Long | 2 | – | – | – | 10 | Evans | 1 | – | – | – | 5 |
| Lowe | 2 | – | – | – | 10 | Weber | 1 | – | – | – | 5 |
| Dixon | 2 | – | – | – | 10 | Buckman | 1 | – | – | – | 5 |
| Emerson | 2 | – | – | – | 10 | | | | | | |
| Snee | – | 4 | – | – | 8 | **Totals** | **28** | **21** | **7** | **0** | **203** |
| T. Vaega | 1 | – | – | – | 5 | | | | | | |
| Renton | 1 | – | – | – | 5 | Opposition scored | 52 | 43 | 16 | 0 | 398 |
| McNicol | 1 | – | – | – | 5 | | | | | | |

## HAWKE'S BAY 2017

| | Southland | Bay of Plenty | Canterbury | Wellington | Otago | Counties Manukau | Taranaki | North Harbour | Northland | Manawatu | TOTALS |
|---|---|---|---|---|---|---|---|---|---|---|---|
| T.J. Falcon | 15 | 15 | 15 | 10 | 10 | 10 | – | 15 | 15 | s | 9 |
| H.W. Hann | 14 | 14 | s | 13 | 13 | – | – | – | s | – | 6 |
| M.R. Emerson | 11 | – | – | – | – | 11 | 11 | 11 | 11 | 11 | 6 |
| T. Vaega | s | s | s | – | s | 14 | – | – | s | s | 7 |
| S.J. McNicol | – | 11 | 11 | 11 | 11 | – | – | – | – | 15 | 5 |
| C.K. Vaega | 13 | 13 | 13 | 12 | 12 | s | 14 | 14 | 14 | 14 | 10 |
| P.M. Dunn | s | s | – | – | – | s | s | s | 12 | – | 6 |
| J.H. Lowe | – | – | 14 | 14 | 14 | 13 | 13 | 13 | 13 | 13 | 8 |
| R.J. Buckman | 12 | 12 | 12 | 15 | 15 | 12 | 12 | 12 | – | 12 | 9 |
| I.T. West | 10 | 10 | 10 | – | – | 15 | 15 | 10 | 10 | 10 | 8 |
| D.R. Snee | – | – | – | s | s | – | 10 | – | – | – | 3 |
| C.G. Eaton | 9 | 9 | 9 | s | – | – | – | – | – | – | 4 |
| Z.G.C. Donaldson | – | s | – | – | – | – | – | – | – | – | 1 |
| B.M. Weber | – | – | s | 9 | 9 | 9 | 9 | 9 | 9 | 9 | 8 |
| E.J. Wilson | – | – | – | – | s | s | s | – | s | s | 5 |
| G.O. Evans | 8 | – | – | – | – | – | – | – | – | 8 | 2 |
| M.E.R. Mikaele-Tu'u | 6 | 8 | 8 | – | 8 | 8 | 8 | 8 | 8 | 6 | 9 |
| T.A. Lamborn | 7 | – | – | 8 | – | 6 | 6 | 7 | 7 | 7 | 7 |
| H.T. Renton | s | – | 6 | 7 | 7 | 7 | 7 | 6 | 6 | s | 9 |
| F. Selesele | – | 7 | 7 | s | s | s | s | s | s | – | 8 |
| B.M. Hamelink | – | s | – | – | – | – | – | – | – | – | 1 |
| L.J. Goodin | – | – | s | 6 | 6 | – | – | – | – | – | 3 |
| R.J. Hayes | – | – | – | s | – | – | – | – | – | – | 1 |
| G.O. Cridge | 5 | 6 | 5 | 5 | – | 5 | 5 | 5 | – | – | 7 |
| M.G. Allardice | 4 | 4 | 4 | – | – | – | 4 | 4 | – | – | 5 |
| N.W. Palmer | s | 5 | s | 4 | 4 | 4 | – | – | 5 | 4 | 8 |
| J.N.R. Eden-Whaitiri | – | s | – | s | 5 | s | s | s | 4 | 5 | 8 |
| B.G. Parsons | – | – | – | – | s | – | – | – | s | s | 3 |
| M.P.J. Kean | 3 | s | – | – | – | – | – | – | – | – | 2 |
| P.G. Rakete-Stones | s | 3 | 3 | s | 3 | 3 | 3 | 3 | 3 | 3 | 10 |
| J.D. Aoake | – | – | s | 3 | s | s | s | s | s | s | 8 |
| J.B. Long | 1 | 1 | 1 | s | 1 | 1 | 1 | 1 | 1 | 1 | 10 |
| M. Braidwood | s | s | s | 1 | s | – | – | – | – | – | 5 |
| T.J. Farrell | – | – | – | – | – | s | s | s | s | s | 5 |
| A.L. Dixon (capt) | 2 | 2 | 2 | – | – | 2 | 2 | 2 | 2 | 2 | 8 |
| J.D. Devery | – | s | s | 2 | s | s | – | – | s | s | 7 |
| J.T. Tangaere | – | – | – | s | 2 | – | – | – | – | – | 2 |

B.M. Weber captained v Wellington and Otago.

## HAWKE'S BAY TEAM RECORD, 2017

Played 10  Won 2  Lost 8  Points for 203  Points against 398

| Date | Opponent | Location | Score | Tries | Con | PG | DG | Referee |
|---|---|---|---|---|---|---|---|---|
| August 19 | Southland (C) | Napier | 24–16 | T. Vaega, Falcon, Mikaele-Tu'u | West (3) | West | | A.W.B. Mabey |
| August 25 | Bay of Plenty (C) | Rotorua | 17–46 | Mikaele-Tu'u, West | West (2) | West | | J.J. Doleman |
| September 1 | Canterbury (P/C) | Napier | 10–53 | Renton | West | West | | C.J. Store |
| September 6 | Wellington (C) | Wellington | 27–40 | C. Vaega, Long, McNicol, Tangaere | Falcon (2) | Falcon | | J.R. Nuttrown |
| September 10 | Otago (C) | Napier | 21–64 | Lowe, Mikaele-Tu'u, Wilson | Snee (3) | | | S.W. McDermott |
| September 17 | Counties Manukau (P/C) | Pukekohe | 14–33 | Dixon, Dunn | West (2) | | | M.G. Lash |
| September 23 | Taranaki (P/C) | Napier | 17–48 | C. Vaega, West, Aoake | Snee | | | S.W. McDermott |
| September 29 | North Harbour (P/C) | Albany | 30–33 | Dixon, C. Vaega, Long | West (3) | West (3) | | R.P. Kelly |
| October 7 | Northland (C) | Whangarei | 7–34 | C. Vaega | West | | | P.M. Williams |
| October 15 | Manawatu (C) | Napier | 36–31 | Emerson (2), Evans, Weber, Buckman, Lowe | West (3) | | | C.J. Stone |

# HOROWHENUA KAPITI

**2017 Status:** Heartland
**Founded 1893.** Affiliated 1893. Name changed
　　　to Horowhenua Kapiti in 1997.
**President:** G.B. (Gerald) De Castro
**Chairman:** J.M. (John) Mowbray
**Chief executive officer:** C.J. (Corey) Kennett
**Coach:** C.R.K. (Chris) Wilton
**Assistant coach:** Katsu Takeuchi
**Main ground:** Levin Park Domain
**Capacity:** 12,000
**Colours:** Red, white and blue

## RECORDS

| | | |
|---|---|---|
| Highest attendance | 6500 | *Hurricanes v Crusaders pre-season, 2014* |
| Most appearances | 153 | *P.M. Hirini, 1986–2000* |
| Most points | 440 | *C.W. Laursen, 1984–89* |
| Most tries | 69 | *D.C. Laursen, 1980–92* |
| | | *P.M. Hirini, 1986–2000* |
| Most points in a season | 136 | *C.J. Spencer, 1993* |
| Most tries in a season | 13 | *D.C. Laursen, 1987* |
| | | *C.J. Kennett, 1993* |
| Most conversions in a season | 26 | *C.J. Spencer, 1993* |
| | | *R.F. Aloe, 2008* |
| Most penalty goals in a season | 29 | *C.W. Laursen, 1987* |
| Most dropped goals in a season | 5 | *M. Liddicoat, 1979* |
| Most points in a match | 29 | *J.P.M. Hamilton v West Coast, 2010* |
| | | *B.C. Laursen v Poverty Bay, 2015* |
| Most tries in a match | 5 | *D.C. Laursen v West Coast, 1991* |
| Most conversions in a match | 9 | *D.P. Nepia v Buller, 1999* |
| | 9 | *R.F. Aloe v East Coast, 2008* |
| Most penalty goals in a match | 6 | *J. Proctor v Wanganui, 2009* |
| | | *J.S. So'oialo v Buller 2017* |
| Highest team score | 73 | *v Buller, 1999* |
| | | *v East Coast, 2008* |
| Record victory (points ahead) | 73 | *73–0 v Buller, 1999* |
| Highest score conceded | 108 | *v Counties, 1994* |
| Record defeat (points behind) | 96 | *12–108 v Counties, 1994* |

Horowhenua Kapiti were the biggest improvers in the 2017 Heartland Championship. With pretty much the same team as last year they not only went all the way to the Meads Cup final for the very first time, but also hosted it. Despite the disappointment of losing to Wanganui, Horowhenua Kapiti finished the season with the much improved record of eight wins from 10 matches, and the satisfaction in winning the coveted Bruce Steel Cup from Wanganui in their round robin clash.

　　The strength of the team was a big forward pack that were able to hold their own against any opposition with impressive set pieces, particularly the scrum, and their pick and go driving and forward rushes. A factor in the performance of the forwards was their managing to stay injury free with six starting in all 10 games and two starting in nine, a consistency of selection that allowed them to develop cohesiveness. While Horowhenua Kapiti may have played a lot of 10-man rugby, it did yield championship points and a place in the final.

In a rugged tight five, captain Ryan Shelford and William Lander were a fine pairing at lock, both giving impetus to the pack, while live-wire hooker Nathan Kendrick got around the field almost like a fourth loose forward. Scott Cameron was a mobile tighthead prop who was strong in the scrum and Robin Praat on the loosehead side also rendered good service. Tyson Maki was a strong running number eight who had a good season.

James So'oialo, playing mainly at first five-eighth, was the star of the backline, controlling play superbly in scoring 133 points including three tries. His goal-kicking was excellent, and the round robin wins over Wanganui and semi-final win over Buller owed much to his penalty goals, which were Horowhenua Kapiti's only scoring in those matches. Wing Willie Paia'aua was again full value and top try-scorer with five tries, but would have benefitted with even more ball as would have fullback Andrew McDougall, who always looked eager.

Higher honours went to:
*New Zealand Heartland*:   S. Cameron, N. Kendrick, W. Paia'aua, E. Pollock

## HOROWHENUA KAPITI REPRESENTATIVES 2017

| | Club | Games for Union | Points for Union | | Club | Games for Union | Points for Union |
|---|---|---|---|---|---|---|---|
| Spencer Bishop | Foxton | 10 | 5 | Willie Paia'aua | Levin College OB | 17 | 37 |
| Scott Cameron | Waikanae | 37 | 38 | Ethan Pollock | Foxton | 17 | 11 |
| Izak Eksteen | Foxton | 3 | 5 | Robin Praat [1] | Massey University [3] | 29 | 0 |
| Kalim Kelemete | Tawa [2] | 9 | 10 | Trent Reti | Waikanae | 13 | 5 |
| Nathan Kendrick | Paraparaumu | 18 | 27 | Ryan Shelford | Paraparaumu | 78 | 22 |
| Aaron Lahmert | Waikanae | 36 | 17 | James So'oialo | Tawa [2] | 10 | 133 |
| William Lander | Athletic | 46 | 11 | Hone Taiapa | Wanderers | 4 | 0 |
| Tyson Maki | Levin College OB | 24 | 22 | Kane Tamou | Foxton | 9 | 0 |
| Andrew McDougall | College OB [3] | 10 | 5 | Dylan Taylor | Paraparaumu | 7 | 0 |
| David McErlean | Foxton | 29 | 25 | Tiwana Thompson-Paringatai | Waikanae | 7 | 0 |
| Luke McMahon | Foxton | 8 | 6 | Louie Tovo | Levin College OB | 25 | 0 |
| Robert Millar | Waikanae | 29 | 15 | Ethan Wade | Shannon | 1 | 0 |

[1] *Player of Origin*   [2] *Wellington RU*   [3] *Manawatu RU*

## INDIVIDUAL SCORING

| | Tries | Con | PG | DG | Points | | Tries | Con | PG | DG | Points |
|---|---|---|---|---|---|---|---|---|---|---|---|
| So'oialo | 3 | 17 | 28 | – | 133 | Eksteen | 1 | – | – | – | 5 |
| Paia'aua | 5 | – | – | – | 25 | Shelford | 1 | – | – | – | 5 |
| Kendrick | 3 | – | – | – | 15 | Millar | 1 | – | – | – | 5 |
| McErlean | 3 | – | – | – | 15 | Bishop | 1 | – | – | – | 5 |
| Kelemete | 2 | – | – | – | 10 | Cameron | 1 | – | – | – | 5 |
| Maki | 2 | – | – | – | 10 | McDougall | 1 | – | – | – | 5 |
| McMahon | – | 3 | – | – | 6 | | | | | | |
| Pollock | 1 | – | – | – | 5 | **Totals** | **27** | **20** | **28** | **0** | **259** |
| Reti | 1 | – | – | – | 5 | | | | | | |
| Lander | 1 | – | – | – | 5 | *Opposition scored* | *17* | *12* | *14* | *1* | *154* |

| HOROWHENUA KAPITI 2017 | North Otago | Poverty Bay | Thames Valley | West Coast | East Coast | Wairarapa Bush | Wanganui | Buller | Buller | Wanganui | TOTALS |
|---|---|---|---|---|---|---|---|---|---|---|---|
| A.J. McDougall | 14 | 15 | 15 | 15 | 15 | 15 | 15 | 15 | 15 | 15 | 10 |
| W.E. Paia'aua | 11 | 11 | 11 | 11 | 11 | 11 | 11 | 11 | 11 | – | 9 |
| I.J. Eksteen | s | 14 | – | 14 | – | – | – | – | – | – | 3 |
| R.N. Millar | – | s | 14 | – | s | s | – | s | s | 11 | 7 |
| D.C. Taylor | – | – | – | s | 14 | 14 | 14 | 14 | 14 | 14 | 7 |
| E.B. Pollock | 13 | 13 | 12 | – | 13 | 13 | 13 | 13 | 13 | 13 | 9 |
| L.R. McMahon | 12 | s | s | 12 | s | s | – | 12 | – | s | 8 |
| K.J.P. Kelemete | 10 | 12 | 13 | 13 | 10 | 10 | 10 | – | 12 | 12 | 9 |
| J.S. So'oialo | 15 | 10 | 10 | 10 | 12 | 12 | 12 | 10 | 10 | 10 | 10 |
| T.C. Reti | 9 | 9 | s | s | 9 | 9 | 9 | 9 | 9 | 9 | 10 |
| K.E.M. Tamou | s | s | 9 | 9 | s | s | – | s | s | s | 9 |
| T.J. Maki | 8 | 8 | 8 | 8 | 8 | 8 | 8 | 8 | 8 | 8 | 10 |
| S.M. Bishop | 7 | 7 | 7 | 7 | 7 | 7 | 7 | 7 | 7 | 7 | 10 |
| A.D. Lahmert | 6 | 6 | 6 | 6 | 6 | 6 | 6 | 6 | 6 | 6 | 10 |
| H.T. Taiapa | – | s | – | – | s | s | – | – | – | s | 4 |
| W.G. Lander | 5 | 5 | 5 | 5 | 5 | 5 | 5 | 5 | 5 | 5 | 10 |
| R.T. Shelford (capt) | 4 | 4 | 4 | 4 | 4 | 4 | 4 | 4 | 4 | 4 | 10 |
| L.L.P. Tovo | s | s | s | s | – | s | s | s | s | s | 9 |
| S.A. Cameron | 3 | 3 | 3 | 3 | 3 | 3 | 3 | 3 | 3 | 3 | 10 |
| R.A. Praat | 1 | 1 | 1 | – | 1 | 1 | 1 | 1 | 1 | 1 | 9 |
| T.S. Thompson-Paringatai | s | s | – | 1 | s | s | – | s | – | s | 7 |
| N.J. Kendrick | 2 | 2 | s | 2 | 2 | 2 | 2 | 2 | 2 | 2 | 10 |
| D.J. McErlean | s | s | 2 | s | s | s | s | s | s | s | 10 |
| E.R. Wade | – | – | – | – | s | – | – | – | – | – | 1 |

## HOROWHENUA KAPITI TEAM RECORD, 2017

Played 10  Won 8  Lost 2  Points for 259  Points against 154

| Date | Opponent | Location | Score | Tries | Con | PG | DG | Referee |
|---|---|---|---|---|---|---|---|---|
| August 26 | North Otago (H) | Levin | 22–19 | So'oialo, Kelemete, Pollock | So'oialo (2) | So'oialo | | N.E.R. Hogan |
| September 2 | Poverty Bay (H) | Gisborne | 39–5 | Paia'aua (2), Reti, Kendrick, So'oialo | So'oialo (4) | So'oialo (2) | | T.M.T. Cottrell |
| September 9 | Thames Valley (H) | Levin | 13–10 | Kelemete | So'oialo | So'oialo (2) | | R.J.M. Gordon |
| September 16 | West Coast (H) | Greymouth | 18–24 | Lander, Eksteen | So'oialo | So'oialo (2) | | T.M.T. Cottrell |
| September 23 | East Coast (H) | Otaki | 52–3 | McErlean (3), Paia'aua, So'oialo, Shelford, Millar | So'oialo (4), McMahon (3) | So'oialo | | T.N. Griffiths |
| October 1 | Wairarapa Bush (H) | Wellington | 38–12 | Maki (2), Kendrick (2), Paia'aua | So'oialo (2) | So'oialo (3) | | J.D. Munro |
| October 7 | Wanganui (H) (BSC) | Levin | 15–8 | | | So'oialo (5) | | M.C.J. Winter |
| October 14 | Buller (H) | Westport | 30–26 | Bishop, Cameron, Paia'aua | So'oialo (3) | So'oialo (3) | | J.D. Murro |
| October 21 | Buller (MC semi-final) | Levin | 18–17 | | | So'oialo (6) | | M.C.J. Winter |
| October 28 | Wanganui (MC final) | Levin | 14–30 | McDougall | | So'oialo (3) | | M.C.J. Winter |

BSC *Bruce Steel Cup*

# KING COUNTRY

**2017 Status:** Heartland
**Founded 1922.** Affiliated 1922
**President:** J.W. (James) Gibb
**Chairman:** I.C. (Ivan) Haines
**General Manager:** S.M. (Susan) Youngman
**Coach:** T.P. (Daniel) Alofa
**Assistant coach:** P.D. (Paul) Olsen
**Main grounds:** Owen Delany Park, Taupo; Rugby Park, Te Kuiti
**Capacity:** 15,000
**Colours:** Gold and maroon

## RECORDS

| | | |
|---|---|---|
| Highest attendance | 12,000 | *King Country v South Africa, 1994 (Taupo)* |
| Most appearances | 147 | *P.L. Mitchell, 1988–2001* |
| Most points | 917 | *H.C. Coffin, 1984–95* |
| Most tries | 46 | *M.R. Kidd, 1974–84* |
| Most points in a season | 230 | *H.C. Coffin, 1992* |
| Most tries in a season | 11 | *D.M. Flavell, 1981* |
| | | *S.J. Bradley, 1992* |
| Most conversions in a season | 40 | *H.C. Coffin, 1992* |
| Most penalty goals in a season | 45 | *H.C. Coffin, 1992* |
| Most dropped goals in a season | 8 | *I.N. Ingham, 1966* |
| Most points in a match | 33 | *H.C. Coffin v Poverty Bay, 1992* |
| Most tries in a match | 4 | *C.A. Crossman v Auckland XV, 1936* |
| | | *J. Haitana & H. Dixon v Thames Valley, 1938* |
| | | *T. Katene v Golden Bay-Motueka, 1955* |
| | | *J.A.W. McIlroy v Horowhenua, 1965* |
| | | *D.W. Koni v Taranaki, 1969* |
| | | *D.M. Flavell v East Coast, 1979* |
| | | *N.A. Harrison v East Coast, 1981* |
| | | *N.A. Harrison v Horowhenua, 1984* |
| | | *J.W. Wells v East Coast, 1992* |
| Most conversions in a match | 10 | *H.C. Coffin v Poverty Bay, 1992* |
| Most penalty goals in a match | 7 | *L.W.T. Peina v Wanganui, 2000* |
| Highest team score | 99 | *v East Coast, 1992* |
| Record victory (points ahead) | 99 | *99–0 v East Coast, 1992* |
| Highest score conceded | 97 | *v Auckland, 1993* |
| Record defeat (points behind) | 94 | *3–97 v Auckland, 1993* |

King Country declined in 2017 with just a sole win against Wairarapa Bush to their credit and suffered a thrashing at the hands of Wanganui. Defence repeatedly let the team down at crucial moments, and in the many close games lost, the trend was either a slow start as against North Otago and Thames Valley or a poor finish as in the Poverty Bay and Mid Canterbury matches.

A number of key players from last year were absent with Zayn Tipping (injured), James Hemara (unavailable), Whakataki Cunningham (Bay of Plenty), Sam Mason, Brian Mansfield, Gene Waller (all retired) and Steve Te Moananui (overseas), while John Koko was only available for one match.

Former All Black halfback Alby Mathewson was residing in Taupo with his partner's parents, after completing the 2016–17 English season with Bristol, when he agreed to join the Rams while looking for another overseas contract. His presence was of huge value to the team, constantly supplying quick ball to the backline. Securing a contract with French club Toulon removed him from the final two matches of the season.

Loan player Reece Macdonald revelled in the service he received from Mathewson, exhibiting a good running and kicking game. Outside him there was a lack of thrust in the midfield which was to the detriment of wingers Dean Church and Alex Thrupp who were both in fine form, particularly Church who was top try-scorer with six.

King Country was well served in the forwards by the versatile Anthony Wise, durable prop Carl Carmichael and centurion Aarin Dunster, who at the age of 39 is still a good lock. Antonie 'Beau' Taylor, who last represented in 2014, was also good value at lock.

No player was called upon for higher honours.

## KING COUNTRY REPRESENTATIVES 2017

| | Club | Games for Union | Points for Union | | Club | Games for Union | Points for Union |
|---|---|---|---|---|---|---|---|
| Sam Adams | Waitete | 4 | 0 | Alby Mathewson | Taupo United | 6 | 5 |
| Robbie Alabaster | Taumarunui RS | 11 | 0 | Stormy McCarthy | Piopio | 12 | 12 |
| Manuele Alofa | Taupo Sports | 16 | 10 | Adam Morris | Taumarunui RS | 26 | 16 |
| Nick Barnes | Taupo Sports | 1 | 0 | Nigel Neustroski | Waitete | 27 | 5 |
| Baven Brown | Waitete | 6 | 5 | Cameron Robinson | Taupo Sports | 3 | 0 |
| Shaun Burr | Waitete | 35 | 20 | Kieron Rollinson | Taupo United | 15 | 43 |
| Carl Carmichael | Taumarunui RS | 19 | 5 | Rob Sherson | Taumarunui RS | 55 | 56 |
| Ethan Christensen | Taupo Sports | 1 | 0 | Nathaniel Smith | Taumarunui Dist | 5 | 0 |
| Dean Church | Waitomo | 67 | 183 | Antonie "Beau" Taylor | Waitete | 65 | 20 |
| Joseva Curuki | Taumarunui Dist | 1 | 0 | Alex Thrupp | Te Puke Sports [2] | 15 | 27 |
| Josh Dais | Taupo Sports | 38 | 5 | Tovia Tufala | Taupo Sports | 2 | 0 |
| Aarin Dunster | Tongariro | 109 | 10 | Stephan Turner | Piopio | 17 | 22 |
| Vaughan Hodgson | Taumarunui Dist | 1 | 0 | Ratu Vosaki | Taupo Sports | 3 | 0 |
| Mike Horrocks | Taumarunui RS | 7 | 0 | Sisa Vosaki | Taupo Sports | 4 | 0 |
| Oliver Kay | Waitomo | 16 | 10 | Sean Wanden | Waitomo | 26 | 22 |
| John Koko | Taupo United | 11 | 30 | Jesse Williams | Waitomo | 21 | 15 |
| Reece Macdonald [1] | Arataki [2] | 6 | 68 | Anthony Wise | Otorohanga [3] | 46 | 57 |

[1] *Player of Origin*   [2] *Bay of Plenty RU*   [3] *Waikato RU*

## INDIVIDUAL SCORING

| | Tries | Con | PG | DG | Points | | Tries | Con | PG | DG | Points |
|---|---|---|---|---|---|---|---|---|---|---|---|
| Macdonald | 3 | 13 | 9 | – | 68 | Carmichael | 1 | – | – | – | 5 |
| Church | 6 | 1 | – | – | 32 | Wanden | 1 | – | – | – | 5 |
| Rollinson | 2 | 4 | 3 | – | 27 | Brown | 1 | – | – | – | 5 |
| Thrupp | 3 | – | – | – | 15 | Kay | 1 | – | – | – | 5 |
| Williams | 3 | – | – | – | 15 | McCarthy | – | 1 | – | – | 2 |
| Turner | 2 | – | – | – | 10 | | | | | | |
| Penalty Try | 1 | – | – | – | 7 | **Totals** | **26** | **19** | **12** | **0** | **206** |
| Sherson | 1 | – | – | – | 5 | | | | | | |
| Mathewson | 1 | – | – | – | 5 | *Opposition scored* | *45* | *29* | *12* | *0* | *323* |

| KING COUNTRY 2017 | West Coast | South Canterbury | Wairarapa Bush | North Otago | Thames Valley | Wanganui | Poverty Bay | Mid Canterbury | TOTALS |
|---|---|---|---|---|---|---|---|---|---|
| D.R. Church | 15 | 15 | 11 | 11 | 15 | 15 | 11 | 15 | 8 |
| A.M. Thrupp | 14 | 14 | 14 | 14 | 11 | 11 | 14 | 13 | 8 |
| B.L. Brown | 11 | 11 | – | – | 14 | 14 | s | 14 | 6 |
| R.S. Vosaki | s | s | s | – | – | – | – | – | 3 |
| C.J. Robinson | – | – | – | – | – | s | – | – | 1 |
| S.K. Turner | 13 | 13 | 13 | 13 | 13 | 13 | 13 | 12 | 8 |
| J.H. Williams | 12 | 12 | 12 | 12 | s | 12 | 12 | 11 | 8 |
| S.T.M.E. McCarthy | s | – | s | s | s | s | s | s | 7 |
| J.P. Koko | – | – | – | – | 12 | – | – | – | 1 |
| R.S. Macdonald | 10 | 10 | 10 | 10 | – | – | 10 | 10 | 6 |
| K.J. Rollinson | – | s | 15 | 15 | 10 | 10 | 15 | s | 7 |
| A.S. Mathewson | 9 | 9 | 9 | 9 | 9 | 9 | – | – | 6 |
| N.K. Smith | s | – | – | – | s | s | 9 | 9 | 5 |
| T. Tufala | – | – | – | – | – | – | s | s | 2 |
| R.L. Sherson (co-capt) | 8 | 8 | 8 | s | s | 8 | 8 | 8 | 8 |
| S.B. Burr | 7 | s | s | – | – | s | 7 | s | 6 |
| O.W. Kay | 6 | 7 | 7 | 7 | 7 | 7 | 6 | 7 | 8 |
| A.E. Wise | 4 | 6 | 6 | 8 | 8 | 6 | 4 | 6 | 8 |
| S. Vosaki | s | s | – | s | 6 | – | – | – | 4 |
| E. Christensen | – | – | – | – | – | – | s | – | 1 |
| M.L. M.L. Horrocks | 5 | 4 | s | 6 | 4 | 5 | – | 4 | 7 |
| V.N. Hodgson | s | – | – | – | – | – | – | – | 1 |
| A.W. Taylor | – | 5 | 4 | 4 | s | 4 | – | s | 6 |
| A.M. Dunster | – | – | 5 | 5 | 5 | – | 5 | 5 | 5 |
| M. Alofa | – | – | – | – | – | s | – | – | 1 |
| S.R.P. Adams | – | – | – | – | – | – | s | – | 1 |
| R.G. Alabaster | 3 | 3 | 3 | 3 | 3 | s | s | – | 7 |
| N.G. Barnes | 1 | – | – | – | – | – | – | – | 1 |
| A.J.D. Morris | s | – | – | s | s | 3 | 3 | 3 | 6 |
| N.R. Neustroski | s | s | – | – | – | s | – | s | 4 |
| C.W. Carmichael | – | 1 | 1 | 1 | 1 | 1 | 1 | 1 | 7 |
| J.K. Curuki | – | – | s | – | – | – | – | – | 1 |
| J.K. Dais (co-capt) | 2 | 2 | 2 | 2 | 2 | 2 | s | s | 8 |
| S.P.B. Wanden | – | – | s | s | s | – | 2 | 2 | 5 |

## KING COUNTRY TEAM RECORD, 2017

Played 8    Won 1    Lost 7    Points for 206    Points against 323

| Date | Opponent | Location | Score | Tries | Con | PG | DG | Referee |
|---|---|---|---|---|---|---|---|---|
| August 26 | West Coast (H) | Taupo | 6–17 | | | Macdonald (2) | | T. Kajiwara *Japan* |
| September 2 | South Canterbury (H) | Timaru | 36–42 | Church (2), Macdonald, Thrupp, Turner | Macdonald (2), Rollinson, Church | Rollinson | | N.J. Webster |
| September 9 | Wairarapa Bush (H) | Te Kuiti | 32–25 | Church (2), Thrupp, Penalty Try | Macdonald (2) | Macdonald (2) | | B.J. Jurlina |
| September 16 | North Otago (H) | Oamaru | 26–28 | Thrupp, Macdonald | Macdonald (2) | Macdonald (4) | | V.F. Ringrose |
| September 23 | Thames Valley (H) | Te Kuiti | 36–45 | Sherson, Mathewson, Rollinson, Turner, Williams | Rollinson (3), McCarthy | Rollinson | | B.J. Jurlina |
| September 30 | Wanganui (H) | Wanganui | 3–80 | | | Rollinson | | T.M.T. Cottrell |
| October 7 | Poverty Bay (H) | Gisborne | 29–43 | Church (2), Carmichael, Williams | Macdonald (3) | Macdonald | | R.J.M. Gordon |
| October 14 | Mid Canterbury (H) | Taupo | 38–43 | Wanden, Williams, Macdonald, Brown, Kay, Rollinson | Macdonald (4) | | | J.T. Bell |

# MANAWATU

**2017 Status:** Mitre 10 Cup Championship
**Founded 1886.** Original member
**President:** J.W. (John) Fisher
**Chairman:** T.J. (Tim) Myers
**Chief executive officer:** J.W. (John) Knowles
**Coach:** J.M. (Jeremy) Cotter
**Assistant coach:** A.J. (Aaron) Good
**Main ground:** Central Energy Trust Arena, Palmerston North
**Capacity:** 17,000
**Colours:** Green and white

**MANAWATU
RUGBY**

## RECORDS

| | | |
|---|---|---|
| Highest attendance | 24,996 | *Manawatu-Horowhenua v British Isles, 1959* |
| Most appearances | 145 | *G.A. Knight, 1975–86* |
| Most points | 641 | *J.J. Holland, 1991–96* |
| Most tries | 66 | *K.W. Granger, 1971–84* |
| Most points in a season | 182 | *J.M. Smith, 1991* |
| Most tries in a season | 14 | *P.L. Alston, 1991* |
| Most conversions in a season | 38 | *D.L. Rollerson, 1981* |
| | | *J.M. Smith, 1991* |
| Most penalty goals in a season | 27 | *M.C. Finlay, 1984* |
| | | *A. McMaster, 1987* |
| Most dropped goals in a season | 9 | *J.P.J. Carroll, 1978* |
| Most points in a match | 35 | *J.M. Smith v Horowhenua, 1992* |
| Most tries in a match | 5 | *J.P. Butt v Wanganui, 1944* |
| | | *N.J. Mears v Horowhenua, 1958* |
| | | *G.P.D. Henare v Horowhenua, 1987* |
| Most conversions in a match | 11 | *J.M. Smith v Poverty Bay, 1991* |
| Most penalty goals in a match | 6 | *M.R. Love v Waikato, 1983* |
| | | *M.C. Finlay v Wanganui, 1984* |
| | | *A. McMaster v Waikato, 1987* |
| | | *J.J. Holland v Counties, 1994* |
| | | *I. Thompson v Northland, 2009* |
| Highest team score | 94 | *v Poverty Bay, 1991* |
| Record victory (points ahead) | 87 | *94–7 v Poverty Bay, 1991* |
| Highest score conceded | 109 | *v British & Irish Lions, 2005* |
| Record defeat (points behind) | 103 | *6–109 v British & Irish Lions, 2005* |

Manawatu had to defeat Hawke's Bay in the last round-robin game to secure a semi-final place but after holding a handy 17–0 halftime lead the team then conceded six tries over the next 20 minutes. Defence had been the team's weakness all season but never as poor as was embarrassingly shown for that quarter at McLean Park. Manawatu had the chance to achieve its first win at Napier since 1955 but blew it. The team had targeted the game as a must win and was prepared to rest several key players for the mid-week game against Taranaki. However, Taranaki had won the Ranfurly Shield the previous weekend and coach Jeremy Cotter had no choice but to field his best in the shield challenge. With only three days to rest, the players showed signs of fatigue at Napier. Had there been no shield challenge Manawatu may well have qualified for the play-offs.

The major loss from 2016 was the departure of experienced captain Callum Gibbins. This was partly offset with the return of former captain Nick Crosswell, who would have been a tremendous asset had he not been injured mid-season. Nehe Milner-Skudder and Ngani Laumape were released from All Blacks duties for two games.

The team's strength was in the forwards where the scrums and lineouts were much improved from 2016. Jackson Hemopo was clearly the standout player, a vigorous lock who consistently produced performances of All Black standard. Fellow lock Tom Parsons had his best season and regularly featured in open play. Fraser Armstrong and Michael Ala'alatoa were a powerful pair at prop, the former must be close to a Super contract. NZ Under 20 rep Sean Paranihi also impressed. Liam Mitchell (lock) and Brayden Iose (loose forward) are promising young players introduced and their futures will be watched with interest.

Kayne Hammington and Jamie Booth are excellent halfbacks, the latter attracting attention with his efforts off the bench. There was little between the two first five-eighths, Otere Black and Jade Te Rure, both fine ball distributors and reliable goalkickers and Te Rure gave such accomplished performances that he gained the edge over Black for the later games. Further out the backline holes in the defensive screen were often exploited by the opposition. Jason Emery, Ambrose Curtis and Newton Tudreu each had their good games but, generally, the midfield and outside backs too seldom clicked sufficiently to produce the sparkling attacking rugby that the Turbos had gained a reputation for in recent years. Kenyan sevens player Willy Ambaka didn't make the impact expected of him. Te Rangatira Waitokia, from Wanganui, is a talent who could make a big impression in 2018.

Higher honours went to:

| | |
|---|---|
| *New Zealand:* | A.W. Cruden, Laumape, Milner-Skudder, A.L. Smith |
| *Maori All Blacks:* | Curtis, Hemopo |
| *New Zealand Sevens:* | Booth, Curtis |

## MANAWATU REPRESENTATIVES 2017

| | Club | Games for Union | Points for Union | | Club | Games for Union | Points for Union |
|---|---|---|---|---|---|---|---|
| Michael Ala'alatoa | FOB Oroua | 27 | 10 | Brice Henderson | College OB | 12 | 0 |
| William Ambaka | FOB Oroua | 5 | 5 | Brayden Iose | Kia Toa | 2 | 0 |
| Fraser Armstrong | OB Marist | 27 | 5 | Antonio Kiri Kiri | OB Marist | 53 | 45 |
| Sione Asi | Kia Toa | 3 | 0 | Ngani Laumape | Kia Toa | 12 | 40 |
| Kurt Baker | Returning | 22 | 25 | Sam Malcolm | University | 9 | 12 |
| Heiden Bedwell-Curtis | Feilding | 50 | 40 | Lewis Marshall | FOB Oroua | 37 | 50 |
| Otere Black | College OB | 39 | 341 | Nehe Milner-Skudder | University | 37 | 35 |
| Jamie Booth | University | 32 | 30 | Liam Mitchell | Te Kawau | 5 | 0 |
| Harrison Brewer | Te Kawau | 13 | 5 | Hamish Northcott | University | 43 | 25 |
| Tim Cadwallader | College OB | 23 | 10 | Sean Paranihi | FOB Oroua | 10 | 0 |
| Nick Crosswell | Feilding | 85 | 15 | Tom Parsons | Te Kawau | 29 | 0 |
| Tom Crozier | Sumner[1] | 5 | 5 | Hunter Prescott | OB Marist | 14 | 5 |
| Ambrose Curtis | OB Marist | 27 | 35 | Tukiterangi Raimona | OB Marist | 17 | 0 |
| Jason Emery | Kia Toa | 56 | 74 | Curtis Reid | College OB | 9 | 5 |
| Liam Hallam-Eames | OB Marist | 9 | 0 | Jade Te Rure | Kia Toa | 29 | 180 |
| Kayne Hammington | Feilding | 30 | 15 | Newton Tudreu | Kia Toa | 36 | 40 |
| Jackson Hemopo | Kia Toa | 20 | 15 | Te Rangatira Waitokia | University | 4 | 0 |

[1] Canterbury RU

## INDIVIDUAL SCORING

| | Tries | Con | PG | DG | Points | | Tries | Con | PG | DG | Points |
|---|---|---|---|---|---|---|---|---|---|---|---|
| Te Rure | 3 | 9 | 11 | – | 66 | Cadwallader | 1 | – | – | – | 5 |
| Black | 1 | 14 | 9 | – | 60 | Crosswell | 1 | – | – | – | 5 |
| Tudreu | 4 | – | – | – | 20 | Crozier | 1 | – | – | – | 5 |
| Booth | 3 | – | – | – | 15 | Hammington | 1 | – | – | – | 5 |
| Curtis | 3 | – | – | – | 15 | Laumape | 1 | – | – | – | 5 |
| Emery | 2 | 1 | – | – | 12 | Milner-Skudder | 1 | – | – | – | 5 |
| Hemopo | 2 | – | – | – | 10 | Prescott | 1 | – | – | – | 5 |
| Marshall | 2 | – | – | – | 10 | Reid | 1 | – | – | – | 5 |
| Northcott | 2 | – | – | – | 10 | | | | | | |
| Ala'alatoa | 1 | – | – | – | 5 | **Totals** | **34** | **24** | **20** | **0** | **278** |
| Ambaka | 1 | – | – | – | 5 | | | | | | |
| Baker | 1 | – | – | – | 5 | Opposition scored | 40* | 23 | 13 | 0 | 287 |
| Brewer | 1 | – | – | – | 5 | | | | | | |

*\* includes one penalty try (7 points)*

## MANAWATU 2017

| | Wellington | Tasman | Otago | Bay of Plenty | Waikato | Northland | Southland | Counties Manukau | Taranaki | Hawke's Bay | TOTALS |
|---|---|---|---|---|---|---|---|---|---|---|---|
| N.R. Milner-Skudder | 15 | – | 14 | – | – | – | – | – | – | – | 2 |
| K.T. Baker | – | 15 | 15 | 15 | 15 | 15 | – | – | 15 | – | 6 |
| Te R.W. Waitokia | – | – | – | – | – | – | 15 | 15 | s | 15 | 4 |
| A.A.D. Curtis | 14 | 14 | 11 | 14 | s | 11 | 11 | 11 | 11 | – | 9 |
| N.W.K. Tudreu | s | s | – | – | 14 | 14 | 14 | 14 | 14 | 14 | 8 |
| W. Ambaka | 11 | 11 | – | 11 | 11 | – | – | – | – | 11 | 5 |
| L.D.P. Marshall | 13 | 13 | s | 13 | 13 | 13 | 13 | 13 | – | 13 | 9 |
| C.B. Reid | 12 | – | – | – | – | – | s | – | – | – | 2 |
| H.C. Northcott | – | 12 | 13 | 12 | s | s | – | s | – | 12 | 7 |
| K.H. Laumape | – | – | 12 | – | – | – | – | – | 12 | – | 2 |
| J.W.C. Emery | – | – | – | s | 12 | 12 | 12 | 12 | 13 | s | 7 |
| O.W. Black | 10 | 10 | 10 | 10 | – | s | s | 10 | 10 | – | 8 |
| J. Te Rure | s | s | s | s | 10 | 10 | 10 | s | s | 10 | 10 |
| K.W. Hammington | 9 | 9 | 9 | 9 | 9 | – | s | 9 | 9 | s | 9 |
| J.P. Booth | s | s | s | s | s | 9 | 9 | s | s | 9 | 10 |
| S.B. Malcolm | – | – | – | – | – | – | s | – | – | – | 1 |
| H.K. Bedwell-Curtis (capt) | 8 | 8 | 8 | 8 | 6 | 6 | 6 | 6 | 6 | 7 | 10 |
| B.W. Henderson | – | s | s | s | 8 | 8 | – | 8 | 8 | – | 7 |
| B.D. Iose | – | – | – | – | – | – | s | – | – | 8 | 2 |
| A.I. Kiri Kiri | 7 | 7 | 7 | 7 | 7 | 7 | 7 | 7 | 7 | s | 10 |
| N.J. Crosswell | 6 | 6 | 6 | 6 | – | – | – | – | – | – | 4 |
| H.P. Brewer | s | – | – | – | s | s | 8 | s | s | 6 | 7 |
| J.N. Hemopo | 5 | 5 | 5 | 5 | 5 | 5 | 5 | 5 | 5 | 5 | 10 |
| T.I. Parsons | 4 | 4 | 4 | 4 | 4 | 4 | 4 | 4 | 4 | 4 | 10 |
| L.J. Hallam-Eames | s | s | s | – | – | – | – | s | s | 5 | 6 |
| L.F. Mitchell | – | – | – | s | s | s | s | – | – | s | 5 |
| S.B. Paranihi | 3 | s | s | s | s | s | 3 | s | s | 3 | 10 |
| M.S. Ala'alatoa | – | 3 | 3 | 3 | 3 | 3 | – | 3 | 3 | s | 8 |
| F.P. Armstrong | 1 | 1 | 1 | 1 | 1 | 1 | s | 1 | 1 | 1 | 10 |
| T.J. Raimona | s | s | s | s | s | s | 1 | s | s | s | 10 |
| S.F. Asi | s | – | – | s | – | – | s | – | – | – | 3 |
| H.W. Prescott | 2 | 2 | 2 | – | – | – | s | s | 2 | – | 6 |
| T.J. Cadwallader | s | s | s | 2 | 2 | 2 | – | – | s | 2 | 8 |
| T.D. Crozier | – | – | – | – | s | s | 2 | 2 | – | s | 5 |

# MANAWATU TEAM RECORD, 2017

**Played 10  Won 4  Lost 6  Points for 278  Points against 287**

| Date | Opponent | Location | Score | Tries | Con | PG | DG | Referee |
|---|---|---|---|---|---|---|---|---|
| August 20 | Wellington (C) | Palmerston North | 29–41 | Ambaka, Reid, Milner-Skudder, Hemopo, Te Rure | Black (2) | | | Shuhei Kubo *Japan* |
| August 27 | Tasman (C/P) | Palmerston North | 35–20 | Crosswell, Baker, Prescott, Northcott | Black (3) | Black (3) | | R.P. Kelly |
| September 2 | Otago (C) | Dunedin | 30–40 | Laumape, Hemopo, Booth | Black (3) | Black (2), Te Rure | | J.D. Munro |
| September 8 | Bay of Plenty (C) | Palmerston North | 17–20 | Black, Marshall | Black (2) | Black | | B.D. O'Keeffe |
| September 16 | Waikato (C/P) | Hamilton | 23–10 | Booth, Brewer | Te Rure (2) | Te Rure (3) | | N.P. Brant |
| September 22 | Northland (C) | Palmerston North | 39–25 | Tudreu (2), Curtis, Northcott | Te Rure (2) | Te Rure (5) | | B.D. O'Keeffe |
| September 30 | Southland (C) | Invercargill | 25–20 | Crozier, Tudreu, Hammington, Emery | Black | Te Rure | | S.W. McDermott |
| October 5 | Counties Manukau (C/P) | Palmerston North | 24–29 | Ala'alatoa, Tudreu, Curtis | Black (3) | Black | | G.W. Jaccson |
| October 11 | Taranaki (C/P, RS) | New Plymouth | 25–46 | Booth, Curtis, Te Rure | Te Rure (2) | Black (2) | | B.D. O'Keeffe |
| October 15 | Hawke's Bay (C) | Napier | 31–36 | Marshall, Cadwallader, Emery, Te Rure | Te Rure (3), Emery | Te Rure | | C.J. Stone |

# MID CANTERBURY

**2017 Status:** Heartland
**Founded 1904** as Ashburton with affiliation to South
Canterbury, 1905–1926 affiliated to Canterbury
as a sub-union. Granted full union status in 1927
as Ashburton County; 1952 name changed to
Mid Canterbury Rugby Football Union.
**President:** J.C. (Jock) Ross
**Chairman:** G.P. (Gerard) Rushton
**Chief executive officer:** I.J. (Ian) Patterson
**Co-coaches:** C.R. (Craig) Dunlea and J.A. (James) Jowsey
**Main ground:** Ashburton Showgrounds
**Capacity:** 10,000
**Colours:** Forest green and gold

## RECORDS

| | | |
|---|---|---|
| **Highest attendance** | 8656 | *Mid Canterbury v British Isles, 1983* |
| **Most appearances** | 158 | *J.C. Ross, 1970–87* |
| **Most points** | 598 | *A.H.A. Smith, 1955–68* |
| **Most tries** | 47 | *G.R. Bryant, 1968–77* |
| **Most points in a season** | 200 | *S.R. Middleton, 1994* |
| **Most tries in a season** | 13 | *M.L. Sau, 2017* |
| **Most conversions in a season** | 34 | *S.R. Middleton, 1994* |
| | | *J.R. Percival, 2017* |
| **Most penalty goals in a season** | 44 | *S.R. Middleton, 1994* |
| **Most dropped goals in a season** | 12 | *M.B. Roulston, 1982* |
| **Most points in a match** | 22 | *M.C. Williams v East Coast, 2014* |
| **Most tries in a match** | 5 | *G.R. Bryant v Nelson Bays, 1977* |
| **Most conversions in a match** | 8 | *S.R. Middleton v West Coast, 1998* |
| **Most penalty goals in a match** | 6 | *S.R. Middleton v Horowhenua Kapiti, 1998* |
| | | *D.J. Maw v West Coast, 2007* |
| | | *M.C. Williams v Wanganui, 2014* |
| **Highest team score** | 90 | *v West Coast, 1998* |
| **Record victory (points ahead)** | 77 | *90–13 v West Coast, 1998* |
| **Highest score conceded** | 99 | *v Hawke's Bay, 2003* |
| **Record defeat (points behind)** | 91 | *8–99 v Hawke's Bay, 2003* |

The Hammers finished the season as Lochore Cup winners in a memorable final against West Coast 47–15 despite having to play with only 14 men for 76 minutes due to a red card, and from 0–10 down.

After losing two of their first three Heartland Championship matches everything suddenly clicked against Wairarapa Bush and from then on Mid Canterbury proved irresistible. Wanganui was defeated in a thriller, but somehow Mid Canterbury contrived to lose to Buller despite leading 29–13 at halftime, and this ultimately cost the Hammers a place in the top four and a shot at the Meads Cup on points differential. Nevertheless, the loss proved to be the only defeat in the final seven matches of the season where they were given licence to attack from anywhere.

Regulars missing from 2016 were Richard Catherwood (Canterbury), Tavita Ula, Jon Dampney (both retired), Kody Nordquist (not playing) and Mike Lynch (returned to Ireland). An arrival with previous first-class experience was Jason Kjestrup who had represented Wairarapa Bush in 2009.

The forwards gave a good account of themselves, although they struggled a bit against the bigger North Otago, South Canterbury and Wanganui packs. Lock Eric Duff was again in excellent form in the lineout and all-round play, and the other outstanding forward was Seta Koroitamana back at flanker, having been placed at wing last year. After shaking off a niggling injury, he turned in a number of fine displays but does need to look at his discipline after picking up three yellow cards to incur an automatic one-game suspension.

Angus Lindsay, in his second season, showed tremendous development at lock, and Sam Finau, Phil Watson and captain Jackson Donlan started every game.

The two stars of the backline were Jarred Percival and Maleli Sau, both showing top form from first game to the last. Percival's attacking game and impressive goal-kicking returned him 140 points. His last-minute penalty goal to win the Wanganui match was from just inside halfway and into the wind. The fast, elusive Sau ended the season scoring 13 tries to set a new season record for Mid Canterbury and was also top try-scorer in the Heartland Championship. Only the red card he sustained in the final, in just the fourth minute, prevented him from adding to his tally of tries and the subsequent three-week suspension forced his withdrawal from the NZ Heartland team.

Wing Willie McGoon made a late start recovering from injury, and although he has lost a little pace, he was still a powerful runner and scored eight tries in his eight matches. Will MacKenzie had a sharp pass at halfback but suffered the misfortune of a broken arm in the semi-final and 19-year-old Tom Hanham-Carter showed a great deal of promise at centre.

Regan King, a 2002 All Black, arrived back in the country at the end of 2016 after a long career overseas and through his friendship with Mid Canterbury co-coach Craig Dunlea, having played together in Wales, linked up with the Southern club who won the Mid Canterbury championship. For the Hammers, King was a very good organiser of the backline, featuring more as a link rather than an attacker, setting up his outsides well. He was unavailable for the last three matches.

Higher honours went to:
**New Zealand Heartland:**   E. Duff, S. Koroitamana, W. McGoon, J. Percival

## MID CANTERBURY REPRESENTATIVES 2017

| | Club | Games for Union | Points for Union | | Club | Games for Union | Points for Union |
|---|---|---|---|---|---|---|---|
| Mark Andrew | Rakaia | 21 | 0 | Will MacKenzie | Southern | 57 | 0 |
| Matt Bentley | Rakaia | 4 | 0 | Isireli Masiwini | Celtic | 6 | 0 |
| Tyler Blackburn | Methven | 17 | 5 | David Maw | Methven | 46 | 340 |
| Nete Caucau | Rakaia | 37 | 35 | Willie McGoon | Rakaia | 21 | 80 |
| Jackson Donlan | Rakaia | 38 | 16 | Phil Mills | Celtic | 11 | 0 |
| Eric Duff | Southern | 40 | 26 | Timoci Nabakeke | Rakaia | 12 | 18 |
| Rupert Elworthy | Lincoln University [2] | 2 | 0 | Jarred Percival | Celtic | 20 | 244 |
| Sam Finau | Mt Wellington [3] | 11 | 20 | Kurt Polson | Celtic | 9 | 5 |
| Dan Fransen | Rakaia | 6 | 5 | Maleli Sau | Rakaia | 17 | 83 |
| Tom Hanham-Carter | Rakaia | 7 | 10 | Adam Stewart | Methven | 10 | 0 |
| Tom Heywood | Rakaia | 7 | 0 | Carisbrook To'omalatai | New Brighton [2] | 7 | 0 |
| Regan King | Southern | 8 | 10 | Christian Vainerere | Celtic | 19 | 33 |
| Jason Kjestrup | Methven | 8 | 5 | Dominic Vesesio | Celtic | 11 | 0 |
| Seta Koroitamana | Rakaia | 41 | 113 | Phil Watson [1] | Shirley [2] | 17 | 6 |
| Angus Lindsay | Celtic | 14 | 20 | Adam Williamson | Southern | 14 | 0 |
| Hamish MacKenzie | Southern | 4 | 0 | | | | |

[1] Player of Origin      [2] Canterbury RU      [3] Auckland RU

## INDIVIDUAL SCORING

| | Tries | Con | PG | DG | Points | | Tries | Con | PG | DG | Points |
|---|---|---|---|---|---|---|---|---|---|---|---|
| Percival | 3 | 34 | 18 | 1 | 140 | Donlan | 1 | – | – | – | 5 |
| Sau | 13 | – | – | – | 65 | Duff | 1 | – | – | – | 5 |
| McGoon | 9 | – | – | – | 45 | Caucau | 1 | – | – | – | 5 |
| Koroitamana | 5 | – | – | – | 25 | Polson | 1 | – | – | – | 5 |
| Finau | 4 | – | – | – | 20 | Blackburn | 1 | – | – | – | 5 |
| Lindsay | 4 | – | – | – | 20 | Fransen | 1 | – | – | – | 5 |
| Vainerere | 3 | – | – | – | 15 | | | | | | |
| King | 2 | – | – | – | 10 | **Totals** | **51** | **35** | **19** | **1** | **385** |
| Hanham-Carter | 2 | – | – | – | 10 | | | | | | |
| Kjestrup | – | 1 | 1 | – | 5 | Opposition scored | 47 | 30 | 11 | 0 | 330 |

## MID CANTERBURY 2017

| | Canterbury | Poverty Bay | North Otago | South Canterbury | Wairarapa Bush | Wanganui | Thames Valley | Buller | King Country | Poverty Bay | West Coast | TOTALS |
|---|---|---|---|---|---|---|---|---|---|---|---|---|
| M.L. Sau | s | 14 | 14 | 14 | 14 | 15 | 15 | 15 | – | 15 | 15 | 10 |
| D.J. Fransen | 14 | s | s | – | – | – | – | – | s | s | s | 6 |
| C.T. Vainerere | 11 | s | 11 | 11 | s | 14 | 14 | 14 | 14 | 14 | 14 | 11 |
| I. Masiwini | s | 11 | – | – | – | – | s | – | s | s | s | 6 |
| T.N. Nabakeke | – | – | s | s | s | – | – | – | – | – | – | 3 |
| W.B. McGoon | – | – | – | s | 11 | 11 | 11 | 11 | 11 | 11 | 11 | 8 |
| R.M. King | 13 | 12 | 12 | 13 | 13 | 13 | 13 | 13 | – | – | – | 8 |
| T.K. Hanham-Carter | – | 13 | 13 | – | – | – | s | s | 13 | 13 | 13 | 7 |
| R.N. Caucau | 12 | – | – | 12 | 12 | 12 | 12 | 12 | 12 | 12 | 12 | 9 |
| J.R. Percival | 15 | 15 | 15 | 15 | 15 | 10 | 10 | 10 | 10 | 10 | 10 | 11 |
| J.N. Kjestrup | 10 | 10 | 10 | 10 | 10 | s | – | s | 15 | – | – | 8 |
| A.W. MacKenzie | 9 | 9 | 9 | – | 9 | 9 | 9 | 9 | 9 | 9 | – | 10 |
| T.A.C. Blackburn | s | s | s | 9 | s | s | s | s | s | s | 9 | 11 |
| D.J. Maw | – | – | – | – | – | – | – | – | – | – | s | 1 |
| V.S. Finau | 8 | 8 | 8 | 8 | 8 | 8 | 8 | 8 | 8 | 8 | 8 | 11 |
| S.S. Koroitamana | 7 | s | s | s | 7 | 7 | 7 | 7 | – | 7 | 7 | 10 |
| K.R. Polson | s | 7 | s | 7 | s | – | s | s | 7 | – | s | 9 |
| H.I. MacKenzie | – | s | 7 | – | – | s | – | – | – | s | – | 4 |
| P.M. Watson | 6 | 6 | 6 | 6 | 6 | 6 | 6 | 6 | 6 | 6 | 6 | 11 |
| A.J. Lindsay | 5 | 5 | 5 | 5 | 5 | 5 | 5 | 5 | 5 | 5 | 5 | 11 |
| E.J. Duff | 4 | 4 | 4 | 4 | 4 | 4 | 4 | 4 | 4 | 4 | 4 | 11 |
| M.J. Bentley | s | – | – | – | – | – | s | – | – | s | s | 4 |
| R.J.C. Elworthy | – | – | – | s | s | – | – | – | – | – | – | 2 |
| A.J. Stewart | 3 | 3 | 3 | 3 | 1 | – | 1 | 1 | 1 | 1 | 1 | 10 |
| M.W. Andrew | 1 | 1 | 1 | – | – | – | – | – | – | – | – | 3 |
| T.J. Heywood | s | – | – | – | – | 1 | s | s | s | s | s | 7 |
| A.C.J. Williamson | s | s | s | 1 | – | – | – | – | – | – | – | 4 |
| D. Vesesio | – | – | – | s | s | s | – | – | – | – | – | 3 |
| C.G. To'omalatai | – | – | – | – | 3 | 3 | 3 | 3 | 3 | 3 | 3 | 7 |
| J.L. Donlan (capt) | 2 | 2 | 2 | 2 | 2 | 2 | 2 | 2 | 2 | 2 | 2 | 11 |
| P.J. Mills | s | s | s | s | s | s | s | s | s | s | s | 11 |

## MID CANTERBURY TEAM RECORD, 2017

Played 11   Won 7   Lost 4   Points for 385   Points against 330

| Date | Opponent | Location | Score | Tries | Con | PG | DG | Referee |
|---|---|---|---|---|---|---|---|---|
| August 4 | Canterbury (RS) | Ashburton | 7–69 | Sau | Kjestrup | | | J.J. Doleman |
| August 26 | Poverty Bay (H) | Ashburton | 34–5 | Koroitamana (2), Sau, Donlan, Percival | Percival (3) | Percival | | J.D. Munro |
| September 2 | North Otago (H) | Oamaru | 25–31 | Sau (2), Finau | Percival (2) | Percival (2) | | R.J.M. Gordon |
| September 9 | South Canterbury (H) (HS) | Ashburton | 16–31 | Duff, Sau | | Percival (2) | | N.J. Webster |
| September 16 | Wairarapa Bush (H) | Masterton | 60–24 | McGoon (2), King (2), Koroitamana, Caucau, Polson, Sau, Lindsay | Percival (6) | Percival | | H.G. Reec |
| September 23 | Wanganui (H) | Ashburton | 40–39 | Sau (2), Vainerere, McGoon | Percival (4) | Percival (4) | | N.J. Webster |
| September 30 | Thames Valley (H) | Paeroa | 25–16 | McGoon, Percival, Vainerere | Percival (2) | Percival (2) | | T.N. Griffiths |
| October 7 | Buller (H) | Ashburton | 32–40 | Sau (3), Lindsay | Percival (3) | Percival, Kjestrup | | B.J. Jurlina |
| October 14 | King Country (H) | Taupo | 43–38 | Lindsay (2), Finau, Hanham-Carter, Percival, McGoon | Percival (5) | Percival | | J.T. Bell |
| October 21 | Poverty Bay (LC semi-final) | Ashburton | 56–22 | McGoon (3), Sau (2), Finau (2), Blackburn | Percival (5) | Percival (2) | | T.N. Griffiths |
| October 29 | West Coast (LC final) | Methven | 47–15 | Koroitamana (2), Hanham-Carter, Vainerere, McGoon, Fransen | Percival (4) | Percival (2) | Percival | J.D. Munro |

RS *Ranfurty Shield* HS *Hanan Shield*

# NORTH HARBOUR

**2017 Status:** Mitre 10 Cup Premiership
**Founded 1985.** Affiliated 1985
**President:** R.J. (Richard) Kidd
**Chairman:** S.R. (Shaun) Nixon
**Chief executive officer:** B.J. (Brett) Hollister (to May)
**General Manager:** D.B. (David) Gibson (from June)
**Coach:** T.J. (Tom) Coventry
**Assistant coach:** D.K. (Daniel) Halangahu
**Main ground:** North Harbour Stadium, Albany
**Capacity:** 25,000
**Colours:** White, black and cardinal

## RECORDS

| | | |
|---|---|---|
| Most appearances | 145 | *Ron Williams, 1985–94* |
| | | *Walter Little, 1987–2000* |
| Most points | 1052 | *Warren Burton, 1990–96* |
| Most tries | 63 | *Richard Kapa, 1985–93* |
| Most points in a season | 258 | *Warren Burton, 1995* |
| Most tries in a season | 16 | *Glenn Davis, 1999* |
| Most conversions in a season | 53 | *Warren Burton, 1991* |
| Most penalty goals in a season | 47 | *Warren Burton, 1995* |
| Most dropped goals in a season | 3 | *Jamie Cameron, 1991* |
| Most points in a match | 34 | *Frano Botica v Queensland Country, 1985* |
| Most tries in a match | 5 | *Glenn Davis v Poverty Bay-East Coast, 1999* |
| | | *Tevita Li v Taranaki, 2017* |
| Most conversions in a match | 10 | *Frano Botica v Taranaki, 1989* |
| | | *Jamie Cameron Cameron v Marlborough, 1990* |
| | | *Warren Burton v Wanganui, 1991* |
| Most penalty goals in a match | 6 | *Warren Burton v Counties, 1990* |
| | | *Warren Burton v Wellington, 1990* |
| | | *Warren Burton v Otago, 1994* |
| | | *Warren Burton v Hawke's Bay, 1996* |
| Highest team score | 99 | *v Horowhenua Kapiti, 2008* |
| Record victory (points ahead) | 93 | *99–6 v Horowhenua Kapiti, 2008* |
| Highest score conceded | 71 | *v Auckland, 1995* |
| Record defeat (points behind) | 55 | *10–65 v Canterbury 2002* |

North Harbour continued its resurgence, following last year's promotion, with a third-place finish in the Premiership round robin. In the semi-final defeat North Harbour caused plenty of problems for eventual champions Canterbury, just as they had done in the round robin match, while the comprehensive win over neighbour Auckland would have been an extremely satisfying result to the union.

Their defence was the best in the Mitre 10 Cup round robin, conceding the least number of tries and points. It was only the fewer bonus points than both Taranaki and Canterbury earned for scoring four tries in a match that accounted for North Harbour finishing behind those two, as all three teams lost just two matches.

The new coach Tom Coventry had the majority of last year's regulars available to him with the only departures being Matthew McGahan, Michael Little, Chris Vui and Nick Mayhew all to overseas. In addition, Rene Ranger returned to Northland having not played a single game for North Harbour in his two years with the union due to injury.

To compensate for each of these losses, the union recruited well with the signings of Shaun Stevenson (Waikato), former Wellington/Highlanders rep Shaun Treeby returned from South Africa during the season, Fijian international Ben Volavola, former All Black Jarrod Hoeata from overseas and Chris Eves (Manawatu) who had made his first-class debut for North Harbour in 2008. Also arriving in were Shane Neville (Northland) and Steven Misa (Waikato).

The forward pack was a very capable one with co-captain and hooker James Parsons leading the forwards by example and part of a front row with props Chris Eves and newcomer Michael Tamoaieta that always gave a good account of itself. Tamoaieta showed great promise, keeping out last year's first-choice tighthead Sione Mafileo. Jarrad Hoeata and Gerard Cowley-Tuioti were a fine locking pair, with Hoeata bringing a good physical edge to endeavours. Brandon Nansen was a useful versatile forward who could cover both lock and loose forward.

Last year's loose forward trio of Murphy Taramai, Connor Collett and Glenn Preston were again to the fore, working hard all year and proving very effective at the breakdown, with Taramai, in particular, standing out.

The backline combined very well together. Halfback Bryn Hall gave some fine displays, proving a splendid link between the forwards and backs. The experienced Chris Smylie was also good value. First five-eighth Bryn Gatland had his best season to date, taking on the line more, quick to get the ball to his outsides and an accurate goal-kicker. He missed the semi-final with injury, although Ben Volavola gave a good account of himself in the match.

Harrison Groundwater started at second five-eighth until injured, which coincided with the arrival of the experienced Shaun Treeby who also then suffered the same fate. Matthew Vaega had a very good season at centre, being able to set up his wings superbly, tackle strongly and score five tries.

The back three of Shaun Stevenson, Matt Duffie and Tevita Li was a very dangerous one with their strong running, counter-attacking and finishing to score 24 of North Harbour's 42 tries between them. Fullback Stevenson showed plenty of enterprise from the back in every match without neglecting defensive duties, while Tevita Li topped the try-scoring in the Mitre 10 competition with 11, including equalling the competition record with five in one game against Taranaki. Co-captain Matt Duffie had a very consistent good all-round season, exhibiting outstanding ability under the high ball, either chasing or defending. He finished well when opportunities presented and his versatility between wing and fullback also helped earn him selection for the All Blacks on the end-of-year tour.

Higher honours went to:
*New Zealand*:          M. Duffie
*New Zealand Maori:*   C. Eves, B. Hall, J. Hoeata, S. Stevenson

## INDIVIDUAL SCORING

| | Tries | Con | PG | DG | Points | | Tries | Con | PG | DG | Points |
|---|---|---|---|---|---|---|---|---|---|---|---|
| Gatland | – | 18 | 20 | – | 96 | Cowley-Tuioti | 1 | – | – | – | 5 |
| Volavola | 3 | 11 | 7 | – | 58 | Groundwater | 1 | – | – | – | 5 |
| Li | 11 | – | – | – | 55 | Hall | 1 | – | – | – | 5 |
| Stevenson | 7 | – | – | – | 35 | Taramai | 1 | – | – | – | 5 |
| Duffie | 6 | – | – | – | 30 | Doolan | – | 2 | – | – | 4 |
| Vaega | 5 | – | – | – | 25 | | | | | | |
| Eves | 2 | – | – | – | 10 | **Totals** | **42** | **31** | **27** | **0** | **355** |
| Parsons | 2 | – | – | – | 10 | | | | | | |
| Penalty Try | 1 | – | – | – | 7 | *Opposition scored* | 29 | 24 | 21 | 0 | 258 |
| Mafileo | 1 | – | – | – | 5 | | | | | | |

## NORTH HARBOUR REPRESENTATIVES 2017

| | Club | Games for Union | Points for Union | | Club | Games for Union | Points for Union |
|---|---|---|---|---|---|---|---|
| Connor Collett | Massey | 19 | 5 | Shane Neville | Takapuna | 7 | 0 |
| Gerard Cowley-Tuioti | Massey | 36 | 10 | James Parsons | Takapuna | 93 | 80 |
| Todd Doolan | Kumeu | 1 | 4 | Glenn Preston | Marist | 25 | 5 |
| Matt Duffie | Takapuna | 21 | 50 | Mark Royal | Massey | 1 | 0 |
| Chris Eves | Kia Toa [1] | 13 | 15 | Adrian Smith | Massey | 27 | 10 |
| Bryn Gatland | Takapuna | 21 | 219 | Chris Smylie | Massey | 71 | 45 |
| Lewis Gjaltema | East Coast Bays | 3 | 0 | Shaun Stevenson | Marist | 11 | 35 |
| Harrison Groundwater | East Coast Bays | 7 | 5 | Michael Tamoaieta | Mahurangi | 11 | 0 |
| Bryn Hall | Northcote | 58 | 62 | Murphy Taramai | Northcote | 22 | 5 |
| Daniel Hilton-Jones | North Shore | 16 | 5 | Mark Telea | Massey | 8 | 0 |
| Jarrad Hoeata | North Shore | 10 | 0 | Shaun Treeby [2] | | 5 | 0 |
| Tevita Li | Massey | 45 | 130 | Karl Tu'inukuafe | Takapuna | 17 | 5 |
| Sione Mafileo | North Shore | 33 | 10 | Josh Tyrell | Takapuna | 10 | 0 |
| Steven Misa | Takapuna | 6 | 0 | Matthew Vaega | Massey | 38 | 67 |
| Hapakuki Moala-Liava'a | Massey | 21 | 0 | Ben Volavola | North Shore | 10 | 58 |
| Brandon Nansen | North Shore | 38 | 5 | | | | |

[1] Manawatu RU     [2] Returned from overseas

| NORTH HARBOUR 2017 | Otago | Southland | Auckland | Counties Manukau | Northland | Canterbury | Hawke's Bay | Tasman | Waikato | Taranaki | Canterbury | TOTALS |
|---|---|---|---|---|---|---|---|---|---|---|---|---|
| S.T. Stevenson | 15 | 15 | 15 | s | 15 | 11 | 15 | 14 | 14 | 15 | 15 | 11 |
| M.D. Duffie (co-capt) | 14 | 14 | 14 | – | 14 | 14 | 14 | 15 | 15 | 14 | 14 | 10 |
| T. Li | 11 | 11 | 11 | 11 | 11 | – | 11 | 11 | 11 | 11 | 11 | 9 |
| M.E. Telea | – | s | – | 14 | – | s | 11 | – | – | – | – | 4 |
| M.D. Vaega | 13 | 13 | 13 | 13 | 13 | 13 | 13 | 13 | 13 | 13 | 13 | 11 |
| D.P. Hilton-Jones | 12 | – | s | s | – | – | – | s | s | 12 | – | 6 |
| H.H. Groundwater | – | 12 | 12 | 12 | 12 | 12 | – | – | – | s | 12 | 7 |
| S.J. Treeby | – | – | – | – | s | s | 12 | 12 | 12 | – | – | 5 |
| B.E.C. Gatland | 10 | 10 | 10 | 10 | 10 | 10 | 10 | s | 10 | – | – | 9 |
| B.T. Volavola | – | s | s | 15 | s | 15 | s | 10 | s | 10 | 10 | 10 |
| T. Doolan | – | – | – | – | – | – | – | – | – | s | – | 1 |
| C.B. Smylie | 9 | s | s | s | – | s | s | 9 | s | s | 9 | 10 |
| L.M. Gjaltema | s | – | – | – | – | – | – | s | – | – | s | 3 |
| B.D. Hall | – | 9 | 9 | 9 | 9 | 9 | 9 | – | 9 | 9 | – | 8 |
| H. Moala-Liava'a | – | – | s | 8 | 8 | 8 | 8 | – | 8 | s | s | 8 |
| J.I. Tyrell | s | s | 8 | – | – | s | – | 8 | – | – | – | 5 |
| M.V.U. Taramai | 8 | 8 | 7 | – | 7 | 7 | s | 7 | 7 | 8 | 8 | 10 |
| C.N.D. Collett | 7 | 7 | – | 7 | s | – | 7 | – | s | 7 | 7 | 8 |
| G.L. Preston | 6 | 6 | 6 | 6 | 6 | 6 | 6 | s | 6 | 6 | 6 | 11 |
| J.M.R.A. Hoeata | 5 | 5 | 5 | 4 | 4 | – | 5 | 5 | 5 | 5 | 5 | 10 |
| G.E. Cowley-Tuioti | 4 | – | 4 | 5 | 5 | 4 | 4 | s | 4 | 4 | – | 9 |
| B.J.T. Nansen | s | 4 | s | s | s | 5 | s | 6 | s | s | 4 | 11 |
| S.G. Neville | – | s | – | s | – | s | – | 4 | – | – | s | 5 |
| M. Tamoaieta | 3 | 3 | 3 | s | 3 | 3 | s | 3 | 3 | 3 | 3 | 11 |
| S.T. Mafileo | s | s | s | 3 | 3 | s | 3 | s | – | – | s | 9 |
| C.I. Eves | 1 | 1 | 1 | 1 | 1 | 1 | s | 1 | 1 | 1 | 1 | 11 |
| M.J.T.K.T.R. Royal | – | s | – | – | – | – | – | – | – | – | – | 1 |
| G.Z.K. Tu'inukuafe | – | – | s | s | s | s | 1 | s | s | s | s | 9 |
| J.W. Parsons (co-capt) | 2 | 2 | 2 | 2 | 2 | 2 | 2 | s | 2 | 2 | 2 | 11 |
| A.A.V. Smith | s | s | s | – | – | – | – | – | s | s | – | 5 |
| S. Misa | – | – | – | s | s | s | – | 2 | s | s | – | 6 |

## NORTH HARBOUR TEAM RECORD, 2017

Played 11  Won 8  Lost 3  Points for 355  Points against 258

| Date | Opponent | Location | Score | Tries | Con | PG | DG | Referee |
|---|---|---|---|---|---|---|---|---|
| August 17 | Otago (P/C) | Albany | 19–17 | Stevenson | Gatland | Gatland (4) | | G.W. Jackson |
| August 24 | Southland (P/C) | Invercargill | 45–20 | Vaega (2), Li (2), Eves, Stevenson | Gatland (2), Volavola | Gatland (2), Volavola | | J.R. Nutbrown |
| September 3 | Auckland (P) | Albany | 57–10 | Stevenson (2), Li (2), Duffie, Parsons, Volavola | Gatland (5) | Gatland (4) | | G.W. Jackson |
| September 7 | Counties Manukau (P) | Pukekohe | 27–18 | Mafileo, Li | Gatland | Volavola (4), Gatland | | J.J. Doleman |
| September 14 | Northland (P/C) | Whangarei | 31–22 | Li, Volavola, Vaega | Gatland (2) | Gatland (4) | | M.C.J. Winter |
| September 23 | Canterbury (P) | Albany | 28–41 | Duffie, Cowley-Tuioti, Groundwater, Stevenson | Gatland (4) | | | A.W.B. Mabey |
| September 29 | Hawke's Bay (P/C) | Albany | 33–30 | Penalty Try, Stevenson, Duffie | Gatland (2) | Gatland (4) | | R.P. Kelly |
| October 4 | Tasman (P) | Blenheim | 14–21 | Duffie, Vaega | Volavola, Gatland | | | J.R. Nutbrown |
| October 8 | Waikato (P) | Hamilton | 13–11 | Duffie | Volavola | Gatland, Volavola | | S.W. McDermott |
| October 15 | Taranaki (P) | Albany | 64–33 | Li (5), Hall, Stevenson, Duffie, Parsons, Vaega | Volavola (5), Doolan (2) | | | S.W. McDermott |
| October 21 | Canterbury (P semi-final) | Christchurch | 24–35 | Volavola, Eves, Taramai | Volavola (3) | Volavola | | B.D. O'Keeffe |

# NORTH OTAGO

**2017 Status:** Heartland
**Founded 1904.** Affiliated 1927
**President:** D.J.L. (David) Douglas
**Chairman:** W.L. (Warren) Prescott
**Chief executive officer:** C.S. (Colin) Jackson
**Coach:** N.G. (Nigel) Walsh
**Assistant coach:** J.A. (Jason) Forrest
**Main ground:** Centennial Park, Oamaru
**Capacity:** 7000
**Colours:** Gold and maroon

## RECORDS

| | | |
|---|---|---|
| Highest attendance | 6500 | *North Otago v Marlborough (Div 3 final), 1997* |
| Most appearances | 123 | *M.J. Mavor, 1995–2009* |
| Most points | 429 | *P.M. Ford, 1964–74* |
| Most tries | 39 | *V.T. Fifita, 2000–04* |
| Most points in a season | 159 | *S.M. Porter, 2002* |
| Most tries in a season | 15 | *V.T. Fifita, 2002* |
| Most conversions in a season | 42 | *M. Adair, 2005* |
| Most penalty goals in a season | 30 | *C.J.W. Finch, 1997* |
| | | *S.M. Porter, 2000* |
| Most dropped goals in a season | 4 | *M.E. Kenworthy, 1986* |
| Most points in a match | 28 | *C.J.W. Finch v Poverty Bay, 1998* |
| | | *S.M. Porter v Poverty Bay, 2000* |
| Most tries in a match | 5 | *L.M. Herden v East Coast, 2010* |
| Most conversions in a match | 9 | *B. Patston v East Coast, 2010* |
| Most penalty goals in a match | 7 | *C.J.W. Finch v South Canterbury, 1998* |
| Highest team score | 116 | *v East Coast, 2010* |
| Record victory (points ahead) | 113 | *116–3 v East Coast, 2010* |
| Highest score conceded | 139 | *v Auckland, 1993* |
| Record defeat (points behind) | 134 | *5–139 v Auckland, 1993* |

North Otago finished the round robin seventh with four wins from eight matches, a small improvement on last year, but their efforts were better than the record suggests. Leads against Horowhenua Kapiti and Buller slipped away in the final few minutes, they were totally dominant in the last 10 minutes against table-topping South Canterbury but just could not score an equalising try, and lost by four points to Wanganui in a very physical match where only one try was scored.

Fielding a bigger pack than in recent years, the forwards laid a good foundation, ensuring plenty of possession. The scrum was one of the best in the Heartland Championship and tighthead prop Meli Kolinisau was one of the best scrummagers in the competition. Loosehead prop Ralph Darling was at his industrious best, making many of his trademark charges. First-choice hooker, and original captain, Sam Sturgess had a season beset with injury.

Josh Clark returned on loan, appearing at both lock and loose forward, and was always full value, winning a lot of lineout ball, while newcomer Tom MacDonald had a satisfactory debut at lock. At number eight Mika Mafi was in devastating form, showing all his strength and experience to regularly get over the advantage line and never shirked his defensive duties.

The backline did suffer from a lack of finishing ability. Former NZ Schools rep Josh Buchan displayed fine all-round form at fullback, scoring four tries, and was also an accomplished goal-kicker. Lemi Masoe is still an able footballer even though he has lost some his pace and had good games against King Country and South Canterbury.

Englishman Dan Lewis started well at first five-eighth until injury struck. Antini Brown took over and displayed good control so that when Lewis returned the coach preferred to use him as impact off the bench. Both were well served by Robbie Smith at halfback.

Higher honours went to:
**New Zealand Heartland:**    R.K. Darling, M. Kolinisau

## NORTH OTAGO REPRESENTATIVES 2017

| | Club | Games for Union | Points for Union | | Club | Games for Union | Points for Union |
|---|---|---|---|---|---|---|---|
| Antini Brown | Athletic Marist | 8 | 5 | Lio Lolo | [3] | 4 | 5 |
| Joshua Buchan [1] | Southern [2] | 9 | 71 | Sosefo Ma'ake | Oamaru Old Boys | 3 | 0 |
| Timoci Bulitavu | Athletic Marist | 1 | 0 | Tom MacDonald | Excelsior | 7 | 0 |
| Joshua Clark | Southern [2] | 25 | 5 | Mikaele Mafi | Southern [2] | 7 | 10 |
| Ralph Darling | Oamaru Old Boys | 91 | 58 | John Marsters | Kurow | 1 | 0 |
| Morgan Dawes | Excelsior | 4 | 0 | Aaron Martin | Excelsior | 5 | 5 |
| Matthew Duff | Excelsior | 41 | 11 | Lemisio Masoe | Oamaru Old Boys | 94 | 124 |
| Junior Fakatoufifita | Athletic Marist | 8 | 10 | Inoke Naufahu | Oamaru Old Boys | 11 | 15 |
| Harvard Fale | Kurow | 3 | 0 | Connor Newlands | Athletic Marist | 5 | 5 |
| Lisala Halaleva | Harbour [2] | 13 | 50 | Robert "Oscar" Pamment | Excelsior | 18 | 15 |
| Adam Johnson | Maheno | 2 | 0 | Joe Pickett | Excelsior | 18 | 6 |
| Anthony Kent | Excelsior | 3 | 0 | Petelo Pouhila | Kurow | 7 | 10 |
| Melikisua Kolinisau | Valley | 26 | 0 | Robert Smith | Maheno | 39 | 37 |
| Mike Lawrence | Maheno | 1 | 0 | Sam Sturgess | Valley | 14 | 15 |
| Dan Lewis | Valley | 7 | 60 | Filipo Veamatahau | Oamaru Old Boys | 26 | 17 |
| Simon Lilicama | Athletic Marist | 11 | 42 | Matthew Vocea | Valley | 23 | 66 |
| Don Lolo | Oamaru Old Boys | 5 | 15 | Jared Whitburn | Athletic Marist | 24 | 11 |

[1] Player of Origin        [2] Otago RU        [3] Arrived from overseas

## INDIVIDUAL SCORING

| | Tries | Con | PG | DG | Points | | Tries | Con | PG | DG | Points |
|---|---|---|---|---|---|---|---|---|---|---|---|
| Buchan | 4 | 15 | 7 | – | 71 | Brown | 1 | – | – | – | 5 |
| Lewis | 4 | 11 | 6 | – | 60 | Martin | 1 | – | – | – | 5 |
| Masoe | 3 | – | 1 | – | 18 | Newlands | 1 | – | – | – | 5 |
| Vocea | 3 | – | – | – | 15 | L. Lolo | 1 | – | – | – | 5 |
| Halaleva | 2 | – | – | – | 10 | Whitburn | 1 | – | – | – | 5 |
| Mafi | 2 | – | – | – | 10 | Naufahu | 1 | – | – | – | 5 |
| Fakatoufifita | 2 | – | – | – | 10 | | | | | | |
| D. Lolo | 2 | – | – | – | 10 | **Totals** | **31** | **26** | **14** | **0** | **249** |
| Pouhila | 2 | – | – | – | 10 | | | | | | |
| Darling | 1 | – | – | – | 5 | Opposition scored | 26 | 18 | 11 | 1 | 202 |

| NORTH OTAGO 2017 | Horowhenua Kapiti | Mid Canterbury | Buller | King Country | South Canterbury | Poverty Bay | East Coast | Wanganui | West Coast | TOTALS |
|---|---|---|---|---|---|---|---|---|---|---|
| J.S. Buchan | 15 | 15 | 15 | 15 | 15 | 15 | 15 | 15 | 15 | 9 |
| J.D. Marsters | 14 | – | – | – | – | – | – | – | – | 1 |
| A.S. Martin | – | 14 | 14 | – | 14 | 14 | – | – | s | 5 |
| A.G. Johnson | – | – | s | 14 | – | – | – | – | – | 2 |
| C. Newlands | – | – | – | – | – | – | 14 | 14 | s | 3 |
| S. Lilicama | – | – | – | – | – | – | – | s | – | 1 |
| M. Vocea | 11 | 11 | 11 | 11 | 11 | 11 | 11 | 11 | 11 | 9 |
| L.O. Halaleva | 13 | 13 | 13 | – | 13 | – | – | – | 14 | 5 |
| L. Masoe | 12 | 12 | s | 13 | 12 | 12 | 12 | 12 | 13 | 9 |
| R.I.J. Pamment | s | s | 12 | – | – | – | s | – | 12 | 5 |
| L. Lolo | – | – | – | 12 | – | 13 | 13 | 13 | – | 4 |
| D.W. Lewis | 10 | 10 | – | – | 10 | s | s | s | 10 | 7 |
| A. Brown | s | s | 10 | 10 | s | 10 | 10 | 10 | – | 8 |
| R.L. Smith | 9 | 9 | 9 | 9 | 9 | 9 | 9 | 9 | 9 | 9 |
| S. Ma'ake | s | s | s | – | – | – | – | – | – | 3 |
| I.L. Naufahu | – | – | – | – | – | – | s | – | – | 1 |
| M.T.T. Mafi | 8 | 8 | 8 | 8 | 8 | – | – | 8 | 8 | 7 |
| M.R.V. Duff | 7 | 7 | s | 7 | 7 | s | 7 | s | 7 | 9 |
| J. Fakatoufifita | 6 | s | 7 | s | s | 6 | s | – | s | 8 |
| F. Veamatahau | s | 6 | 6 | s | – | s | 8 | 6 | 6 | 8 |
| M.A. Dawes | – | s | – | – | – | 7 | 6 | 7 | – | 4 |
| J.A. Clark | 5 | 5 | 5 | 6 | 6 | 8 | 5 | 5 | 5 | 9 |
| T. MacDonald | 4 | 4 | 4 | 4 | 4 | 4 | – | 4 | – | 7 |
| D.E. Lolo | s | – | – | 5 | 5 | – | – | – | – | 3 |
| J.P. Whitburn | – | – | – | – | s | 5 | 4 | s | – | 4 |
| J.H. Fale | – | – | – | – | – | – | – | – | 4 | 1 |
| M. Lawrence | – | – | – | – | – | – | – | – | s | 1 |
| M. Kolinisau | 3 | 3 | 3 | 3 | 3 | 3 | 3 | 3 | 3 | 9 |
| R.K. Darling | 1 | 1 | 1 | 1 | 1 | 1 | 1 | 1 | 1 | 9 |
| P. Pouhila | s | s | s | s | s | 2 | – | – | s | 7 |
| A. Kent | – | – | – | – | s | – | s | – | s | 3 |
| S.W. Sturgess | 2 | – | 2 | – | – | s | 2 | 2 | – | 5 |
| J.D. Pickett | s | 2 | s | 2 | 2 | – | s | s | 2 | 8 |
| T. Bulitavu | – | s | – | – | – | – | – | – | – | 1 |

S.W. Sturgess captained v Horowhenua Kapiti; R.L. Smith and R.K. Darling co-captained the next four matches, with Darling sole captain in the final four matches.

## NORTH OTAGO TEAM RECORD, 2017

| | | | Played 9 | Won 4 | Lost 5 | Points for 249 | | Points against 202 |
|---|---|---|---|---|---|---|---|---|
| Date | Opponent | Location | Score | Tries | Con | PG | DG | Referee |
| August 26 | Horowhenua Kapiti (H) | Levin | 19–22 | Halaleva | Buchan | Buchan (3), Lewis | | N.E.R. Hogan |
| September 2 | Mid Canterbury (H) | Oamaru | 31–25 | Lewis (2), Masoe, Mafi | Lewis (4) | Lewis | | R.J.M. Gordon |
| September 9 | Buller (H) | Westport | 31–33 | Darling, Fakatouffita, Buchan, Brown | Buchan (4) | Buchan | | T.M.T. Cottrell |
| September 16 | King Country (H) | Oamaru | 28–26 | D. Lolo (2), Buchan | Lewis (2) | Lewis (3) | | V.F. Ringrose |
| September 23 | South Canterbury (H) (HS) | Timaru | 29–36 | Masoe (2), Lewis, Halaleva | Lewis (3) | Lewis | | R.J.M. Gordon |
| September 30 | Poverty Bay (H) | Oamaru | 34–12 | Pouhila, Vocea, Martin, Fakatouffita | Buchan (4) | Buchan, Masoe | | V.F. Ringrose |
| October 7 | East Coast (H) | Oamaru | 57–14 | Buchan (2), Vocea (2), Newlands, L. Lolo, Whitburn, Naufahu, Lewis | Buchan (6) | | | T.N. Griffiths |
| October 14 | Wanganui (H) | Wanganui | 6–10 | | | Buchan (2) | | T.M.T. Cottrell |
| October 21 | West Coast (LC semi-final) | Greymouth | 14–24 | Pouhila, Mafi | Lewis (2) | | | J.D. Munro |

HS *Hanan Shield*

# NORTHLAND

**2017 Status:** Mitre 10 Cup Championship
**Founded 1920** as North Auckland. Affiliated 1920.
Name changed to Northland 1994
**President:** S.L. (Sharon) Morgan
**Chairman:** A.C. (Ajit) Balasingham
**Chief executive officer:** A.K. (Alister) McGinn
**Coach:** D.J.C. (Derren) Witcombe
**Assistant coach:** D.J. (Dale) MacLeod
**Main ground:** Okara Park, Whangarei
**Capacity:** 24,000
**Colours:** Cambridge blue and navy blue

## RECORDS

| | | |
|---|---|---|
| Most appearances | 165 | *Joe Morgan, 1967–81* |
| Most points | 1656 | *Warren Johnston, 1986–97* |
| Most tries | 71 | *Norman Berryman, 1991–2003* |
| Most points in a season | 283 | *David Holwell, 1997* |
| Most tries in a season | 21 | *Norman Berryman, 1994* |
| Most conversions in a season | 85 | *David Holwell, 1997* |
| Most penalty goals in a season | 34 | *Warren Johnston, 1989* |
| Most dropped goals in a season | 10 | *Eddie Dunn, 1979* |
| Most points in a match | 38 | *David Holwell v Thames Valley, 1997* |
| Most tries in a match | 7 | *Norman Berryman v Wairarapa Bush, 1994* |
| Most conversions in a match | 14 | *David Holwell v Thames Valley, 1997* |
| Most penalty goals in a match | 6 | *Chippie Semenoff v Thames Valley, 1978* |
| | | *Warren Johnston v Wairarapa Bush, 1993* |
| | | *Warren Johnston v France, 1994* |
| | | *Warren Johnston v Wairarapa Bush, 1995* |
| | | *Ash Moeke v North Harbour, 2012* |
| | | *Dan Hawkins v North Harbour, 2014* |
| | | *Peter Breen v Otago, 2017* |
| Highest team score | 113 | *v Thames Valley, 1997* |
| Record victory (points ahead) | 99 | *113–14 v Thames Valley, 1997* |
| Highest score conceded | 84 | *v Otago, 1998* |
| Record defeat (points behind) | 74 | *10–84 v Otago, 1998* |

With four wins in 11 matches, Northland made a big improvement on the dismal performances of the two previous seasons when they had won just once in 20 matches. A spot in the Championship playoffs was achieved when Manawatu failed to beat Hawke's Bay on the last day of the regular season, and even though the semi-final ended in defeat to Wellington, the union and supporters will have been heartened by the team's efforts in 2017.

The side's best performance, for the second year in a row, was the convincing win over premiership team Waikato, while the loss to Manawatu was the most disappointing effort. The playing record could have been even better if it were not for a two-point loss to Auckland in a low-scoring game and a win against North Harbour slipping away upon conceding two converted tries in the last five minutes when leading 22–17.

Returning coach Derren Witcombe, last in the role in 2014, deserves much of the credit for the improved showing, with the major improvements in the team being the defence, the performance of the tight five, and the midfield. There was also more depth and experience to call on as of the 33 players used just seven were new to Northland colours, and four of those had previous first-class rugby with other provinces.

The scrum was one of the best in the Mitre 10 Cup, with the front row of Ross Wright, Matt Moulds and Ropate Rinakama all proving very effective at set piece and general play. Loosehead prop Wright has now played 82 games for Northland and was the outstanding forward to deservedly earn Maori All Blacks selection for the first time at the end of the year. Rinakama had last appeared in first-class rugby in 2013 for North Harbour and played so well at tighthead prop that he debuted for Fiji on their end-of-year tour. Being relieved of the captaincy seemed to energise Matt Moulds who was a good all-round mobile hooker.

Imports Tim Bond and Murray Douglas were an industrious pair at lock, and received good support from Josh Goodhue. Once again, the efforts of the loose forwards Dan and Kara Pryor, Jack Ram and Matt Matich was a strong point with all of them taking turns to shine during the course of the season.

The backline played very expansively with Solomon Alaimalo a very potent attacker from fullback who always seemed to find gaps and make a lot of metreage. Left wing Jone Macilai showed pace and strength to be top try-scorer while Jordan Hyland was a much improved player on the right wing.

Jack Goodhue was the star of the backline at second five-eighth, proving elusive on attack, solid in the tackle, and excellent in his distributing to earn All Blacks selection at the end of the year. Rene Ranger used all his considerable experience at centre to full advantage, their partnership in the midfield being a formidable one. At halfback Sam Nock had his best season yet, and combined well with both first five-eighths used in Dan Hawkins and Peter Breen.

Of last year's regulars, Warren Dunn (police force), Tom Robinson (injured), Shane Neville (North Harbour), Matt Talaese (France) and Waisea Lawabuka (visa issues) were all absent. All the signings in proved to be of good value: Rene Ranger (from North Harbour back to the province he represented with success 2006–13), Jack Goodhue (from Canterbury back to the province of his birth and early schooling), Tim Bond (Bay of Plenty), Ropate Rinakama (Auckland B last year), and Scotsman Murray Douglas (Melbourne Rebels).

Higher honours went to:

| | |
|---|---|
| **New Zealand:** | Jack Goodhue |
| **New Zealand Maori:** | D. Pryor, R. Wright |
| **New Zealand Under 20:** | T. Tua |

## NORTHLAND REPRESENTATIVES 2017

| | Club | Games for Union | Points for Union | | Club | Games for Union | Points for Union |
|---|---|---|---|---|---|---|---|
| Solomon Alaimalo | Otamatea | 21 | 30 | Matt Matich | Western Sharks | 19 | 20 |
| Chris Apoua | Mid Northern | 6 | 0 | Jaycob Matiu | Hora Hora | 17 | 0 |
| Tim Blundell | Mid Western | 3 | 2 | Matt Moulds | Otamatea | 45 | 15 |
| Tim Bond | Hikurangi | 8 | 5 | Sam Nock | Kerikeri | 27 | 17 |
| Peter Breen | OB Marist | 17 | 136 | Jordan Olsen | Mid Northern | 27 | 5 |
| Murray Douglas | Awanui | 10 | 0 | Emil Pittman | Mid Western | 2 | 0 |
| Michael Faleafa | Hikurangi | 12 | 10 | Dan Pryor | OB Marist | 63 | 65 |
| Jack Goodhue | United Kawakawa | 9 | 15 | Kara Pryor | OB Marist | 38 | 15 |
| Joshua Goodhue | Kamo | 22 | 15 | Jack Ram | Kerikeri | 40 | 35 |
| Dan Hawkins | Otamatea | 47 | 329 | Rene Ranger | Wellsford | 76 | 130 |
| Blake Hohaia | Kamo | 5 | 5 | Ropate Rinakama | Waipu | 10 | 0 |
| Jordan Hyland | Wellsford | 29 | 30 | Howard Sililoto | OB Marist | 31 | 10 |
| Phil Kite | OB Marist | 18 | 10 | Tamati Tua | Hikurangi | 16 | 0 |
| Josh Larsen | Mid Northern | 10 | 5 | Namatahi Wa'a | Hikurangi | 29 | 10 |
| Jone Macilai | Awanui | 36 | 60 | Matt Wright | Wellsford | 39 | 73 |
| Malcolm MacLeod | Mid Northern | 10 | 0 | Ross Wright | Wellsford | 82 | 25 |
| Matthew Markwick | OB Marist | 11 | 0 | | | | |

## INDIVIDUAL SCORING

| | Tries | Con | PG | DG | Points |
|---|---|---|---|---|---|
| Hawkins | – | 15 | 12 | – | 66 |
| Breen | – | 8 | 13 | – | 55 |
| Macilai | 5 | – | – | – | 25 |
| Ram | 4 | – | – | – | 20 |
| Hyland | 4 | – | – | – | 20 |
| Alaimalo | 4 | – | – | – | 20 |
| Jack Goodhue | 3 | – | – | – | 15 |
| D. Pryor | 3 | – | – | – | 15 |
| Nock | 2 | 1 | – | – | 12 |
| Sililoto | 1 | – | – | – | 5 |
| M. Wright | 1 | – | – | – | 5 |

| | Tries | Con | PG | DG | Points |
|---|---|---|---|---|---|
| Olsen | 1 | – | – | – | 5 |
| R.Wright | 1 | – | – | – | 5 |
| Hohaia | 1 | – | – | – | 5 |
| Ranger | 1 | – | – | – | 5 |
| Bond | 1 | – | – | – | 5 |
| Blundell | – | 1 | – | – | 2 |
| **Totals** | **32** | **25** | **25** | **0** | **285** |
| Opposition scored | 31 | 23 | 23 | 0 | 270 |

### NORTHLAND 2017

| | Bay of Plenty | Auckland | Southland | Waikato | North Harbour | Manawatu | Otago | Counties Manukau | Hawkes Bay | Wellington | Wellington | TOTALS |
|---|---|---|---|---|---|---|---|---|---|---|---|---|
| M.K. Wright | 15 | 15 | – | – | – | – | – | 15 | 11 | – | – | 4 |
| S. Alaimalo | 11 | 11 | 15 | 15 | 15 | 15 | 15 | 11 | 15 | 15 | 15 | 11 |
| J.S.C. Hyland | 14 | – | 14 | 14 | 14 | 14 | 14 | 14 | 14 | 14 | 14 | 10 |
| J. Macilai | s | s | 11 | 11 | 11 | 11 | 11 | – | – | 11 | 11 | 9 |
| R.M.N. Ranger | 13 | 14 | 13 | 13 | 13 | s | 13 | 13 | 13 | 13 | 13 | 11 |
| T.R. Tua | 12 | 12 | – | – | – | – | – | s | 12 | s | s | 7 |
| E. Jack Goodhue | – | 13 | 12 | 12 | 12 | 13 | 12 | – | 12 | 12 | 12 | 9 |
| B.M. Hohaia | – | – | s | s | s | 12 | – | s | – | – | – | 5 |
| D.C. Hawkins | 10 | s | 10 | 10 | 10 | 10 | – | – | s | 10 | 10 | 9 |
| P.J.L. Breen | s | 10 | – | – | s | s | 10 | 10 | 10 | s | s | 9 |
| T.P. Blundell | – | – | s | s | – | – | – | s | – | – | – | 3 |
| M.D.G. Markwick | 9 | – | s | s | s | s | s | – | – | – | – | 6 |
| M.A. MacLeod | s | s | – | – | – | – | – | – | – | – | – | 2 |
| S.J. Nock | – | 9 | 9 | 9 | 9 | 9 | 9 | 9 | 9 | 9 | 9 | 10 |
| E. Pittman | – | – | – | – | – | – | – | – | – | s | s | 2 |
| M.E.S. Matich | s | s | 8 | 8 | – | – | 8 | 8 | 8 | 8 | 8 | 9 |
| J. Matiu | – | – | s | s | 8 | 8 | – | s | – | – | – | 5 |
| D.J. Pryor | 8 | 8 | – | 7 | 7 | 7 | 7 | – | 7 | 7 | 6 | 9 |
| K.A. Pryor | 7 | 7 | s | – | – | s | s | 7 | s | s | 7 | 9 |
| J.D. Ram | s | 6 | 7 | 6 | 6 | 6 | 6 | 6 | – | s | s | 10 |
| M.J. Faleafa | – | – | – | – | s | – | s | s | s | – | s | 5 |
| M.I. Douglas | 6 | 5 | 6 | 5 | 4 | s | 5 | – | 6 | 6 | 5 | 10 |
| T.O. Bond | 5 | 4 | 5 | 4 | 5 | – | – | 5 | 5 | 5 | – | 8 |
| Joshua K Goodhue | 4 | s | 4 | – | – | 5 | 4 | 4 | 4 | 4 | 4 | 9 |
| J.S. Larsen | – | – | – | s | s | 4 | – | – | – | – | – | 3 |
| N.T. Wa'a | 3 | 3 | – | – | – | – | – | – | – | – | – | 2 |
| R.R. Rinakama | s | s | – | 3 | 3 | 3 | 3 | 3 | 3 | 3 | 3 | 10 |
| P.D.M. Kite | – | – | 3 | s | s | s | s | s | s | s | s | 9 |
| H.J.F. Sililoto | 1 | 1 | s | s | s | – | – | – | – | – | – | 5 |
| R.G. Wright | s | s | 1 | 1 | 1 | 1 | 1 | 1 | 1 | 1 | 1 | 11 |
| C. Apoua | – | – | s | – | – | s | – | s | – | s | s | 5 |
| M.G. Moulds (capt) | 2 | 2 | 2 | 2 | 2 | 2 | 2 | 2 | 2 | 2 | 2 | 11 |
| J.D. Olsen | s | s | s | s | s | s | s | s | s | s | s | 11 |

## NORTHLAND TEAM RECORD, 2017

**Played 11   Won 5   Lost 6   Points for 285   Points against 270**

| Date | Opponent | Location | Score | Tries | Con | PG | DG | Referee |
|---|---|---|---|---|---|---|---|---|
| August 20 | Bay of Plenty (C) | Whangarei | 28–23 | Siiiloto, Ram, M. Wright, Macilai | Hawkins (2), Breen (2) | | | B.E. Pickerill |
| August 26 | Auckland (P/C) | Auckland | 8–10 | Macilai | | Breen | | S. Kuho *Japan* |
| September 2 | Southland (C) | Invercargill | 44–13 | Jack Goodhue, Hyland, Nock, Macilai, Alaimalo, Olsen | Hawkins (4) | Hawkins (2) | | P.M. Williams |
| September 9 | Waikato (P/C) | Whangarei | 37–7 | Alaimalo, R. Wright, Ram, Jack Goodhue, Macilai | Hawkins (2), Blundell | Hawkins (2) | | M.G. Lash |
| September 14 | North Harbour (P/C) | Whangarei | 22–31 | Hyland | Breen | Hawkins (3), Breen (2) | | M.C.J. Writer |
| September 22 | Manawatu (C) | Palmerston North | 25–39 | Ram (2), D. Pryor | Hawkins (2) | Hawkins (2) | | B.D. O'Keeffe |
| September 27 | Otago (C) | Whangarei | 32–30 | Alaimalo, Macilai | Breen (2) | Breen (6) | | N.P. Brian |
| October 1 | Counties Manukau (P/C) | Pukekohe | 16–25 | Hohaia | Breen | Breen (3) | | M.I. Fraser |
| October 7 | Hawke's Bay (C) | Whangarei | 34–7 | D. Pryor (2), Ranger, Bond | Breen (2), Hawkins (2) | Breen, Hawkins | | P.M. Williams |
| October 12 | Wellington (C) | Wellington | 18–36 | Hyland, Jack Goodhue | Hawkins | Hawkins (2) | | R.P. Kelly |
| October 20 | Wellington (C semi-final) | Wellington | 21–49 | Hyland, Alaimalo, Nock | Hawkins (2), Nock | | | G.W. Jackson |

# OTAGO

**2017 Status:** Mitre 10 Cup Championship
**Founded 1881.** Affiliated 1895
**President:** D.G. (Des) Smith
**Chairman:** K.T. (Keith) Cooper
**General Manager:** R.P. (Richard) Kinley
**Coach:** C.N. (Corey) Brown
**Assistant coach:** T.J.S. (Tom) Donnelly
**Main ground:** Forsyth Barr Stadium
**Capacity:** 28,000
**Colours:** Dark blue and gold

## RECORDS

| | | |
|---|---|---|
| **Most appearances** | 170 | *Richard Knight, 1981–92* |
| **Most points** | 1520 | *Greg Cooper, 1984–96* |
| **Most tries** | 73 | *Paul Cooke, 1990–96* |
| **Most points in a season** | 279 | *Greg Cooper, 1991* |
| **Most tries in a season** | 16 | *John Timu, 1988* |
| | | *John Timu, 1990* |
| | | *Paul Cooke, 1995* |
| | | *Brendon Laney, 1998* |
| **Most conversions in a season** | 50 | *Greg Cooper, 1998* |
| **Most penalty goals in a season** | 54 | *Greg Cooper, 1989* |
| **Most dropped goals in a season** | 9 | *Lee Smith, 1986* |
| **Most points in a match** | 39 | *Paul Turner v East Coast, 1986* |
| **Most tries in a match** | 5 | *George Owles v South Canterbury, 1920* |
| | | *Bill Meates v South Canterbury, 1948* |
| | | *Bruce Hunter v Marlborough, 1969* |
| | | *Graham Sims v West Coast, 1972* |
| **Most conversions in a match** | 14 | *Paul Turner v East Coast, 1986* |
| **Most penalty goals in a match** | 7 | *Greg Cooper v NZ Combined Services, 1989* |
| | | *Greg Cooper v Canterbury, 1991* |
| | | *Blair Feeney v Wellington, 2002* |
| **Highest team score** | 91 | *v East Coast, 1986* |
| **Record victory (points ahead)** | 85 | *88–3 v North Otago, 1983* |
| **Highest score conceded** | 68 | *v Wellington, 2007* |
| **Record defeat (points behind)** | 61 | *7–68 v Wellington, 2007* |

After just missing promotion to the Premiership last year, Otago's record of four wins in 11 games in 2017 was a disappointing one. The side still made the playoffs, but produced their worst defensive effort of the year when losing to Bay of Plenty in the Championship semi-final.

The North Harbour, Tasman and Northland matches were all lost by just two points and the losses sustained to Canterbury in the Ranfurly Shield challenge and to Wellington were very spirited performances in thrilling encounters. While a losing bonus point was earned for all five of these narrow losses, the side just did not have the ability to claim victory in any of the tight matches. By contrast, all four wins achieved were ones where Otago was not in any real danger of losing in the last 10 minutes.

Coach Cory Brown had the misfortune to lose the experienced players Michael Collins and captain Liam Coltman for the whole season to injury, while Matthew Faddes and Hayden Parker only appeared four times and twice respectively for the same reason. A serious loss was the transfer of outstanding lock Tom Franklin to Bay of Plenty, and other 2016 regulars that had departed were Fa'asiu Fuatai, Jack Wilson, Paul Grant and Fiji international Naulia Dawai all overseas, while Lee Allan had retired due to concussion and Shaun Eade returned to Southland.

The exciting teenager Vilimoni Koroi was signed straight from school in Manawatu late last year and made a big impression with the NZ Sevens team this year. In the transition back to fifteens he started the Mitre 10 Cup campaign at fullback, but the majority of his appearances in the second half of the season were off the bench, providing particularly good impact in the semi-final. Fletcher Smith had a poor opening game at first five-eighth and lost his place. When Koroi was a late withdrawal from the Hawke's Bay match, Smith was placed at fullback and responded with a man-of-the-match performance scoring three tries in a 34-point haul. The rest of his appearances, except for one, remained at fullback and topped the points table with 116, including five tries.

Debutant Jona Nareki was the best of the wings with nine tries in nine matches, having a standout match against Manawatu when he scored three tries among a number of strong runs. It was a pity he missed the semi-final as his finishing ability was a big loss. The best player in the backline was Tei Walden who showed plenty of endeavour on attack and was strong in defence. He was well supported in the midfield by Petelesio Tomkinson in an effective partnership.

There were contrasting styles in the halfbacks, with Jonathan Ruru having a good running game and Josh Renton prominent with a crisp pass and good kick, Ruru being favoured with the starts at the business end of the season. Josh Ioane had a satisfactory debut season at first five-eighth, revealing much promise in general play but his goal-kicking was below par.

James Lentjes and Dillon Hunt were a lively pair of openside flankers, and the coach decided to utilise them both in the starting fifteens. This worked well until Lentjes had his season end with injury against Northland. Hunt carried on the good form to gain selection in the All Blacks' end-of-year tour. Adam Knight also performed well at loose forward in roles at number eight and blindside flanker.

Josh Furno at lock was another to debut satisfactorily, showing good skill in the lineout, and together with the industrious Josh Dickson were a fine locking pair. The scrum was very good; it even got the better of the much vaunted Canterbury scrum. All four props used were very effective in the front row, with Craig Millar in particular a powerful loosehead and a workhorse in the tight exchanges. Sam Anderson-Heather was a capable hooker, bringing up 50 games for Otago, and took over the captaincy.

Higher honours went to:

| | |
|---|---|
| *New Zealand:* | D. Hunt, B. Smith |
| *New Zealand Maori:* | J. Ruru, T. Walden |
| *New Zealand Under 20:* | J. Nareki |
| *New Zealand Sevens:* | F. Fuatai, V. Koroi |

## OTAGO REPRESENTATIVES 2017

| | Club | Games for Union | Points for Union | | Club | Games for Union | Points for Union |
|---|---|---|---|---|---|---|---|
| Sam Anderson–Heather | Dunedin | 57 | 45 | Jona Nareki | Alhambra Union | 9 | 45 |
| Jonah Aoina | Kaikorai | 3 | 10 | Hayden Parker | Taieri | 47 | 442 |
| George Bower | Harbour | 2 | 0 | Sekonaia Pole | Harbour | 25 | 5 |
| Donald Brighouse | Dunedin | 41 | 5 | Josh Renton | Kaikorai | 38 | 10 |
| Josh Dickson | University | 32 | 10 | Tom Rowe | Zingari Richmond | 6 | 0 |
| Matthew Faddes | University | 37 | 55 | Jonathan Ruru | Napier Pirates [1] | 22 | 15 |
| Josh Furno | Taieri | 10 | 15 | Yoshihisa Sasagi | Southern | 35 | 0 |
| Kurt Hammer | Taieri | 1 | 0 | Mitchell Scott | Taieri | 17 | 25 |
| Dillon Hunt | University | 13 | 10 | Aki Seiuli | Taieri | 57 | 25 |
| Josh Ioane | Southern | 11 | 42 | Fletcher Smith | University | 34 | 287 |
| Ricky Jackson | University | 1 | 0 | Sione Teu | University | 13 | 10 |
| Adam Knight | Southern | 27 | 15 | Josh Timu | University | 2 | 0 |
| Joketani Koroi | Harbour | 2 | 0 | Petelesio Tomkinson | Harbour | 26 | 25 |
| Vilimoni Koroi | Alhambra Union | 9 | 15 | Blair Tweed | Kaikorai | 25 | 5 |
| James Lentjes | Taieri | 31 | 35 | Latu Vaeno | Spotswood United [2] | 7 | 5 |
| Mikaele Mafi | Southern | 12 | 5 | Leroy van Dam | Dunedin | 5 | 0 |
| Slade McDowall | Kaikorai | 6 | 0 | Teihorangi Walden | Southern | 46 | 45 |
| Craig Millar | Southern | 45 | 20 | | | | |

[1] *Hawke's Bay RU*   [2] *Taranaki RU*

## INDIVIDUAL SCORING

| | Tries | Con | PG | DG | Points | | Tries | Con | PG | DG | Points |
|---|---|---|---|---|---|---|---|---|---|---|---|
| Smith | 5 | 26 | 13 | – | 116 | Hunt | 1 | – | – | – | 5 |
| Nareki | 9 | – | – | – | 45 | Pole | 1 | – | – | – | 5 |
| Ioane | 1 | 8 | 7 | – | 42 | Seiuli | 1 | – | – | – | 5 |
| Tomkinson | 5 | – | – | – | 25 | Faddes | 1 | – | – | – | 5 |
| Scott | 4 | – | – | – | 20 | Vaeno | 1 | – | – | – | 5 |
| Ruru | 3 | – | – | – | 15 | Aoina | 1 | – | – | – | 5 |
| Anderson-Heather | 3 | – | – | – | 15 | | | | | | |
| Furno | 3 | – | – | – | 15 | **Totals** | **47** | **34** | **20** | **0** | **363** |
| Walden | 3 | – | – | – | 15 | | | | | | |
| V. Koroi | 3 | – | – | – | 15 | Opposition scored | 40 | 24 | 21 | 0 | 317 |
| Teu | 2 | – | – | – | 10 | | | | | | |

| OTAGO 2017 | North Harbour | Canterbury | Manawatu | Hawke's Bay | Tasman | Auckland | Northland | Wellington | Bay of Plenty | Southland | Bay of Plenty | TOTALS |
|---|---|---|---|---|---|---|---|---|---|---|---|---|
| V.T. Koroi | 15 | 15 | 15 | – | s | s | 15 | s | 14 | – | s | 9 |
| F.H. Smith | 10 | s | s | 15 | 15 | 15 | 10 | 15 | 15 | s | s | 11 |
| M.A. Faddes | 13 | – | – | – | – | – | – | – | s | 15 | 15 | 4 |
| M.J. Scott | 14 | 14 | 14 | – | 14 | 14 | – | – | – | 14 | 14 | 7 |
| J.M. Nareki | s | 11 | 11 | 11 | – | 11 | 11 | 11 | 11 | 11 | – | 9 |
| L. van Dam | – | – | s | 14 | s | s | s | – | – | – | – | 5 |
| L.M. Vaeno | – | – | – | s | 11 | – | 14 | 14 | s | s | 11 | 7 |
| P.F. Tomkinson | 11 | 13 | 13 | 13 | 13 | 13 | – | 13 | 13 | 13 | 13 | 10 |
| J.C. Timu | – | – | – | s | – | – | 13 | – | – | – | – | 2 |
| T.T. Walden | 12 | 12 | 12 | 12 | 12 | 12 | – | 12 | 12 | 12 | 12 | 10 |
| J.R. Ioane | s | 10 | 10 | 10 | 10 | 10 | 12 | 10 | 10 | 10 | 10 | 11 |
| H.J. Parker | – | – | – | – | – | – | s | s | – | – | – | 2 |
| J.D. Renton | 9 | s | s | 9 | 9 | 9 | 9 | s | – | s | s | 10 |
| J.L. Ruru | s | 9 | 9 | s | s | s | s | 9 | 9 | 9 | 9 | 11 |
| K.M. Hammer | – | – | – | – | – | – | – | – | s | – | – | 1 |
| S.F.F. Teu | 8 | s | s | s | s | 8 | 8 | – | – | 8 | 8 | 9 |
| M.T.T. Mafi | – | – | – | – | – | s | – | 8 | 8 | – | – | 3 |
| S.R. McDowall | – | – | – | – | – | s | s | s | s | s | s | 6 |
| J.A.R. Lentjes | 7 | 7 | 7 | 7 | 7 | 7 | 7 | – | – | – | – | 7 |
| D. Hunt | 6 | 6 | 6 | 6 | 6 | – | – | – | 7 | 7 | 7 | 8 |
| A.G. Knight | s | 8 | 8 | 8 | 8 | 6 | 6 | 7 | 6 | 6 | 6 | 11 |
| T.B. Rowe | 5 | s | s | – | – | 5 | – | – | – | – | – | 4 |
| J.M. Dickson | s | 5 | 5 | 5 | – | – | 5 | 5 | 5 | 5 | 5 | 9 |
| B.R. Tweed | 4 | – | – | s | 5 | – | s | 4 | – | 4 | 4 | 7 |
| J.R. Furno | – | 4 | 4 | 4 | 4 | 4 | 4 | 6 | 4 | s | s | 10 |
| J.R. Koroi | – | – | – | – | – | – | – | s | s | – | – | 2 |
| D.I.M. Brighouse | 3 | 3 | s | s | s | 3 | 3 | s | s | 3 | 3 | 11 |
| G.G. Bower | s | – | – | – | – | – | – | – | – | – | – | 1 |
| Y. Sasagi | – | s | 3 | 3 | 3 | s | s | 3 | 3 | s | s | 10 |
| A. Seiuli | 1 | 1 | 1 | s | s | 1 | 1 | s | s | – | s | 10 |
| C.W. Millar | s | s | s | 1 | 1 | s | s | 1 | 1 | 1 | 1 | 11 |
| J.T. Aoina | – | – | – | – | – | – | – | – | – | s | – | 1 |
| S.G. Anderson-Heather (capt) | 2 | 2 | 2 | 2 | 2 | 2 | s | – | 2 | 2 | 2 | 10 |
| S.J. Pole | s | s | s | s | s | s | 2 | 2 | – | s | s | 10 |
| R.D. Jackson | – | – | – | – | – | – | – | s | – | – | – | 1 |

J.A.R. Lentjes captained v Northland; T.T. Walden v Wellington.

## OTAGO TEAM RECORD, 2017

**Played 11  Won 4  Lost 7  Points for 363  Points against 317**

| Date | Opponent | Location | Score | Tries | Con | PG | DG | Referee |
|---|---|---|---|---|---|---|---|---|
| August 17 | North Harbour (P/C) | Albany | 17–19 | Ruru, Scott | Ioane (2) | Ioane | | G.W. Jackson |
| August 27 | Canterbury (P/C) (RS) | Christchurch | 24–30 | Ioane, Scott, Anderson-Heather, Nareki | Smith (2) | | | P.M. Williams |
| September 2 | Manawatu (C) | Dunedin | 40–30 | Nareki (3), Ruru, Scott, Anderson-Heather | Smith (2) | Ioane, Smith | | J.D. Munro |
| September 10 | Hawke's Bay (C) | Napier | 64–21 | Smith (3), Furno (2), Hunt, Tomkinson, Pole, Seiuli | Smith (8) | Smith | | S.W. McDermott |
| September 16 | Tasman (P/C) | Dunedin | 27–29 | Walden, Tomkinson, Teu | Smith (3) | Smith (2) | | M.I. Fraser |
| September 21 | Auckland (P/C) | Dunedin | 34–26 | Nareki (2), Tomkinson (2), Furno | Smith (3) | Smith | | G.W. Jackson |
| September 27 | Northland (C) | Whangarei | 30–32 | Smith, V. Koroi, Nareki | Smith (3) | Smith (3) | | N.P. Briant |
| October 1 | Wellington (C) | Wellington | 24–27 | Ruru, V. Koroi | Smith | Smith (4) | | J.R. Nutbrown |
| October 7 | Bay of Plenty (C) | Dunedin | 28–36 | Smith, Nareki, Faddes | Smith, Ioane | Ioane (2), Smith | | B.D. O'Keeffe |
| October 14 | Southland (C) | Dunedin | 43–19 | Scott, Tomkinson, Nareki, Walden, Vaeno, Aoina | Ioane (5) | Ioane | | A.W.B. Mabey |
| October 21 | Bay of Plenty (C semi-final) | Tauranga | 32–48 | Anderson-Heather, Teu, V. Koroi, Walden | Smith (3) | Ioane (2) | | B.E. Pickerill |

RS *Ranfurly Shield*

# POVERTY BAY

**2017 Status:** Heartland
**Founded 1890. Affiliated 1893**
**President:** K.H. (Kevin) Joblin
**Chairman:** George Brown
**Chief executive officer:** M.L. (Marty) Davis
**Coach:** K.M.F. (Mana) Otai
**Assistant coach:** D.E. (Dwayne) Russell
**Main ground:** Rugby Park, Gisborne
**Capacity:** 18,000
**Colour:** Scarlet

## RECORDS

| | | |
|---|---|---|
| Highest attendance | 15,000 | *Poverty Bay-East Coast v British Isles, 1971* |
| Most appearances | 149 | *S.T. Ngatu, 2003–2017* |
| Most points | 791 | *S.C. Leighton, 2004–12* |
| Most tries | 35 | *P.S.R. Ransley, 1961–74* |
| Most points in a season | 144 | *S.C. Leighton, 2007* |
| Most tries in a season | 11 | *J. Moeke, 1997;* |
| | | *J. Stewart, 2010* |
| | | *J. Stewart, 2011* |
| Most conversions in a season | 30 | *S.C. Leighton, 2007* |
| Most penalty goals in a season | 27 | *D.M. Boyle, 1999* |
| Most dropped goals in a season | 3 | *G.B. Ross, 1976; J. Whittle, 1979* |
| Most points in a match | 35 | *S.C. Leighton v Thames Valley, 2007* |
| Most tries in a match | 4 | *J.L. Penny v Olympians Club, 1953* |
| | | *K.A. Twigley v East Coast, 1966* |
| | | *I.A. Kirkpatrick v East Coast, 1971* |
| | | *K.D. Ferris v East Coast, 1983* |
| | | *A.B. Hansen v North Otago, 1987* |
| Most conversions in a match | 9 | *R.P. Owen v East Coast, 1983* |
| Most penalty goals in a match | 7 | *S.P. Parkes v Buller, 2013* |
| Highest team score | 75 | *v East Coast, 1980* |
| Record victory (points ahead) | 75 | *75–0 v East Coast, 1980* |
| Highest score conceded | 121 | *v Waikato, 1998* |
| Record defeat (points behind) | 121 | *0–121 v Waikato, 1998* |

After a slow start to the Heartland Championship where they lost their first three matches, Poverty Bay improved as the season went on to earn four victories in their final six matches. The final round robin match against Thames Valley was the defining moment of the season as the 36–35 win meant both teams finished level on 20 points, but Poverty Bay finished eighth due to winning the match to claim the last spot for the Lochore Cup.

The mobile forward pack was well led by 21-year-old captain James Grogan who was a very lively flanker and always in the thick of things. Continuing on from last year, Siosiua Moala was again an outstanding performer on both attack and defence at number eight. They received good support in the loose forward department from Willis Tamatea until his injury.

Everard Reid was the main lineout winner and also made a solid contribution in the tight work, while at the age of 36 Sione Ngatu continued to increase his appearance record and serve his union well.

At fullback Ethine Reeves was the star of the backline. He showed plenty of attacking enterprise in every match, was a very capable defender, which he showed in the King Country match, and kicked goals as well. Andrew Tauatevalu, a 20-year-old wing, showed promise in the seven matches he played with five tries and some good goal-kicking.

There was not much between the two first five-eighths Kelvin Smith and Jake Holmes with both able in taking on the line, while Mario Counsell established himself as the number one halfback in the second half of the season with some fine displays.

Of last year's regulars Kieran Short (overseas), Isaia Leach (Tasman) and Tamati Samuels (Hawke's Bay) had moved on, although Leach did return as a loan player until injured, while Ken Houkamau, Murray Hewson and Geoff Pari were not favoured by the new coach Mana Otai.

Higher honours went to:
*New Zealand Heartland:* S. Moala, E. Reeves, E. Reid

## POVERTY BAY REPRESENTATIVES 2017

| | Club | Games for Union | Points for Union | | Club | Games for Union | Points for Union |
|---|---|---|---|---|---|---|---|
| Semisi Akana | Ngatapa | 14 | 10 | Korey Love | Gisborne HSOB | 2 | 5 |
| Juston Allen | Pirates | 16 | 15 | Mike MacDonald | Gisborne OB Marist | 1 | 0 |
| Mekepio Brown | YMP | 8 | 0 | Karl MacPherson | Ngatapa | 7 | 15 |
| Jacob Cook | Gisborne OB Marist | 18 | 6 | Matekairoa McGuire | Giaborne HSOB | 7 | 0 |
| Mario Counsell | Waikohu | 37 | 10 | Siosiua Moala | Gisborne HSOB | 27 | 55 |
| Ratu Daurua | Whakatane Marist [2] | 13 | 48 | Efoti Moimoi | Gisborne OB Marist | 14 | 0 |
| Jesse Fleming | Waikohu | 7 | 5 | Sione Ngatu | Ngatapa | 149 | 81 |
| James Grogan | Gisborne OB Marist | 24 | 16 | Ethine Reeves | Waikohu | 41 | 87 |
| William Grogan | Gisborne OB Marist | 20 | 0 | Everard Reid | Pirates | 26 | 54 |
| George Halley | Gisborne HSOB | 4 | 6 | Pamona Samupo | Pirates | 11 | 0 |
| Tamanui Hill | Gisborne HSOB | 20 | 20 | Kelvin Smith | Waikohu | 32 | 41 |
| Leslie Hills | Gisborne HSOB | 18 | 11 | Tawhao Stewart | Waikohu | 7 | 5 |
| Sandy Hohipa–Campbell | Waikohu | 6 | 0 | Willis Tamatea | YMP | 34 | 5 |
| Jake Holmes | Gisborne OB Marist | 16 | 20 | Andrew Tauatevalu | Gisborne HSOB | 7 | 53 |
| Tipuna Jones | YMP | 2 | 0 | Jody Tuhaka | Gisborne HSOB | 19 | 5 |
| Anthony Karauria | Ngatapa | 10 | 5 | Isaia Vuki | Whakatane Marist [2] | 16 | 103 |
| Brody Lam | Eden [3] | 6 | 20 | Ricky Waitoa | Pirates | 4 | 0 |
| Isaiah Leach [1] | Wanderers [4] | 13 | 6 | Fawn White | YMP | 8 | 0 |
| Alesana Leatio'o | East Tamaki [3] | 2 | 0 | | | | |

[1] *Player of Origin*  [2] *Bay of Plenty RU*  [3] *Auckland RU*  [4] *Tasman RU*

## INDIVIDUAL SCORING

| | Tries | Con | PG | DG | Points |
|---|---|---|---|---|---|
| Tauatelavu | 5 | 8 | 4 | – | 53 |
| Reeves | 2 | 10 | 1 | – | 33 |
| Holmes | 4 | – | – | – | 20 |
| Moala | 4 | – | – | – | 20 |
| Lam | 4 | – | – | – | 20 |
| Reid | 4 | – | – | – | 20 |
| Vuki | 2 | 2 | 1 | – | 17 |
| MacPherson | 3 | – | – | – | 15 |
| Smith | 1 | 3 | – | – | 11 |
| Akana | 2 | – | – | – | 10 |
| Penalty Try | 1 | – | – | – | 7 |
| Counsell | 1 | – | – | – | 5 |
| Hills | 1 | – | – | – | 5 |

| | Tries | Con | PG | DG | Points |
|---|---|---|---|---|---|
| Hill | 1 | – | – | – | 5 |
| Love | 1 | – | – | – | 5 |
| Tuhaka | 1 | – | – | – | 5 |
| Stewart | 1 | – | – | – | 5 |
| Fleming | 1 | – | – | – | 5 |
| J. Grogan | 1 | – | – | – | 5 |
| Karauria | 1 | – | – | – | 5 |
| Ngatu | 1 | – | – | – | 5 |
| **Totals** | **42** | **23** | **6** | **0** | **276** |
| Opposition scored | 42 | 28 | 16 | 0 | 314 |

## POVERTY BAY 2017

| | East Coast | Wairarapa Bush | Mid Canterbury | Horowhenua Kapiti | Wanganui | East Coast | West Coast | North Otago | King Country | Thames Valley | Mid Canterbury | TOTALS |
|---|---|---|---|---|---|---|---|---|---|---|---|---|
| K.D. Love | 15 | – | – | – | – | – | – | – | – | s | – | **2** |
| E.S. Reeves | – | – | 15 | 15 | – | 15 | 15 | 15 | 15 | 15 | 15 | **8** |
| T. Jones | 14 | – | – | – | – | – | – | – | – | – | – | **1** |
| K.K. MacPherson | 11 | 14 | 14 | 14 | – | – | – | – | 14 | 14 | 14 | **7** |
| G.W.W. Halley | – | 11 | s | – | 11 | – | – | – | – | – | – | **3** |
| R.T. Daurua | – | – | 11 | 11 | – | – | – | 13 | – | – | – | **3** |
| A.H. Tauatevalu | – | – | – | – | 14 | 11 | 14 | 14 | 11 | 13 | 13 | **7** |
| B.M. Lam | – | – | – | – | – | 14 | 11 | 11 | s | 11 | 11 | **6** |
| J. Fleming | 13 | – | – | 12 | 13 | 12 | 12 | 12 | 13 | – | – | **7** |
| I.U. Vuki | – | 15 | 13 | s | 15 | 13 | 13 | – | – | – | – | **6** |
| T.M.T.I.W. Stewart | – | 13 | 12 | 13 | s | – | s | – | – | s | s | **7** |
| A.T. Karauria | 12 | 12 | – | – | 12 | s | s | s | 12 | 12 | 12 | **9** |
| M. McDonald | s | – | – | – | – | – | – | – | – | – | – | **1** |
| P. Samupo | – | s | – | – | – | – | – | – | – | – | – | **1** |
| K.M. Smith | 10 | s | s | s | 10 | 10 | s | s | 10 | 10 | 10 | **11** |
| J.G. Holmes | s | 10 | 10 | 10 | s | s | 10 | 10 | s | s | s | **11** |
| M.B. Counsell | 9 | s | 9 | s | s | s | 9 | 9 | 9 | 9 | 9 | **11** |
| W.D. Grogan | s | 9 | 9 | 9 | 9 | s | s | s | s | s | s | **11** |
| S. Moala | 8 | 8 | 8 | 8 | – | 8 | 8 | 8 | 8 | 8 | 8 | **10** |
| F.D. White | 7 | – | – | s | 7 | s | s | s | – | 6 | 6 | **8** |
| J.R. Grogan (capt) | – | 7 | 7 | 7 | 8 | 7 | 7 | 7 | 7 | 7 | 7 | **10** |
| E.K. Moimoi | s | – | – | – | – | – | – | – | – | – | – | **1** |
| W.T. Tamatea | – | 5 | 4 | 4 | 6 | 6 | 6 | 6 | 6 | – | – | **8** |
| L.P. Hills | 6 | 6 | 6 | 6 | 4 | – | – | 4 | 4 | 4 | 4 | **9** |
| J.M. Allen | 5 | s | s | – | – | – | s | – | – | s | s | **6** |
| J.E. Cook | 4 | 4 | 5 | 5 | s | 4 | 4 | s | s | – | s | **10** |
| M.N. Brown | s | s | s | – | s | s | – | s | s | s | – | **8** |
| R.J.S. Waitoa | – | s | – | – | – | – | – | – | – | – | – | **1** |
| E.J. Reid | – | – | s | s | 5 | 5 | 5 | 5 | 5 | 5 | 5 | **9** |
| S.T. Ngatu | 3 | 3 | 3 | 3 | 3 | 3 | 3 | 3 | 3 | 1 | 1 | **11** |
| T.G. Hill | s | 1 | 1 | 1 | 1 | 1 | 2 | 1 | 1 | 2 | 2 | **11** |
| S.M. Akana | – | s | s | s | s | s | 1 | s | s | 3 | 3 | **10** |
| A. Leatio'o | – | – | – | – | – | – | s | – | – | s | – | **2** |
| M.W.E. McGuire | 2 | 2 | 2 | 2 | 2 | – | – | – | – | – | – | **5** |
| J.K. Tuhaka | s | – | – | – | – | – | – | – | – | – | – | **1** |
| S.T.T.P. Hohipa-Campbell | 1 | – | – | s | s | s | – | – | s | – | s | **6** |
| I. Leach | – | – | – | – | – | 2 | – | 2 | 2 | – | – | **3** |

J. Fleming captained in first match v East Coast.

## POVERTY BAY TEAM RECORD, 2017

**Played 11  Won 6  Lost 5  Points for 276  Points against 314**

| Date | Opponent | Location | Score | Tries | Con | PG | DG | Referee |
|---|---|---|---|---|---|---|---|---|
| June 3 | East Coast | Gisborne | 38–23 | Counsell, MacPherson, Hills, Hill, Love, Tuhaka | Smith (2), Holmes (2) | | | R.J.M. Gordon |
| August 12 | Wairarapa Bush | Gisborne | 31–6 | Stewart, Moala, MacPherson | Holmes, Vuki | Holmes (3), Vuki | | H.G. Reed |
| August 26 | Mid Canterbury (H) | Ashburton | 5–34 | Moala | | | | J.D. Munro |
| September 2 | Horowhenua Kapiti (H) | Gisborne | 5–39 | Vuki | | | | T.M.T. Cottrell |
| September 9 | Wanganui (H) | Wanganui | 14–25 | Tauatelavu, Holmes | Vuki, Tauatelavu | | | H.G. Reed |
| September 16 | East Coast (H) | Gisborne | 35–15 | Lam (2), Fleming, Vuki, Reid | Reeves (2) | Tauatevalu (2) | | N.E.R. Hogan |
| September 23 | West Coast (H) | Gisborne | 36–19 | Tauatelavu (2), Moala, J. Grogan, Karauria | Tauatelavu (3), Smith | Tauatelavu | | H.G. Reed |
| September 30 | North Otago (H) | Oamaru | 12–34 | Reid, Reeves | Tauatevalu | | | V.F. Ringrose |
| October 7 | King Country (H) | Gisborne | 43–29 | Tauatelavu, Ngatu, Moala, Smith, Penalty Try, Akana | Tauatevalu (3), Reeves | Tauatevalu | | R.J.M. Gordon |
| October 14 | Thames Valley (H) | Te Aroha | 35–34 | Reid (2), Tauatevalu, MacPherson, Reeves | Reeves (5) | | | V.F. Ringrose |
| October 21 | Mid Canterbury (LC semi-final) | Ashburton | 22–56 | Lam (2), Akana | Reeves (2) | Reeves | | T.N. Griffiths |

# SOUTH CANTERBURY

**2017 Status:** Heartland
**Founded 1888.** Original member
**President:** M.G. (Murray) Roberts
**Chairman:** R.T. (Ray) Teahen
**Chief Executive Officer:** C.W. (Craig) Calder
**Coach:** B.A. (Barry) Matthews
**Assistant coach:** G.W. (Grant) McFarlane
**Main ground:** Alpine Energy Stadium, Timaru
**Capacity:** 17,000
**Colours:** Emerald green and black

## RECORDS

| | | |
|---|---|---|
| Highest attendance | 17,000 | *South Canterbury v France, 1961* |
| Most appearances | 152 | *S.J. Todd, 1986–2001* |
| Most points | 1048 | *B.J. Fairbrother, 1981–92* |
| Most tries | 60 | *S.J. Todd 1986–2001* |
| Most points in a season | 175 | *B.J. Fairbrother, 1991* |
| Most tries in a season | 13 | *J.S. Ellery, 1960* |
| | | *C.J. Dorgan, 1992* |
| | | *B.J. Laney, 1992* |
| Most conversions in a season | 31 | *B.J. Fairbrother, 1989* |
| Most penalty goals in a season | 31 | *B.J. Fairbrother, 1990* |
| Most dropped goals in a season | 8 | *B.J. Fairbrother, 1987* |
| | | *B.J. Fairbrother, 1991* |
| Most points in a match | 32 | *G.I. Dempster v Wairarapa Bush, 1996* |
| Most tries in a match | 4 | *G.V. Gerard v Southland, 1926* |
| | | *E.W. Ryan v Ashburton County, 1935* |
| | | *E.W. Ryan v Wellington XV, 1937* |
| | | *J.M. Cole v North Otago, 1958* |
| | | *E.C. Smith v Nelson, 1961* |
| | | *B.J. Matthews v North Otago, 1992* |
| | | *D.J. Hunter v Poverty Bay, 1993* |
| | | *I.G. Howden v Marlborough, 1996* |
| | | *S. Kiole v West Coast, 2002* |
| | | *E. Tau v Poverty Bay, 2015* |
| Most conversions in a match | 8 | *B.J. Fairbrother v West Coast, 1989* |
| | | *B.J. Fairbrother v North Otago, 1991* |
| | | *B.J. Fairbrother v North Otago, 1992* |
| | | *C.S. Gard v North Otago, 1993* |
| | | *B.J. Laney v North Otago, 1994* |
| | | *G.I. Dempster v Wairarapa Bush, 1996* |
| Most penalty goals in a match | 7 | *B.J. Fairbrother v East Coast, 1990* |
| Highest team score | 94 | *v North Otago, 1994* |
| Record victory (points ahead) | 87 | *94–7 v North Otago, 1994* |
| Highest score conceded | 103 | *v Canterbury, 2001* |
| Record defeat (points behind) | 103 | *0–103 v Canterbury, 2001* |

South Canterbury's season ended in disappointment with a home Meads Cup semi-final defeat to Wanganui whom they had defeated 21–17 earlier in the competition. Despite plenty of possession on the day, the attack could not translate this into enough points. After an opening round loss to Buller, South Canterbury won seven straight games to top the points table in the round robin for the second time in three years. Attack was a strength of the side, but defence and the lineout were variable.

Regular local players from last year who had departed were John Dyer (Bay of Plenty) and Taione Ratu (Wanganui), while the experienced Setefano Sauqaqa arrived from Buller and former Highlanders rep Juan-Pierre Koen arrived from Southland. A number of last year's locals did not regain selection in 2017.

Kalavini Leatigaga was an exciting wing, having speed, an ability to beat a man and finish off and midfielder Vatiliai Tora was a very hard man to stop with ball in hand. Halfback Willie Wright was a solid and dependable halfback, having an outstanding game against West Coast when he scored 30 points, including three tries. His goal-kicking was excellent and topped 100 points for the season. Nineteen-year-old wing Sireli Bulirarua, in his first season, showed potential.

Four players were tried at fullback. Great things were expected of Liam Edwards on his much anticipated return after his two superb years in 2012 and 2013, but injury restricted him to just two appearances. Shayne Anderson and Setefano Sauqaqa also had injury-plagued seasons. In a bit of a gamble, the coach Barry Matthews selected all three for the semi-final despite their having missed the lead-up matches. First-choice first five-eighth Miles Medlicott also suffered injury with a broken thumb against West Coast, ending his season.

By comparison, the forward pack was a more settled unit. Openside flanker Nick Strachan was in tremendous form and number eight Brad Hemopo was always prominent with ball carrying and defence. Whether at loose forward or lock, captain Kieran Coll led by example and Luke Brice, who had last appeared in 2012, made a good contribution at lock. The front row of Juan-Pierre Koen, Marac Beckham and Matt Fetu was a very capable one, with Beckham proving a very mobile hooker.

Higher honours went to:
**New Zealand Heartland:**   K. Coll, M. Fetu, N. Strachan, W. Wright

## SOUTH CANTERBURY REPRESENTATIVES 2017

| | Club | Games for Union | Points for Union | | Club | Games for Union | Points for Union |
|---|---|---|---|---|---|---|---|
| Sakenasa Aca | Saracens [2] | 3 | 0 | Jack Kingsford | Pleasant Point | 1 | 0 |
| Shayne Anderson | Marist Albion [2] | 5 | 0 | Juan-Pierre Koen | Pleasant Point | 8 | 5 |
| Jonny Andrews | Mackenzie | 26 | 5 | Kalavini Leatigaga | Temuka | 14 | 71 |
| Marac Beckham | Geraldine | 9 | 15 | Viliame Logavatu [3] | | 9 | 23 |
| Luke Brice | Pleasant Point | 25 | 10 | Miles Medlicott | Waimate | 41 | 28 |
| Henry Bryce | Waimate | 2 | 0 | Kevin Moore | Pleasant Point | 7 | 5 |
| Sireli Bulirarua | Harlequins | 8 | 5 | Leone Nawalu | Harlequins | 3 | 5 |
| Kieran Coll | Pleasant Point | 28 | 53 | Brad Oliver | Geraldine | 8 | 0 |
| Keith Darby | Temuka | 1 | 0 | Setefano Sauqaqa | Mackenzie | 5 | 0 |
| Theo Davidson [3] | | 26 | 25 | Stephen Smith | Waimate | 3 | 0 |
| Liam Edwards | Napier OB Marist [4] | 20 | 284 | Nick Strachan | Celtic | 71 | 52 |
| Matthew Fetu | Celtic | 93 | 35 | Glen Sturgess | Timaru Old Boys | 4 | 5 |
| Siaosi "George" Folau | Mackenzie | 14 | 25 | Junior Taia | Shirley [2] | 2 | 0 |
| Jared Gilmore | Celtic | 2 | 0 | Vatiliai Tora | Harlequins | 8 | 35 |
| Ken Hellier | Harlequins | 1 | 0 | Loni Toumohuni | Waimate | 10 | 20 |
| Brad Hemopo | Canterbury University [2] | 6 | 25 | Jared Trevathan | Mackenzie | 49 | 146 |
| Philip Henderson [1] | Burnside [2] | 8 | 0 | Josateki Veikune | Harlequins | 21 | 0 |
| Ben Hewitson | Pleasant Point | 54 | 5 | Willie Wright | Celtic | 28 | 130 |
| Will Joines | Celtic | 17 | 6 | | | | |

[1] *Player of Origin*   [2] *Canterbury RU*   [3] *Returned from overseas*   [4] *Hawke's Bay RU*

## INDIVIDUAL SCORING

| | Tries | Con | PG | DG | Points | | Tries | Con | PG | DG | Points |
|---|---|---|---|---|---|---|---|---|---|---|---|
| Wright | 7 | 30 | 2 | – | 101 | Logovatu | 1 | – | – | – | 5 |
| Tora | 7 | – | – | – | 35 | Bulirua | 1 | – | – | – | 5 |
| Leatigaga | 7 | – | – | – | 35 | Nawalu | 1 | – | – | – | 5 |
| Hemopo | 5 | – | – | – | 25 | Sturgess | 1 | – | – | – | 5 |
| Toumohuni | 4 | – | – | – | 20 | Moore | 1 | – | – | – | 5 |
| Coll | 3 | – | – | – | 15 | Trevathan | – | 2 | – | – | 4 |
| Beckham | 3 | – | – | – | 15 | | | | | | |
| Strachan | 2 | – | – | – | 10 | **Totals** | **45** | **33** | **2** | **0** | **297** |
| Medlicott | 1 | 1 | – | – | 7 | | | | | | |
| Koen | 1 | – | | – | 5 | Opposition scored | 25 | 20 | 18 | 0 | 219 |

## SOUTH CANTERBURY 2017

| | Buller | King Country | Mid Canterbury | Wanganui | North Otago | West Coast | Wairarapa Bush | East Coast | Wanganui | TOTALS |
|---|---|---|---|---|---|---|---|---|---|---|
| S.W. Anderson | 15 | 15 | 13 | 13 | – | – | – | – | 12 | 5 |
| J.D. Trevathan | 10 | – | 15 | 15 | – | s | 15 | 10 | 10 | 7 |
| L.J. Edwards | – | – | – | – | 15 | – | – | – | 15 | 2 |
| S.T. Sauqaqa | 14 | 11 | – | 14 | – | 13 | – | – | 14 | 5 |
| S.T. Folau | 11 | – | – | s | – | – | s | 14 | – | 4 |
| K.V. Leatigaga | s | 14 | 14 | 11 | 11 | 11 | 11 | 11 | 11 | 9 |
| S.K. Bulirarua | – | s | 11 | s | 14 | 14 | 14 | 15 | s | 8 |
| J. Taia | 13 | 12 | – | – | – | – | – | – | – | 2 |
| L. Toumohuni | 12 | s | s | s | 13 | – | s | 12 | s | 8 |
| V.T. Tora | – | 13 | 12 | 12 | 12 | 12 | 12 | 13 | 13 | 8 |
| S.S. Aca | – | – | – | – | s | 15 | 13 | – | – | 3 |
| K.E. Hellier | – | – | – | – | – | s | – | – | – | 1 |
| M.W. Medlicott | s | 10 | 10 | 10 | 10 | 10 | – | – | – | 6 |
| T.R. Davidson | – | – | – | – | – | s | 10 | – | – | 2 |
| W.A. Wright | 9 | 9 | 9 | 9 | 9 | 9 | 9 | 9 | 9 | 9 |
| G.D. Sturgess | – | s | s | s | s | s | – | s | – | 4 |
| K.P. Coll (capt) | 8 | 8 | 6 | – | 6 | 4 | 4 | 8 | 4 | 8 |
| B.C.M. Hemopo | – | – | 8 | 8 | 8 | 8 | 8 | – | 8 | 6 |
| N.J.C. Strachan | 7 | 7 | 7 | 7 | 7 | 7 | 7 | – | 7 | 8 |
| K.M. Moore | 6 | – | – | – | – | – | – | s | s | 3 |
| B.J. Oliver | s | – | s | 6 | s | 6 | s | 7 | 6 | 8 |
| S. Smith | – | s | s | s | – | – | – | – | – | 3 |
| L.B. Nawalu | – | – | – | – | s | – | 6 | 6 | – | 3 |
| J. Kingsford | – | – | – | – | – | – | s | – | – | 1 |
| L.J. Brice | 5 | 5 | 5 | 5 | 5 | – | 5 | 5 | 5 | 8 |
| J.F. Veikune | 4 | 6 | – | – | 4 | – | – | – | – | 3 |
| P.J. Henderson | s | 4 | 4 | 4 | s | 5 | s | 4 | – | 8 |
| K.J. Darby | – | s | – | – | – | – | – | – | – | 1 |
| W.J. Joines | – | – | – | – | – | s | – | s | – | 2 |
| J-P. Koen | 3 | s | 3 | 3 | 3 | 3 | 3 | – | 3 | 8 |
| M. Fetu | 1 | 1 | 1 | 1 | 1 | – | – | 1 | 1 | 7 |
| V.N. Logavatu | s | 3 | – | – | – | – | – | – | – | 2 |
| H.J. Bryce | – | – | – | – | – | – | s | s | – | 2 |
| B.C. Hewitson | 2 | s | s | s | s | 1 | 1 | 3 | s | 9 |
| M.E.L. Beckham | s | 2 | 2 | 2 | 2 | 2 | 2 | 2 | 2 | 9 |
| J.K. Gilmore | – | – | s | – | – | s | – | – | – | 2 |
| J.W. Andrews | – | – | – | – | – | – | – | s | – | 1 |

N.J.C. Strachan captained in first match v Wanganui.

## SOUTH CANTERBURY TEAM RECORD, 2017

**Played 9**    **Won 7**    **Lost 2**    **Points for 297**    **Points against 219**

| Date | Opponent | Location | Score | Tries | Con | PG | DG | Referee |
|------|----------|----------|-------|-------|-----|----|----|---------|
| August 26 | Buller (H) | Westport | 24–27 | Koen, Coll, Toumohuni, Logavatu | Wright, Medlicott | | | V.F. Ringrose |
| September 2 | King Country (H) | Timaru | 42–36 | Coll (2), Beckham, Medlicott, Strachan, Tora | Wright (6) | | | N.J. Webster |
| September 9 | Mid Canterbury (H) (HS) | Ashburton | 31–16 | Hemopo (2), Strachan, Leatigaga, Tora | Wright (3) | | | N.J. Webster |
| September 16 | Wanganui (H) | Timaru | 21–17 | Beckham, Leatigaga, Hemopo | Wright (3) | | | T.N. Griffiths |
| September 23 | North Otago (H) (HS) | Timaru | 36–29 | Leatigaga (3), Wright, Hemopo, Tora | Wright (3) | | | R.J.M. Gordon |
| September 30 | West Coast (H) | Greymouth | 45–38 | Wright (3), Leatigaga (2), Tora | Wright (6) | Wright | | N.E.R. Hogan |
| October 7 | Wairarapa Bush (H) | Timaru | 29–20 | Wright (2), Buliarua, Hemopo, Tora | Wright (2) | | | N.E.R. Hogan |
| October 14 | East Coast (H) | Ruatoria | 45–7 | Toumohuni (3), Tora (2), Nawalu, Sturgess | Wright (3), Trevathan (2) | | | M.C.J. Winter |
| October 21 | Wanganui (MC semi-final) | Timaru | 24–29 | Wright, Moore, Beckham | Wright (3) | Wright | | N.J. Webster |

HS *Hanan Shield*

# SOUTHLAND

**2017 Status:** Mitre 10 Cup Championship
**Founded 1887.** Affiliated 1894
**President:** K.I. (Kim) McDowall
**Chairman:** J.R. (Jason) Franklin
**General Manager:** A.I. (Andrew) Moreton
**Coach:** H.J. (Hoani) MacDonald
**Assistant coaches:** J.M. (Jason) Kawau, Clarke Dermody
**Main ground:** Rugby Park Stadium, Invercargill
**Capacity:** 20,200
**Colours:** Maroon, blue and white

**RUGBY SOUTHLAND**

## RECORDS

| | | |
|---|---|---|
| Most appearances | 139 | *Jason Rutledge, 2000–2016* |
| Most points | 976 | *Simon Culhane, 1988–98* |
| Most tries | 46 | *Bruce Pascoe, 1983–89* |
| Most points in a season | 194 | *Simon Culhane, 1994* |
| Most tries in a season | 13 | *Simon Forrest, 1992* |
| Most conversions in a season | 38 | *Simon Culhane, 1997* |
| Most penalty goals in a season | 41 | *Eion Crossan, 1989* |
| Most dropped goals in a season | 10 | *Brian McKechnie, 1977* |
| Most points in a match | 37 | *Simon Culhane v Manawatu, 1994* |
| Most tries in a match | 5 | *Simon Forrest v Poverty Bay, 1992* |
| Most conversions in a match | 11 | *Simon Culhane v Malborough, 1997* |
| Most penalty goals in a match | 8 | *Simon Culhane v Manawatu, 1994* |
| Highest team score | 92 | *v Marlborough, 1997* |
| Record victory (points ahead) | 74 | *79–5 v Poverty Bay, 1992* |
| Highest score conceded | 95 | *v Waikato, 1998* |
| Record defeat (points behind) | 88 | *7–95 v Waikato, 1998* |

The 2017 season was a disastrous one for Southland, losing all 10 games. The Stags gave a reasonable account of themselves against Hawke's Bay, Manawatu and Auckland, but in the remaining matches were outclassed.

After the 0–57 loss to Bay of Plenty the union's management and board took the unusual step of issuing a statement to their supporters on the current state of rugby within the province, outlining issues on and off the field, all being reflected in the performance of the representative team. The union also introduced a policy this year that new players arriving in to the province had to be playing club rugby in the province by the second Saturday in June to be eligible for Southland selection, with only exceptional circumstances allowed after that.

Missing from last year were Jimmy Cowan (retired), Dylan Collier (Waikato), Kieran Moffat, Wharenui Hawera, Pene Ravai, Matthew Phillip (all overseas), Josh Clark (Otago), Jaye Thompson-Te Muunu (unavailable), and Tauasosi Tuimavave (injured).

Imports with previous first-class experience were former Hawke's Bay rep Ryan Tongia from overseas and the return from Otago of Scott Eade. Two players with international sevens experience arrived in Neria Fomai (Samoa) and Lewis Ormond (New Zealand).

At number eight, Elliot Dixon set a fine example to the rest of his forwards with his driving play and work rate and was also the main lineout winner. He received good support from Phil Halder who continues to progress. Sadly, Tim Boys was not as effective as previous years but has remained a loyal servant, having now played 127 games for the union. Nineteen-year-old debutant hooker Flynn Thomas gave a glimpse of future potential with a good performance against Tasman.

The best of the backs was undoubtedly debutant second five-eighth Matthew Johnson who provided a cutting edge that has been missing in the midfield for a while and also the best tackler in the backline. Another 19-year-old debutant Jay Renton ended the season as first-choice halfback and looked distinctly promising.

Higher honours went to:
*New Zealand:*    L. Sopoaga
*New Zealand Maori:*    E. Dixon
*New Zealand Sevens:*    D. Collier (to June).

## SOUTHLAND REPRESENTATIVES 2017

| Name | Club | Games for Union | Points for Union | Name | Club | Games for Union | Points for Union |
|---|---|---|---|---|---|---|---|
| Tim Boys | Midlands | 127 | 50 | Aleki Morris | Woodlands | 12 | 10 |
| Jack Capil | Star | 1 | 0 | Nelson "Junior" Ngaluafe | Star | 37 | 25 |
| Elliot Dixon | Blues | 65 | 65 | Lewis Ormond | Woodlands | 9 | 10 |
| Greg Dyer | Pirates OB | 12 | 21 | Jay Renton | Blues | 7 | 0 |
| Scott Eade | Marist | 58 | 249 | James Schrader | Pirates OB | 23 | 20 |
| Neria Fomai | Woodlands | 8 | 5 | Manaaki Selby-Rickit | Star | 6 | 5 |
| Ben Fotheringham | Marist | 1 | 0 | Tupou Sopoaga | Woodlands | 9 | 0 |
| Bill Fukofuka | Blues | 38 | 20 | Sam Stewart | Star | 1 | 0 |
| Phil Halder | Marist | 19 | 0 | Shaun Stodart | Marist | 12 | 0 |
| Liam Howley | Pirates OB | 15 | 10 | William Talataina-Mu | Midlands | 5 | 0 |
| Matthew Johnson | Marist | 10 | 10 | Flynn Thomas | Marist | 10 | 0 |
| Michael McKee | Waikaia | 20 | 5 | Tepasu Thomas | Star | 8 | 0 |
| Guy Millar | Marist | 30 | 5 | Ryan Tongia | Marist | 9 | 3 |
| Brayden Mitchell | Star | 45 | 15 | Jahvis Wallace | Waikaka White Star | 7 | 5 |
| Morgan Mitchell | Albion Excelsior | 31 | 0 | Joseph Walsh | Woodlands | 19 | 0 |
| Michael Molloy | Pirates OB | 23 | 25 | | | | |

## INDIVIDUAL SCORING

| | Tries | Con | PG | DG | Points | | Tries | Con | PG | DG | Points |
|---|---|---|---|---|---|---|---|---|---|---|---|
| Eade | – | 11 | 11 | – | 55 | Selby-Rickit | 1 | – | – | – | 5 |
| Johnson | 2 | – | – | – | 10 | Fukofuka | 1 | – | – | – | 5 |
| Howley | 2 | – | – | – | 10 | Boys | 1 | – | – | – | 5 |
| Morris | 2 | – | – | – | 10 | McKee | 1 | – | – | – | 5 |
| Ormond | 2 | – | – | – | 10 | Schrader | 1 | – | – | – | 5 |
| Dyer | – | 3 | – | – | 6 | Tongia | – | – | 1 | – | 3 |
| Ngaluafe | 1 | – | – | – | 5 | | | | | | |
| Fomai | 1 | – | – | – | 5 | **Totals** | **18** | **14** | **12** | **0** | **154** |
| B. Mitchell | 1 | – | – | – | 5 | | | | | | |
| Molloy | 1 | – | – | – | 5 | *Opposition scored* | 66 | 46 | 10 | 0 | 454 |
| Dixon | 1 | – | – | – | 5 | | | | | | |

## SOUTHLAND 2017

| | Hawke's Bay | North Harbour | Northland | Canterbury | Auckland | Bay of Plenty | Tasman | Manawatu | Wellington | Otago | TOTALS |
|---|---|---|---|---|---|---|---|---|---|---|---|
| L.H. Ormond | 15 | 15 | 15 | 15 | 15 | 15 | 13 | – | 11 | 15 | **9** |
| R.P. Tongia | 14 | 14 | 14 | s | – | s | 15 | 15 | 15 | 14 | **9** |
| A.M. Morris | 11 | 11 | 11 | s | 11 | 11 | 11 | 11 | 14 | 11 | **10** |
| M.J. Molloy | – | s | s | 11 | 14 | 14 | 14 | 14 | s | – | **8** |
| N.S. Ngaluafe | – | – | – | 14 | s | – | – | – | – | – | **2** |
| N. Fomai | 13 | – | – | 13 | 13 | 13 | s | 13 | 13 | 13 | **8** |
| W.D.J. Talataina-Mu | s | s | – | – | s | s | s | – | – | – | **5** |
| M. Johnson | 12 | 13 | 13 | 12 | 12 | 12 | 12 | 12 | 12 | 12 | **10** |
| J.W. Schrader | s | 12 | 12 | – | – | – | – | s | s | s | **6** |
| S.D. Eade | 10 | 10 | 10 | 10 | 10 | 10 | 10 | 10 | s | 10 | **10** |
| G.I. Dyer | s | – | s | s | s | – | s | s | 10 | s | **7** |
| J.L. Renton | 9 | s | – | – | – | s | 9 | 9 | 9 | 9 | **7** |
| L.O. Howley | – | 9 | 9 | 9 | 9 | 9 | – | s | – | s | **7** |
| J.D. Wallace | – | – | s | – | – | – | – | – | – | – | **1** |
| E.C. Dixon | 8 | 8 | 8 | 8 | – | 8 | 8 | 8 | – | – | **8** |
| T.P. Boys | 7 | 7 | 7 | 7 | s | s | 7 | 7 | s | 7 | **10** |
| P.W. Halder | 6 | 6 | 6 | 6 | 7 | 7 | – | 6 | 7 | 6 | **9** |
| T.T. Sopoaga | – | s | s | s | 6 | 6 | 6 | s | 6 | 8 | **9** |
| M.W.H. Selby-Rickit | 5 | s | – | – | s | – | 5 | 4 | 4 | – | **6** |
| M.J.F. McKee | 4 | 4 | 4 | s | 4 | s | 4 | 5 | 5 | 5 | **10** |
| T.R. Thomas | s | – | s | 4 | 5 | 5 | s | – | s | 4 | **8** |
| B.S. Fukofuka | s | 5 | 5 | 5 | 8 | 4 | s | s | 8 | s | **10** |
| J.W. Capil | – | – | – | – | – | – | s | – | – | – | **1** |
| B.J. Fotheringham | – | – | – | – | – | – | – | – | – | s | **1** |
| G.P. Millar | 3 | 3 | 3 | s | s | 3 | 3 | 3 | 3 | 3 | **10** |
| M.D. Mitchell | s | s | s | 3 | 3 | s | s | s | s | s | **10** |
| J.S. Walsh | 1 | 1 | 1 | 1 | 1 | 1 | s | 1 | 1 | 1 | **10** |
| S.D.G. Stodart | s | s | s | s | s | s | 1 | s | s | s | **10** |
| B.T. Mitchell (capt) | 2 | 2 | 2 | 2 | 2 | 2 | s | 2 | 2 | – | **9** |
| F.C. Thomas | s | s | s | s | s | s | 2 | s | s | 2 | **10** |
| S.W. Stewart | – | – | – | – | – | – | – | – | – | s | **1** |

E.C. Dixon captained v Tasman; G.P. Millar v Otago.

## SOUTHLAND TEAM RECORD, 2017

**Played 10  Won 0  Lost 10  Points for 154  Points against 454**

| Date | Opponent | Location | Score | Tries | Con | PG | DG | Referee |
|------|----------|----------|-------|-------|-----|-----|-----|---------|
| August 19 | Hawke's Bay (C) | Napier | 16–24 | Johnson | Eade | Eade (3) | | A.W.B. Mabey |
| August 24 | North Harbour (P/C) | Invercargill | 20–45 | Johnson, Howley | Eade (2) | Tongia, Eade | | J.R. Nutbrown |
| September 2 | Northland (C) | Invercargill | 13–44 | Morris | Dyer | Eade (2) | | P.M. Williams |
| September 8 | Canterbury (P/C) (RS) | Christchurch | 20–78 | Ngaluafe, Fomai | Eade (2) | Eade (2) | | N.P. Briant |
| September 15 | Auckland (P/C) | Invercargill | 17–27 | B. Mitchell, Howley | Eade (2) | Eade | | J.D. Munro |
| September 20 | Bay of Plenty (C) | Rotorua | 0–57 | | | | | P.M. Williams |
| September 24 | Tasman (P/C) | Nelson | 17–50 | Molloy, Morris, Dixon | Eade | | | J.J. Doleman |
| September 30 | Manawatu (C) | Invercargill | 20–25 | Selby-Rickit, Fukofuka | Eade (2) | Eade (2) | | S.W. McDermott |
| October 7 | Wellington (C) | Invercargill | 12–61 | Boys, McKee | Dyer | | | M.G. Lash |
| October 14 | Otago (C) | Dunedin | 19–43 | Ormond (2), Schrader | Eade, Dyer | | | A.W.B. Mabey |

RS *Ranfurly Shield*

# TARANAKI

**2017 Status:** Mitre 10 Cup Premiership
**Founded 1889.** Original member
**President:** Murray Wills
**Chairman:** Lindsay Thomson
**Chief executive officer:** Mike Collins
**Coach:** Colin Cooper
**Assistant coach:** Willie Rickards, Paul Tito
**Main ground:** Yarrow Stadium, New Plymouth
**Capacity:** 23,000
**Colours:** Amber and black

## RECORDS

| | | |
|---|---|---|
| **Most appearances** | 222 | *Ian Eliason, 1964–81* |
| **Most points** | 1723 | *Kieran Crowley, 1980–94* |
| **Most tries** | 64 | *Kieran Crowley, 1980–94* |
| **Most points in a season** | 233 | *Jamie Cameron, 1995* |
| **Most tries in a season** | 13 | *Charlie McAlister, 1985* |
| **Most conversions in a season** | 49 | *Kieran Crowley, 1983* |
| **Most penalty goals in a season** | 39 | *Jamie Cameron, 1995* |
| **Most dropped goals in a season** | 11 | *Ross Brown, 1964* |
| **Most points in a match** | 34 | *Jamie Cameron v Nelson Bays, 1995* |
| **Most tries in a match** | 5 | *George Loveridge v Wanganui, 1913* |
| | | *Dave Vesty v Thames Valley, 1971* |
| | | *Mark Robinson v Southland, 1997* |
| **Most conversions in a match** | 13 | *Kieran Crowley v East Coast, 1983* |
| **Most penalty goals in a match** | 9 | *Beauden Barrett v Bay of Plenty, 2011* |
| **Highest team score** | 104 | *v Nelson Bays, 1995* |
| **Record victory (points ahead)** | 97 | *97–0 v East Coast, 1983* |
| **Highest score conceded** | 80 | *v Otago, 1996* |
| **Record defeat (points behind)** | 60 | *16–76 v North Harbour, 1989* |

Winning the Ranfurly Shield for the sixth time and with a record high winning score meant that this year will be remembered as one of the most successful for Taranaki. The Ranfurly Shield challenge against Canterbury will be recorded as one of the greatest of all-time. Down 0–24 after 20 minutes and 21–38 early in the second half, and then to lead 55–38 shortly before fulltime is probably without precedent in any form of rugby. The last round robin game against North Harbour was sacrificed but will still be recorded as the highest score against a Ranfurly Shield-holding team. The sacrifice was in vain however, as in spite of scoring twice as many tries as Tasman, the lack of discipline cost them victory. This was an unfortunate end for a team which had not scored fewer than four tries in every game throughout the season and was rightly seeded top team at the end of the round robin.

Marty McKenzie was the regular fullback and goal kicker, bringing up a century of points for the second consecutive year. His seven conversions for the challenging team in the Ranfurly Shield match is a new record. Declan O'Donnell was an improved wing, being the only player to appear in every game. Seta Tamanivalu was a strong running centre or wing. Sean Wainui continues to improve in the midfield. Charlie Ngatai added excellence to every game he played. Young Stephen Perofeta is already among the top bracket of first five eighths in the country. Te Toiroa Tahuriorangi gave a number of mature performances.

Toa Halafihi started ten games at number eight which was equal most by a forward. It was a surprise that he was not selected for a Super Rugby team. Lachlan Boshier had a great season which included tries against the big three – Auckland, Canterbury and Wellington – a rare feat. Adrian Wyrill had his biggest season yet. Pita Sowakula, a blindside flanker, was one of the most improved first year forwards in the country. Leon Power was the most used lock with Finn Hoeata – younger brother of former All Black and Taranaki lock Jarrad – being an impressive debutant. The return of Angus Ta'avoa, plus Mitch Graham's recovery from a broken leg, and the return to his home team by Ricky Riccitelli meant for a formidable front row.

Charlie Ngatai captained against Waikato, Wellington, Counties Manukau and North Harbour. Angus Ta'avoa captained the remaining games.

Higher honours went to:

**New Zealand:** B. Barrett, J. Barrett, S. Barrett, W. Naholo, S. Tamanivalu

**New Zealand Under 20:** C. Matoe, S. Perofeta

**Maori All Blacks:** C. Ngatai, L. Price, T. Tahuriorangi, S. Wainu

**New Zealand Sevens:** I. Iopu-Aso, L. Ormond, B. Waaka

## TARANAKI REPRESENTATIVES 2017

| | Club | Games for Union | Points for Union | | Club | Games for Union | Points for Union |
|---|---|---|---|---|---|---|---|
| Lachlan Boshier | New Plymouth OB | 26 | 30 | Jackson Ormond | Southern | 56 | 60 |
| Logan Crowley | Coastal | 4 | 0 | Stephen Perofeta | Clifton | 21 | 54 |
| Johnny Fa'auli | Coastal | 16 | 20 | Leon Power | Coastal | 38 | 0 |
| Tom Florence | New Plymouth OB | 2 | 0 | Leighton Price | Tukapa | 19 | 5 |
| Mitchell Graham | Spotswood | 44 | 5 | Jared Proffitt | Spotswood | 15 | 5 |
| Toa Halafihi | Spotswood | 34 | 55 | Ricky Riccitelli | Tukapa | 9 | 15 |
| Finn Hoeata | New Plymouth OB | 10 | 0 | Brad Slater | New Plymouth OB | 1 | 0 |
| Mike Kainga | Coastal | 9 | 0 | Pita Sowakula | Spotswood | 8 | 15 |
| Warwick Lahmert | Spotswood | 3 | 0 | Asaeli Sorovaki | Spotswood | 5 | 0 |
| Sione Lea | Clifton | 52 | 5 | Angus Ta'avoa | – | 31 | 5 |
| Avon Lewis | Inglewood | 4 | 5 | Te Toiroa Tahuriorangi | New Plymouth OB | 31 | 20 |
| Donald Maka | Stratford | 8 | 0 | Seta Tamanivalu | Spotswood | 52 | 115 |
| Manasa Mataele | Spotswood | 13 | 15 | Kane Thompson | (Wellington) | 6 | 0 |
| Ciarahn Matoe | Coastal | 3 | 20 | Micaiah Torrance | Spotswood | 1 | 0 |
| Marty McKenzie | Clifton | 36 | 392 | Brad Tucker | New Plymouth OB | 7 | 0 |
| Waisake Naholo | Spotswood | 35 | 95 | Latu Vaeno | Spotswood | 17 | 15 |
| Charlie Ngatai | Spotswood | 28 | 73 | Beaudein Waaka | Clifton | 19 | 7 |
| Declan O'Donnell | Clifton | 20 | 30 | Sean Wainui | New Plymouth OB | 34 | 50 |
| Kylem O'Donnell | Clifton | 33 | 15 | Daniel Waite | New Plymouth OB | 1 | 0 |
| Reuben O'Neil | New Plymouth Old Boys | 18 | 5 | Adrian Wyrill | Tukapa | 15 | 15 |

## INDIVIDUAL SCORING

| | Tries | Con | PG | DG | Points |
|---|---|---|---|---|---|
| McKenzie | 1 | 34 | 9 | – | 100 |
| Perofeta | 3 | 3 | 1 | 1 | 27 |
| Boshier | 5 | – | – | – | 25 |
| Naholo | 5 | – | – | – | 25 |
| Ngatai | 5 | – | – | – | 25 |
| Tamanivalu | 5 | – | – | – | 25 |
| Wainui | 5 | – | – | – | 25 |
| D. O'Donnell | 4 | – | – | – | 20 |
| Matoe | 2 | 5 | – | – | 20 |
| Halafihi | 3 | – | – | – | 15 |
| Riccitelli | 3 | – | – | – | 15 |
| Sowakula | 3 | – | – | – | 15 |
| Wyrill | 3 | – | – | – | 15 |
| Mataele | 2 | – | – | – | 10 |

| | Tries | Con | PG | DG | Points |
|---|---|---|---|---|---|
| K. O'Donnell | 2 | – | – | – | 10 |
| Tahuriorangi | 2 | – | – | – | 10 |
| penalty try | 1 | – | – | – | 7 |
| Fa'auli | 1 | – | – | – | 5 |
| Graham | 1 | – | – | – | 5 |
| Lea | 1 | – | – | – | 5 |
| Price | 1 | – | – | – | 5 |
| Proffitt | 1 | – | – | – | 5 |
| Waaka | 1 | – | – | – | 5 |
| **Totals** | **60** | **42** | **10** | **1** | **419** |
| *Opposition scored* | *46* | *32* | *18* | *0* | *348* |

## TARANAKI 2017

| | Waikato | Wellington | Counties Manukau | Auckland | Bay of Plenty | Hawke's Bay | Tasman | Canterbury | Manawatu | North Harbour | Tasman | TOTALS |
|---|---|---|---|---|---|---|---|---|---|---|---|---|
| M.R. McKenzie | 15 | – | 15 | 15 | 15 | 10 | 15 | 15 | 15 | – | 15 | 9 |
| D.P.T.K. O'Donnell | 14 | 14 | s | 14 | 14 | 14 | 14 | 14 | s | 11 | 14 | 11 |
| W.R. Naholo | – | s | 14 | – | – | – | – | – | 14 | – | – | 3 |
| J.T. Ormond | – | – | – | – | – | – | – | – | – | 14 | – | 1 |
| M.M.B.T. Mataele | – | – | 11 | 11 | s | 11 | s | 11 | 11 | – | – | 7 |
| S. Tamanivalu | 11 | – | 13 | 13 | 11 | – | 11 | 13 | 13 | – | 11 | 8 |
| L. Vaeno | s | – | – | – | – | – | – | – | – | – | – | 1 |
| A.P. Lewis | – | – | – | – | – | – | – | – | – | s | – | 1 |
| B. Waaka | s | – | – | – | – | – | – | – | – | – | – | 1 |
| S.T. Wainui | 13 | 13 | – | 12 | 13 | 13 | 13 | 12 | 12 | – | 13 | 9 |
| C.J. Ngatai | 12 | 15 | 12 | s | 12 | – | – | s | s | 15 | 12 | 9 |
| J.F. Fa'auli | – | 12 | – | s | s | 12 | 12 | – | – | 13 | – | 6 |
| D.S. Waite | – | – | – | – | – | – | – | – | – | 12 | – | 1 |
| S. Perofeta | 10 | 10 | 10 | 10 | 10 | 15 | 10 | 10 | 10 | – | 10 | 10 |
| C.R. Matoe | – | – | – | – | – | s | s | – | – | 10 | – | 3 |
| T.T.H. Tahuriorangi | 9 | 9 | 9 | 9 | 9 | s | 9 | 9 | 9 | – | 9 | 10 |
| L.E. Crowley | s | – | – | – | – | – | s | s | – | s | – | 4 |
| K.F.T. O'Donnell | – | s | s | s | s | 9 | – | – | s | 9 | s | 8 |
| W.H. Lahmert | – | – | – | – | – | – | – | – | – | s | – | 1 |
| S.T. Halafihi | 8 | 8 | 8 | 8 | 8 | 8 | 8 | 8 | 8 | – | 8 | 10 |
| T.H.T. Florence | – | – | – | – | – | s | – | – | – | 8 | – | 2 |
| L.S. Boshier | 7 | 6 | 7 | 7 | 7 | s | 7 | 7 | 7 | – | 7 | 10 |
| A.E. Wyrill | s | 7 | – | s | s | 7 | s | s | s | 7 | s | 10 |
| P-G. Sowakula | 6 | – | – | 6 | 6 | 6 | 6 | 6 | 6 | – | 6 | 8 |
| L.W. Power | 5 | 5 | 5 | – | s | 5 | 5 | 5 | 5 | s | 5 | 10 |
| F.W.S.P. Hoeata | – | s | s | 5 | 5 | s | s | s | s | 6 | s | 10 |
| M. Torrance | – | – | – | – | – | – | – | – | – | 5 | – | 1 |
| B.C. Tucker | s | 4 | 4 | 4 | 4 | – | – | s | – | 4 | – | 7 |
| L.T. Price | 4 | – | – | – | – | – | – | – | – | – | – | 1 |
| K.G. Thompson | – | – | – | s | – | 4 | 4 | 4 | 4 | – | 4 | 6 |
| A.Ta'avao | 3 | 3 | – | 3 | 3 | 3 | 3 | 3 | 3 | – | 3 | 9 |
| M.Z.H. Kainga | s | s | 3 | – | – | – | s | – | – | s | – | 5 |
| A.S. Sorovaki | – | – | s | – | s | – | – | – | – | s | – | 3 |
| R.G. O'Neill | – | – | – | s | – | – | – | – | s | 3 | – | 5 |
| M.B. Graham | 1 | 1 | 1 | 1 | 1 | 1 | 1 | 1 | 1 | – | 1 | 10 |
| J.P. Proffitt | s | s | – | s | – | s | s | s | s | 1 | s | 9 |
| S.M. Lea | 2 | 2 | s | – | s | s | – | – | – | – | – | 6 |
| J.R. Riccitelli | – | s | 2 | 2 | 2 | 2 | 2 | 2 | 2 | – | 2 | 9 |
| D.S.K. Maka | s | s | – | s | – | – | s | s | s | 2 | s | 8 |
| B.A. Slater | – | – | – | – | – | – | – | – | – | s | – | 1 |

## TARANAKI TEAM RECORD 2017

Played 11  Won 8  Lost 3  Points for 419  Points against 348

| Date | Opponent | Location | Score | Tries | Con | PG | DG | Referee |
|---|---|---|---|---|---|---|---|---|
| August 19 | Waikato (P) | New Plymouth | 34–29 | Price, Ngatai, Perofeta, Wainui, Tamanivalu, Waaka | McKenzie (2) | | | N. Briant |
| August 26 | Wellington (C) | Wellington | 26–42 | Ngatai, Wainui, Boshier, Naholo | Perofeta (3) | | | M. Lash |
| September 2 | Counties Manukau (P) | New Plymouth | 30–27 | Naholo (2), Ngatai, Riccitelli | McKenzie (2) | McKenzie (2) | | A.Mabey |
| September 9 | Auckland (P) | Auckland | 49–38 | D. O'Donnell, Halafihi, Perofeta, Tahuriorangi, Boshier, K. O'Donnell | McKenzie (5) | McKenzie (2) Perofeta | | M. Fraser |
| September 15 | Bay of Plenty (C) | New Plymouth | 29–7 | D. O'Donnell, Graham, Mataele, Lea | McKenzie (3) | McKenzie | | J. Nutbrown |
| September 23 | Hawke's Bay (C) | Napier | 48–17 | Halafihi, McKenzie, Riccitelli, penalty try, Sowakula, Wainui, Wyrill | McKenzie (3) Matoe | McKenzie | | S. McDermott |
| September 28 | Tasman (P) | New Plymouth | 40–26 | Wainui (2), Fa'auli, Boshier, Sowakula, Halafihi | McKenzie (5) | McKenzie | | A.Mabey |
| October 6 | Canterbury (RS) (P) | Christchurch | 55–43 | Boshier (2), Tamanivalu, Perofeta, Sowakula, Riccitelli, Mataele | McKenzie (7) | McKenzie | Perofeta | M. Fraser |
| October 11 | Manawatu (RS) (C) | New Plymouth | 46–25 | Naholo (2), Tamanivalu (2), Ngatai, K. O'Donnell, Wyrill | McKenzie (4) | McKenzie | | B. O'Keeffe |
| October 15 | North Harbour (P) | Albany | 33–64 | Matoe (2), D. O'Donnell, Proffitt, Wyrill | Matoe (4) | | | S. McDermott |
| October 22 | Tasman (P semi-final) | New Plymouth | 29–30 | D. O'Donnell, Ngatai, Tahurirangi, Tamanivalu | McKenzie (3) | McKenzie | | M. Briant |

# TASMAN

**2017 Status:** Mitre 10 Cup Premiership
**Founded and affiliated** 2005 (December)
**President:** J.R.J. (John) Tapp
**Chairman:** K.J. (Ken) Beams
**Chief executive officer:** A.J.F. (Tony) Lewis
**Coach:** L.R. (Leon) MacDonald
**Assistant coach:** L.B. (Leo) Crowley
**Main ground:** Trafalgar Park, Nelson
**Capacity:** 18,000
**Colours:** Navy blue and red

## RECORDS

| | | |
|---|---|---|
| Most appearances | 104 | *Robbie Malneek, 2006–2017* |
| Most points | 628 | *Marty Banks, 2013–2016* |
| Most tries | 25 | *Robbie Malneek* |
| Most points in a season | 173 | *Marty Banks, 2014* |
| Most tries in a season | 10 | *Peter Playford, 2006* |
| Most conversions in a season | 37 | *Marty Banks, 2014* |
| Most penalty goals in a season | 33 | *Marty Banks, 2016* |
| Most dropped goals in a season | 1 | *by five players* |
| Most points in a match | 28 | *Marty Banks v Northland, 2013* |
| Most tries in a match | 4 | *Peter Playford v Canada A, 2006* |
| | | *Peter Playford v Northland, 2006* |
| Most conversions in a match | 7 | *Aaron Kimura v Northland, 2006* |
| | | *Marty Banks v Manawatu, 2013* |
| Most penalty goals in a match | 8 | *Tom Marshall v Bay of Plenty, 2010* |
| Most dropped goals in a match | 1 | *by five players* |
| Highest team score | 64 | *v Waikato, 2013* |
| Record victory (points ahead) | 56 | *56-0 v Southland, 2016* |
| Highest score conceded | 52 | *v Counties Manukau, 2017* |
| Record defeat (points behind) | 42 | *7–49 v Auckland, 2007* |

For the third time in the last four years Tasman went all the way to the Premiership final to indicate a successful season, but it was one of mixed effort. There was a slow start with two opening defeats followed by a win over Waikato when Waikato missed a last-minute conversion to draw. From the Wellington match onwards the side hit form, coming from 13–28 down to win 37–35 and inflict the only defeat of the season on the rampant eventual Championship winners. The defeat to Counties Manukau in the final round robin match was endured with a semi-final spot already assured and a number of leading players being rested. The semi-final win against their more fancied opponents Taranaki at New Plymouth was a very gutsy effort; however, the performance in the final was below expectations.

With the departure overseas of Marty Banks, Mitchell Hunt stepped into first five-eighth having played most of his rugby for Tasman previously at fullback. He grew in stature the more the season progressed, culminating in a standout performance in the semi-final win over Taranaki, ending the season as one of the better first five-eighths in the Mitre 10 Cup.

The exciting 19-year-old Will Jordan, in his debut season, caught the eye with his speed and penetration at fullback. Another newcomer, Levi Aumua impressed at centre with strong running and powerful tackling. He had a memorable match against Otago when he shrugged off six tackles to score a try followed by a later red card for a dump tackle and subsequent three-match suspension. Alex Nankivell had a steady season at second five-eighth, missing just one match.

James Lowe was the best of the wings, being back to his effervescent best after last year's injury woes while David Havili only managed one appearance due to All Blacks duty. Billy Guyton was in fine form at halfback, having a good combination with Mitchell Hunt, and it was a pity he was injured at the tail end of the season.

Losing captain Shane Christie for the season due to injury was a real blow, but the loose forward combinations of Jordan Taufua, Peter Samu, Vernon Fredericks and Ethan Blackadder competed well, with Taufua and Blackadder to the fore. At lock Alex Ainley, at the age of 36, was playing as well as ever, and with Quinten Strange affected by a shoulder injury, the versatile lock/loose forward Shannon Frizzell stepped up very ably in partnering Ainley.

Tim Perry was a solid scrummager at loosehead prop who missed the final due to All Blacks call-up. Tighthead prop Siosiua Halanukonuka had an injury-plagued season, but this allowed 21-year-old Tyrel Lomax, son of Kiwis rugby league rep John Lomax, who arrived from Australia with a promising reputation, to make a good impression. In Andrew Makalio and the returning Ti'i Paulo, Tasman had two capable hookers, with Makalio showing up well against North Harbour and in the semi-final.

Regulars from 2016 who did not return were Kieron Fonotia, Marty Banks, Tevita Koloamatangi, Ross Geldenhuys (all overseas) and Caleb Makene (Canterbury). This was balanced by the return of Ti'i Paulo and Robbie Malneek from overseas, and Jordan Taufua from Counties Manukau, while New Zealand-born Levi Aumua arrived from Brisbane and Tyrel Lomax from Super Rugby team Melbourne Rebels.

Higher honours went to:

| | |
|---|---|
| *New Zealand:* | K. Hames, D. Havili, T. Perry, L. Squire |
| *New Zealand Maori:* | K. Hames, T. Lomax, J. Lowe |
| *New Zealand Under 20:* | L. Fainga'anuku, W. Jordan |
| *New Zealand Sevens:* | T. Joass, A. Knewstubb, T. Ng Shiu |

## TASMAN REPRESENTATIVES 2017

| | Club | Games for Union | Points for Union |
|---|---|---|---|
| Alex Ainley | Wanderers | 90 | 45 |
| Tomas Aoake | Stoke | 2 | 0 |
| Brendon Asomua-Goodman | Nelson | 1 | 0 |
| Levi Aumua | Riwaka | 8 | 15 |
| Ethan Blackadder | Nelson | 20 | 15 |
| Finlay Christie | Harlequins | 22 | 5 |
| Te Ahiwaru Cirikidaveta | Stoke | 1 | 0 |
| Ryan Coxon | Central | 2 | 0 |
| Lotima Fainga'anuku | Nelson | 17 | 15 |
| Ben Finau | Moutere | 1 | 0 |
| Vernon Fredericks | Moutere | 55 | 20 |
| Shannon Frizell | Marist | 23 | 25 |
| Michael Green | Sydenham [1] | 1 | 5 |
| Billy Guyton | Waimea OB | 52 | 90 |
| Siosiua Halanukonuka | Wanderers | 46 | 5 |
| Kane Hames | Marist | 15 | 0 |
| David Havili | Nelson | 32 | 72 |
| James Hawkey | Marist | 2 | 0 |
| Tom Hill | Stoke | 10 | 0 |
| Mitchell Hunt | Stoke | 23 | 124 |
| Trael Joass | Wanderers | 22 | 0 |
| Will Jordan | Nelson | 10 | 25 |

| | Club | Games for Union | Points for Union |
|---|---|---|---|
| Viliami Lolohea | Harlequins | 17 | 30 |
| Tyrel Lomax | [2] | 8 | 0 |
| James Lowe | Waimea OB | 46 | 100 |
| Andrew Makalio | Harlequins | 21 | 15 |
| Robbie Malneek | Central | 104 | 125 |
| Samiuela Moli | Harlequins | 1 | 0 |
| Alex Nankivell | Stoke | 27 | 30 |
| Tone Ng Shiu | Wanderers | 3 | 0 |
| Tim O'Malley | Waitohi | 11 | 31 |
| Pari Pari Parkinson | Stoke | 10 | 0 |
| Rupena Parkinson | Stoke | 1 | 0 |
| Ti'i Paulo | Renwick | 21 | 5 |
| Tim Perry | Harlequins | 60 | 25 |
| Andrew Petelo | Wanderers | 1 | 0 |
| Isaac Salmon | Nelson | 6 | 0 |
| Peter Samu | Waimea OB | 40 | 65 |
| Willis Scott | Nelson | 1 | 0 |
| Braden Stewart | Central | 4 | 0 |
| Jack Straker | Sydenham [1] | 3 | 0 |
| Quinten Strange | Nelson | 16 | 10 |
| Jordan Taufua | Riwaka | 20 | 15 |

[1] Canterbury RU      [2] arrived from overseas

## INDIVIDUAL SCORING

| | Tries | Con | PG | DG | Points |
|---|---|---|---|---|---|
| Hunt | 4 | 15 | 15 | – | 95 |
| Jordan | 5 | – | – | – | 25 |
| O'Malley | 1 | 7 | 2 | – | 25 |
| Guyton | 2 | 7 | – | – | 24 |
| Lowe | 3 | – | – | – | 15 |
| Aumua | 3 | – | – | – | 15 |
| Blackadder | 3 | – | – | – | 15 |
| Nankivell | 3 | – | – | – | 15 |
| Penalty Try | 2 | – | – | – | 14 |
| Ainley | 2 | – | – | – | 10 |
| Fredericks | 2 | – | – | – | 10 |
| Taufua | 2 | – | – | – | 10 |

| | Tries | Con | PG | DG | Points |
|---|---|---|---|---|---|
| Lolohea | 2 | – | – | – | 10 |
| Frizell | 2 | – | – | – | 10 |
| Green | 1 | – | – | – | 5 |
| Perry | 1 | – | – | – | 5 |
| Samu | 1 | – | – | – | 5 |
| Makalio | 1 | – | – | – | 5 |
| Fainga'anuku | 1 | – | – | – | 5 |
| **Totals** | **41** | **29** | **17** | **0** | **318** |
| Opposition scored | 51 | 37 | 13 | 0 | 370 |

## TASMAN 2017

| | Canterbury | Manawatu | Waikato | Wellington | Otago | Southland | Taranaki | North Harbour | Auckland | Counties Manukau | Taranaki | Canterbury | TOTALS |
|---|---|---|---|---|---|---|---|---|---|---|---|---|---|
| W.T. Jordan | – | 15 | 15 | 15 | 15 | 15 | 15 | 15 | 15 | – | 15 | 15 | 10 |
| R.T. Malneek | – | – | – | – | – | s | s | – | – | – | – | – | 2 |
| J. Hawkey | – | – | – | – | – | – | – | – | s | s | – | – | 2 |
| J.F.R. Lowe | 15 | – | 11 | 11 | 11 | 11 | 11 | 11 | 11 | – | 11 | 11 | 10 |
| V. Lolohea | 14 | 14 | – | – | – | 14 | 14 | – | – | – | – | – | 4 |
| L.T. Fainga'anuku | 11 | 11 | 14 | 14 | 14 | – | – | 14 | 14 | 15 | 14 | – | 9 |
| M.D. Green | – | s | – | – | – | – | – | – | – | – | – | – | 1 |
| T. Aoake | – | – | – | – | – | – | – | – | – | 14 | – | 14 | 2 |
| A.P. Nankivell | 13 | 13 | 13 | 12 | 12 | 12 | 12 | 12 | – | 12 | 12 | 12 | 11 |
| L. Aumua | s | – | s | 13 | 13 | – | – | – | 13 | 11 | 13 | 13 | 8 |
| R. Parkinson | – | – | – | – | – | – | – | – | – | s | – | – | 1 |
| T.J. Joass | 12 | 12 | – | s | s | 13 | 13 | 13 | 12 | 13 | s | s | 11 |
| D.K. Havili | – | – | 12 | – | – | – | – | – | – | – | – | – | 1 |
| M.J. Hunt | 10 | 10 | 10 | 10 | 10 | s | 10 | 10 | 10 | – | 10 | 10 | 11 |
| T.P. O'Malley | s | s | – | – | s | 10 | s | s | s | 10 | s | s | 10 |
| F.T. Christie | 9 | 9 | s | s | s | 9 | s | s | s | 9 | 9 | 9 | 12 |
| B.I. Finau | s | – | – | – | – | – | – | – | – | – | – | – | 1 |
| B-J.A. Guyton | – | s | 9 | 9 | 9 | s | 9 | 9 | 9 | s | – | s | 10 |
| S.J. Taufua | – | 8 | 8 | 8 | 8 | 8 | 8 | 8 | 8 | – | 8 | 8 | 10 |
| P. Samu | 7 | 7 | s | s | s | 7 | s | 7 | – | 8 | 7 | s | 11 |
| V.J. Fredericks | – | s | 7 | 7 | 7 | s | 7 | – | 7 | 7 | – | 7 | 9 |
| E.J. Blackadder | 6 | – | 6 | 6 | 6 | 6 | 6 | 6 | 6 | 6 | 6 | 6 | 11 |
| W.T. Scott | s | – | – | – | – | – | – | – | – | – | – | – | 1 |
| B. Stewart | – | – | – | – | – | – | – | – | s | s | s | – | 3 |
| S.M. Frizell | 8 | 6 | 5 | 5 | s | 4 | s | 4 | 4 | – | 5 | 5 | 11 |
| Q.J. Strange | 5 | 5 | – | – | 5 | 5 | 5 | – | – | – | – | – | 5 |
| A.N. Ainley (capt) | 4 | 4 | 4 | 4 | 4 | – | 4 | – | s | 4 | 4 | 4 | 10 |
| T.J. Ng Shiu | s | – | – | – | – | – | s | – | – | – | – | – | 2 |
| P.P.M. Parkinson | – | s | s | – | – | s | – | 5 | 5 | 5 | – | s | 7 |
| T.A. Cirikidaveta | – | – | – | – | – | – | – | – | – | s | – | – | 1 |
| S. Halanukonuka | 3 | – | – | – | – | s | 3 | s | s | s | s | 1 | 8 |
| K.S. Hames | s | – | – | – | – | – | – | – | – | – | – | – | 1 |
| I. Salmon | – | 3 | 3 | 3 | 3 | – | – | s | s | – | – | – | 6 |
| J.J. Straker | – | s | s | s | – | – | – | – | – | – | – | – | 3 |
| T.S. Lomax | – | – | – | – | s | 3 | s | 3 | 3 | 3 | 3 | 3 | 8 |
| T.G. Perry | 1 | 1 | 1 | 1 | – | 1 | 1 | 1 | 1 | – | 1 | – | 9 |
| T.R. Hill | s | s | s | s | 1 | s | s | – | – | s | – | s | 9 |
| A.A. Petelo | – | – | – | – | s | – | – | – | – | – | – | – | 1 |
| R.C. Coxon | – | – | – | – | – | – | – | – | – | 1 | – | s | 2 |
| A. Makalio | 2 | – | s | 2 | 2 | 2 | 2 | 2 | 2 | – | 2 | 2 | 10 |
| T.T. Paulo | s | 2 | 2 | s | s | s | s | s | s | 2 | s | s | 12 |
| B.J. Asomua-Goodman | – | s | – | – | – | – | – | – | – | – | – | – | 1 |
| S. Moli | – | – | – | – | – | – | – | – | – | s | – | – | 1 |

T.G. Perry captained v Southland, North Harbour and Auckland.

# TASMAN TEAM RECORD, 2017

**Played 12  Won 7  Lost 5  Points for 318  Points against 370**

| Date | Opponent | Location | Score | Tries | Con | PG | DG | Referee |
|---|---|---|---|---|---|---|---|---|
| August 18 | Canterbury (P) | Nelson | 0–39 | | | | | B.D. O'Keeffe |
| August 27 | Manawatu (P/C) | Palmerston North | 20–35 | Ainley, Green | Hunt (2) | Hunt (2) | | R.P. Kelly |
| September 3 | Waikato (P) | Hamilton | 31–29 | Guyton, Fredericks, Jordan, Taufua | Hunt (4) | Hunt | | J.J. Doleman |
| September 10 | Wellington (P/C) | Blenheim | 37–35 | Perry, Jordan, Lowe, Hunt | Hunt (4) | Hunt (3) | | B.E. Pickerill |
| September 16 | Otago (P/C) | Dunedin | 29–27 | Jordan, Lowe, Aumua, Penalty Try | Hunt (2) | Hunt | | M.I. Fraser |
| September 24 | Southland (P/C) | Nelson | 50–17 | Lolohea (2), Samu, Lowe, Blackadder, Taufua, Nankivell, Hunt | O'Malley (4), Hunt | | | J.J. Doleman |
| September 28 | Taranaki (P) | New Plymouth | 26–40 | Makalio, Nankivell, Ainley, Hunt | Guyton (2), O'Malley | | | A.W.B. Mabey |
| October 4 | North Harbour (P) | Blenheim | 21–14 | Penalty Try, Jordan, Frizell | Guyton (2) | | | J.R. Nutbrown |
| October 8 | Auckland (P) | Nelson | 31–18 | Fredericks, Guyton, Blackadder, Jordan, Frizell | Guyton (3) | | | B.E. Pickerill |
| October 14 | Counties Manukau (P) | Pukekohe | 30–52 | O'Malley, Blackadder, Aumua, Nankivell | O'Malley (2) | O'Malley (2) | | P.M. Williams |
| October 21 | Taranaki (P semi-final) | New Plymouth | 30–29 | Fainga'anuku, Hunt | Hunt | Hunt (6) | | N.P. Briart |
| October 28 | Canterbury (P final) | Christchurch | 13–35 | Aumua | Hunt | Hunt (2) | | M.I. Fraser |

# THAMES VALLEY

**2017 Status:** Heartland
**Founded and affiliated 1922**
**President:** K.J. (Kelly) Plummer
**Chairman:** G.W. (Graham) Hallett
**Chief executive officer:** Edmond Leahy
**Coach:** M.W. (Matthew) Bartleet
**Assistant coaches:** D.P. (David) Harrison,
J.R. (Joe) Murray
**Main ground:** Paeroa Domain
**Capacity:** 3000
**Colours:** Black and gold and red

## RECORDS

| | | |
|---|---|---|
| Highest attendance | 7000 | *Thames Valley v Auckland (Ranfurly Shield), 1989* |
| Most appearances | 144 | *B.C. Duggan, 1970–84* |
| Most points | 665 | *D.P. Harrison, 2004–15* |
| Most tries | 42 | *I.F. Campbell, 1981–94* |
| Most points in a season | 127 | *J.R. Reynolds, 2011* |
| Most tries in a season | 14 | *I.F. Campbell, 1988* |
| Most conversions in a season | 30 | *D.B. McCallum, 1995* |
| Most penalty goals in a season | 25 | *J.R. Reynolds, 2011* |
| Most dropped goals in a season | 4 | *T.E. Shaw, 1962* |
| | | *R.W. Kemp, 1968* |
| Most points in a match | 27 | *D.B. McCallum v East Coast, 1995* |
| | | *M. Griffin v King Country, 2003* |
| Most tries in a match | 4 | *I.F. Campbell v North Otago, 1990* |
| | | *G.A. Ellis v North Otago, 1994* |
| | | *G.W. McLiver v Marlborough, 1995* |
| Most conversions in a match | 8 | *G.A. Ellis v West Coast, 1994* |
| | | *M.A. Handley v North Otago, 1994* |
| Most penalty goals in a match | 7 | *D.P. Harrison v Mid Canterbury, 2009* |
| | 7 | *J.R. Reynolds v East Coast, 2011* |
| Highest team score | 86 | *v North Otago, 1994* |
| Record victory (points ahead) | 79 | *86–7 v North Otago, 1994* |
| Highest score conceded | 113 | *v Northland, 1997* |
| Record defeat (points behind) | 99 | *14–113 v Northland, 1997* |

After five rounds of the 2017 Mitre 10 Heartland Championship Thames Valley were third equal on the points table and had a top four play-off position firmly in their sights. However, the only return from the final three games was three bonus points and consequently they fell back to eighth equal position with Poverty Bay. On the strength of their 36¬–35 victory over the Swamp Foxes it was Poverty Bay who progressed to the semi-finals of the Lochore Cup. For the first time in the history of the competition, 20 points were not enough for a team to gain a semi-final position.

For their efforts on the paddock Thames Valley deserved greater rewards. In a warm-up match the Auckland Colts were defeated 27–20 and then in competition games their biggest loss was by only nine points. In fact, three games were lost by one, two and three points, including the Meads Cup finalists, Wanganui and Horowhenua-Kapiti whose victories were by the 'skin of their teeth'. A powerful scrum was the strength of the team. It was never mastered and proved to be a huge challenge for all opposition.

Matt Bartleet, who had previously served four years as assistant coach to Roger Wilton, was appointed as head coach and he was ably assisted by two recent players, Joe Murray and David Harrison. This group developed into a very strong coaching combination. They produced effective game plans and the team was strengthened by the astute recruitment of loan players.

Former Chiefs and Waikato player, Alex Bradley was a great source of inspiration and the young Mt Maunganui forward, Aaron Carrol is an excellent example of the modern lock with his strength in the tight and ability on attack. The Melville outside back, Harry Lafituanai, was a strong runner with the ball in hand. However, the player of the year was Brett Ranga, returning in his original role to have an outstanding season on the side of the scrum. New player, Travis Scott, together with George Lelenoa (formerly a No. 8) and co-captain, Hayden Wisnewski at hooker formed a formidable front row. Although not a big man, the former Irish Under 20 Representative Rory Moloney served the side effectively as openside flanker and he was well backed up by the promising Matt Hart. The other key forward was Connor McVerry who handled the transition from flanker to lock with aplomb.

At halfback, Ben Bonnar did not have the impact of the previous season and he shared the position with newcomer Jonty Wood. The veteran Chris Doak was a tradesman-like first five-eighth with the young Jarod Goodhall also gaining valuable experience as his understudy. Thames Valley were well served in the midfield with co-captain Shaun Hill (who had previously represented in 2014) and newcomer Sam McCahon forming a strong partnership. When given room to move the team's speedsters, Tyrone Keith and Lafituanai were a threat to all opponents and it is disappointing that more attacking opportunities were not created for this pair. Josh Law returned to the side after a year's absence to cover the fullback position.

After four competition matches Thames Valley had scored 14 tries and conceded only five. It was therefore disappointing that their defence faded in the final four matches as they let in 17 tries and only managed one further victory. However, as evidence of the competitive nature of this team, it was Valley's best ever season for scoring bonus points (eight). Thirty-two players were used, with half making their Thames Valley debuts and a core group of 24 appearing the most often. If the majority of these players are available in 2018 then the side will be in a strong position to make further progress.


No player was called upon for higher honours.

## THAMES VALLEY REPRESENTATIVES 2017

| | Club | Games for Union | Points for Union | | Club | Games for Union | Points for Union |
|---|---|---|---|---|---|---|---|
| Hayden Anderson | Te Puke Sports [2] | 6 | 10 | Joshua Law | Thames | 30 | 20 |
| Jarred Bayliss | Te Aroha COB | 1 | 5 | Siaosi "George" Lelenoa | Waihou | 19 | 30 |
| Ben Bonnar | Waihou | 17 | 18 | Keegan Lewis | Waihou | 3 | 0 |
| Alex Bradley | United Matamata Sports [3] | 8 | 15 | Logan Matai-Povey | Thames | 1 | 0 |
| Roger Cairns | Thames | 1 | 0 | Sam McCahon | Waihou | 8 | 0 |
| Aaron Carroll | Mt Maunganui Sports [2] | 6 | 15 | Eden McLean | Mercury Bay | 6 | 0 |
| Chris Doak | Waihou | 34 | 43 | Connor McVerry | Mercury Bay | 19 | 0 |
| Lance Easton | Paeroa West | 65 | 97 | Rory Moloney | Hauraki North | 8 | 5 |
| Tim Erceg | Waihou | 8 | 0 | Brett Ranga [1] | Mt Maunganui Sports [2] | 34 | 20 |
| Jarrod Goodall | Thames | 6 | 34 | Matthew Rolston | Waihou | 14 | 0 |
| Beau Hamilton | Mercury Bay | 21 | 23 | Ethan Roycroft | Te Aroha COB | 14 | 0 |
| Matthew Hart | Waihi | 8 | 5 | Travis Scott | Waihou | 7 | 0 |
| Shaun Hill | Hauraki North | 8 | 10 | Sitiveni Topou | Thames | 5 | 0 |
| Tyrone Keith | Te Aroha COB | 21 | 46 | Rupeni Voyocaki | Thames | 5 | 0 |
| Harry Laufituanai | Melville [3] | 8 | 15 | Hayden Wisnewski | Waihou | 33 | 54 |
| Eli Lavery | Hauraki North | 1 | 0 | Jonty Wood | Waihi | 7 | 0 |

[1] *Player of Origin*      [2] *Bay of Plenty RU*      [3] *Waikato RU*

## INDIVIDUAL SCORING

| | Tries | Con | PG | DG | Points | | Tries | Con | PG | DG | Points |
|---|---|---|---|---|---|---|---|---|---|---|---|
| Doak | – | 8 | 7 | – | 37 | Hamilton | – | – | 2 | – | 6 |
| Goodall | 1 | 10 | 3 | – | 34 | Bayliss | 1 | – | – | – | 5 |
| Lelenoa | 4 | – | – | – | 20 | Hart | 1 | – | – | – | 5 |
| Wisnewski | 3 | – | – | – | 15 | Moloney | 1 | – | – | – | 5 |
| Keith | 3 | – | – | – | 15 | Law | 1 | – | – | – | 5 |
| Bradley | 3 | – | – | – | 15 | | | | | | |
| Carroll | 3 | – | – | – | 15 | **Totals** | **27** | **18** | **12** | **0** | **209** |
| Lafituanai | 3 | – | – | – | 15 | | | | | | |
| Hill | 2 | – | – | – | 10 | *Opposition scored* | *22* | *17* | *10* | *0* | *174* |
| Penalty Try | 1 | – | – | – | 7 | | | | | | |

| THAMES VALLEY 2017 | East Coast | Wanganui | Horowhenua Kapiti | Buller | King Country | Mid Canterbury | West Coast | Poverty Bay | TOTALS |
|---|---|---|---|---|---|---|---|---|---|
| H.K. Laufituanai | 15 | 13 | 15 | 15 | 11 | 15 | 15 | 11 | 8 |
| J.D. Law | s | 15 | s | s | 15 | s | s | 15 | 8 |
| T.G.B. Keith | 14 | 14 | 14 | – | 14 | – | 14 | 14 | 6 |
| R. Voyocaki | 11 | 11 | – | 11 | – | 11 | 11 | – | 5 |
| L.C. Easton | – | s | 11 | – | – | 14 | – | s | 4 |
| E.S. McLean | – | – | – | 14 | – | – | – | – | 1 |
| S.M. McCahon | 13 | 12 | 12 | 13 | 13 | 13 | 13 | 13 | 8 |
| S.M.G. Hill (co-capt) | 12 | – | 13 | 12 | 12 | 12 | 12 | 12 | 7 |
| C.H. Doak | 10 | – | 10 | – | – | 10 | 10 | 10 | 5 |
| J.M. Goodall | s | 10 | s | 10 | 10 | – | s | – | 6 |
| B.R. Hamilton | – | s | – | s | s | s | – | s | 5 |
| B.T. Bonnar | 9 | s | s | s | 9 | s | 9 | 9 | 8 |
| J.B. Bayliss | s | – | – | – | – | – | – | – | 1 |
| J.S. Wood | – | 9 | 9 | 9 | s | 9 | s | s | 7 |
| A.J. Bradley | 8 | 8 | 8 | 8 | 8 | 8 | 8 | 8 | 8 |
| R.C. Moloney | 7 | 7 | 7 | 7 | 7 | 7 | 7 | 7 | 8 |
| B.D. Ranga | 6 | 6 | 6 | 6 | 6 | 6 | 6 | 6 | 8 |
| M.J. Hart | s | s | s | s | s | s | s | s | 8 |
| M.J. Rolston | 5 | – | – | 4 | 4 | – | s | s | 5 |
| A. Carroll | 4 | 4 | 4 | – | – | 4 | 4 | 4 | 6 |
| C.E. McVerry | s | 5 | 5 | 5 | 5 | – | 5 | 5 | 7 |
| K.S. Lewis | – | s | s | – | – | 5 | – | – | 3 |
| T.M.A. Erceg | – | – | – | s | s | s | – | – | 3 |
| R. Cairns | 3 | – | – | – | – | – | – | – | 1 |
| S.K. Lelenoa | s | 3 | 3 | 3 | 3 | 3 | 3 | 3 | 8 |
| T.S. Scott | 1 | 1 | 1 | – | 1 | s | 1 | 1 | 7 |
| E.D. Lavery | – | s | – | – | – | – | – | – | 1 |
| S.V. Topou | – | – | s | s | – | 1 | s | s | 5 |
| H.T. Anderson | – | – | – | 1 | – | – | – | – | 1 |
| H.A. Wisnewski (co-capt) | 2 | 2 | 2 | 2 | 2 | 2 | 2 | 2 | 8 |
| E.T. Roycroft | s | s | s | – | s | s | s | s | 7 |
| L.T. Matai-Povey | – | – | – | s | – | – | – | – | 1 |

## THAMES VALLEY TEAM RECORD, 2017

Played 8    Won 3    Lost 5    Points for 209    Points against 174

| Date | Opponent | Location | Score | Tries | Con | PG | DG | Referee |
|---|---|---|---|---|---|---|---|---|
| August 26 | East Coast (H) | Ruatoria | 42–13 | Wisnewski, Hill, Keith, Bradley, Bayliss, Hart | Doak (2), Goodall | Doak (2) | | M.C.J. Winter |
| September 2 | Wanganui (H) | Paeroa | 19–21 | Carroll, Lelenoa, Maloney | Goodall (2) | | | B.J. Jurlina |
| September 9 | Horowhenua Kapiti (H) | Levin | 10–13 | Lelenoa | Doak | Doak | | R.J.M. Gordon |
| September 16 | Buller (H) | Paeroa | 26–7 | Lafituanai, Bradley, Wisnewski, Lelenoa | Goodall (3) | | | R.J.M. Gordon |
| September 23 | King Country (H) | Te Kuiti | 45–36 | Lelenoa, Goodall, Wisnewski, Lafituanai, Keith | Goodall (4) | Goodall (2), Hamilton (2) | | B.J. Jurlina |
| September 30 | Mid Canterbury (H) | Paeroa | 16–25 | Bradley | Doak | Doak (3) | | T.N. Griffiths |
| October 7 | West Coast (H) | Greymouth | 17–24 | Keith, Penalty Try | Doak | Goodall | | N.J. Webster |
| October 14 | Poverty Bay (H) | Te Aroha | 34–35 | Carroll (2), Lafituanai, Law, Hill | Doak (3) | Doak | | V.F. Ringrose |

# WAIKATO

**2017 Status:** Mitre 10 Cup Premiership
**Founded 1909** as South Auckland.
**Affiliated 1909.** Name changed to Waikato 1921
**President:** Duane Monkley
**Chairman:** Colin Groves
**Chief executive officer:** Blair Foote
**Coach:** Sean Botherway
**Assistant coaches:** Carl Hoeft, Paul Williams
**Main ground:** FMG Stadium, Hamilton
**Capacity:** 27,000
**Colours:** Red, yellow and black

## RECORDS

| | | |
|---|---|---|
| Most appearances | 148 | *Ian Foster, 1985–98* |
| Most points | 1604 | *Matthew Cooper, 1990–99* |
| Most tries | 70 | *Bruce Smith, 1979–84* |
| Most points in a season | 269 | *Brett Craies, 1989* |
| Most tries in a season | 17 | *Bruce Smith, 1981* |
| Most conversions in a season | 69 | *Brett Craies, 1989* |
| Most penalty goals in a season | 57 | *Matthew Cooper, 1993* |
| Most dropped goals in a season | 10 | *John Boe, 1981* |
| Most points in a match | 35 | *Bruce Reihana v North Otago, 2000* |
| Most tries in a match | 5 | *Gary Major v East Coast, 1981* |
| | | *Bruce Smith v Nadi, 1982* |
| | | *Bruce Smith v South Australia, 1983* |
| | | *Ian Wilson v South Canterbury, 1984* |
| | | *Rob Gordon v Southland, 1990* |
| | | *Roger Randle v Poverty Bay, 1998* |
| | | *Sitiveni Sivivatu v Auckland, 2004* |
| Most conversions in a match | 12 | *Matthew Cooper v Wairarapa Bush, 1990* |
| | | *Glen Jackson v West Coast, 2000* |
| Most penalty goals in a match | 7 | *Andrew Strawbridge v Wellington, 1985* |
| | | *Trent Renata v Bay of Plenty, 2013* |
| Highest team score | 121 | *v Poverty Bay, 1998* |
| Record victory (points ahead) | 121 | *121–0 v Poverty Bay, 1998* |
| Highest score conceded | 96 | *v Harlequins Invitation XV, 1995* |
| Record defeat (points behind) | 71 | *25–96 v Harlequins Invitation XV, 1995* |

Beginning the season with two modest wins from their first three games was as good as it got for Waikato as seven consecutive losses followed with relegation to the Championship Division for next year. Team selections were reasonably consistent, but apart from the five tries scored by Jordan Manihera in the first two games it was difficult to recall a memorable moment.

Former All Black, the nomadic Zac Guildford was the regular fullback, but we didn't see that explosive speed remembered from early in his career. Returning from Japan, Dwayne Sweeney was to be captain, but was restricted to just four appearances. Last year's leading tryscorer, Iliesa Tavuyara, failed to get on the scoreboard in eight games this year. Speedy Sevu Reece promised much more than he actually delivered. Bailyn Sullivan is a player to watch out for in the future.

Sam Christie and Matty Lansdown covered the first-five eighth position, but rarely controlled games up to expectation. A rare occurrence – that of having a current All Black playing provincial rugby – occurred with the appearance of Tawera Kerr-Barlow in a game against Tasman. This was to be his last game for Waikato as he is heading overseas. Samoan international Pele Cowley and local boy Harrison Levien covered most of the halfback duties.

Adam Burn and Jordan Manihera were industrious number eights. On the flanks together for the first time were the Jacobson brothers, Luke and Mitch. Luke had captained the champion New Zealand Under 20 side earlier in the year. Both look set to serve Waikato well over the next few years. James Tucker, playing mostly at lock, was the only player to start in every game. Jacob Skeen was his most regular locking partner.

Highly promising prop Atu Moli was only available for the latter half of the season. Sefo Kautai had earlier given good service at tighthead. Ayden Johnstone is developing into a most useful loosehead prop. Hame Fiva started his seven games as hooker, but Samisoni Taukei'aho got to play in all ten games and was the only tight forward to have scored more than one try this year.

Waikato captains this year were – Sweeney v Taranaki, Counties Manukau, Tasman and Canterbury, Tucker v Wellington, Northland and Bay of Plenty, Burn v Auckland and Manawatu, and Skeen v North Harbour.

Higher honours went to:

| | |
|---|---|
| *New Zealand:* | A. Lienert-Brown, T. Kerr-Barlow, D. McKenzie, A. Moli |
| *New Zealand Under 20:* | S. Caird, R. Coxon, L. Jacobson |
| *Maori All Blacks:* | Kerr-Barlow, McKenzie, J. Manihera, L. Messam |
| *New Zealand Sevens:* | D. Collier, T. Mikkelson, I. Te Tamaki |

## WAIKATO REPRESENTATIVES 2017

| | Club | Games for Union | Points for Union | | Club | Games for Union | Points for Union |
|---|---|---|---|---|---|---|---|
| Pita Ah Ki | – | 6 | 20 | Matty Lansdown | Fraser Tech | 10 | 37 |
| Jahrome Brown | Melville | 1 | 0 | Laghlan McWhannell | Hautapu | 2 | 5 |
| Adam Burn | Hamilton Old Boys | 43 | 15 | Jordan Manihera | Hamilton Old Boys | 20 | 40 |
| Sam Caird | Hautapu | 7 | 0 | Atu Moli | University | 16 | 10 |
| Tyler Campbell | University | 13 | 10 | Sekope Moli | Hautapu | 9 | 5 |
| Sam Christie | Fraser Tech | 64 | 34 | Duke Nginingini | Hamilton Old Boys | 4 | 0 |
| Pele Cowley | Fraser Tech | 16 | 0 | Sevu Reece | Hamilton Old Boys | 22 | 64 |
| Hame Faiva | University | 41 | 40 | Jacob Skeen | University | 31 | 0 |
| Leva Fifita | Hamilton Old Boys | 13 | 5 | Bailyn Sullivan | Hamilton Marist | 7 | 10 |
| Zac Guildford | Hamilton Old Boys | 7 | 5 | Dwayne Sweeney | Morrinsville Sports | 82 | 117 |
| Joshua Iosefa-Scott | Melville | 8 | 0 | Raniera Takarangi | Hamilton Old Boys | 1 | 0 |
| Luke Jacobson | Hautapu | 10 | 0 | Latu Talakai | Fraser Tech | 37 | 25 |
| Mitch Jacobson | Hautapu | 26 | 5 | Tevita Taufui | Melville | 18 | 10 |
| Ayden Johnstone | Hautapu | 9 | 0 | Samisoni Taukei'aho | Fraser Tech | 11 | 15 |
| Sefo Kautai | Hamilton Marist | 20 | 5 | Ilisesa Tavuyara | Hamilton Old Boys | 19 | 55 |
| Tawera Kerr-Barlow | Hautapu | 45 | 15 | James Tucker | Hamilton Marist | 22 | 10 |
| Harrison Levien | Hamilton Marist | 18 | 0 | Loni Uhila | Hamilton Marist | 28 | 30 |

## INDIVIDUAL SCORING

| | Tries | Con | PG | DG | Points |
|---|---|---|---|---|---|
| Reece | 5 | 3 | 1 | – | 34 |
| Manihera | 6 | – | – | – | 30 |
| Lansdown | 1 | 4 | 5 | – | 28 |
| Ah Ki | 3 | 1 | 1 | – | 20 |
| Sweeney | – | 7 | 1 | – | 17 |
| Taukei'aho | 3 | – | – | – | 15 |
| Sullivan | 2 | – | – | – | 10 |
| Uhila | 2 | – | – | – | 10 |
| penalty try | 1 | – | – | – | 7 |
| Burn | 1 | – | – | | 5 |
| Campbell | 1 | – | – | – | 5 |

| | Tries | Con | PG | DG | Points |
|---|---|---|---|---|---|
| Guildford | 1 | – | – | – | 5 |
| M. Jacobson | 1 | – | – | – | 5 |
| Kerr-Barlow | 1 | – | – | – | 5 |
| McWhannell | 1 | – | – | – | 5 |
| S. Moli | 1 | – | – | – | 5 |
| Tucker | 1 | – | – | – | 5 |
| Christie | – | 1 | – | – | 2 |
| **Totals** | **31** | **16** | **8** | **0** | **213** |
| Opposition scored | 38 | 29 | 15 | 0 | 293 |

## WAIKATO 2017

| | Taranaki | Counties Manukau | Auckland | Tasman | Northland | Manawatu | Wellington | Canterbury | North Harbour | Bay of Plenty | TOTALS |
|---|---|---|---|---|---|---|---|---|---|---|---|
| Z.R. Guildford | 15 | 15 | 15 | 15 | 15 | 15 | – | – | – | 14 | **7** |
| T.A.J. Campbell | s | 14 | 11 | 11 | 11 | s | 15 | 15 | 15 | 15 | **10** |
| I.R. Tavuyara | 14 | s | 14 | 14 | 14 | – | 14 | – | 14 | s | **8** |
| S.L. Reece | 11 | 11 | s | 13 | 13 | 11 | 11 | 11 | 11 | 11 | **10** |
| B.W.M. Sullivan | 13 | 13 | 13 | – | s | 14 | 13 | 14 | – | – | **7** |
| P.J. Ah Ki | – | – | – | – | s | 13 | s | 13 | 13 | 13 | **6** |
| D.W.H. Sweeney | 12 | 12 | – | 12 | – | – | – | 12 | – | – | **4** |
| T. Taufui | s | s | 12 | – | – | 12 | 12 | s | 12 | 12 | **8** |
| S.J. Christie | 10 | 10 | s | 10 | 10 | 10 | 10 | 10 | s | 10 | **10** |
| M.R.T. Lansdown | – | – | 10 | s | s | s | s | s | 10 | s | **8** |
| P.Z. Cowley | 9 | 9 | 9 | – | 9 | s | 9 | s | s | s | **9** |
| T.N.J. Kerr-Barlow | – | – | – | 9 | – | – | – | – | – | – | **1** |
| H.C. Levien | s | – | – | – | s | 9 | s | 9 | 9 | 9 | **7** |
| R. Takarangi | – | s | – | – | – | – | – | – | – | – | **1** |
| J.M. Manihera | 6 | 8 | 6 | 8 | 8 | s | 8 | 8 | 8 | 8 | **10** |
| A.N. Burn | s | s | 8 | s | s | 8 | s | s | s | s | **10** |
| M.L. Jacobson | 7 | 7 | – | 7 | 7 | 7 | 7 | 7 | 7 | 7 | **9** |
| J.D.R. Brown | – | – | 7 | – | – | – | – | – | – | – | **1** |
| L.B. Jacobson | s | 6 | s | 6 | 6 | 6 | 6 | 6 | 6 | 6 | **10** |
| S.H.L. Fifita | 5 | s | 5 | s | s | 4 | 4 | – | 4 | – | **8** |
| J.F. Tucker | 8 | 5 | 4 | 5 | 5 | 5 | 5 | 5 | 5 | 5 | **10** |
| L.E. McWhannell | – | – | s | – | – | – | – | – | – | s | **2** |
| J.M. Skeen | 4 | 4 | – | 4 | 4 | – | 4 | – | 4 | – | **5** |
| S.W. Caird | – | – | – | – | – | s | s | s | s | 4 | **5** |
| S.S.V. Kautai | 3 | 3 | 3 | 3 | 3 | 3 | s | s | s | – | **9** |
| J.Z.A. Iosefo-Scott | s | s | – | – | – | – | – | – | – | – | **2** |
| S.L. Moli | – | – | s | – | – | – | – | – | – | – | **1** |
| A.Moli | – | – | – | – | – | s | 3 | 3 | 3 | 3 | **5** |
| D.A. Nginingini | – | – | s | s | s | – | – | – | – | – | **3** |
| S.L. Talakai | 1 | – | s | s | – | s | – | – | – | – | **4** |
| L. Uhila | – | 1 | – | 1 | 1 | 1 | s | s | s | s | **8** |
| C.A. Johnstone | s | s | 1 | – | s | – | 1 | 1 | 1 | 1 | **8** |
| E.H. Faiva | 2 | 2 | – | 2 | 2 | 2 | 2 | – | – | – | **7** |
| S.F. Taukei'aho | s | s | 2 | s | s | s | s | s | 2 | 2 | **10** |

## WAIKATO TEAM RECORD 2017

Played 10    Won 2    Lost 8    Points for 213    Points against 293

| Date | Opponent | Location | Score | Tries | Con | PG | DG | Referee |
|---|---|---|---|---|---|---|---|---|
| August 19 | Taranaki (P) | New Plymouth | 29–34 | Manihera (3), M. Jacobson | Sweeney (3) | Sweeney | | N. Briant |
| August 25 | Counties Manukau (P) | Hamilton | 33–21 | Manihera (2), Sullivan, Tucker, Taukei'aho | Sweeney (4) | | | M. Fraser |
| August 30 | Auckland (P) | Auckland | 35–27 | Campbell, Manihera, penalty try, Reece | Lansdown, Christie | Lansdown (3) | | R. Kelly |
| September 3 | Tasman (P) | Hamilton | 29–31 | Uhila, Reece, Taukei'aho, Guildford, Kerr-Barlow | Lansdown (2) | | | J. Doleman |
| September 9 | Northland (C) | Whangarei | 7–37 | Burn | Lansdown | | | M. Lash |
| September 16 | Manawatu (C) | Hamilton | 10–23 | Ah Ki, Taukei'aho | | | | N. Briant |
| September 23 | Wellington (C) | Hamilton | 10–34 | Sullivan | Reece | Reece | | C. Stone |
| September 30 | Canterbury (P) | Christchurch | 17–37 | Reece (2), Ah Ki | Reece | | | G. Jackson |
| October 8 | North Harbour (P) | Hamilton | 11–13 | Lansdown | | Lansdown (2) | | S. McDermott |
| October 14 | Bay of Plenty (C) | Tauranga | 32–26 | A.Moli, Reece, Ah Ki, McWhannell, Uhila | Ah Ki, Recce | Ah Ki | | J. Doleman |

# WAIRARAPA BUSH

**2017 Status:** Heartland
**Founded:** Wairarapa 1886 and original member.
Bush 1890 and affiliated 1893. Amalgamated 1971.
**President:** R.A. (Richard) Dahlberg
**Chairman:** T.H.G. (Tim) Nathan
**Chief executive officer:** A.R. (Tony) Hargood
**Coach:** J.R. (Joe) Harwood
**Assistant coach:** J.C. (James) Bruce
**Main ground:** Memorial Park, Masterton
**Capacity:** 10,000
**Colours:** Green and red

## RECORDS

| | | |
|---|---|---|
| Highest attendance | 12,000 | *Wairarapa Bush v British Isles, 1971 and 1983* |
| Most appearances | 132 | *G.K. McGlashan, 1971–83* |
| Most points | 561 | *P. Harding-Rimene, 1999–2008* |
| Most tries | 43 | *M.T. Foster, 1984–92* |
| Most points in a season | 166 | *G.M. Walters, 2012* |
| Most tries in a season | 14 | *S.F. Simanu, 2005* |
| Most conversions in a season | 28 | *M.F.C. Benton, 1987* |
| Most penalty goals in a season | 34 | *G.M. Walters, 2012* |
| Most dropped goals in a season | 7 | *K.W. Carter, 1985* |
| Most points in a match | 26 | *M.J. Berry v South Canterbury, 1995* |
| Most tries in a match | 4 | *G.I. Karaitiana v Hawke's Bay, 1985* |
| | | *M.T. Foster v Horowhenua, 1987* |
| | | *C.I. Sullivan v Mid Canterbury, 1995* |
| Most conversions in a match | 11 | *M.F.C. Benton v Horowhenua, 1987* |
| Most penalty goals in a match | 6 | *J.T. Te Huia v Buller, 2010* |
| | | *G.M. Walters v South Canterbury, 2012* |
| Highest team score | 82 | *v Horowhenua, 1987* |
| Record victory (points ahead) | 73 | *82–9 v Horowhenua, 1987* |
| Highest score conceded | 96 | *v Canterbury, 2006* |
| Record defeat (points behind) | 86 | *10–96 v Canterbury, 2006* |

Wairarapa Bush's fortunes fell dramatically in 2017, from last year's fourth position with six wins and a Meads Cup semi-final appearance, down to 11th on the table and a solitary win against East Coast who finished below them in last place. Injuries and form did affect the squad with 35 players used, only 16 returning from last year, and the depth was not adequate locally. Lack of fitness may have been an issue as well.

The new coach Joe Harwood discarded a number of the 2016 local regulars in Cameron Hayton, Andrew Smith and Richard Puddy, while elsewhere went Glen Walters (Wellington), Zac Guildford (Waikato) and Andy Humberstone had returned to England. Former Waikato/Counties Manukau/Thames Valley rep Armyn Sanders was an arrival in. Experienced campaigners Nick Olsen and James Goodger only appeared once due to injuries.Former All Black halfback Piri Weepu was a marquee signing, having returned from France. Although heavier than his All Black days, his experience was invaluable to the young team around him. He missed the final match due to a rib injury and then announced his retirement.

In a mobile forward pack that suffered with size and height in comparison to some other

Heartland teams, the loose forwards Brendon Campbell, captain Eddie Cranston, Chris Raymond and Epeli Rayaqayaqa all functioned together quite well. Rayaqayaqa's play, in particular, was quite outstanding. Lock Sam Gammie only made four appearances but exhibited good hard running in the tight.

Of the backs, 20-year-old wing Soli Malatai looked promising, and Tipene Haira appeared in four different positions. It was a blow when concussion ended Sam Monaghan's season early.

In November 2016 the union announced that from 2019 loan players would not be chosen and only local club players and players of origin would be selected for the representative team.

No player was called upon for higher honours.

## WAIRARAPA BUSH REPRESENTATIVES 2017

| | Club | Games for Union | Points for Union | | Club | Games for Union | Points for Union |
|---|---|---|---|---|---|---|---|
| Robbie Anderson | Eketahuna | 21 | 26 | Matthew McCrae | Gladstone | 2 | 0 |
| Cyrus Baker [1] | College Old Boys [2] | 16 | 10 | Corey McFadzean | Carterton | 19 | 5 |
| Brendon Campbell | Eketahuna | 28 | 0 | Lachie McFadzean | Carterton | 34 | 0 |
| Eddie Cranston | Gladstone | 19 | 45 | Andrew McLean | Gladstone | 74 | 26 |
| Nikora Ewe | Pioneer | 7 | 10 | Sam Monaghan | Eketahuna | 23 | 52 |
| Gerard Faitotoa | Northern United [3] | 4 | 0 | Nick Olson | Greytown | 79 | 110 |
| Sam Gammie | Eketahuna | 14 | 12 | James Pakoti | Martinborough | 9 | 5 |
| James Goodger | Marist | 40 | 54 | Daryl Pickering | Carterton | 4 | 0 |
| Tipene Haira | Martinborough | 21 | 20 | Regan Pope | Greytown | 7 | 0 |
| Nick Hohepa | Greytown | 16 | 0 | Tim Priest | Martinborough | 29 | 223 |
| Jacko Hull | Carterton | 20 | 0 | Epeli Rayaqayaqa | East Coast | 6 | 25 |
| Tavita Isaac | Greytown | 7 | 5 | Chris Raymond | Martinborough | 17 | 15 |
| Inia Katia | Gladstone | 63 | 55 | Armyn Sanders | Martinborough | 1 | 0 |
| Matthew Kawana | Pioneer | 25 | 5 | Pu'a Tafa | Marist | 2 | 0 |
| Blane Kete | Greytown | 2 | 0 | Sosaia Tufui | Petone [3] | 6 | 0 |
| Soli Malaitai | Marist | 9 | 15 | Hone Vella | Carterton | 2 | 0 |
| Jayden Mason | Pioneer | 6 | 0 | Piri Weepu [4] | | 8 | 5 |
| Chaz Matthews | Greytown | 1 | 0 | | | | |

[1] Player of Origin  [2] Manawatu RU  [3] Wellington RU  [4] Arrived from overseas

## INDIVIDUAL SCORING

| | Tries | Con | PG | DG | Points | | Tries | Con | PG | DG | Points |
|---|---|---|---|---|---|---|---|---|---|---|---|
| Priest | – | 16 | 7 | – | 53 | Anderson | 1 | – | – | – | 5 |
| Rayaqayaqa | 5 | – | – | – | 25 | Pakoti | 1 | – | – | – | 5 |
| Raymond | 3 | – | – | – | 15 | Baker | 1 | – | – | – | 5 |
| Malaitai | 3 | – | – | – | 15 | Weepu | 1 | – | – | – | 5 |
| Cranston | 3 | – | – | – | 15 | Goodger | – | 1 | – | – | 2 |
| Ewe | 2 | – | – | – | 10 | | | | | | |
| Monaghan | 2 | – | – | – | 10 | **Totals** | **25** | **17** | **7** | **0** | **180** |
| Isaac | 1 | – | – | – | 5 | | | | | | |
| Katia | 1 | – | – | – | 5 | *Opposition scored* | *46* | *32* | *16* | *0* | *344* |
| C. McFadzean | 1 | – | – | – | 5 | | | | | | |

| WAIRARAPA BUSH 2017 | Poverty Bay | Wanganui | East Coast | King Country | Mid Canterbury | Buller | Horowhenua Kapiti | South Canterbury | West Coast | TOTALS |
|---|---|---|---|---|---|---|---|---|---|---|
| S.J. Monaghan | 10 | 15 | 15 | 15 | 15 | – | – | – | – | 5 |
| N.K. Olson | 14 | – | – | – | – | – | – | – | – | 1 |
| S. Malatai | s | 14 | 14 | 14 | s | s | s | 14 | 14 | 9 |
| N.V. Ewe | – | 11 | 11 | 11 | – | 11 | 11 | 11 | s | 7 |
| C.A. McFadzean | – | s | s | s | 14 | 14 | 14 | s | 11 | 8 |
| M.W.D. McCrae | s | 13 | – | – | – | – | – | – | – | 2 |
| R.J. Anderson | s | – | – | – | 13 | 13 | 13 | 13 | – | 5 |
| T.T. Haira | – | s | 13 | 13 | 11 | 15 | 15 | 10 | 10 | 8 |
| C.C. Baker | 13 | 12 | 12 | 12 | 12 | 12 | 12 | 12 | 13 | 9 |
| A.C. Sanders | 12 | – | – | – | – | – | – | – | – | 1 |
| T.C. Priest | 15 | 10 | 10 | 10 | 10 | 10 | 10 | 15 | 15 | 9 |
| P.A.T. Weepu | 9 | 9 | 9 | 9 | s | 9 | 9 | 9 | – | 8 |
| I.S.T. Katia | 11 | s | s | s | 9 | s | s | s | 9 | 9 |
| D.J. Pickering | – | – | – | – | – | – | – | – | s | 1 |
| B.J.W. Campbell | 8 | 8 | 6 | 6 | 6 | 8 | 8 | 8 | 8 | 9 |
| C.R. Matthews | – | s | – | – | – | – | – | – | – | 1 |
| T.A. Isaac | – | – | 8 | 8 | 8 | – | s | s | s | 6 |
| E.J. Cranston (capt) | 7 | 6 | 7 | 7 | 7 | 7 | 7 | s | 12 | 9 |
| C.C. Raymond | 6 | 7 | s | s | s | s | 6 | 6 | 6 | 9 |
| E. Rayaqayaqa | – | – | s | s | s | 6 | – | 7 | 7 | 6 |
| A.R. McLean | 5 | 5 | 5 | 5 | 5 | 4 | 5 | 5 | 5 | 9 |
| L.J.M. McFadzean | 4 | 4 | 4 | 4 | 4 | – | – | – | – | 5 |
| R.S. Pope | s | s | s | – | – | s | s | s | s | 7 |
| S.G. Gammie | – | – | – | s | – | 5 | 4 | 4 | – | 4 |
| J.W.P.R. Goodger | – | – | – | – | – | – | – | – | 4 | 1 |
| G.Z. Faitotoa | 3 | – | – | 3 | – | s | s | – | – | 4 |
| J.M. Mason | – | s | 3 | – | 3 | 3 | 3 | – | 3 | 6 |
| J.T. Hull | 1 | 3 | – | – | – | – | – | – | – | 2 |
| M.H. Kawana | s | – | s | s | 1 | s | s | 3 | – | 7 |
| N.J. Hohepa | – | 1 | 1 | 1 | s | 1 | 1 | 1 | 1 | 8 |
| B. Kete | – | – | – | – | – | – | – | s | s | 2 |
| J.E. Pakoti | 2 | 2 | 2 | 2 | 2 | s | 2 | 2 | 2 | 9 |
| H.J. Vella | s | s | – | – | – | – | – | – | – | 2 |
| S.M. Tufui | – | – | s | s | s | 2 | s | – | s | 6 |
| P. Tafa | – | – | – | – | – | – | – | s | s | 2 |

B.J.W. Campbell captained the final two matches.

## WAIRARAPA BUSH TEAM RECORD, 2017

Played 9   Won 1   Lost 8   Points for 180   Points against 344

| Date | Opponent | Location | Score | Tries | Con | PG | DG | Referee |
|---|---|---|---|---|---|---|---|---|
| August 12 | Poverty Bay | Gisborne | 6–31 | | | Priest (2) | | H.G. Reed |
| August 26 | Wanganui (H) (BSC) | Wanganui | 7–79 | Ewe | Priest | | | T.N. Griffiths |
| September 2 | East Coast (H) | Masterton | 36–10 | Isaac, Raymond, Malatai, Katia, Cranston | Priest (4) | Priest | | T. Kajiwara *Japan* |
| September 9 | King Country (H) | Te Kuiti | 25–32 | Monaghan (2), Rayaqayaqa | Priest (2) | Priest (2) | | B.J. Jurlina |
| September 16 | Mid Canterbury (H) | Masterton | 24–60 | Cranston, Rayaqayaqa, Malatai, C. McFadzean | Priest (2) | | | H.G. Reed |
| September 23 | Buller (H) | Westport | 24–29 | Rayaqayaqa, Anderson, Malatai, Pakoti | Priest (2) | | | N.E.R. Hogan |
| October 1 | Horowhenua Kapiti (H) | Wellington | 12–38 | Raymond, Baker | Priest | | | J.D. Munro |
| October 7 | South Canterbury (H) | Timaru | 20–29 | Weepu, Rayaqayaqa | Priest (2) | Priest (2) | | N.E.R. Hogan |
| October 14 | West Coast (H) | Masterton | 26–36 | Rayaqayaqa, Raymond, Cranston, Ewe | Priest (2), Goodger | | | N.J. Webster |

BSC *Bruce Steel Cup*

# WANGANUI

**2017 Status:** Heartland
**Founded 1888.** Original member
**President:** D.R. (David) Hoskin
**Chairman:** J.M. (Jeff) Phillips
**Chief executive officer:** B.S. (Bridget) Belsham
**Coach:** J.M. (Jason) Caskey
**Assistant coaches:** J.P. (Jason) Hamlin
**Main ground:** Cooks Gardens
**Capacity:** 15,000
**Colours:** Royal blue, black and white

## RECORDS

| | | |
|---|---|---|
| Highest attendance | 6500 | *Wanganui v Scotland, 1996* |
| Most appearances | 146 | *T.T.T. Olney, 1973–90* |
| Most points | 980 | *R.B. Barrell, 1963–77* |
| Most tries | 48 | *J.D. Hainsworth, 1984–95* |
| Most points in a season | 184 | *G.R.J. Lennox, 1994* |
| Most tries in a season | 14 | *H.S. Gordon, 1988* |
| | 14 | *P. Fetuia, 2006* |
| Most conversions in a season | 44 | *M.K. Davis, 2008* |
| Most penalty goals in a season | 39 | *R.B. Barrell, 1975* |
| Most dropped goals in a season | 6 | *L.T. Head, 1952* |
| Most points in a match | 32 | *K.H. Chase v East Coast, 1989* |
| Most tries in a match | 6 | *D.F. Philipson v Taranaki, 1919* |
| Most conversions in a match | 10 | *L.K. Harding v West Coast, 1993* |
| | | *G.R.J. Lennox v Buller, 1994* |
| Most penalty goals in a match | 6 | *R.B. Barrell v Manawatu, 1971* |
| | | *R.B. Barrell v Taranaki, 1975* |
| | | *M.K. Davis v East Coast, 2011* |
| Highest team score | 81 | *v West Coast, 1993* |
| | | *v Buller, 1994* |
| Record victory (points ahead) | 77 | *80–3 v King Country, 2017* |
| Highest score conceded | 88 | *v Taranaki, 2000* |
| Record defeat (points behind) | 84 | *0–84 v Taranaki, 1995* |

After qualifying for the Meads Cup playoffs in a somewhat fortunate fourth place on points differential over Mid Canterbury and West Coast, Wanganui then proceeded to move through the semi-final and final in convincing fashion and claim the Meads Cup as Heartland Champion for an unprecedented three-peat. Their considerable experience in playoff football counted for much in winning both matches at the business end against opponents they had lost to in the round robin. At their free-flowing best Wanganui crushed Wairarapa Bush and King Country but in wet conditions looked vulnerable in defeating Thames Valley and losing to Horowhenua Kapiti.

A rebuild job was necessary with a number of the 2016 Invincibles having moved on. Asalemo Malo, Karl Parker and last year's captain Peter Rowe all retired after the Ranfurly Shield challenge against Canterbury. Rowe had retired after last year's Meads Cup final but came back to play for the NZ Provincial Barbarians against the British and Irish Lions. Others not to reappear were Te Rangatira Waitokia, Kameli Kuruyubaki (both Manawatu), Kane Tamou (Horowhenua Kapiti), Gavin Thornbury (back in Ireland), Michael Nabuliwaqa, Malakai Volau (both back in Fiji) and Tietie Tuimauga (injured).

Gains with previous first-class experience were Taione Ratu (South Canterbury) and Sekonaia Kalou who had represented Fiji at the 2011 World Cup and prior to that had played for North Otago and Otago under the name of Sekonaia Qaranaqio.

Newcomer Timoci Seruwalu was the team's outstanding back, topping the try-scoring with nine. He was a constant threat to opposing defences and played in the final with a well-strapped broken hand. Cameron Crowley missed early matches while recovering from injury, but by season's end had scored five tries, showing great determination on attack and defence. Nick Harding, who had last appeared in 2012, gave good service at fullback, fielding safely, tackling solidly and attacking well.

Whether at first five-eighth or midfield, Craig Clare gave some high-class displays in marshalling the backline with good tactical sense, and experienced halfback Lindsay Horrocks was another to end the season in the ascendancy after indifferent form in the middle of the season.

Lock Sam Madams stood out in the pack for his skills in the lineout and forceful play around the field, and with Campbell Hart they dominated the Horowhenua Kapiti lineout jumpers in the final. Prop Viki Tofa was always good value and he was well supported by newcomer Hamish Mellow who gave of his best at all times. Bryn Hudson was a fine forward at number eight.

The two experienced hookers and co-captains Cole Baldwin and Roman Tutauha passed 100 games and 50 games for Wanganui respectively during the season. Baldwin announced his retirement after the final, having participated in all six of Wanganui's Meads Cup final victories, a fine record.

Higher honours went to:
***New Zealand Heartland:*** C. Clare, C. Crowley, B. Hudson

## WANGANUI REPRESENTATIVES 2017

| | Club | Games for Union | Points for Union | | Club | Games for Union | Points for Union |
|---|---|---|---|---|---|---|---|
| Cole Baldwin | Border | 105 | 97 | Kamipeli Latu [2] | | 25 | 10 |
| Craig Clare | Ruapehu | 17 | 143 | Sam Madams | Marist | 40 | 10 |
| Cameron Crowley | Marist | 45 | 135 | Asalemo Malo | Kaierau | 85 | 243 |
| Kaveni Dabenaise | Border | 11 | 20 | Hamish Mellow | Border | 21 | 0 |
| Sam Dawson | Kaierau | 1 | 0 | Angus Middleton | Border | 10 | 10 |
| Simon Dibben | Marist | 48 | 87 | Karl Parker | Ruapehu | 9 | 5 |
| Tremaine Gilbert | Taihape | 37 | 47 | Taione Ratu | Marist | 3 | 0 |
| Gabriel Hakaraia | Ruapehu | 7 | 5 | Cade Robinson | Kaierau | 3 | 0 |
| Fraser Hammond | Ruapehu | 60 | 30 | Ethan Robinson | Kaierau | 2 | 0 |
| Nick Harding | Border | 13 | 83 | Peter Rowe | Ruapehu | 120 | 20 |
| Campbell Hart | Ruapehu | 15 | 6 | Jona Sawailau | Suburbs [3] | 5 | 25 |
| Cody Hemi | Wanganui Collegiate | 8 | 10 | Timoci Seruwalu | Ngamatapouri | 9 | 45 |
| Lindsay Horrocks | Border | 51 | 47 | Tom Stewart [1] | Feilding OB-Oroua [4] | 10 | 0 |
| Bryn Hudson | Ngamatapouri | 35 | 46 | Ranato Tikoisolomone | Border | 16 | 11 |
| Jamie Hughes | Ruapehu | 20 | 28 | Viki Tofa | Marist | 38 | 10 |
| Fa'alele Iosua | Pirates | 1 | 0 | Bruno Tuivai | Suburbs [3] | 4 | 0 |
| Sokonaia Kalou | Border | 7 | 0 | Roman Tutauha | Ruapehu | 58 | 26 |
| Samu Kubunavanua | Ngamatapouri | 32 | 76 | Dane Whale | Taihape | 27 | 59 |
| Josh Lane | Kaierau | 2 | 0 | | | | |

[1] *Player of Origin*   [2] *Returned from overseas*   [3] *Auckland RU*   [4] *Manawatu RU*

## WANGANUI 2017

| | Canterbury | Wairarapa Bush | Thames Valley | Poverty Bay | South Canterbury | Mid Canterbury | King Country | Horowhenua Kapiti | North Otago | South Canterbury | Horowhenua Kapiti | TOTALS |
|---|---|---|---|---|---|---|---|---|---|---|---|---|
| A. Malo | 15 | – | – | – | – | – | – | – | – | – | – | 1 |
| C.T.A.M. Hemi | – | s | s | 15 | – | s | 10 | 10 | 10 | s | – | 8 |
| J.B. Sawailau | – | – | – | 13 | 15 | 15 | 14 | 14 | – | – | – | 5 |
| N.R. Harding | – | – | – | – | – | s | 15 | 15 | 15 | 15 | 15 | 6 |
| S.M. Kubunavanua | 14 | 15 | 15 | – | – | 14 | – | s | s | s | s | 8 |
| S.K. Dibben | s | 14 | 14 | 14 | 14 | – | – | – | 14 | 14 | 14 | 8 |
| C.J. Crowley | 13 | – | – | s | s | 11 | 11 | 11 | 11 | 11 | 11 | 9 |
| B.M. Tuivai | – | 11 | 11 | 11 | 11 | – | – | – | – | – | – | 4 |
| K. Dabenaise | 11 | 13 | 13 | – | 13 | 13 | s | s | 13 | 13 | 13 | 10 |
| T.S. Seruwalu | 12 | 12 | 12 | 12 | 12 | 12 | 12 | 12 | – | – | s | 9 |
| E. Robinson | – | – | – | – | – | – | – | – | s | 12 | – | 2 |
| C.D. Clare | 10 | 10 | 10 | 10 | 10 | 10 | 13 | 13 | – | – | 12 | 9 |
| D.J. Whale | s | s | s | s | s | – | s | – | 12 | 10 | 10 | 9 |
| L.D. Horrocks | 9 | 9 | 9 | s | 9 | 9 | 9 | 9 | 9 | 9 | 9 | 11 |
| F. Iosua | s | – | – | – | – | – | – | – | – | – | – | 1 |
| T.F. Stewart | – | s | s | 9 | s | s | s | s | s | s | s | 10 |
| B.D. Hudson | 8 | 8 | 8 | 8 | 8 | 8 | 8 | 8 | 8 | 8 | 8 | 11 |
| R. Tikoisolomone | s | – | – | – | – | – | – | – | – | – | – | 1 |
| P.G. Rowe | 7 | – | – | – | – | – | – | – | – | – | – | 1 |
| J.N. Hughes | s | 7 | 7 | s | 7 | s | s | s | 7 | 7 | 7 | 11 |
| A.H. Middleton | – | s | s | 7 | s | 7 | 7 | 7 | s | s | s | 10 |
| F.C. Hammond | – | 6 | 6 | – | – | – | – | – | – | – | – | 2 |
| T.J. Gilbert | – | s | s | 6 | 6 | 6 | 6 | 6 | 6 | 6 | 6 | 10 |
| C. Robinson | – | – | – | – | – | s | – | – | – | s | s | 3 |
| T. Ratu | 6 | – | – | s | s | – | – | – | – | – | – | 3 |
| S. Kalou | 5 | 4 | 4 | – | 5 | 5 | 5 | 5 | – | – | – | 7 |
| S.A. Madams | 4 | 5 | 5 | 4 | 4 | 4 | 4 | 4 | 4 | 4 | 4 | 11 |
| C.J. Hart | – | – | – | 5 | – | – | – | s | 5 | 5 | 5 | 5 |
| J. Lane | – | – | – | – | – | – | s | – | s | – | – | 2 |
| H.B. Mellow | 3 | 1 | 1 | 1 | 1 | – | 1 | 1 | s | 3 | 3 | 10 |
| V.M. Tofa | 1 | 3 | 3 | 3 | 3 | 3 | 3 | 3 | – | – | 1 | 10 |
| K.W. Parker | s | – | – | – | – | – | – | – | – | – | – | 1 |
| S.R. Dawson | s | – | – | – | – | – | – | – | – | – | – | 1 |
| G.T.E. Hakaraia | – | s | s | s | s | 1 | – | – | – | s | – | 6 |
| K.T. Latu | – | – | – | – | – | s | s | s | 1 | 1 | s | 6 |
| C. Baldwin (co-capt) | 2 | s | s | 2 | s | 2 | 2 | 2 | 2 | 2 | 2 | 11 |
| R.B.K. Tutauha (co-capt) | s | 2 | 2 | s | 2 | s | s | s | s | s | s | 11 |

## INDIVIDUAL SCORING

| | Tries | Con | PG | DG | Points | | Tries | Con | PG | DG | Points |
|---|---|---|---|---|---|---|---|---|---|---|---|
| Clare | 3 | 17 | 16 | – | 97 | Hemi | 2 | – | – | – | 10 |
| Seruwalu | 9 | – | – | – | 45 | Hammond | 1 | – | – | – | 5 |
| Harding | 1 | 7 | 7 | – | 40 | Hakaraia | 1 | – | – | – | 5 |
| Sawailau | 5 | – | – | – | 25 | Baldwin | 1 | – | – | – | 5 |
| Crowley | 5 | – | – | – | 25 | Hughes | 1 | – | – | – | 5 |
| Dabenaise | 4 | – | – | – | 20 | Hudson | 1 | – | – | – | 5 |
| Whale | – | 4 | – | 1 | 11 | Kubunavanua | 1 | – | – | – | 5 |
| Horrocks | 2 | – | – | – | 10 | | | | | | |
| Gilbert | 2 | – | – | – | 10 | **Totals** | **43** | **28** | **23** | **1** | **343** |
| Dibben | 2 | – | – | – | 10 | | | | | | |
| Middleton | 2 | – | – | – | 10 | *Opposition scored* | *27* | *24* | *17* | *0* | *234* |

## WANGANUI TEAM RECORD, 2017

**Played 11    Won 7    Lost 4    Points for 343    Points against 234**

| Date | Opponent | Location | Score | Tries | Con | PG | DG | Referee |
|---|---|---|---|---|---|---|---|---|
| June 21 | Canterbury (RS) | Christchurch | 5–71 | Seruwalu | | | | R.P. Kelly |
| August 26 | Wairarapa Bush (H) (BSC) | Wanganui | 79–7 | Seruwalu (3), Clare, Horrocks, Dabenaise, Gilbert, Hammond, Dibben, Middleton | Clare (6), Whale (4) | Clare (3) | | T.N. Griffiths |
| September 2 | Thames Valley (H) | Paeroa | 21–19 | Seruwalu, Dabenaise | Clare | Clare (3) | | B.J. Jurlina |
| September 9 | Poverty Bay (H) | Wanganui | 25–14 | Clare, Hakaraia, Sawailau | Clare (2) | Clare (2) | | H.G. Reed |
| September 16 | South Canterbury (H) | Timaru | 17–21 | Seruwalu | | Clare (4) | | T.N. Griffiths |
| September 23 | Mid Canterbury (H) | Ashburton | 39–40 | Crowley (2), Sawailau, Seruwalu, Dabenaise, Clare | Clare (3) | Clare | | N.J. Webster |
| September 30 | King Country (H) | Wanganui | 80–3 | Sawailau (2), Seruwalu (2), Hemi (2), Crowley (2), Middleton, Horrocks, Baldwin, Hughes, Harding | Clare (4) Harding (2) | Harding Clare | | T.M.T. Cottrell |
| October 7 | Horowhenua Kapiti (H) (BSC) | Levin | 8–15 | Sawailau | | Harding | | M.C.J. Winter |
| October 14 | North Otago (H) | Wanganui | 10–6 | Gilbert | Harding | Harding | | T.M.T. Cottrell |
| October 21 | South Canterbury (MC semi-final) | Timaru | 29–24 | Dibben, Hudson | Harding (2) | Harding (5) | | N.J. Webster |
| October 28 | Horowhenua Kapiti (MC final) | Levin | 30–14 | Dabenaise, Kubunavanua, Crowley | Harding (2), Clare | Clare (2) | Whale | M.C.J. Winter |

BSC *Bruce Steel Cup* RS *Ranfurly Shield*

# WELLINGTON

**2017 Status:** Mitre 10 Cup Championship
**Founded 1879.** Original member
**President:** B.F. (Brendan) Gard'ner
**Chairman:** I.G. (Iain) Potter
**Chief Executive Officer:** S.P. (Steve) Rogers
**Coach:** C.J. (Chris) Gibbes
**Assistant coaches:** A.H.R. (Andre) Bell, Rodney So'oialo
**Main ground:** Westpac Stadium, Wellington
**Capacity:** 34,500
**Colours:** Black and gold

## RECORDS

| | | |
|---|---|---|
| Most appearances | 174 | *Graham Williams, 1964–76* |
| Most points | 909 | *Allan Hewson, 1977–86* |
| Most tries | 105 | *Bernie Fraser, 1975–86* |
| Most points in a season | 199 | *John Gallagher, 1987* |
| Most tries in a season | 24 | *Bernie Fraser, 1981* |
| Most conversions in a season | 47 | *Jackson Garden-Bachop, 2017* |
| Most penalty goals in a season | 38 | *Jon Preston, 1994* |
| Most dropped goals in a season | 7 | *John Dougan, 1971* |
| Most points in a match | 34 | *David Holwell v Bay of Plenty, 2002* |
| Most tries in a match | 7 | *Nigel Geany v Wanganui, 1991* |
| Most conversions in a match | 14 | *Peter O'Shaughnessy, v Horowhenua, 1988* |
| | | *Simon Mannix v Rosario, 1995* |
| Most penalty goals in a match | 7 | *Jackson Garden-Bachop v North Harbour, 2016* |
| Highest team score | 118 | *v Rosario, 1995* |
| Record victory (points ahead) | 101 | *118–17 v Rosario, 1995* |
| Highest score conceded | 82 | *v Otago, 1998* |
| Record defeat (points behind) | 72 | *10–82 v Otago, 1998* |

Wellington won promotion back to the Premiership after rampaging through the Championship, winning 11 of their 12 games. During the course of the season the 74 tries scored by the Lions was a new first division record.

The only defeat of the season was to premiership team Tasman 35–37, conceding a last-minute converted try after leading 28–13, while the demolition of eventual national champions Canterbury 60–14 was the result of the season. With wins over premiership heavyweights Taranaki and Canterbury in 2017, Wellington can look forward to the 2018 Premiership with a lot of confidence.

Missing from last year were Peter Umaga-Jensen, Matt Proctor, Greg Foe, Reg Goodes (all injured), Mark Reddish (retired after an overseas stint), Jason Woodward, Hoani Matenga (both overseas) and Shaun Treeby (North Harbour). Signings were Trent Renata (overseas, having previously represented Waikato/Otago/Tasman), Ben Lam (Auckland), Daniel Kirkpatrick (overseas, last representing Wellington 2009) and Tolu Fahamokioa (returned from Hawke's Bay).

Wellington had a powerhouse pair of wingers in former NZ Sevens rep Ben Lam and discarded All Black Julian Savea who scored six and seven tries respectively. While these are good totals, Savea's form was not deemed sufficient enough by the All Blacks selectors to earn a recall for the end-of-year tour, but did stand out in the semi-final.

Wes Goosen was a success at centre with his elusive running and pace for finishing off tries.

Thomas Umaga-Jensen made a belated debut during the season and played so well, particularly on attack, that at season end he had displaced Regan Verney as starting second five-eighth.

Jackson Garden-Bachop, after a season with the Melbourne Rebels in Super Rugby, displayed great confidence. His running game was a revelation and he had a superb all-round season. With his excellent goal-kicking, he finished the season with 142 points. He was well served by halfbacks Sheridan Rangihuna and Kemara Hauiti-Parapara, with Rangihuna's experience giving him the nod in the playoffs.

Wellington had much depth in all positions of the forward pack. In the loose forwards 20-year-old Du Plessis Kirifi in his debut season was a very energetic openside flanker who showed much skill at the breakdown, winning turnovers and tackling superbly. Captain Brad Shields suffered from injuries, but there was no doubting his ability in the games he played.

Sam Lousi's good form for the Hurricanes carried over into the Mitre 10 Cup for Wellington at lock where James Blackwell gave good support in having his best season yet.

The front row contained two vastly improved young players in tighthead prop Alex Fidow and hooker Asafo Aumua, both 20 years old, who scored eight and seven tries respectively. Their scrum and lineout work developed well from last year and with ball in hand were very hard to stop. Aumua's spectacular try against Canterbury, running 60 metres down the left touchline and going around the fullback to score, was a try of which any winger would have been proud.

Higher honours went to:

| | |
|---|---|
| *New Zealand:* | A. Aumua, D. Coles, V. Fifita, T.J. Perenara, A. Savea, J. Savea, J. To'omaga-Allen |
| *New Zealand Maori:* | J. Garden-Bachop, M. Proctor |
| *New Zealand Under 20:* | A. Aumua, A. Fidow, K. Hauiti-Parapara, C. Price, T. Umaga-Jensen, I. Walker-Leawere |

## WELLINGTON REPRESENTATIVES 2017

| | Club | Games for Union | Points for Union | | Club | Games for Union | Points for Union |
|---|---|---|---|---|---|---|---|
| Ha'amea Ahio | Marist St Pats | 5 | 0 | Sam Lousi | Marist St Pats | 19 | 15 |
| Joe Apikitoa | Hutt OB Marist | 22 | 0 | Will Mangos | Old Boys University | 10 | 5 |
| Leni Apisai | Northern United | 30 | 25 | Chris Middleton | Northern United | 5 | 5 |
| Asafo Aumua | Avalon | 20 | 65 | Sitiveni Paongo | Tawa | 12 | 15 |
| Teariki Ben-Nicholas | Old Boys University | 7 | 0 | Carlos Price | Petone | 2 | 0 |
| James Blackwell | Petone | 20 | 10 | Billy Proctor | Marist St Pats | 3 | 0 |
| Alex Dalzell | Wellington | 2 | 0 | Sheridan Rangihuna | Hutt OB Marist | 27 | 10 |
| Tolu Fahamokioa | Tawa | 23 | 25 | Trent Renata | Oriental Rongotai | 7 | 21 |
| Alex Fidow | Oriental Rongotai | 19 | 50 | Vince Sakaria | Marist St Pats | 19 | 0 |
| Vaea Fifita | Wellington | 30 | 50 | Julian Savea | Oriental Rongotai | 32 | 75 |
| Losi Filipo | Petone | 4 | 5 | Brad Shields | Petone | 60 | 30 |
| Jackson Garden-Bachop | Northern United | 41 | 309 | Galu Taufale | Poneke | 17 | 15 |
| Wes Goosen | Old Boys University | 30 | 70 | Jeffrey To'omaga-Allen | Marist St Pats | 34 | 30 |
| Levi Harmon | Poneke | 2 | 0 | James Tuiatua | Marist St Pats | 4 | 0 |
| Kamara Hauiti-Parapara | Tawa | 12 | 5 | Malo Tuitama | Oriental Rongtotai | 17 | 35 |
| Mateaki Kafatolu | Petone | 7 | 5 | Thomas Umaga-Jensen | Wainuiomata | 8 | 25 |
| Du Plessis Kirifi | Fraser Tech [1] | 10 | 5 | Regan Verney | Old Boys University | 11 | 20 |
| Dan Kirkpatrick | Petone | 30 | 166 | Isaia Walker-Leawere | Poneke | 12 | 10 |
| Ben Lam | Tawa | 11 | 30 | Andrew Wells | Marist St Pats | 5 | 0 |

[1] Waikato RU

## INDIVIDUAL SCORING

| | Tries | Con | PG | DG | Points | | Tries | Con | PG | DG | Points |
|---|---|---|---|---|---|---|---|---|---|---|---|
| Garden-Bachop | 3 | 47 | 11 | – | 142 | Walker-Leawere | 2 | – | – | – | 10 |
| Fidow | 8 | – | – | – | 40 | Rangihuna | 1 | – | – | – | 5 |
| Savea | 7 | – | – | – | 35 | Blackwell | 1 | – | – | – | 5 |
| Aumua | 7 | – | – | – | 35 | Filipo | 1 | – | – | – | 5 |
| Lam | 6 | – | – | – | 30 | Kirifi | 1 | – | – | – | 5 |
| Goosen | 6 | – | – | – | 30 | Kafatolu | 1 | – | – | – | 5 |
| Tuitama | 5 | – | – | – | 25 | Mangos | 1 | – | – | – | 5 |
| Umaga-Jensen | 5 | – | – | – | 25 | Hauiti-Parapara | 1 | – | – | – | 5 |
| Renata | 3 | 3 | – | – | 21 | Shields | 1 | – | – | – | 5 |
| Verney | 4 | – | – | – | 20 | | | | | | |
| Kirkpatrick | 1 | 3 | 2 | – | 17 | **Totals** | **74** | **53** | **13** | **0** | **515** |
| Paongo | 3 | – | – | – | 15 | | | | | | |
| Lousi | 3 | – | – | – | 15 | *Opposition scored* | *37* | *26* | *12* | *0* | *273* |
| Fahamokioa | 3 | – | – | – | 15 | | | | | | |

| WELLINGTON 2017 | Manawatu | Taranaki | Bay of Plenty | Hawke's Bay | Tasman | Canterbury | Waikato | Otago | Southland | Northland | Northland | Bay of Plenty | TOTALS |
|---|---|---|---|---|---|---|---|---|---|---|---|---|---|
| T.W.K. Renata | 15 | 15 | – | – | – | – | – | 15 | 15 | 15 | 15 | 15 | 7 |
| A.T. Wells | – | – | 15 | 15 | – | – | – | – | – | – | – | – | 2 |
| S.J. Savea | 14 | 14 | – | 14 | 14 | 14 | 14 | 14 | – | 14 | 14 | 14 | 10 |
| M.B. Lam | 11 | 11 | 11 | 11 | 15 | 15 | 15 | 11 | – | 11 | 11 | 11 | 11 |
| M. Tuitama | s | s | 14 | s | – | 11 | 11 | – | 14 | s | s | s | 10 |
| L.F. Filipo | – | – | s | – | 11 | – | – | s | 11 | – | – | – | 4 |
| W.T. Goosen | 13 | 13 | 13 | 13 | 13 | – | – | – | s | 13 | 13 | 13 | 9 |
| L. Harmon | – | – | – | – | s | s | – | – | – | – | – | – | 2 |
| B.D. Proctor | – | – | – | – | – | – | s | s | 13 | – | – | – | 3 |
| R.D. Verney | 12 | 12 | 12 | – | 12 | 12 | 12 | 12 | s | s | s | s | 11 |
| T.N.M. Umaga-Jensen | – | – | – | 12 | – | 13 | 13 | 13 | 12 | 12 | 12 | 12 | 8 |
| J.K. Garden-Bachop | 10 | 10 | 10 | 10 | 10 | 10 | s | 10 | 10 | 10 | 10 | 10 | 12 |
| D.J.P. Kirkpatrick | s | s | s | s | – | s | 10 | – | – | – | – | – | 6 |
| S.M. Rangihuna | 9 | s | – | 9 | – | s | 9 | s | 9 | – | 9 | 9 | 9 |
| K.H. Hauiti-Parapara | s | 9 | 9 | s | 9 | 9 | s | 9 | s | 9 | s | s | 12 |
| C.T. Price | – | – | s | – | – | – | – | – | – | s | – | – | 2 |
| B.D.F. Shields (capt) | 8 | 6 | 8 | – | 8 | – | – | – | – | 8 | 6 | 8 | 7 |
| T.G. Ben-Nicholas | s | 8 | – | 8 | – | 8 | 8 | s | 8 | – | – | – | 7 |
| D.P.A. Kirifi | 7 | 7 | – | 7 | 7 | s | 7 | 7 | s | – | s | s | 10 |
| G.F. Taufale | 6 | s | 7 | 6 | – | – | s | 8 | 6 | – | 8 | s | 9 |
| V.T.L. Fifita | – | – | 6 | – | – | – | – | – | – | 6 | – | – | 2 |
| J. Tuiatua | – | – | s | s | – | – | – | – | 7 | s | – | – | 4 |
| M. Kafatolu | – | – | – | – | s | 7 | 6 | 6 | – | 7 | 7 | 7 | 7 |
| J. Blackwell | 5 | 5 | – | 5 | 5 | 6 | – | – | – | 5 | 5 | 6 | 8 |
| S.T. Lousi | 4 | 4 | 5 | – | 4 | 4 | 4 | – | – | 4 | 4 | 4 | 9 |
| I.E.T. Walker-Leaware | s | s | 4 | 4 | s | 5 | – | – | – | – | – | – | 6 |
| W.K. Mangos | – | – | s | s | 6 | s | 5 | 5 | 5 | s | s | 5 | 10 |
| C.K. Middleton | – | – | – | – | – | – | s | 4 | 4 | – | – | – | 3 |
| A.J. Dalzell | – | – | – | – | – | – | – | s | s | – | – | – | 2 |
| A.F. Fidow | 3 | 3 | s | 3 | 3 | s | 3 | 3 | – | 3 | 3 | 3 | 11 |
| S.J.L. Apikitoa | s | s | – | s | – | – | s | s | 3 | s | s | s | 9 |
| J.L. To'omaga-Allen | – | – | 3 | – | – | 3 | – | – | – | – | – | – | 2 |
| U.H. Ahio | – | – | – | – | – | – | – | – | s | – | – | – | 1 |
| O.A. Fahamokioa | 1 | 1 | 1 | 1 | 1 | 1 | s | 1 | 1 | 1 | 1 | 1 | 12 |
| V.V.S. Sakaria | s | s | s | s | – | – | – | – | s | s | s | s | 8 |
| A. Aumua | 2 | 2 | 2 | – | s | 2 | 2 | s | 2 | s | 2 | – | 10 |
| S.F. Paongo | – | s | s | 2 | s | s | 1 | s | s | 2 | s | s | 11 |
| L.C.A. Apisai | – | – | – | s | 2 | s | s | 2 | – | – | – | 2 | 6 |

J. Blackwell captained v Hawke's Bay; S.J. Savea v Canterbury, Waikato, and Otago; G.F. Taufale v Southland.

## WELLINGTON TEAM RECORD, 2017   Played 12   Won 11   Lost 1   Points for 515   Points against 273

| Date | Opponent | Location | Score | Tries | Con | PG | DG | Referee |
|---|---|---|---|---|---|---|---|---|
| August 20 | Manawatu (C) | Palmerston North | 41–29 | Rangihuna, Fidow, Garden-Bachop, Renata, Savea, Tuitama | Garden-Bachop (4) | Kirkpatrick | | S. Kubo *Japan* |
| August 26 | Taranaki (P/C) | Wellington | 42–26 | Aumua (2), Lam, Savea, Verney | Garden-Bachop (3), Kirkpatrick | Garden-Bachop (3) | | M.G. Lash |
| August 31 | Bay of Plenty (C) | Rotorua | 31–10 | Tuitama, Walker-Leawere, Lam, Goosen, Aumua | Garden-Bachop (3) | | | M.C.J. Winter |
| September 6 | Hawke's Bay (C) | Wellington | 40–27 | Fidow (2), Savea, Paongo, Goosen, Tuitama | Garden-Bachop (4), Kirkpatrick | | | J.R. Nutbrown |
| September 10 | Tasman (P/C) | Blenheim | 35–37 | Fidow, Lam, Lousi, Blackwell, Filipo | Garden-Bachop (5) | | | B.E. Pickerill |
| September 17 | Canterbury (P/C) | Wellington | 60–14 | Tuitama (2), Savea, Aumua, Walker-Leawere, Kirifi, Lam, Verney | Garden-Bachop (7) | Garden-Bachop (2, | | R.P.Kelly |
| September 23 | Waikato (P/C) | Hamilton | 34–10 | Lousi, Kirkpatrick, Kafatolu, Umaga-Jensen, Fidow | Garden-Bachop (2), Kirkpatrick | Kirkpatrick | | C.J Stone |
| October 1 | Otago (C) | Wellington | 27–24 | Lam (2), Fidow, Savea | Garden-Bachop (2) | Garden-Bachop | | J.R. Nutbrown |
| October 7 | Southland (C) | Invercargill | 61–12 | Renata, Mangos, Garden-Bachop, Aumua, Umaga-Jensen, Goosen, Verney, Paongo, Hauiti-Parapara | Garden-Bachop (5), Renata (3) | | | M.G. Lash |
| October 12 | Northland (C) | Wellington | 36–18 | Aumua (2), Umaga-Jensen, Garden-Bachop, Fidow, Savea | Garden-Bachop (3) | Garden-Bachop | | R.P. Kelly |
| October 20 | Northland (C semi-final) | Wellington | 49–21 | Goosen (2), Umaga-Jensen, Renata, Fahamokioa, Verney | Garden-Bachop (5) | Garden-Bachop (3) | | G.W. Jackson |
| October 27 | Bay of Plenty (C final) | Wellington | 59–45 a.e.t. | Fahamokioa (2), Umaga-Jensen, Lousi, Shields, Fidow, Goosen, Paongo, Savea | Garden-Bachop (4) | Garden-Bachop (2) | | P.M. Williams |

a.e.t. *after extra time*

# WEST COAST

**2017 Status:** Heartland
**Founded 1890.** Affiliated 1893
**President:** J.G. (John) Torrance (resigned July)
**Chairman:** M.J. (Mike) Meehan
**Chief executive officer:** Mike Connors
**Coach:** S.J. (Sean) Cuttance
**Assistant coach:** N.J. (Nick) Makea
**Main ground:** Rugby Park, Greymouth
**Capacity:** 8000
**Colours:** Red and white

## RECORDS

| | | |
|---|---|---|
| Highest attendance | 5500 | *West Coast v British Isles, 1983* |
| Most appearances | 92 | *M.T. Mudu, 2004–2017* |
| Most points | 712 | *M.A. Foster, 1992–2000* |
| Most tries | 27 | *K.J.J. Beams, 1965–78* |
| Most points in a season | 176 | *M.A. Foster, 1999* |
| Most tries in a season | 9 | *P.A. Teen, 1975* |
| Most conversions in a season | 20 | *M.A. Foster, 1999* |
| Most penalty goals in a season | 38 | *M.A. Foster, 1999* |
| Most dropped goals in a season | 9 | *A.P. O'Regan, 1987* |
| Most points in a match | 24 | *M.A. Foster v Horowhenua Kapiti, 1999* |
| Most tries in a match | 4 | *K. McNee v Buller, 1964* |
| | | *F.P. O'Donnell v Buller, 1970* |
| | | *P.A. Teen v Nelson Bays, 1975* |
| Most conversions in a match | 6 | *L.T. Martyn v Golden Bay-Motueka, 1933* |
| Most penalty goals in a match | 6 | *P.W. Hutchison v East Coast, 1991* |
| | | *C.N. Simpson v South Canterbury, 2007* |
| Highest team score | 54 | *v North Otago, 2016* |
| Record victory (points ahead) | 42 | *45–3 v Golden Bay-Motueka, 1933* |
| Highest score conceded | 128 | *v Canterbury, 1992* |
| Record defeat (points behind) | 128 | *0–128 v Canterbury, 1992* |

Fielding one of their best sides for a while, West Coast ended the season with six wins in 10 games, narrowly failing to make the top four but qualifying for the Lochore Cup. After an indifferent first five matches, in the next four matches, starting with the narrow defeat to top of the table South Canterbury, West Coast played its best rugby of the season.

In the final against Mid Canterbury, West Coast were 10–0 up after just four minutes and playing against 14 men for the remainder of the game, but were unable to press home the advantage. The big forward pack performed very well throughout the season, with the driving maul from a lineout being a particularly successful tactic. Locks Lawrence Babe, Isei Lewaqai and Joshua Manning were all skilful lineout jumpers, with Lewaqai also very prominent around the field. It was a shame that Babe left mid-season for a contract overseas.New props Dylan Turnbull and Daniel Davis along with experienced hooker Troy Tauwhare handled the front-row duties in the scrum soundly. The loose forward unit of Amenatave Tukana, Steven Soper and Brad Tauwhare was just as capable as any other in the Heartland Championship.

In a backline where finishing remained variable throughout the season, the best were halfback Jarrod Ferguson, first five-eighth Tom Reekie and fullback Nick Cumming. Ferguson and

Cumming both missed the semi-final and final due to injury, which was a blow. With Ferguson's unavailability, assistant coach Nick Makea took over in the pivot position.Wing Maleli Mudu set a new appearance record of 92 during the season, having debuted in 2004. Although he has lost some of his pace, he scored a fine try against Buller.

West Coast had the services of ex-All Black Corey Flynn who had returned from playing in Scotland, honouring a handshake made with West Coast CEO Mike Connors back in 2014. He resided in Christchurch and drove to Greymouth every Friday, and his vast experience added much to the team. He missed the final due to playing for a World XV in Japan and then announced his retirement.

Two players who reappeared after absence were loose forwards Brad Tauwhare and Rowan O'Gorman, having last appeared in 2000 and 2014 respectively. O'Gorman scored his 26th try for West Coast which leaves him just one short of the current record.

West Coast challenged Nelson Bays for the Seddon Shield on 5 August and lost 15–32 at Murchison.

Higher honours went to:
**New Zealand Heartland:**   T. Reekie

## WEST COAST REPRESENTATIVES 2017

| | Club | Games for Union | Points for Union | | Club | Games for Union | Points for Union |
|---|---|---|---|---|---|---|---|
| Lawrence Babe | Blaketowm | 4 | 5 | Maleli Mudu | Marist | 92 | 131 |
| Simon Cameron | South Westland | 2 | 0 | Rowan O'Gorman | Marist | 51 | 130 |
| David Crouchley | Grey Valley | 43 | 16 | Jesse Pitman-Joass | Wanderers [4] | 4 | 0 |
| Nick Cumming [1] | Sumner [2] | 23 | 144 | Pieter Prinsloo | Blaketown | 2 | 0 |
| Daniel Davis | South Westland | 9 | 5 | Kelly Rasmussen | Kiwi | 7 | 0 |
| Gilbert Fahey | Marist | 1 | 0 | Tom Reekie | Marist | 10 | 30 |
| Jarrod Ferguson | Kiwi | 14 | 15 | Steven Soper | Wanderers [4] | 10 | 15 |
| Corey Flynn | [3] | 7 | 0 | Regan Stanton | Blaketown | 31 | 57 |
| Dan Foord | Kiwi | 9 | 5 | Todd Struthers | Kiwi | 3 | 10 |
| Nathaniel Hamilton | Wests | 6 | 0 | Brad Tauwhare | Kiwi | 33 | 35 |
| Logan Heath | Grey Valley | 16 | 22 | Troy Tauwhare | Kiwi | 56 | 44 |
| Isei Lewaqai | Marist | 14 | 30 | Peter Te Rakau | Kiwi | 13 | 10 |
| Jesse MacRae | South Westland | 17 | 0 | Robert Thomson | Blaketown | 51 | 5 |
| Nick Makea | – | 30 | 10 | Joshua Tomlinson | Wests | 3 | 0 |
| Thor Manawatu | Grey Valley | 1 | 0 | Amenatave Tukana | Belfast [2] | 16 | 16 |
| Joshua Manning | Marist Albion [2] | 23 | 10 | Dylan Turnbull | Marist | 8 | 0 |
| Sean McClure | Kiwi | 43 | 59 | Noah Waaka | Grey Valley | 1 | 0 |

[1] *Player of Origin*      [2] *Canterbury RU*      [3] *Arrived from overseas*      [4] *Tasman RU*

## INDIVIDUAL SCORING

| | Tries | Con | PG | DG | Points | | Tries | Con | PG | DG | Points |
|---|---|---|---|---|---|---|---|---|---|---|---|
| Cumming | 3 | 11 | 1 | – | 40 | O'Gorman | 1 | – | – | – | 5 |
| Reekie | 1 | 8 | 2 | 1 | 30 | Mudu | 1 | – | – | – | 5 |
| B. Tauwhare | 4 | – | '– | – | 20 | Babe | 1 | – | – | – | 5 |
| Soper | 3 | – | – | – | 15 | Foord | 1 | – | – | – | 5 |
| Stanton | 3 | – | – | – | 15 | Te Rakau | 1 | – | – | – | 5 |
| Lewaqai | 3 | – | – | – | 15 | Davis | 1 | – | – | – | 5 |
| Penalty Try | 2 | – | – | – | 14 | Crouchley | 1 | – | – | – | 5 |
| Struthers | 2 | – | – | – | 10 | McClure | – | 2 | – | – | 4 |
| Ferguson | 2 | – | – | – | 10 | | | | | | |
| Tukana | 2 | – | – | – | 10 | **Totals** | **38** | **21** | **3** | **1** | **248** |
| Manning | 2 | – | – | – | 10 | | | | | | |
| Heath | 2 | – | – | – | 10 | *Opposition scored* | 33 | 25 | 13 | 2 | 262 |
| T. Tauwhare | 2 | – | – | – | 10 | | | | | | |

## WEST COAST 2017

| | King Country | Buller | East Coast | Horowhenua Kapiti | Poverty Bay | South Canterbury | Thames Valley | Wairarapa Bush | North Otago | Mid Canterbury | TOTALS |
|---|---|---|---|---|---|---|---|---|---|---|---|
| J. Pitman-Joass | 15 | 15 | 14 | 14 | – | – | – | – | – | – | 4 |
| N.K. Cumming | – | s | 15 | 15 | 15 | 15 | 15 | 15 | – | – | 7 |
| N.F. Hamilton | 14 | – | – | – | – | s | 14 | s | s | s | 6 |
| R.J. Stanton | s | – | s | s | 14 | 14 | – | 14 | 14 | 14 | 8 |
| T.R. Struthers | 11 | – | – | 11 | 11 | – | – | – | – | – | 3 |
| M.T. Mudu | – | 14 | 11 | – | s | – | s | s | s | s | 7 |
| P.E. Te Rakau | – | 11 | s | – | s | 11 | 11 | 11 | 11 | 11 | 8 |
| S.R. McClure | 13 | 13 | 13 | 13 | 13 | 13 | 13 | 13 | 13 | 13 | 10 |
| L.A. Heath | 12 | 12 | 12 | 12 | 12 | 12 | – | 12 | 12 | 12 | 9 |
| N.M. Waaka | – | – | – | – | – | – | 12 | – | – | – | 1 |
| T.J. Reekie | 10 | 10 | 10 | 10 | 10 | 10 | 10 | 10 | 10 | 10 | 10 |
| J.C. Ferguson | 9 | 9 | 9 | 9 | 9 | 9 | 9 | 9 | – | – | 8 |
| P. Prinsloo | s | – | s | – | – | – | – | – | – | – | 2 |
| T.H. Manawatu | – | s | – | – | – | – | – | – | – | – | 1 |
| N.J. Makea | – | – | – | – | – | – | – | – | 9 | 9 | 2 |
| G.J. Fahey | – | – | – | – | – | – | – | – | – | s | 1 |
| A.V. Tukana | – | – | 8 | 8 | 8 | 8 | 8 | 8 | 8 | 8 | 8 |
| R.P. Thomson | s | – | s | s | s | s | s | s | 15 | 15 | 9 |
| S.G. Soper | 7 | 7 | 7 | 7 | 7 | 7 | 7 | 7 | 7 | 7 | 10 |
| B.G. Tauwhare | 8 | 8 | s | 6 | 6 | 6 | 6 | 6 | 6 | 6 | 10 |
| R.P. O'Gorman | 6 | 6 | – | – | – | s | – | – | s | s | 5 |
| S.D-R. Cameron | – | – | s | – | s | – | – | – | – | – | 2 |
| J.P. Tomlinson | – | – | – | – | – | – | – | s | s | s | 3 |
| L.W. Babe | 5 | 5 | 5 | 5 | – | – | – | – | – | – | 4 |
| J.J. Manning | 4 | 4 | – | – | 4 | 4 | 4 | 4 | 4 | 4 | 8 |
| I.N.T. Lewaqai | s | s | 4 | 4 | – | 5 | 5 | 5 | 5 | 5 | 9 |
| K.R. Rasmussen | – | – | – | – | 5 | – | – | – | – | – | 1 |
| D.J. Davis | 3 | 3 | – | 3 | 3 | 3 | 3 | 3 | 3 | 3 | 9 |
| D.J. Turnbull | 1 | 1 | 1 | – | s | s | – | 1 | 1 | 1 | 8 |
| D.J. Crouchley | s | s | s | – | s | 1 | 1 | s | s | s | 9 |
| D.M. Foord | s | – | 3 | 1 | 1 | – | – | – | – | – | 4 |
| J.S. MacRae | – | – | – | s | – | – | s | s | s | s | 5 |
| T.K. Tauwhare | 2 | 2 | 2 | 2 | 2 | 2 | 2 | 2 | 2 | 2 | 10 |
| C.R. Flynn | s | s | 6 | s | s | – | – | s | s | – | 7 |

## WEST COAST TEAM RECORD, 2017

**Played 10  Won 6  Lost 4  Points for 248  Points against 262**

| Date | Opponent | Location | Score | Tries | Con | PG | DG | Referee |
|---|---|---|---|---|---|---|---|---|
| August 26 | King Country (H) | Taupo | 17–6 | Penalty Try, Struthers, O'Gorman | | | | T. Kajiwara *Japan* |
| September 2 | Buller (H) | Greymouth | 19–34 | Soper, B. Tauwhare, Mudu | Reekie (2) | | | H.G. Reed |
| September 9 | East Coast (H) | Ruatoria | 32–19 | Cumming (2), Babe, Reekie, Soper | Reekie (2) | | Reekie | V.F. Ringrose |
| September 16 | Horowhenua Kapiti (H) | Greymouth | 24–18 | Ferguson (2), Foord, Stanton | McClure (2) | | | T.M.T. Cottrell |
| September 23 | Poverty Bay (H) | Gisborne | 19–36 | Tukana, Struthers, Soper | Cumming (2) | | | H.G. Reed |
| September 30 | South Canterbury (H) | Greymouth | 38–45 | Te Rakau, Manning, Davis, Stanton, Heath | Cumming (5) | Cumming | | N.E.R. Hogan |
| October 7 | Thames Valley (H) | Greymouth | 24–17 | Tukana, Crouchley, B. Tauwhare, Cumming | Cumming (2) | | | N.J. Webster |
| October 14 | Wairarapa Bush (H) | Masterton | 36–26 | B. Tauwhare (2), Lewaqai, T. Tauwhare, Heath | Cumming (2), Reekie (2) | Reekie | | N.J. Webster |
| October 21 | North Otago (LC semi-final) | Greymouth | 24–14 | Manning, Stanton, T. Tauwhare, Lewaqai | Reekie (2) | | | J.D. Munro |
| October 29 | Mid Canterbury (LC final) | Methven | 15–47 | Penalty Try, Lewaqai | | Reekie | | J.D. Munro |

# RANFURLY SHIELD 2017

For the 12th successive year, the Ranfurly Shield changed hands, with Taranaki taking it from Canterbury in an extraordinary match. Canterbury made a blistering start with their fourth try coming in just the 27th minute to lead 31–7. Incredibly, Taranaki not only levelled at 38–38 with a 58th minute penalty goal, but with two more converted tries followed by a 77th minute drop goal, went out to a 55–38 lead.

Canterbury scored the final points with a try on fulltime but surrendered the Shield 43–55.

Taranaki's 55 points is the highest ever score by a challenger, and their seven tries equals the record of most tries scored by a challenger, matching the efforts of Waikato against North Harbour in 2007 and against Taranaki in 2012, when also winning the Ranfurly Shield on both occasions.

Canterbury's 43 points is the highest ever score by a holder losing the Ranfurly Shield, while their six tries is also the most tries scored by a holder when losing the Ranfurly Shield.

*Results*

**Canterbury**

| June 21 | v Wanganui | Christchurch | won | 71–5 |
|---|---|---|---|---|
| August 4 | v Mid Canterbury | Ashburton | won | 69–7 |
| August 27 | v Otago | Christchurch | won | 30–24 |
| September 8 | v Southland | Christchurch | won | 78–20 |
| September 13 | v Counties Manukau | Christchurch | won | 78–5 |
| September 30 | v Waikato | Christchurch | won | 37–17 |
| October 6 | v Taranaki | Christchurch | lost | 43–55 |

**Taranaki**

| October 11 | v Manawatu | New Plymouth | won | 46–25 |
|---|---|---|---|---|

| First and most recent Ranfurly Shield match | Played | Won | Lost | Drawn as holder | Drawn as challenger | Points for | Points against |
|---|---|---|---|---|---|---|---|
| Auckland (1904–2015) | 203 | 158 | 39 | 5 | 1 | 5849 | 2220 |
| Bay of Plenty (1920–2015) | 24 | 2 | 23 | – | – | 328 | 655 |
| Buller (1907–2001) | 12 | – | 11 | – | 1 | 36 | 328 |
| Bush (1927–1968) | 7 | – | 7 | – | – | 41 | 285 |
| Canterbury (1920–2017) | 195 | 148 | 40 | 6 | 1 | 5676 | 2501 |
| Counties Manukau (1958–2017) | 33 | 7 | 24 | – | 2 | 566 | 872 |
| East Coast (1953–2013) | 7 | – | 7 | – | – | 22 | 430 |
| Golden Bay-Motueka (1958) | 1 | – | 1 | – | – | 8 | 56 |
| Hawke's Bay (1905–2015) | 95 | 61[1] | 30 | 3 | 1 | 2016 | 1432 |
| Horowhenua Kapiti (1914–2015) | 10 | – | 10 | – | – | 92 | 563 |
| King Country (1922–2016) | 20 | – | 20 | – | – | 120 | 664 |
| Manawatu (1914–2017) | 37 | 14 | 22 | – | 1 | 490 | 687 |
| Manawhenua (1927–29) | 6 | 3 | 3 | – | – | 84 | 110 |
| Marlborough (1908–2005) | 20 | 7 | 13 | – | – | 245 | 539 |
| Mid Canterbury (1933–2017) | 15 | – | 15 | – | – | 111 | 620 |
| Nelson (1924–1959) | 2 | – | 2 | – | – | 17 | 66 |
| Nelson Bays (1973–2005) | 6 | – | 6 | – | – | 46 | 334 |
| North Harbour (1986–2016) | 20 | 4 | 16 | – | – | 462 | 608 |
| North Otago (1938–2011) | 13 | – | 13 | – | – | 78 | 738 |
| Northland (1935–2015) | 48 | 17 | 30 | 1 | – | 715 | 1053 |
| Otago (1904–2017) | 82 | 36 | 43 | 1 | 2 | 1170 | 1128 |
| Poverty Bay (1911–2008) | 16 | – | 16 | – | – | 78 | 712 |
| South Auckland (1911) | 1 | – | 1 | – | – | 5 | 21 |
| South Canterbury (1920–2006) | 26 | 3 | 23 | – | – | 263 | 821 |
| Southland (1906–2017) | 72 | 30 | 39 | – | 3 | 1061 | 1356 |
| Taranaki (1906–2017) | 96 | 46 | 44 | 3 | 3 | 1460 | 1554 |
| Tasman (2008–2012) | 2 | – | 2 | – | – | 60 | 75 |
| Thames Valley (1951–2016) | 15 | – | 15 | – | – | 76 | 665 |
| Waikato (1932–2017) | 104 | 64 | 36 | 3 | 1 | 3002 | 1593 |
| Wairarapa (1905–1969) | 30 | 12 | 17 | – | 1 | 431 | 504 |
| Wairarapa Bush (1973–2015) | 9 | – | 9 | – | – | 67 | 491 |
| Wanganui (1907–2017) | 30 | – | 29 | – | 1 | 229 | 952 |
| Wellington (1904–2014) | 98 | 50 | 42 | 1 | 5 | 1545 | 1343 |
| West Coast (1932–2000) | 15 | – | 15 | – | – | 107 | 588 |

[1] includes one game where shield did not change hands because of a residential breach.

## HIGHEST WINNING MARGIN BY A SHIELD HOLDER
134 points
Auckland 139          North Otago 5 at Oamaru 1993

## HIGHEST WINNING MARGIN BY A CHALLENGER
45 points
Waikato 52          North Harbour 7 at Albany 2007

## INDIVIDUAL PERFORMANCES

| | | |
|---|---|---|
| **Most matches** | 57 | *G.J. Fox, Auckland* |
| **Most points** | 932 | *G.J. Fox, Auckland* |
| **Most tries** | 53 | *T.J. Wright, Auckland* |
| **Most conversions** | 233 | *G.J. Fox, Auckland* |
| **Most penalty goals** | 142 | *G.J. Fox, Auckland* |
| **Most dropped goals** | 14 | *R.H. Brown, Taranaki;* |
| | | *D. Trevathan, Otago* |
| **Most goals from a mark** | 3 | *J.H. Dufty, Auckland* |
| **Most points in a match** | 40 | *J.J. Kirwan, Auckland v North Otago, 1993* |
| **Most tries in a match** | 8 | *J.J. Kirwan, Auckland v North Otago, 1993* |
| **Most conversions in a match** | 12 | *B.M. Craies, Auckland v Horowhenua,1986;* |
| | | *G.J. Fox, Auckland v Nelson Bays, 1991;* |
| | | *G.W. Jackson, Waikato v West Coast, 2000;* |
| | | *L.H. Munro, Auckland v North Otago, 2008* |
| **Most penalty goals in a match** | 7 | *R.M. Deans, Canterbury v Counties, 1984* |
| | | *C.J. McIntyre, Canterbury v Wellington, 2003* |
| **Most dropped goals in a match** | 3 | *R.H. Brown, Taranaki v Wanganui, 1964;* |
| | | *R.H. Brown, Taranaki v North Auckland, 1964;* |
| | | *G.P. Coffey, Canterbury v Auckland, 1990;* |
| | | *A.P. Mehrtens, Canterbury v Southland, 1995* |

## SUCCESSFUL CHALLENGES

| | | | | | | | | |
|---|---|---|---|---|---|---|---|---|
| Auckland | 15 | | Otago | 5 | | Marlborough | 1 | |
| Canterbury | 15 | | Hawke's Bay | 5 | | Manawatu | 1 | |
| Wellington | 10 | | Northland | 4 | | Bay of Plenty | 1 | |
| Waikato | 9 | | Wairarapa | 3 | | North Harbour | 1 | |
| Southland | 7 | | South Canterbury | 2 | | Counties Manukau | 1 | |
| Taranaki | 6 | | Manawhenua | 1 | | | | |

*Auckland were also the first holders, presented the Shield by the NZRFU in 1902 for having the best record that year.*

## TENURES

| Longest tenure | Challenges resisted | | Shortest tenure | | Days |
|---|---|---|---|---|---|
| Auckland | 1985–93 | 61 | Hawke's Bay | 2013 | 6 |
| Auckland | 1960–63 | 25 | Wellington | 1963 | 7 |
| Canterbury | 1982–85 | 25 | Waikato | 2007 | 7 |
| Hawke's Bay | 1922–27 | 24 | Otago | 2013 | 9 |
| Auckland | 1905–13 | 23 | Auckland | 1972 | 10 |
| Canterbury | 1953–56 | 23 | North Auckland | 1960 | 11 |
| Canterbury | 2000–03 | 23 | Wairarapa | 1950 | 14 |
| Hawke's Bay | 1966–69 | 21 | South Canterbury | 1950 | 14 |
| Waikato | 1997–00 | 21 | Auckland | 1952 | 14 |

*North Auckland resisted one challenge;*
*the other unions were defeated by the first challenger.*

# HAPPENINGS

When the British and Irish Lions last toured New Zealand in 2005, they played 11 matches. 183 players appeared against them in the 11 matches, with just two of those 183 players appearing against the British and Irish Lions in 2017 — Jerome Kaino and Cory Jane. Kaino played for Auckland in 2005 and the All Blacks (three times) in 2017 while Jane played for Wellington in 2005 and the Hurricanes in 2017, each time as a substitute.

•  •  •

The opening match of the British and Lions tour pitted the tourists against a NZ Provincial Barbarians team, and featured father against son. Warren Gatland coached the British and Irish Lions against his son Bryn who played at first five-eighth for the NZ Provincial Barbarians. This has occurred at least once previously at first-class level in New Zealand. In 2009 when Taranaki hosted Hawke's Bay, Adrian Kennedy coached Taranaki against his son Ross who played at lock for Hawke's Bay.

•  •  •

The 31–31 draw between the British and Irish Lions and the Hurricanes was the highest-scoring drawn match for both teams. The British and Irish Lions previous highest drawn result was the 25–25 score against Argentina in 2005, while the Hurricanes previous highest drawn result were the 26–26 draws against the Blues in 2004 and Crusaders in 2010.

•  •  •

Celtic won the South Canterbury club championship for the ninth year in a row, defeating Harlequins 25–10 in the final. Three Celtic players have played in all nine winning finals — Nick Strachan, Matt Fetu and Kali Latu.

•  •  •

In the Mitre 10 Cup the average age of the players was 24 years old. By province the average age was: Auckland 23, Bay of Plenty 24, Canterbury 23, Counties Manukau 25, Hawke's Bay 24, Manawatu 23, North Harbour 24, Northland 25, Otago 23, Southland 23, Taranaki 23, Tasman 25, Waikato 23, Wellington 23.

In the Heartland Championship the average age of the players was 26 years old. By province the average was: Buller 27, East Coast 26, Horowhenua Kapiti 25, King Country 28, Mid Canterbury 25, North Otago 24, Poverty Bay 25, South Canterbury 27, Thames Valley 25, Wairarapa Bush 25, Wanganui 26, West Coast 26.

•  •  •

Five players represented two provinces during 2017: Michael Green — Canterbury, Tasman (on loan). Mikaele Mafi — Otago, North Otago (on loan). Joshua Manning — Canterbury, West Coast (on loan). Jack Straker — Canterbury, Tasman (on loan). Latu Vaeno — Taranaki, Otago (on loan). Mafi played all four opening matches for North Otago and was then recalled by Otago for their match against Auckland on Thursday, 21 September. Two days later he turned out again for North Otago, against South Canterbury.

•  •  •

Otane Sports won the Hawke's Bay second division championship on 5 August, defeating Porangahau 12–5 in the final. The match was notable for 43-year-old Kelly Graham playing his 450th consecutive game for Otane Sports first team in his 26th season, all games consecutive from his debut in 1992. Otane Sports declined promotion to the Hawke's Bay premier division for 2018, but have participated in the premier division previously.

• • •

Asafo Aumua was selected for the All Blacks end-of-year tour without having played any Super Rugby. Since the advent of Super Rugby in 1996, Aumua is now the eighth player to have played for the All Blacks before appearing in Super Rugby. The eight are:

Todd Miller 1997, Daniel Braid 2002, Regan King 2002, Ben Atiga 2003, Saimone Taumoepeau 2004, Jason Eaton 2005, Isaia Toeava 2005, Asafo Aumua 2017.

• • •

In the 28 crossover matches between Premiership and Championship teams in the Mitre 10 Cup, there were 19 wins to Premiership teams, eight wins to Championship teams, and one draw. Since the advent of the Premiership/Championship split in 2011, the overall results per year have been:

| Year | Wins by Premiership teams | Wins by Championship teams | Draws |
|------|---------------------------|----------------------------|-------|
| 2011 | 19 | 9 | 0 |
| 2012 | 21 | 7 | 0 |
| 2013 | 17 | 11 | 0 |
| 2014 | 18 | 10 | 0 |
| 2015 | 19 | 8 | 1 |
| 2016 | 20 | 7 | 1 |
| 2017 | 19 | 8 | 1 |

• • •

Beauden Barrett was World Rugby's 2017 Player of the Year. Among his 2017 achievements were:

- Top points scorer in international rugby with 168 points — which was nearly 30 per cent more than second place.
- His 168 points follows his 152 points in 2016, which makes him the first player in history to exceed 150 points in consecutive years.
- He established a new world record of converting 45 tries against top tier teams in a calendar year.
- His 45 conversions follow his record 40 conversions in 2016 to become the first player in history to kick 40 or more conversions in consecutive years.
- He kicked a record seven conversions in a test against Australia.
- He kicked a record seven conversions in a test against South Africa.
- Including the Samoan game, he kicked seven conversions in three different test matches.
- He has currently kicked 11 consecutive conversions against Australia.
- He kicked a record seven penalty goals in a test against the British and Irish Lions.
- Only considering games where the player was selected as a designated goal-kicker, he has converted 20–25% more tries per match than any other player.

| Player | Tests | Conv | Conv per test |
|--------|-------|------|---------------|
| Barrett | 30 | 95 | 3.2 |
| Carter | 112 | 293 | 2.6 |
| Fox | 46 | 118 | 2.6 |
| Mehrtens | 70 | 169 | 2.4 |
| Clarke | 31 | 33 | 1.1 |
| McCormick | 16 | 23 | 1.4 |
| Wilkinson | 91 | 162 | 1.8 |

- This could be a function of the fact that his teams score more tries.
- His six tries scored in test matches is the fourth most by any test player in 2017.
- Barrett has scored the third most tries in history by a first five-eighth.

| Player | Tests | Tries |
|--------|-------|-------|
| Carter | 94 | 24 |
| Larkham | 84 | 20 |
| Barrett | 30 | 17 |

• • •

At the South Canterbury annual meeting the team manager was elected a life member of the union. Cedric John Coll chalked up 160 games as senior manager during the 2016 season and was reappointed for 2017. His tenure spanned over 20 years. He was colts manager for three years during the early 1980s before his first stint as Heartland manager in 1985–91 followed by terms during 1993–96, 2001–03 and 2015–17.

• • •

Australian Amy Perrett is the first female to officiate as an assistant referee in a Super Rugby fixture. In 2016 Perrett officiated during the Rebels v Stormers match and in 2017 the Reds v Hurricanes match, played at Brisbane on 1 April.

• • •

Feilding High School was well represented in the All Blacks final international of the year when former pupils Sam (as captain) and Luke Whitelock, Codie Taylor and Aaron Smith were in the starting XV for the test against Wales. At the women's Rugby World Cup three former pupils appeared in the final, Sarah Goss and Crystal Mayes for the Black Ferns while Amy Cokayne opposed them as hooker for England. Vilimoni Koroi was a member of the All Blacks Sevens team. At the NZR annual awards Sam Whitelock won the Kelvin R. Tremain Memorial Trophy (Player of the Year) and Sarah Goss won the women's Player of the Year. Goss, who captained the Black Ferns Sevens team to win the world series, was awarded the Oceania athlete of the year trophy at the Association of National Olympic Committee's awards function at Prague. Feilding High School is the only secondary school in Feilding, a small Manawatu town with a population of 14,000.

• • •

Two former *Rugby Almanack* Promising Players of the Year appeared for Italy during 2017. Dean Budd, with six tests, and Jayden Hayward, three tests, were both selected as Promising Players in 2008.

• • •

The 2017 ASB Rugby Awards were held at SKY City Convention Centre, Auckland, on 14 December. The winners are recorded elsewhere in this publication, but we record here the finalists for some of the awards (**winner in bold**).
- Sky Television Fans Try of the Year — Hannah Brough (Waikato), Toni Pulu (Chiefs), **Portia Woodman** (Black Ferns).
- Charles Monro Rugby Volunteer of the Year — Nick Mulvaney (North Harbour), Slade Sturmey (Horowhenua Kapiti), **Sid Tatana** (Wairarapa Bush).
- New Zealand Rugby Referee of the Year — Glen Jackson, **Ben O'Keeffe**, Paul Williams.
- New Zealand Rugby Age Grade Player of the Year — **Asafo Aumua**, Braydon Ennor, Will Jordan.

- Mitre 10 Heartland Championship Player of the Year — **Scott Cameron**, Eric Duff, Bryn Hudson.
- Richard Crawshaw Memorial All Blacks Sevens Player of the Year — **DJ Forbes**, Vilimoni Koroi, Regan Ware.
- Black Ferns Sevens Player of the Year — Tyla Nathan-Wong, **Ruby Tui**, Portia Woodman.
- Duane Monkley Medal (formerly the Mitre 10 Cup player of the Year) — Asafo Aumua, Mike Delany, **Jack Goodhue**.
- Fiao'o Fa'amausili Medal (new for 2017) — Morgan Henderson, **Hazel Tubic**, Selica Winiata.
- Investec Super Rugby Player of the Year — Ngani Laumape, Richie Mo'unga, **Sam Whitelock**.
- Tom French Memorial Maori Player of the Year — **Rieko Ioane**, Charlie Ngatai, Liam Squire.
- ASB Coach of the Year — **Glenn Moore** (Black Ferns), Craig Philpott (Under 20), Scott Robertson (Crusaders).
- New Zealand Rugby Women's Player of the Year — Aldora Itunu, **Sarah Goss**, Portia Woodman.
- Kelvin R. Tremain Memorial Player of the Year — Sarah Goss, Rieko Ioane, **Sam Whitelock**.
- adidas Team of the Year — **Black Ferns**, Crusaders, U20s.

• • •

The Ranfurly Shield has been to many weird and wonderful places during its 115 years of existence. During 2017 it spent 14 days out of the country and, as far as we are aware, this is the first time the Ranfurly Shield has left New Zealand.

Canterbury RU 2016 Volunteer of the year Julie Patterson is also Human Resources manager at Antarctica NZ in Christchurch, with Christchurch one of just five gateway cities to Antarctica. As the Ranfurly Shield would be residing in Canterbury over the 2016-2017 summer and with Scott Base in Antarctica celebrating 60 years in January 2017, the idea occurred to Julie to tie the two events together and take the Shield down to Scott Base at McMurdo Sound, Antarctica.

After receiving the required permission from the Canterbury RU, Julie and the Ranfurly Shield left Christchurch in a US airforce C17 Globemaster on 27 January and five hours later touched down at new Phoenix Ice runway at McMurdo Sound, the first scheduled flight on the new runway.

The Ranfury Shield returned to Christchurch on 9 February. At the 2017 Canterbury RU AGM Julie was elected vice-President of the union, a two-year position, and on course to be Canterbury RU President in 2019.

# 2017 SEASON'S STATISTICS

## LEADING SCORERS IN ALL FIRST-CLASS MATCHES IN NEW ZEALAND AND FOR NEW ZEALAND TEAMS OVERSEAS

*(Record: 519, G.J. Fox, 1989 in 32 games, 2 Tries, 122 Con, 88 PG, 1 DG)*

|  | Teams | M | Tries | Con | PG | DG | Total |
|---|---|---|---|---|---|---|---|
| R. Mo'unga | Crusaders/Canterbury/UK Barbarians/ New Zealand | 26 | 8 | 80 | 35 | 0 | 305 |
| B.J. Barrett | Hurricanes/New Zealand | 29 | 10 | 65 | 18 | 0 | 234 |
| D.S. McKenzie | Chiefs/NZ Maori/New Zealand | 28 | 11 | 23 | 23 | 0 | 170 |
| J.R. Percival | Mid Canterbury/NZ Heartland | 12 | 4 | 38 | 19 | 1 | 156 |
| M.J. Hunt | Crusaders/Tasman | 24 | 6 | 30 | 20 | 1 | 153 |
| J.K. Garden-Bachop | Wellington/NZ Maori | 14 | 4 | 48 | 12 | 0 | 152 |
| J.M. Barrett | Hurricanes/New Zealand | 20 | 8 | 38 | 11 | 0 | 149 |
| J.J. Lash | Buller | 9 | 6 | 27 | 19 | 2 | 147 |
| I.T. West | Blues/NZ Maori/Hawke's Bay | 19 | 4 | 36 | 17 | 0 | 143 |
| J.S. So'oialo | Horowhenua Kapiti | 10 | 3 | 17 | 28 | 0 | 133 |
| F.H. Smith | Highlanders/Otago | 19 | 5 | 29 | 15 | 0 | 128 |
| M. Banks | Highlanders | 15 | 1 | 36 | 16 | 0 | 125 |
| T.J. Falcon | NZ Under 20/Hawke's Bay | 16 | 3 | 35 | 12 | 0 | 121 |
| M.R. McKenzie | Crusaders/Taranaki | 14 | 1 | 39 | 9 | 0 | 110 |
| B.E.C. Gatland | Blues/NZ Provincial Barbarians/ North Harbour | 14 | 0 | 20 | 23 | 0 | 109 |
| C.D. Clare | Wanganui/NZ Heartland | 10 | 5 | 17 | 16 | 0 | 107 |
| W.A. Wright | South Canterbury/NZ Heartland | 10 | 8 | 30 | 2 | 0 | 106 |
| W.R. Naholo | Highlanders/New Zealand/Taranaki | 22 | 21 | 0 | 0 | 0 | 105 |
| R.E. Ioane | Blues/NZ Maori/New Zealand | 27 | 21 | 0 | 0 | 0 | 105 |
| V. Aso | Hurricanes/Auckland/UK Barbarians | 28 | 21 | 0 | 0 | 0 | 105 |
| L.Z. Sopoaga | Highlanders/New Zealand | 21 | 2 | 23 | 15 | 0 | 101 |
| K.H. Laumape | Hurricanes/New Zealand/Manawatu | 27 | 20 | 0 | 0 | 0 | 100 |

## LEADING TRY-SCORERS

*(Record: 36, J.J. Kirwan, 1987 in 32 games)*

| Tries | Games |  | Teams |
|---|---|---|---|
| 21 | 22 | W.R. Naholo | Highlanders/New Zealand/Taranaki |
| 21 | 27 | R.E. Ioane | Blues/NZ Maori/New Zealand |
| 21 | 28 | V. Aso | Hurricanes/Auckland/UK Barbarians |
| 20 | 27 | K.H. Laumape | Hurricanes/New Zealand/Manawatu |
| 18 | 31 | G.C. Bridge | Crusaders/Canterbury/UK Barbarians |
| 15 | 21 | T. Li | Highlanders/North Harbour |
| 15 | 21 | W.T. Goosen | Hurricanes/Wellington |
| 15 | 26 | S. Tamanivalu | Crusaders/Taranaki/New Zealand |
| 15 | 29 | S.J. Savea | Hurricanes/New Zealand/Wellington/UK Barbarians |
| 14 | 15 | B.M. Ennor | NZ Under 20/Canterbury |
| 14 | 17 | W.T. Jordan | NZ Under 20/Tasman |
| 14 | 27 | J.F.R. Lowe | Chiefs/NZ Maori/Tasman |
| 13 | 10 | M.L. Sau | Mid Canterbury |

| 13 | 17 | A. Aumua | NZ Under 20/Wellington |
|----|----|----------|------------------------|
| 12 | 20 | T.E.S. Bateman | Crusaders/Canterbury/NZ Maori |
| 12 | 26 | M.D. Duffie | Blues/North Harbour/New Zealand |
| 12 | 29 | M.D. Drummond | Crusaders/Canterbury/UK Barbarians/New Zealand |
| 12 | 31 | S.T. Stevenson | Chiefs/North Harbour/NZ Maori |
| 11 | 12 | J.M. Nareki | NZ Under 20/Otago |
| 11 | 28 | D.S. McKenzie | Chiefs/NZ Maori/New Zealand |
| 10 | 24 | R. Thompson | Highlanders/NZ Maori/Canterbury |
| 10 | 29 | B.J. Barrett | Hurricanes/New Zealand |

## THREE (or more) TRIES IN A MATCH
*(Record: 8, T.R. Heeps, New Zealand v Northern NSW, 1962;*
*J.J. Kirwan, Auckland v North Otago, 1993)*

| 5 | T. Li | North Harbour v Taranaki |
|---|-------|---------------------------|
| 4 | B.M. Ennor | Canterbury v Southland |
| 4 | M.D. Drummond | Canterbury v Counties Manukau |
| 3 | R.E. Ioane | Blues v Rebels |
| 3 | N. Milner-Skudder | Hurricanes v Rebels |
| 3 | M.M.B.T. Mataele | Crusaders v Sunwolves |
| 3 | V. Aso | Hurricanes v Brumbies |
| 3 | G.C. Bridge | Crusaders v Stormers |
| 3 | W.T. Jordan | New Zealand Under 20 v Fiji Under 20 |
| 3 | G.C. Bridge | Crusaders v Cheetahs |
| 3 | V. Aso | Hurricanes v Cheetahs |
| 3 | L.T. Fainga'anuku | New Zealand Under 20 v Scotland Under 20 |
| 3 | J.F.R. Lowe | Chiefs v Waratahs |
| 3 | C.B. Clarke | New Zealand Under 20 v Ireland Under 20 |
| 3 | W.T. Jordan | New Zealand Under 20 v Ireland Under 20 |
| 3 | A. Aumua | New Zealand Under 20 v England Under 20 |
| 3 | J.M. Manihera | Waikato v Taranaki |
| 3 | T.S. Seruwalu | Wanganui v Wairarapa Bush |
| 3 | J.M. Nareki | Otago v Manawatu |
| 3 | G.C. Bridge | Canterbury v Southland |
| 3 | V. Aso | Auckland v Taranaki |
| 3 | F.H. Smith | Otago v Hawke's Bay |
| 3 | T.E.S. Bateman | Canterbury v Counties Manukau |
| 3 | D.J. McErlean | Horowhenua Kapiti v East Coast |
| 3 | K.V. Leatigaga | South Canterbury v North Otago |
| 3 | W.A. Wright | South Canterbury v West Coast |
| 3 | M.L. Sau | Mid Canterbury v Buller |
| 3 | L. Toumohuni | South Canterbury v East Coast |
| 3 | W.B. McGoon | Mid Canterbury v Poverty Bay, 21 October |

## 21 (or more) POINTS IN A MATCH

*(Record: 45, S.D. Culhane, New Zealand v Japan, 1995, 1 try, 20 conversions)*

| | | |
|---|---|---|
| 34 | T.H. Smith | Otago v Hawke's Bay, 3t, 8c, 1pg |
| 30 | W.A. Wright | South Canterbury v West Coast, 3t, 6c, 1pg |
| 26 | C.D. Clare | Wanganui v Wairarapa Bush, 1t, 6c, 3pg |
| 25 | J.J. Lash | Buller v Mid Canterbury, 1t, 4c, 4pg |
| 25 | T. Li | North Harbour v Taranaki, 5t |
| 25 | M.J. Hunt | Tasman v Taranaki, 21 October, 1t, 1c, 6pg |
| 25 | R. Mo'unga | Canterbury v Tasman, 28 October, 2t, 3c, 3pg |
| 23 | B.D. Cameron | Canterbury v Hawke's Bay, 1t, 6c, 2pg |
| 23 | R. Mo'unga | Canterbury v Southland, 2t, 5c, 1pg |
| 23 | J.J. Lash | Buller v North Otago, 1t, 3c, 3pg, 1dg |
| 23 | R. Mo'unga | Canterbury v Counties Manukau, 10c, 1pg |
| 22 | B.E.C. Gatland | North Harbour v Auckland, 5c, 4pg |
| 22 | M.J. Hunt | Tasman v Wellington, 1t, 4c, 3pg |
| 22 | P.J.L. Breen | Northland v Otago, 2c, 6pg |
| 22 | J.S. Buchan | North Otago v East Coast, 2t, 6c |
| 21 | B.J. Barrett | New Zealand v British & Irish Lions, 1 July, 7pg |
| 21 | D.W. Lewis | North Otago v Mid Canterbury, 2t, 4c, 1pg |
| 21 | R.S. Macdonald | King Country v North Otago, 1t, 2c, 4pg |
| 21 | A. Tauatevalu | Poverty Bay v West Coast, 2t, 4c, 1pg |
| 21 | R. Mo'unga | Canterbury v North Harbour, 1t, 5c, 2pg |

## SIX (or more) PENALTY GOALS IN A MATCH

*(Record: 9, A.P. Mehrtens, New Zealand v Australia, at Auckland, 1999;*
*A.P. Mehrtens, New Zealand v France, at Paris, 2000;*
*B.J. Barrett, Taranaki v Bay of Plenty, 2011)*

| | | |
|---|---|---|
| 7 | B.J. Barrett | New Zealand v British & Irish Lions, 1 July |
| 6 | S.L. Halfpenny | British & Irish Lions v New Zealand Maori |
| 6 | P.J.L. Breen | Northland v Otago |
| 6 | J.S. So'oialo | Horowhenua Kapiti v Buller, 21 October |
| 6 | M.J. Hunt | Tasman v Taranaki, 21 October |

## SIX (or more) CONVERSIONS IN A MATCH
*(Record: 20, J.P. Preston, Canterbury v West Coast, 1992;*
*S.D. Culhane, New Zealand v Japan, 1995)*

| | | |
|---|---|---|
| 10 | R. Mo'unga | Canterbury v Counties Manukau |
| 9 | O.W. Black | Hurricanes v Sunwolves |
| 8 | F.H. Smith | Otago v Hawke's Bay |
| 7 | J.M. Barrett | Hurricanes v Brumbies |
| 7 | T.J. Falcon | New Zealand Under 20 v Ireland Under 20 |
| 7 | S. Perofeta | New Zealand Under 20 v England Under 20 |
| 7 | B.J. Barrett | New Zealand v Samoa |
| 7 | B.D. Cameron | Canterbury v Wanganui |
| 7 | B.J. Barrett | New Zealand v Australia, 19 August |
| 7 | J.K. Garden-Bachop | Wellington v Canterbury |
| 7 | B.J. Barrett | New Zealand v South Africa, 16 September |
| 7 | J.J. Lash | Buller v East Coast |
| 7 | M.R, McKenzie | Taranaki v Canterbury |
| 6 | I.T. West | Blues v Rebels |
| 6 | B.J. Barrett | Hurricanes v Rebels |
| 6 | R. Mo'unga | Crusaders v Stormers |
| 6 | C.R. Matoe | New Zealand Under 20 v Samoa Under 20 |
| 6 | M. Banks | Highlanders v Cheetahs |
| 6 | C.D. Clare | Wanganui v Wairarapa Bush |
| 6 | B.D. Cameron | Canterbury v Hawke's Bay |
| 6 | W.A. Wright | South Canterbury v King Country |
| 6 | J.R. Percival | Mid Canterbury v Wairarapa Bush |
| 6 | W.A. Wright | South Canterbury v West Coast |
| 6 | J.S. Buchan | North Otago v East Coast |

## TWO (or more) DROPPED GOALS IN A MATCH
*(Record: 5, M.K. Sisam, Hawke's Bay v East Coast, 1979)*

No player drop kicked more than one goal in a match in 2017

## SCORED IN ALL FOUR WAYS

| | |
|---|---|
| J.J. Lash | Buller v North Otago, 1t, 3c, 3pg, 1dg |
| N. Sanchez | Argentina v New Zealand, 9 September, 1t, 1c, 2pg, 1dg |

# CURRENT PLAYER STATISTICS

## CAREER RECORDS OF PLAYERS APPEARING IN FIRST-CLASS RUGBY IN NEW ZEALAND, 2017

### 100 GAMES OF FIRST-CLASS RUGBY

| | | | | | |
|---|---|---|---|---|---|
| W.W.V. Crockett | 339 | T.N.J. Kerr-Barlow | 168 | A.N. Ainley | 130 |
| L.J. Messam | 310 | L.G. Brownlee | 167 | J.L. To'omaga-Allen | 130 |
| K.J. Read | 300 | T.E.S. Bateman | 165 | R.J. Buckman | 128 |
| C.R. Flynn | 289 | T.T.R. Perenara | 164 | G. Moala | 128 |
| P.A.T. Weepu | 284 | L. Romano | 163 | J.P.T. Moody | 127 |
| J. Kaino | 283 | R.M.N. Ranger | 162 | A.S. Savea | 126 |
| H.T.P. Elliot | 261 | E.C. Dixon | 161 | I.T. West | 125 |
| C.S. Jane | 257 | C.J. Retallick | 160 | M.F. Fekitoa | 123 |
| O.T. Franks | 252 | B.D.F. Shields | 159 | A.Malo | 123 |
| S.R. Donald | 241 | P.J. Beveridge | 156 | A.O.H.M. Tu'ungafasi | 122 |
| B.R. Smith | 239 | L.C. Whitelock | 156 | A.M. Dunster | 122 |
| S.L. Whitelock | 238 | B.C.F. Funnell | 155 | S.M.J. Prattley | 122 |
| R.J. Crotty | 235 | S.T. Ngatu | 155 | M.P. Delany | 121 |
| A.L. Smith | 231 | L.Z. Sopoaga | 153 | C.J. Gibbins | 118 |
| D.S. Coles | 228 | T.T. Nanai-Williams | 152 | B.D. Hall | 118 |
| I.J.A. Dagg | 228 | J.M.R.A. Hoeata | 151 | C.I. Eves | 118 |
| C.S. Smylie | 228 | J.T. Wheeler | 150 | C. Baldwin | 116 |
| C.C. Faumuina | 203 | P. Manu | 149 | B-J. A. Guyton | 116 |
| A.W. Cruden | 201 | C.J. Ngatai | 149 | W.R. Naholo | 113 |
| M.B. Todd | 197 | L.J. Coltman | 143 | P. Osborne | 110 |
| Z.R. Guildford | 196 | A.W. Pulu | 142 | C.J. Taylor | 110 |
| B. May | 196 | D.W.H. Sweeney | 142 | B.M. Weber | 108 |
| S.J. Savea | 195 | P.G. Rowe | 141 | S.J. Tupou | 107 |
| B.J. Barrett | 193 | C.G. Eaton | 140 | N.E. Laulala | 106 |
| A.S. Mathewson | 193 | S.J. Taufua | 134 | J.F.R. Lowe | 106 |
| T.P. Boys | 191 | D.J. Bird | 133 | S. Williams | 105 |
| A.L. Dixon | 178 | R.T. Malneek | 132 | D.J. Pryor | 103 |
| J.W. Parsons | 178 | S.J. Treeby | 132 | G.O. Evans | 102 |
| S.J. Cane | 174 | T.S.G. Franklin | 132 | M.P. Proctor | 101 |
| B.A. Retallick | 169 | D.S. Luatua | 131 | T. Li | 100 |

### 500 POINTS IN FIRST-CLASS RUGBY

| | | | | | |
|---|---|---|---|---|---|
| S.R. Donald | 1839 | M. Banks | 932 | H.J. Parker | 616 |
| B.J. Barrett | 1682 | M.P. Delany | 761 | S.J. Savea | 575 |
| A.W. Cruden | 1462 | R. Mo'unga | 715 | M.R. McKenzie | 549 |
| L.Z. Sopoaga | 1379 | P.A.T. Weepu | 713 | J.J. Lash | 509 |
| I.T. West | 1099 | D.S. McKenzie | 678 | | |

### 50 TRIES IN FIRST-CLASS RUGBY

| | | | | | |
|---|---|---|---|---|---|
| S.J. Savea | 115 | B.R. Smith | 75 | K.J. Read | 58 |
| Z.R. Guildford | 96 | W.R. Naholo | 72 | G. Moala | 54 |
| C.S. Jane | 87 | S.R. Donald | 69 | J.F.R. Lowe | 52 |
| I.J.A. Dagg | 76 | B.J. Barrett | 58 | T. Li | 51 |
| L.J. Messam | 76 | T.T.R. Perenara | 58 | T.T. Nanai-Williams | 50 |

# FIRST-CLASS STATISTICS

*to January 1, 2018*

## 250 GAMES OF FIRST-CLASS RUGBY

| | | | | | |
|---|---|---|---|---|---|
| K.F. Mealamu | 2000–15 | 384 | A.P. Mehrtens | 1993–2005 | 282 |
| C.E. Meads | 1955–74 | 361 | A.J. Wyllie | 1964–80 | 279 |
| S.B.T. Fitzpatrick | 1983–97 | 346 | A.M. Stone | 1980–94 | 275 |
| W.W.V. Crockett | 2005–17 | 339 | C.J. Spencer | 1992–2005 | 273 |
| R.H. McCaw | 2000–15 | 334 | J.A. Collins | 1994–2010 | 273 |
| T.D. Woodcock | 2000–15 | 331 | M.J.A. Cooper | 1985–99 | 270 |
| M.A. Nonu | 2002–15 | 330 | D.E. Holwell | 1995–2010 | 270 |
| J.F. Umaga | 1994–2011 | 329 | J.M. Muliaina | 1999–2014 | 270 |
| A.M. Haden | 1971–86 | 327 | B.G. Williams | 1968–84 | 269 |
| Q.J. Cowan | 2000–16 | 326 | K.R. Tremain | 1957–72 | 268 |
| R.W. Loe | 1980–97 | 321 | J.J. Kirwan | 1983–94 | 267 |
| G.W. Whetton | 1979–95 | 313 | A.M. Ellis | 2004–16 | 266 |
| Z.V. Brooke | 1985–97 | 311 | L.R. MacDonald | 1994–2009 | 266 |
| A.K. Hore | 1999–2016 | 311 | C.G. Smith | 2003–15 | 265 |
| W.F. McCormick | 1958–78 | 310 | G.L. Slater | 1991–2005 | 262 |
| L.J. Messam | 2003–17 | 310 | R.D. Thorne | 1996–2 | 262 |
| C.S. Ralph | 1996–2008 | 306 | H.T.P. Elliot | 2005–17 | 261 |
| G.J. Fox | 1982–95 | 303 | K.J. Crowley | 1980–94 | 260 |
| K.J. Read | 2005–17 | 300 | T.J. Blackadder | 1990–2001 | 260 |
| A.D. Oliver | 1993–2007 | 298 | C.H. Hoeft | 1993–2005 | 260 |
| N.J. Hewitt | 1988–2001 | 296 | I.A. Eliason | 1964–82 | 259 |
| S.C. McDowell | 1982–98 | 294 | E. Clarke | 1990–2005 | 259 |
| R.M. Brooke | 1987–2001 | 289 | S.J. Bachop | 1986–99 | 257 |
| C.R. Flynn | 2001–17 | 289 | C.S. Jane | 2003–17 | 257 |
| D.W. Carter | 2002–15 | 287 | G.A. Knight | 1972–86 | 254 |
| I.D. Jones | 1988–2000 | 287 | G.M. Somerville | 1997–2008 | 254 |
| I.A. Kirkpatrick | 1966–79 | 285 | I.J. Clarke | 1951–63 | 253 |
| J.W. Marshall | 1992–2005 | 284 | O.T. Franks | 2007–17 | 252 |
| P.A.T. Weepu | 2003–17 | 284 | S.M. Going | 1962–78 | 251 |
| J. Kaino | 2003–17 | 283 | C.R. Jack | 1998–11 | 250 |
| W.K. Little | 1988–2000 | 283 | B.J. Robertson | 1971–84 | 250 |

## 1000 POINTS IN FIRST-CLASS RUGBY

| | Career | Games | Tries | Con | PG | DG/Mark | Points |
|---|---|---|---|---|---|---|---|
| G.J. Fox | 1982–95 | 303 | 29 | 901 | 683 | 47 | 4112 |
| D.W. Carter | 2002–2015 | 287 | 78 | 649 | 646 | 19 | 3683 |
| A.P. Mehrtens | 1993–2005 | 282 | 40 | 556 | 572 | 54 | 3190 |
| M.J.A. Cooper | 1985–99 | 270 | 79 | 475 | 420 | 2 | 2577 |
| K.J. Crowley | 1980–94 | 260 | 86 | 375 | 376 | 9 | 2261 |
| G.J.L Cooper | 1984–96 | 188 | 60 | 385 | 388 | 14 | 2221 |
| D.E. Holwell | 1995–2010 | 270 | 39 | 451 | 366 | 2 | 2201 |
| W.B. Johnston | 1986–2001 | 220 | 29 | 421 | 396 | 5 | 2179 |
| R.M. Deans | 1979–90 | 187 | 45 | 390 | 370 | 1 | 2073 |
| W.F. McCormick | 1958–78 | 310 | 57 | 457 | 314 | 9 | 2065 |
| T.E. Brown | 1995–2011 | 211 | 29 | 345 | 373 | 14 | 1996 |
| A.R. Cashmore | 1992–2005 | 185 | 64 | 351 | 290 | 2 | 1898 |
| C.J. Spencer | 1992–2005 | 273 | 101 | 329 | 222 | 11 | 1860 |
| D.B. Clarke | 1951–64 | 226 | 22 | 365 | 318 | 28/3 | 1851 |
| S.R. Donald | 2001–17 | 241 | 68 | 337 | 273 | 2 | 1839 |
| B.J. Barrett | 2010–17 | 193 | 58 | 321 | 249 | 1 | 1682 |
| S.D. Culhane | 1988–99 | 155 | 20 | 292 | 312 | 19 | 1671 |
| J.B. Cunningham | 1990–98 | 136 | 52 | 316 | 226 | 1 | 1569 |
| B.A. Blair | 1999–2006 | 148 | 59 | 302 | 221 | – | 1562 |
| A.W. Cruden | 2008–17 | 201 | 33 | 245 | 267 | 2 | 1462 |
| G.W. Jackson | 1996–2004 | 175 | 41 | 267 | 215 | 8 | 1408 |
| D.W. Hill | 1997–2006 | 177 | 30 | 279 | 230 | 1 | 1401 |
| L.Z. Sopoaga | 2010–17 | 153 | 22 | 258 | 246 | 5 | 1379 |
| A.R. Hewson | 1973–88 | 154 | 19 | 247 | 229 | 17 | 1308 |
| J.P. Preston | 1987–98 | 171 | 21 | 242 | 231 | – | 1281 |
| M. Williment | 1958–68 | 121 | 17 | 296 | 188 | 16 | 1255 |
| F.M. Botica | 1985–2001 | 149 | 37 | 262 | 171 | 7 | 1213 |
| L.W. Mains | 1967–76 | 142 | 13 | 213 | 227 | 13 | 1193 |
| E.J. Crossan | 1987–96 | 91 | 29 | 189 | 220 | – | 1157 |
| G.D. Rowlands | 1969–82 | 179 | 41 | 198 | 186 | 15 | 1151 |
| C.L. McAlister | 2002–11 | 151 | 19 | 205 | 207 | 1 | 1129 |
| J.W. Wilson | 1992–2002 | 233 | 151 | 76 | 68 | 4 | 1123 |
| W.J. Burton | 1990–96 | 93 | 10 | 215 | 204 | 5 | 1099 |
| I.T. West | 2012–17 | 125 | 26 | 219 | 175 | 2 | 1099 |
| J.A. Gallagher | 1984–90 | 139 | 67 | 196 | 144 | 1 | 1095 |
| J.A. Gopperth | 2002–09 | 125 | 27 | 228 | 167 | 2 | 1094 |
| B.J.W. Fairbrother | 1981–92 | 118 | 20 | 132 | 183 | 61 | 1076 |
| R.B. Barrell | 1963–79 | 147 | 20 | 125 | 225 | 10 | 1030 |
| D.P. Lilley | 1993–2003 | 162 | 41 | 139 | 176 | 6 | 1029 |
| G.W. Anscombe | 2010–14 | 83 | 27 | 163 | 182 | 1 | 1010 |

## 100 TRIES IN FIRST-CLASS RUGBY

| | Games | Tries | | Games | Tries |
|---|---|---|---|---|---|
| J.J. Kirwan | 267 | 199 | I.A. Kirkpatrick | 285 | 114 |
| T.J. Wright | 217 | 177 | N.R. Berryman | 188 | 114 |
| D.C. Howlett | 240 | 173 | J. Vidiri | 154 | 112 |
| B.G. Fraser | 201 | 171 | E. Clarke | 259 | 111 |
| C.M. Cullen | 233 | 164 | C.I. Green | 159 | 111 |
| Z.V. Brooke | 311 | 161 | J.T. Rokocoko | 214 | 111 |
| J.F. Umaga | 329 | 156 | H.E. Gear | 228 | 111 |
| J.W. Wilson | 233 | 151 | G.B. Batty | 142 | 109 |
| R.A. Jarden | 134 | 145 | B.R. Ford | 196 | 109 |
| R.Q. Randle | 188 | 141 | J.K.R. Timu | 182 | 108 |
| B.G. Williams | 269 | 137 | R.L. Gear | 197 | 108 |
| K.R. Tremain | 268 | 136 | T.W. Mitchell | 155 | 106 |
| P.J. Cooke | 192 | 134 | S.S. Wilson | 202 | 106 |
| C.S. Ralph | 306 | 133 | E.J. Rush | 196 | 104 |
| J.T. Lomu | 203 | 126 | B.W. Smith | 146 | 102 |
| S.W. Sivivatu | 191 | 125 | R.M. Smith | 152 | 102 |
| M. Clamp | 141 | 123 | A.R. Sutherland | 208 | 102 |
| A.E. Cooke | 131 | 119 | P. Bale | 129 | 101 |
| M.A. Nonu | 330 | 117 | C.J. Spencer | 273 | 101 |
| S.J. Savea | 195 | 115 | | | |

## MOST DROPPED GOALS IN FIRST-CLASS RUGBY

| | | | | | |
|---|---|---|---|---|---|
| B.J.W. Fairbrother | 61 | M.A. Herewini | 47 | P. Martin | 34 |
| A.P. Mehrtens | 54 | R.J. Preston | 39 | B.J. McKechnie | 33 |
| M.B. Roulston | 49 | J.W. Boe | 37 | E.J. Dunn | 32 |
| G.J. Fox | 47 | R.H. Brown | 35 | D. Trevathan | 31 |

## MOST POINTS IN A FIRST-CLASS MATCH

| | Match | Tries | Con | PG | DG | Total |
|---|---|---|---|---|---|---|
| S.D. Culhane | New Zealand v Japan, 1995 | 1 | 20 | – | – | 45 |
| J.P. Preston | Canterbury v West Coast, 1992 | 1 | 20 | – | – | 44 |
| R.M. Deans | New Zealand v South Australia, 1984 | 3 | 14 | 1 | – | 43 |
| A.R. Cashmore | Auckland v Mid Canterbury, 1995 | 5 | 9 | – | – | 43 |
| J.F. Karam | New Zealand v South Australia, 1974 | 2 | 15 | 1 | – | 41 |
| J.J. Kirwan | Auckland v North Otago, 1993 | 8 | – | – | – | 40 |
| P.W. Turner | Otago v East Coast, 1986 | 2 | 14 | 1 | – | 39 |
| J.W. Wilson | New Zealand Colts v Thames Valley, 1993 | 4 | 5 | 3 | – | 39 |
| D.J. Kellett | Western Samoa v Marlborough, 1993 | 3 | 12 | – | – | 39 |
| R.A. Jarden | New Zealand v Central West (Aust), 1951 | 6 | 10 | – | – | 38 |
| D.E. Holwell | Northland v Thames Valley, 1997 | 2 | 14 | – | – | 38 |
| B.A. Blair | New Zealand v Ireland A, 2001 | 3 | 4 | 5 | – | 38 |
| J.L. Graham | Counties v East Coast, 1972 | – | 14 | 3 | – | 37 |
| S.D. Culhane | Southland v Manawatu, 1994 | 1 | 1 | 8 | 2 | 37 |
| J.B. Cunningham | Central Vikings v South Canterbury, 1997 | 3 | 11 | – | – | 37 |
| B.A. Blair | Canterbury v Counties Manukau, 1999 | 3 | 11 | – | – | 37 |

# REFEREES

*by Chris Jansen*

## 2017 NEW ZEALAND RUGBY NATIONAL REFEREE SQUAD

| | Union | Squad Debut | Tests | S15 | N1 | N2 | Sevens | Nat[1] | Prov[2] | RS[3] | Total |
|---|---|---|---|---|---|---|---|---|---|---|---|
| N.P. Briant | Bay of Plenty | 2009 | 7 | 41 | 49 | 10 | 26 | 15 | – | 9 | 148 |
| T.M.T. Cottrell* | Hawke's Bay | 2017 | – | – | – | 5 | – | – | 1 | – | 6 |
| J.J. Doleman | Auckland | 2014 | – | – | 8 | 16 | 4 | 1 | – | 1 | 29 |
| M.I. Fraser | Wellington | 2007 | 4 | 40 | 52 | 16 | 5 | 16 | 1 | 8 | 134 |
| R.J.M. Gordon* | Wellington | 2015 | – | – | – | 18 | – | 1 | – | – | 19 |
| T.N. Griffiths* | Manawatu | 2016 | – | – | – | 11 | – | – | – | – | 11 |
| N.E.R. Hogan* | Wellington | 2017 | – | – | – | 5 | – | – | – | – | 5 |
| G.W. Jackson | Bay of Plenty | 2010 | 25 | 65 | 49 | 7 | – | 6 | 1 | 5 | 153 |
| B.J. Jurlina* | Northland | 2016 | – | – | – | 8 | – | – | – | – | 8 |
| R.P. Kelly | Taranaki | 2009 | – | – | 40 | 10 | 39 | 4 | 3 | 2 | 96 |
| M.G. Lash | Tasman | 2013 | – | – | 20 | 7 | – | 6 | – | 2 | 33 |
| A.W.B. Mabey | Auckland | 2014 | – | – | 15 | 14 | – | 2 | – | 1 | 31 |
| S.W. McDermott | Bay of Plenty | 2006 | – | – | 40 | 32 | – | 5 | 5 | 2 | 82 |
| J.D. Munro | Canterbury | 2011 | – | – | 2 | 9 | – | – | – | – | 11 |
| J.R. Nutbrown | Canterbury | 2014 | – | 8 | 15 | 4 | – | 6 | – | 1 | 33 |
| Dr. B.D. O'Keeffe | Wellington | 2012 | 8 | 24 | 33 | 6 | – | 1 | 5 | 5 | 77 |
| B.E. Pickerill | North Harbour | 2012 | 1 | 12 | 31 | 6 | – | 9 | – | 2 | 59 |
| H.G. Reed* | Hawke's Bay | 2016 | – | – | – | 8 | – | 1 | – | – | 9 |
| V.F. Ringrose* | Wellington | 2014 | – | – | – | 21 | – | – | 2 | – | 23 |
| C.J. Stone | Taranaki | 2012 | – | – | 11 | 18 | – | – | 1 | – | 30 |
| N.J. Webster* | North Otago | 2016 | – | – | – | 10 | – | – | – | – | 10 |
| M.C.J. Winter | Waikato | 2015 | – | – | 2 | 16 | – | – | – | – | 18 |
| P.M. Williams | Taranaki | 2014 | 5 | 11 | 20 | 7 | – | 5 | 1 | 2 | 49 |

N1    Mitre 10 Cup (total includes former ITM Cup fixtures)
N2    Heartland Championship
[1]NZR appointment — international tour, Ranfurly Shield (non-Mitre 10 Cup), national trial, and women's international.
[2]interprovincial (non-Mitre 10 Cup, non-Heartland Championship, non-Ranfurly Shield)
[3]Ranfurly Shield — also included within N1 or Nat (if a non-Mitre 10 Cup match)
* NZR Referee Development Squad

## REFEREE APPOINTMENTS 2017

**Jamie Bell** (Bay of Plenty)

| October | 14 | N2 | King Country v Mid Canterbury | Taupo |
|---|---|---|---|---|

**Nick Briant**

| February | 24 | S18 | Reds v Sharks | Brisbane |
|---|---|---|---|---|
| March | 11 | S18 | Jaguares v Lions | Buenos Aires |
| April | 1 | S18 | Chiefs v Bulls | Hamilton |
| | 8 | S18 | Brumbies v Reds | Canberra |
| | 30 | S18 | Brumbies v Blues | Canberra |
| May | 27 | S18 | Blues v Chiefs | Auckland |
| June | 3 | S18 | Brumbies v Rebels | Canberra |
| | 9 | S18 | Hurricanes v Chiefs | Wellington |
| | 16 | | Tonga v Wales | Auckland |
| July | 8 | RWCQ | Fiji v Tonga | Suva |
| August | 19 | N1 | Taranaki v Waikato | New Plymouth |
| September | 8 | N1/RS | Canterbury vs Southland | Christchurch |
| | 16 | N1 | Waikato v Manawatu | Hamilton |
| | 27 | N1 | Northland v Otago | Whangarei |

| October | 7 | JTL | Ricoh Black Rams v Toyota Verblitz | Morioka City |
|---|---|---|---|---|
| | 15 | JTL | Munakata Sanix Blues v Canon Eagles | Hiroshima |
| | 22 | N1 s-f | Taranaki v Tasman | New Plymouth |
| November | 4 | | Japan v Australia | Yokohama |

**Tipene Cottrell**

| September | 2 | N2 | Poverty Bay v Horowhenua Kapiti | Gisborne |
|---|---|---|---|---|
| | 9 | N2 | Buller v North Otago | Westport |
| | 16 | N2 | West Coast v Horowhenua Kapiti | Greymouth |
| | 30 | N2 | Wanganui v King Country | Wanganui |
| October | 14 | N2 | Wanganui v North Otago | Wanganui |

**James Doleman**

| January | 14/15 | * | National Sevens | Rotorua |
|---|---|---|---|---|
| | 28/29 | | New Zealand World Rugby Sevens | Wellington |
| February | 4/5 | | Australia World Rugby Sevens | Sydney |
| May | 13/14 | | France World Rugby Sevens | Paris |
| | 20/21 | | England World Rugby Sevens | London |
| August | 4 | RS | Canterbury v Mid Canterbury | Ashburton |
| | 25 | N1 | Bay of Plenty v Hawke's Bay | Rotorua |
| September | 3 | N1 | Waikato v Tasman | Hamilton |
| | 7 | N1 | Counties Manukau v North Harbour | Pukekohe |
| | 23 | N1 | Tasman v Southland | Nelson |
| October | 14 | N1 | Bay of Plenty v Waikato | Tauranga |

**Mike Fraser**

| February | 24 | S18 | Highlanders v Chiefs | Dunedin |
|---|---|---|---|---|
| March | 18 | S18 | Lions v Reds | Johannesburg |
| | 24 | S18 | Jaguares v Reds | Buenos Aires |
| April | 15 | S18 | Blues v Hurricanes | Auckland |
| | 29 | S18 | Force v Lions | Perth |
| May | 19 | S18 | Chiefs v Crusaders | Suva |
| | 27 | S18 | Jaguares v Brumbies | Buenos Aires |
| July | 14 | S18 | Highlanders v Reds | Duenedin |
| August | 25 | N1 | Waikato v Counties Manukau | Hamilton |
| September | 9 | N1 | Auckland v Taranaki | Auckland |
| | 16 | N1 | Otago v Tasman | Dunedin |
| October | 1 | N1 | Counties Manukau v Northland | Pukekohe |
| | 6 | N1/RS | Canterbury v Taranaki | Christchurch |
| | 28 | N1 p-f | Canterbury v Tasman | Christchurch |

**Richard Gordon**

| June | 3 | | Poverty Bay vs East Coast | Gisborne |
|---|---|---|---|---|
| September | 2 | N2 | North Otago v Mid Canterbury | Oamaru |
| | 9 | N2 | Horowhenua Kapiti v Thames Valley | Levin |
| | 16 | N2 | Thames Valley v Buller | Paeroa |
| | 23 | N2 | South Canterbury v North Otago | Timaru |
| October | 7 | N2 | Poverty Bay v King Country | Gisborne |

**Tim Griffiths**

| August | 26 | N2 | Wanganui v Wairarapa Bush | Wanganui |
|---|---|---|---|---|
| September | 16 | N2 | South Canterbury v Wanganui | Timaru |
| | 23 | N2 | Horowhenua Kapiti v East Coast | Levin |
| | 30 | N2 | Thames Valley v Mid Canterbury | Paeroa |

| October | 7 | N2 | North Otago v East Coast | Oamaru |
|---|---|---|---|---|
| | 21 | N2 s-f | Mid Canterbury v Poverty Bay | Ashburton |

**Nick Hogan**

| August | 26 | N2 | Horowhenua Kapiti v North Otago | Levin |
|---|---|---|---|---|
| September | 16 | N2 | Poverty Bay v East Coast | Gisborne |
| | 23 | N2 | Buller v Wairarapa Bush | Westport |
| | 30 | N2 | West Coast v South Canterbury | Greymouth |
| October | 7 | N2 | South Canterbury v Wairarapa Bush | Timaru |

**Glen Jackson**

| February | 11 | 6N | Italy v Ireland | Rome |
|---|---|---|---|---|
| | 25 | S18 | Crusaders v Brumbies | Christchurch |
| March | 11 | S18 | Blues v Highlanders | Auckland |
| | 18 | S18 | Waratahs vs Brumbies | Sydney |
| April | 15 | S18 | Rebels v Brumbies | Melbourne |
| | 28 | S18 | Highlanders v Stormers | Dunedin |
| May | 5 | S18 | Hurricanes v Stormers | Wellington |
| | 27 | S18 | Rebels v Crusaders | Melbourne |
| June | 3 | S18 | Crusaders v Highlanders | Christchurch |
| | 10 | | South Africa v France | Pretoria |
| July | 15 | S18 | Hurricanes v Crusaders | Wellington |
| | 21 | S18 q-f | Brumbies vs Hurricanes | Canberra |
| | 29 | S18 s-f | Crusaders v Chiefs | Christchurch |
| August | 17 | N1 | North Harbour v Otago | Albany |
| September | 3 | N1 | North Harbour v Auckland | Albany |
| | 9 | RC | Australia v South Africa | Perth |
| | 21 | N1 | Otago v Auckland | Dunedin |
| | 30 | N1/RS | Canterbury v Waikato | Christchurch |
| October | 5 | N1 | Manawatu v Counties Manukau | Palmerston North |
| | 20 | N1 s-f | Wellington v Northland | Wellington |
| November | 11 | | Wales v Australia | Cardiff |

**Boris Jurlina**

| September | 2 | N2 | Thames Valley v Wanganui | Paeroa |
|---|---|---|---|---|
| | 9 | N2 | King Country v Wairarapa Bush | Te Kuiti |
| | 23 | N2 | King Country v Thames Valley | Te Kuiti |
| | 30 | N2 | East Coast v Buller | Ruatoria |
| October | 7 | N2 | Mid Canterbury v Buller | Ashburton |

**Richard Kelly**

| January | 14/15 | * | National Sevens | Rotorua |
|---|---|---|---|---|
| | 28/29 | | New Zealand World Rugby Sevens | Wellington |
| February | 4/5 | | Australia World Rugby Sevens | Sydney |
| March | 3–5 | | USA World Rugby Sevens | Las Vegas |
| | 11/12 | | Canada World Rugby Sevens | Vancouver |
| April | 7–9 | | Hong Kong World Rugby Sevens | Hong Kong |
| | 15/16 | | Singapore World Rugby Sevens | Singapore |
| May | 13/14 | | France World Rugby Sevens | Paris |
| | 20/21 | | England World Rugby Sevens | London |
| June | 21 | RS | Canterbury v Wanganui | Christchurch |
| August | 27 | N1 | Manawatu v Tasman | Palmerston North |
| | 30 | N1 | Auckland v Waikato | Auckland |
| September | 17 | N1 | Wellington v Canterbury | Wellington |

|  | 29 | N1 | North Harbour v Hawke's Bay | Albany |
| October | 12 | N1 | Wellington v Northland | Wellington |
| December | 1–2 |  | Dubai World Rugby Sevens | Dubai |
|  | 9/10 |  | South Africa World Rugby Sevens | Cape Town |

**Mike Lash**

| January | 14/15 | * | National Sevens | Rotorua |
| April | 29 |  | NZ Universities v Kanto | Hamilton |
| August | 26 | N1 | Wellington v Taranaki | Wellington |
| September | 9 | N1 | Northland v Waikato | Whangarei |
|  | 17 | N1 | Counties Manukau v Hawke's Bay | Pukekohe |
|  | 24 | N1 | Bay of Plenty v Counties Manukau | Tauranga |
| October | 7 | N1 | Southland v Wellington | Invercargill |

**Angus Mabey**

| August | 19 | N1 | Hawke's Bay v Southland | Napier |
| September | 2 | N1 | Taranaki v Counties Manukau | New Plymouth |
|  | 23 | N1 | North Harbour v Canterbury | Albany |
|  | 28 | N1 | Taranaki v Tasman | New Plymouth |
| October | 14 | N1 | Otago v Southland | Dunedin |

**Shane McDermott**

| September | 10 | N1 | Hawke's Bay v Otago | Napier |
|  | 23 | N1 | Hawke's Bay v Taranaki | Napier |
|  | 30 | N1 | Southland v Manawatu | Invercargill |
| October | 8 | N1 | Waikato v North Harbour | Hamilton |
|  | 15 | N1 | North Harbour v Taranaki | Albany |

**James Munro**

| January | 14/15 | * | National Sevens | Rotorua |
| August | 26 | N2 | Mid Canterbury v Poverty Bay | Ashburton |
| September | 2 | N1 | Otago v Manawatu | Dunedin |
|  | 15 | N1 | Southland v Auckland | Invercargill |
|  | 30 | N2 | Wairarapa Bush v Horowhenua Kapiti | Masterton |
| October | 14 | N2 | Buller v Horowhenua Kapiti | Westport |
|  | 21 | N2 s-f | West Coast v North Otago | Greymouth |
|  | 29 | LC f | Mid Canterbury v West Coast | Methven |

**Jamie Nutbrown**

| March | 17 | S18 | Bulls v Sunwolves | Pretoria |
| April | 8 | S18 | Highlanders v Blues | Dunedin |
|  | 22 | S18 | Highlanders v Sunwolves | Invercargill |
| May | 6 | S18 | Chiefs v Reds | New Plymouth |
| June | 3 | JWC | Argentina U20 v France U20 | Tbilisi |
|  | 8 | JWC | Wales U20 v Samoa U20 | Tbilisi |
|  | 18 | JWC | Scotland U20 v Australia U20 | Tbilisi |
|  | 30 | S18 | Jaguares v Kings | Buenos Aires |
| August | 24 | N1 | Southland v North Harbour | Invercargill |
| September | 6 | N1 | Wellington v Hawke's Bay | Wellington |
|  | 15 | N1 | Taranaki v Bay of Plenty | New Plymouth |
| October | 1 | N1 | Wellington v Otago | Wellington |
|  | 4 | N1 | Tasman v North Harbour | Blenheim |
| November | 4 |  | NZ Heartland XV v NZ Marist XV | Timaru |

## Ben O'Keeffe

| February | 25 | S18 | Waratahs v Force | Sydney |
|---|---|---|---|---|
| March | 3 | S18 | Chiefs v Blues | Waikato |
| | 11 | 6N | Italy v France | Rome |
| April | 15 | S18 | Bulls v Jaguares | Pretoria |
| | 22 | S18 | Bulls v Cheetahs | Pretoria |
| May | 13 | S18 | Jaguares v Force | Buenos Aires |
| | 27 | S18 | Highlanders v Waratahs | Dunedin |
| June | 2 | S18 | Blues vs Reds | Apia |
| | 17 | | South Africa v France | Durban |
| July | 8 | S18 | Waratahs v Jaguares | Sydney |
| | 15 | S18 | Chiefs vs Brumbies | Hamilton |
| August | 18 | N1 | Tasman v Canterbury | Nelson |
| September | 8 | N1 | Manawatu v Bay of Plenty | Palmerston North |
| | 22 | N1 | Manawatu v Northland | Palmerston North |
| | 30 | RC | South Africa v Australia | Bloemfontein |
| October | 7 | N1 | Otago v Bay of Plenty | Dunedin |
| | 11 | RS/N1 | Taranaki v Manawatu | New Plymouth |
| | 21 | N1 s-f | Canterbury v North Harbour | Christchurch |
| November | 11 | | Ireland v South Africa | Dublin |
| | 18 | | England v South Africa | London |

## Brendon Pickerill

| March | 10 | S18 | Chiefs v Hurricanes | Hamilton |
|---|---|---|---|---|
| | 17 | S18 | Crusaders v Blues | Christchurch |
| | 24 | S18 | Rebels v Waratahs | Melbourne |
| April | 21 | S18 | Hurricanes v Brumbies | Napier |
| May | 12 | S18 | Blues v Cheetahs | Auckland |
| | 26 | S18 | Reds v Force | Brisbane |
| July | 7 | S18 | Reds v Brumbies | Brisbane |
| August | 20 | N1 | Northland v Bay of Plenty | Whangarei |
| September | 10 | N1 | Tasman v Wellington | Blenheim |
| | 13 | N1/RS | Canterbury v Counties Manukau | Christchurch |
| October | 8 | N1 | Tasman v Auckland | Nelson |
| | 13 | N1 | Auckland v Canterbury | Auckland |
| | 21 | N1 s-f | Bay of Plenty v Otago | Tauranga |
| | 28 | | Australia v Barbarians | Sydney |
| November | 18 | | Germany v USA | Wiesbaden |

## Hugh Reed

| August | 12 | | Poverty Bay v Wairarapa Bush | Gisborne |
|---|---|---|---|---|
| September | 2 | N2 | West Coast v Buller | Greymouth |
| | 9 | N2 | Wanganui v Poverty Bay | Wanganui |
| | 16 | N2 | Wairarapa Bush v Mid Canterbury | Masterton |
| | 23 | N2 | Poverty Bay v West Coast | Gisborne |

## Vincent Ringrose

| January | 14/15 | * | National Sevens | Rotorua |
|---|---|---|---|---|
| August | 26 | N2 | Buller v South Canterbury | Westport |
| September | 9 | N2 | East Coast v West Coast | Ruatoria |
| | 16 | N2 | North Otago v King Country | Oamaru |
| | 30 | N2 | North Otago v Poverty Bay | Oamaru |

**Cameron Stone**

| August | 19 | N1 | Counties Manukau v Auckland | Pukekohe |
|---|---|---|---|---|
| September | 1 | N1 | Hawke's Bay v Canterbury | Napier |
| | 23 | N1 | Waikato v Wellington | Hamilton |
| | 30 | N1 | Auckland v Bay of Plenty | Auckland |
| October | 15 | N1 | Hawke's Bay v Manawatu | Napier |

**Michael Winter**

| January | 14/15 | * | National Sevens | Rotorua |
|---|---|---|---|---|
| August | 26 | N2 | East Coast v Thames Valley | Ruatoria |
| | 31 | N1 | Bay of Plenty v Wellington | Rotorua |
| September | 14 | N1 | Northland v North Harbour | Whangarei |
| October | 7 | N2 | Horowhenua Kapiti v Wanganui | Levin |
| | 14 | N2 | East Coast v South Canterbury | Ruatoria |
| | 21 | N2 s-f | Horowhenua Kapiti v Buller | Levin |
| | 28 | MC f | Horowhenua Kapiti v Wanganui | Levin |

**Nick Webster**

| September | 2 | N2 | South Canterbury v King Country | Timaru |
|---|---|---|---|---|
| | 9 | N2 | Mid Canterbury v South Canterbury | Ashburton |
| | 23 | N2 | Mid Canterbury v Wanganui | Ashburton |
| October | 7 | N2 | West Coast v Thames Valley | Greymouth |
| | 14 | N2 | Wairarapa Bush v West Coast | Masterton |
| | 21 | N2 s-f | South Canterbury v Wanganui | Timaru |

**Paul Williams**

| March | 4 | S18 | Highlanders v Crusaders | Dunedin |
|---|---|---|---|---|
| | 18 | S18 | Jaguares v Cheetahs | Buenos Aires |
| April | 22 | S18 | Crusaders v Stormers | Christchurch |
| | 29 | S18 | Reds v Waratahs | Brisbane |
| May | 12 | S18 | Brumbies v Lions | Canberra |
| June | 3 | S18 | Chiefs v Waratahs | Hamilton |
| | 10 | | Italy v Scotland | Singapore |
| | 17 | | Fiji v Italy | Suva |
| July | 15 | RWCQ | Samoa v Fiji | Apia |
| August | 27 | N1/RS | Canterbury v Otago | Christchurch |
| September | 2 | N1 | Southland v Northland | Whangarei |
| | 20 | N1 | Bay of Plenty v Southland | Rotorua |
| October | 7 | N1 | Northland v Hawke's Bay | Whangarei |
| | 14 | N1 | Counties Manukau v Tasman | Pukekohe |
| | 27 | N1 c-f | Wellington v Bay of Plenty | Wellington |
| November | 18 | | Ireland v Fiji | Dublin |

\*    *Non first-class appointment*
*RWCQ  Rugby World Cup Qualifier*
*JWC    Junior World Championship*
*RC     Rugby Championship*
*6N     Six Nations*

**Two overseas referees controlled two Mitre 10 Cup & two
Heartland Championship fixtures:**
*Shuhei Kubo (Japan)* Aug 20: Manawatu v Wellington, Aug 26: Auckland v Northland,
*Teru Kajiwara (Japan)* Aug 26: King Country v West Coast, Sep 2: Wairarapa Bush v East Coast,

## INTERNATIONAL ASSISTANT REFEREES AND
## TELEVISION MATCH OFFICIALS

### Nick Brlant

| | | | | | |
|---|---|---|---|---|---|
| February | 4 | 6N | Scotland v Ireland | | Edinburgh |
| | 11 | 6N | Wales v England | | Cardiff |
| July | 1 | RWCQ | Samoa v Tonga | | Apia |
| | 15 | RWCQ | Samoa v Fiji | | Apia |

### Mike Fraser

| | | | | | |
|---|---|---|---|---|---|
| June | 10 | | Italy v Scotland | | Singapore |
| | 16 | | Tonga v Wales | | Auckland |
| | 24 | | Samoa v Wales | | Apia |
| November | 4 | | Japan v Australia | | Yokohama |

### Glen Jackson

| | | | | | |
|---|---|---|---|---|---|
| February | 4 | 6N | England v France | | London |
| June | 17 | | South Africa v France | | Durban |
| | 24 | | South Africa v France | | Johannesburg |
| September | 16 | RC | Australia v Argentina | | Canberra |
| November | 18 | | Italy v Argentina | | Florence |

### Shane McDermott

| | | | | | |
|---|---|---|---|---|---|
| June | 17 | | Australia v Scotland | (TMO) | Sydney |

### Glenn Newman

| | | | | | |
|---|---|---|---|---|---|
| February | 4 | 6N | Scotland v Ireland | (TMO) | Edinburgh |
| | 11 | 6N | Wales v England | (TMO) | Cardiff |
| June | 10 | | Japan v Romania | (TMO) | Kumamoto |
| | 17 | | Japan v Ireland | (TMO) | Shizuoka |
| | 24 | | Japan v Ireland | (TMO) | Tokyo |
| August | 19 | RC | South Africa v Argentina | (TMO) | Port Elizabeth |
| | 26 | RC | Argentina v South Africa | (TMO) | Salta |

### Ben O'Keeffe

| | | | | | |
|---|---|---|---|---|---|
| March | 18 | 6N | France v Wales | | Paris |
| June | 10 | | South Africa v France | | Pretoria |
| | 24 | | South Africa v France | | Johannesburg |

### Aaron Paterson

| | | | | | |
|---|---|---|---|---|---|
| June | 10 | | Argentina v England | (TMO) | San Juan |
| | 17 | | Argentina v England | (TMO) | Santa Fe |
| | 24 | | Argentina v Georgia | (TMO) | Jujuy |

### Brendon Pickerill

| | | | | | |
|---|---|---|---|---|---|
| June | 10 | | Australia v Fiji | | Melbourne |
| | 17 | | Australia v Scotland | | Sydney |
| | 24 | | Australia v Italy | | Brisbane |
| November | 11 | | Italy v Fiji | | Catania |

### Ben Skeen

| | | | | | |
|---|---|---|---|---|---|
| March | 10 | 6N | Wales v Ireland | (TMO) | Cardiff |
| | 11 | 6N | England v Scotland | (TMO) | London |

|  | 18 | 6N | Ireland v England | (TMO) | Dublin |
| June | 10 | | Australia v Fiji | (TMO) | Melbourne |
|  | 16 | | Tonga v Wales | (TMO) | Auckland |
|  | 24 | | Australia v Italy | (TMO) | Brisbane |
| September | 9 | RC | Australia v South Africa | (TMO) | Perth |
|  | 16 | RC | Australia v Argentina | (TMO) | Canberra |
| November | 4 | | Japan v Australia | (TMO) | Yokohama |

**Cameron Stone**

| June | 16 | Tonga v Wales | Auckland |

**Paul Williams**

| June | 16 | | Tonga v Wales | Auckland |
| July | 1 | RWCQ | Samoa v Tonga | Apia |
|  | 8 | RWCQ | Fiji v Tonga | Suva |
| September | 9 | RC | Australia v South Africa | Perth |
|  | 16 | RC | Australia v Argentina | Canberra |
| November | 11 | | Scotland v Samoa | Edinburgh |

*(TMO) Television Match Official*
*JWC Junior World Championship*
*PNC Pacific Nations Cup*
*RC Rugby Championship*
*6N Six Nations*

## 2017 INTERNATIONAL REFEREES

N.P. Briant 2014: Fiji v Cook Islands (RWCQ), Romania v Canada; 2016: Georgia v Tonga, Tonga v USA; 2017: Tonga v Wales, Fiji v Tonga (RWCQ), Japan v Australia;

G.W. Jackson 2012: England v Fiji, Georgia v Japan; 2013: Italy v Australia, France v Tonga; 2014: Argentina v Ireland, South Africa v Scotland, Australia v Argentina, France v Fiji, Ireland v Australia; 2015: France v Scotland, Wales v Ireland, Argentina v South Africa, Ireland v Canada (RWC), Australia v Fiji (RWC), Tonga v Namibia (RWC), USA v Japan (RWC); 2016: Italy v England, Scotland v France, South Africa v Ireland, South Africa v Argentina, France v Australia; 2017: Italy v Ireland, South Africa v France, Australia v South Africa, Wales v Australia;

Dr B.D. O'Keeffe 2016: Samoa v Georgia, Japan v Scotland, Scotland v Argentina; 2017: Italy v France, South Africa v France, South Africa v Australia, Ireland v South Africa, England v Australia;

B.E. Pickerill 2017: Germany v USA;

P.M. Williams 2016: Romania v USA; 2017: Italy v Scotland, Fiji v Italy, Samoa vs Fiji (RWCQ), Ireland v Fiji;

# INTERNATIONAL REFEREES
*to 1 January, 2018*

| | | | |
|---|---|---|---|
| Bishop, D.J. (Southland) 1986–95 | 26 | McKenzie, E. (Wairarapa) 1921 | 1 |
| Bray, L.E. (Wellington) 2001–08 | 9 | McKenzie, H.J. (Wairarapa) 1936 | 1 |
| Briant, N.P. (Bay of Plenty) 2014–17 | 7 | McLachlan, L.L. (Otago) 1989–94 | 7 |
| Brown, K.W. (Southland) 2008–11 | 8 | McMullen, R.F. (Auckland) 1973 | 1 |
| Campbell, A. (Auckland) 1908 | 2 | Matheson, A.M. (Taranaki) 1946 | 1 |
| Dainty, C.J. (Wellington) 1982–86 | 2 | Millar, D.H. (Otago) 1965–78 | 8 |
| Deaker, K.M. (Hawke's Bay) 2001–08 | 23 | Moffit, J. (Wellington) 1936 | 1 |
| Doocey, T.F. (Canterbury) 1976–83 | 3 | Munro, V.G. (Canterbury) 2009–10 | 2 |
| Downes, A.D. (Otago) 1913 | 1 | Murphy, J.P. (North Auckland) 1959–69 | 13 |
| Duffy, B.W. (Taranaki) 1977 | 1 | Neilson, A.E. (Wellington) 1921 | 2 |
| Duncan, J. (Otago) 1908 | 1 | Nicholson, G.W. (Auckland) 1913 | 1 |
| Evans, F.T. (Canterbury) 1904 | 1 | O'Brien, P.D. (Southland) 1994–2005 | 37 |
| Farquahar, A.B. (Auckland) 1961–64 | 6 | O'Keeffe, Dr B.D. (Wellington) 2016–17 | 8 |
| Fleury, A.L. (Otago) 1959 | 1 | Parkinson, F.G.M. (Manawatu) 1955–56 | 3 |
| Fong, A.S. (West Coast) 1946–50 | 2 | Pickerill, B.E. (North Harbour) 2017 | 1 |
| Forsyth, R.A. (Taranaki) 1958 | 1 | Pollock, C.J. (Hawke's Bay) 2005–15 | 22 |
| Francis, R.C. (Wairarapa Bush) 1984–86 | 10 | Pring, J.P.G. (Auckland) 1966–72 | 8 |
| Fraser, M.I. (Wellington) 2013–14 | 4 | Robson, C.F. (Waikato) 1963 | 1 |
| Fright, W.A. (Canterbury) 1956 | 2 | Simpson, J.L. (Wellington) 1913 | 1 |
| Frood, J. (Otago) 1952 | 1 | Skeen, B.D. (Auckland) 2008–09 | 2 |
| Garrard, W.G. (Canterbury) 1899 | 1 | Sullivan, G. (Taranaki) 1950 | 1 |
| Gillies, C.R. (Waikato) 1958–59 | 4 | Sutherland, F.E. (Auckland) 1930 | 1 |
| Griffiths, A.A. (Waikato) 1952 | 1 | Taylor, A.R. (Canterbury) 1965–72 | 3 |
| Harrison, G.L. (Wellington) 1979–83 | 4 | Thompson, M.W. (Auckland) 1983 | 2 |
| Hawke, C.J. (South Canterbury) 1990–2001 | 24 | Tindill, E.W.T. (Wellington) 1950–55 | 3 |
| Hill, E.D. (Auckland) 1949 | 1 | Wahlstrom, G.K. (Auckland) 1994–97 | 6 |
| Hollander, S. (Canterbury) 1930–31 | 4 | Walsh, L. (Canterbury) 1949 | 1 |
| Honiss, P.G. (Canterbury & Waikato) 1997–2008 | 46 | Walsh, S. (Wellington) 1994–97 | 5 |
| Jackson, G.W. (Bay of Plenty) 2012–17 | 25 | Walsh, S.R. (North Harbour) 1998–2008 | 33 |
| King, J.S. (Wellington) 1937 | 2 | White, J.M (Auckland) 2013 | 2 |
| Lawrence, B.J. (Bay of Plenty) 2005–11 | 25 | Williams, J. (Otago) 1905 | 1 |
| Lawrence, K.H. (Bay of Plenty) 1985–91 | 13 | Williams, P.M. (Taranaki) 2016–17 | 5 |
| Macassey, L.E. (Otago) 1937 | 1 | Williamson G.L. (Wellington) 2010–13 | 2 |
| McAuley, C.J. (Otago) 1962 | 1 | Wise, G.J. (Hawke's Bay) 2004 | 1 |
| McDavitt, P.A. (Wellington) 1972–77 | 5 | Wolstenholme, B. (Poverty Bay) 1955 | 1 |

## SEVENTY-FIVE AND MORE FIRST-CLASS MATCHES
### to 1 January, 2018

| | | | | | | |
|---|---|---|---|---|---|---|
| P.D. O'Brien | 1988–2005 | 221 | D.J. Bishop | 1976–1995 | 114 |
| P.G. Honiss | 1992–2008 | 220 | K.W. Brown | 1999–2012 | 111 |
| S.R. Walsh | 1994–2008 | 210 | G.J. Wise | 1996–2007 | 109 |
| B.J. Lawrence | 1997–2012 | 201 | K.H. Lawrence | 1971–1992 | 99 |
| C.J. Pollock | 2000–2016 | 201 | S. Walsh | 1980–2000 | 99 |
| K.M. Deaker | 1996–2008 | 178 | R.P. Kelly | 2009-2017 | 96 |
| C.J. Hawke | 1983–2001 | 175 | V.G. Munro | 2001–2012 | 87 |
| G.W. Jackson | 2010–2017 | 153 | S.W. McDermott | 2006-2017 | 82 |
| N.P. Briant | 2009–2017 | 148 | R.C. Francis | 1967–1988 | 81 |
| L.E. Bray | 1991–2008 | 140 | K.R. McBride | 2006-2016 | 81 |
| M.I. Fraser | 2007–2017 | 134 | T.F. Doocey | 1973–1988 | 79 |
| G.K. Wahlstrom | 1985–2002 | 127 | Dr. B.D. O'Keeffe | 2012–2017 | 77 |
| G.L. Williamson | 2003–2014 | 116 | J.P.G. Pring | 1955–1980 | 77 |
| J.M. White | 2000–2013 | 115 | A.G. Riley | 1986–1998 | 77 |

## MOST INTERNATIONAL APPOINTMENTS BY REFEREES

| | | | | | | | |
|---|---|---|---|---|---|---|---|
| N. Owens | Wales | 2003–17 | 80 | D.T.M. McHugh | Ireland | 1994–2004 | 29 |
| W. Barnes | England | 2006–17 | 76 | D. Pearson | England | 2003–12 | 28 |
| J.I. Kaplan | South Africa | 1996–2013 | 70 | J.D. Lacey | Ireland | 2010–17 | 28 |
| C.P. Joubert | South Africa | 2003–16 | 69 | W.J. Erickson | Australia | 1994–2002 | 27 |
| A.C.P. Rolland | Ireland | 2001–14 | 67 | A.J. Watson | South Africa | 1996–2004 | 27 |
| S.R. Walsh | New Zealand/ | | | S.M. Lawrence | South Africa | 2000–11 | 27 |
| | Australia | 1998–2014 | 60 | D.J. Bishop | New Zealand | 1986–1995 | 26 |
| R. Poite | France | 2006–17 | 55 | B. Gabbei | Germany | 1993–2006 | 26 |
| C.R. White | England | 1998–2009 | 51 | S.M. Young | Australia | 1994–2006 | 26 |
| S.J. Dickinson | Australia | 1997–2011 | 47 | K.V.J. Fitzgerald | Australia | 1985–1991 | 25 |
| P.G. Honiss | New Zealand | 1997–2008 | 46 | C. Norling | Wales | 1978–1991 | 25 |
| D.A. Lewis | Ireland | 1998–2010 | 45 | B.J. Lawrence | New Zealand | 2005–11 | 25 |
| G.J. Clancy | Ireland | 2006–16 | 45 | M. Jonker | South Africa | 2005–14 | 25 |
| W.D. Bevan | Wales | 1985–2000 | 44 | G.W. Jackson | New Zealand | 2012–17 | 25 |
| J.M. Fleming | Scotland | 1985–2001 | 41 | C.J. Hawke | New Zealand | 1990–2001 | 24 |
| A.J. Spreadbury | England | 1990–2008 | 41 | D.G. Walters | Wales | 1959–66 | 23 |
| J. Garces | France | 2010–17 | 40 | K.D. Kelleher | Ireland | 1959–71 | 23 |
| J.D. Peyper | South Africa | 2011–17 | 39 | K.M. Deaker | New Zealand | 2001–08 | 23 |
| E.F. Morrison | England | 1991–2001 | 38 | J.P. Doyle | England | 2009–17 | 23 |
| P.D. O'Brien | New Zealand | 1994–2005 | 37 | M. Joseph | Wales | 1966–77 | 22 |
| J. Jutge | France | 1996–2007 | 35 | J. Dume | France | 1993–2003 | 22 |
| P. Gauzere | France | 2010–17 | 32 | C.J. Pollock | New Zealand | 2005–15 | 22 |
| A.J. Cole | Australia | 1997–2005 | 31 | R.C. Williams | Ireland | 1957–64 | 21 |
| P.L. Marshall | Australia | 1993–2003 | 30 | F.A. Howard | England | 1984–92 | 20 |

# SEVENS RUGBY
## NEW ZEALAND SEVENS SQUADS 2017

Competition in the World Series became increasingly even during 2017 with six nations sharing the ten Cup titles during the calendar year. 2016/17 series winners South Africa dominated with five titles while the other five Cup titles were shared between England, Fiji, Canada, Scotland and New Zealand, each with won tournament win. New coach Clark Laidlaw took charge in June and improved results were immediate. After 14 tournaments when the All Blacks Sevens failed to reach a Cup final, Clark's squad made the final at the Oceania event in Fiji and also the first two rounds of the 2017/18 Series tournaments, the win at Cape Town being a pleasing finish to the year.

| | | New Zealand | Australia | USA | Canada | Hong Kong | Singapore | France | England | Fiji | Dubai | South Africa | TOTALS |
|---|---|---|---|---|---|---|---|---|---|---|---|---|---|
| Kurt Baker | Manawatu | – | – | – | – | – | – | – | – | – | – | * | 1 |
| Jamie Booth | Manawatu | – | – | – | – | – | – | * | * | – | – | – | 2 |
| Dylan Collier | Southland/Waikato | * | * | * | * | * | – | – | – | * | * | * | 8 |
| Scott Curry (capt) | Bay of Plenty | * | * | – | * | – | – | – | – | * | * | * | 6 |
| Ambrose Curtis | Manawatu | – | – | s | * | – | – | – | – | – | – | – | 2 |
| Sam Dickson | Canterbury | – | – | – | – | * | * | * | * | – | * | * | 6 |
| DJ Forbes | Counties Manukau | * | * | * | * | * | * | * | * | – | – | – | 8 |
| Fa'asiu Fuatai | Otago | – | – | – | – | – | – | * | * | – | – | – | 2 |
| Jesse Houston | Canterbury | – | – | – | – | – | – | – | * | – | – | – | 1 |
| Iopu Iopu-Aso | Taranaki | * | * | * | * | * | * | – | – | – | – | – | 6 |
| Trael Joass | Tasman | – | * | * | * | * | * | * | * | – | – | – | 7 |
| Rocky Khan | Auckland | * | * | – | – | – | – | * | – | – | – | – | 3 |
| Andrew Knewstubb | Tasman | – | * | * | * | s | * | – | * | * | * | * | 9 |
| Vilimoni Koroi | Otago | * | * | * | * | * | * | – | – | – | * | * | 8 |
| Tim Mikkelson | Waikato | * | * | * | – | * | – | * | – | * | * | * | 8 |
| Sione Molia | Counties Manukau | * | * | * | * | * | * | * | – | * | * | * | 10 |
| Tone Ng Shiu | Tasman | * | – | * | s | – | * | * | * | * | * | – | 8 |
| Lewis Ormond | Taranaki | – | – | – | – | – | s | * | * | – | – | – | 3 |
| Joe Ravouvou | Auckland | – | – | – | – | * | * | – | – | * | * | * | 5 |
| Tamati Samuels | Hawke's Bay | – | – | – | – | – | – | – | * | – | – | – | 1 |
| Bailey Simonsson | Bay of Plenty | – | – | – | – | – | – | – | * | – | – | – | 1 |
| Teddy Stanaway | Bay of Plenty | – | – | – | – | – | – | – | * | – | – | * | 2 |
| Sherwin Stowers | Counties Manukau | * | * | * | * | – | – | s | * | – | – | – | 6 |
| Isaac Te Tamaki | Waikato | * | s | * | * | * | – | – | – | * | * | s | 8 |
| Beaudein Waaka | Taranaki | – | – | * | * | * | * | – | – | – | – | – | 4 |
| Regan Ware | Bay of Plenty | * | * | – | – | * | * | * | – | * | * | * | 8 |
| Joe Webber | Bay of Plenty | – | – | – | – | – | * | * | * | * | * | * | 6 |

Forbes was captain at Las Vegas, Hong Kong, Singapore, Paris and London.

**Coaches:** Scott Waldrom (*Wellington*); Clark Laidlaw (*Otago*) from June
**Manager:** Ross Everiss *(Bay of Plenty)*
**Physiotherapist:** Katherine Rottier (*Taranaki*); Damian Banks (*Bay of Plenty*) from November

## INDIVIDUAL SCORING

| | Tries | Con | Points | | Tries | Con | Points |
|---|---|---|---|---|---|---|---|
| Ware | 24 | – | 120 | Joass | 5 | – | 25 |
| Koroi | 12 | 28 | 116 | Curtis | 3 | – | 15 |
| Ravouvou | 21 | – | 105 | Houston | 3 | – | 15 |
| Molia | 19 | – | 95 | Iopu-Aso | 3 | – | 15 |
| Mikkelson | 18 | 1 | 92 | Ormond | 3 | – | 15 |
| Knewstubb | 10 | 19 | 88 | Simonsson | 3 | – | 15 |
| Waaka | 6 | 28 | 86 | Fuatai | 2 | – | 10 |
| Webber | 9 | 20 | 85 | Stanaway | 2 | – | 10 |
| Te Tamaki | 10 | 14 | 78 | penalty try | 1 | – | 7 |
| Curry | 13 | 1 | 67 | Baker | 1 | – | 5 |
| Forbes | 13 | – | 65 | Booth | 1 | – | 5 |
| Collier | 12 | – | 60 | Samuels | – | 1 | 2 |
| Dickson | 11 | – | 55 | | | | |
| Khan | 3 | 20 | 55 | **TOTALS** | **226\*** | **132** | **1396** |
| Stowers | 11 | – | 55 | *Opposition scored 802 points* | | | |
| Ng Shiu | 7 | – | 35 | | | | |

\* From the commencement of the 2016/17 series a penalty try is worth seven points with no conversion attempt required.

*Final points for 2016/17 World Rugby Sevens Series:* South Africa 192, England 164, Fiji 150, New Zealand 137, USA 129, Australia 113, Scotland 109, Canada 98, Argentina 90, Wales 73, France 66, Kenya 63, Samoa 51, Russia 29, Japan 20, Chile 6, Uganda 4, Papua New Guinea 2, Spain 2, Hong Kong 1, South Korea 1. The series was held over ten tournaments between December 2016 and May 2017.

*Previous winners:* New Zealand 2000, 2001, 2002, 2003, 2004, 2005, 2007, 2008, 2011, 2012, 2013, 2014; Fiji 2006, 2015, 2016; South Africa 2009; Samoa 2010.

*World Rugby Sevens Series Cup championship titles (1999 to 1 January 2018):* New Zealand 51, Fiji 31, South Africa 25, England 19, Samoa 10, Australia 6, Argentina 2, Scotland 2, France 1, United States 1, Kenya 1, Canada 1.

## NEW ZEALAND AT NEW ZEALAND SEVENS
### Westpac Stadium, Wellington                    January 28/29, 2017

| Date | Opponent | Result | Tries | Conversions |
|---|---|---|---|---|
| Jan 28 | Samoa | won 33–7 | Curry (2), Stowers, Mikkelson, Forbes | Khan (4) |
| Jan 28 | France | won 21–14 | Khan, Stowers, Molia | Khan (3) |
| Jan 28 | USA | won 24–12 | Te Tamaki (2), Koroi, Mikkelson | Koroi, Khan |
| Jan 29 | Fiji (Cup q-f) | lost 10–26 | Forbes, Mikkelson | |
| Jan 29 | England (s-f for 5th) | won 24–0 | Curry, Ware, Iopu-Aso, Stowers | Koroi, Te Tamaki |
| Jan 29 | Argentina (final for 5th) | lost 12–17 | Ware, Curry | Te Tamaki |

South Africa defeated Fiji 26–5 in the Cup final

## NEW ZEALAND AT AUSTRALIA SEVENS
### Allianz Stadium, Sydney                    February 4/5, 2017

| Date | Opponent | Result | Tries | Conversions |
|---|---|---|---|---|
| Feb 4 | Australia | won 26–14 | Koroi, Mikkelson, Stowers, Khan | Koroi (2), Khan |
| Feb 4 | Papua New Guinea | won 31–7 | Molia, Knewstubb, Stowers, Collier, Ware | Khan (2), Mikkelson |
| Feb 4 | Scotland | won 14–7 | Curry, Mikkelson | Koroi (2) |
| Feb 5 | Fiji (Cup q-f) | won 24–21 | Iopu-Aso, Ware, Stowers, Molia | Koroi, Khan |
| Feb 5 | England (Cup s-f) | lost 5–12 | Ware | |
| Feb 5 | Australia (for 3rd ) | won 29–14 | Khan, Collier, Forbes, Joass, Ware | Khan, Te Tamaki |

South Africa defeated England 29–14 in the Cup final.

## NEW ZEALAND AT USA SEVENS
### Sam Boyd Stadium, Las Vegas                    March 3–5, 2017

| Date | Opponent | Result | Tries | Conversions |
|---|---|---|---|---|
| Mar 3 | Kenya | won 24–7 | Stowers, Mikkelson, Collier, Molia | Koroi, Waaka |
| Mar 3 | Russia | won 19–5 | Waaka, Te Tamaki, Forbes | Waaka (2) |
| Mar 4 | Argentina | lost 10–12 | Forbes, Te Tamaki | |
| Mar 4 | England (Cup qf | won 19–0 | Mikkelson (2), Forbes | Te Tamaki (2) |
| Mar 5 | Fiji (Cup s-f) | lost 14–19 | penalty try*, Te Tamaki | Te Tamaki |
| Mar 5 | USA (for 3rd) | lost 15–19 | Forbes, Mikkelson, Molia | |

South Africa defeated Fiji 19–12 in the Cup final
* penalty try worth seven points

## NEW ZEALAND AT CANADA SEVENS
### BC Place Stadium, Vancouver                                   March 11/12, 2017

| Date | Opponent | Result | Tries | Conversions |
|---|---|---|---|---|
| Mar 11 | Russia | won 40–0 | Knewstubb (2), Joass, Stowers, Curry, Curtis | Waaka (4), Koroi |
| Mar 11 | Scotland | won 33–12 | Curtis (2), Curry, Collier, Te Tamaki | Koroi (3), Te Tamaki |
| Mar 11 | Canada | won 15–14 | Koroi (2), Curry | |
| Mar 12 | England (Cup q-f) | lost 12–14 | Forbes, Curry | Waaka |
| Mar 12 | Australia (s-f for 5th) | won 21–0 | Curry, Waaka, Knewstubb | Waaka (3) |
| Mar 12 | Argentina (for 5th) | won 17–14 | Waaka, Te Tamaki, Koroi | Waaka |

England defeated South Africa 19–7 in the Cup final

## NEW ZEALAND AT HONG KONG SEVENS
### Hong Kong Stadium, Hong Kong                                   April 7–9, 2017

| Date | Opponent | Result | Tries | Conversions |
|---|---|---|---|---|
| Apr 7 | Wales | won 19–7 | Mikkelson, Forbes, Waaka | Te Tamaki, Waaka |
| Apr 8 | Japan | won 40–14 | Collier (2), Ravouvou (2), Dickson, Te Tamaki | Waaka (5) |
| Apr 8 | Fiji | lost 14–17 | Ravouvou, Ware | Koroi, Te Tamaki |
| Apr 9 | South Africa (Cup q-f) | lost 19–21 | Ware, Molia, Dickson | Koroi, Waaka |
| Apr 9 | England (s-f for 5th) | won 21–7 | Ravouvou (2), Molia | Waaka (3) |
| Apr 9 | Argentina (for 5th) | won 10–7 | Ravouvou, Dickson | |

Fiji defeated South Africa 22–0 in the Cup final

## NEW ZEALAND AT SINGAPORE SEVENS
### National Stadium, Singapore                                   April 15/16, 2017

| Date | Opponent | Result | Tries | Conversions |
|---|---|---|---|---|
| Apr 15 | Scotland | won 22–21 | Ware, Ravouvou, Joass, Ng Shiu | Waaka |
| Apr 15 | Wales | won 36–14 | Molia (2), Webber, Iopu-Aso, Ravouvou, Waaka | Koroi (2), Waaka |
| Apr 15 | USA | won 21–14 | Ware (2), Dickson | Koroi (2), Waaka |
| Apr 16 | Canada (Cup q-f) | lost 14–26 | Ware, Joass | Koroi (2) |
| Apr 16 | Kenya (s-f for 5th) | won 24–21 | Ormond (2), Joass, Waaka | Waaka (2) |
| Apr 16 | South Africa (for 5th) | won 17–12 | Ravouvou, Molia, Koroi | Waaka |

Canada defeated USA 26–19 in the Cup final

## *NEW ZEALAND AT FRANCE SEVENS*
### Stade Jean Bouin, Paris                                     May 13/14, 2017

| Date | Opponent | Result | Tries | Conversions |
|------|----------|--------|-------|-------------|
| May 13 | Wales | won 26–7 | Mikkelson, Forbes, Ware, Molia | Khan (3) |
| May 13 | Argentina | won 21–14 | Ware, Mikkelson, Dickson | Khan (3) |
| May 13 | USA | won 27–14 | Ware (2), Booth, Fuatai, Ng Shiu | Khan |
| May 14 | France (Cup q-f) | won 14–0 | Forbes, Molia | Webber (2) |
| May 14 | South Africa (Cup s-f) | lost 5–26 | Ware | |
| May 14 | England (for 3rd) | won 12–5 | Dickson, Stowers | Webber |

South Africa defeated Scotland 15–5 in the Cup final.

## *NEW ZEALAND AT ENGLAND SEVENS*
### Twickenham, London                                          May 20/21, 2017

| Date | Opponent | Result | Tries | Conversions |
|------|----------|--------|-------|-------------|
| May 20 | Japan | won 33–7 | Houston (2), Stowers, Dickson, Forbes | Webber (3), Samuels |
| May 20 | Canada | won 19–14 | Dickson, Stowers, Ng Shiu | Webber (2) |
| May 20 | Fiji | won 27–21 | Webber (2), Forbes, Ormond, Houston | Webber |
| May 21 | Scotland (Cup q-f) | lost 21–24 | Dickson, Fuatai, Knewstubb | Webber (3) |
| May 21 | Australia (s-f for 5th) | lost 7–40 | Ng Shiu | Webber |

Scotland defeated England 12–7 in the Cup final

## *NEW ZEALAND AT OCEANIA SEVENS*
### ANZ Stadium, Suva, Fiji                                November 10/11, 2017

| Date | Opponent | Result | Tries | Conversions |
|------|----------|--------|-------|-------------|
| Nov 10 | Nauru | won 46–0 | Ware (3), Stanaway (2), Simonsson, Knewstubb, Webber | Te Tamaki (2), Webber |
| Nov 10 | Cook Islands | won 36–0 | Ravouvou (2), Collier, Webber, Mikkelson, Ng Shiu | Knewstubb (3) |
| Nov 11 | American Samoa (Cup q-f) | won 58–0 | Ravouvou (3), Ng Shiu (2), Simonsson (2), Webber, Curry, Te Tamaki | Webber (3), Knewstubb |
| Nov 11 | Australia (Cup s-f) | won 29–0 | Knewstubb, Molia, Mikkelson, Te Tamaki | Knewstubb, Te Tamaki |
| Nov 11 | Fiji (Cup final) | lost 0–26 | | |

## NEW ZEALAND AT DUBAI SEVENS
### The Sevens, Dubai
**December 1/2, 2017**

| Date | Opponent | Result | Tries | Conversions |
|------|----------|--------|-------|-------------|
| Dec 1 | Samoa | won 24–12 | Ware, Collier, Curry, Molia | Knewstubb (2) |
| Dec 1 | Argentina | won 21–19 | Koroi, Webber, Molia | Knewstubb, Koroi, Te Tamaki |
| Dec 1 | USA | won 22–12 | Molia (2), Ravouvou, Ware | Webber |
| Dec 2 | Kenya (Cup q-f) | won 14–12 | Collier, Knewstubb | Koroi, Knewstubb |
| Dec 2 | England (Cup s-f) | won 14–5 | Ravouvou (2) | Knewstubb (2) |
| Dec 2 | South Africa (Cup final) | lost 12–24 | Knewstubb, Curry | Knewstubb |

## NEW ZEALAND AT SOUTH AFRICA SEVENS
### Cape Town Stadium, Cape Town
**December 9/10, 2017**

| Date | Opponent | Result | Tries | Conversions |
|------|----------|--------|-------|-------------|
| Dec 9 | USA | lost 0–22 | | |
| Dec 9 | Spain | won 50–0 | Mikkelson (2), Dickson (2), Webber, Baker, Ware, Koroi | Koroi (3), Webber, Knewstubb |
| Dec 9 | Australia | won 35–12 | Collier (2), Koroi (2), Molia | Koroi (2), Curry, Webber, Knewstubb |
| Dec 10 | England (Cup q-f) | won 17–12 | Knewstubb, Collier, Ravouvou | Knewstubb |
| Dec 10 | South Africa (Cup s-f) | won 19–12 | Mikkelson, Koroi, Webber | Koroi, Knewstubb |
| Dec 10 | Argentina (Cup final) | won 38–14 | Ravouvou (2), Koroi, Mikkelson, Ware, Molia, | Knewstubb (3), Te Tamaki |

\* Penalty try worth seven points.

## PLAYING RECORD OF NEW ZEALAND SEVENS TEAMS

| | Tournaments | | | Games | | | | Points | |
|---|---|---|---|---|---|---|---|---|---|
| | Attended | Won | Runner-up | Played | Won | Draw | Lost | For | Against |
| 1973 | 1 | – | – | 3 | 2 | – | 1 | 58 | 50 |
| 1983 | 1 | – | – | 5 | 4 | – | 1 | 114 | 4 |
| 1984 | 1 | – | 1 | 5 | 4 | – | 1 | 74 | 40 |
| 1985 | 1 | – | – | 4 | 3 | – | 1 | 88 | 18 |
| 1986 | 3 | 3 | – | 16 | 15 | – | 1 | 414 | 72 |
| 1987 | 2 | 1 | 1 | 11 | 10 | – | 1 | 284 | 66 |
| 1988 | 2 | 1 | 1 | 11 | 10 | – | 1 | 274 | 37 |
| 1989 | 2 | 2 | – | 11 | 11 | – | – | 316 | 71 |
| 1990 | 1 | – | 1 | 5 | 4 | – | 1 | 134 | 44 |
| 1991 | 1 | – | 1 | 5 | 4 | – | 1 | 150 | 18 |
| 1992 | 1 | – | 1 | 5 | 4 | – | 1 | 130 | 34 |
| 1993 | 3 | – | – | 17 | 12 | – | 5 | 420 | 175 |
| 1994 | 2 | 1 | – | 10 | 9 | – | 1 | 361 | 89 |
| 1995 | 5 | 2 | 1 | 22 | 19 | – | 3 | 681 | 182 |
| 1996 | 5 | 3 | 2 | 29 | 27 | – | 2 | 1263 | 236 |
| 1997 | 4 | 1 | 1 | 21 | 18 | – | 3 | 670 | 287 |
| 1998 | 11 | 6 | 2 | 59 | 54 | – | 5 | 2134 | 473 |
| 1999 | 10 | 7 | 2 | 54 | 49 | 1 | 4 | 1574 | 426 |
| 2000 | 10 | 6 | 3 | 59 | 55 | – | 4 | 2048 | 354 |
| 2001 | 10 | 7 | 1 | 60 | 56 | – | 4 | 2042 | 330 |
| 2002 | 13 | 8 | 2 | 75 | 68 | 1 | 6 | 2377 | 565 |
| 2003 | 7 | 1 | 3 | 40 | 34 | – | 6 | 1285 | 411 |
| 2004 | 8 | 3 | 2 | 46 | 39 | – | 7 | 1396 | 395 |
| 2005 | 8 | 3 | 1 | 48 | 41 | – | 7 | 1509 | 441 |
| 2006 | 9 | 2 | 1 | 48 | 36 | 2 | 10 | 1380 | 551 |
| 2007 | 8 | 4 | – | 44 | 40 | – | 4 | 1391 | 355 |
| 2008 | 8 | 4 | 2 | 47 | 43 | – | 4 | 1350 | 367 |
| 2009 | 9 | 2 | 2 | 49 | 37 | – | 12 | 1262 | 514 |
| 2010 | 9 | 2 | 2 | 51 | 43 | 1 | 7 | 1531 | 541 |
| 2011 | 9 | 4 | 1 | 50 | 43 | – | 7 | 1479 | 519 |
| 2012 | 9 | 3 | 4 | 54 | 46 | – | 8 | 1375 | 556 |
| 2013 | 10 | 3 | 4 | 60 | 52 | – | 8 | 1651 | 584 |
| 2014 | 10 | 4 | 3 | 60 | 50 | – | 10 | 1645 | 511 |
| 2015 | 8 | 1 | 3 | 47 | 33 | 1 | 13 | 1039 | 692 |
| 2016 | 11 | 3 | 1 | 64 | 45 | 3 | 16 | 1357 | 860 |
| 2017 | 11 | 1 | 2 | 64 | 48 | – | 16 | 1396 | 802 |
| **TOTALS** | **223** | **88** | **51** | **1259** | **1068** | **9** | **182** | **36652** | **11670** |

# SEVENS RECORDS
*to January 1, 2018*

## *BY NEW ZEALAND TEAMS*

| | | |
|---|---|---|
| Most successive wins | 47 | 2007–08 |
| Most successive tournament wins | 7 | 2007–08 |
| Most successive appearances in finals | 12 | 1986–92 |

### Tournament records
| | | |
|---|---|---|
| Most points | 463 | Portugal, 1996 |
| Most tries | 69 | Portugal, 1996 |
| Most conversions | 59 | Portugal, 1996 |

### Match records
| | | |
|---|---|---|
| Highest team score | 94 | v Moldova, Portugal, 1996 |
| Record victory (*points ahead*) | 94 | 94–0, v Moldova, 1996 |
| Highest score conceded | 61 | v Fiji, Japan, 1996 |
| Record defeat (*points behind*) | 56 | 5–61, v Fiji, Japan, 1996 |
| Most tries | 14 | v Moldova, Portugal, 1996 |
| Most conversions | 12 | v Moldova, Portugal, 1996 |
| | | v Hungary, Portugal, 1996 |

## *BY THE PLAYERS*

### Career records
| | | |
|---|---|---|
| Attended most tournaments | 94 | DJ Forbes |
| Most points | 2122 | T. Cama |
| Most tries | 208 | T.J. Mikkelson |

### Tournament records
| | | |
|---|---|---|
| Most points | 136 | C.M. Cullen, Hong Kong, 1996 |
| Most tries | 20 | B.R.M. Fleming, Portugal, 1996 |
| Most conversions | 28 | D.A. Smith, Portugal, 1996 |

### Match records
| | | |
|---|---|---|
| Most points | 37 | C.M. Cullen, v Sri Lanka, Hong Kong, 1996 |
| Most tries | 7 | C.M. Cullen, v Sri Lanka, Hong Kong, 1996 |
| Most conversions | 9 | T.J. Wright, v Korea, Sydney, 1989 |
| | | M. Ashford, v Sri Lanka, Dubai, 2001 |

## NEW ZEALAND SEVENS REPRESENTATIVES, 1973–2017

| | *Tournaments* |
|---|---|
| **Ahki, P.J.** (*North Harbour*) 2013– | |
| 14–16 | 7 |
| **Ai'i, O.** | |
| (*Auckland*) 1999–00–01–02–04–05 | 25 |
| **Alley, G.** (*North Harbour*) 1992–93 | 2 |
| **Andrews, L.S.** (*Otago*) 1999 | 2 |
| **Anesi, S.R.** (*Waikato*) 2004–06 | 7 |
| **Arnold, T.C.** (*Bay of Plenty*) | |
| 2009–10–11–12 | 19 |
| **Ashford, M.R.** (*Auckland*) 2001–05 | 10 |
| **Atiga, B.A.C.** (*Auckland*) 2007 | 1 |
| **Austin, H.S.E.** (*Taranaki*) 1999 | 1 |
| **Auva'a, O.J.** (*Auckland*) 2006–09 | 5 |
| | |
| **Bachop, G.T.M.** | |
| (*Canterbury*) 1990–91–92–94 | 5 |
| **Baker, K.T.** (*Manawatu*) 2008–09–17 | |
| (*Taranaki*) 2010–12–13–14–16 | 29 |
| **Bale, P.** (*Canterbury*) 1990–92–93 | 3 |
| **Barrett, B.J.** (*Taranaki*) 2010 | 2 |
| **Batty, G.B.** (*Wellington*) 1973 | 1 |
| **Baxter, C.N.O.** | |
| (*Bay of Plenty*) 2003–06–07 | 9 |
| **Berryman, N.R.** (*Northland*) 1997 | 1 |
| **Blackadder, T.J.** (*Canterbury*) 1993 | 2 |
| **Blackie, J.M.** (*Otago*) 2002–03– | |
| 04–05–06 | 12 |
| **Blowers, A.F.** (*Auckland*) 1995 | 3 |
| **Blythe, T.G.** (*Waikato*) 1999 | |
| (*Bay of Plenty*) 2001 | 3 |
| **Booth, J.P.** (*Manawatu*) 2017 | 2 |
| **Botica, F.M.** | |
| (*North Harbour*) 1985–86–87–88 | 8 |
| **Bourke, C.R.** (*Hawke's Bay*) 2004 | 3 |
| **Brooke, Z.V.** | |
| (*Auckland*) 1986–87–88–89–90 | 10 |
| **Brooke-Cowden, M.** | |
| (*Auckland*) 1986–87 | 5 |
| **Bruning, K.T.** (*Waikato*) 1994 | |
| (*Nelson Bays*) 1995 | 3 |
| **Bryant, R.J.** (*Taranaki*) 1997 | 1 |
| **Bunce, F.E.** (*North Harbour*) 1993 | 2 |
| **Bunce; J.F.** (*Manawatu*) 2015 | 2 |
| **Bunting, A.M.** | |
| (*Bay of Plenty*) 2002–03 | 6 |
| **Cama, T.** (*Manawatu*) 2005–07–08– | |
| 09–10–11–12–13–14 | 63 |

| | *Tournaments* |
|---|---|
| **Camburn, M.** | |
| (*North Harbour*) 2005 | 3 |
| **Cashmore, A.R.** (*Auckland*) 1995 | 4 |
| **Christie, S.A.** (*Tasman*) 2011 | 2 |
| **Clamp, M.** (*Wellington*) 1984–85–86 | 4 |
| **Clarke, E.** (*Auckland*) 1993 | 1 |
| **Clutterbuck, M.J.** | |
| (*Bay of Plenty*) 2014 | 1 |
| **Cocker, E.** (*Otago*) 2005–06–07 | |
| (*Auckland*) 2008–09 | 28 |
| **Collier, D.J.** (*Waikato*) 2015–16–17 | 23 |
| **Colling, G.L.** (*Otago*) 1973 | 1 |
| **Collins, N.I.** (*Bay of Plenty*) 2001–02 | 6 |
| **Crowley, A.E.** | |
| (*Taranaki*) 1987–88–89–91 | 6 |
| **Cullen, C.M.** (*Manawatu*) 1995–96 | |
| (*Wellington*) 1998–00 | 7 |
| **Curry, S.B.** (*Manawatu*) 2010–12–13 | |
| (*Bay of Plenty*) 2011–14–15–16–17 | 41 |
| **Curtis, A.A.D.** (*Wellington*) 2013–14–15 | |
| (*Manawatu*) 2017 | 19 |
| | |
| **Dagg, I.J.A.** (*Hawke's Bay*) 2007–08 | 6 |
| **Daniel, B.W.** (*Bay of Plenty*) 1997 | 2 |
| **Dauwai, A.** (*Thames Valley*) 2006 | 2 |
| **Dawson, A.J.** (*Counties*) 1983–85 | 2 |
| **De Goldi, C.D.** | |
| (*Bay of Plenty*) 1998–99–00 | |
| (*Auckland*) 2001–02–03–04 | 41 |
| **Dickson, S.N.** (*Canterbury*) 2012–13– | |
| 14–15–16–17 | 38 |
| **Donald, A.J.** (*Wanganui*) 1983 | 1 |
| **Duggan, R.J.L.** (*Waikato*) 1997 | 1 |
| | |
| **Ellis, M.C.G.** (*Otago*) 1993 | 1 |
| **Ellison, T.E.** (*Wellington*) 2005–06 | 5 |
| **Ensor A.C.** (*Otago*) 2014 | 1 |
| **Erenavula, L.** (*Counties*) 1994 | 2 |
| **Evans, N.J.** (*North Harbour*) 2002 | 8 |
| | |
| **Faddes, M.A.** (*Otago*) 2013 | 3 |
| **Farani, D.** (*Wellington*) 1997 | 1 |
| **Flavell, T.V.** (*North Harbour*) 1998 | 2 |
| **Fleming, B.R.M.** | |
| (*Bay of Plenty*) 1995 | |
| (*Canterbury*) 1996–97–98 | |
| (*Wellington*) 1998–99–00–01–02 | |
| (*Otago*) 2003–04 | 35 |

¹Tournament reserve players called upon when injuries prevented New Zealand from having fit reserves for the final.

# NEW ZEALAND INTERNATIONAL SEVENS

Westpac Stadium, Wellington                                      January 28–29, 2017

## POOL PLAY

A    *Argentina 17, Kenya 12; England 40, Papua New Guinea 0; Kenya 47, Papua New Guinea 5;*
     *England 26, Argentina 7; Argentina 41, Papua New Guinea 14; England 31, Kenya 12.*

B    *Fiji 26, Australia 12; South Africa 33, Japan 0; Fiji 56, Japan 0;*
     *South Africa 28, Australia 0; Australia 33, Japan 12; South Africa 31, Fiji 12.*

C    *USA 21, France 21; New Zealand 33, Samoa 7; USA 24, Samoa 12;*
     *New Zealand 21, France 14; France 28, Samoa 5; New Zealand 24, USA 12.*

D    *Wales 33, Russia 0; Canada 28, Scotland 19; Canada 28, Wales 5;*
     *Scotland 12, Russia 5; Canada 29, Russia 0; Scotland 31, Wales 7.*

## CUP CHAMPIONSHIP

| | |
|---|---|
| *Quarter-finals* | Scotland 14, England 12; Fiji 26, New Zealand 10; |
| | Canada 17, Argentina 12; South Africa 45, France 0. |
| *Semi-finals* | Fiji 19, Scotland 12; South Africa 21, Canada 5. |
| *Final* | South Africa 26, Fiji 5. |
| *Play off for 3rd* | Scotland 28, Canada 22. |
| *5th place semi-final* | New Zealand 24, England 0; Argentina 19, France 14. |
| *5th place play-off* | Argentina 17, New Zealand 12. |

## CHALLENGE TROPHY

| | |
|---|---|
| *Quarter-finals* | Kenya 24, Russia 5; USA 19, Japan 14; |
| | Wales 29, Papua New Guinea 7; Australia 17, Samoa 14. |
| *Semi-finals* | Kenya 19, USA 12; Australia 24, Wales 10. |
| *Final* | Kenya 19, Australia 13. |
| *Play off for 3rd* | Scotland 28, Canada 22. |
| *13th place semi-final* | Russia 15, Japan 5; Samoa 35, Papua New Guinea 7. |
| *13th place play-off* | Samoa 19, Russia 12. |

*Tournament referees:* James Doleman (*New Zealand*), Nori Hashimoto (*Japan*), Richard Kelly (*New Zealand*), Damon Murphy (*Australia*), Rasta Rasivhenge (*South Africa*), Matt Rodden (*Hong Kong*), Tevita Rokovereni (*Fiji*), Kaveni Talemaivavalagi (*Fiji*), Jordan Way (*Australia*).

Previous New Zealand International Sevens Tournaments (*at Westpac Stadium, Wellington*)

| | Cup final | Plate winner | Bowl winner | Shield winner |
|---|---|---|---|---|
| 2000 | Fiji 24, New Zealand 14 | Canada | France | |
| 2001 | Australia19, Fiji 17 | Samoa | South Africa | Japan |
| 2002 | South Africa 17, Samoa 14 | Argentina | France | Cook Is |
| 2003 | New Zealand 38, England 26 | Samoa | Canada | Tonga |
| 2004 | New Zealand 33, Fiji 15 | Tonga | Argentina | USA |
| 2005 | New Zealand 31, Argentina 7 | Australia | Kenya | Niue |
| 2006 | Fiji 27, South Africa 22 | England | Scotland | Tonga |
| 2007 | Samoa 17, Fiji 14 | England | Argentina | Portugal |
| 2008 | New Zealand 22, Samoa 7 | South Africa | England | USA |
| 2009 | England 19, New Zealand 17 | South Africa | Cook Is | Scotland |
| 2010 | Fiji 19, Samoa 14 | Australia | Wales | USA |
| 2011 | New Zealand 29, England 14 | Fiji | Kenya | USA |
| 2012 | New Zealand 24, Fiji 7 | South Africa | Kenya | Scotland |
| 2013 | England 24, Kenya 19 | Australia | Canada | Wales |
| 2014 | New Zealand 21, South Africa 0 | Australia | Kenya | USA |
| 2015 | New Zealand 27, England 21 | Fiji | France | Canada |
| 2016 | New Zealand 24, South Africa 21 | Australia | Samoa | France |

| | Cup final | Challenge Trophy winner |
|---|---|---|
| 2017 | South Africa 26, Fiji 5 | Kenya |

## NEW ZEALAND DEVELOPMENT TEAM

This squad travelled to California and participated at the Silicon Valley Sevens held during November 4/5 at Avaya Stadium, San Jose.

*Squad:* Mason Emerson (*Hawke's Bay*), Levi Harmon (*Wellington*), Jesse Houston (*Canterbury*), Jordan Hyland (*Northland*), Luteru Laulala (*Counties Manukau*), Luke Masirewa (*Bay of Plenty*), Whiria Meltzer (*Northland*), Salesi Rayasi (*Auckland*), Mark Telea (*North Harbour*), Chase Tiatia (*Bay of Plenty*), TJ Vaega (*Hawke's Bay*), Te Rangatira Waitokia (*Manawatu*).

Coach: Tomasi Cama
Assistant coach: PJ Williams
Trainer: Andrew Keene
Physiotherapist: Ema Pene
Manager: Dean Watkins

*Results:*
Day 1 – lost to Chile 0–7, lost to USA 12–24.
Day 2 – defeated Tonga 34–0, lost to Australia 7–40, lost to Fiji 15–26, defeated Japan 26–5.
*Editors regret full details could not be supplied in time for inclusion in this publication.*

# NATIONAL SEVENS

Rotorua International Stadium                              January 14–15, 2017

## POOL PLAY

A      Waikato 24, Southland 14; Hawke's Bay 31, North Harbour 7;
       Waikato 17, North Harbour 10; Hawke's Bay 24, Southland 21;
       Waikato 28, Hawke's Bay 5; North Harbour 21, Southland 14.

B      Northland 24, South Canterbury 7; Counties Manukau 26, Manawatu 7;
       Northland 33, Manawatu 5; Counties Manukau 55, South Canterbury 0;
       Counties Manukau 15, Northland 14; Manawatu 29, South Canterbury 12.

C      Canterbury 19, Bay of Plenty 17; Tasman 28, Taranaki 19;
       Taranaki 33, Canterbury 5; Bay of Plenty 28, Tasman 17;
       Taranaki 21, Bay of Plenty 17; Tasman 17, Canterbury 14.

D      Wellington 31, Horowhenua Kapiti 7; Auckland 19, Otago 12;
       Wellington 17, Otago 10; Auckland 40, Horowhenua Kapiti 12;
       Otago 29, Horowhenua Kapiti 12; Auckland 12, Wellington 5.

## CUP CHAMPIONSHIP

| | |
|---|---|
| *Quarter-finals* | Waikato 12, Northland 7; Taranaki 22, Auckland 17;Wellington 14, Tasman 10; Counties Manukau 22, Hawke's Bay 0. |
| *Semi-finals* | Waikato 31, Taranaki 7; Counties Manukau 15, Wellington 12. |
| *Final* | Counties Manukau 14, Waikato 7. |

## PLATE CHAMPIONSHIP

| | |
|---|---|
| *Semi-finals* | Auckland 14, Northland 7; Tasman 14, Hawke's Bay 7. |
| *Final* | Auckland 28, Tasman 21 |

## BOWL CHAMPIONSHIP

| | |
|---|---|
| *Quarter-finals* | North Harbour 19, South Canterbury 12; Bay of Plenty 26, Otago 17; Canterbury 19, Horowhenua Kapiti 0; Manawatu 27, Southland 19. |
| *Semi-finals* | Bay of Plenty 33, North Harbour 0; Canterbury 36, Manawatu 17. |
| *Final* | Bay of Plenty 19, Canterbury 14. |

## SHIELD CHAMPIONSHIP

| | |
|---|---|
| *Semi-finals* | Otago 31, South Canterbury 7; Southland 17, Horowhenua Kapiti 12. |
| *Final* | Otago 28, Southland 0. |

*Tournament referees:* James Doleman, Richard Kelly, Michael Lash, James Munro, Vincent Ringrose, Michael Winter.

**Joe Tauiwi Memorial Trophy** *(Player of the Tournament)*
2001 Rua Tipoki (*North Harbour*), 2002 Tafai Ioasa (*Wellington*), 2004 Rudi Wulf (*North Harbour*), 2005 Amasio Valence (*Auckland*), 2006 Gary Saifoloi (*Auckland*), 2007 Tomasi Cama (*Manawatu*), 2008 David Raikuna (*Counties Manukau*), 2009 Luke Hamilton (*North Harbour*), 2010 Ben Souness (*Taranaki*), 2011 Malakai Fekitoa (*Auckland* , *2012 Buxton Popoaili'i (Otago*), 2013 David Raikuna (*North Harbour*), 2014 George Tilsley (*Manawatu*), 2015 Luke Masirewa (*Waikato*), 2016 Augustine Pulu (*Counties Manukau*) , 2017 Andrew Knewstubb (*Tasman*).

# NATIONAL SEVENS
## *TOURNAMENT TROPHY WINNERS*

| | Venue | Cup | Plate | Bowl | Shield |
|---|---|---|---|---|---|
| 1975 | Auckland | Marlborough | | | |
| 1976 | Christchurch | Marlborough | | | |
| 1977 | Blenheim | Manawatu | | | |
| 1978 | Hamilton | Manawatu | | | |
| 1979 | Palmerston Nth | Manawatu | | | |
| 1980 | Palmerston Nth | Auckland | | | |
| 1981 | Palmerston Nth | Taranaki | | | |
| 1982 | Feilding | Taranaki | | | |
| 1983 | Feilding | Auckland | | | |
| 1984 | Feilding | Auckland | | | |
| 1985 | Feilding | Counties | | | |
| 1986 | Feilding | Nth Harbour | | | |
| 1987 | Christchurch | Nth Harbour | Canterbury | Horowhenua | |
| 1988 | Pukekohe | Auckland | Manawatu | Wai Bush | |
| 1989 | Palmerston Nth | Auckland | Taranaki | Wanganui | Hawke's Bay |
| 1990 | Palmerston Nth | Canterbury | Bay of Plenty | Wanganui | Manawatu B |
| 1991 | Palmerston Nth | Auckland | Counties | Canterbury | East Coast |
| 1992 | Palmerston Nth | Nth Harbour | Counties | Auckland | Manawatu B |
| 1993 | Palmerston Nth | Canterbury | Nth Harbour | Taranaki | King Country |
| 1994 | Palmerston Nth | Counties | Nth Harbour | Canterbury | Manawatu B |
| 1995 | Palmerston Nth | Counties | Wellington | King Country | Manawatu B |
| 1996 | (*Mar*) Palm Nth | Waikato | C'nties M'kau | Wai Bush | Poverty Bay |
| 1996 | (*Nov*) Palm Nth | Waikato | Wellington | Wai Bush | Wanganui |
| 1997 | Rotorua | Waikato | Auckland | Otago | Wai Bush |
| 1998 | Rotorua | Waikato | Canterbury | Wai Bush | Otago |
| 1999 | Palmerston Nth | Nth Harbour | Canterbury | King Country | Nelson Bays |
| 2000 | Palmerston Nth | Nth Harbour | Wanganui | Nelson Bays | Southland |
| 2001 | Palmerston Nth | Nth Harbour | C'nties M'kau | Manawatu | West Coast |
| 2002 | Palmerston Nth | Wellington | Waikato | Marlborough | West Coast |
| 2004 | Queenstown | Nth Harbour | Auckland | Canterbury | Manawatu |
| 2005 | Queenstown | Auckland | Wellington | Otago | Manawatu |
| 2006 | Queenstown | Auckland | Bay of Plenty | Southland | Cantabrians |
| 2007 | Queenstown | Auckland | C'nties M'kau | Wellington | Northland |

| | Venue | Cup | Plate | Bowl | Shield |
|---|---|---|---|---|---|
| 2008 | Queenstown | Auckland | Manawatu | Wellington | Tasman |
| 2009 | Queenstown | Nth Harbour | Wellington | Otago | Southland |
| 2010 | Queenstown | Waikato | Nth Harbour | Horo' Kapiti | Tasman |
| 2011 | Queenstown | Auckland | Nth Harbour | Manawatu | Canterbury |
| 2012 | Queenstown | Auckland | Taranaki | Tasman | Bay of Plenty |
| 2013 | Queenstown | Taranaki | Auckland | Hawke's Bay | C'nties M'kau |
| 2014 | Rotorua | Wellington | Manawatu | Nth Harbour | Waikato |
| 2015 | Rotorua | Waikato | Taranaki | NthHarbour | Canterbury |
| 2016 | Rotorua | C'nties M'kau | Auckland | Northland | Wanganui |
| 2017 | Rotorua | C'nties M'kau | Auckland | Bay of Plenty | Otago |

# NEW ZEALAND DEAF
# RUGBY FOOTBALL UNION 2017

*Founded 1991*

The national team visited England for the first time and met England Deaf in three internationals played in the London area.

| TEAM 2017 | | England | England | England | TOTALS |
|---|---|---|---|---|---|
| Matt Hollis | Poneke, Wellington | 15 | 15 | 15 | 3 |
| Herbie Agnew | Linwood, Canterbury | – | 9 | 14 | 3 |
| Michael May | Linwood, Canterbury | s | – | s | 2 |
| Joseph Konelio | Suburbs, Auckland | 11 | 11 | – | 3 |
| Petaera Meihana | Feilding OB Oroua, Manawatu | 13 | 13 | 13 | 3 |
| Darryl Alexander | Johnsonville, Wellington | 12 | 12 | – | 3 |
| James Copeland | College Rifles, Auckland | 10 | 10 | 10 | 3 |
| Kamau Wise | Southern United, Waikato | 9* | – | s | 3 |
| Mark Lewis | Matamata, Waikato | s | s | 9 | 3 |
| Mitchell MacPherson | Silverdale, North Harbour | 8 | 8 | 8 | 3 |
| Reuben Buzzard (vice-capt) | Christchurch, Canterbury | 7 | 7 | 7 | 3 |
| Brandon Lochore | Northern United, Wellington | 6* | s | s | 3 |
| Theodore Waterhouse | Marist St Pat's, Wellington | s | 6 | 6* | 3 |
| Patrick Stokell | Linwood, Canterbury | – | – | s | 1 |
| Paul Rautao | Johnsonville, Wellington | 5 | 5* | s | 3 |
| Samuel Lane | Kaierau, Wanganui | s | – | 5* | 2 |
| Toby Agnew (capt) | Linwood, Canterbury | 4* | 4 | 4* | 3 |
| Mihaka Lemon | Kaikohe, Northland | 3* | – | s | 2 |
| Maara Tuare | Celtic, Mid Canterbury | s | 3 | 3* | 3 |
| David Dayberg | East Tamaki, Auckland | 1* | 1 | 1* | 3 |
| Sailusi Toalima | College Rifles, Auckland | s | – | s | 2 |
| Ashley Bensley | Linwood, Canterbury | 2* | 2* | s | 3 |
| Ben Webb | Northern United, Wellington | s | s | 2* | 3 |

*Manager:* Gregory Pateman (Christchurch)
*Assistant manager:* Evelyn Pateman (Christchurch)
*Coach:* Clive Morgan (Wellington)
*Assistant coach:* Ben Robertson (Christchurch)
*Physiotherapist:* Dina Lewis (Waikato)
*Sign language interpreter:* Fiona Love (Wellington)

November 4 v **England Deaf,** at Blackheath RFC, London. Lost 27–36. Hollis, H. Agnew, Konelio, Bensley tries; Copeland 2 conversions and penalty goal. Referee: Michael Woods. November 8 v **England Deaf,** at Latton Park, Harlow RFC, Essex. Lost 20–22. Meihana, Wise, MacPherson tries; Copeland conversion and penalty goal. Referee: Calum Howard. November 12 v **England Deaf,** at Barking RFC, Dagenham, Essex. Lost 18–31. Lewis, MacPherson tries; Copeland conversion and 2 penalty goals. Referee: Alexis Manley.

Before leaving for England the team played Wainuiomata RFC on October 30 at Mary Crowther Park, Lower Hutt. NZ Deaf won 29–20 with Wise, H. Agnew, MacPherson, Waterhouse and Copeland scoring tries and Copeland 2 conversions. On arrival in London the team played a Bromley RFC Invitation XV on November 1 at Bromley. NZ Deaf lost 17–43 with May and Copeland scoring tries and Copeland 2 conversions and a penalty goal.

## INTERNATIONAL MATCH RECORD

| 1995 | v South Africa | Christchurch | lost | 15 | 22 |
|------|----------------|--------------|------|----|----|
|      | v South Africa | Palmerston North | won | 17 | 8 |
|      | v South Africa | Takapuna | lost | 0 | 46 |
| 1998 | v Wales | Newport | won | 35 | 10 |
|      | v Wales | Neath | won | 55 | 3 |
|      | v Wales | Llanelli | won | 57 | 5 |
| 2001 | v Australia | Sydney | won | 25 | 0 |
|      | v Australia | Sydney | lost | 12 | 15 |
| 2002 | v Australia | Sydney | won | 19 | 17 |
|      | v Wales (WC) | Auckland | lost | 5 | 11 |
|      | v Australia (WC) | Auckland | won | 23 | 13 |
|      | v Wales (WC final) | Auckland | lost | 14 | 28 |
| 2005 | v Australia | Wanganui | lost | 10 | 22 |
|      | v Australia | Christchurch | won | 10 | 8 |
| 2012 | v Australia | Auckland | lost | 20 | 22 |
| 2013 | v Australia | Canberra | won | 30 | 13 |
| 2015 | v Australia | Christchurch | lost | 13 | 15 |
| 2016 | v Argentina | Cordoba | won | 19 | 15 |
|      | v Argentina | San Salvador de Jujuy | won | 18 | 16 |
| 2017 | v England | London | lost | 27 | 36 |
|      | v England | London | lost | 20 | 22 |
|      | v England | London | lost | 18 | 31 |

*WC    World Cup*

The 24th national Deaf tournament between the three zones was held at Jerry Collins Stadium, Porirua, Wellington during April 14–16. The results were: Central Zone 20 Northern 20; Southern 29 Central 13; Southern 17 Northern 10. Southern Zone was awarded the NZ Rugby Shield.

# CLUB FINALS

Results of the 2017 senior club finals.

## Auckland — Gallaher Shield:

29 July: University 39 v Suburbs 18
*Halftime: 13-5. Six tries to three.*

## Bay of Plenty — Baywide Premier Trophy:

29 July: Mount Maunganui 41 v Rotoiti 8
*Halftime: 13-8. Mount Maunganui took advantage of a yellow card to Rotoiti to score two tries in three minutes and extend to 23-8.*

## Buller — Senior Shield:

22 July: White Star 27 v Westport 25
*A last-minute try from a tap-kick penalty by Josh Tuidriva, for his third try of the day, gave White Star the victory. Westport led three times.*

## Canterbury

### Ellesmere-Mid Canterbury-North Canterbury combined — Luisetti Cup:
13 June: Southbridge 13 v Rakaia 12
*A penalty goal from Shannon Donald with three minutes left gave Southbridge the lead for the first time.*

### Metropolitan — Hawkins Trophy:
30 July: Lincoln University 25 v Canterbury University 19
*Lincoln, down 3–5 at halftime, went 25–5 ahead after 61 minutes. Canterbury University closed to 25–19 with three minutes left. Third title in a row for Lincoln.*

### Ellesmere sub union — Coleman Shield:
5 August: Southbridge 16 v Darfield 15
*Darfield led 12–0 during the first half, but a 79ᵗʰ minute penalty goal from Shannon Donald edged Southbridge in front.*

### North Canterbury sub union — Hunnibel Memorial Trophy:
5 August: Saracens 21 v Oxford 16
*Down 3–9 at halftime, Saracens went out to 21–9 after 60 minutes. Saracens, down to 14 men, conceded a late converted try.*

## Counties Manukau — McNamara Cup:

22 July: Bombay 32 v Karaka 24
*Halftime: 17–17. Bombay's fourth title in a row. Each side scored four tries.*

## East Coast — Rangiora Keelan Memorial Shield:

29 July: Tihirau Victory Club 24 a.e.t. v Hikurangi 21 a.e.t.
*Rapata Haerewa kicked a penalty goal with the last kick of the game to give TVC their first ever title. He had missed a penalty two minutes earlier. 14–14 after 80 minutes.*

## Hawke's Bay — Maddison Trophy:

5 August: Napier OB Marist 31 v Clive 26
*Second title in a row for OB Marist, completing a perfect season 20 wins from 20 matches. Joe Penitito played for OB Marist, his brother Duff played for Clive.*

**Wairoa sub union — Garry Allen Memorial Shield**
12 August – 23 September: 1st YMP 18 points, 2nd Tapuae 11 points
*Played after the Hawke's Bay and Poverty Bay competitions were completed, YMP won all four of their matches for second title in a row (shared last year with TKT). YMP also won the HB division three title in 2017.*

## Horowhenua Kapiti — Ramsbottom Cup:

22 July: Waikanae 11 v Paraparaumu 6
*Lincoln Timoteo scored the only try of the game with ten minutes left to put Waikanae 8–6 in front.*

## King Country — Meads Shield:

29 July: Taumarunui RS 25 v Waitete 13
*Taumarunui RS led 25–3 after 55 minutes.*

## Manawatu — Hankins Shield:

22 July: Old Boys Marist 28 v Kia Toa 27
*First title for the amalgamated club, and fourth year in a row Kia Toa have been beaten in the final. From 13–20 down at halftime, OB Marist went out to 28–20 after 60 minutes.*

## Mid Canterbury — Watters Cup:

23 July: Southern 35 v Rakaia 21
*Second year in a row the teams have met in the final. Rakaia led 11–8 at halftime. The match was postponed from the previous day due to bad weather.*

## Northland

**Northland Premiership — Joe Morgan Memorial Trophy:**
29 July: Old Boys Marist 34 v Mid Northern 25
*Renata Tenana scored four of OB Marist's five tries, his last in the final minute made the game safe.*

**Bay of Islands sub union — Championship Shield:**
5 August: Moerewa-United Kawakawa 32 v Kaikohe 14
*Debut season of the combined team.*

**Mangonui sub union — Bell Shield:**
5 August: Eastern United 26 v Awanui 23
*Down 14–23, Eastern United scored two tries in the final ten minutes with just 13 men to win, the last try to Billy Ray Murphy from a tap penalty in the final play of the game. Awanui had won both previous matches this year.*

## North Harbour — A.S.B. Cup:

22 July: Northcote 17 v Takapuna 15
*Ben Searle kicked the winning penalty goal with the last kick of the game, for Northcote's first title since 2010. Only one try was scored in the match.*

## North Otago — Citizen's Shield:

5 August: Old Boys 20 v Valley 13
*Ahead 15–13, Old Boys scored an unconverted try with four minutes left.*

## Otago

### Metropolitan — Speight's Championship Shield:
29 July: Southern 24 v Harbour 15
*On as an injury replacement after just two minutes, MacKenzie Haugh scored three of Southern's four tries for their first title since 2007.*

### Central Region — Super Liquor Trophy:
29 July: Wakatipu 13 v Arrowtown 10
*Halftime: 0–0. Arrowtown scored two tries to one and missed a last minute penalty to force extra time.*

### Southern Region — Speight's Cup:
29 July: Clutha 60 v Crescent 12
*Third title in a row for Clutha.*

### Central Region-Southern Region — Countrywide Shield:
5 August: Clutha 71 v Wakatipu 7
*Tyler Bichan scored three tries as Clutha won their third title in a row and completed a perfect season 17 wins from 17 games.*

## Poverty Bay — Lee Brothers Shield:

22 July: High School Old Boys 34 v Waikohu 3
*Third title in a row for High School Old Boys. Waikohu's first ever final.*

## Southland — Galbraith Shield:

15 July: Marist 26 v Star 15
*Marist led 23–3 halfway through the second half to claim their first title since 2001.*

## South Canterbury — Hamersley Cup:

29 July: Celtic 25 v Harlequins 10
*Ninth title in a row for Celtic, after leading 13–7 at halftime.*

## Taranaki — McMasters Shield:

15 July: Tukapa 17 v Coastal 14
*A last minute converted try to Adrian Wyrill saw Tukapa win the title for the second year in succession. Coastal had won their two previous meetings this year.*

## Tasman — Tasman Trophy:

5 June: Waimea OB 31 a.e.t v Nelson 28 a.e.t.
*In the final minute of extra time a converted Daniel Hytongue try won the game for Waimea OB. 21–21 after 80 minutes.*

### Marlborough sub union — Champion of Champions Trophy:
22 July: Moutere 22 v Renwick 19
*Moutere led 17–14 at halftime, and 22–19 after 60 minutes.*

**Nelson Bays sub union — Strange Memorial Cup+Centennial Cup:**
22 July: Nelson 41 v Wanderers 19
*Nelson led 41–5 after 65 minutes.*

## Thames Valley — McClinchy Cup:

29 July: Hauraki North 28 v Waihi Athletic 27
*Brook Campbell kicked a 79th minute penalty goal to put Hauraki North in front. He had also kicked an 80th minute penalty goal to win their semi-final 26–23 against Mercury Bay. Waihi Athletic won all three previous encounters in 2017.*

## Waikato — Breweries Shield:

July 29: Hamilton Old Boys 38 v Otorohanga 16
*Hamilton Old Boys were down 14–16 at halftime. Otorohanga won both previous encounters in 2017.*

## Wanganui — President's Rosebowl:

29 July: Ruapehu 28 v Border 26
*A last minute drop goal by Craig Clare gave Ruapehu victory, after leading 18–3 after 35 minutes.*

## Wairarapa Bush — Tui Cup:

29 July: Gladstone 25 v Martinborough 12
*Gladstone led 15–7 at halftime, and 25–7 going into the final minute, for their first title since 2011.*

## Wellington — Jubilee Cup:

5 August: Old Boys University 32 v Hutt OB Marist 19
*Halftime: 24–14. Five tries to three.*

## West Coast — Taylorville Wallsend Trophy:

22 July: Kiwi 22 v Blaketown 15
*Kiwi scored four tries to nil for their second title in a row.*

## Most consecutive championships:

*14 Star (Southland) 1890–1903
10 Athletic (North Otago) 1906–1915
9 Celtic (South Canterbury) 2009–2017
8 Star (Southland) 1919–1926; Westport (Buller) 1963–1970; Invercargill (Southland) 1987–1994; Ponsonby (Auckland) 2004-2011

## Sub Union championships:

13 Mahia (Wairoa) 1981–1993
11 Dannevirke O.B. (Dannevirke) 1946–1955, (Central HB-Dannevirke) 1956

*Previously recorded as 16 consecutive titles 1888–1903, investigation has established that Pirates were Southland champions in 1889 with 8 points followed by Star 6 points and Invercargill 0 points.

# JOCK HOBBS MEMORIAL NATIONAL UNDER 19 TOURNAMENT

The fourth edition of this tournament was played from 10–16 September, and again held at Owen Delany Park, Taupo. Four of the 24 matches were shown live on Sky TV. The matches are not of first-class status.

Each squad was made up of 25 players who were registered to play club rugby in their Provincial Union and who were under 19 as at 1 January 2017.

The seedings for the National Tournament, based on placings in tournaments held within each Super Rugby franchise (Crusaders and Highlanders combined), were:

**Premiership** (top eight) — Graham Mourie Cup
Auckland *(Blues 1)*; Bay of Plenty *(Chiefs 1)*; Canterbury *(Southern 2)*; Manawatu *(Hurricanes 2)*; North Harbour *(Blues 2)*; Tasman *(Southern 1)*; Waikato *(Chiefs 2)*; Wellington *(Hurricanes 1)*.

**Championship** (bottom eight) – Michael Jones Trophy
Auckland Development *(Blues 3)*; Counties Manukau *(Chiefs 4)*; Hawke's Bay *(Hurricanes 3)*; Heartland Team; Northland *(Blues 4)*; Otago *(Southern 3)*; Southland *(Southern 4)*; Taranaki *(Chiefs 3)*.

The Heartland team was again invited into the Michael Jones Trophy competition. Buller was the only Heartland union not represented due to a late withdrawal.

## 2017 RESULTS
### PREMIERSHIP — GRAHAM MOURIE CUP (1ST–8TH)
**Day One: Se**ptember 10
Waikato 28–Tasman 11; North Harbour 30–Wellington 27; Canterbury 23–Bay of Plenty 21; Auckland 71–Manawatu 5
**Day Two:** September 13
*Semi-finals:* Waikato 27–North Harbour 20; Auckland 44–Canterbury 10
*Ranking:* Tasman 38–Wellington 26; Bay of Plenty 54–Manawatu 7
**Day Three:** September 16
*1st/2nd Final:* Auckland 30–Waikato 17
*3rd/4th* North Harbour 24–Canterbury 17; *5th/6th* Bay of Plenty 74–Tasman 10;
*7th/8th* Wellington 24–Manawatu 20

### CHAMPIONSHIP — MICHAEL JONES TROPHY (9TH–16TH)
**Day** One: September 10
Hawke's Bay 25–Northland 14; Counties Manukau 15–Otago 13;
Heartland 19–Auckland Development 16; Southland 32–Taranaki 28
**Day Two:** September 13
*Semi-finals:* Counties Manukau 20–Hawke's Bay 3; Southland 36–Heartland 8
*Ranking:* Otago 52–Northland 9; Taranaki 34–Auckland Development 26
**Day Three:** September 16
*9th/10th Final:* Counties Manukau 33–Southland 31
*11th/12th* Hawke's Bay 26–Heartland 16; *13th/14th* Otago 36–Taranaki 31;
*15th/16th* Northland 27–Auckland Development 19

# 2016 RESULTS:

The 2017 *Almanack* inadvertently repeated the 2015 match results instead of presenting the 2016 match results. The 2016 match results are recorded here.

## PREMIERSHIP — GRAHAM MOURIE CUP (1ST—8TH)

**Day One:** September 15
Canterbury 57–Manawatu 10; Waikato 41–Auckland B 0; Wellington 37–Otago 14;
Auckland A 36–Taranaki 11
**Day Two:** September 18
*Semi-finals:* Waikato 32–Canterbury 21; Auckland A 19–Wellington 17
*Ranking:* Manawatu 52–Auckland B 10; Otago 62–Taranaki 23
**Day Three:** September 21
*1st/2nd Final:* Waikato 25–Auckland A 22
*3rd/4th* Wellington 31–Canterbury 24; *5th/6th* Otago 13–Manawatu 13 aet\*;
*7th/8th* Auckland B 29–Taranaki 27
\*Otago won the match on the tiebreak of scoring the first try.

## CHAMPIONSHIP — MICHAEL JONES TROPHY (9TH—16TH)

**Day One:** September 15
Counties Manukau 45–Northland 17; Hawke's Bay 41–Southland 24; Bay of Plenty 39–North Harbour 31; Tasman 20–Heartland 17
**Day Two:** September 18
*Semi-finals:* Bay of Plenty 31–Hawke's Bay 8; Counties Manukau 22–Tasman 11
*Ranking:* North Harbour 36–Southland 24; Northland 18–Heartland 8
**Day Three:** September 21
*9th/10th Final:* Counties Manukau 35–Bay of Plenty 20
*11th/12th* Tasman 32–Hawke's Bay 20; *13th/14th* North Harbour 27–Northland 0;
*15th/16th* Heartland 32–Southland 5

## D.J. GRAHAM AWARD (PLAYER OF THE TOURNAMENT)

| | | |
|---|---|---|
| 2014 | Mitchell Karpik | (*Auckland A*) |
| 2015 | Charlie Gamble | (*Canterbury*) |
| 2016 | Luke Jacobson | (*Waikato*) |
| 2017 | Sione Talitui | (*Auckland*) |

**Top Try-scorer**

| | | |
|---|---|---|
| 2014 | (4) | Setariki Koroitamana (*Heartland*) |
| 2015 | (5) | Jonathan Taumateine (*Counties Manukau*) |
| 2016 | (5) | Salimoni Tukania (*Counties Manukau*) |
| 2017 | (4) | Ajay Mua (*Bay of Plenty*), Jaya More (*Southland*) |

**Top Points-scorer**

| | | |
|---|---|---|
| 2014 | (46) | Jaye Thompson (*Southland*) |
| 2015 | (69 | Jonathan Taumateine (*Counties Manukau*) |
| 2016 | (51) | Mathew Lansdown (*Waikato*) |
| 2017 | (60) | Harry Plummer (*Auckland*) |

## FINISHING POSITIONS

|  | 2014 | 2015 | 2016 | 2017 |
|---|---|---|---|---|
| Auckland | 3 | 7 | 2 | 1 |
| Auckland Development | 13 | 16 | 7 | 16 |
| Bay of Plenty | 8 | 13 | 10 | 5 |
| Canterbury | 2 | 1 | 4 | 4 |
| Counties Manukau | 16 | 9 | 9 | 9 |
| Hawke's Bay | 12 | 12 | 12 | 11 |
| Heartland | 11 | 15 | 15 | 12 |
| Manawatu | 10 | 8 | 6 | 8 |
| North Harbour | 7 | 6 | 13 | 3 |
| Northland | 15 | 14 | 14 | 15 |
| Otago | 5 | 4 | 5 | 13 |
| Southland | 9 | 11 | 16 | 10 |
| Taranaki | 6 | 3 | 8 | 14 |
| Tasman | 14 | 10 | 11 | 6 |
| Waikato | 4 | 2 | 1 | 2 |
| Wellington | 1 | 5 | 3 | 7 |

## *2017 SQUADS (APPEARANCES IN BRACKETS):*

**Auckland:** *Captain:* Waimana Riedlinger-Kapa          *Coach:* Andrew Hewetson
John Akauola-Laula (3); Caleb Clarke (3); Robert Cobb (3); Aleks Dabek (3); Caleb Fa'alili (0); Wiseguy Faiane (3); Penisoni Fineanganofo (3); Alexander Lam (1); Harry Plummer (3); Waimana Riedlinger-Kapa (3); Benjamin Sa'u (3); Kaynan Siteine-Tua (3); Hoskins Sotutu (3); Matthew Storm (3); Cameron Suafoa (3); Rilloy Suesue (3); Sione Talitui (3); Te Ariki Te Puni (2); Tanielu Tele'a (3); Fe'ao Teutau (3); Godinet Tinei (3); Siave Togoiu (3); Anzelo Tuitavuki (2); Seleti Tu'ungafasi (2); Sebastian Visinia (2).

**Auckland Development:** *Captain:* Matangireia Yates-Francis          *Coach:* Joe Snee
Nofo Amituanai (2); Sean Cassidy (3); McCarthy Cocker-Filikitonga (1); Solomone Fonda (2); Spencer Fruean (3); Hugo Garcia-Rafael (3); Nicholas Laufoli (3); Paula Maama (3); Bryan Malitalo (1); Santana Marshall-Baker (3); Zachery Martin (3); Darius Mauga (2); JP Ngatokoroa (0); Michael Palmer (2); Richmond Patea-Seve (3); Otanuku Pauta (3); Obey Samate (3); Matthew Sowter (3); Joseph Tangulu (3); Gabriel Te Kani (3); Simon-Peter Toleafoa (3); Sila Ukugia (2); Andy Williams (3); Roni Wright (3); Matangireia Yates-Francis (3).

**Bay of Plenty:** *Captain:* Joseph Johnston          *Coach:* Mike Rogers
Ratu Aca (3); Champ Betham (3); Rewita Biddle (3); Sam Bright (3); Jarryd Broughton (2); Oisin Clarken (3); Cheyenne Dalley (3); Manaia Harawira (2); Mitchell Holton (2); Joseph Johnston (3); Charles Lawrence (3); Tevita Mafileo (3); Ajay Mua (2); Will Ngatai (3); Sua Selau (1); Bailey Simonsson (3); Aaron Tait (1); Kaleb Trask (3); Sione Tuputupu (3); Uliti Uilou (1); Ricky van der Heyden (3); Stan van der Hoven (3); Matthew van Leeuwen (1); Raniera Whakataka (3); Tera Whata (3); Keita Yamamoto (2).

**Canterbury:** *Captain:* Tom Christie (2); Milan Bonkovich (1). *Coach:* Mark Brown
Josh Archer (3); Logan Bell (3); Milan Bonkovich (3); Tom Christie (2); Connor Collins (3); Dominic Devine (3); Connor Garden-Bachop (3); Sam Gilbert (3); Connor Gordon (3); Perry Karati (3); Sam Lester (1); Atu Manu (3); Sam Matenga (3); Tom McKay (2); Zac McKay (3); Dallas McLeod (3); Josef Meek (2); Ryan Neill (0); Rameka Poihipi (2); Ngane Punavai (3); Ben Renton (0); Joseph Robins (3); Cameron Russell (2); Kale Thatcher (2); Will Tucker (3); Sean Youngman (3).

**Counties Manukau:** *Captain:* Jamie Orr *Coach:* Mark Selwyn
Fuifatu Asomua (3); Suetena Asomua (3); Joshua Baverstock (3); Dylan du Plessis (3); Lionel Evans (1); Logan Fonoti (3); Alamoti Funaki (3); Joshua Gray (3); Matthew Hill (3); Tahu Hollis (3); Petelo Ikenasio (3); Hunter Jack (2); Marcellus Lei Sam (0); Lesili Manu (3); Katetistoti Nginingini (3); Jamie Orr (3); Davin Paea (2); Prince Saumani (3); Liumeione Silinu'u (0); Zuriel Togiatama (2); Alex Tuiloma (3); Reuben Unga (2); Cole Watson (3); Dylan Watters (3); Paul Wolfgramm (3).

**Hawke's Bay:** *Captain:* Angus McKnight *Coach:* Blair Cross
Nathan Burton (2); Jackman Byrne (3); Kaine Cargill-Isaacs (1); Mitchell Drew (2); Asotasi Faavae (1); Tim Farrell (1); Ethan Flanders (2); Will Gunson (3); Bronson Hokianga (3); Mark Huata (0); Felise Iopu-Tavae (3); Sam Lewis (2); Angus McKnight (3); Al Momoisea (2); McKenzie Oliver (3); Raniera Petersen (2); Cameron Pratt (2); Tyler Simon-Burke (3); Jesse Sipaia (3); Isaac Thomas (2); Will Tremain (2); Tuamelie Ulupano (3); Alex Wainwright (1); Benjamin Weeks (3); Jack White (3); Jasper Wylie (3).

**Heartland:** *Captain:* Dylan Bowater (2), Nathaniel Smith (1) *Coach:* Mark Rutene
Bryan Arnold *Wairarapa Bush* (1); Hamish Bennett *Wanganui* (3); Dylan Bowater *Wanganui* (2); Chris Breuer *Wanganui* (3); Baven Brown *King Country* (2); Xavier Conrad *King Country* (3); Gordon Coogan *Wanganui* (0); Hurakia Firth *Thames Valley* (3); Tristan Flutey *Wairarapa Bush* (3); Kelepi Funaki *North Otago* (3); Dylan Gallien *Wanganui* (2); Brad Griffith *Wairarapa Bush* (3); Tomas Hanham-Carter *Mid Canterbury* (2); Ryan Hargood *Wairarapa Bush* (3); Alec Hendricksen *Wairarapa Bush* (3); Fabyan Kahaki *East Coast* (3); Taina Keelan *Horowhenua Kapiti* (3); Jack Loader *Wairarapa Bush* (3); Ngahiwi Manuel *Poverty Bay* (3); Nathaniel Payton *Horowhenua Kapiti* (1); Kurt Prendeville *South Canterbury* (3); Dylan Robinson *Thames Valley* (3); Nathaniel Smith *King Country* (3); Harry Symes *Wanganui* (3); Jayden Tegg *Thames Valley* (3); Josh Tomlinson *West Coast* (3).

**Manawatu:** *Captain:* Ueta Tufuga *Coach:* Shane Ratima
Jacob Ackerman (3); Daniel Artz (1); Sione Asi (3); Adam Boult (3); Brayden Cunningham (3); Zane Dallinger (3); Jeremy David (0); Tevita Fehoko (2); Brad Fountain (3); Tyler Goodwin (3); Jarrod Harawira (3); James Holland (3); Braydon Iose (3); Ben McColgan (3); Josh McIntyre (3); Te Anini Pardoe (2); Leighton Ralph (3); Geordie Redfearn (2); Matene Ruawai (3); Nathan Smith (3); Gene Syminton (3); Ueta Tufuga (3); Hunter Waller (3); Tobias Wickham-Manuel (3); Liam Younger (3).

**North Harbour:** *Captain:* Luteru Tolai *Coach:* Greg Aldous
Sam Babb (0); Declan Barbarich (2); Jack Bergin (3); Leon Bongare (2); Nicholas Burns (1); Joe Clarkson (1); Jack Heighton (3); Cameron Hey (3); Matthew Jerlina (3); Logan Lawrence (2); Zak Martin (2); Finlay McBrearty (3); Grecia McNamara-Teale (2); Josiah Ngatipa (2); Isaac Nonoa (2); Max Parekura (3); Mackenave Pisi (3); Jacob Ridling (2); Kai Stroem (0); Leon Thambiran (3); Sebastian Tielu (3); Luteru Tolai (3); Salyn Tonu'u (3); Nathan Va'atausili (3); Harrison Windleburn (3).

**Northland:** *Captain:* Samuel McNamara                    *Coach:* Mark Seymour
Paora Allen (3); Thomas Barlow (3); Sam Bean (1); Kahu Boyd (3); Jackson Brott (3); Cullen Curtis (3); Mikael-Jones Daniela (3); James Dempster (2); Scott Gregory (2); Logan Groome (3); Lyrik Joyce (2); Jayden Leaupepe (3); Samuel McNamara (3); Tom Morrison (3); Waitangi Neho (2); Denver Patua (3); Raymond Rakete (2); Mitchell Reader (3); Javahn Repia (3); Taine Rogers (3); Ngapuhi Simeon (3); Hayden Sloper (3); Kepa Wiki (3); James Witihera (3).

**Otago:** *Captain:* Slade McDowall                    *Coach:* Luke Herden
Corrie Barrett (3); William Boswell (3); Sam Dickson (3); Angus Gray (1); Josh Hill (3); Daniel Hogan (2); Tim Hogan (3); Ricky Jackson (1); William Kirkwood (3); Kilipati Lea (3); Patrick McCurran (3); Slade McDowall (3); Jack McHugh (3); Kieran McLea (2); Alex Niedzwiecki (0); Keegan O'Donnell (3); Chase Owen (3); Sam Pene (3); Tatai Proctor (3); Tainc Rarere (1); Trevor Smith (1); Mamea Taimalie (3); George Thomas (3); Isimeli Tuivaga (3); Jake Turrell (2); George Witana (3); Tom Yarrall (2).

**Southland:** *Captain:* Jaya More                    *Coach:* Daryl Thompson
Sam Calder (2); Henry Earland (3); Hunter Hape-Crammond (2); Connor Harvey (1); Ben Holland (1); Kaydis Hona (1); Shane Johnston (1); Logan Jones (3); Sione Kaufononga (3); Jake Lawlor (2); Jaya More (3); Ryan Nicholson (3); Albert Qoro (3); Jay Renton (3); Tokahirere Sopoaga (3); Caleb Stevenson (3); Mitchell Taylor (3); Stewart Thomson (3); Daniel Thwaites (3); Viliami Tosi (3); James Wairau (3); Nathan Wairau (2); Sy Waiti (3); Regan Wilson (3).

**Taranaki:** *Captain:* Bradley Slater                    *Coach:* Tim Stuck
Toby Burkett (2); Joel Chard (3); Cody Chilcott (2); Luke Dravitski (3); Louis Duffels-Des Forge (2); Tom Florence (3); Luke Fowler (3); Jesse Goodwin (3); Matthew Guthrie (3); Salese Havea (2); Zac Henderson (2); Maioha Kershaw (1); Brodie Lilley (3); Ciarahn Matoe (3); Michael McDonald (2); Alex Mitchell (2); Brayton Northcott-Hill (3); Josh Perrett (2); Chad Peterson (3); Bradley Slater (3); Patrick Stark (3); Kyle Stewart (3); Josh Thomson (2); Jahmarl Weir (3); Michael Winter (2).

**Tasman:** *Captain:* Rupena Parkinson                    *Coach:* Mike Fraser
Tom Allen (1); Mitchell Amberger (3); Eden Beech (3); Joe Brady (2); Isaac Briggs (0); Lemeki Cagialau (3); Te Ahiwaru Cirikidaveta (3); Harrrison Curtis (2); Jakob Dabinet (2); Ryan Dafel (3); Jack Grooby (3); Quinn Harrison-Jones (3); William Havili (3); Vito Lammers (3); Isaiah Miller (2); Samiuela Moli (3); Rupena Parkinson (3); Tyler Power (2); Tim Sail (3); Teu Sami (2); Jamie Spowart (3); Culainn Stringer (3); Timoci Tavatavanawai (3); Sosefo Vaka (3); Mitchell Walsh (3).

**Waikato:** *Captain:* Morgan Jackson (2), Jacob Norris (1)                    *Coach:* Alf Daniels
Nico Anadewiel (3); Josh Balme (3); Kauri Coffin (1); Liam Coombes-Fabling (3); Rhys Dickinson (3); Ezra Dunlop (3); Benjamin Engels (0); Sosaia Fale (3); JJ Havea (0); Xavier Hill (2); Tom Jordan (3); Josh Kaho (3); Kieran Lee (3); Niven Longapoa (3); Laghlan McWhannell (3); Josh Moorby (3); Jackson Morgan (3); Jacob Norris (1); Jonty Powers (3); Xavier Roe (3); Shammah Solomona (3); Tuipulotu Tapa (3); Maioro Taylor (3); Sheldon Tovio (3); Joedici Waru-Savage (0).

**Wellington:** *Co-Captains:* Billy Proctor (3), Naera Tipoki (1)                    *Coach:* Zak Feaunati
Ben Aumua-Peseta (3); Eamonn Carr (3); Adam Clark (2); Meinrad Fitisemanu (3); Junior Foaitua (2); William Heather (3); Chris Hicks (3); George Jacobs (3); Esi Komoaisavai (3); Roy Maiva (3); Jahzeel Marais (1); Sione Ma'u (3); Angus Morton (3); Jacob Mua (2); Xavier Numia (3); Carlos Price (3); Billy Proctor (3); Jake Quin (3); Regan Sword (2); Naera Tipoki (1); Denny To'o (3); Pasi Uluilakepa (3); Malachi Unasa (3); Callum Watts-Pointer (2); Grayson Whitman (2).

# SECONDARY SCHOOLS RUGBY

Following a development camp when 49 players gathered at the Massey University Sport & Rugby Institute 22–24 September the NZ Schools squad was chosen to visit Australia and the Barbarians Schools squad chosen to play two games. Both squads were undefeated. In Sydney, the NZ Schools games were played at Knox Grammar School. Devan Flanders was awarded the Bronze Boot.

## *NEW ZEALAND SCHOOLS, 2017*

|  | School | Date of birth | Height | Weight |
|---|---|---|---|---|
| Naitoa Ah Kuoi | Wellington College | 7/10/99 | 194 | 107 |
| Charles Alaimalo | Hamilton BHS | 14/6/99 | 195 | 103 |
| Sam Cooper | St Paul's Collegiate | 26/10/99 | 183 | 93 |
| George Dyer | St Paul's Collegiate | 22/10/99 | 189 | 115 |
| Leicester Fainga'anuku | Nelson College | 11/10/99 | 188 | 101 |
| Devan Flanders | Hastings BHS | 20/7/99 | 192 | 98 |
| Taufa Funaki– | Sacred Heart College | 29/7/00 | 175 | 87 |
| Cullen Grace | Timaru BHS | 20/12/99 | 192 | 97 |
| Tauterangimarie Kapea | Hamilton BHS | 16/6/99 | 187 | 104 |
| Shilo Klein | St Andrew's College | 4/5/99 | 179 | 107 |
| Lincoln McClutchie | Hastings BHS | 12/4/99 | 169 | 81 |
| Jeriah Mua | Hastings BHS | 11/10/99 | 180 | 88 |
| Etene Nanai | St Kentigern College | 20/8/99 | 179 | 90 |
| Kiniviliame Nasolo | Hastings BHS | 16/4/99 | 178 | 86 |
| Fatongia Paea | Sacred Heart College | 9/4/99 | 179 | 116 |
| Abraham Pole | Otago BHS | 28/6/99 | 184 | 111 |
| Isaiah Punivai | Christ's College | 1/12/00 | 187 | 92 |
| Rivez Reihana | St Kentigern College | 25/5/00 | 186 | 88 |
| Humphrey Sheild | Napier BHS | 10/2/99 | 169 | 76 |
| Joshua Southall | St Patrick's C, Silverstream | 23/6/00 | 179 | 94 |
| Quade Tapsell | Gisborne BHS | 4/4/99 | 186 | 98 |
| Josiah Tavita-Metcalfe | Hastings BHS | 4/2/99 | 182 | 116 |
| Danny Toala | Hastings BHS | 26/3/99 | 179 | 95 |
| Quinn Tupaea (captain) | Hamilton BHS | 10/5/99 | 187 | 102 |
| Tupou Vaa'i | Wesley College | 27/1/00 | 197 | 122 |
| Tamati Williams | St Kentigern College | 10/8/00 | 194 | 121 |

**Coaches:** Jason Holland (*Hurricanes*), Tom Cairns (*assistant, Gisborne BHS*)
**Manager:** Nick Reid (*Awatapu College*)
**Strength & conditioning coach:** Ewan Brumwell (*Otago*)
**Physiotherapist:** Karl Houltham (*Highlanders*)
**Performance analyst:** Peter Bowden (*Canterbury*)

## INDIVIDUAL SCORING

| | Tries | Con | PG | DG | Points |
|---|---|---|---|---|---|
| Fainga'anuku | 5 | 1 | 1 | – | 30 |
| Toala | | 9 | – | – | 18 |
| Nanai | 3 | – | – | – | 15 |
| Ah Kuoi | 2 | – | – | – | 10 |
| Pole | 2 | – | – | – | 10 |
| Punivai | 2 | – | – | – | 10 |
| Tupaea | 2 | – | – | – | 10 |
| Vaa'i | 2 | – | – | – | 10 |
| Cooper | 1 | – | – | – | 5 |
| Dyer | 1 | – | – | – | 5 |
| McClutchie | 1 | – | – | – | 5 |
| Mua | 1 | – | – | – | 5 |
| Reihana | – | 2 | – | – | 4 |
| **TOTALS** | **22** | **12** | **1** | **0** | **137** |
| Opposition scored | 2 | 1 | 4 | 0 | 24 |

## NEW ZEALAND SCHOOLS 2017

| | Fiji | Australia Schools Barbarians | Australia | TOTALS |
|---|---|---|---|---|
| Nanai | 15 | 14 | 15 | 3 |
| Toala | – | 15 | s | 2 |
| Nasolo | 14 | – | 14 | 2 |
| Fainga'anuku | 11 | 11 | 11 | 3 |
| Kapea | 13 | – | – | 1 |
| Punivai | s | 13 | 13 | 3 |
| Tupaea | 12 | 12 | 12 | 3 |
| Rehana | 10 | s | 10 | 3 |
| McClutchie | s | 10 | s | 3 |
| Funaki | 9 | s | 9 | 3 |
| Sheild | s | 9 | s | 3 |
| Flanders | 8 | 8 | 8 | 3 |
| Mua | 7 | s | 7 | 3 |
| Southall | s | 7 | s | 3 |
| Alaimalo | 6 | s | 6 | 3 |
| Tapsell | s | 6 | s | 3 |
| Vaa'i | 5 | 5 | 5 | 3 |
| Ah Kuoi | 4 | s | 4 | 3 |
| Grace | – | 4 | – | 1 |
| Tavita-Metcalfe | 3 | – | s | 2 |
| Dyer | s | 3 | 3 | 3 |
| Williams | 1 | s | 1 | 3 |
| Paea | s | 1 | s | 3 |
| Cooper | 2 | s | 2 | 3 |
| Klein | – | 2 | s | 2 |
| Pole | s | s | – | 2 |

## NEW ZEALAND SCHOOLS, 2017

Played 3 — Won 3 — Points for 137 — Points against 24

| Date | Opponent | Location | Score | Tries | Con | PG | DG | Referee |
|---|---|---|---|---|---|---|---|---|
| September 28 | Fiji Schools | Sydney | 54–7 | Fainga'anuku (3), Ah Kuoi (2), Tupaea (2), Cooper, Pole | Reihana (2), Fainga'anuku | Fainga'anuku | | Dru Tonks |
| October 2 | Australia Schools Barbarians | Sydney | 49–6 | Nanai (2), Punivai, Dyer, Vaa'i, Fainga'anuku, Pole | Toala (7) | | | Lincoln Sto lery |
| October 7 | Australia Schools | Sydney | 34–11 | Mua, Vaa'i, Nanai, Fainga'anuku, Punivai, McClutchie | Toala (2) | | | Dru Tonks |

## NEW ZEALAND BARBARIANS SCHOOLS

*Results:*
September 28 v **Tonga Schools**, at Sport & Rugby Institute, Palmerston North. Won 33–19.
Norris, Syme, Chapman, Talamahina, Burke tries; Burke 4 conversions.

October 2 v **NZ Maori Under 18**, at Sport & Rugby Institute, Palmerston North. Won 28–24.
Higgins 2, Burke, Seti tries; Burke 4 conversions.

**Backs:** TJ Ane (*De La Salle College*), Fergus Burke (*St Paul's Collegiate*), Louie Chapman (*Christchurch BHS*), Luke Donaldson (*St Paul's Collegiate*), Kienan Higgins (*St Patrick's College, Silverstream*), Josiah Maraku (*Feilding HS*), Lemeki Namoa (*Sacred Heart College*), Siave Seti (*St John's College*), James Stratton (*Palmerston North BHS*), Rico Syme (*Christchurch BHS*), Kaleb Talamahina (*Southland BHS*). Namoa was injured in the first game and replaced for the second game by Ane.

**Forwards:** Joshua Bokser (*Napier BHS*), Tovo Faleafa (*Auckland Grammar*), Samipeni Finau (*St Peter's College, Cambridge*), Ethan McQuinlan (*Feilding HS*), Saula Mau (*Auckland Grammar*), David Meki (*Rosmini College*), Oliver Norris (*St Peter's College, Cambridge*), Simon Parker (*Otamatea College*), Taine Plumtree (*Wellington College*), Tane Te Aho (*captain, Hamilton BHS*), Taine Te Whata (*Otago BHS*), Patrick Thacker (*Christ's College*), James Thompson (*St Peter's College, Cambridge*).

| | |
|---|---|
| **Coach:** Brad Mooar | **Assistant coach:** Sam Moore |
| **Manager:** Cam Kilgour | **Trainer:** Joel Marshall |
| **Analyst:** Doug Neilson | **Physiotherapist:** Andy McGregor |

## NATIONAL UNDER 18 MAORI TEAM

A squad of Maori under-18 players was assembled for two fixtures. The players were mainly high school students with a few club players.

October 2 v **New Zealand Barbarians Schools**, at Sport & Rugby Institute, Palmerston North. Lost 24–28.

October 6 v **Tonga Schools**, at Porirua Park, Wellington. Won 38–26.

**Squad:** Shamara Brooks (*Hastings BHS*), Austin Brown (*Gisborne BHS*), John Cooper (*Westlake BHS*), Stewart Cruden (*Palmerston North BHS*), Tanara Haenga (*Wainuiomata College*), Josh Hill (*Otago Univ*), Cameron Huata (*Napier BHS*), Tahu Kaa (*Christchurch BHS*), Coel Kerr (*Paeroa College*), Tamarau McGahan (*Rosmini College*), Nikau McGregor (*Napier BHS*), Donovan Mataira (*Hastings BHS*), Terrell Peita (*Mt Albert Grammar*), Jacob Pepper-Edwards (*Ashley RFC*), Jonas Pomare (*Hamilton BHS*), Billy Priestley (*Gisborne BHS*), Robert Rush (*St Kentigern College*), James Simpson-Te Pairi (*King's HS*), Sam Smith (*Wairarapa College*), Ben Strowger-Turnock (*Wellington College*), Eru Tahuri (*Ashburton Celtic RFC*), Te Ariki Te Puni (*Auckland Univ*), Jaylen Tuapola (*Scots College*), Keelan Whitman (*St Patrick's College, Wellington*), Tobias Wickham-Manuel (*Kia Toa RFC, Manawatu*).

**Coach:** Rua Wanoa
**Assistant coaches:** Kahu Carey, Stacey Grant, Anthony Rehutai, Jeremy Wara

## *NEW ZEALAND BARBARIANS AREA SCHOOLS*

Selected from the smaller country high schools, this squad was brought together for two fixtures in Canterbury.

*Results:*
September 26 v **North Canterbury Secondary Schools**, at Oxford RFC. Won 33–22. Enosi-Tuipulotu, Hawley, Morrison-Sheridan, Hemana-Brown, Walden tries; Broughton 4 conversions.

September 30 v **Canterbury Country Under 18**, at Rangiora. Lost 38–22. Leef, Hawley, Matthews, Hemana-Brown tries; Broughton conversion.

**Squad:** Ilai Arona (*Abundant Christian Life, Northland*), Kyhia Bovill (*Onewhero Area Sch, Counties*), Cyrus Broughton (*Taipa Area Sch, Northland*), Jarod Bryant (*Rai Valley Area Sch, Tasman*), Flynn Crean (*Hurunui College, Canterbury*), Brayden Crowne (*Cheviot Area Sch, Canterbury*), Robin Enosi-Tuipulotu (*Akaroa Area Sch, Canterbury*), Nathan Hawley (*Murchison Area Sch, Buller*), Cahrydge Hemana-Brown (*Te Kaokaoroa o Petetere Area Sch, Waikato*), Danny Henderson (*Tauraroa Area Sch, Northland*), Liam Henderson (*Tauraroa Area Sch, Northland*), Angus Johns (*Amuri Area Sch, Canterbury*), Henry Leef (*Cheviot Area Sch, Canterbury*), Roscoe Matthews (*Panguru Area Sch, Northland*), Henare Maxwell (*TKKM o Horouta Wanaga, East Coast*), Chase Morrison-Sheridan (*Tolaga Bay Area Sch, East Coast*), Blair Norton (*Hurunui College, Canterbury*), Connor Quest (*Tauraroa Area Sch, Northland*), Zhane Taikato (*Whangamata Area Sch, Thames Valley*), Jesse Te Kani (*Onewhero Area Sch, Counties*), Kayleb te Whare (*TKKM o Horouta Wanaga, East Coast*), Mark James Tupawa (*Tolaga Bay Area Sch, East Coast*), Sean Vincent (*Abundant Christian Life, Northland*), Jordan Walden (*Onewhero Area Sch, Counties*).

**Coach:** Justin Marsh (*Tongariro Area Sch*)
**Assistant coaches:** Steve Beck (*Hurunui College*), Hone Manuel (*Coromandel Area Sch*), Ratu Taira (*Raglan Area Sch*).
**Manager:** Michael Smith (*Mercury Bay Area Sch*).

# SCHOOLS RUGBY REVIEW
*by Adam Julian*

## HIGHLIGHTS

- Kini Naholo (*brother of All Black Waisake Naholo*) scored 41 tries for Hastings Boys' High School. Naholo captured national headlines with his prolific scoring feats. His big hauls included six tries against St Pats Town (*subbed at halftime*), five against Wellington College and Palmerston North Boys' High School and three against Kelston Boys' High School, Wellington College, King's College, Rongotai College and Mount Albert Grammar School.
- St Pats Silverstream enjoyed an imperious season in Wellington, winning 17 out of 18 games and establishing a school record for most points scored in a season (*982*). Silverstream won the WelTec Premiership, beating Wellington College 17–11 in the final. Such was their dominance they didn't attempt a single penalty goal all season.
- Timaru Boys' High School made the final of the UC Championship for the first time, but was beaten 18–10 by Christchurch Boys' High School who captured honours for the 10th time. Rico Syme, who started the season in the 7th XV, was the player of the final and later made the NZ Barbarians and featured on One News.
- Wesley College won the Central North Island title for the first time, recovering from a 28–11 deficit to topple Feilding High School 32–28 in the final. Wesley ended the 29-game unbeaten streak of Hamilton's St Paul's Collegiate.
- Rosmini College won the North Harbour 1A title for the eighth time, foiling Westlake Boys' High School 18–12 in the final. Diminutive fullback Seamus O'Reilly was the hero improbably beating four defenders en route to scoring the winning try.
- King's High School, Dunedin won the Otago Secondary Schools competition undefeated and held the Trustbank Cup, typically contested in every game involving a fellow South Island school.

## HASTINGS, UNBEATEN WINNERS OF THE TOP FOUR

A month out from this tournament many were confidently predicting a final between Hastings Boys' High School and Hamilton Boys' High School. Those forecasts proved accurate as both schools enjoyed comfortable semi-finals wins. Hastings disposed of Auckland champions St Kentigern College 29–10. Hastings used a sizeable breeze to build a 19–3 halftime lead which they never looked like relinquishing. Fullback Danny Toala scored 19 points.

Hamilton trounced Southland 49–0, establishing a record for the biggest win at the tourney, despite missing their last six conversions. Wing Emoni Narawa scored three of his side's nine tries.

With three minutes remaining in the final, Hastings was ahead 18–17 and Hamilton had the ball 10 metres shy of halfway. Hastings captain and loosehead prop Kianu Kereru-Symes won an inspirational penalty with a crunching tackle and steal at the ruck. Hastings kicked inside the Hamilton 22 and, after a maul, prop Josiah Tavita-Metcalfe stormed ahead 10 metres for the winning try. It was a great final with six lead changes and high-quality attacking play on a heavy surface.

Hastings was unbeaten in 21 games this year and scored 1035 points. In the past two seasons Hastings has lost only once in 40 matches. Hastings became the 13th unbeaten winner of the National Top Four. In the playoff for third, St Kentigern beat Southland 21–3 in a lacklustre affair.

*Final Summary:* Hastings Boys' High School 25 (Kini Naholo, Shamara Brooks, Josiah Tavita-Metcalfe tries; Danny Toala 2 con, 2 pen) defeated Hamilton Boys' High School 17 (Josh Calvert try; Coby Miln 3 pen, Fletcher Morgan pen) HT: 15–14.

## ST PETER'S WIN CO-ED CROWN

St Peter's Cambridge won the title for the first time with commanding victories over St Andrew's College, Christchurch, 48–15 in the semi-final and 29–3 over defending champions Feilding High School in the decider. St Peter's hit the ground running, leading 41–0 at halftime in the semi-final. Halfback Cam Roigard scored four tries and Bodie Mechell crossed for a double.

The final failed to soar to any great heights. St Peter's were ahead 24–3 when they were reduced to 13 players with 20 minutes to go, but Feilding lacked polish all afternoon and conceded the last try on fulltime. Centre PJ Latu scored the best of St Peter's four tries when he dashed 65 metres following an offload from standout No.8 Andrew Viane.

Feilding had beaten Rangitoto College from North Harbour 44–3 in the semi-finals. Griffin Culver scored two tries. In the playoff for third St Andrew's beat Rangitoto 27–17.

*Final Summary:* St Peters Cambridge 29 (Devin Gregory, PJ Latu, Kaea Hongara, Sean Chenery tries; Bodie Mechell 3 con, pen, Jacob Smyth con) defeated Feilding High School 3 (Drew Wild pen) HT: 17–3.

## ST MARY'S CELEBRATE STELLAR SEASON

By September, St Mary's College, Wellington, had confirmed their status as the best girls team in the country. The school held the Condor and World Sevens titles in addition to the National top four crown. Two years ago St Mary's was in the second division of the Wellington competition. St Mary's 22–17 win over Auckland champions Southern Cross Campus in the semi-finals on the Friday suggested they would struggle to go one better than their second placing a year earlier. In tough conditions, St Mary's played poorly and only a spectacular solo try to Dhys Faleafaga foiled a stubborn opponent. Tilila Hifo was outstanding for Southern Cross and scored two tries.

By contrast, Hamilton Girls' thrashed 2016 champions Southland Girls' High School 51–12 in the other semi-final. The game was close approaching halftime when Hamilton only led 12–7, but a 100-metre individual try to Jazmine Hotham opened the floodgates for Hamilton.

In blustery, soggy conditions, St Mary's and Hamilton produced an excellent spectacle in the final which was closer than the final scoreline of 29–12 suggested. The decisive moment of the match occurred six minutes into the second half. Hamilton was hot on attack inside the St Mary's 22 and surrendered a tighthead. Powerful runs by St Mary's centres Dhys Faleafaga and Ana Puleiata were followed by a storming charge by loosehead Marianive Leota who rampaged 20 metres to the tryline to make it 22–5. The 17-point margin was never lost by St Mary's, despite conceding the next try to Hamilton hooker Lena Mitchell. In the playoff for third Southland beat Southern Cross 14–5.

*Final Summary:* St Mary's College 29 (Ainsleyana Pulieta 2, Te Araroa Sopoaga, Dhys Faleafaga, Marianne Leota tries; Cheyne Copeland 2 con) defeated Hamilton Girls' High School 12 (Paj Walker, Lena Mitchell tries; Nyesha Hamilton con) HT: 17–5.

## MOASCAR CUP

Nelson College became the first team since Hamilton Boys' High School in 2009 to defend the Moascar Cup for an entire season. Nelson repelled nine challenges this year and have held the trophy for 12 defences since lifting it from Timaru Boys' High School in late 2016. The record for most defences is held by Christchurch Boys' High School with 22 between 2004 and 2007. In 2017, Timaru would prove to be Nelson's toughest defence with a late penalty goal required to secure the win 21–20. In the first game of the UC championship Nelson resisted a dogged challenge from Christ's College to eventually prevail 22–21. Leicester Faingaanuku scored two tries against Christ's and the first try against Timaru. Nelson also beat Christ's 29–7 in the annual quadrangular final, which was another defence, as was the 24–5 triumph over Wellington College in the same tournament. Nelson's other defences were against Lincoln High School (*55–5*), Burnside High School (*74–7*), Marlborough Boys' College (*35–15*), Rangiora High School (*22–10*) and St Bede's College (*64–17*).

## CONDOR SEVENS

The 31st annual Youthtown Condor Sevens were held on rock hard grounds at Sacred Heart College, Auckland in December. The Under-15 event was held over two days and featured 32 boys and 16 girls' teams. Kerikeri High School were the surprise winners of the girls' event, pipping Hamilton Girls' High School 21–20 in the final. Kelston Boys' High School beat New Plymouth Boys' High School 19–10 in the male decider.

In the open event, which featured 32 boys and 20 female teams, Hamilton Boys' High School joined Kelston Boys' High School as the only school to win the title three times in a row, defeating Scots College, Wellington, 21–10 in the final. Hamilton Girls' made it a double for the Waikato province when they foiled Christchurch Girls High School 20–5 in the final.

Leroy Carter (*Tauranga Boys' College*) and Arorangi Totorewa-Tauranga (*Hamilton Girls' High School*) were the respective players of the tournament.

# WOMEN'S RUGBY

## SEASON IN REVIEW
*By Melodie Robinson*

The year 2017 was the most significant one for New Zealand women's rugby in the history of the game, culminating with the Black Ferns winning the prestigious Team of the Year at the World Rugby Awards. They became the first women's team to take out the category, signalling a change of attitude towards female rugby players.

The year started with the English XVs players making history by being paid to train fulltime from January to prepare for the Women's Rugby World Cup being played in Ireland during August. This was a luxury the Kiwi girls would have loved to have had. The English RFU were sounding a warning that they were serious about retaining the silverware by making their players fulltime professionals and prioritising XVs over sevens.

In late January, however, the attention went back to the seven-aside World Rugby Series in Sydney. Olympic gold medallists Australia were so confident of victory they'd nominated their home tournament as the one in which if they won, they'd get a big cash bonus from the Australian Rugby Union. They choked under the pressure, coming in fourth, New Zealand beating them for bronze, with the new sevens darlings Canada taking down the United States in the final 21–17.

The Black Ferns sevens, though, bounced back well in their next tournaments in Las Vegas in March and Kitakyushu, Japan, in April. The consistent selection policy of coach Allan Bunting contributed to their increasing dominance. The New Zealanders were not only playing the wide game well, but they were far more physical than most.

During May, however, some of the big names of the sevens campaign switched to the Black Ferns XVs campaign: Sarah Goss, Portia Woodman, Kelly Brazier, Stacey Waaka, Theresa Fitzpatrick, and Renee Wickliffe were all fulltime contractors who had been given the go-ahead to represent New Zealand in Ireland. Not that it impeded the sevens team, who won the leg in Canada with their new-look team – including Tyla Nathan-Wong captaining for the first time. They wrapped up the World Series in France in style a month later, taking down the Aussies 22–7. It was 21-year-old Michaela Blyde's best season – the wing finishing with 40 tries. Rewind to a year ago and she was the non-travelling reserve to the Olympics after coach Sean Horan had switched her to prop, a position that never really suited her.

Back to XVs and in June England and Canada came to New Zealand to take on the Black Ferns as part of their preparation for the World Cup. In the first test in Wellington – a curtain-raiser to the Hurricanes vs Chiefs Super Rugby match – the Kiwis took out Canada easily enough, 28–16. That was despite the assertion from the groundsman at Westpac Stadium that they weren't allowed to warm up on the pitch, even though two games were about to be played there.

But at Rotorua it was a different story, with ill-discipline being a major factor in a forward-dominated victory by England 29–21 over the hosts. It was a loss that led to Black Ferns coach Glenn Moore changing a number of moves and tactics before heading to Ireland in August.

Dublin was the host for the pool matches of the 2017 Women's Rugby World Cup, with the field at University College Dublin superb. Only up to 3500 seats were available, which meant a great atmosphere and sold-out crowds. The Black Ferns were on fire from the start with Portia Woodman always dangerous in their win over Wales, 44–12. Fullback Selica Winiata nabbed a hat-trick. In the next game, the Black Ferns' 121 to nil thrashing of Hong Kong was soundly condemned by commentators as symbolic of the lack of depth in the women's game. The criticism conveniently overlooked the All Blacks' 145-point win over Japan in 1995 and the Wallabies' 142-point winning margin over Namibia in 2003. Considering the first official Women's World

Cup wasn't until 1998, it makes sense that development worldwide needs to continue.

The Black Ferns' final pool game was won 48–5 over world number 3 Canada, showing how much improvement the Ferns had made since June. The other two sides to watch were England and France, neither of whom were particularly troubled in their pool matches. Those teams, along with the USA, had made it through to the semis. True to form, New Zealand weren't too troubled by the powerful United States at Kingspan Stadium in Belfast, winning 45–12, but England had a fight on their hands against France before winning 20–3.

So the two old foes were to meet in the final. It was to be the fully professional outfit, England, against a group of mums or youngsters, with at least half of the squad employed in vocations such as the police, fire service, graphic design, teaching and more. It was quite simply the best final world rugby has seen for many years – it wasn't women's rugby; it was rugby at its finest. The New Zealanders played a tactical game, with kicks for territory dominating their first half. Most fans watching were confused as it seemed to play right into England's hands, with the superb Emily Scarratt picking up every ball and making the Kiwis pay.

After the break, England went ahead with speedster Lydia Thompson flat-footing Portia Woodman, but soon after New Zealand completely changed their tack and used the power of their forwards to take on England. It worked. They absolutely monstered the previously vaunted English pack, and Toka Natua became the first prop in World Cup history to score a hat-trick. It was all over after the third quarter – England grabbed a late try, but the Black Ferns took home their fifth World Cup title, 41–32.

The peak television audience of the final was 2.6 million, proving that women's rugby at this level really does have a huge appeal. But perhaps what happened after the final whistle was the story of the year as traditional rugby reporters started to ask why women rugby players are not paid. While many jumped on the pay-parity bandwagon, the real question is: when do the women's players get more and better competition? The answer to that may come later in 2018 if New Zealand Rugby Chairman Brent Impey has anything to do with it. Sources have confirmed that a competition similar to the AFL's women's league is being investigated, and the New Zealand Rugby Players Association is currently looking at what professional contracts would realistically look like, considering they'd need new commercial partners to make it happen.

Meanwhile, the Farah Palmer Cup got under way without any of the fulltime sevens players and with the majority of the Black Ferns slow to come back. It was the first time Tasman was to join the competition with a premiership and championship competition structure to make sure the games were even. The lack of big-name players meant new names stunned onlookers at times. While the Bay of Plenty and Tasman sides hardly kicked the ball, their skill-sets and speed were breathtaking. High schooler Risi Pouri-Lane has already represented New Zealand in judo and touch rugby and competes at nationals in sprinting and javelin. She was the only teenager selected for the New Zealand sevens development side in 2017 and is a 'watch this space' with an exclamation point. For the Bay of Plenty, you could take your pick of talent, but wing Autumn-Rain Stephens-Daly stands out consistently.

During the round robin it was difficult to predict which side might meet a dominant Counties in the final, but the work done quietly in the background by the Canterbury Rugby Union in developing players over the last three seasons was coming to fruition. Coaches Wayne Love and former Black Ferns captain Melissa Ruscoe had their side playing an expansive style that was balanced with a good kicking game, and they were led from the front by halfback Kendra Cocksedge, one of the first Black Ferns back into action. Canterbury lost to the Auckland Storm in week two, but the Storm's young squad had started to lose confidence after a 12–36 loss to Counties. Canterbury meanwhile found their mojo in a 40–10 win over Manawatu and then a surprise win, 32–29, over Counties in week four, winning the JJ Stewart Trophy. The Counties team had actually forgotten to bring the trophy and had to hand it over later.

From there the momentum continued to build. Tasman, Waikato and then the Mooloos again in the semi-final all fell to the red and blacks, setting up a final against a seething Counties team who still couldn't believe they'd lost in round four. The two styles were contrasting when they clashed in the final at Pukekohe. The big power players from Counties tried to intimidate the Cantabs, while the visitors' speed and fitness were their weapons as they withstood pounding after pounding of big runs at their defence. A try to Rebecca Todd in the 78th minute and Cocksedge's accurate boot meant Canterbury won their first ever national championship title – especially sweet for captain Stephanie Te Ohaere-Fox who had played in seven finals and never won.

The final chapter for 2017 for women's rugby in New Zealand concluded in Monaco at the World Rugby Awards. The women cleaned up. Michaela Blyde was awarded Sevens Player of the Year over teammate Ruby Tui, and Portia Woodman won Women's Player of the Year after her standout statistics for the Black Ferns – with Kelly Brazier another of the finalists there. And, as mentioned, to top it off the Black Ferns took out Team of the Year over the All Blacks and England, an achievement that will remain in the history books as the first women's team to win.

# NEW ZEALAND BLACK FERNS

## NEW ZEALAND, 2017

| | Union | Date of Birth | Height | Weight | Tests at 1/1/17 |
|---|---|---|---|---|---|
| C.H. (Chelsea) Alley | Waikato | 7/11/92 | 1.78 | 81 | 12 |
| E.S. (Eloise) Blackwell | Auckland | 28/12/90 | 1.82 | 89 | 24 |
| K.A. (Kelly) Brazier | Bay of Plenty | 28/10/89 | 1.70 | 68 | 29 |
| K.M. (Kendra) Cocksedge | Canterbury | 1/7/88 | 1.57 | 61 | 34 |
| R.P. (Rawinia) Everitt | Counties Manukau | 4/9/86 | 1.72 | 76 | 19 |
| F.M. (Fiao'o) Fa'amausili (capt) | Auckland– | 30/9/80 | 1.63 | 76 | 44 |
| T.M. (Theresa) Fitzpatrick | Auckland | 25/2/95 | 1.69 | 76 | 0 |
| S.L. (Sarah) Goss | Manawatu | 9/12/92 | 1.74 | 80 | 2 |
| C.P.T. (Charlene) Gubb | Auckland | 17/1/88 | 1.71 | 89 | 5 |
| A.H. (Honey) Hireme | Waikato | 3/5/81 | 1.72 | 78 | 15 |
| C.G. (Carla) Hohepa | Waikato | 27/7/85 | 1.75 | 73 | 14 |
| A.T. (Aldora) Itunu | Auckland | 28/6/91 | 1.78 | 110 | 8 |
| L.F. (Linda) Itunu | Auckland | 21/11/84 | 1.73 | 83 | 29 |
| L.T. (Lesley) Ketu | Waikato | 10/1/87 | 1.66 | 62 | 3 |
| P.E.A. (Phillipa) Love | Canterbury | 8/4/90 | 1.73 | 88 | 1 |
| C.J. (Charmaine) McMenamin | Auckland | 13/5/90 | 1.73 | 84 | 7 |
| A.K. (Aotearoa) Mata'u | Counties Manukau | 5/2/97 | 1.85 | 133 | 5 |
| T.I. (Toka) Natua | Waikato | 22/11/91 | 1.70 | 101 | 8 |
| A.P. (Aleisha) Nelson | Auckland | 2/3/90 | 1.82 | 104 | 20 |
| T.R. (Te Kura) Ngata-Aerengamate | Counties Manukau | 21/10/91 | 1.64 | 96 | 11 |
| A. (Aroha) Savage | Counties Manukau | 10/3/90 | 1.78 | 85 | 22 |
| C.B. (Charmaine) Smith | North Harbour | 15/11/90 | 1.83 | 77 | 8 |
| V.S. (Victoria) Subritzky-Nafatali | Counties Manukau | 2/12/91 | 1.66 | 101 | 11 |
| K.J. (Kristina) Sue | Manawatu | 13/3/87 | 1.60 | 63 | 4 |
| S.J. (Sosoli) Talawadua | Waikato | 30/1/89 | 1.60 | 90 | 1 |
| H.S. (Hazel) Tubic | Counties Manukau | 31/12/90 | 1.65 | 69 | 10 |
| S.J.A.K. (Stacey) Waaka | Waikato | 3/11/95 | 1.70 | 72 | 3 |
| R.W.M. (Renee) Wickliffe | Counties Manukau | 30/5/87 | 1.64 | 66 | 24 |
| S.C. (Selica) Winiata | Manawatu | 14/11/86 | 1.55 | 55 | 24 |
| R.J. (Rebecca) Wood | North Harbour | 8/8/87 | 1.80 | 83 | 0 |
| P.L. (Portia) Woodman | Counties Manukau | 12/7/91 | 1.70 | 74 | 8 |

Original selection for RWC Rawinia Everitt withdrew and was replaced by Gubb.

**Coach:** Glenn Moore  
**Assistant coach:** Wesley Clarke, Grant Keenan  
**Manager:** Lauren Cournane  
**Campaign manager:** Hannah Porter  
**Physiotherapist:** Isobel Freeman  
**Doctor:** Deb Robinson  
**Strength & conditioning coach:** Jamie Tout

# NEW ZEALAND IN NEW ZEALAND AND AT RUGBY WORLD CUP, 2017

| BLACK FERNS 2017 | Canada | Australia | England | Wales | Hong Kong | Canada | USA | England | TOTALS |
|---|---|---|---|---|---|---|---|---|---|
| Winiata | 15 | 15* | 15 | 15 | – | 15 | 15 | 15 | 7 |
| Tubic | – | – | – | – | 15 | – | – | – | 1 |
| Woodman | 14 | 11 | 14 | 14 | 14 | 14 | 14 | 14 | 8 |
| Hireme | s | 14 | s | – | – | – | – | – | 3 |
| Wickliffe | 11* | – | 11* | 11* | – | 11* | 11* | 11* | 6 |
| Hohepa | – | – | s | 11* | s | s | s | 5 |
| Waaka | 13 | 13 | 13 | 13 | s | 13* | 13* | 13* | 8 |
| Brazier | 12 | 10 | 10 | 12 | s | 12 | 12 | 12 | 8 |
| Fitzpatrick | s | 12* | – | s | 13 | s | s | s | 7 |
| Alley | – | s | 12* | – | 12* | – | – | – | 3 |
| Subritzki-Nafatali | 10* | s | s | 10* | 10* | 10 | 10 | 10 | 8 |
| Cocksedge | 9* | 9* | 9* | 9* | 9 | 9* | 9 | 9* | 8 |
| Sue | s | s | s | s | – | s | – | s | 6 |
| Savage | 8* | – | – | 8* | s | 8 | 8* | 8 | 6 |
| McMenamin | – | 8 | s | s | 8 | 6* | 6* | 6* | 7 |
| L. Itunu | s | s | 8* | – | – | s | s | 5 |
| Goss | 7 | 7* | 7 | 7 | 6* | 7 | 7 | 7 | 8 |
| Everitt | 6* | – | 6* | – | – | – | – | – | 2 |
| Ketu | s | s | – | s | 7 | – | s | s | 6 |
| Smith | 5 | 6 | 5 | 6 | 5* | 5 | 5* | 5* | 8 |
| Wood | – | 5 | s | 5* | s | s | s | s | 7 |
| Blackwell | 4 | 4* | 4 | 4 | s | 4* | 4 | 4 | 8 |
| Gubb | – | – | – | – | 4* | – | – | – | 1 |
| Nelson | 3* | s | s | – | 3* | – | s | s | 6 |
| A. Itunu | s | 3* | 3* | 3* | – | 3* | 3* | 3* | 7 |
| Love | 1* | – | – | – | – | – | – | – | 1 |
| Natua | s | 1* | 1* | 1* | s | 1* | 1 | 1* | 8 |
| Talawadua | – | s | s | s | 1* | s | s | s | 7 |
| Mata'u | – | – | – | s | s | s | – | – | 3 |
| Fa'amausili | 2* | 2* | 2* | 2* | 2 | 2* | 2* | 2* | 8 |
| Ngata-Aerengamate | s | s | s | s | s | s | s | s | 8 |

## INDIVIDUAL SCORING

| | Tries | Con | PG | DG | Points | | Tries | Con | PG | DG | Points |
|---|---|---|---|---|---|---|---|---|---|---|---|
| Cocksedge | 6 | 31 | 2 | – | 98 | Alley | 1 | – | – | – | 5 |
| Woodman | 16 | – | – | – | 80 | Blackwell | 1 | – | – | – | 5 |
| Winiata | 9 | – | – | – | 45 | Hohepa | 1 | – | – | – | 5 |
| Natua | 4 | – | – | – | 20 | Ketu | 1 | – | – | – | 5 |
| Brazier | 3 | 2 | – | – | 19 | McMenamin | 1 | – | – | – | 5 |
| Fa'amausili | 3 | – | – | – | 15 | Ngata-Aerengamate | 1 | – | – | – | 5 |
| A. Itunu | 3 | – | – | – | 15 | Talawadua | 1 | – | – | – | 5 |
| Waaka | 3 | – | – | – | 15 | Tubic | 1 | – | – | – | 5 |
| Wickliffe | 3 | – | – | – | 15 | | | | | | |
| Fitzpatrick | 2 | – | – | – | 10 | **Totals** | **64** | **33** | **2** | **0** | **392** |
| Smith | 2 | – | – | – | 10 | | | | | | |
| Subritzky-Nafatali | 2 | – | – | – | 10 | Opposition scored | 19* | 7 | 4 | 0 | 123 |

* Includes 1 penalty try (7 points)

## NEW ZEALAND IN NEW ZEALAND AND AT RUGBY WORLD CUP 2017

**Played 8    Won 7    Lost 1    Points for 392    Points against 123**

| Date | Opponent | Location | Score | Tries | Con | PG | DG | Referee |
|---|---|---|---|---|---|---|---|---|
| June 9 | Canada | Wellington | 28–16 | Cocksedge (2), Fa'amausili, Winiata | Cocksedge (4), | | | Tim Baker *Hong Kong* |
| June 13 | Australia | Christchurch | 44–17 | Winiata (2), Woodman (2), Fa'amausili, Natua, Cocksedge, Smith | Cocksedge (2) | | | Tim Baker *Hong Kong* |
| June 17 | England | Rotorua | 21–29 | Cocksedge, Woodman, Subritzky-Nafatali | Cocksedge (2), Brazier | | | Amy Perrett *Australia* |
| August 9 | Wales (RWC) | Dublin | 44–12 | Winiata (3), Wickliffe (2), Waaka, Woodman, Blackwell | Cocksedge (2) | | | Ian Tempest *England* |
| August 13 | Hong Kong (RWC) | Dublin | 121–0 | Woodman (8), Fitzpatrick (2), Hohepa, Cocksedge, McMenamin, Alley, Tubic, Talawadua, Brazier, Waaka, Ketu | Cocksedge (13) | | | Sara Cox *England* |
| August 17 | Canada (RWC) | Dublin | 48–5 | A. Itunu (3), Winiata, Waaka, Brazier, Fa'amausili, Wickliffe | Cocksedge (3), Brazier | | | Alhambra Nievas *Spain* |
| August 22 | USA (semi-final) | Belfast | 45–12 | Woodman (4), Subritzky-Nafatali, Ngata-Aerengamate, Brazier | Cocksedge (2) | Cocksedge (2) | | Alhambra Nievas *Spain* |
| August 26 | England (final) | Belfast | 41–32 | Natua (3), Winiata (2), Smith, Cocksedge | Cocksedge (3) | | | Joy Neville *Ireland* |

# RUGBY WORLD CUP SEMI-FINAL
# NEW ZEALAND V USA

Kingspan Stadium, Belfast                               August 22, 2017

Won by New Zealand 45–12

## NEW ZEALAND

Selica Winiata

Renee Wickliffe            Stacey Waaka            Portia Woodman

Kelly Brazier

Victoria Subritzky-Nafatali

Kendra Cocksedge

Aroha Savage

Sarah Goss        Charmaine Smith        Eloise Blackwell        Charmaine McMenamin

Aldora Itunu            Fiao'o Fa'amausili (capt)            Toka Natua

Catherine Benson            Kathryn Augustyn            Tiffany Faaee (capt)

Sara Parsons        Stacey Bridges        Alycia Washington        Kate Zackary

Jordan Gray

Deven Owsiany

Kimber Rozier

Alev Kelter

Kris Thomas            Nicole Heavirland            Naya Tapper

Cheta Emba

## UNITED STATES OF AMERICA

*Reserves:* New Zealand – Te Kura Ngata-Aerengamate (sub Fa'amausili 70m), Sosoli Talawadua (sub Natua 66m), Aleisha Nelson (sub A. Itunu 60m), Rebecca Wood (sub Smith 68m), Lesley Ketu (sub McMenamin 60m), Linda Itunu (sub Savage 60m), Theresa Fitzpatrick (sub Waaka 74m), Carla Hohepa (sub Wickliffe 60m).

USA – Sam Pankey (sub Augustyn 70m), Hope Rogers (sub Faaee 47m), Nicole James (sub Benson 56m), Abby Gustaitis (sub Bridges 66m), Kristine Sommer (sub Zachary 76m), Kayla Canett (sub Owsiany 70m), Tess Feury (sub Rozier 74m), Jess Wooden (sub Thomas 74m).

*Referee:* Alhambra Nievas (*Spain*)
*Assistant Referees:* Sean Gallagher (*Ireland*)
Rose LaBreche (*Canada*)

*Scorers:*    *New Zealand:*                          *USA:*
        *Tries:* Woodman (4),              *Tries:* Thomas, Kelter
        Subritzky-Nafatali,              *Conversion:* Kelter
        Ngata-Aerengamate, Brazier
        *Conversions:* Cocksedge (2)
        *Penalty goals:* Cocksedge (2)

*Scoring:*

First half: 3m Subritzky-Nafatali try 5–0, 15m Thomas try, Kelter conversion 5–7, 19m Cocksedge penalty goal 8–7, 25m Woodman try, Cocksedge conversion 15–7.

Second half: 48m Woodman try 20–7, 55m Cocksedge penalty goal 23–7, 58m Kelter try 23–12, 62m Woodman try 28–12, 71m Woodman try 33–12, 75m Ngata-Aerengamate try 38–12, 77m Brazier try, Cocksedge conversion 45–12.

*Yellow card* — L. Itunu 66m.

# RUGBY WORLD CUP FINAL
# NEW ZEALAND V ENGLAND

Kingspan Stadium, Belfast                                    August 26, 2017

## Won by New Zealand 41–32

### *NEW ZEALAND*

Selica Winiata

Renee Wickliffe                Stacey Waaka                Portia Woodman

Kelly Brazier

Victoria Subritzky-Nafatali

Kendra Cocksedge

Aroha Savage

Sarah Goss          Charmaine Smith          Eloise Blackwell          Charmaine McMenamin

Aldora Itunu          Fiao'o Fa'amausili (capt)          Toka Natua

Vickii Cornborough          Amy Cokayne          Sarah Bern

Alex Matthews          Abbie Scott          Tamara Taylor          Marlie Packer

Sarah Hunter (capt)

Natasha Hunt

Katy Mclean

Alev Kelter

Kay Wilson                Megan Jones                Lydia Thompson

Emily Scarratt

### *ENGLAND*

*Reserves: New Zealand* – Te Kura Ngata-Aerengamate (sub Fa'amausili 79m), Sosoli Talawadua (sub Natua 77m), Aleisha Nelson (sub Itunu 67m), Rebecca Wood (sub Smith 74m), Lesley Ketu (sub McMenamin 71m), Kristina Sue (sub Cocksedge 79m), Theresa Fitzpatrick (sub Waaka 64m), Carla Hohepa (sub Wickliffe 59m).

*England* – Vicky Fleetwood (sub Cokayne 57m), Rochelle Clark (sub Cornborough 57m), Justine Lucas (sub Bern 57m), Harriet Millar-Mills (sub Taylor 64m), Isabelle Noel-Smith (sub Packer 60m), La Toya Mason (sub Hunt 59m), Amber Reed (sub Burford 55m), Amy Wilson Hardy (sub Thompson 71m).

*Referee:* Joy Neville (*Ireland*)
*Assistant Referees:* Graham Cooper (*Australia*)

Hollie Davidson (*Scotland*)

| *Scorers:* | *New Zealand* | *England* |
|---|---|---|
| | *Tries:* Natua (3), Winiata (2), | *Tries:* Thompson (2), Noel-Smith, |
| | Smith, Cocksedge | penalty try |
| | *Conversions:* Cocksedge (3) | *Conversions:* Scarratt (2) |
| | | *Penalty goals:* Scarratt (2) |

*Scoring:*

First half: 8m Winiata try 5–0, 15m Scarratt penalty goal 5–3, 25m England penalty try 5–10, 32m Thompson try, Scarratt conversion 5–17, 39m Natua try 10–17.

Second half: 45m Natua try, Cocksedge conversion 17–17, 51m Scarratt penalty goal 17–20, 53m Smith try, Cocksedge conversion 24–20, 55m Thompson try 24–25, 58m Natua try, Cocksedge conversion 31–25, 63m Cocksedge try 36–25, 69m Winiata try 41–25, 77m Noel-Smith try, Scarratt conversion 41–32.

*Yellow card* — Goss 20m, Ketu 71m.

## *RUGBY WORLD CUP RESULTS*

| | | | | | | | |
|---|---|---|---|---|---|---|---|
| Aug 9 | B | | England | 56 | Spain | 5 | UCD Bowl, Dublin |
| | A | | New Zealand | 44 | Wales | 12 | Billings Park UCD, Dublin |
| | B | | USA | 24 | Italy | 12 | UCD Bowl, Dublin |
| | A | | Canada | 98 | Hong Kong | 0 | Billings Park UCD, Dublin |
| | C | | Ireland | 19 | Australia | 17 | UCD Bowl, Dublin |
| | C | | France | 72 | Japan | 14 | Billings Park UCD, Dublin |
| Aug 13 | A | | New Zealand | 121 | Hong Kong | 0 | Billings Park UCD, Dublin |
| | B | | England | 56 | Italy | 13 | Billings Park UCD, Dublin |
| | B | | USA | 43 | Spain | 0 | UCD Bowl, Dublin |
| | A | | Canada | 15 | Wales | 0 | Billings Park UCD, Dublin |
| | C | | Ireland | 24 | Japan | 14 | UCD Bowl, Dublin |
| | C | | France | 48 | Australia | 0 | UCD Bowl, Dublin |
| Aug 17 | A | | New Zealand | 48 | Canada | 5 | Billings Park UCD, Dublin |
| | B | | England | 47 | USA | 26 | Billings Park UCD, Dublin |
| | B | | Spain | 22 | Italy | 8 | UCD Bowl, Dublin |
| | C | | Australia | 29 | Japan | 15 | Billings Park UCD, Dublin |
| | A | | Wales | 39 | Hong Kong | 15 | UCD Bowl, Dublin |
| | C | | France | 21 | Ireland | 5 | UCD Bowl, Dublin |
| Aug 22 | s-f for 9th | | Italy | 22 | Japan | 0 | Queen's University, Belfast |
| | s-f for 9th | | Spain | 31 | Hong Kong | 7 | Queen's University, Belfast |
| | s-f for 5th | | Australia | 36 | Ireland | 24 | Kingspan Stadium, Belfast |
| | s-f for 5th | | Canada | 52 | Wales | 0 | Queen's University, Belfast |
| | s-f for Cup | | New Zealand | 45 | USA | 12 | Kingspan Stadium, Belfast |
| | s-f for Cup | | England | 20 | France | 3 | Kingspan Stadium, Belfast |
| Aug 26 | Play-off for 11th | | Japan | 44 | Hong Kong | 5 | Queen's University, Belfast |
| | Play-off for 9th | | Italy | 20 | Spain | 15 | Queen's University, Belfast |
| | Play-off for 7th | | Wales | 27 | Ireland | 17 | Queen's University, Belfast |
| | Play-off for 5th | | Canada | 43 | Australia | 12 | Kingspan Stadium, Belfast |
| | Play-off for 3rd | | France | 31 | USA | 23 | Kingspan Stadium, Belfast |
| | Cup final | | New Zealand | 41 | England | 32 | Kingspan Stadium, Belfast |

# NEW ZEALAND WOMEN'S REPRESENTATIVES, 1989–2017

| | Internationals | |
| --- | --- | --- |
| | Games | Points |
| **Aiatu, Muteremoana S.** 1981– | | |
| (Wellington) 2011 | 1 | – |
| **Alley, Chelsea H.** 1992– | | |
| (Waikato) 2013–14 (North Harbour) | | |
| 2015–16-17 | 15 | 15 |
| **Andrew, Shannon R.** 1972– | | |
| (Auckland) 1996 | 2 | – |
| **Aniseko, Fa'anati** 1989– | | |
| (Auckland) 2007 | 2 | 5 |
| **Apiata, Jacquileen W.** 1966– | | |
| (Canterbury) 1989–90–91– | | |
| 92–93–94–95 | 5 | – |
| **Atkins, Leanne T.** 1976– | | |
| (Northland) 1994 | – | – |
| **Baker, Lise** | | |
| (Wellington) 1990 | – | – |
| **Baker, Miriama** 1962– | | |
| (Auckland) 1989–91 | – | – |
| **Baker, Shakira J.** 1992– | | |
| (Wellington) 2011 | | |
| (Manawatu) 2012–14 | 13 | 40 |
| **Ballinger, Shona** 1970– | | |
| (Wellington) 1990–91 | – | – |
| **Barclay, F.J.** *see* **King, F.J.** | | |
| **Berry, Zoey P.** 1987– (Canterbury) | | |
| 2012 | 1 | – |
| **Blackledge, V.E.** *see* **Grant, V.E.** | | |
| **Blackwell, Eloise S.** 1990– (Auckland) | | |
| 2011–12–13–14–15–16-17 | 32 | 15 |
| **Blyde, Cherrie** | | |
| (Taranaki) 1992 | – | – |
| **Borthwick, Nicole M.** 1980– | | |
| (Auckland) 2005 | 2 | 7 |
| **Bosman** (nee Ngatai), **Melodie**, 2010. | | |
| *see* **Ngatai, M.M.** | | |
| **Brazier, Kelly A.** 1989– | | |
| (Otago) 2009–10–12–13–14–16 | | |
| (Canterbury) 2011 | | |
| (Bay of Plenty) 2017 | 37 | 190 |
| **Brett, Lesley** 1968– | | |
| (Canterbury) 1990–91 | 3 | 12 |
| **Broughton, Florence** | | |
| (Wellington) 1990 | – | – |
| **Canterbury, Marina R.** 1984– | | |
| (Hawke's Bay) 2005 | 5 | 10 |
| **Chase, Debbie P.M.** 1966– | | |
| (Canterbury) 1990–91–93 | 3 | 12 |
| **Chittock, Barbara J.** 1985– | | |
| (Canterbury) 2009 | – | – |

| | Internationals | |
| --- | --- | --- |
| | Games | Points |
| **Coady, Olivia R.** 1990– | | |
| (Canterbury) 2008–09 | 4 | 5 |
| **Cobley, Rhonda J.** 1971– | | |
| (Canterbury) 1992–94 | – | – |
| **Cocksedge, Kendra M.** 1988– | | |
| (Canterbury) 2007–08–09–10–11– | | |
| 12–13–14–15–16-17 | 42 | 225 |
| **Codling, Monalisa M.** 1977– | | |
| (Otago) 1998 | | |
| (Auckland) 1999–02–03–04–05– | | |
| 06–07–08-10 | 30 | 25 |
| **Cootes, Vanessa** 1969– | | |
| (Waikato) 1995–96–97–98–00– | | |
| 01–02 | 16 | 215 |
| **Crossman, Lydia J.** 1986– | | |
| (Hawke's Bay) 2011 | | |
| (Auckland) 2012 | 5 | – |
| **Cunningham, Vicky** | | |
| (Auckland) 1997 | 1 | – |
| **Davie, Mary** | | |
| (Canterbury) 1992–93 | – | – |
| **Dawson, Susan** 1971– | | |
| (Northland) 1999–00–02 | 4 | 5 |
| **de Jong, Catherine L.** 1984– | | |
| (Otago) 2005 | 1 | – |
| **Demant, Kiritapu W.** 1996– | | |
| (Auckland) 2015 | 2 | – |
| **Edwards** (*nee* Shelford), | | |
| **Exia T.** 1975– | | |
| (Bay of Plenty) 1998–99–00– | | |
| 01–02–03–04–05–06 | 27 | 90 |
| **Edwards, Maree** 1975– | | |
| (Otago) 1998–00 | | |
| (Canterbury) 2003 | 4 | 5 |
| **Edwards, Tangaloa** | | |
| (Auckland) 1989 | – | – |
| **Ellis, Judith M.** 1966– | | |
| (Canterbury) 1993–94–95 | 1 | – |
| **Engebretsen, Lauren J.** 1983– | | |
| (Waikato) 2004 | 3 | – |
| **Epiha, Eva A.** 1974– | | |
| (Auckland) 1994 | – | – |
| **Everitt, Rawinia P.** 1986– | | |
| (Auckland) 2011–12 | | |
| (Counties Manukau) 2013–14–16-17 | 21 | 25 |
| **Ewe, Donna** 1964– | | |
| (Auckland) 1990–91 | 3 | – |
| **Fa'amausili, Fiao'o** 1980– | | |
| (Auckland) 2002–03–05–06–07– | | |
| 08–09–10–11–12–13–14–15–16-17 | 52 | 60 |
| **Fa'aope, Lili** | | |
| (Canterbury) 1989–90 | – | – |

| | Internationals | |
|---|---|---|
| | Games | Points |
| **Farr, Amy M.** 1982– | | |
| (Wellington) 2007 | 1 | 0 |
| **Fereti** (nee Patea), **Jackie S.** see | | |
| **Patea, J.S.** | | |
| **Fitzgibbon, Maree** 1966– | | |
| (Canterbury) 1989–90–91 | 3 | – |
| **Fitzpatrick, Theres M.** 1995- | | |
| (Auckland) 2017 | 7 | 10 |
| **Ford, Amanda** 1970– | | |
| (Canterbury) 1990–91 | 1 | 4 |
| **Ford, Deborah** 1965– | | |
| (Canterbury) 1989–90–91 | – | – |
| **Frost, Seuga** 1966– | | |
| (Canterbury) 1990–91 | – | – |
| **Garden, Susan** 1961–2008 | | |
| (Canterbury) 1989–90–91 | | |
| (Otago) 1992 | – | – |
| **Gavet, Sandra** 1961– | | |
| (Auckland) 1990–92 | – | – |
| **Goss, Sarah L.** 1992– (Manawatu) | | |
| 2016 -17 | 10 | 5 |
| **Grant (***nee* **Blackledge),** | | |
| **Victoria E.** 1982– | | |
| (Auckland) 2006–07–08–09–10–11 | | |
| (Waikato) 2013 | 17 | 30 |
| **Gray, Isabel** 1974– | | |
| (Wellington) 1999–02–05 | 5 | 5 |
| **Gubb** (nee Halapua), **Charlene P.T.** | | |
| see **Halapua, C.P.T.** | | |
| **Halapua, Charlene P.T.** 1988– | | |
| (Auckland) 2015–16–17 | 9 | 5 |
| **Harrison, Sarah** | | |
| (Wellington) 1999 | 2 | – |
| **Hayes, Carol** 1970– | | |
| (Southland) 1989–91–92–93 | – | – |
| **Heenan, Janet M.** 1969– | | |
| (Northland) 1996–98 | 5 | – |
| **Heighway, Victoria L** 1980– | | |
| (Auckland) 2000–01–02–03–04– | | |
| 05–06–07–08–09–10 | 32 | 10 |
| **Hiemer, Riki** | | |
| (Wellington) 1997 | 2 | – |
| **Hina, Trisha R.** 1977– | | |
| (Auckland) 2010 | 4 | – |
| **Hireme, A. Honey 1981–** (Waikato) | | |
| 2014–15–16–17 | 18 | 75 |
| **Hirovanaa, Monique J.** 1966– | | |
| (Auckland) 1994–95–96–97– | | |
| 98–99–00–01–02 | 24 | 65 |
| **Hohepa, Carla G.** 1985– | | |
| (Otago) 2007–08–09–10 | | |
| (Waikato) 2016-17 | 19 | 80 |
| **Hull, R.M.** *see* **Mahoney, R.M.** | | |
| **Hopkins, Anna** 1970– | | |
| (Wellington) 1991 | – | – |

| | Internationals | |
|---|---|---|
| | Games | Points |
| **Huxford, Sarah** | | |
| (Wellington) 1993 | – | – |
| **Inwood, Nicola A.** 1970– | | |
| (Canterbury) 1989–90–91 | 3 | – |
| **Itunu, Aldora T.** 1991– | | |
| (Auckland) 2015–16-17 | 15 | 15 |
| **Itunu, Linda F.** 1984– | | |
| (Auckland) 2003–04–06–07–08– | | |
| 09–10–14–15-17 | 34 | 10 |
| **Jensen, Emma M.** 1977– | | |
| (Waikato) 2002–03–04 | | |
| (Auckland) 2005–06–07–08–09– | | |
| 10–11–12–13–14–15 | 49 | 53 |
| **John, Chris** | | |
| (Canterbury) 1990 | – | – |
| **Johnson, Fiona C.** 1970– | | |
| (Wellington) 1990 | – | – |
| **Kahura, Dianne M.T.** 1969– | | |
| (Auckland) 1998–99–00–02 | 12 | 95 |
| **Kay, Rhonda** 1976– | | |
| (Waikato) 2000 | 1 | – |
| **Ketu, Lesley T.** 1987– | | |
| (Waikato) 2015-17 | 9 | 5 |
| **King (***nee* **Barclay), Fiona J.** 1972– | | |
| (Otago) 1996–97–98–99–00– | | |
| 01–02 | 18 | 5 |
| **Kingi, Mere A.** 1974– | | |
| (Auckland) 2003–04 | 5 | 10 |
| **Kiwi, Kellie H.** 1972– | | |
| (Bay of Plenty) 1996–97–98 | 8 | 15 |
| **Knight, Neroli** 1974– | | |
| (Wellington) 1990–91–99–00–01 | 4 | – |
| **Konui, Toni R.H.** 1966– | | |
| (Auckland) 1998 | 3 | – |
| **Kupa, Mel** | | |
| (Hawke's Bay) 1997 | 2 | – |
| **Lavea, Justine** 1984– | | |
| (Auckland) 2004–05–07–09–10– | | |
| 11–12–13–14 | | |
| 14 (Counties Manukau) 2015 | 34 | 30 |
| **Lavea, Vaniya N.H.** 1981– | | |
| (Auckland) 2003–04–07 | 5 | – |
| **Leiataua, Onjeurlina F.** 1995– | | |
| (Auckland) 2013 | 1 | – |
| **Lemon, Tracey M.** 1970–2012 | | |
| (Auckland) 1991–94–95 | 2 | – |
| **Lene, Stacey O.** 1980– | | |
| (Canterbury) 2003–04–05 | 7 | 35 |
| **Levave, Sanita D.** 1988– | | |
| (Wellington) 2014 | 5 | – |
| **Lili'i, Adrienne P.** 1970– | | |
| (Auckland) 1999–02–03–04 | | |
| (Waikato) 2000 | 12 | 5 |

|  | Internationals Games | Points |
|---|---|---|
| **Littleworth, Helen M.** 1966– | | |
| (Canterbury) 1989–90–91–92–93–94 | | |
| (Otago) 1995–96 | 8 | 20 |
| **Liua'ana, Rebecca** 1970– | | |
| (Wellington) 1999–00–01–02 | 10 | 10 |
| **Lotui'iga, L. Brigitta** 1968– | | |
| (Auckland) 1998 | 5 | – |
| **Love, Phillipa E.A.** 1990– | | |
| (Otago) 2014 | | |
| (Canterbury) 2017 | 2 | – |
| **McKay, K. Ruth** 1986– | | |
| (Manawatu) 2007–08–09–10–12–13–14 | 25 | – |
| **McKenzie, Margaret J.** 1970– | | |
| (Otago) 2000–05 | 5 | 5 |
| **McMenamin, Charmaine J.** 1990– | | |
| (Auckland) 2013–16-17 | 14 | 5 |
| **Mahon, Helen L.** 1968– | | |
| (Canterbury) 1989 | | |
| (Wellington) 1991 | | |
| (Waikato) 1992 | 3 | 12 |
| **Mahoney (*nee* Hull), Rebecca M.** 1983– | | |
| (Manawatu) 2004–08 | | |
| (Hawke's Bay) 2006 | | |
| (Wellington) 2009–10–11 | 16 | 25 |
| **Makata, Rachel J.** 1974– | | |
| (Auckland) 2006 | 2 | 5 |
| **Maliukaetau, F. Diane L.** 1986– | | |
| (Auckland) 2005–06 | 6 | 5 |
| **Mallard, Beth L.** 1981– | | |
| (Otago) 2006–07–08–09 | 8 | – |
| **Manuel, Huriana R.** 1986– | | |
| (Auckland) 2005–06–07–08–09–10–14 | 25 | 70 |
| **Marsh, A.** *see* **Rule, A.** | | |
| **Martin, Rochelle L.** 1973– | | |
| (Wellington) 1994–95 | | |
| (Auckland) 1996–97–98–99–00–02–04–05–06 | 32 | 70 |
| **Matapo, P.E.A. 'Kelani'** 1983– | | |
| (Auckland) 2011 | 1 | – |
| **Mata'u, Aotearoa K.** 1997– | | |
| (Counties Manukau) 2016-17 | 8 | 5 |
| **Mihinui, M.T. Eliza** 1960– | | |
| (Auckland) 1994 | – | – |
| **Moore, Aroha** 1978– | | |
| (Auckland) 2004 | 3 | – |
| **Mortimer, Stephanie A.** 1981– | | |
| (Canterbury) 2003–04–05–06 | 11 | 50 |
| **Mulipola, Tala** 1981– | | |
| (Auckland) 2000–01–03 | 7 | 5 |
| **Murphy, Amanda J.** 1985– | | |
| (Canterbury) 2009–11 | 2 | – |
| **Myers, H.J.** *see* **Porter, H.J.** | | |
| **Natua Toka I.** 1991– | | |
| (Waikato) 2015–16-17 | 16 | 25 |

|  | Internationals Games | Points |
|---|---|---|
| **Nelson, Aleisha P.** 1990– | | |
| (Auckland) 2012–14–15–16-17 | 26 | 10 |
| **Nemaia, Ana** | | |
| (Auckland) 1989 | – | – |
| **Nesbit, Joanne** | | |
| (Canterbury) 1989 | – | – |
| **Ngata-Aerengamate, Te Kura R.** 1991– | | |
| (Counties Manukau) 2014–15–16-17 | 19 | 5 |
| **Ngatai, Melodie M.** 1976– | | |
| (Auckland) 2004 | | |
| (Waikato) 2005 | | |
| (Hawke's Bay) 2006–11 | | |
| (Canterbury) 2010–13 | 17 | – |
| **Nielsen, Jacinta** 1972– | | |
| (Otago) 1997–98–00 | 7 | – |
| **O'Leary, Pauline** | | |
| (Wanganui) 1993 | – | – |
| **O'Reilly, Lauren M.** 1967– | | |
| (Canterbury) 1992–93–94 | 1 | – |
| **Paasi, Poinisitia** 1970– | | |
| (Wellington) 2001–07 | 4 | – |
| **Paitai, Elsie** 1963– | | |
| (Auckland) 1990–91 | – | – |
| **Palmer, Farah R.** 1972– | | |
| (Otago) 1996–98–99–00 | | |
| (Waikato) 1997 | | |
| (Manawatu) 2001–02–03–04–05–06 | 35 | 25 |
| **Papalii, Christine** 1962– | | |
| (Auckland) 1989–90–92 | – | – |
| **Patea, Jackie S.** 1986– | | |
| (Wellington) 2012–13–14–16 | 12 | – |
| **Paul, Geraldine** 1965– | | |
| (Bay of Plenty) 1991–97 | | |
| (Taranaki) 1994 | 4 | 10 |
| **Paul, Tamaku** 1979– | | |
| (Bay of Plenty) 2001 | 1 | – |
| **Penetito, Karina E.** *see* **Stowers, K.E.** | | |
| **Piho, Mata** 1972– | | |
| (Otago) 1998–00 | 3 | – |
| **Porter (*nee* Myers), Hannah J.** 1979– | | |
| (Otago) 2000–02 | | |
| (Auckland) 2003–04–05–06–08 | 22 | 169 |
| **Reader, Heidi C.** 1971– | | |
| (Otago) 1993 | | |
| (Waikato) 1994–96 | | |
| (Bay of Plenty) 1995 | 3 | 38 |
| **Rees, Vivian L.** 1971– | | |
| (Wellington) 1993–94–95 | 2 | 2 |
| **Rere (Ratu), Ericka** 1963– | | |
| (Wellington) 1990–91–92 | | |
| (Bay of Plenty) 1993 | 3 | – |
| **Reynolds, Julie** 1966– | | |
| (Canterbury) 1993–94 | – | – |

|  | Internationals Games | Points |
|---|---|---|
| **Richards, Anna M.** 1964–<br>(Auckland) 1990–91–92–93–94–<br>96–97–98–99–00–01–02–03–04–<br>05–06–07–08–10 | 49 | 89 |
| **Richards, Fiona C.** 1970–<br>(Canterbury) 1993–94–95–96<br>(Auckland) 1997–98–99 | 14 | – |
| **Richardson, Claire** 1984–<br>(Otago) 2003–04–05–06–07–12<br>(Auckland) 2013–14 | 23 | 54 |
| **Rikihana-Broughton, Julie**<br>(Wellington) 1990 | – | – |
| **Robertson, Casey J.** 1981–<br>(Canterbury) 2002–03–04–05–06–<br>09–10–11–12–13–14 | 38 | 10 |
| **Robinson, Melodie C.** 1973–<br>(Wellington) 1996–97–98–99<br>(Auckland) 2001–02 | 18 | 20 |
| **Robinson, Vita J.** 1982–<br>(Auckland) 2007–09–10–11–13 | 14 | – |
| **Rodd, Christine A.** 1959–<br>(Canterbury) 1990–91 | 2 | – |
| **Ross, L. Christine** 1964–<br>(Mid C'bury) 1989–92–96<br>(Canterbury) 1990–91 | 5 | 52 |
| **Rowat, Claire L.** 1983–<br>(Wellington) 2009 | – | – |
| **Rule (*nee* Marsh), Amiria** 1983–<br>(Canterbury) 2000–01–02–03–5–<br>06–09–11–13–14 | 34 | 75 |
| **Ruscoe, Melissa J.** 1976–<br>(Canterbury) 2004–05–06–07–<br>08–10 | 22 | 32 |
| **Rush, Annaleah M.** 1976–<br>(Otago) 1996–97–98–99<br>(Auckland) 2000–01–02 | 20 | 156 |
| **Rush, Erin** 1970–<br>(Wellington) 2003 | 2 | – |
| **Savage, Aroha** 1990–<br>(Auckland) 2010–11–12<br>(Counties Manukau) 2013–14–16-17 | 28 | 20 |
| **Sheck, Regina** 1969–<br>(Auckland) 1994–96–97–98<br>(Waikato) 1999–00–01–02–03–04 | 25 | 25 |
| **Shelford, Exia T.** *see* **Edwards, E.T.** | | |
| **Shortland, Suzanne** 1974–<br>(Auckland) 1997–98–99–00–01–02 | 18 | 20 |
| **Simpson-Brown, Lenadeen H.** 1964–<br>(Canterbury) 1994<br>(Waikato) 1995–96–97 | 8 | 15 |
| **Sio, Nina** 1963–<br>(Auckland) 1989–91–92<br>(Waikato) 1994 | 4 | – |
| **Sione, Joan L.** 1986–<br>(Auckland) 2005–10 | 6 | 5 |
| **Sisifa, Angelene A.F.** 1989–<br>(Otago) 2015–16 | 7 | – |

|  | Internationals Games | Points |
|---|---|---|
| **Smith, Charmaine B.** 1990–<br>(North Harbour) 2015–16-17 | 16 | 15 |
| **Smith, Kimberly M.** 1985–<br>(Canterbury) 2005–06–07–08–09 | 11 | – |
| **Solomon, Pikihuia P.** 1983–<br>(Otago) 2005 | 2 | 10 |
| **Stowers, Karina E. (*nee* Penetito)**<br>1986–<br>(Auckland) 2005–09–10–11–12–13 | 18 | – |
| **Su'a, S.M.A. 'Nara'** 1969–<br>(Auckland) 1996 | 2 | 5 |
| **Suasua-White, D.** *see* **White, D.M.** | | |
| **Subritzky-Nafatali, Victoria S.** 1991–<br>(Otago) 2012–14<br>(Counties Manukau) 2015–16-17 | 19 | 34 |
| **Sue, Kristina J.** 1987–<br>(Manawatu) 2016-17 | 10 | – |
| **Sutorius, Aimee E.** 1979–<br>Wellington) 2007–08–09 | 3 | – |
| **Tahu, Bella M.** 1970–<br>(Auckland) 1996 | 3 | – |
| **Talawadua, Sosoli J.** 1989–<br>(Waikato) 2016-17 | 8 | 5 |
| **Tamihana, Florence**<br>(Wellington) 1995 | 1 | – |
| **Taufateau, Doris J.T.** 1987–<br>(Auckland) 2008–10–11 | 5 | – |
| **Taylor, Karen** 1968–<br>(Bay of Plenty) 1996 | 2 | 5 |
| **Teddy, Waimania L.** 1979–<br>(Auckland) 2005–06–07 | 6 | – |
| **Te Tamaki, Teresa K.** 1981–<br>(Auckland) 2007–08–11<br>(Waikato) 2012–15 | 10 | – |
| **Tekeu, No'o**<br>(–) 1990 | – | – |
| **Te Ohaere-Fox,<br>Stephanie A.** 1985–<br>(Canterbury) 2008–09–10–12–<br>13–14<br>(Wasps) 2011 | 24 | – |
| **Thomas, Emma H.** 1958–<br>(Bay of Plenty) 1996–97–98 | 9 | – |
| **Tiplady, Anika M.** 1980–<br>(Manawatu) 2007<br>(Canterbury) 2009 | 2 | – |
| **Tiplady-Hurring, Halie A.** 1986–<br>(Canterbury) 2008–10–14<br>(Otago) 2012 | 13 | 15 |
| **Tiriamai, Kimi** 1964–<br>(Auckland) 1990–91 | 2 | – |
| **Tubic, Hazel S.** 1990–<br>(Auckland) 2011–12<br>(Counties Manukau) 2016-17 | 11 | 12 |
| **Va'aga, Helen** 1977–<br>(Auckland) 2002–03–05–06 | 10 | 10 |
| **Vaeteru, Teina**<br>(–) 1990 | – | – |

|  | Internationals Games | Points |
|---|---|---|
| **Vaughan, Janna M.** 1988– |  |  |
| (Manawatu) 2015–16 | 6 | 10 |
| **Waaka, Cheryl M.** 1970– |  |  |
| (Auckland) 1997–98–00–01–02– 03–04 |  |  |
| (Northland) 1999 | 20 | 35 |
| **Waaka, Stacey J.A.K.** 1995– |  |  |
| (Waikato) 2015-17 | 11 | 20 |
| **Wall, Louisa H.** 1972– |  |  |
| (Waikato) 1994 |  |  |
| (Auckland) 1995–96–97–98–99 | 15 | 95 |
| **Waters, Tracey J.R.** 1973– |  |  |
| (Canterbury) 1995–96–98 | 10 | 5 |
| **Wharton, Julie** |  |  |
| (Auckland) 1990 | – | – |
| **Whata-Simpkins, Katarina R.** 1990– |  |  |
| (Wellington) 2011 | 1 | 0 |
| **White, Davida M.** 1967– |  |  |
| (Auckland) 1993–94–95–96– 98–00 | 13 | 0 |
| **Wickliffe, Renee W.M.** 1987– |  |  |
| (Auckland) 2009–10–11 |  |  |
| (Counties Manukau) 2013–14–15– 16-17 | 30 | 65 |

|  | Internationals Games | Points |
|---|---|---|
| **Wihongi, Kamila T.** 1982– |  |  |
| (Otago) 2005 | 1 | – |
| **Williams, Amy L.** 1986– |  |  |
| (Hawke's Bay) 2005–06 | 6 | – |
| **Williams, Tasha H.** 1973– |  |  |
| (Manawatu) 1994 | 1 | 10 |
| **Willoughby, Shannon M.** 1982– |  |  |
| (Otago) 2005–06 | 8 | – |
| **Wilson, Tammi** 1973– |  |  |
| (Auckland) 1998–99–00–01–02 | 16 | 196 |
| **Wilton, Kathleen A.** 1984– |  |  |
| (Otago) 2007–11–12–13–14 | 18 | – |
| **Winiata, Selica C.** 1986– |  |  |
| (Manawatu) 2008–12–13–14–15– 16-17 | 31 | 175 |
| **Wong, Natasha A.** 1967– |  |  |
| (Canterbury) 1990–91–92–93–94 | 3 | – |
| **Wood, Rebecca J.** 1987- |  |  |
| (North Harbour) 2017 | 7 | – |
| **Woodman, Portia L.** 1991– |  |  |
| (Auckland) 2013 |  |  |
| (Counties Manukau) 2016-17 | 16 | 110 |
| **Woodman, Sharnita K.** 1986– |  |  |
| (Counties Manukau) 2016 | 2 | – |
| **Yates, Sandy** 1979– |  |  |
| (Counties Manukau) 2001 | 1 | – |

# BLACK FERNS RECORDS

## NEW ZEALAND INTERNATIONAL CAPTAINS

| | | |
|---|---|---|
| Farah Palmer | 1997–2006 | 30 |
| Fiao'o Fa'amausili | 2012–17 | 30 |
| Melissa Ruscoe | 2007–10 | 8 |
| Lenadeen Simpson-Brown | 1994–96 | 6 |
| Helen Littleworth | 1991 | 3 |
| Victoria Grant | 2010–11 | 3 |
| Rochelle Martin | 2005–06 | 2 |
| Victoria Heighway | 2009 | 2 |
| Davida White | 1998 | 1 |
| Anna Richards | 2005 | 1 |
| Casey Robertson | 2011 | 1 |
| Amiria Rule | 2014 | 1 |

## MOST APPEARANCES IN INTERNATIONALS

| | | | | | | |
|---|---|---|---|---|---|---|
| F.M. Fa'amausili | 2002–17 | 52 | C.J. Robertson | 2002–14 | 38 |
| A.M. Richards | 1991–10 | 49 | K.A. Brazier | 2009–17 | 37 |
| E.M. Jensen | 2002–15 | 49 | F.R. Palmer | 1996–06 | 35 |
| K.M. Cocksedge | 2007–17 | 42 | | | |

## MOST SUCCESSIVE INTERNATIONALS

| | | |
|---|---|---|
| E.M. Jensen | 2003–15 | 44 |

## MOST POINTS IN INTERNATIONALS

| | Tries | Con | PG | DG | Total | | Tries | Con | PG | DG | Total |
|---|---|---|---|---|---|---|---|---|---|---|---|
| K.M. Cocksedge | 13 | 56 | 16 | – | 225 | K.A. Brazier | 11 | 45 | 15 | – | 190 |
| V. Cootes | 43 | – | – | – | 215 | S.C. Winiata | 35 | – | – | – | 175 |
| T. Wilson | 21 | 29 | 11 | – | 196 | A.M. Rush | 14 | 34 | 6 | – | 156 |
| H.J. Porter | 5 | 42 | 20 | – | 169 | | | | | | |

## MOST POINTS IN AN INTERNATIONAL

| | | | |
|---|---|---|---|
| V. Cootes | v France, 1996 | 45 | (9 tries) |
| P.L. Woodman | v Hong Kong, 2017 | 40 | (8 tries) |
| T. Wilson | v USA, 1999 | 36 | (6 tries, 3 conversions) |
| L.C. Ross | v France, 1996 | 34 | (2 tries, 12 conversions) |
| K.M. Cocksedge | v Hong Kong, 2017 | 31 | (1 try, 13 conversions) |
| T. Wilson | v Germany, 1998 | 30 | (4 tries, 5 conversions) |

## MOST TRIES IN AN INTERNATIONAL

| | | | | | |
|---|---|---|---|---|---|
| V. Cootes | v France, 1996 | 9 | V. Cootes | v USA, 1998 | 5 |
| P.L. Woodman | v Hong Kong, 2017 | 8 | V. Cootes | v Germany, 2002 | 5 |
| T. Wilson | v USA, 1999 | 6 | S.C. Winiata | v Samoa, 2014 | 5 |
| V. Cootes | v USA, 1996 | 5 | | | |

## MOST PENALTY GOALS IN AN INTERNATIONAL

| | | | | | |
|---|---|---|---|---|---|
| K.A. Brazier | v England, 2013 | 4 | K.M. Cocksedge | v England, 2015 | 4 |

## MOST CONVERSIONS IN AN INTERNATIONAL

| | | | | | |
|---|---|---|---|---|---|
| K.M. Cocksedge | v Hong Kong, 2017 | 13 | L.C. Ross | v Canada, 1996 | 9 |
| L.C. Ross | v France, 1996 | 12 | H.C. Reader | v USA, 1996 | 8 |

## INTERNATIONAL MATCH RECORD

| 1991 | v Canada[1] | Glamorgan | won | 24 | 8 |
|---|---|---|---|---|---|
| | v Wales[1] | Llanharen | won | 24 | 6 |
| | v USA[1] (semi-final) | Cardiff | lost | 0 | 7 |
| 1994 | v Australia | Sydney | won | 37 | 0 |
| 1995 | v Australia | Auckland | won | 64 | 0 |
| 1996 | v Australia | Sydney | won | 28 | 5 |
| | v Canada | St Albert | won | 88 | 3 |
| | v USA | Edmonton | won | 86 | 8 |
| | v France | Edmonton | won | 109 | 0 |
| 1997 | v England | Burnham | won | 67 | 0 |
| | v Australia | Dunedin | won | 40 | 0 |
| 1998 | v Germany[1] | Amsterdam | won | 134 | 6 |
| | v Scotland[1] | Amsterdam | won | 76 | 0 |
| | v Spain[1] (quarter-final) | Amsterdam | won | 46 | 3 |
| | v England[1] (semi-final) | Amsterdam | won | 44 | 11 |
| | v USA[1] (final) | Amsterdam | won | 44 | 12 |
| | v Australia | Sydney | won | 27 | 3 |
| 1999 | v Canada | Palmerston North | won | 73 | 0 |
| | v USA | Palmerston North | won | 65 | 5 |
| 2000 | v Canada | Winnipeg | won | 41 | 0 |
| | v USA | Winnipeg | won | 45 | 0 |
| | v England | Winnipeg | won | 32 | 13 |
| 2001 | v England | Rotorua | won | 15 | 10 |
| | v England | Albany | lost | 17 | 22 |
| 2002 | v Germany[1] | Barcelona | won | 117 | 0 |
| | v Australia[1] | Barcelona | won | 36 | 3 |
| | v France[1] (semi-final) | Barcelona | won | 30 | 0 |
| | v England[1] (final) | Barcelona | won | 19 | 9 |
| 2003 | v World XV | Auckland | won | 37 | 0 |
| | v World XV | Whangarei | won | 38 | 19 |
| 2004 | v Canada | Vancouver | won | 32 | 5 |
| | v USA | Calgary | won | 35 | 0 |
| | v England | Edmonton | won | 38 | 0 |
| 2005 | v Scotland | Ottawa | won | 30 | 9 |
| | v Canada | Ottawa | won | 43 | 3 |
| | v Canada | Ottawa | won | 32 | 5 |
| | v England | Auckland | won | 33 | 8 |
| | v England | Hamilton | won | 24 | 15 |
| 2006 | v Canada[1] | Edmonton | won | 66 | 7 |
| | v Samoa[1] | Edmonton | won | 50 | 0 |
| | v Scotland[1] | Edmonton | won | 21 | 0 |
| | v France[1] (semi-final) | Edmonton | won | 40 | 10 |
| | v England[1] (final) | Edmonton | won | 25 | 17 |
| 2007 | v Australia | Wanganui | won | 21 | 11 |
| | v Australia | Wellington | won | 29 | 12 |
| 2008 | v Australia | Canberra | won | 37 | 3 |
| | v Australia | Canberra | won | 22 | 16 |
| 2009 | v England | London | won | 16 | 3 |
| | v England | London | lost | 3 | 10 |

| | | | | | | |
|---|---|---|---|---|---|---|
| **2010** | v | South Africa[1] | London | won | 55 | 3 |
| | v | Australia[1] | London | won | 32 | 5 |
| | v | Wales[1] | London | won | 41 | 8 |
| | v | France[1] (semi-final) | London | won | 45 | 7 |
| | v | England[1] (final) | London | won | 13 | 10 |
| **2011** | v | England | London | lost | 0 | 10 |
| | v | England | London | lost | 7 | 21 |
| | v | England | London | draw | 8 | 8 |
| **2012** | v | England | Esher | lost | 13 | 16 |
| | v | England | Aldershot | lost | 8 | 17 |
| | v | England | London | lost | 23 | 32 |
| **2013** | v | England | Auckland | won | 29 | 10 |
| | v | England | Hamilton | won | 14 | 9 |
| | v | England | Pukekohe | won | 29 | 8 |
| **2014** | v | Australia | Rotorua | won | 38 | 3 |
| | v | Samoa | Auckland | won | 90 | 12 |
| | v | Canada | Tauranga | won | 16 | 8 |
| | v | Canada | Whakatane | won | 33 | 21 |
| | v | Kazakhstan[1] | Marcoussis | won | 79 | 5 |
| | v | Ireland[1] | Marcoussis | lost | 14 | 17 |
| | v | USA[1] | Marcoussis | won | 34 | 3 |
| | v | Wales[1] | Paris | won | 63 | 7 |
| | v | USA[1] | Paris | won | 55 | 5 |
| **2015** | v | Canada | Calgary | won | 40 | 22 |
| | v | England | Red Deer | won | 26 | 7 |
| | v | USA | Edmonton | won | 49 | 14 |
| **2016** | v | Australia | Auckland | won | 67 | 3 |
| | v | Australia | Albany | won | 29 | 3 |
| | v | England | London | won | 25 | 20 |
| | v | Canada | Dublin | won | 20 | 10 |
| | v | Ireland | Dublin | won | 38 | 8 |
| **2017** | v | Canada | Wellington | won | 28 | 16 |
| | v | Australia | Christchurch | won | 44 | 17 |
| | v | England | Rotorua | lost | 21 | 29 |
| | v | Wales[1] | Dublin | won | 44 | 12 |
| | v | Hong Kong[1] | Dublin | won | 121 | 0 |
| | v | Canada[1] | Dublin | won | 48 | 5 |
| | v | USA[1] (semi-final) | Belfast | won | 45 | 12 |
| | v | England[1] (final) | Belfast | won | 41 | 32 |

[1]World Cup

## SUMMARY OF INTERNATIONALS

| | | | |
|---|---|---|---|
| Played: | 88 | Points for: | 3525 |
| Won: | 77 | Points against: | 748 |
| Lost: | 10 | | |
| Drawn: | 1 | | |

# RESULTS FROM 2017 FIRST-CLASS
# SEASON IN NEW ZEALAND
## AND TEAMS OF NEW ZEALANDERS OVERSEAS

Key:

| | | |
|---|---|---|
| | RWC | Rugby World Cup |
| | P | Farah Palmer Cup Premiership |
| | C | Farah Palmer Cup Championship |
| | P/C | Crossover match between teams from the FPC |
| | | Premiership and Championship divisions |
| | st | semi-final |
| | f | final |
| | ST | J.J. Stewart Trophy |
| | * | not first-class |

**January**

| Sat/Sun | 14/15 * | | National Sevens | | | | Rotorua |
|---|---|---|---|---|---|---|---|

**February**

| Fri/Sat | 3/4 | * | Australia WR Sevens | | | | Sydney |
|---|---|---|---|---|---|---|---|

**March**

| Fri/Sat | 3/4 | * | USA WR Sevens | | | | Las Vegas |
|---|---|---|---|---|---|---|---|

**April**

| Sat/Sun | 22/23 * | | Japan WR Sevens | | | | Kitakyushu |
|---|---|---|---|---|---|---|---|

**May**

| Sat/Sun | 27/28 * | | Canada WR Sevens | | | | Victoria |
|---|---|---|---|---|---|---|---|

**June**

| Fri | 9 | | England | 53 | Australia | 10 | Porirua |
|---|---|---|---|---|---|---|---|
| | | | New Zealand | 28 | Canada | 16 | Wellington |
| Tue | 13 | | England | 27 | Canada | 20 | Christchurch |
| | | | New Zealand | 44 | Australia | 17 | Christchurch |
| Sat | 17 | | Canada | 45 | Australia | 5 | Rotorua |
| | | | England | 29 | New Zealand | 21 | Rotorua |
| Sat/Sun | 24/25 * | | France WR Sevens | | | | Clermont-Ferrand |

**August**

| | 9 | RWC | New Zealand | 44 | Wales | 12 | Dublin |
|---|---|---|---|---|---|---|---|
| | 13 | RWC | New Zealand | 121 | Hong Kong | 0 | Dublin |
| | 17 | RWC | New Zealand | 48 | Canada | 5 | Dublin |
| | 22 | RWC | New Zealand | 45 | USA | 12 | Belfast |
| | 26 | RWC | New Zealand | 41 | England | 32 | Belfast |

**September**

| | 2 | P/C | Bay of Plenty | 10 | Auckland | 10 | Whakatane |
|---|---|---|---|---|---|---|---|
| | | P/C | Wellington | 42 | Hawke's Bay | 10 | Porirua |
| | | P/C | Waikato | 25 | Tasman | 17 | Blenheim |
| | | P/C, ST | Counties Manukau | 84 | North Harbour | 7 | Pukekohe |

| | 3 | P/C | Canterbury | 20 | Otago | 7 | Christchurch |
|---|---|---|---|---|---|---|---|
| | 7 | P, ST | Counties Manukau | 48 | Waikato | 0 | Pukekohe |
| | 9 | P | Auckland | 41 | Canterbury | 12 | Auckland |
| | | P | Manawatu | 35 | Wellington | 27 | Petone |
| | | C | Bay of Plenty | 24 | Hawke's Bay | 10 | Napier |
| | | C | Otago | 82 | Tasman | 0 | Dunedin |
| | 16 | C | Otago | 39 | Hawke's Bay | 17 | Napier |
| | | P | Counties Manukau | 36 | Auckland | 12 | Pakuranga |
| | | P | Canterbury | 40 | Manawatu | 10 | Christchurch |
| | | P | Wellington | 11 | Waikato | 5 | Hamilton |
| | | C | Bay of Plenty | 34 | North Harbour | 12 | Rotorua |
| | 22 | P | Waikato | 36 | Manawatu | 28 | Palmerston North |
| | 23 | P, ST | Canterbury | 32 | Counties Manukau | 29 | Papakura |
| | | C | North Harbour | 20 | Hawke's Bay | 0 | Albany |
| | | P | Auckland | 31 | Wellington | 30 | Porirua |
| | | C | Bay of Plenty | 38 | Tasman | 15 | Tauranga |
| | 29 | P/C | Auckland | 37 | North Harbour | 5 | Albany |
| | 30 | P/C | Wellington | 41 | Otago | 19 | Dunedin |
| | | P/C | Manawatu | 86 | Hawke's Bay | 8 | Napier |
| | | P/C | Waikato | 19 | Bay of Plenty | 17 | Hamilton |
| | | P/C, ST | Canterbury | 67 | Tasman | 12 | Christchurch |

**October**

| | 7 | P | Counties Manukau | 43 | Wellington | 13 | Porirua |
|---|---|---|---|---|---|---|---|
| | | C | Bay of Plenty | 27 | Otago | 17 | Dunedin |
| | | P | Manawatu | 15 | Auckland | 15 | Palmerston North |
| | 8 | C | North Harbour | 25 | Tasman | 12 | Nelson |
| | | P | Canterbury | 31 | Waikato | 20 | Hamilton |
| | 14 | P, ST | Canterbury | 55 | Wellington | 34 | Christchurch |
| | | P | Counties Manukau | 48 | Manawatu | 0 | Palmerston North |
| | | P | Waikato | 43 | Auckland | 34 | Pakuranga |
| | | C | Tasman | 24 | Hawke's Bay | 12 | Nelson |
| | 15 | C | Otago | 34 | North Harbour | 15 | Albany |
| | 21 | P sf | Counties Manukau | 22 | Auckland | 17 | Pukekohe |
| | | P sf | Canterbury | 60 | Waikato | 26 | Christchurch |
| | | C sf | Otago | 39 | North Harbour | 12 | Dunedin |
| | 28 | C f | Bay of Plenty | 7 | Otago | 5 | Mt Maunganui |
| | 29 | P f | Canterbury | 13 | Counties Manukau | 7 | Pukekohe |

**November**

| | 10/11 * | | Oceania Sevens | | | | Suva |
|---|---|---|---|---|---|---|---|
| | 30/1 * | | Dubai WR Sevens | | | | Dubai |

# WOMEN'S CLUB FINALS

Results of the 2017 senior club finals. Counties Manukau and North Harbour clubs participated in the Auckland competition.

| Union | Winner | | Runner-up | |
|-------|--------|-----|-----------|-----|
| Auckland | Marist | 15 | College Rifles | 10 |
| Bay of Plenty | Waikite | 21 | Rangataua | 10 |
| Canterbury | Christchurch | 28 | Cant. University | 18 |
| Hawke's Bay | Clive | 23 | Taradale | 7 |
| Manawatu | Kia Toa | 24 | Feilding OB Oroua | 19 |
| Otago | Pirates | 27 | University | 10 |
| Tasman | Moutere | 37 | Marist | 5 |
| Waikato | Hamilton OB | 19 | University | 10 |
| Wellington | Oriental Rongotai | 63 | OB University | 8 |

# FARAH PALMER CUP

The number of teams competing in the Farah Palmer Cup increased by two with the return of Hawke's Bay and the introduction of Tasman for the first time. Teams were ranked based on the 2016 results with the top six teams playing in the premiership division and the remaining five in the championship division. Similar to the men's competition, crossover games were played with each team playing two teams from the other division. However, Counties Manukau and Manawatu each had only one crossover game and awarded five championship points for the bye round.

Defending champions Counties Manukau were again a powerful force. But having lifted the JJ Stewart Trophy from Auckland in the third round, Counties Manukau then lost the trophy the following week to Canterbury. The southerners suffered a big loss to Auckland in round two but won the remaining seven games. Canterbury added the Farah Palmer Cup and the Stewart trophy to the union's bulging trophy cabinet.

In the Championship division top qualifiers Bay of Plenty had a direct route to the final while Otago and North Harbour played in the semi-final.

*Final standings after round robin:*

| | P | W | D | L | B⁴ | B⁷ | Pts | T | C | PG | DG | Total | T | C | PG | DG | Total |
|---|---|---|---|---|---|---|---|---|---|---|---|---|---|---|---|---|---|
| | | | | | | | | | | FOR | | | | | AGAINST | | |
| **PREMIERSHIP DIVISION** | | | | | | | | | | | | | | | | | |
| Counties Manukau | 6 | 5 | - | 1 | 6 | 1 | 32 | 45* | 26 | 3 | - | 288 | 11 | 3 | 1 | - | 64 |
| Canterbury | 7 | 6 | - | 1 | 5 | - | 29 | 40 | 21 | 5 | - | 257 | 26 | 10 | 1 | - | 153 |
| Waikato | 7 | 4 | - | 3 | 3 | 1 | 20 | 23 | 9 | 5 | - | 148 | 28 | 14 | 6 | - | 186 |
| Auckland | 7 | 3 | 2 | 2 | 4 | - | 20 | 31 | 11 | 1 | - | 180 | 23 | 12 | 4 | - | 151 |
| Manawatu | 6 | 2 | 1 | 3 | 3 | - | 18 | 26 | 16 | 4 | - | 174 | 27 | 9 | 7 | - | 174 |
| Wellington | 7 | 3 | - | 4 | 5 | 1 | 18 | 32* | 9 | 6 | - | 198 | 29* | 21 | 3 | - | 198 |
| **CHAMPIONSHIP DIVISION** | | | | | | | | | | | | | | | | | |
| Bay of Plenty | 6 | 4 | 1 | 1 | 4 | 1 | 23 | 26 | 10 | - | - | 150 | 14 | 5 | 1 | - | 83 |
| Otago | 6 | 3 | - | 3 | 3 | - | 15 | 31* | 19 | 1 | - | 198 | 20* | 6 | 2 | - | 120 |
| North Harbour | 6 | 2 | - | 4 | 1 | - | 9 | 13 | 5 | 3 | - | 84 | 35 | 13 | - | - | 201 |
| Tasman | 6 | 1 | - | 5 | - | - | 4 | 13 | 6 | 1 | - | 80 | 39 | 24 | 2 | - | 249 |
| Hawke's Bay | 6 | - | - | 6 | - | - | 0 | 9 | 3 | 2 | - | 57 | 37* | 18 | 4 | - | 235 |
| **TOTALS** | | | | | | | | 289 | 135 | 31 | 0 | 1814 | 289 | 135 | 31 | 0 | 1814 |

B⁴ *bonus points for four or more tries in a match.*
B⁷ *bonus points for loss by seven or fewer points.*
\* *includes one penalty try (7 points)*

## PREMIERSHIP

**Semi-finals:**   Counties Manukau 22, Auckland 17, at Pukekohe
Canterbury 60, Waikato 26, at Christchurch

**Final:**   Canterbury 13, Counties Manukau 7, at Pukekohe

## CHAMPIONSHIP

**Semi-final:**   Otago 39, North Harbour 12, at Dunedin

**Final:**   Bay of Plenty 7, Otago 5, at Mount Maunganui

### LEADING POINTS-SCORERS

| Hazel Tubic | Counties Manukau | 78 |
|---|---|---|
| Kendra Cocksedge | Canterbury | 73 |
| Elizabeth Goulden | Manawatu | 44 |

### LEADING TRY-SCORERS

| Luka Connor | Bay of Plenty | 8 |
|---|---|---|
| Kilisitina Moata'ane | Otago | 7 |

# CAREER CHAMPIONSHIP RECORDS

**Points**
| 684 | Kendra Cocksedge (Canterbury) |
|---|---|
| 524 | Emma Jensen (Waikato/Auckland) |
| 398 | Selica Winiata (Manawatu) |

**Games**
| 106 | Emma Jensen (Waikato/Auckland) |
|---|---|
| 102 | Fiao'o Fa'amausili (Auckland) |
| 98 | Justine Lavea (Auckland/Counties Manukau) |

**Tries**
| 62 | Selica Winiata (Manawatu) |
|---|---|
| 45 | Victoria Grant (Nth Harb/Auckland) |
| 45 | Fiao'o Fa'amausili (Auckland) |

# GRAND FINAL RESULTS

| | Winner | | Runner-up | | Venue |
|---|---|---|---|---|---|
| 1999 | Auckland | 22 | Wellington | 0 | Wellington |
| 2000 | Auckland | 22 | Otago | 12 | Auckland |
| 2001 | Auckland | 28 | Wellington | 3 | Auckland |
| 2002 | Auckland | 53 | Wellington | 3 | Auckland |
| 2003 | Auckland | 35 | Wellington | 0 | Auckland |
| 2004 | Auckland | 29 | Canterbury | 10 | Auckland |
| 2005 | Auckland | 36 | Canterbury | 3 | Auckland |
| 2006 | Wellington | 11 | Auckland | 10 | Auckland |
| 2007 | Auckland | 32 | Otago | 27 | Auckland |
| 2008 | Auckland | 13 | Canterbury | 12 | Auckland |
| 2009 | Auckland | 24 | Canterbury | 20 | Christchurch |
| 2011 | Auckland | 34 | Wellington | 8 | Hamilton |
| 2012 | Auckland | 38 | Canterbury | 12 | Christchurch |
| 2013 | Auckland | 20 | Canterbury | 10 | Wellington |
| 2014 | Auckland | 28 | Waikato | 14 | New Plymouth |
| 2015 | Auckland | 39 | Wellington | 9 | Napier |
| 2016 | Counties Manukau | 41 | Auckland | 22 | Pukekohe |
| 2017 | Canterbury | 13 | Counties Manukau | 7 | Pukekohe |

# CHAMPIONSHIP RECORDS

## BY THE TEAMS

| | BEST PERFORMANCE 2017 | RECORD |
|---|---|---|
| **Season Totals** | | |
| Most points | 330 by Canterbury | 413 by Auckland, 2014 |
| Most tries | 51 by Canterbury | 68 by Auckland, 2015 |
| Most conversions | 29 by Counties Manukau | 33 by Auckland, 2014 |
| Most penalty goals | 6 by Canterbury; Wellington | 14 by Otago, 2013 |
| Most dropped goals | 1 by Canterbury | 2 by Manawatu, 2002; Auckland, 2012 |
| **Match Records** | | |
| Most points | 86 by Manawatu v Hawke's Bay | 116 by Auckland v North Harbour, 1999 |
| Most tries | 14 by Counties Manukau v North Harbour | 18 by Auckland v North Harbour, 1999 |
| Most conversions | 11 by Otago v Tasman | 13 by Auckland v North Harbour, 1999 |
| Most penalty goals | 3 by Canterbury v Manawatu; Waikato v Manawatu | 13 by Auckland v North Harbour, 1999 |
| Most dropped goals | 1 by Canterbury v Counties Manukau | 1 on seven occasions |
| Biggest winning margin | 82 by Otago v Tasman (82–0) | 116 by Auckland v North Harbour (116–0), 1999 |

## BY THE PLAYERS

| | BEST PERFORMANCE 2017 | | RECORD | |
|---|---|---|---|---|
| **Season Totals** | | | | |
| Most points | 78 | Hazel Tubic (Counties Manukau) | 110 | Selica Winiata (Manawatu) 2012 |
| Most tries | 8 | Luka Connor (Bay of Plenty) | 16 | Mele Hufanga (Auckland) 2015 |
| Most conversions | 28 | Hazel Tubic (Counties Manukau) | 28 | Hazel Tubic (Counties Manukau) 2017 |
| Most penalty goals | 6 | Acacia Te Iwimate (Wellington) | 12 | Chelsea Alley (Waikato) 2013 |
| Most dropped goals | 1 | Charntay Poko (Canterbury) | 2 | Rebecca Hull (Manawatu), 2002; Bella Milo (Auckland) 2012 |
| **Match Totals** | | | | |
| Most points | 25 | Kendra Cocksedge (Canterbury) v Wellington; Kilisitina Moata'ane (Otago) v Tasman | 45 | Kelly Brazier (Otago) v Hawke's Bay, 2012 |
| Most tries | 5 | Kilisitina Moata'ane (Otago) v Tasman | 8 | Annaleah Rush (Otago) v Hanan Shield Districts, 1999 |
| Most conversions | 9 | Elizabeth Goulden (Manawatu) v Hawke's Bay; Olivia Waldron (Otago) v Tasman | 13 | Tammi Wilson (Auckland) v Nth Harbour, 1999 |
| Most penalty goals | 3 | by three players | 6 | Annaleah Rush (Auckland) v Wellington, 2001 |
| Most dropped goals | 1 | Charntay Poko (Canterbury) v Counties Manukau | 1 | by six players on nine occasions |

# AUCKLAND STORM

**2017 Status:** Premiership
**NPC participation:** 1999–
**Coach:** John Fa'amausili
**Assistant coaches:** Chris Tautiaga, Waisake Sotutu
**Home grounds:** Eden Park; Bell Park, Pakuranga

## RECORDS

| | | |
|---|---|---|
| Most appearances | 102 | *Fiao'o Fa'amausili, 1999-2017* |
| Most points | 452 | *Emma Jensen, 2004–17* |
| Most tries | 45 | *Fiao'o Fa'amausili, 1999-2017* |
| Most points in a season | 101 | *Tammi Wilson, 1999* |
| Most tries in a season | 16 | *Mele Hufanga 2015* |
| Most conversions in a season | 27 | *Bella Milo, 2012* |
| Most penalty goals in a season | 9 | *Emma Jensen, 2014* |
| Most dropped goals in a season | 2 | *Bella Milo, 2012* |
| Most points in a match | 31 | *Tammi Wilson v North Harbour, 1999* |
| Most tries in a match | 4 | *Louisa Wall v North Harbour, 1999;* |
| | | *v Northland, 1999;* |
| | | *Victoria Grant v Otago, 2008;* |
| | | *Jade Le Pesq v Manawatu, 2012* |
| | | *Mele Hufanga v Wellington, 2014;* |
| | | *v Hawke's Bay, 2014;* |
| | | *v Canterbury 2015;* |
| | | *Natahlia-Debnorah Moors v Bay of Plenty 2015* |
| Most conversions in a match | 13 | *Tammi Wilson v North Harbour, 1999* |
| Most penalty goals in a match | 6 | *Annaleah Rush v Wellington, 2001* |
| Highest team score | 116 | *v North Harbour, 1999* |
| Record victory (points ahead) | 116 | *116-0 v North Harbour, 1999* |
| Highest score conceded | 43 | *34-43 v Waikato, 2017* |
| Record defeat (points behind) | 24 | *12-36 v Counties Manukau, 2017* |

Auckland had appeared in every championship final since the competition commenced in 1999 and had lost only two of the 17 finals — to Wellington in 2006, and to Counties Manukau in 2016. But, for the first time, the 2017 final was played without Auckland present. Counties Manukau, who had defeated Auckland in the 2016 final, comfortably beat their northern neighbours 36–12 in the round robin and carried away the JJ Stewart Trophy. Counties Manukau again defeated Auckland, in a much closer contest, in the semi-final. The drawn game against Bay of Plenty was a surprising result; so too the drawn game against Manawatu. The best result was against Canterbury, won 41–12, when the eventual champions suffered their only loss of the season.

Despite having many players involved in the Black Ferns Sevens and at the Rugby World Cup, Auckland had many experienced players for the championship campaign, including Emma Jensen, Mele Hufanga and Karina Stowers. The Black Ferns had just arrived home from their successful World Cup tournament when the Farah Palmer Cup commenced. When the Black Ferns deserved a well-earned rest, they were brought back into service for the Storm to help steady a battling team. Finishing fourth after the round robin was the Storm's poorest result ever, but it reflects the rising standard of other unions more so than any lowering of Auckland's standard of play.

During the season Black Ferns Rugby World Cup-winning captain Fiao'o Fa'amausili became the first to play 100 championship games for a union.

## AUCKLAND REPRESENTATIVES 2017

| | Club | Games for Union | Points for Union | | Club | Games for Union | Points for Union |
|---|---|---|---|---|---|---|---|
| Jacqui Aiono | Marist | 2 | 0 | Hasting Leiataua | Marist | 12 | 20 |
| Eloise Blackwell | Ponsonby | 45 | 50 | Onjeurlina Leiataua | Marist | 44 | 45 |
| Rebecca Burch | College Rifles | 16 | 0 | Ricshay Lemanu | Papatoetoe | 2 | 0 |
| Kalo Cuthers | Marist | 2 | 0 | Charmaine McMenamin | Ponsonby | 42 | 45 |
| Ruahei Demant | College Rifles | 22 | 60 | Lose Mafi | Marist | 10 | 10 |
| Fiao'o Fa'amausili | Marist | 102 | 225 | Corina Nanai | College Rifles | 3 | 0 |
| Joanna Fanene | Marist | 6 | 15 | Aleisha Nelson | Ponsonby | 54 | 60 |
| Moana Fineaso-Levi | Marist | 6 | 10 | Tiana Ngawati | College Rifles | 17 | 20 |
| Chinatsu Fukuda | Ponsonby | 1 | 0 | Bridie Reeves | College Rifles | 3 | 0 |
| Charlene Gubb | College Rifles | 38 | 45 | Maki Saena | Marist | 3 | 0 |
| Vicky Henry | Waitakere | 2 | 0 | Fa'asea Sao-Taliu | College Rifles | 8 | 0 |
| Mele Hufanga | Marist | 41 | 180 | Karina Stowers | Marist | 75 | 55 |
| Manutalaaho Huni | Marist | 2 | 0 | Leanne Thompson | College Rifles | 16 | 15 |
| Aldora Itunu | Ponsonby | 31 | 65 | Malia Tova | Marist | 12 | 30 |
| Linda Itunu | Ponsonby | 47 | 45 | Clementine Varea | College Rifles | 4 | 0 |
| Emma Jensen | College Rifles | 82 | 452 | Aeron Warbrooke | Ponsonby | 16 | 0 |
| Eleni Leiataua | Marist | 8 | 0 | Hinemoa Watene | College Rifles | 4 | 10 |

## INDIVIDUAL SCORING

| | Tries | Con | PG | DG | Points | | Tries | Con | PG | DG | Points |
|---|---|---|---|---|---|---|---|---|---|---|---|
| Jensen | 1 | 11 | 1 | – | 30 | Fineaso-Levi | 2 | – | – | – | 10 |
| Gubb | 4 | – | – | – | 20 | Stowers | 2 | – | – | – | 10 |
| Nelson | 4 | – | – | – | 20 | Watene | 2 | – | – | – | 10 |
| Fanene | 3 | – | – | – | 15 | Fa'amausili | 1 | – | – | – | 5 |
| Hufanga | 3 | – | – | – | 15 | O. Leiataua | 1 | – | – | – | 5 |
| H. Laiataua | 3 | – | – | – | 15 | | | | | | |
| Ngawati | 3 | – | – | – | 15 | **Totals** | **34** | **12** | **1** | **0** | **197** |
| Thompson | 3 | – | – | – | 15 | | | | | | |
| Demant | 2 | 1 | – | – | 12 | Opposition scored | 26 | 14 | 5 | 0 | 173 |

Higher honours went to:

**New Zealand:** Blackwell, Fa'amausili, T.M. Fitzpatrick, Gubb, A. Itunu, L. Itunu, McMenamin, Nelson

**New Zealand Sevens:** T.M. Fitzpatrick, K.M. McAlister, T.B. Nathan-Wong, N.L.V. Williams

| AUCKLAND 2017 | Bay of Plenty | Canterbury | Counties Manukau | Wellington | North Harbour | Manawatu | Waikato | Counties Manukau | TOTALS |
|---|---|---|---|---|---|---|---|---|---|
| H. Leiataua | 15 | 15 | 15 | – | – | – | – | – | 3 |
| T.A. Ngawati | 11 | – | 14 | 15 | 15 | 15 | – | 15 | 6 |
| L. Mafi | 14 | – | s | 14 | – | – | 14 | – | 4 |
| C. Nanai | – | 14 | s | – | – | – | – | s | 3 |
| R.L.V. Lemanu | – | – | – | – | 11 | – | s | – | 2 |
| H.H. Watene | – | – | – | – | s | 11 | 15 | 11 | 4 |
| E. Leiataua | s | 11 | 11 | 11 | 13 | 13 | 12 | 12 | 8 |
| M.M. Hufanga (co-capt) | 12 | 13 | 13 | 13 | 14 | 14 | 13 | 14 | 8 |
| O.F. Leiataua | 13 | 12 | 12 | 12 | 12 | 12 | 11 | 13 | 8 |
| M.K. Tova | 10 | – | – | – | s | – | – | – | 2 |
| D.R. Demant | – | 10 | 10 | 10 | 10 | – | 10 | 10 | 6 |
| C. Fukuda | – | s | – | – | – | – | – | – | 1 |
| E.M. Jensen | 9 | 9 | 9 | 9 | 9 | 10 | 9 | 9 | 8 |
| A.K. Warbrooke | – | – | – | – | s | 9 | – | s | 3 |
| J. Fanene | 8 | 8 | – | 6 | 6 | 6 | s | – | 6 |
| J.F. Aiono | s | s | – | – | – | – | – | – | 2 |
| C. Varea | s | s | 8 | – | – | – | s | – | 4 |
| C.J. McMenamin | – | – | s | 8 | 8 | s | 8 | 7 | 6 |
| L.F. Itunu | – | – | – | – | s | 8 | – | 8 | 3 |
| A. Fineasi-Levi | 7 | 7 | 7 | 7 | – | s | 6 | – | 6 |
| L.P. Thompson | 6 | 6 | 6 | s | 7 | 7 | 7 | s | 8 |
| B. Reeves | 5 | s | – | s | – | – | – | – | 3 |
| C.P.T. Gubb | s | 5 | 5 | 5 | 5 | 5 | 5 | 5 | 8 |
| R.M. Burch | 4 | 4 | 4 | 4 | s | 4 | – | s | 7 |
| M.H. Huni | s | s | – | – | – | – | – | – | 2 |
| E.S. Blackwell | – | – | s | – | 4 | – | 4 | 4 | 4 |
| A.T. Cuthers | 3 | 3 | – | – | – | – | – | – | 2 |
| A.P. Nelson | – | – | – | 3 | 3 | 3 | 3 | 3 | 5 |
| F. Sao-Taliu | 1 | 1 | 3 | 1 | s | s | 1 | s | 8 |
| V. Henry | s | s | – | – | – | – | – | – | 2 |
| A.T. Itunu | – | – | 1 | s | s | 1 | s | 1 | 6 |
| M. Saena | – | – | s | s | – | s | – | – | 3 |
| K.E. Stowers (co-capt) | 2 | 2 | 2 | 2 | 1 | 2 | 2 | 2 | 8 |
| F.M. Fa'amausili | – | s | s | – | 2 | – | s | 6 | 5 |

## AUCKLAND TEAM RECORD, 2017

**Played 8    Won 3    Drew 2    Lost 3    Points for 197    Points against 173**

| Date | Opponent | Location | Score | Tries | Con | PG | DG | Referee |
|---|---|---|---|---|---|---|---|---|
| September 2 | Bay of Plenty (P/C) | Whakatane | 10–10 | Stowers, Thompson | | | | B. Roberts |
| September 9 | Canterbury (P, ST) | Auckland | 41–12 | H. Leiataua (2), Fineaso-Levi (2), Fanene, Hufanga, Gubb | Jensen (3) | | | S.B. Fellows |
| September 16 | Counties Manukau (P, ST) | Pakuranga | 12–36 | H. Leiataua, Ngawati | Demant | | | R.G. Borthwick |
| September 23 | Wellington (P) | Porirua | 31–30 | Ngawati (2), Gubb, O. Leiataua, Fanene | Jensen (3) | | | M.J. McEwen |
| September 29 | North Harbour (P/C) | Albany | 37–5 | Gubb, Demant, Fanene, Hufanga, Nelson, Thompson, Fa'amausili | Jensen | | | R.M. Mahoney |
| October 7 | Manawatu (P) | Palmerston North | 15–15 | Thompson, Nelson, Gubb | | | | L.A. Jenner |
| October 14 | Waikato (P) | Pakuranga | 34–43 | Nelson (2), Watene, Stowers, Demant | Jensen (3) | Jensen | | L.A. Jenner |
| October 21 | Counties Manukau (semi-final) | Pukekohe | 17–22 | Watene, Jensen, Hufanga | Jensen | | | R.G. Borthwick |

ST Stewart Trophy

# BAY OF PLENTY VOLCANIX

**2017 Status:** Championship
**NPC participation:** 1999–2005, 2014–
**Coach:** Brendon Webby
**Assistant coaches:** Zane Winslade, Mike Lewis
**Home Grounds:** Rotorua International Stadium; Rugby Park,
Whakatane; Tauranga Domain; Blake Park,
Mount Maunganui

## RECORDS

| | | |
|---|---|---|
| **Most appearances** | 35 | *Lisa Mansell, 1999–2015* |
| **Most points** | 90 | *Tamaku Paul, 1999–2002* |
| **Most tries** | 18 | *Tamaku Paul, 1999–2002* |
| **Most points in a season** | 55 | *Tamaku Paul, 1999* |
| **Most tries in a season** | 11 | *Tamaku Paul, 1999* |
| **Most conversions in a season** | 12 | *Puawai Hohepa, 2004* |
| **Most penalty goals in a season** | 3 | *Puawai Hohepa, 2000;* |
| | | *Exia Shelford, 2003* |
| | | *Kymbillie Raynes, 2016* |
| **Most dropped goals in a season** | 1 | *Puawai Hohepa, 2000* |
| **Most points in a match** | 20 | *Tamaku Paul v Counties Manukau, 1999* |
| **Most tries in a match** | 4 | *Tamaku Paul v Counties Manukau, 1999* |
| **Most conversions in a match** | 5 | *Exia Shelford v Counties Manukau, 2003* |
| **Most penalty goals in a match** | 2 | *Heidi Reader v Northland, 1999;* |
| | | *Puawai Hohepa v Waikato, 2000* |
| | | *Kymbillie Raynes v North Harbour, 2016* |
| **Highest team score** | 60 | *v Counties Manukau, 1999* |
| **Record victory (points ahead)** | 60 | *60–0 v Counties Manukau, 1999* |
| **Highest score conceded** | 101 | *v Auckland, 2015* |
| **Record defeat (points behind)** | 101 | *0–101 v Auckland, 2015* |

The Volcanix made a strong statement in the opening round by drawing with Auckland, then marched on to win four of the remaining five games in the Championship division. The only loss, by just two points, was to Waikato. Finishing top of the Championship ladder the Volcanix, by competition regulations, went directly to the final. Having had a bye in the last round, and not having to play a semi-final, the team sat out two weekends before meeting Otago in the final. Defeating Otago 7–5 to claim the Championship trophy, Bay of Plenty enjoyed a remarkable season, considering only one win had been registered in the previous three seasons. They played very attractive rugby, and promotion to the Premiership division for 2018 is the reward for a fine season.

There was not a lot of experience within the squad, but they had the services of former Black Fern Lesley Elder for the later games and also fullback Crystal Mayes, a former Manawatu player who had moved north as a Black Ferns Sevens contracted player. Luka Connor, the Volcanix's most experienced representative, was the team's standout performer. Only 20 years of age, yet in her fourth season in the team, Connor scored tries in each of the first five games and finished the season with eight tries, the most by anyone in the 2017 Farah Palmer Cup. What makes her feat more remarkable is that she played at prop. Wing Autumn Stephens-Daly was another player to impress among a squad that has rapidly lifted women's rugby in the Bay to become a team to be respected by the larger unions.

## BAY OF PLENTY REPRESENTATIVES 2017

| | Club | Games for Union | Points for Union |
|---|---|---|---|
| Amanda Aldridge | Rangiuru | 5 | 0 |
| Seqouia Autumn Te Aonui | Waikite | 7 | 5 |
| Julia Buescher | Rangataua | 7 | 0 |
| Brigid Cameron | Rangataua | 1 | 0 |
| Aryahn Clarke | Rangiuru | 11 | 15 |
| Luka Connor | Waikite | 25 | 50 |
| Christine Corbett | Whakarewarewa | 3 | 0 |
| Makayla Daysh | Rangataua | 5 | 0 |
| Lesley Elder (nee Ketu) | Rangataua | 3 | 0 |
| Lily Florence | Whakarewarewa | 13 | 0 |
| Kate Henwood | Rangataua | 13 | 0 |
| Kororia Heyblom | Rangiuru | 2 | 0 |
| Baye Jacob | Rangiuru | 12 | 0 |
| Kaci James | Whakarewarewa | 19 | 0 |
| Sarah Kay | Rangataua | 1 | 0 |
| Julie Lewis (nee Howard) | Whakarewarewa | 10 | 0 |

| | Club | Games for Union | Points for Union |
|---|---|---|---|
| Crystal Mayes | Kia Toa[1] | 7 | 23 |
| Polly Playle | Rotoiti | 6 | 0 |
| Tania-Rose Raharuhi | Whakarewarewa | 7 | 0 |
| Kendra Reynolds | Rangiuru | 19 | 0 |
| Zaan Scott | Rangataua | 5 | 0 |
| Autumn Stephens-Daly | Waikite | 17 | 20 |
| Nadine Stone | Whakarewarewa | 8 | 0 |
| Sapphire Tapsell | Rangiuru | 13 | 15 |
| Teilani Thompson | Rotoiti | 1 | 0 |
| Jade Tuilaepa | Rangataua | 4 | 5 |
| Braxton Walker | Rangiuru | 3 | 0 |
| Shaye Whareaorere | Rangiuru | 11 | 4 |
| Ereti Williams | Rangiuru | 17 | 15 |
| Ora Williams | Rotoiti | 6 | 15 |
| Christie Yule | Rangiuru | 12 | 0 |

[1] Manawatu RU

## INDIVIDUAL SCORING

| | Tries | Con | PG | DG | Points |
|---|---|---|---|---|---|
| Connor | 8 | – | – | – | 40 |
| Mayes | 1 | 9 | – | – | 23 |
| Stephens-Daly | 4 | – | – | – | 20 |
| Clarke | 3 | – | – | – | 15 |
| Tapsell | 3 | – | – | – | 15 |
| E. Williams | 3 | – | – | – | 15 |
| O. Williams | 3 | – | – | – | 15 |

| | Tries | Con | PG | DG | Points |
|---|---|---|---|---|---|
| Autumn Te Aonui | 1 | – | – | – | 5 |
| Tuilaepa | 1 | – | – | – | 5 |
| Whareaorere | – | 2 | – | – | 4 |
| **Totals** | **27** | **11** | **0** | **0** | **157** |
| Opposition scored | 15 | 5 | 1 | 0 | 88 |

Higher honours went to:
**New Zealand:** K.A. Brazier
**New Zealand Sevens:** M.G. Blyde, K.A. Brazier

### BAY OF PLENTY 2017

| | Auckland | Hawke's Bay | North Harbour | Tasman | Waikato | Otago | Otago | TOTALS |
|---|---|---|---|---|---|---|---|---|
| C.A.M. Mayes | 15 | 15 | 15 | 15 | 15 | 15 | 15 | 7 |
| S.N.K. Tapsell | 14 | 14 | 11 | 11 | 14 | 11 | 14 | 7 |
| A-R. Stephens-Daly | 11 | 11 | 14 | 14 | 11 | 14 | 11 | 7 |
| Z. Scott | s | s | s | s | – | s | – | 5 |
| N.M.M. Stone | – | – | – | s | – | – | – | 1 |
| A.T. Clarke | 13 | 13 | 13 | 13 | 13 | 13 | 13 | 7 |
| S-M.L. Whareaorere | 12 | 12 | 12 | s | 10 | 10 | 10 | 7 |
| T-R.N. Raharuhi | s | s | s | 12 | 12 | 12 | 12 | 7 |
| K.F. Heyblom | – | – | – | – | – | s | s | 2 |
| O.P.R. Williams | 10 | 10 | 10 | 10 | – | 9 | 9 | 6 |
| P-J.M. Playle | 9 | – | – | – | – | – | – | 1 |
| B.I. Cameron | s | – | – | – | – | – | – | 1 |
| J.U. Tuilaepa | – | 9 | 9 | 9 | 9 | – | – | 4 |
| S.L. Kay | – | – | s | – | – | – | – | 1 |
| S. Autumn Te Aonui | 8 | 8 | 8 | 8 | 8 | 8 | 8 | 7 |
| K.L. Reynolds | 7 | – | 7 | 7 | 7 | 6 | – | 5 |
| L-A.T. Elder | – | – | – | – | s | 7 | 7 | 3 |
| C.E. Yule (co-capt) | 6 | 6 | 6 | 6 | 6 | 4 | 6 | 7 |
| C. James (co-capt) | 5 | 5 | 5 | 5 | 5 | 5 | 5 | 7 |
| K.K. Henwood | 4 | – | – | – | – | – | – | 1 |
| J.M. Buescher | s | 4 | 4 | 4 | 4 | s | 4 | 7 |
| M.A. Daysh | s | s | s | s | – | – | – | 4 |
| A. Aldridge | – | s | s | s | s | s | – | 5 |
| T.V. Thompson | – | – | – | – | – | s | – | 1 |
| B.L. Jacob | 3 | 3 | – | – | – | – | – | 2 |
| E.R.R. Williams | 2 | 2 | 3 | 3 | 3 | 3 | – | 6 |
| C.A. Corbett | – | s | s | s | – | – | – | 3 |
| B.M.M. Walker | – | – | – | – | s | s | 3 | 3 |
| L. Connor | 1 | 1 | 1 | 1 | 1 | 1 | 1 | 7 |
| J.A. Lewis | s | s | 2 | 2 | s | s | s | 7 |
| L.J. Florence | s | 7 | s | s | 2 | 2 | 2 | 7 |

## BAY OF PLENTY TEAM RECORD, 2017

Played 7  Won 5  Drew 1  Lost 1  Points for 157  Points against 88

| Date | Opponent | Location | Score | Tries | Con | PG | DG | Referee |
|---|---|---|---|---|---|---|---|---|
| September 2 | Auckland (C/P) | Whakatane | 10–10 | Connor, E. Williams | | | | B. Roberts |
| September 9 | Hawke's Bay (C) | Napier | 24–10 | Connor (2), Tuilaepa, Clarke | Whareaorere (2) | | | M. Cogger-Orr |
| September 16 | North Harbour (C) | Rotorua | 34–12 | Connor (2), Stephens-Daly (2), E. Williams, Mayes | Mayes (2) | | | M. Cogger-Orr |
| September 24 | Tasman (C) | Tauranga | 38–15 | Stephens-Daly (2), O. Williams, Connor, Tapsell, Autumn Te Aonui | Mayes (4) | | | L.A. Jenner |
| September 30 | Waikato (C/P) | Hamilton | 17–19 | Connor (2), Tapsell | Mayes | | | L.A. Jenner |
| October 7 | Otago (C) | Dunedin | 27–17 | Clarke (2), O. Williams (2), E. Williams | Mayes | | | N.M. Ganley |
| October 28 | Otago (C final) | Mt Maunganui | 7–5 | Tapsell | Mayes | | | M. Cogger-Orr |

# CANTERBURY

*2017 Status:* Premiership
*NPC participation:* 1999–
*Coach:* Wayne Love
*Assistant coaches:* Kieran Kite, Melissa Ruscoe
*Home Ground:* Linfield Park; AMI Stadium
(v Tasman and Waikato)

## RECORDS

| | | |
|---|---|---|
| Most appearances | 81 | *Stephanie Te Ohaere-Fox, 2004-17* |
| Most points | 684 | *Kendra Cocksedge, 2007-17* |
| Most tries | 43 | *Kendra Cocksedge, 2007-17* |
| Most points in a season | 107 | *Kendra Cocksedge, 2016* |
| Most tries in a season | 8 | *Kendra Cocksedge, 2016* |
| Most conversions in a season | 24 | *Kendra Cocksedge, 2014* |
| Most penalty goals in a season | 11 | *Kendra Cocksedge, 2014* |
| Most dropped goals in a season | 1 | *Charntay Poko, 2017* |
| Most points in a match | 30 | *Kendra Cocksedge, v Taranaki, 2013* |
| | | *v North Harbour, 2016* |
| Most tries in a match | 4 | *Stephanie Mortimer v Waikato, 2004;* |
| | | *Kendra Cocksedge, v Taranaki, 2013* |
| Most conversions in a match | 8 | *Kendra Cocksedge v Hawke's Bay, 2012* |
| Most penalty goals in a match | 5 | *Kendra Cocksedge v Auckland, 2009* |
| | | *v Waikato, 2016* |
| Highest team score | 92 | *v Taranaki, 2013* |
| Record victory (points ahead) | 80 | *92–12 v Taranaki, 2013* |
| Highest score conceded | 70 | *v Auckland, 2015* |
| Record defeat (points behind) | 62 | *8–70 v Auckland, 2015* |

Canterbury had taken part in six championship finals but each time was defeated by Auckland. And it was Auckland again that inflicted Canterbury's only defeat of 2017. Canterbury was in commanding form through the other round-robin games and included the winning of the Stewart Trophy (the Ranfurly Shield of women's rugby) from Counties Manukau, at Papakura, and two successful defences at home. Having comfortably disposed of Waikato in a semi-final, Canterbury returned north for the final against defending Cup holders Counties Manukau. The final was won 13–7 and the Canterbury union added the Farah Palmer Cup to its trophy cabinet alongside the Mitre 10 Cup won by the men the previous day.

Experienced halfback Kendra Cocksedge returned from the Black Ferns triumph in Ireland and again played a major role in Canterbury's backline play. An astute playmaker, she extended her remarkable points-scoring records in provincial rugby. Stephanie Te Ohaere-Fox again led the team and the championship success was of immense satisfaction to her considering she had played in each of the previous six finals defeats. Canterbury was a team of few stars but was very efficient and controlled, and players emerged who will become contenders for Black Ferns honours.

## CANTERBURY REPRESENTATIVES 2017

| | Club | Games for Union | Points for Union |
|---|---|---|---|
| Lucy Anderson | Christchurch | 29 | 45 |
| Alana Bremner | Lincoln Univ | 24 | 0 |
| Chelsea Bremner | Lincoln Univ | 9 | 5 |
| Grace Brooker | Christchurch | 7 | 25 |
| Kendra Cocksedge | Canterbury Univ | 67 | 684 |
| Sam Curtis | Christchurch | 12 | 35 |
| Taylor Curtis | Christchurch | 6 | 0 |
| Becky Davidson | Lincoln Univ | 8 | 20 |
| Kate Ebrahim | Lincoln Univ | 3 | 0 |
| Catriona Greenslade | Burnside-Dunsandel-Irwell | 4 | 0 |
| Jess Hansen | Canterbury Univ | 22 | 15 |
| Lucy Jenkins | Christchurch | 8 | 0 |
| Zoe Johnson | Christchurch | 3 | 0 |
| Rosie Kelly | HSOB | 4 | 0 |
| Phillipa Love | Christchurch | 21 | 35 |

| | Club | Games for Union | Points for Union |
|---|---|---|---|
| Olivia McGoverne | Canterbury Univ | 19 | 57 |
| Sui Pauaraisa | Suburbs | 17 | 5 |
| Elizabeth Pera | Canterbury Univ | 28 | 35 |
| Charntay Poko | Suburbs | 32 | 65 |
| Nina Poletti | Christchurch | 8 | 10 |
| Melanie Puckett | Canterbury Univ | 5 | 10 |
| Nicole Purdom | Canterbury Univ | 20 | 20 |
| Cassie Siataga | Lincoln Univ | 8 | 7 |
| Usipua Simaile | Christchurch | 8 | 0 |
| Kaylee Tavendale | Christchurch | 13 | 0 |
| Stephanie Te Ohaere-Fox | Christchurch | 81 | 75 |
| Charna Thompson | Christchurch | 11 | 0 |
| Rebecca Todd | Christchurch | 16 | 20 |
| Estelle Uren | Christchurch | 29 | 50 |
| Corrina Whiley | Suburbs | 24 | 65 |

## INDIVIDUAL SCORING

| | Tries | Con | PG | DG | Points |
|---|---|---|---|---|---|
| Cocksedge | 5 | 21 | 2 | – | 73 |
| S. Curtis | 6 | – | – | – | 30 |
| Whiley | 6 | – | – | – | 30 |
| Brooker | 5 | – | – | – | 25 |
| Purdom | 4 | – | – | – | 20 |
| Todd | 4 | – | – | – | 20 |
| Poko | – | 4 | 3 | 1 | 20 |
| Anderson | 3 | – | – | – | 15 |
| Davidson | 3 | – | – | – | 15 |
| Hansen | 2 | – | – | – | 10 |
| Love | 2 | – | – | – | 10 |

| | Tries | Con | PG | DG | Points |
|---|---|---|---|---|---|
| Poletti | 2 | – | – | – | 10 |
| Puckett | 2 | – | – | – | 10 |
| Te Ohaere-Fox | 2 | – | – | – | 10 |
| Uren | 2 | – | – | – | 10 |
| McGoverne | 1 | 1 | 1 | – | 10 |
| Siataga | 1 | 1 | – | – | 7 |
| C. Bremner | 1 | – | – | – | 5 |
| **Totals** | **51** | **27** | **6** | **1** | **330** |
| Opposition scored | 31 | 14 | 1 | 0 | 186 |

Higher honours went to:
*New Zealand:* Cocksedge, Love
*New Zealand Sevens:* R. Tui

## CANTERBURY 2017

| | Otago | Auckland | Manawatu | Counties Manukau | Tasman | Waikato | Wellington | Waikato | Counties Manukau | TOTALS |
|---|---|---|---|---|---|---|---|---|---|---|
| O.B. McGoverne | 15 | 15 | – | – | 15 | s | s | 15 | 15 | 7 |
| G.E. Brooker | – | – | 15 | 15 | s | 15 | 15 | 11 | 11 | 7 |
| S.G.B. Curtis | 14 | – | 14 | 14 | 14 | 14 | 14 | 14 | – | 7 |
| B.L. Davidson | 11 | – | – | – | 11 | 11 | – | – | – | 3 |
| T.R.B. Curtis | s | 11 | s | – | – | – | – | – | – | 3 |
| M.C. Puckett | – | – | 11 | 11 | – | – | 11 | s | 14 | 5 |
| C. Siataga | 13 | s | s | s | s | 10 | 10 | s | – | 8 |
| C. Whiley | s | 13 | – | – | – | 13 | 13 | 13 | 13 | 6 |
| E.P. Pera | s | 14 | 13 | 13 | 13 | s | – | – | – | 6 |
| Z.K. Johnson | – | s | – | – | – | – | – | – | – | 1 |
| L.E. Anderson | 12 | 12 | 12 | 12 | 12 | 12 | 12 | 12 | 12 | 9 |
| C.E. Poko | 10 | 10 | 10 | 10 | 10 | – | – | 10 | 10 | 7 |
| K. Ebrahim | 9 | 9 | 9 | – | – | – | – | – | – | 3 |
| R. Kelly | – | – | s | – | s | s | – | s | – | 4 |
| K.M. Cocksedge | – | – | – | 9 | 9 | 9 | 9 | 9 | 9 | 6 |
| R.A. Todd | 2 | 2 | 8 | 8 | 8 | 8 | 8 | 8 | 8 | 9 |
| S. Pauaraisa | 7 | – | s | – | – | – | 7 | s | – | 4 |
| L.V.M. Jenkins | 6 | 7 | 7 | 7 | 7 | 7 | – | 7 | 7 | 8 |
| N.J. Purdom | 8 | 8 | 6 | 6 | 6 | 6 | 6 | 6 | 6 | 9 |
| C.J. Thompson | s | 6 | – | s | s | s | s | s | s | 8 |
| C.J. Greenslade | – | s | – | – | – | – | – | – | – | 1 |
| C.J. Bremner | 5 | s | s | – | s | s | 5 | s | s | 8 |
| E.D. Uren | – | 5 | 5 | 5 | 5 | 5 | – | 5 | 5 | 7 |
| A.J. Bremner | 4 | 4 | 4 | 4 | – | 4 | 4 | 4 | 4 | 8 |
| K.V. Tavendale | s | s | – | – | 4 | – | s | – | – | 4 |
| S.A. Te Ohaere-Fox (capt) | 3 | – | 3 | 3 | 3 | 3 | 3 | 3 | 3 | 8 |
| P.E.A. Love | – | 1 | 1 | 1 | s | 1 | 1 | 1 | 1 | 8 |
| U. Simaile | s | s | s | – | 1 | s | s | – | – | 6 |
| J.E. Hansen | 1 | 3 | 2 | 2 | 2 | 2 | 2 | 2 | 2 | 9 |
| N.J.N. Poletti | s | s | s | – | s | s | s | s | s | 8 |

Todd was captain v Auckland.

## CANTERBURY TEAM RECORD, 2017

**Played 9   Won 8   Lost 1   Points for 330   Points against 186**

| Date | Opponent | Location | Score | Tries | Con | PG | DG | Referee |
|---|---|---|---|---|---|---|---|---|
| September 3 | Otago (P/C) | Christchurch | 20–7 | Todd, Purdom, Poletti | Poko | McGoverne | | K. Hancox |
| September 9 | Auckland (P) | Auckland | 12–41 | Love, McGoverne | McGoverne | | | S.B. Fellows |
| September 16 | Manawatu (P) | Christchurch | 40–10 | Brooker (2), Anderson, Puckett, Purdom | Poko (2), Siataga Poko (3) | | | K. Hancox |
| September 23 | Counties Manukau (P, ST) | Papakura | 32–29 | S. Curtis (2), Puckett, Todd, Cocksedge, Brooker | Cocksedge | | | N.M. Ganley |
| September 30 | Tasman (P/C, ST) | Christchurch | 67–12 | Davidson (3), Hansen (2), S. Curtis (2), Uren, Purdom, C. Bremner, Siataga | Cocksedge (5), Poko | | | M. Togger-Orr |
| October 8 | Waikato (P) | Hamilton | 31–20 | Whiley (2), Todd, Cocksedge, Poletti | Cocksedge (3) | | | B. Roberts |
| October 14 | Wellington (P, ST) | Christchurch | 55–34 | Anderson (2), Whiley (2), Cocksedge (2), TeOhaere-Fox, Purdom | Cocksedge (6) | Cocksedge | | R.J.M Gordon |
| October 21 | Waikato (semi-final) | Christchurch | 60–26 | S. Curtis (2), Brooker (2), Whiley (2), Uren, Love, Cocksedge, TeOhaere-Fox | Cocksedge (5) | | | N.M. Ganley |
| October 29 | Counties Manukau (final) | Pukekohe | 13–7 | Todd | Cocksedge | Cocksedge | Poko | N.M. Ganley |

ST Stewart Trophy

# COUNTIES MANUKAU HEAT

*2017 Status:* Premiership
*NPC participation:* 1999–2005, 2013–
*Coach:* Davida White
*Assistant coaches:* Josh Levi, Jeremy Clark
*Home grounds:* ECO Light Stadium, Pukekohe;
Massey Park, Papakura

## RECORDS

| | | |
|---|---|---|
| Most appearances | 37 | *Arihiana Marino 2013-17* |
| Most points | 210 | *Hazel Tubic, 2005-17* |
| Most tries | 24 | *Te Kura Ngata-Aerengamate, 2013-17* |
| Most points in a season | 78 | *Hazel Tubic, 2017* |
| Most tries in a season | 10 | *Renee Wickliffe, 2015* |
| Most conversions in a season | 28 | *Hazel Tubic 2017* |
| Most penalty goals in a season | 8 | *Hazel Tubic, 2013* |
| Most dropped goals in a season | 0 | |
| Most points in a match | 27 | *Hazel Tubic v Taranaki, 2013* |
| Most tries in a match | 4 | *Renee Wickliffe v Otago, 2015* |
| | | *Portia Woodman v Wellington 2016* |
| Most conversions in a match | 7 | *Hazel Tubic v Taranaki, 2013* |
| Most penalty goals in a match | 4 | *Hazel Tubic v Auckland, 2013* |
| Highest team score | 84 | *v North Harbour, 2017* |
| Record victory (points ahead) | 77 | *84-7 v North Harbour, 2017* |
| Highest score conceded | 65 | *v Auckland B, 2005* |
| Record defeat (points behind) | 65 | *0–65 v Auckland B, 2005* |

Like Auckland, Counties Manukau Heat was well represented in the Black Ferns World Cup squad and the returning players were quickly brought into the squad for the Farah Palmer Cup campaign. The defending champions commenced in convincing fashion, scoring 130 points in the first two games while conceding only one try. The JJ Stewart Trophy was won off Auckland, then surprisingly lost the following week to challengers Canterbury. Finishing at the top of the table after the round robin, the team defeated Auckland in the home semi-final but then lost the final, played at home, to a well-drilled Canterbury team.

Missing from the 2017 squad were Rawinia Everitt (injured), Renee Wickliffe and Portia Woodman, the latter two returning to the Black Ferns Sevens programme upon their arrival back from the successful World Cup campaign. Halfback Arihiana Marino was again a fine captain. Victoria Subritzky-Nafatali has proven to be more than just a strong ball carrier as she impressed with her sound tactical kicking both at the World Cup and for the Heat. Hazel Tubic involved herself in attacking play as well as being a reliable goal-kicker. Her outstanding season was rewarded when she became the first recipient of the Fiao'o Fa'amausili Medal for the Farah Palmer Cup player of the year. The solid forward pack wore down all opposition except Canterbury. The front row of Te Kura Ngata-Aerengamate, Aotearoa Matau and Leilani Perese was a formidable combination.

## COUNTIES MANUKAU REPRESENTATIVES 2017

| | Club | Games for Union | Points for Union | | Club | Games for Union | Points for Union |
|---|---|---|---|---|---|---|---|
| Utumalama Atonio | Ardmore Marist | 7 | 10 | Serai Murray-Wihongi | Manurewa | 6 | 5 |
| Hanna Brough | Ardmore Marist | 31 | 5 | Te Kura Ngata-Aerengamate | Ardmore Marist | 36 | 120 |
| Stacey Brown | Manurewa | 26 | 5 | Yuki Ono | Ardmore Marist | 10 | 15 |
| Grace Gago | Manurewa | 6 | 0 | Isabel Ozorio | Ardmore Marist | 8 | 2 |
| Aroha Heta | Manurewa | 2 | 20 | Leilani Perese | Manurewa | 15 | 15 |
| Harono Iringa | Manurewa | 8 | 5 | Hinewai Pomare | Manurewa | 25 | 20 |
| Emily Kitson | Ardmore Marist | 4 | 5 | Bernadette Robertson | Ardmore Marist | 8 | 25 |
| Justine Lavea | Ardmore Marist | 17 | 15 | Lauryn Steed | Ardmore Marist | 7 | 5 |
| Timara Leaf | Manurewa | 17 | 15 | Victoria Subritzky-Nafatali | Ardmore Marist | 16 | 67 |
| Georgina Lidgard | Manurewa | 4 | 0 | Amiria Te Iringa | Manurewa | 3 | 0 |
| Larissa Lima E Silva | Ardmore Marist | 8 | 0 | Hazel Tubic | Manurewa | 28 | 210 |
| Arihiana Marino | Manurewa | 37 | 168 | Lanulangi Veainu | Ardmore Marist | 14 | 45 |
| Kate Matau | Ardmore Marist | 28 | 50 | Cindy Wong | Ardmore Marist | 3 | 0 |
| Victoria Meki | Ardmore Marist | 21 | 0 | | | | |

## INDIVIDUAL SCORING

| | Tries | Con | PG | DG | Points | | Tries | Con | PG | DG | Points |
|---|---|---|---|---|---|---|---|---|---|---|---|
| Tubic | 2 | 28 | 4 | – | 78 | Perese | 2 | – | – | – | 10 |
| Matau | 5 | – | – | – | 25 | penalty try | 1 | – | – | – | 7 |
| Robertson | 5 | – | – | – | 25 | Brough | 1 | – | – | – | 5 |
| Heta | 4 | – | – | – | 20 | Brown | 1 | – | – | – | 5 |
| Marino | 4 | – | – | – | 20 | Iringa | 1 | – | – | – | 5 |
| Ngata-Aerengamate | 4 | – | – | – | 20 | Kitson | 1 | – | – | – | 5 |
| Subritzky-Nafatali | 4 | – | – | – | 20 | Murray-Wihongi | 1 | – | – | – | 5 |
| Leaf | 3 | – | – | – | 15 | Ozorio | – | 1 | – | – | 2 |
| Ono | 3 | – | – | – | 15 | | | | | | |
| Veainu | 3 | – | – | – | 15 | **Totals** | **49\*** | **29** | **4** | **0** | **317** |
| Atonio | 2 | – | – | – | 10 | | | | | | |
| Lavea | 2 | – | – | – | 10 | Opposition scored | 15 | 5 | 2 | 1 | 94 |

Higher honours went to:

**New Zealand:** R.P. Everitt, Mata'u, Ngata-Aerengamate, Savage, Subritzky-Nafatali, Tubic, R.W.M. Wickliffe, P.L. Woodman

**New Zealand Sevens:** R.W.M. Wickliffe, P.L. Woodman

## COUNTIES MANUKAU 2017

| | North Harbour | Waikato | Auckland | Canterbury | Wellington | Manawatu | Auckland | Canterbury | TOTALS |
|---|---|---|---|---|---|---|---|---|---|
| H.S. Tubic | 15 | 15 | 15 | 15 | 15 | 15 | 15 | 15 | 8 |
| Y. Ono | 14 | 14 | 14 | – | 9 | 11 | s | 9 | 7 |
| S.R. Murray-Wihongi | s | s | s | 14 | 14 | – | – | s | 6 |
| E.F. Kitson | s | – | – | s | s | 14 | – | – | 4 |
| L. Veainu | – | – | 11 | – | – | – | 14 | 14 | 3 |
| M.B.J. Robertson | 11 | 11 | 13 | 11 | 11 | 13 | 11 | 11 | 8 |
| U. Atonio | 13 | 13 | – | 13 | 13 | s | 13 | 13 | 7 |
| T.R. Leaf | 12 | 12 | 12 | 12 | s | 12 | 12 | 12 | 8 |
| I.B. Ozorio | s | s | s | s | s | s | s | s | 8 |
| V.S. Subritzky-Nafatali | 10 | 10 | 10 | 10 | 10 | 10 | 10 | – | 7 |
| A.A.H. Marino (capt) | 9 | 9 | 9 | 9 | 12 | 9 | 9 | 10 | 8 |
| A. Heta | 8 | s | – | – | – | – | – | – | 2 |
| J. Lavea | 7 | 8 | 8 | 8 | 7 | 7 | 7 | 8 | 8 |
| L. Lima E Silva | 6 | 7 | 7 | 7 | s | s | s | 7 | 8 |
| S.J. Brown | s | 6 | 6 | 6 | 6 | 6 | 6 | 6 | 8 |
| V. Meki | – | – | s | – | – | – | – | – | 1 |
| A. Te Iringa | – | – | s | s | – | s | – | – | 3 |
| H.L. Brough | 5 | 5 | 5 | 5 | 4 | 4 | 4 | 4 | 8 |
| G. Lidgard | – | s | s | – | 5 | 5 | – | – | 4 |
| C.B. Wong | – | – | – | – | s | s | 5 | – | 3 |
| H. Iringa | 4 | 4 | 4 | 4 | 8 | 8 | 8 | 5 | 8 |
| L. Steed | 3 | s | – | s | s | s | – | s | 6 |
| L.R.R. Perese | 1 | 3 | 3 | 1 | 1 | 1 | 1 | 1 | 8 |
| A.K. Matau | s | 1 | 1 | 3 | 3 | 3 | 3 | 3 | 8 |
| H. Pomare | s | – | s | – | – | – | – | – | 2 |
| G.L.F. Gago | 2 | s | s | s | s | s | – | | 6 |
| T.R. Ngata-Arengamate | s | 2 | 2 | 2 | 2 | 2 | 2 | 2 | 8 |

## COUNTIES MANUKAU TEAM RECORD, 2017

Played 8    Won 6    Lost 2    Points for 317    Points against 94

| Date | Opponent | Location | Score | Tries | Con | PG | DG | Referee |
|------|----------|----------|-------|-------|-----|-----|-----|---------|
| September 2 | North Harbour (P/C) | Pukekohe | 84–7 | Heta (3), Robertson (3), Ono (2), Lavea, Subritzky-Nafatali, Matau, Ngata-Aerengamate, Brough, Leaf | Tubic (6), Ozorio | | | K.C. Lagerwall |
| September 7 | Waikato (P) | Pukekohe | 48–0 | Marino (2), Atonio, Leaf, Matau, Brown, Heta | Tubic (5) | Tubic | | M.E. Playle |
| September 16 | Auckland (P, ST) | Pakuranga | 36–12 | Veainu (2), Tubic, Marino, Robertson | Tubic (4) | Tubic | | R.G. Borthwick |
| September 23 | Canterbury (P, ST) | Papakura | 29–32 | Murray-Wihongi, Matau, Atonio, Marino, Ngata-Aerengamate | Tubic (2) | | | N.M. Canley |
| October 7 | Wellington (P) | Porirua | 43–13 | Subritzky-Nafatali (3), Lavea, Perese, penalty try | Tubic (4) | Tubic | | Rachel Horton (Australia) |
| October 14 | Manawatu (P) | Palmerston North | 48–0 | Matau (2), H. Iringa, Kitson, Ngata-Aerengamate, Robertson, Tubic, Ono | Tubic (4) | | | N.M. Ganley |
| October 21 | Auckland (semi-final) | Pukekohe | 22–17 | Ngata-Aerengamate, Perese, Leaf | Tubic (2) | Tubic | | R.G. Borthwick |
| October 29 | Canterbury (final) | Pukekohe | 7–13 | Veainu | Tubic | | | N.M. Ganley |

ST Stewart Trophy

# HAWKE'S BAY TUIS

*2017 Status:* Championship
*NPC participation:* 1999–2012, 2014–2015, 2017
*Coach:* Terangi Maeva
*Home grounds:* Tremain Field, Park Island, Napier

## RECORDS

| | | |
|---|---|---|
| Most appearances | 64 | *Chanel Huddleston, 2001–14* |
| Most points | 192 | *Nerina Hawkins, 1999–2004* |
| Most tries | 21 | *Deidre Hakopa, 1999–2009* |
| Most points in a season | 61 | *Nerina Hawkins, 2003* |
| Most tries in a season | 9 | *Deidre Hakopa, 2003* |
| Most conversions in a season | 16 | *Nerina Hawkins, 2003* |
| Most penalty goals in a season | 8 | *Nerina Hawkins, 2003* |
| Most dropped goals in a season | 0 | |
| Most points in a match | 25 | *Deidre Hakopa v Southland, 2003* |
| Most tries in a match | 5 | *Deidre Hakopa v Southland, 2003* |
| Most conversions in a match | 7 | *Nerina Hawkins v Poverty Bay, 2000* |
| Most penalty goals in a match | 4 | *Nerina Hawkins v Auckland, 2003* |
| Highest team score | 100 | *v Southland, 2003* |
| Record victory (points ahead) | 95 | *100–5 v Southland, 2003* |
| Highest score conceded | 93 | *v Auckland, 2014* |
| Record defeat (points behind) | 93 | *0–93 v Auckland, 2014* |

The Hawke's Bay Tuis returned after a year's absence but had a poor season in the Farah Palmer Cup. All six matches were lost and the team scored the fewest tries and fewest points of all 11 teams. Hawke's Bay was hampered by injuries as not once was the side able to field a full complement of seven substitutes on the bench. There were reasonable efforts in the Bay of Plenty, North Harbour and Tasman matches but suffered a thrashing at the hands of Manawatu in a dire performance. The team has not won a game since 2014.

The best of the backline were experienced halfback Gemma Woods and former Black Fern Amy Williams at first five-eighth who were a good combination. Second five-eighth Renee Holmes showed future potential, but it was a blow that Krysten Cottrell could only appear once. Niamh Jefferson did not get many opportunities to shine at centre but was effective at flanker, and number eight Awhina Tangen-Wainohu was a strong ball carrier.

In the match against Otago, Julie Ferguson-Ngawaka and her daughter Teilah Ferguson appeared together.

## NDIVIDUAL SCORING

| | Tries | Con | PG | DG | Points | | Tries | Con | PG | DG | Points |
|---|---|---|---|---|---|---|---|---|---|---|---|
| Woods | 2 | – | – | – | 10 | Powdrell | 1 | – | – | – | 5 |
| Williams | – | 2 | 1 | – | 7 | Tipiwai | 1 | – | – | – | 5 |
| Bennett | 1 | – | – | – | 5 | Whaitiri | 1 | – | – | – | 5 |
| Cotton | 1 | – | – | – | 5 | | | | | | |
| Greville | 1 | – | – | – | 5 | **Totals** | **9** | **3** | **2** | **0** | **57** |
| Holmes | – | 1 | 1 | – | 5 | | | | | | |
| MacGregor | 1 | – | – | – | 5 | *Opposition scored* | *37\** | *18* | *4* | *0* | *235* |

\* *Includes one penalty try (7 points)*

## HAWKE'S BAY REPRESENTATIVES 2017

| | Club | Games for Union | Points for Union |
|---|---|---|---|
| Jessica Bennett | Clive | 12 | 5 |
| Laurae Blake | Clive | 21 | 5 |
| Forne Burkin | Taradale | 12 | 5 |
| Natalie Cotton | Taradale | 38 | 5 |
| Krysten Cottrell (nee Duffill) | Taradale | 19 | 12 |
| Luana Eden | Taradale | 19 | 5 |
| Tamia Edwards | MAC | 7 | 0 |
| Teilah Ferguson | Hastings R&S | 2 | 0 |
| Julie Ferguson-Ngawaka | Hastings R&S | 39 | 80 |
| Natasha Greville | Taradale | 4 | 5 |
| Hope Hakopa | Petone[1] | 9 | 0 |
| Charlie Hoggard | Clive | 1 | 0 |
| Renee Holmes | Hastings R&S | 5 | 5 |
| Rebekah Hurae | Clive | 11 | 0 |
| Niamh Jefferson | Clive | 5 | 0 |
| Kristen Kirkpatrick | Clive | 5 | 0 |
| Christine Lauvao | MAC | 3 | 0 |
| Te Maari McGregor | Clive | 39 | 79 |
| Whitney Olsen | Taradale | 1 | 0 |
| Danielle Pomare-Mackay | Clive | 5 | 0 |
| Felicity Powdrell | Taradale | 11 | 5 |
| Awhina Tangen-Wainohu | MAC | 6 | 0 |
| Jasmine Taukamo-Apiata | Taradale | 1 | 0 |
| Shaylee Tipiwai | Clive | 26 | 25 |
| Yarnisae Whaitiri | Clive | 11 | 5 |
| Amy Williams | Clive | 56 | 121 |
| Gemma Woods | Taradale | 41 | 35 |

[1] *Wellington RU*

### HAWKE'S BAY 2017

| | Wellington | Bay of Plenty | Otago | North Harbour | Manawatu | Tasman | TOTALS |
|---|---|---|---|---|---|---|---|
| J.M. Ferguson-Ngawaka | 15 | 14 | 11 | – | – | 11 | 4 |
| F.R. Powdrell | 14 | 15 | 15 | 15 | 15 | 15 | 6 |
| T.N.W. Ferguson | – | – | s | 14 | – | – | 2 |
| T.T. Edwards | – | – | – | s | 14 | 12 | 3 |
| S.T. Tipiwai | 11 | 13 | 13 | – | – | – | 3 |
| D.J. Pomare-Mackay | – | 11 | 14 | 13 | 10 | 14 | 5 |
| N.D.D. Greville | – | s | s | 11 | 12 | – | 4 |
| Te M.T. MacGregor | – | – | – | – | – | 13 | 1 |
| R.M.M. Holmes | 12 | 12 | 12 | 12 | 11 | – | 5 |
| A.L. Williams (capt) | 10 | 10 | 10 | 10 | 9 | 10 | 6 |
| K.J. Cottrell | s | – | – | – | – | – | 1 |
| G.L. Woods | 9 | 9 | 9 | 9 | 6 | 9 | 6 |
| C.J. Hoggard | – | – | – | s | – | – | 1 |
| L.M. Eden | 8 | 8 | 6 | – | – | – | 3 |
| A.K. Tangen-Wainohu | 1 | 1 | 8 | 8 | 8 | 8 | 6 |
| L.M.A. Blake | 7 | 7 | s | 7 | – | 7 | 5 |
| J. Taukamo-Apiata | 6 | – | – | – | – | – | 1 |
| N.W. Jefferson | 13 | 6 | 7 | – | 13 | 6 | 5 |
| H.L. Hakopa | s | 4 | s | 6 | 7 | – | 5 |
| C. Lauvao | 5 | – | – | s | s | – | 3 |
| R.K. Hurae | – | 5 | 5 | 5 | 5 | 5 | 5 |
| K.D.F. Kirkpatrick | 4 | – | 4 | 4 | 4 | 4 | 5 |
| W.A.M. Olsen | – | – | – | – | – | s | 1 |
| Y.R. Whaitiri | 3 | 3 | 3 | 3 | 3 | – | 5 |
| N.J. Cotton | s | s | s | s | s | 3 | 6 |
| J.L. Bennett | s | s | 1 | 1 | 1 | 1 | 6 |
| F.K. Burkin | 2 | 2 | 2 | 2 | 2 | 2 | 6 |

## HAWKE'S BAY TEAM RECORD, 2017

**Played 6  Lost 6  Points for 57  Points against 235**

| Date | Opponent | Location | Score | Tries | Con | PG | DG | Referee |
|---|---|---|---|---|---|---|---|---|
| September 2 | Wellington (C/P) | Porirua | 10–42 | Tipiwai | Williams | Williams | | M.J. McEwen |
| September 9 | Bay of Plenty (C) | Napier | 10–24 | Whaitiri, Cotton | | | | M. Cogger-Orr |
| September 16 | Otago (C) | Napier | 17–39 | Woods (2), Bennett | Holmes | | | S.C. Catley |
| September 23 | North Harbour (C) | Albany | 0–20 | | | | | Amber Hibbard Australia |
| September 30 | Manawatu (C/P) | Napier | 8–86 | Greville | | Holmes | | H.G. Reed |
| October 14 | Tasman (C) | Nelson | 12–24 | MacGregor, Powdrell | Williams | | | L.K. Moore |

# MANAWATU CYCLONES

*2017 Status:* Premiership
*NPC participation:* 1999–
*Coach:* Fusi Feaunati
*Assistant coach:* Scott Lewis
*Home grounds:* Central Energy Trust Arena

**MANAWATU RUGBY**

## RECORDS

| | | |
|---|---|---|
| Most appearances | 71 | *Selica Winiata, 2002–17* |
| Most points | 398 | *Selica Winiata, 2002–17* |
| Most tries | 62 | *Selica Winiata, 2002–17* |
| Most points in a season | 110 | *Selica Winiata, 2012* |
| Most tries in a season | 14 | *Selica Winiata, 2012* |
| Most conversions in a season | 17 | *Selica Winiata, 2012* |
| Most penalty goals in a season | 8 | *Anika Tiplady, 2004* |
| Most dropped goals in a season | 2 | *Rebecca Hull, 2002* |
| Most points in a match | 38 | *Selica Winiata v Waikato, 2012* |
| Most tries in a match | 4 | *Catherine Doyle v Poverty Bay-East Coast, 2002;* |
| | | *Selica Winiata v Waikato, 2012;* |
| | | *Selica Winiata v Wellington, 2012* |
| Most conversions in a match | 9 | *Elizabeth Goulden v Hawke's Bay 2017* |
| Most penalty goals in a match | 4 | *Anika Tiplady v Bay of Plenty, 2004* |
| Highest team score | 86 | *v Hawke's Bay, 2017* |
| Record victory (points ahead) | 78 | *86-8 v Hawke's Bay, 2017* |
| Highest score conceded | 70 | *v Auckland, 2011* |
| Record defeat (points behind) | 65 | *5-70 v Auckland, 2011* |

The Manawatu Cyclones were well represented in Black Ferns and Black Ferns Sevens teams, although unfortunately several were unavailable for the Farah Palmer Cup games. Sarah Goss, Crystal Mayes, Rebekah Tufuga and Kristina Sue are all quality players, but only Sue made an appearance and only for two games before injury ended her season. Selica 'Shorty' Winiata, in her seventeenth year of representative rugby, shows no sign of slowing up. Her blistering speed and anticipation of play resulted in an extension of her remarkable try-scoring record and she was a finalist for the Fiao'o Fa'amausili Medal for the Farah Palmer Cup player of the year. Her omission from The Black Ferns Sevens squad was difficult to understand but the Cyclones benefitted immensely from her presence.

An encouraging win over Wellington in the first game was followed by a thumping from Canterbury, and another thumping in the final game, from Counties Manukau. A big win over Hawke's Bay preceded a magnificent 15-15 draw against Auckland. The accurate goal-kicking of former Wellington representative Lizzie Goulden was the crucial factor in the Cyclones' best ever result against Auckland. Her experience at first five-eighth combined well with equally experienced midfielders Whanda Leota and Janna Vaughan. Nicole Dickins was again a grand forward leader. Ruci Malanicagi was a strong running wing. Among the younger brigade to impress were 17-year-old loose forward Georgia Ponsonby and 19-year-old wing Lauren Balsillie.

Higher honours went to:
*New Zealand:* S.L. Goss, Sue, Winiata
*New Zealand Sevens:* S.L. Goss, C.A.M. Mayes, T. Reti, R. Tufuga

## MANAWATU REPRESENTATIVES 2017

| | Club | Games for Union | Points for Union | | Club | Games for Union | Points for Union |
|---|---|---|---|---|---|---|---|
| Lauren Balsillie | FOB Oroua | 15 | 40 | Loa Nimarota | Kia Toa | 5 | 0 |
| Anna Darling | OB Univ[1] | 4 | 0 | Aroha Nuku | FOB Oroua | 27 | 25 |
| Nicole Dickins | FOB Oroua | 43 | 10 | Jayme Nuku | Kia Toa | 16 | 0 |
| Jessica Fagan-Pease | Kia Toa | 5 | 5 | Mahalia Polson | Kia Toa | 12 | 0 |
| Rhiarna Ferris | FOB Oroua | 10 | 5 | Georgia Ponsonby | FOB Oroua | 6 | 5 |
| Ruby Finau | Kia Toa | 1 | 0 | Rikki-Lee Rawleigh | University | 16 | 0 |
| Elizabeth Goulden | Kia Toa | 6 | 44 | Kristina Sue | FOB Oroua | 50 | 25 |
| Sequita Hemingway | Kia Toa | 3 | 0 | Kendall Templeman | Kia Toa | 18 | 20 |
| Ashleigh Knight | FOB Oroua | 3 | 0 | Kahli Tipene | Kia Toa | 25 | 0 |
| Whanda Leota | Kia Toa | 38 | 5 | Samantha Tipene | Kia Toa | 23 | 10 |
| Stacey Littleworth | University | 2 | 0 | Fononga Veikoso | Kia Toa | 4 | 0 |
| Stacey Loye | Kia Toa | 14 | 0 | Janna Vaughan | Kia Toa | 34 | 80 |
| Samantha McIntosh | FOB Oroua | 17 | 25 | Paige Walker | Kia Toa | 8 | 0 |
| Ruci Malanicagi | Kia Toa | 4 | 20 | Corrineke Windle | University | 9 | 5 |
| Jaymi Ngaia | Stratford[2] | 14 | 5 | Selica Winiata | Kia Toa | 71 | 398 |

[1] *Wellington RU*    [2] *Taranaki RU*

## INDIVIDUAL SCORING

| | Tries | Con | PG | DG | Points | | Tries | Con | PG | DG | Points |
|---|---|---|---|---|---|---|---|---|---|---|---|
| Goulden | – | 16 | 4 | – | 44 | Ponsonby | 1 | – | – | – | 5 |
| Winiata | 5 | – | – | – | 25 | Sue | 1 | – | – | – | 5 |
| Malanicagi | 4 | – | – | – | 20 | S. Tipene | 1 | – | – | – | 5 |
| Vaughan | 4 | – | – | – | 20 | Windle | 1 | – | – | – | 5 |
| Templeman | 3 | – | – | – | 15 | | | | | | |
| Balsillie | 2 | – | – | – | 10 | **Totals** | **26** | **16** | **4** | **0** | **174** |
| McIntosh | 2 | – | – | – | 10 | | | | | | |
| Fagan-Pease | 1 | – | – | – | 5 | *Opposition scored* | *27* | *9* | *7* | *0* | *174* |
| Ferris | 1 | – | – | – | 5 | | | | | | |

| MANAWATU 2017 | Wellington | Canterbury | Waikato | Hawke's Bay | Auckland | Counties Manukau | TOTALS |
|---|---|---|---|---|---|---|---|
| S.C. Winiata (capt) | 15 | 15 | 15 | 15 | 15 | 10 | 6 |
| L.N.Y. Balsillie | 14 | 14 | 11 | – | – | 14 | 4 |
| K.L. Templeman | – | s | 14 | 14 | s | 11 | 5 |
| R.L. Malanicagi | 11 | – | – | 11 | 11 | 15 | 4 |
| L.I. Nimarota | s | 11 | – | s | 14 | 13 | 5 |
| S.R. Finau | – | – | – | – | – | s | 1 |
| J.M. Vaughan | 13 | 13 | 13 | 13 | 13 | – | 5 |
| M.S. Leota | 12 | 12 | 12 | 12 | 12 | 12 | 6 |
| P.M. Walker | s | – | s | s | s | s | 5 |
| E.L.M. Goulden | 10 | 10 | 10 | 10 | 10 | 9 | 6 |
| K.J. Sue | 9 | 9 | – | – | – | – | 2 |
| C.M. Windle | – | s | 9 | 9 | 9 | – | 4 |
| S.M. McIntosh | 8 | – | s | s | 8 | s | 5 |
| G.R.A. Ponsonby | s | 8 | 8 | 8 | s | 8 | 6 |
| S.J. Tipene | 7 | 7 | s | 7 | 7 | 7 | 6 |
| S.A. Loye | 6 | s | – | – | – | 5 | 3 |
| J.R. Te O. Nuku | s | s | 6 | s | s | s | 6 |
| N.H. Dickins | – | 6 | 7 | 6 | 6 | 6 | 5 |
| J.K. Fagan-Pease | 5 | s | s | 4 | 5 | – | 5 |
| R.R. Ferris | – | 5 | 5 | 5 | – | 4 | 4 |
| M.R. Polson | 4 | 4 | 4 | – | 4 | – | 4 |
| A.J. Knight | – | – | s | s | s | – | 3 |
| A.S. Darling | 3 | – | s | 3 | – | 3 | 4 |
| J.A. Ngaia | s | 3 | – | 1 | 1 | 1 | 5 |
| K.M. Tipene | s | – | 3 | 2 | 3 | s | 5 |
| R-L. Rawleigh | 1 | 1 | 1 | – | – | s | 4 |
| F.M. Veikoso | – | s | – | s | s | s | 4 |
| S.M. Hemingway | – | – | s | s | s | – | 3 |
| A.M. Nuku | 2 | 2 | 2 | – | 2 | 2 | 5 |
| S.M. Littleworth | s | s | – | – | – | – | 2 |

## MANAWATU TEAM RECORD, 2017

| | | | Played 6 | Won 2 | Drew 1 | Lost 3 | Points for 174 | | Points against 174 |
|---|---|---|---|---|---|---|---|---|---|
| Date | Opponent | Location | Score | Tries | | Con | PG | DG | Referee |
| September 9 | Wellington (P) | Petone | 35–27 | Balsillie (2), Malanicagi, Sue, Winiata | | Goulden (5) | | | R.M. Mahoney |
| September 16 | Canterbury (P) | Christchurch | 10–40 | Vaughan, Winiata | | | | | K. Hancox |
| September 22 | Waikato (P) | Palmerston North | 28–36 | Templeman (2), Fagan-Pease, McIntosh | | Goulden | Goulden (2) | | R.M. Mahoney |
| September 30 | Hawke's Bay (P/C) | Napier | 86–8 | Vaughan (3), Winiata (3), Ponsonby, Templeman, S. Tipene, Windle, Malanicagi, Ferris, McIntosh | | Goulden (9) | Goulden | | H.G. Reed |
| October 7 | Auckland (P) | Palmerston North | 15–15 | Malanicagi (2) | | Goulden | Goulden | | L.A. Jenner |
| October 14 | Counties Manukau (P) | Palmerston North | 0–48 | | | | | | N.M. Ganley |

# NORTH HARBOUR HIBISCUS

*2017 Status:* Championship
*NPC participation:* 1999–2005, 2016–
*Coach:* Bill Wigglesworth
*Assistant coach:* Jared Letham
*Home grounds:* QBE Stadium, Albany

## RECORDS

| | | |
|---|---|---|
| **Most appearances** | 23 | *Joanne Cherrington 1999–2004* |
| **Most points** | 34 | *Chelsea Alley, 2016* |
| **Most tries** | 6 | *Anita Harris, 2002–04* |
| **Most points in a season** | 34 | *Chelsea Alley, 2016* |
| **Most tries in a season** | 5 | *Caitlyn Cox, 2017* |
| **Most conversions in a season** | 10 | *Chelsea Alley, 2016* |
| **Most penalty goals in a season** | 7 | *Rachel Howard, 2003* |
| **Most dropped goals in a season** | 0 | |
| **Most points in a match** | 12 | *Chelsea Alley v Otago, 2016* |
| **Most tries in a match** | 2 | *by six players* |
| **Most conversions in a match** | 3 | *by three players* |
| **Most penalty goals in a match** | 3 | *Rachel Howard v Auckland B, 2003* |
| **Highest team score** | 39 | *v Otago, 2016* |
| **Record victory (points ahead)** | 32 | *39–7 v Otago, 2016* |
| **Highest score conceded** | 116 | *v Auckland, 1999* |
| **Record defeat (points behind)** | 116 | *0–116 v Auckland, 1999* |

In only its second year back in the competition, the North Harbour Hibiscus is still adjusting to rep rugby and has some way to go before it can be promoted to the premier division. The departure of Chelsea Alley, back to Waikato, was a loss for the union. The union's two Black Ferns, Charmaine Smith and Rebecca Wood, each made only two appearances.

Games were won over winless Hawke's Bay and competition newcomers Tasman. Of note among the try-scorers was 18-year-old wing Caitlyn Cox who crossed the line in five games. First five-eighth Claudia McMeekin won the Hibiscus Player of the Year award.

This union will be looking to attract home several players who in past years have crossed the harbour bridge to play in Auckland.

Higher honours went to:
*New Zealand:* Smith, Wood

## NORTH HARBOUR REPRESENTATIVES 2017

| | Club | Games for Union | Points for Union | | Club | Games for Union | Points for Union |
|---|---|---|---|---|---|---|---|
| Caitlyn Cox | East Coast Bays | 7 | 25 | Jemma Palmer | East Coast Bays | 12 | 5 |
| Natasha Dallow | Glenfield | 7 | 0 | Maryke Penman | East Coast Bays | 11 | 0 |
| Rachel Dunn | Glenfield | 3 | 0 | Amy Robertshaw | East Coast Bays | 5 | 0 |
| Claire Erasmus | Glenfield | 4 | 5 | Charmaine Smith | East Coast Bays | 8 | 10 |
| Sophie Fisher | East Coast Bays | 7 | 24 | Pia Tapsell | East Coast Bays | 13 | 15 |
| Alexa Fraser | Massey | 7 | 5 | Cristo Tofa | Ponsonby[1] | 7 | 0 |
| Louise Halaleva | East Coast Bays | 1 | 0 | Tuiala To'o | College Rifles[1] | 7 | 0 |
| Emma Iversen | East Coast Bays | 12 | 0 | Te Hine-ngaro Tuterangiwhiu | Glenfield | 5 | 0 |
| Billy-Jo Jones | East Coast Bays | 10 | 0 | Mispah Vunga-Ilaiu | College Rifles[1] | 3 | 0 |
| Laishon Jones | Ponsonby[1] | 6 | 5 | Justine Vizirgianakis | Glenfield | 12 | 5 |
| Kelvery Longopoa | Ponsonby[1] | 2 | 0 | Olivia Ward-Duin | East Coast Bays | 13 | 5 |
| Cesca Luafaleauo | Suburbs[1] | 7 | 0 | Cheyenne Wikaira | Massey | 7 | 0 |
| Claudia McMeekin | East Coast Bays | 13 | 17 | Kate Williams | East Coast Bays | 5 | 5 |
| Briar-Anne McNamara | East Coast Bays | 13 | 22 | Rebecca Wood | East Coast Bays | 8 | 0 |
| Nikita Ngarongo-Porima | Glenfield | 5 | 0 | | | | |

[1] Auckland RU

## INDIVIDUAL SCORING

| | Tries | Con | PG | DG | Points | | Tries | Con | PG | DG | Points |
|---|---|---|---|---|---|---|---|---|---|---|---|
| Cox | 5 | – | – | – | 25 | Vizirgianakis | 1 | – | – | – | 5 |
| Fisher | 1 | 5 | 3 | – | 24 | Ward-Duin | 1 | – | – | – | 5 |
| McMeekin | 1 | 1 | – | – | 7 | Williams | 1 | – | – | – | 5 |
| Erasmus | 1 | – | – | – | 5 | | | | | | |
| Fraser | 1 | – | – | – | 5 | **Totals** | **15** | **6** | **3** | **0** | **96** |
| L. Jones | 1 | – | – | – | 5 | | | | | | |
| Smith | 1 | – | – | – | 5 | *Opposition scored* | 42 | 15 | 0 | 0 | 240 |
| Tapsell | 1 | – | – | – | 5 | | | | | | |

| **NORTH HARBOUR 2017** | Counties Manukau | Bay of Plenty | Hawke's Bay | Auckland | Tasman | Otago | Otago | **TOTALS** |
|---|---|---|---|---|---|---|---|---|
| B. McNamara | 15 | 15 | 15 | 15 | 15 | s | 15 | **7** |
| M. Vunga-Ilaiu | s | – | s | s | – | – | – | **3** |
| C.R. Cox | 14 | 14 | 14 | 14 | 14 | 14 | 14 | **7** |
| J. Vizirgianakis | 11 | s | 11 | 11 | 11 | 11 | 11 | **7** |
| L. Halaleva | – | – | – | – | – | – | s | **1** |
| T. To'o | 13 | 13 | s | s | s | s | s | **7** |
| N. Dallow | s | – | – | s | – | s | – | **3** |
| E.A.A. Iversen | – | 11 | 13 | 13 | 13 | .13 | 13 | **6** |
| C. Erasmus | 12 | 12 | – | – | s | 15 | – | **4** |
| L. Jones | – | s | 12 | 12 | 12 | 12 | 12 | **6** |
| C. McMeekin | 10 | 10 | 10 | 10 | 10 | 10 | 10 | **7** |
| C. Luafaleauo | 9 | 9 | 9 | 9 | 9 | 9 | 9 | **7** |
| N.D. Ngarongo-Porima | s | s | s | s | – | s | s | **5** |
| J. Palmer | 8 | 8 | – | 8 | 8 | 8 | 8 | **6** |
| K.R. Williams | 7 | 7 | – | – | 7 | 7 | 7 | **5** |
| P.H. Tapsell | 6 | 6 | 8 | 6 | 6 | 5 | 5 | **7** |
| A.S. Fraser | s | s | s | s | s | 6 | s | **7** |
| K. Longopoa | s | – | – | – | – | – | s | **2** |
| M.S. Penman | 5 | 5 | 7 | 7 | 5 | – | 6 | **6** |
| R.J. Wood | – | s | 5 | – | – | – | – | **2** |
| C.B. Smith | – | – | 6 | 5 | – | – | – | **2** |
| S.R. Fisher | 4 | 4 | 4 | 4 | 4 | 4 | 4 | **7** |
| R.A. Dunn | – | – | – | – | s | s | s | **3** |
| O.Y. Ward-Duin | 3 | 3 | 3 | 3 | 3 | 3 | 3 | **7** |
| C.L. Tofa | 1 | 1 | 1 | 1 | 1 | 1 | 1 | **7** |
| C. Wikaira | s | s | s | s | s | s | s | **7** |
| A.G. Robertshaw (capt) | 2 | – | 2 | 2 | 2 | – | 2 | **5** |
| B-J. Jones | s | 2 | – | s | – | s | s | **5** |
| Te H.U. Tuterangiwhiu | – | s | s | s | s | 2 | – | **5** |

Palmer was captain v Bay of Plenty and Otago (i)

## NORTH HARBOUR TEAM RECORD, 2017

|  |  |  | Played 7 | Won 2 | Lost 5 | Points for 96 |  | Points against 240 |
|---|---|---|---|---|---|---|---|---|
| Date | Opponent | Location | Score | Tries | Con | PG | DG | Referee |
| September 2 | Counties Manukau (C/P) | Pukekohe | 7–84 | Cox | Fisher |  |  | K.C. Lagerwall |
| September 16 | Bay of Plenty (C) | Rotorua | 12–34 | Cox, McMeekin | Fisher |  |  | M. Cogger-Orr |
| September 23 | Hawke's Bay (C) | Albany | 20–0 | Vizirgianakis, Cox, Smith | Fisher | Fisher |  | Amber Hibbard Australia |
| September 29 | Auckland (C/P) | Albany | 5–37 | Tapsell |  |  |  | R.M. Mahoney |
| October 8 | Tasman (C) | Nelson | 25–12 | Cox, Ward-Duin, Williams, L. Jones | McMeekin | Fisher |  | V.F. Ringrose |
| October 15 | Otago (C) | Albany | 15–34 | Erasmus, Cox | Fisher | Fisher |  | M. Cogger-Orr |
| October 21 | Otago (semi-final) | Dunedin | 12–39 | Fisher, Fraser | Fisher |  |  | L.A. Jenner |

# OTAGO SPIRIT

**2017 Status:** Championship
**NPC participation:** 1999–
**Coach:** Kane Jury
**Assistant coaches:** Warren Kearney
**Home grounds:** Forsyth Barr Stadium;
Logan Park (v Tasman) .

## RECORDS

| | | |
|---|---|---|
| Most appearances | 47 | *Beth Mallard 1999–2011;* |
| | | *Angie Sisifa, 2011-17* |
| Most points | 221 | *Claire Richardson, 2002–12* |
| Most tries | 25 | *Carla Hohepa, 2006–09* |
| Most points in a season | 70 | *Kelly Brazier, 2012* |
| Most tries in a season | 11 | *Annaleah Rush, 1999* |
| Most conversions in a season | 17 | *Kelly Brazier, 2012* |
| Most penalty goals in a season | 12 | *Hannah Myers, 2000* |
| Most dropped goals in a season | 0 | |
| Most points in a match | 45 | *Kelly Brazier v Hawke's Bay, 2012* |
| Most tries in a match | 8 | *Annaleah Rush v Mid/South Canterbury, 1999* |
| Most conversions in a match | 10 | *Kelly Brazier v Hawke's Bay, 2012* |
| Most penalty goals in a match | 5 | *Anika Tiplady v Auckland, 2013* |
| Highest team score | 85 | *v Hawke's Bay, 2012* |
| Record victory (points ahead) | 82 | *82–0 v Mid/South Canterbury, 1999;* |
| | | *82-0 v Tasman 2017* |
| Highest score conceded | 86 | *v Auckland, 2011* |
| Record defeat (points behind) | 81 | *5–86 v Auckland, 2011* |

Otago Spirit progressed to the Championship final before bowing to Bay of Plenty 7-5 at Mount Maunganui. Losses to Canterbury and Wellington showed that the team was off the pace against the Premiership division teams, but there were several fine wins against Championship sides. The season included a record-equalling score against debutants Tasman, during which Kilistina Moata'ane scored five tries. There were also high scores against Hawke's Bay and twice against North Harbour.The experienced former Black Fern Angie Sisifa captained the team, as she had since 2014. Sheree Hume, Greer Muir, Olivia Waldron and Zoe Whatarau were backs with considerable rep experience while in the forwards were seasoned campaigners Julia Gorinski, Leyhana van Vliet and Georgia Mason. Teenager Morgan Henderson was a lively flanker, and her impressive performances were rewarded when she was a finalist for the Fiao'o Fa'amausili Medal for the Farah Palmer Cup Player of the Year. Sam Hollows was selected for the national sevens development team.

## OTAGO REPRESENTATIVES 2017

| | Club | Games for Union | Points for Union | | Club | Games for Union | Points for Union |
|---|---|---|---|---|---|---|---|
| Catarina Antunes | North Otago | 4 | 0 | Gemma Millar | Pirates | 3 | 0 |
| Sarah Crabbe | North Otago | 2 | 0 | Kilisitina Moata'ane | Pirates | 26 | 50 |
| Cheyenne Cunningham | North Otago | 7 | 15 | Greer Muir | Pirates | 45 | 100 |
| Michaela Day | Pirates | 5 | 0 | Syreeta Norris | Pirates | 17 | 0 |
| Eilis Doyle | Alhambra Union | 19 | 0 | Isla Pringle | University | 6 | 0 |
| Julia Gorinski | University | 23 | 10 | Angie Sisifa | Pirates | 47 | 65 |
| Laura Harrison | University | 1 | 0 | Kate Smith | University | 13 | 0 |
| Morgan Henderson | North Otago | 8 | 15 | Lauren Tye | University | 2 | 0 |
| Sam Hollows | University | 5 | 20 | Soraya Umaga-Jensen | Pirates | 6 | 5 |
| Tegan Hollows | University | 19 | 0 | Annemieke van Vliet | Alhambra Union | 12 | 10 |
| Sheree Hume | Pirates | 33 | 31 | Leyhana van Vugt | University | 28 | 25 |
| Saane Kaufanga | Pirates | 1 | 0 | Olivia Waldron | University | 27 | 31 |
| Jessica Kendall | University | 13 | 5 | Morgan Walker | North Otago | 8 | 0 |
| Nicole Kennedy | University | 8 | 10 | Kiana Wereta | Alhambra Union | 9 | 0 |
| Georgia Mason | University | 24 | 25 | Zoe Whatarau | Alhambra Union | 24 | 0 |

## INDIVIDUAL SCORING

| | Tries | Con | PG | DG | Points | | Tries | Con | PG | DG | Points |
|---|---|---|---|---|---|---|---|---|---|---|---|
| Moata'ane | 7 | – | – | – | 35 | van Vugt | 2 | – | – | – | 10 |
| Waldron | – | 14 | 1 | – | 31 | penalty try | 1 | – | – | – | 7 |
| Muir | 5 | – | – | – | 25 | Gorinsky | 1 | – | – | – | 5 |
| S. Hollows | 4 | – | – | – | 20 | Kendall | 1 | – | – | – | 5 |
| Sisifa | 4 | – | – | – | 20 | Kennedy | 1 | – | – | – | 5 |
| Hume | 1 | 7 | – | – | 19 | Umaga-Jensen | 1 | – | – | – | 5 |
| Cunningham | 3 | – | – | – | 15 | | | | | | |
| Henderson | 3 | – | – | – | 15 | **Totals** | **39\*** | **21** | **1** | **0** | **242** |
| Mason | 3 | – | – | – | 15 | | | | | | |
| van Vliet | 2 | – | – | – | 10 | *Opposition scored* | *23\** | *8* | *2* | *0* | *139* |

## OTAGO 2017

| | Canterbury | Tasman | Hawke's Bay | Wellington | Bay of Plenty | North Harbour | North Harbour | Bay of Plenty | TOTALS |
|---|---|---|---|---|---|---|---|---|---|
| S.J. Hume | 15 | 15 | 10 | 15 | 15 | 15 | 15 | 10 | **8** |
| C.S.R. Antunes | 14 | 14 | 11 | – | – | – | s | – | **4** |
| K.M.P.Y. Wereta | s | – | 14 | – | – | s | – | – | **3** |
| S.M. Hollows | 13 | – | s | 14 | 14 | 14 | – | – | **5** |
| C.B. Cunningham | s | 11 | 15 | – | s | s | 11 | 15 | **7** |
| N. Kennedy | – | s | – | 11 | 11 | 11 | 14 | 14 | **6** |
| I.S. Kaufanga | – | s | – | – | – | – | – | – | **1** |
| G.A. Muir | 12 | 13 | 13 | 13 | 13 | 13 | 13 | 13 | **8** |
| K. Moata'ane | 11 | 12 | 12 | 12 | 12 | – | s | 11 | **7** |
| S.T. Umaga-Jensen | – | – | s | s | s | 12 | 12 | 12 | **6** |
| O.N. Waldron | 10 | 10 | – | 10 | 10 | 10 | 10 | s | **7** |
| Z.J.T. Whatarau | 9 | 9 | 9 | 9 | 9 | 9 | 9 | 9 | **8** |
| L.S. Tye | s | – | – | s | – | – | – | – | **2** |
| L.R. van Vugt | – | s | s | s | s | s | s | s | **7** |
| A.A.F. Sisifa (capt) | 8 | 8 | 8 | 8 | 8 | 8 | 8 | 8 | **8** |
| G.E. Mason | 7 | 7 | 7 | 7 | 7 | 7 | 7 | 7 | **8** |
| M.A. Henderson | 6 | 6 | 6 | 6 | 6 | 6 | 6 | 6 | **8** |
| S.E. Crabbe | s | – | s | – | – | – | – | – | **2** |
| K.E. Smith | 5 | s | s | s | s | 4 | 4 | 4 | **8** |
| M. Day | s | 5 | – | s | – | s | s | – | **5** |
| A.A. van Vliet | s | s | 5 | 1 | s | s | s | s | **8** |
| J.F. Gorinski | – | – | – | 5 | 5 | 5 | 5 | 5 | **5** |
| J.B. Kendall | 4 | 4 | 4 | 4 | 4 | – | s | s | **7** |
| S.R. Norris | 3 | 3 | 3 | – | 3 | 3 | – | s | **6** |
| I.R. Pringle | – | s | s | – | s | s | 3 | 3 | **6** |
| E.O. Doyle | 1 | 1 | 1 | 3 | 1 | 1 | 1 | 1 | **8** |
| L.M. Harrison | – | – | – | s | – | – | – | – | **1** |
| M.J. Walker | 2 | – | – | s | – | s | s | 2 | **5** |
| T.J. Hollows | s | 2 | 2 | 2 | 2 | 2 | 2 | – | **7** |
| G.A. Millar | – | s | s | – | s | – | – | – | **3** |

## OTAGO TEAM RECORD, 2017

**Played 8　　Won 4　　Lost 4　　Points for 242　　Points against 139**

| Date | Opponent | Location | Score | Tries | Con | PG | DG | Referee |
|---|---|---|---|---|---|---|---|---|
| September 3 | Canterbury (C/P) | Christchurch | 7–20 | Cunningham | Hume | | | K. Hancox |
| September 9 | Tasman (C) | Dunedin | 82–0 | Moata'ane (5), Muir (2), Sisifa (2), Cunningham, Henderson, van Vugt | Waldron (9), Hume (2) | | | B.A. Malcolm |
| September 16 | Hawke's Bay (C) | Napier | 39–17 | Cunningham, Mason, penalty try, van Vliet, Muir, van Vugt, S. Hollows | Hume | | | S.C. Catley |
| September 30 | Wellington (C/P) | Dunedin | 19–41 | Kendall, Henderson, Hume | Waldron (2) | | | B.A. Malcolm |
| October 7 | Bay of Plenty (C) | Dunedin | 17–27 | Gorinsky, van Vliet | Waldron, Hume | Waldron | | N.M. Ganley |
| October 15 | North Harbour (C) | Albany | 34–15 | S. Hollows (3), Kennedy, Umaga-Jensen, Muir | Waldron, Hume | | | M. Cogger-Orr |
| October 21 | North Harbour (semi-final) | Dunedin | 39–12 | Sisifa (2), Mason (2), Moata'ane (2), Muir | Waldron, Hume | | | L.A. Jenner |
| October 28 | Bay of Plenty (final) | Mt Maunganui | 5–7 | Henderson | | | | M. Cogger-Orr |

# TASMAN MAKO

*2017 Status:* Championship
*NPC participation:* 2017–
*Coach:* Martyn O'Cain
*Assistant coach:* Mark Kelly
*Home Grounds:* Lansdowne Park, Blenheim;
Trafalgar Park, Nelson

Tasman was a welcome addition to a steadily expanding competition. The debutants produced a very encouraging result in the opening game, against Waikato, then took a hammering from Otago in the second round. The win in the final game, against Hawke's Bay, would have installed much confidence in the team for 2018. The squad contained several secondary school pupils from Motueka High School, and it could take several years for the union to develop a squad of seasoned campaigners. However, the relatively new Tasman union has achieved remarkable success in a short time with its Makos and one cannot dismiss the possibility of the women's team meeting similar success. The team did play attractive running rugby.

While nearly all the squad were new to first-class rugby, centre Wairakau Greig had played three years with Manawatu. Jess Foster captained the team and showed good leadership and form, having played for the Bay of Plenty Volcanix, as a loan player, in 2016. Stars of the team were 17-year-old Risi Pouri-Lane and outside back Jess Drummond, both of whom made trips to Japan and Australia with the national development sevens team. Pouri-Lane has already represented New Zealand at judo and touch and this multi-talented sportswoman, from the very successful Motueka High School sevens team, looks to have a Black Ferns shirt within her grasp. Rosie Buchanan-Brown showed promise at halfback; she's another 17-year-old with a bright future in the game.

Higher honours went to:
*New Zealand Sevens:* Drummond

## INDIVIDUAL SCORING

| | Tries | Con | PG | DG | Points |
|---|---|---|---|---|---|
| Greig | 4 | – | – | – | 20 |
| Pouri-Lane | 1 | 5 | 1 | – | 18 |
| Drummond | 2 | – | – | – | 10 |
| Foster | 1 | 1 | – | – | 7 |
| Buchanan-Brown | 1 | – | – | – | 5 |
| Curry | 1 | – | – | – | 5 |
| Mitchell | 1 | – | – | – | 5 |

| | Tries | Con | PG | DG | Points |
|---|---|---|---|---|---|
| Nathan | 1 | – | – | – | 5 |
| Wilson | 1 | – | – | – | 5 |
| **Totals** | **13** | **6** | **1** | **0** | **80** |
| Opposition scored | 39 | 24 | 2 | 0 | 249 |

## TASMAN REPRESENTATIVES 2017

| | Club | Games for Union | Points for Union | | Club | Games for Union | Points for Union |
|---|---|---|---|---|---|---|---|
| Pippa Andrews | Moutere | 5 | 0 | Helen Leota | Moutere | 1 | 0 |
| Shelly Barry | Marist | 3 | 0 | Stephani Mitchell | Waimea OB | 6 | 5 |
| Rosie Buchanan-Brown | Moutere | 6 | 5 | Ashleigh Nathan | Moutere | 1 | 5 |
| Courtney Clarke | Motueka HS | 6 | 0 | Raelene Olsen | Moutere | 2 | 0 |
| Kelly Couper | Moutere | 6 | 0 | Risi Pouri-Lane | Motueka HS | 4 | 18 |
| Michelle Curry | Marist | 6 | 5 | Niska Scott | Moutere | 5 | 0 |
| Stacey Davis | Waimea OB | 6 | 0 | Lina Sekai | Moutere | 1 | 0 |
| Jess Drummond | Motueka HS | 4 | 10 | Lyric Siaki | Motueka HS | 3 | 0 |
| Jessica Foster | Waimea OB | 6 | 7 | Tamara Silcock | Marist | 6 | 0 |
| Leti Fotumoala | Moutere | 5 | 0 | Kelly Stanford | Moutere | 6 | 0 |
| Hannah Gillespie | Moutere | 6 | 0 | Naomi Tiumalu | Moutere | 5 | 0 |
| Wairakau Greig | Moutere | 4 | 20 | Shayla Tuitupou | Marist | 2 | 0 |
| Fern Hoskin | Marist | 6 | 0 | Sydnee Wilkins | Motueka HS | 3 | 0 |
| Staci Kohe | Marist | 6 | 0 | Dana Wilson | Marist | 5 | 5 |
| Ashley Ulutupu | Marist | 5 | 0 | | | | |

## TASMAN 2017

| | Waikato | Otago | Bay of Plenty | Canterbury | North Harbour | Hawke's Bay | TOTALS |
|---|---|---|---|---|---|---|---|
| S.L. Wilkins | 15 | – | – | – | 15 | 15 | 3 |
| J.A. Drummond | – | – | 15 | 15 | 13 | 14 | 4 |
| F. Hoskin | 14 | 14 | s | 14 | 14 | s | 6 |
| P.S. Andrews | 11 | 15 | 14 | 11 | s | – | 5 |
| M.A. Curry | s | 11 | 11 | s | 11 | 11 | 6 |
| R. Olsen | s | s | – | – | – | – | 2 |
| L.L. Fotumoala | – | s | s | s | s | s | 5 |
| W. Greig | 13 | – | 13 | 13 | – | 13 | 4 |
| S.E. Kohe | 12 | 13 | 12 | 12 | 12 | 12 | 6 |
| L.M.B.A. Siaki | s | 12 | – | s | – | – | 3 |
| H. Leota | – | s | – | – | – | – | 1 |
| R.I.R. Pouri-Lane | 10 | – | 10 | – | 10 | 10 | 4 |
| D.L. Wilson | – | 10 | s | 10 | s | s | 5 |
| R.M.E. Buchanan-Brown | 9 | 9 | 9 | 9 | 9 | 9 | 6 |
| J. E-M. Foster (capt) | 8 | 8 | 8 | 8 | 8 | 8 | 6 |
| K.A. Stanford | 7 | 7 | 7 | 7 | 7 | 7 | 6 |
| T. Silcock | 6 | 6 | 6 | 6 | 6 | 6 | 6 |
| S.E. Barry | – | – | s | s | – | s | 3 |
| A. Nathan | – | – | s | – | – | – | 1 |
| C.E. Clarke | 5 | 5 | 5 | 5 | 5 | 5 | 6 |
| N.M. Scott | s | s | – | s | s | s | 5 |
| H.E. Gillespie | 4 | 4 | 4 | 4 | 4 | 4 | 6 |
| S.L. Davis | 3 | 3 | 1 | 3 | 3 | s | 6 |
| A. Ulutupu | – | s | s | s | s | 3 | 5 |
| K.M. Couper | 1 | 1 | 3 | 1 | 1 | s | 6 |
| N.M.A. Tiumalu | s | s | s | – | s | 1 | 5 |
| S.Te A. Tuitupou | s | s | – | – | – | – | 2 |
| L.B. Sekai | – | – | – | s | – | – | 1 |
| S.L. Mitchell | 2 | 2 | 2 | 2 | 2 | 2 | 6 |

## TASMAN TEAM RECORD, 2017

Played 6 · Won 1 · Lost 5 · Points for 80 · Points against 249

| Date | Opponent | Location | Score | Tries | Con | PG | DG | Referee |
|---|---|---|---|---|---|---|---|---|
| September 2 | Waikato (C/P) | Blenheim | 17–25 | Curry, Buchanan-Brown, Greig | Pouri-Lane | | | M. Cogger-Orr |
| September 9 | Otago (C) | Dunedin | 0–82 | | | | | B.A. Malcolm |
| September 24 | Bay of Plenty (C) | Tauranga | 15–38 | Greig (2), Nathan | | | | L.A. Jenner |
| September 30 | Canterbury (C/P, ST) | Christchurch | 12–67 | Greig, Drummond | Foster | | | M. Cogger-Orr |
| October 8 | North Harbour (C) | Nelson | 12–25 | Drummond, Foster | Pouri-Lane | | | V.F. Ringrose |
| October 14 | Hawke's Bay (C) | Nelson | 24–12 | Mitchell, Pouri-Lane, Wilson | Pouri-Lane (3) | Pouri-Lane | | L.K. Moore |

ST Stewart Trophy

# WAIKATO

**2017 Status:** Premiership
**NPC participation:** 1999–2005, 2012–
**Coach:** Wayne Maxwell
**Assistant coach:** James Semple
**Home Grounds:** Marist Rugby Club (v Wellington);
Beetham Park (v Bay of Plenty);
FMG Stadium Waikato (v Canterbury).

**W.R.U**

## RECORDS

| | | |
|---|---|---|
| Most appearances | 40 | *Regina Sheck, 1999–2012* |
| Most points | 212 | *Chelsea Alley, 2012–17* |
| Most tries | 19 | *Honey Hireme, 2001–16* |
| Most points in a season | 81 | *Chelsea Alley, 2014* |
| Most tries in a season | 11 | *Stacey Waaka, 2014* |
| Most conversions in a season | 21 | *Chelsea Alley, 2014* |
| Most penalty goals in a season | 12 | *Chelsea Alley, 2013* |
| Most dropped goals in a season | 1 | *Emma Jensen, 2000* |
| Most points in a match | 18 | *C. Alley v Bay of Plenty, 2014* |
| Most tries in a match | 3 | *Jordon Webber v Manawatu, 2012;* |
| | | *Honey Hireme v Manawatu, 2014;* |
| | | *Stacey Waaka v Canterbury, 2014;* |
| | | *v Bay of Plenty 2015* |
| Most conversions in a match | 5 | *C. Alley v Manawatu, 2014;* |
| | | *v Bay of Plenty, 2014* |
| Most penalty goals in a match | 4 | *Emma Jensen v Northland, 2000* |
| | | *Tenika Willison v North Harbour, 2016* |
| Highest team score | 48 | *v Bay of Plenty, 2014* |
| Record victory (points ahead) | 48 | *48–0 v Bay of Plenty, 2014* |
| Highest score conceded | 78 | *v Auckland, 2002* |
| Record defeat (points behind) | 78 | *0–78 v Auckland, 2002* |

Waikato finished third on the ladder but suffered big losses to Counties Manukau (0–48) and, in the semifinal, to Canterbury (26–60). The squad was missing several of its Black Ferns and some other players had gained sevens contracts. The team fielded a large forward pack led by hooker Sosoli Talawadua. Victoria Edmonds finished the season one short of Regina Sheck's record 40 appearances for the union. Chelsea Alley returned after two years with North Harbour. The team's top try-scorer was 17-year-old wing Hannah Brough.

Higher honours went to:
*New Zealand:* Alley, A.H. Hireme, C.G. Hohepa, L.T. Ketu, Natua, Talawadua, S.J.A.K. Waaka
*New Zealand Sevens:* S.J. Baker, C.R.A. Robins-Reti, T.L.R. Te Tamaki, S.J.A.K. Waaka,
T.R. Willison

## WAIKATO REPRESENTATIVES 2017

| | Club | Games for Union | Points for Union |
|---|---|---|---|
| Chelsea Alley | University | 25 | 212 |
| Kate Anderson | University | 4 | 0 |
| Ariana Bayler | Hamilton OB | 23 | 27 |
| Hannah Brough | Otorohanga Sports | 7 | 25 |
| Natalie Delamere | University | 13 | 20 |
| Victoria Edmonds | University | 39 | 10 |
| Karli Faneva | Marist | 4 | 10 |
| Donna Fermanis | Hamilton OB | 6 | 5 |
| Huia Harding | Marist | 22 | 25 |
| Ryleigh Hayes | Marist | 8 | 10 |
| Emma-Lee Heta | University | 9 | 10 |
| Grace Houpapa-Barrett | Marist | 15 | 15 |
| Stephanie Hyde-Richards | University | 21 | 0 |
| Tanya Kalounivale | Hamilton OB | 7 | 0 |

| | Club | Games for Union | Points for Union |
|---|---|---|---|
| Lydia King | University | 1 | 0 |
| Leomie Kloppers | Hamilton OB | 5 | 0 |
| Michelle Montague | Hamilton OB | 26 | 5 |
| Toka Natua | Southern United | 21 | 10 |
| Rina Paraone | University | 8 | 10 |
| Myron Rapana-Barrett | University | 5 | 0 |
| Tyler Reid | Hamilton OB | 4 | 0 |
| Makaia Riki-Te Kanawa | Hamilton OB | 16 | 25 |
| Veronica Sue | Hamilton OB | 1 | 5 |
| Mikhayla Tainui Mclean | Otorohanga Sports | 3 | 0 |
| Sosoli Talawadua | University | 27 | 15 |
| Teirea Te Aho | Hamilton OB | 20 | 5 |
| Lacy Tomu | Marist | 15 | 0 |
| Calista Wihone | University | 7 | 15 |

## INDIVIDUAL SCORING

| | Tries | Con | PG | DG | Points |
|---|---|---|---|---|---|
| Brough | 5 | – | – | – | 25 |
| Delamere | 4 | – | – | – | 20 |
| Alley | 1 | 3 | 3 | – | 20 |
| Wihine | 1 | 2 | 2 | – | 15 |
| Bayler | – | 7 | – | – | 14 |
| Faneva | 2 | – | – | – | 10 |
| Hayes | 2 | – | – | – | 10 |
| Heta | 2 | – | – | – | 10 |
| Houpapa-Barrett | 2 | – | – | – | 10 |
| Paraone | 2 | – | – | – | 10 |

| | Tries | Con | PG | DG | Points |
|---|---|---|---|---|---|
| Talawadua | 2 | – | – | – | 10 |
| Fermanis | 1 | – | – | – | 5 |
| Natua | 1 | – | – | – | 5 |
| Riki-Te Kanawa | 1 | – | – | – | 5 |
| Sue | 1 | – | – | – | 5 |
| **Totals** | **27** | **12** | **5** | **0** | **174** |
| *Opposition scored* | *38* | *19* | *6* | *0* | *246* |

| WAIKATO 2017 | Tasman | Counties Manukau | Wellington | Manawatu | Bay of Plenty | Canterbury | Auckland | Canterbury | TOTALS |
|---|---|---|---|---|---|---|---|---|---|
| M. Riki-Te Kanawa | 15 | 15 | 15 | 15 | 15 | 15 | 15 | 15 | 8 |
| V. Sue | s | – | – | – | – | – | – | – | 1 |
| H. Brough | 14 | 14 | 11 | 14 | – | 11 | 14 | 14 | 7 |
| H.R. Harding | – | – | – | – | 14 | 14 | 11 | 11 | 4 |
| M. Rapana-Barrett | 11 | s | – | s | – | s | s | – | 5 |
| D. Fermanis | s | 11 | 14 | 11 | 11 | – | – | s | 6 |
| R. Paraone | 13 | 13 | 13 | 13 | 13 | 13 | 13 | 13 | 8 |
| R. Hayes | 12 | 12 | 12 | 12 | 12 | 12 | 12 | 12 | 8 |
| C. Wihone | 10 | 10 | 10 | – | 10 | 10 | s | s | 7 |
| C.H. Alley | – | – | – | 10 | – | s | 10 | 10 | 4 |
| A.J. Bayler | 9 | 9 | 9 | s | s | s | 9 | 9 | 8 |
| T. Te Aho | s | s | s | 9 | 9 | 9 | s | s | 8 |
| N. Delamere | 8 | s | 8 | 8 | 8 | 2 | 2 | 2 | 8 |
| T.I. Natua | – | 8 | – | s | s | – | 8 | 8 | 5 |
| L. Tomu | 7 | 7 | s | 6 | 6 | s | s | s | 8 |
| E-L. Heta | s | s | 7 | 7 | 7 | 7 | 7 | 7 | 8 |
| M. Montague | 6 | 4 | 6 | s | s | 6 | 6 | 6 | 8 |
| V.R. Edmonds | s | 6 | 5 | 5 | 5 | 8 | – | – | 6 |
| S. Hyde-Richards | 5 | 5 | 4 | 4 | 4 | 4 | 4 | 4 | 8 |
| L. Kloppers | s | s | – | – | – | 5 | 5 | 5 | 5 |
| L. King | 4 | – | – | – | – | – | – | – | 1 |
| M. Tainui Mclean | – | s | – | – | – | s | – | s | 3 |
| K. Faneva | – | – | – | – | – | s | s | s | 3 |
| G. Houpapa-Barrett | 3 | 3 | 1 | 1 | 1 | 1 | 1 | 1 | 8 |
| T. Reid | – | 1 | 3 | 3 | 3 | – | – | – | 4 |
| T. Kalounivale | 1 | – | s | s | s | 3 | 3 | 3 | 7 |
| K. Anderson | s | s | – | – | – | s | – | s | 4 |
| S.J. Talawadua (capt) | 2 | 2 | 2 | 2 | 2 | – | – | – | 5 |

Edmonds captained the team against Canterbury and Alley was captain in the final two games.

# WAIKATO TEAM RECORD, 2017

Played 8   Won 4   Lost 4   Points for 174   Points against 246

| Date | Opponent | Location | Score | Tries | Con | PG | DG | Referee |
|------|----------|----------|-------|-------|-----|----|----|---------|
| September 2 | Tasman (P/C) | Blenheim | 25–17 | Riki-Te Kanawa, Houpapa-Barrett, Sue, Brough | Bayler | Wihone | | M. Cogger-Orr |
| September 7 | Counties Manukau (P) | Pukekohe | 0–48 | | | | | M.E. Playle |
| September 16 | Wellington (P) | Hamilton | 5–11 | Fermanis | | | | R.M. Mahoney |
| September 22 | Manawatu (P) | Palmerston North | 36–28 | Talawadua (2), Heta, Delamere, Natua | Alley | Alley (3) | | R.M. Mahoney |
| September 30 | Bay of Plenty (P/C) | Hamilton | 19–17 | Delamere (2), Wihone | Wihone (2) | | | L.A. Jenner |
| October 8 | Canterbury (P) | Hamilton | 20–31 | Brough, Delamere, Alley | Alley | Wihone | | B. Roberts |
| October 14 | Auckland (P) | Pakuranga | 43–34 | Paraone (2), Faneva (2), Brough, Houpapa-Barrett, Hayes | Bayler (4) | | | L.A. Jenner |
| October 21 | Canterbury (semi-final) | Christchurch | 26–60 | Brough (2), Hayes (2), Heta | Bayler (2), Alley | | | N.M. Ganley |

# WELLINGTON PRIDE

*2017 Status:* Premiership
*NPC participation:* 1999–
*Coach:* Ross Bond
*Assistant coaches:* Gary Hilsdon, Matt Poutua
*Home ground:* Porirua Park; Petone Recreation Ground

## RECORDS

| | | |
|---|---|---|
| Most appearances | 58 | *Rebecca Liua'ana, 1999–2012* |
| Most points | 184 | *Elizabeth Goulden 2012–16* |
| Most tries | 18 | *Ayesha Leti-I'iga 2015–17* |
| Most points in a season | 69 | *Elizabeth Goulden, 2015* |
| Most tries in a season | 10 | *Shakira Baker, 2011* |
| Most conversions in a season | 21 | *Elizabeth Goulden 2015* |
| Most penalty goals in a season | 11 | *Elizabeth Goulden, 2014* |
| Most dropped goals in a season | 0 | |
| Most points in a match | 20 | *Huia Paul v Otago, 2011;* |
| | | *Helen Collins v Hawke's Bay, 2012* |
| Most tries in a match | 4 | *Huia Paul v Otago, 2011;* |
| | | *Helen Collins v Hawke's Bay, 2012* |
| Most conversions in a match | 8 | *Neroli Knight v Poverty Bay, 1999* |
| Most penalty goals in a match | 5 | *Elizabeth Goulden v Taranaki, 2013* |
| Highest team score | 81 | *v Poverty Bay, 1999* |
| Record victory (points ahead) | 76 | *81–5 v Poverty Bay, 1999* |
| Highest score conceded | 65 | *v Auckland, 2012* |
| Record defeat (points behind) | 65 | *0–65 v Auckland, 2012* |

Wellington Pride finished at the foot of the Premiership division, the team's best results perhaps being the win over Waikato and the one-point loss to Auckland. The union had lost experienced first five-eight Lizzie Goulden to Manawatu, but several regulars from previous years maintained a balanced team. Jackie Patea-Fereti captained the team from the back of the scrum. Other seasoned forwards included Kiri Mei, Gina Williamson, Sanita Levave (sister of Faifili Levave) and Joanah Ngan-Woo. Among the backs were halfback Acacia Te Iwimate (nee Claridge), 18-year-old wing Ayesha Leti-I'iga who was the top points-scorer, and utility Vaine Marsters.

New coach Ross Bond had previous first-class coaching experience when in charge of the Horowhenua Kapiti Heartland team. Wellington drops to the Championship division for 2018.

Higher honours went to:
*New Zealand Sevens:* K.R. Whata-Simpkins

## WELLINGTON REPRESENTATIVES 2017

| | Club | Games for Union | Points for Union |
|---|---|---|---|
| Jane Bryce | Marist St Pats | 5 | 11 |
| Sherri Burgess | OB University | 1 | 0 |
| Tawny Burgess | OB University | 5 | 0 |
| Cheyne Copeland | Marist St Pats | 2 | 9 |
| Susannah Crawford | OB University | 1 | 0 |
| Dhys Faleafaga | Northern United | 3 | 10 |
| Selestina Hamlin | Marist St Pats | 5 | 0 |
| Patricia Kalolo-Apolinario | Poneke | 4 | 0 |
| Petra Kriklanova | Petone | 8 | 0 |
| Toreka Leti | Northern United | 6 | 0 |
| Ayesha Leti-l'iga | Oriental Rongotai | 19 | 90 |
| Sanita Levave | Northern United | 39 | 20 |
| Raylene Lolo | Oriental Rongotai | 14 | 10 |
| Kauna Lopa | Oriental Rongotai | 18 | 0 |
| Holly MacDonald | OB University | 6 | 0 |
| Lilian Mapu | Oriental Rongotai | 8 | 0 |
| Vaine Marsters | Northern United | 33 | 35 |

| | Club | Games for Union | Points for Union |
|---|---|---|---|
| Kiri Mei | Wainuiomata | 30 | 50 |
| Joanah Ngan-Woo | Oriental Rongotai | 34 | 30 |
| Jackie Patea-Fereti | Wainuiomata | 49 | 40 |
| Alicia Print | Oriental Rongotai | 20 | 0 |
| Rosie Stirling | Hutt OB Marist | 8 | 0 |
| Tove Svanborg | Paremata-Plimmerton | 4 | 5 |
| Monica Tagoai | Marist St Pats | 9 | 5 |
| Elieta Taito | Avalon | 13 | 10 |
| Brooke Tauaneai | Wainuiomata | 10 | 5 |
| Janet Taumoli | Oriental Rongotai | 15 | 5 |
| Acacia Te Iwimate | Petone | 42 | 41 |
| Sinead To'oala-Ryder | Marist St Pats | 4 | 5 |
| Saua Ualesi | Poneke | 5 | 5 |
| Angelica Uila | Petone | 7 | 15 |
| Rejieli Uluinayau | Oriental Rongotai | 11 | 15 |
| Gina Williamson | OB University | 27 | 5 |

## INDIVIDUAL SCORING

| | Tries | Con | PG | DG | Points |
|---|---|---|---|---|---|
| Leti-l'iga | 6 | – | – | – | 30 |
| Te Iwimate | – | 4 | 6 | – | 26 |
| Mei | 3 | – | – | – | 15 |
| Patea-Fereti | 3 | – | – | – | 15 |
| Uila | 3 | – | – | – | 15 |
| Bryce | 1 | 3 | – | – | 11 |
| Faleafaga | 2 | – | – | – | 10 |
| Lolo | 2 | – | – | – | 10 |
| Marsters | 2 | – | – | – | 10 |
| Uluinayau | 2 | – | – | – | 10 |
| Copeland | 1 | 2 | – | – | 9 |

| | Tries | Con | PG | DG | Points |
|---|---|---|---|---|---|
| penalty try | 1 | – | – | – | 7 |
| Levave | 1 | – | – | – | 5 |
| Svanborg | 1 | – | – | – | 5 |
| Tagoai | 1 | – | – | – | 5 |
| To'oala-Ryder | 1 | – | – | – | 5 |
| Ualesi | 1 | – | – | – | 5 |
| Williamson | 1 | – | – | – | 5 |
| **Totals** | **32\*** | **9** | **6** | **0** | **198** |
| Opposition scored | 29* | 21 | 3 | 0 | 198 |

\* Includes one penalty try (7 points)

## WELLINGTON 2017

| | Hawke's Bay | Manawatu | Waikato | Auckland | Otago | Counties Manukau | Canterbury | TOTALS |
|---|---|---|---|---|---|---|---|---|
| R. Uluinayau | 15 | 15 | 15 | 15 | 15 | s | 9 | 7 |
| C. Copeland | – | – | s | – | – | – | 15 | 2 |
| T.A. Svanborg | 14 | 14 | 11 | s | – | – | – | 4 |
| S. Burgess | s | – | – | – | – | – | – | 1 |
| T.L. Leti | – | – | 14 | – | – | – | – | 1 |
| D. Faleafaga | – | – | – | – | s | 14 | 14 | 3 |
| A. Leti-I'iga | 11 | – | – | 11 | 11 | 11 | 11 | 5 |
| V.A. Marsters | 13 | 13 | 12 | 14 | 14 | 15 | 12 | 7 |
| M. Tagoai | – | – | 13 | 13 | 13 | 13 | 13 | 5 |
| T. Burgess | 12 | 12 | – | s | s | 12 | – | 5 |
| J. Bryce | – | 11 | s | 12 | 12 | s | – | 5 |
| K. Lopa | 10 | 10 | 10 | 10 | – | – | s | 5 |
| S. Hamlin | – | s | – | s | 10 | 10 | s | 5 |
| A.M. Te Iwimate | 9 | 9 | 9 | 9 | 9 | 9 | 10 | 7 |
| J.S. Patea-Fereti (capt) | 8 | 8 | 8 | 8 | 8 | 8 | 8 | 7 |
| G.M. Williamson | 7 | 7 | 7 | – | – | – | – | 3 |
| S. To'oala-Ryder | – | – | – | 7 | 7 | 7 | 7 | 4 |
| K.R.W. Mei | 6 | 6 | 6 | 6 | 6 | 6 | 6 | 7 |
| S. Ualesi | s | s | s | – | s | s | – | 5 |
| L.P. Mapu | s | s | – | – | – | – | s | 3 |
| S.D. Levave | 5 | – | 5 | 5 | 5 | 5 | 5 | 6 |
| P. Kriklanova | 4 | 4 | 4 | 4 | – | – | – | 4 |
| J.M.P. Ngan-Woo | s | 5 | s | s | 4 | 4 | s | 7 |
| H. MacDonald | s | s | – | s | s | s | 4 | 6 |
| P. Kalolo-Apolinario | 3 | 3 | – | – | – | – | – | 2 |
| S. Crawford | – | s | – | – | – | – | – | 1 |
| B. Tauaneai | – | – | 3 | – | 3 | 3 | s | 4 |
| J. Taumoli | – | – | s | 3 | – | s | 3 | 4 |
| E. Taito | – | – | – | – | s | – | – | 1 |
| A. Uila | 1 | – | 1 | 1 | s | s | s | 6 |
| R. Lolo | s | 1 | s | s | 1 | 1 | 1 | 7 |
| A. Print | 2 | 2 | 2 | 2 | s | 2 | 2 | 7 |
| R. Stirling | s | s | s | s | 2 | s | s | 7 |

## WELLINGTON TEAM RECORD, 2017

Played 7   Won 3   Lost 4   Points for 198   Points against 198

| Date | Opponent | Location | Score | Tries | Con | PG | DG | Referee |
|---|---|---|---|---|---|---|---|---|
| September 2 | Hawke's Bay (P/C) | Porirua | 42–10 | Mei (2), Uluinayau (2), Leti-I'iga, Uila, Lolo | Te Iwimate (2), Bryce | Te Iwimate | | M.J. McEwen |
| September 9 | Manawatu (P) | Petone | 27–35 | Marsters, Williamson, Ualesi, Svanborg, Bryce | Bryce | | | R.M. Mahoney |
| September 16 | Waikato (P) | Hamilton | 11–5 | Levave | | Te Iwimate (2) | | R.M. Mahoney |
| September 23 | Auckland (P) | Porirua | 30–31 | Leti-I'iga (2), Marsters, Uila | Te Iwimate (2) | Te Iwimate (2) | | M.J. McEwen |
| September 30 | Otago (P/C) | Dunedin | 41–19 | Lolo, penalty try, To'oala-Ryder, Patea-Fereti, Leti-I'iga, Faleafaga, Tagoai | Bryce (2) | | | B.A. Malcolm |
| October 7 | Counties Manukau (P) | Porirua | 13–43 | Mei, Uila | | Te Iwimate | | Rachel Horton Australia |
| October 14 | Canterbury (P, ST) | Christchurch | 34–55 | Patea-Fereti (2), Leti-I'iga (2), Copeland, Faleafaga | Copeland (2) | | | R.J.M. Gordon |

ST Stewart Trophy

# WOMEN'S FIRST-CLASS STATISTICS

*to January 1, 2018*

## 75 GAMES IN FIRST-CLASS RUGBY

| | Career | Games | | Career | Games |
|---|---|---|---|---|---|
| Emma Jensen | 1999–2017 | 157 | Karina Stowers | 2004–17 | 95 |
| Fiao'o Fa'amausili | 1999–2017 | 155 | Monalisa Codling | 1998–2008 | 91 |
| Justine Lavea | 2001–17 | 136 | Victoria Heighway | 1999–2009 | 90 |
| Anna Richards | 1990–2011 | 125 | Linda Itunu | 2003–17 | 83 |
| Casey Robertson | 1999–2014 | 118 | Teresa Te Tamaki | 2002–15 | 81 |
| Stephanie Te Ohaere-Fox | 2003–17 | 111 | Aleisha Nelson | 2008–17 | 80 |
| Kendra Cocksedge | 2007–17 | 110 | Claire Richardson | 2001–14 | 79 |
| Selica Winiata | 2001–17 | 102 | Eloise Blackwell | 2009–17 | 77 |
| Amiria Rule | 1999–2014 | 98 | Kelly Brazier | 2005–17 | 75 |

## 275 POINTS IN FIRST-CLASS RUGBY

| | Career | Games | Tries | Con | PG | DG | Points |
|---|---|---|---|---|---|---|---|
| Kendra Cocksedge | 2007–17 | 110 | 57 | 205 | 73 | – | 914 |
| Emma Jensen | 1999–2017 | 157 | 11 | 143 | 79 | 1 | 581 |
| Selica Winiata | 2001–17 | 102 | 97 | 29 | 10 | – | 573 |
| Hannah Porter | 1999–2008 | 59 | 20 | 115 | 61 | – | 513 |
| Tammi Wilson | 1998–2001 | 45 | 40 | 92 | 24 | 1 | 459 |
| Kelly Brazier | 2005–17 | 75 | 35 | 84 | 27 | – | 424 |
| Claire Richardson | 2001–14 | 79 | 36 | 33 | 25 | – | 321 |
| Hazel Tubic | 2005–17 | 57 | 18 | 83 | 19 | – | 313 |
| Fiao'o Fa'amausili | 1999–2017 | 155 | 57 | – | – | – | 285 |
| Annaleah Rush | 1996–2002 | 40 | 29 | 44 | 15 | – | 278 |
| Chelsea Alley | 2011–17 | 51 | 16 | 53 | 30 | – | 276 |

## 40 TRIES IN FIRST-CLASS RUGBY

| | Tries | Games | | Tries | Games |
|---|---|---|---|---|---|
| Selica Winiata | 97 | 102 | Victoria Grant | 51 | 69 |
| Fiao'o Fa'amausili | 57 | 155 | Louisa Wall | 48 | 32 |
| Kendra Cocksedge | 57 | 110 | Carla Hohepa | 45 | 44 |
| Vanessa Cootes | 54 | 50 | Monique Hirovanaa | 43 | 62 |
| Dianne Kahura | 53 | 35 | Tammi Wilson | 40 | 45 |

## MOST DROPPED GOALS IN FIRST-CLASS RUGBY

| | DG | Games |
|---|---|---|
| Rebecca Mahoney (*nee* Hull) | 4 | 69 |

## 100 POINTS IN A SEASON

| | Teams | M | Tries | Con | PG | DG | Total |
|---|---|---|---|---|---|---|---|
| Kendra Cocksedge | Canterbury/NZ, 2017 | 14 | 11 | 52 | 4 | – | 171 |
| Tammi Wilson | Auckland/NZ, 1999 | 10 | 15 | 34 | 4 | – | 155 |
| Kendra Cocksedge | Canterbury/NZ, 2016 | 12 | 11 | 32 | 12 | – | 155 |
| Kendra Cocksedge | Canterbury/NZ, 2014 | 17 | 5 | 32 | 16 | – | 137 |
| Tammi Wilson | Auckland/NZ, 2002 | 11 | 8 | 20 | 14 | 1 | 125 |
| Selica Winiata | Manawatu/NZ, 2012 | 9 | 15 | 17 | 2 | – | 115 |
| Hannah Myers | Auckland/NZ, 2003 | 7 | 6 | 25 | 9 | – | 107 |
| Hannah Myers | Auckland/NZ, 2005 | 12 | 4 | 27 | 11 | – | 107 |

## MOST TRIES IN A SEASON

| | Teams | Tries | Games |
|---|---|---|---|
| Dianne Kahura | Auckland/NZ, 2002 | 19 | 11 |
| Vanessa Cootes | New Zealand, 1996 | 18 | 3 |
| Selica Winiata | Manawatu/NZ, 2016 | 18 | 11 |
| Mele Hufanga | Auckland 2015 | 16 | 7 |
| Portia Woodman | New Zealand, 2017 | 16 | 8 |
| Tammi Wilson | Auckland/NZ, 1999 | 15 | 10 |
| Selica Winiata | Manawatu/NZ, 2012 | 15 | 9 |
| Selica Winiata | Manawatu/NZ, 2014 | 15 | 13 |

## MOST POINTS IN A GAME

| | Match | Tries | Con | PG | DG | Points |
|---|---|---|---|---|---|---|
| Vanessa Cootes | New Zealand v France, 1996 | 9 | – | – | – | 45 |
| Kelly Brazier | Otago v Hawke's Bay, 2012 | 5 | 10 | – | – | 45 |
| Annaleah Rush | Otago v Hanan Shield Unions, 1999 | 8 | 1 | – | – | 42 |
| Portia Woodman | New Zealand v Hong Kong, 2017 | 8 | – | – | – | 40 |
| Selica Winiata | Manawatu v Waikato, 2012 | 4 | 6 | 2 | – | 38 |
| Tammi Wilson | New Zealand v USA, 1999 | 6 | 3 | – | – | 36 |
| Christine Ross | New Zealand v France, 1996 | 2 | 12 | – | – | 34 |
| Kelly Brazier | Otago v Manawatu, 2009 | 4 | 7 | – | – | 34 |
| Tammi Wilson | Auckland v North Harbour, 1999 | 1 | 13 | – | – | 31 |
| Kendra Cocksedge | New Zealand v Hong Kong | 1 | 13 | – | – | 31 |
| Tammi Wilson | New Zealand v Germany, 1998 | 4 | 5 | – | – | 30 |
| Kendra Cocksedge | Canterbury v Taranaki, 2013 | 4 | 5 | – | – | 30 |
| Kendra Cocksedge | Canterbury v North Harbour, 2016 | 4 | 5 | – | – | 30 |

## MOST TRIES IN A GAME

| | Match | Tries |
|---|---|---|
| Vanessa Cootes | New Zealand v France, 1996 | 9 |
| Annaleah Rush | Otago v Hanan Shield Unions, 1999 | 8 |
| Portia Woodman | New Zealand v Hong Kong, 2017 | 8 |
| Tammi Wilson | New Zealand v USA, 1999 | 6 |
| Helen Reader | New Zealand v New South Wales, 1994 | 5 |
| Vanessa Cootes | New Zealand v USA, 1996 | 5 |
| Vanessa Cootes | New Zealand v USA, 1998 | 5 |
| Vanessa Cootes | New Zealand v Germany, 2002 | 5 |
| Deidre Hakopa | Hawke's Bay v Southland, 2003 | 5 |
| Kelly Brazier | Otago v Hawke's Bay, 2012 | 5 |
| Selica Winiata | New Zealand v Samoa, 2014 | 5 |
| Kilisitina Moata'ane | Otago v Tasman, 2017 | 5 |

## MOST CONVERSIONS IN A GAME

| | Match | Con |
|---|---|---|
| Tammi Wilson | Auckland v North Harbour, 1999 | 13 |
| Kendra Cocksedge | New Zealand v Hong Kong, 2017 | 13 |
| Christine Ross | New Zealand v France, 1996 | 12 |
| Kelly Brazier | Otago v Hawke's Bay, 2012 | 10 |
| Christine Ross | New Zealand v Canada, 1996 | 9 |
| Elizabeth Goulden | Manawatu v Hawke's Bay, 2017 | 9 |
| Olivia Waldron | Otago v Tasman, 2017 | 9 |

## MOST PENALTY GOALS IN A GAME

| | Match | PG |
|---|---|---|
| Annaleah Rush | Auckland v Wellington, 2001 | 6 |
| Kendra Cocksedge | Canterbury v Auckland, 2009 | 5 |
| Elizabeth Goulden | Wellington v Taranaki, 2013 | 5 |
| Kendra Cocksedge | Canterbury v Waikato, 2016 | 5 |

## HIGHEST TEAM SCORES

| Score | Match | Result |
|---|---|---|
| 134 | New Zealand v Germany, 1998 | 134–6 |
| 121 | New Zealand v Hong Kong, 2017 | 121–0 |
| 117 | New Zealand v Germany, 2002 | 117–0 |
| 116 | Auckland v North Harbour, 1999 | 116–0 |
| 109 | New Zealand v France, 1996 | 109–0 |
| 101 | Auckland v Bay of Plenty 2015 | 101–0 |
| 100 | Hawke's Bay v Southland, 2003 | 100–5 |

# WOMEN'S RUGBY REFEREES 2017

*by Chris Jansen*

## WOMEN'S RUGBY REFEREE SQUAD 2017

|              |                  |      | Tests | Nat[1] | NC[2] | Sevens | Total |
|--------------|------------------|------|-------|-------|------|--------|-------|
| B.J. Andrew  | Manawatu         | 2015 | –     | –     | 8    | –      | 8     |
| M. Cogger-Orr| Auckland         | 2017 |       |       | 6    |        | 6     |
| N.M. Ganley  | North Harbour    | 2013 | –     | –     | 16   | –      | 16    |
| L.A. Jenner  | Counties Manukau | 2017 | –     | –     | 5    | –      | 5     |
| R.M. Mahoney | Wairarapa Bush   | 2015 | 1     | 1     | 13   | 3      | 18    |
| L.K. Moore   | Southland        | 2017 |       |       | 1    |        | 1     |

*Nat[1] Tour fixture      NC[2] National Provincial Championship (Farah Palmer Cup)*

## REFEREE APPOINTMENTS 2017

**Brittany Andrew**

| January | 14/15 | * | National Sevens | Rotorua |
|---------|-------|---|-----------------|---------|

**Maggie Cogger – Orr**

| September | 2  | NC     | Tasman v Waikato          | Blenheim     |
|-----------|----|--------|---------------------------|--------------|
|           | 9  | NC     | Hawke's Bay v Bay of Plenty | Napier     |
|           | 16 | NC     | Bay of Plenty v North Harbour | Rotorua  |
|           | 30 | NC     | Canterbury v Tasman       | Christchurch |
| October   | 14 | NC     | North Harbour v Otago     | Albany       |
|           | 28 | NC c-f | Bay of Plenty v Otago     | Mt Maunganui |

**Natarsha Ganley**

| January   | 14/15 | *      | National Sevens             | Rotorua          |
|-----------|-------|--------|-----------------------------|------------------|
| September | 23    | NC     | Counties Manukau v Canterbury | Papakura       |
| October   | 7     | NC     | Otago v Bay of Plenty       | Dunedin          |
|           | 14    | NC     | Manawatu v Counties Manukau | Palmerston North |
|           | 21    | NC s-f | Canterbury v Waikato        | Christchurch     |
|           | 29    | NC p-f | Counties Manukau v Canterbury | Pukekohe       |

**Lauren Jenner**

| January   | 14/15 | *      | National Sevens       | Rotorua          |
|-----------|-------|--------|-----------------------|------------------|
| September | 24    | NC     | Bay of Plenty v Tasman | Tauranga        |
|           | 30    | NC     | Waikato v Bay of Plenty | Hamilton       |
| October   | 7     | NC     | Manawatu v Auckland   | Palmerston North |
|           | 14    | NC     | Auckland v Waikato    | Pakuranga        |
|           | 21    | NC s-f | Otago v North Harbour | Dunedin          |

**Rebecca Mahoney**

| January   | 14/15 | *    | National Sevens                      | Rotorua     |
|-----------|-------|------|--------------------------------------|-------------|
| February  | 4/5   |      | Australia World Rugby Women's Sevens | Sydney      |
| April     | 6/7   | RWCQ | World Rugby Women's Sevens Qualifier | Hong Kong   |
|           | 22/23 |      | Japan World Rugby Women's Sevens     | Kitakyushu  |
| September | 9     | NC   | Wellington v Manawatu                | Petone      |
|           | 16    | NC   | Waikato v Wellington                 | Hamilton    |

| 22 | NC | Manawatu v Waikato | Palmerston North |
|----|----|-----|------|
| 29 | NC | North Harbour v Auckland | Albany |

**Louise Moore**

| October | 14 | NC | Tasman v Hawke's Bay | Nelson |
|---------|----|----|-----|------|

| * | Non first-class appointment |
|---|---|
| NC | National provincial championship (Farah Palmer Cup) |
| RWCQ | Rugby World Cup Qualifying |
| s-f | semi-final |
| p-f | premiership final |
| c-f | championship final |

### One overseas referee controlled National Sevens fixtures:
*Tyler Miller (Australia)*

### Two overseas referees controlled Farah Palmer Cup fixtures:
***Amber Hibbard*** *(Australia)* Sep 23 North Harbour v Hawke's Bay.
***Rachel Horton*** *(Australia)* Oct 7 Wellington v Counties Manukau.

### Twelve males refereed Farah Palmer Cup fixtures:
***Brandon Roberts*** *(Counties Manukau)* Sep 2 Bay of Plenty v Auckland, Oct 8:
    Waikato v Canterbury
***Matthew McEwen*** *(Manawatu)* Sep 2: Wellington v Hawke's Bay, Sep 23:
    Wellington v Auckland
***Kyle Lagerwall*** *(North Harbour)* Sep 2: Counties Manukau v North Harbour
***Karl Hancox*** *(Canterbury)* Sep 3: Canterbury v Otago, Sep 16: Canterbury v Manawatu
***Marcus Playle*** *(Auckland)* Sep 7: Counties Manukau v Waikato
***Sam Fellows*** *(Bay of Plenty)* Sep 9: Auckland v Canterbury
***Blair Malcolm*** *(North Otago)* Sep 9: Otago v Tasman, Sep 30: Otago v Wellington
***Ryan Borthwick*** *(Counties Manukau)* Sep 16: Auckland v Counties Manukau,
    Oct 21: Counties Manukau v Auckland
***Stu Catley*** *(Hawke's Bay)* Sep 16: Hawke's Bay v Otago
***Hugh Reed*** *(Hawke's Bay)* Sep 30: Hawke's Bay v Manawatu
***Vincent Ringrose*** *(Wellington)* Oct 8: Tasman v North Harbour
***Richard Gordon*** *(Wellington)* Oct 14: Canterbury v Wellington

*Note:* men refereeing Farah Palmer Cup fixtures are not credited with a first-class appointment.

## INTERNATIONAL ASSISTANT REFEREES

**Brittany Andrew**

| | | | | |
|---|---|---|---|---|
| June | 9 | New Zealand v Canada | | Wellington |
| | 13 | New Zealand v Australia | | Christchurch |

**Natarsha Ganley**

| | | | | |
|---|---|---|---|---|
| June | 9 | Australia v England | | Porirua |
| | 13 | Canada v England | | Christchurch |
| | 17 | New Zealand v England | | Rotorua |

**Lee Jeffrey**

| | | | | |
|---|---|---|---|---|
| June | 9 | New Zealand v Canada | (TMO) | Wellington |
| | 13 | New Zealand v Australia | (TMO) | Christchurch |
| | 17 | New Zealand v England | (TMO) | Rotorua |

**Lauren Jenner**

| | | | | |
|---|---|---|---|---|
| June | 17 | Australia v Canada | | Rotorua |

**Rebecca Mahoney**

| | | | | |
|---|---|---|---|---|
| June | 9 | Australia v England | | Porirua |
| | 13 | Canada v England | | Christchurch |
| | 17 | Australia v Canada | | Rotorua |

*(TMO) Television Match Official*

## INTERNATIONAL REFEREES
### *to 1 January, 2018*

| | |
|---|---|
| Beard, J.D.L. (Counties Manukau) 2014–16 | 10 |
| Inwood, N.A. (Wanganui & Canterbury) 2002–14 | 32 |
| Mahoney, R.M. (Wairarapa Bush) 2016 | 1 |
| Mellor, K.E. (North Harbour) 2006 | 1 |

## TWENTY-FIVE AND MORE FIRST-CLASS MATCHES
### *to 1 January, 2018*

| | | | | | |
|---|---|---|---|---|---|
| N.A. Inwood | 2000–14 | 85 | L. Jeffrey | 2003–16 | 42 |
| J.D.L. Beard | 2012–16 | 49 | C.F. Gurr | 2011–16 | 34 |

# WOMEN'S SEVENS RUGBY

The Black Ferns Sevens won the 2016/17 HSBC Sevens Series with five Cup titles from the six tournaments which commenced in December 2016. Late in the year the team won the Oceania Sevens in Fiji which prepared the side for the first round of the 2017/18 series in Dubai. However, having comfortably defeated USA in the final pool game New Zealand suffered a shock loss to the same opponent in the Cup quarter-final.

| | | Australia | USA | Japan | Canada | France | Fiji | Dubai | TOTALS |
|---|---|---|---|---|---|---|---|---|---|
| Shakira Baker | Waikato | – | – | – | * | * | – | – | 2 |
| Michaela Blyde | Taranaki/Bay of Plenty | * | * | * | * | * | * | * | 7 |
| Kelly Brazier | Bay of Plenty | * | * | * | – | – | – | – | 3 |
| Gayle Broughton | Taranaki | – | – | – | – | * | * | * | 3 |
| Jess Drummond | Tasman | – | – | – | * | * | – | – | 2 |
| Theresa Fitzpatrick | Auckland | * | * | – | * | – | * | * | 5 |
| Sarah Goss (capt) | Manawatu | * | * | * | – | – | * | * | 5 |
| Kayla McAlister | Auckland | – | – | – | – | – | * | – | 1 |
| Crystal Mayes | Manawatu | – | – | – | * | * | – | – | 2 |
| Tyla Nathan-Wong | Auckland | * | * | * | * | * | * | * | 7 |
| Tayla Reti | Wellington | – | – | – | – | * | – | – | 1 |
| Cheyelle Robins-Reti | Waikato | – | * | * | * | – | – | – | 3 |
| Alena Saili | Southland | * | * | * | * | * | * | * | 7 |
| Terina Te Tamaki | Waikato | * | * | – | – | * | * | – | 4 |
| Rebekah Tufuga | Manawatu | – | – | * | * | – | – | – | 2 |
| Ruby Tui | Canterbury | * | * | * | * | * | * | * | 7 |
| Stacey Waaka | Waikato | – | – | – | – | – | * | * | 2 |
| Katarina Whata-Simpkins | Wellington | * | – | * | * | * | – | * | 5 |
| Renee Wickliffe | Counties Manukau | * | * | – | – | – | * | – | 3 |
| Niall Williams | Auckland | * | * | * | * | * | – | * | 6 |
| Tenika Willison | Waikato | – | – | * | – | – | * | – | 2 |
| Portia Woodman | Counties Manukau | * | * | * | – | – | * | * | 5 |

Nathan-Wong was captain at Canada and France.

*Coach:* Allan Bunting
*Assistant coach:* Cory Sweeney, Stu Ross
*Manager:* Jenelle Strickland
*Strength & conditioning trainer:* Brad Anderson
*Video analyst:* Stu Ross
*Physiotherapist:* Nicole Armstrong, Paul Cameron

## INDIVIDUAL SCORING

| | Tries | Con | Points | | Tries | Con | Points |
|---|---|---|---|---|---|---|---|
| Nathan-Wong | 7 | 85 | 205 | Goss | 4 | – | 20 |
| Blyde | 40 | – | 200 | McAlister | 4 | – | 20 |
| Woodman | 35 | – | 175 | Wickliffe | 4 | – | 20 |
| Williams | 12 | – | 60 | Robins-Reti | 2 | 4 | 18 |
| Tui | 11 | – | 55 | Baker | 3 | – | 15 |
| Saili | 9 | – | 45 | Mayes | 3 | – | 15 |
| Whata-Simpkins | 7 | 4 | 43 | Waaka | 2 | – | 10 |
| Broughton | 7 | – | 35 | Drummond | 1 | – | 5 |
| Brazier | 6 | 1 | 32 | | | | |
| Willison | 1 | 10 | 25 | **Totals** | **162** | **104** | **1018** |
| Fitzpatrick | 4 | – | 20 | | | | |

*Opposition scored 251 points*

*Final points for 2016/17 World Rugby Sevens Series:* New Zealand 116, Australia 100, Canada 98, Fiji 66, Russia 66, United States 62, France 60, England 37, Ireland 34, Spain 19, Brazil 13, South Africa 6, Japan 4, Papua New Guinea 1, Netherlands 1, Argentina 1. The series was held over six tournaments from December 2016 to June 2017.

*Previous winners:* New Zealand 2013, 2014, 2015; Australia 2016.
*World Rugby Sevens Series Cup championship titles (2012 to 1 January 2018):* New Zealand 15, Australia 7, Canada 3, England 2.

## NEW ZEALAND AT AUSTRALIA SEVENS
### Allianz Stadium, Sydney                                    February 3/4, 2017

| Date | Opponent | Result | Tries | Conversions |
|---|---|---|---|---|
| Feb 3 | Papua New Guinea | won 34–5 | Blyde (3), Wickliffe, Woodman, Saili | Nathan-Wong, Brazier |
| Feb 3 | France | won 14–12 | Brazier (2) | Nathan-Wong (2), |
| Feb 3 | Canada | won 31–10 | Woodman (2), Brazier, Blyde, Fitzpatrick | Nathan-Wong (3) |
| Feb 4 | France (Cup q-f) | won 24–5 | Whata-Simpkins, Woodman, Williams, Blyde | Nathan-Wong (2) |
| Feb 4 | USA (Cup s-f) | lost 12–19 | Whata-Simpkins, Nathan-Wong | Nathan-Wong |
| Feb 4 | Australia (for 3rd place) | won 19–0 | Blyde (2), Woodman | Nathan-Wong (2) |

Canada defeated USA 21–17 in the Cup final

## NEW ZEALAND AT USA SEVENS
### Sam Boyd Stadium, Las Vegas      March 3/4, 2017

| Date | Opponent | Result | Tries | Conversions |
|---|---|---|---|---|
| Mar 3 | Brazil | won 24–0 | Blyde (2), Woodman, Nathan-Wong | Nathan-Wong (2) |
| Mar 3 | England | won 27–5 | Goss, Woodman, Saili, Brazier, Blyde | Nathan-Wong |
| Mar 3 | Australia | won 21–14 | Woodman (2), Blyde | Nathan-Wong (3) |
| Mar 4 | Russia (Cup q-f) | won 26–5 | Blyde (2), Tui, Woodman | Nathan-Wong (3) |
| Mar 4 | USA (Cup s-f) | won 12–7 | Blyde, Williams | Nathan-Wong |
| Mar 4 | Australia (Cup final) | won 28–5 | Tui, Nathan-Wong, Woodman, Saili | Nathan-Wong (4) |

## NEW ZEALAND AT JAPAN SEVENS
### Mikuni World Stadium, Kitakyushu      April 22/23, 2017

| Date | Opponent | Result | Tries | Conversions |
|---|---|---|---|---|
| Apr 22 | Japan | won 31–0 | Woodman, Brazier, Whata-Simpkins, Robins-Reti, Saili | Robins-Reti (3) |
| Apr 22 | France | won 19–14 | Williams (2), Nathan-Wong | Nathan-Wong (2) |
| Apr 22 | Russia | won 22–7 | Woodman (2), Williams, Tui | Nathan-Wong |
| Apr 23 | England (Cup q-f) | won 21–5 | Woodman, Blyde, Williams | Nathan-Wong (3) |
| Apr 23 | Fiji (Cup s-f) | won 21–0 | Woodman (2), Brazier | Nathan-Wong (3) |
| Apr 23 | Canada (Cup final) | won 17–14 | Williams, Woodman, Blyde | Nathan-Wong |

## NEW ZEALAND AT CANADA SEVENS
### Westhills Stadium, Langford, Victoria, British Columbia      May 27/28, 2017

| Date | Opponent | Result | Tries | Conversions |
|---|---|---|---|---|
| May 27 | Netherlands | won 17–10 | Blyde, Baker, Robins-Reti | Robins-Reti |
| May 27 | USA | won 7–0 | Baker | Nathan-Wong |
| May 27 | England | won 43–7 | Blyde (5), Tui, Drummond, | Nathan-Wong (4) |
| May 28 | Russia (Cup q-f) | won 24–0 | Saili, Tui, Blyde, Mayes | Nathan-Wong (2) |
| May 28 | France (Cup s-f) | won 28–5 | Mayes, Blyde, Williams, Whata-Simpkins | Nathan-Wong (4) |
| May 28 | Canada (Cup final) | won 17–7 | Blyde, Nathan-Wong, Saili | Nathan-Wong |

## NEW ZEALAND AT FRANCE SEVENS
### Stade Gabriel-Montpied, Clermont-Ferrand    June 24/25, 2017

| Date | Opponent | Result | Tries | Conversions |
|---|---|---|---|---|
| June 24 | Japan | won 21–10 | Tui, Williams, Nathan-Wong | Nathan-Wong (3) |
| June 24 | Ireland | won 26–5 | Blyde (2), Saili, Williams | Nathan-Wong (3) |
| June 24 | USA | won 19–14 | Nathan-Wong, Broughton, Whata-Simpkins | Nathan-Wong (2) |
| June 25 | Fiji (Cup q-f ) | won 31–7 | Saili (2), Whata-Simpkins, Blyde, Mayes | Nathan-Wong (3) |
| June 25 | France (Cup s-f ) | won 21–7 | Blyde, Tui, Whata-Simpkins | Nathan-Wong (3) |
| June 25 | Australia (Cup final) | won 22–7 | Tui, Williams, Blyde, Baker | Nathan–Wong |

## NEW ZEALAND AT OCEANIA SEVENS
### ANZ Stadium, Suva, Fiji    November 10/11, 2017

| Date | Opponent | Result | Tries | Conversions |
|---|---|---|---|---|
| Nov 10 | Tahiti | won 70–0 | Wickliffe (3), Goss (2), Woodman (2), Willison, Fitzpatrick, Blyde | Willison (10) |
| Nov 10 | Cook Islands | won 26–5 | Woodman (2), Blyde, Waaka | Nathan-Wong (3) |
| | Papua New Guinea | won 15–0 | Woodman (3) | |
| Nov 11 | Fiji(s-f ) | won 24–0 | Fitzpatrick, Woodman, Blyde, Broughton | Nathan-Wong (2) |
| Nov 11 | Australia (final) | won 12–5 | Tui, Broughton | Nathan-Wong |

## NEW ZEALAND AT DUBAI SEVENS
### The Sevens, Dubai    November 30/1, 2017

| Date | Opponent | Result | Tries | Conversions |
|---|---|---|---|---|
| Nov 30 | South Africa | won 40–0 | Blyde, Woodman, Broughton, McAlister, Fitzpatrick, Waaka | Nathan-Wong (4), Whata-Simpkins |
| Nov 30 | France | won 28–7 | Woodman (2), Blyde, McAlister | Nathan-Wong (4) |
| Nov 30 | USA | won 45–14 | Woodman (2), Blyde, Tui, Goss, McAlister, Broughton | Nathan-Wong (4), Whata-Simpkins |
| Dec 1 | USA (Cup q-f ) | lost 12–14 | Broughton, Woodman | Nathan-Wong |
| Dec 1 | Spain (s-f for 5th) | won 43–0 | Blyde (3), Tui, Williams, McAlister, Broughton | Nathan-Wong (2), Whata-Simpkins (2) |
| Dec 1 | France (final for 5th place) | won 24–0 | Woodman (3), Blyde | Nathan-Wong (2) |

Australia defeated USA 34–0 in the Cup final

# SEVENS RECORDS

*to January 1, 2018*

## BY NEW ZEALAND TEAMS

| | | |
|---|---|---|
| Most successive wins | 44 | 2014–15 |
| Most successive tournament wins | 7 | 2014–15 |
| Most successive appearances in finals | 10 | 2013–15 |

**Tournament records**

| | | |
|---|---|---|
| Most points | 293 | Hong Kong 2000 |
| Most tries | 47 | Hong Kong 2000 |
| Most conversions | 30 | New Zealand 2001 |

**Match records**

| | | |
|---|---|---|
| Highest team score | 83 | v International Selection, Japan 2001 |
| Record victory (points ahead) | 83 | 83–0 v International Selection, Japan 2001 |
| Highest score conceded | 35 | v Australia (final), Dubai 2013 |
| Record defeat (points behind) | 29 | 5–34 v USA, Amsterdam 2015; |
| Most tries | 13 | v International Selection, Japan 2001 |
| Most conversions | 10 | v Tahiti, Fiji 2017 |

## BY THE PLAYERS

**Career records**

| | | |
|---|---|---|
| Attended most tournaments | 31 | S.L. Goss |
| Most points | 910 | P.L. Woodman |
| Most tries | 182 | P.L. Woodman |
| Most conversions | 291 | T.B. Nathan-Wong |

**Tournament records**

| | | |
|---|---|---|
| Most points | 70 | P.L. Woodman, USA 2015 |
| Most tries | 14 | P.L. Woodman, USA 2015 |
| Most conversions | 29 | A.M. Richards, New Zealand 2001 |

**Match records**

| | | |
|---|---|---|
| Most points | 25 | M. Blyde, v Samoa, Noosa 2013 |
| | | P.L. Woodman v France, Brazil 2015; |
| | | P.L. Woodman v USA, USA 2015 |
| | | M. Blyde v England, Canada 2017; |
| | | T.R. Willison v Tahiti, Fiji 2017 |
| Most tries | 5 | M. Blyde, v Samoa, Noosa 2013 |
| | | P.L. Woodman v France, Brazil 2015; |
| | | P.L. Woodman v USA, USA 2015 |
| | | M. Blyde v England, Canada 2017 |
| Most conversions | 10 | T.R. Willison v Tahiti, Fiji 2017 |

## NEW ZEALAND SEVENS REPRESENTATIVES, 2000–17

# NATIONAL SEVENS

Rotorua International Stadium                    **January 14–15, 2017**

## POOL

A    Manawatu 33, North Harbour 5; Waikato 12, Otago 12;
     Manawatu 20, Otago 10; Waikato 22, North Harbour 10;
     Manawatu 17, Waikato 12; Otago 38, North Harbour 12.

B    Wellington 41, Hawke's Bay 0; Bay of Plenty 24, Auckland 19;
     Auckland 31, Wellington 0; Bay of Plenty 42, Hawke's Bay 5;
     Auckland 43, Hawke's Bay 0; Bay of Plenty 33, Wellington 0.

C    Counties Manukau 40, Taranaki 5; Canterbury 25, Tasman 0;
     Counties Manukau 45, Tasman 0; Canterbury 24, Taranaki 10;
     Tasman 34, Taranaki 5; Counties Manukau 35, Canterbury 12.

## CUP CHAMPIONSHIP

*Quarter-finals*        Manawatu 26, Wellington 10; Waikato 19, Bay of Plenty 0;
                        Counties Manukau 24, Otago 7; Auckland 17, Canterbury 5.
*Semi-finals*           Manawatu 12, Auckland 7; Counties Manukau 33, Waikato 0.
*Final*                 Counties Manukau 24, Manawatu 17.
*Play-off for 3rd/4th*  Auckland 28, Waikato 5.

## PLATE CHAMPIONSHIP

*Semi-finals*           Canterbury 19, Wellington 17; Bay of Plenty 33, Otago 5.
*Final (5th/6th)*       Bay of Plenty 17, Canterbury 12.
*Play-off for 7th/8th*  Wellington 21, Otago 19.

## BOWL FINAL

*Semi-finals*           Tasman 15, Hawke's Bay 0; Taranaki 22, North Harbour 17.
*Final*                 Taranaki 24, Tasman 19.
*Play-off for 11th/12th*  North Harbour 29, Hawke's Bay 12.

*Tournament referees:* Brittany Andrew, Natarsha Ganley, Lauren Jenner, Rebecca Mahoney, Tyler Miller (*Australia*).

**Anna Richards Trophy** (*Player of the Tournament*):

2013    Selica Winiata (*Manawatu*)
2014    Hazel Tubic (*Counties Manukau*)
2015    Kayla McAlister (*Auckland*)
2016    Katarina Whata-Simpkins (*Wellington*)
2017    Kelly Brazier (*Bay of Plenty*)

## TOURNAMENT TROPHY WINNERS

| | Venue | Cup | Plate | Bowl |
|---|---|---|---|---|
| 1998 | Rotorua | Auckland | | |
| 1999 | Palmerston North | Wellington | | |
| 2000 | Palmerston North | Bay of Plenty | | |
| 2001 | Palmerston North | Auckland | | |
| 2002 | Palmerston North | Canterbury | | |
| 2013 | Queenstown | Manawatu | | |
| 2014 | Rotorua | Manawatu | Taranaki | Canterbury |
| 2015 | Rotorua | Auckland | Wellington | Otago |
| 2016 | Rotorua | Manawatu | Waikato | Tasman |
| 2017 | Rotorua | Counties Manukau | Bay of Plenty | Taranaki |

## PLAYING RECORD OF NEW ZEALAND SEVENS TEAMS

| | Tournaments | | | Games | | | | Points | |
|---|---|---|---|---|---|---|---|---|---|
| | Attended | Won | Runner-up | Played | Won | Draw | Lost | For | Against |
| 2000 | 1 | 1 | – | 7 | 7 | – | – | 293 | 20 |
| 2001 | 3 | 3 | – | 15 | 15 | – | – | 661 | 17 |
| 2008 | 1 | – | 1 | 6 | 4 | – | 2 | 174 | 57 |
| 2009 | 1 | – | 1 | 6 | 5 | – | 1 | 177 | 37 |
| 2012 | 2 | 2 | – | 12 | 10 | 2 | – | 378 | 69 |
| 2013 | 6 | 3 | 1 | 36 | 30 | – | 6 | 958 | 279 |
| 2014 | 6 | 5 | 1 | 37 | 36 | – | 1 | 1102 | 262 |
| 2015 | 6 | 3 | – | 36 | 30 | – | 6 | 1011 | 402 |
| 2016 | 6 | 1 | 3 | 36 | 30 | – | 6 | 915 | 279 |
| 2017 | 7 | 5 | – | 41 | 39 | – | 2 | 1018 | 251 |
| **TOTALS** | **39** | **23** | **7** | **232** | **206** | **2** | **24** | **5772** | **1673** |

## NEW ZEALAND DEVELOPMENT SEVENS SQUAD

This squad took part in three tournaments, two in Japan and one in Australia. The first event in Japan took place during March 16/17. The second trip to Japan was September 9/10 at a tournament at the Hokkaido Barbarians Jozankei Ground. *Editors regret results from these two tournaments could not be supplied in time for inclusion in this publication.*

| | | Japan | Japan | Australia | TOTALS |
|---|---|---|---|---|---|
| Shakira Baker | Waikato | * | * | – | 2 |
| Sam Curtis | Canterbury | – | * | * | 2 |
| Rebecca Davidson | Canterbury | – | * | * | 2 |
| Jessica Drummond | Tasman | * | * | * | 3 |
| Rhiarna Ferris | Manawatu | – | * | * | 2 |
| Huia Harding | Waikato | – | – | * | 1 |
| Sam Hollows | Otago | – | * | * | 2 |
| Jazmin Hotham | Waikato | – | – | * | 1 |
| Rebecca Kersten | Bay of Plenty | * | – | * | 2 |
| Crystal Mayes | Manawatu | * | – | – | 1 |
| Natahlia Moors | Auckland | * | * | * | 3 |
| Danielle Paenga | Waikato | * | * | * | 3 |
| Risaleanna Pouri-Lane | Tasman | * | * | * | 3 |
| Tayla Reti | Wellington | – | * | – | 1 |
| Kendra Reynolds | Bay of Plenty | * | * | – | 2 |
| Leanna Ryan | Waikato | – | * | * | 2 |
| Autumn Stephens | Bay of Plenty | * | – | – | 1 |
| Monica Tagoa'i | Wellington | * | – | – | 1 |
| Rebekah Tufuga | Manawatu | * | – | – | 1 |
| Ora Williams | Bay of Plenty | * | – | – | 1 |

*Coach:* Kane Jury
*Assistant coach:* Victoria Grant (March event); Stu Ross
*Manager:* Hannah Catchpole
*Strength & conditioning trainer:* Michael Jacobs
*Video analyst:* PJ Williams
*Physiotherapist:* Kendall Elliot

## NEW ZEALAND DEVELOPMENT AT CENTRAL COAST SEVENS
### Wyong Rugby League Club, Kanwal, NSW                    October 28/29, 2017

| Date | Opponent | Result | Tries | Conversions |
|---|---|---|---|---|
| Oct 28 | ACT Brumbies | won 36–7 | Ryan, Drummond, Ferris, Davidson, Kersten, Holtham | Pouri-Lane (3) |
| Oct 28 | Pride Sevens | won 26–0 | Drummond (2), Kersten, Holtham | Pouri-Lane (3) |
| Oct 28 | Randwick | won 33–0 | Ryan (3), Drummond, Moors | Pouri-Lane (4) |
| Oct 29 | Sunnybank | won 17–7 | Ryan, Hotham, Moors | Pouri-Lane |
| Oct 29 | Australia (s-f ) | lost 12–34 | Curtis, Pouri-Lane | Pouri-Lane |
| Oct 29 | Stars (for 3rd place) | won 45–0 | Ryan (2), Holtham (2), Drummond, Hollows, Moors | Pouri-Lane (5) |

# CHRONICLE OF EVENTS

## JANUARY 2017

**1** In Auckland Ardie and Julian Savea play a charity tennis match with Serena and Venus Williams that raises $63,000 for the Kaikoura earthquake appeal.

**11** Halberg Awards finalists are named. Steve Hansen is a finalist for coach of the year.

**18** Aaron Cruden has signed a three-year deal with French club Montpellier, and will leave after the Super 18 season.

**24** NZR confirms the All Blacks on last year's end-of-year tour are not available to play for their franchises at the Brisbane Global Tens on 11–12 February, to the consternation of event organisers Duco Events who believed the squads would be at full strength and had even used some of the All Blacks to promote the event. The NZR/NZRPA Players' Agreement stipulates the All Blacks involved have a 12-week stand-down from the end of last year's tour, which goes to 18–19 February.

**27** The Blues announce they will play their 2 June home match against the Reds in Apia. The cost will be underwritten by the Samoan Government.

**28–29** The Wellington Sevens attracts a combined total of 20,000 spectators for the two days, less than one-third capacity, the lowest ever in the history of the event.

**30** The All Blacks of last year's end-of-year tour report for Super Rugby training with their franchises . . . SANZAAR announces a change to the Super 18 playoffs structure. The semi-finals match-ups will now be predetermined with the quarter-final winner of 1 v 8 playing the quarter-final winner of 4 v 5, and the winner of quarter-final 2 v 7 playing the quarter-final winner of 3 v 6. The semi-final host teams will be the highest ranked winners from the respective quarter-finals. This new structure creates more certainty for scheduling and travelling. The new structure means teams seeded 3 to 8 now have two possible semi-final destinations, whereas last year third seed had two options, fifth seed had three options, and teams seeded fourth, sixth, seventh and eighth had four options.

## FEBRUARY

**2** The Te Papapa Onehunga club premier team is suspended from the Auckland premier competition for all of 2017 after having played a player in one or three matches last year who had been given a life ban in 2011, and for providing false details on the teamsheet. The club had sacked the coach at the time after becoming aware of the situation. Other teams fielded by the club are not affected.

**5** NZR/NZRPA confirm Patrick Tuipulotu is currently under suspension, which is why he has not turned up for the Blues pre-season training. He returned home early from the All Blacks end-of-year tour before the final test, which was announced then as for 'personal reasons' but actually was due to a positive drugs test.

**6** SANZAAR announces the 19-man referees' panel for Super Rugby. The seven from New Zealand are: Nick Briant, Mike Fraser, Glen Jackson, Jamie Nutbrown, Ben O'Keeffe, Brendon Pickerill and Paul Williams.

**7** New South Wales police announce they have charged a security consultant with public mischief in their investigation of a listening device being found in the All Blacks hotel meeting room before the test in Sydney last August. The person concerned is a director of a security/investigations firm that the All Blacks have regularly used.

**8** A training squad of 51 is announced for the Black Ferns as part of a regional training programme designed to identify and develop the best players in the country.

**9** Tuipulotu has his suspension removed after his B sample comes back negative . . . At the Halberg Awards Steve Hansen is unsuccessful.

**13** Steven Luatua has signed for English club Bristol and will leave after the Super 18 season.

**15** Jane Duncan is elected Chairman of the Buller RU, becoming the first woman Chair of a NZ provincial union.

**16** SANZAAR announces a number of changes for Super Rugby. To improve consistency, a permanent three-man judiciary panel (Nigel Hampton, NZ; John Langford, Australia; Stefan Terblanche, South Africa; with a fourth person in reserve) has been appointed; the judiciary can open, or reopen, a case of foul play if new evidence becomes available at any time (not now restricted to the deadline of 12 hours after a match); bye rounds will not count towards weeks served in a suspension. In an attempt to speed up TMO referrals, if a referee refers an incident to the TMO, the referee will now have to give his decision on what he has seen before the TMO views it, and the TMO can only overturn the referee's call if evidence shows it. A foul play incident can still be referred to the TMO without the referee giving a decision on what he/she has seen.

**18** Steve Hansen confirms the Blues and Crusaders will have their All Blacks available to play for them against the British and Irish Lions. The All Blacks squad will assemble on 11 June, the day after the Crusaders match.

**22** Mid Canterbury rep Kolinio Tamanitoakula pleads guilty to the charge of assault with intent to commit sexual violation in Gisborne after their match in Ruatoria against East Coast last October. He is remanded for sentencing.

**23** The Commerce Commission refuses permission for Sky TV and Vodafone NZ to merge their New Zealand operations. Sky TV planned to buy Vodafone NZ with a mixture of cash, loan from Vodafone NZ, and issue of new shares, which would leave Vodafone NZ with 51 per cent of the new entity in a reverse takeover. Sky TV's dominance of live sport was a major factor in the Commerce Commission's decision. Internet NZ and Vodafone's rivals Spark and 2degrees opposed the merger in their submissions . . . After appealing the severity of their ban, the Te Papapa Onehunga club is allowed to field a team in the Auckland premier competition in 2017. Their ban is reduced to 33 weeks and backdated to 13 August 2016, the date of the initial judicial hearing.

**25** Bay of Plenty coach Clayton McMillan will coach the NZ Barbarians against the British and Irish Lions.

**27** Canterbury makes a profit of $2372 . . . Hawke's Bay a profit of $202,248.

## MARCH

**1** The Black Ferns will participate in a Four Nations series in NZ with Canada, England and Australia in June, as preparation for the World Cup in August . . . Manawatu records a profit of $93,900.

**2** ACC announces it will spend more on funding NZR's Rugby Smart programme. For the next four years the funding will be $1.75 million per year, up from the current $300,000 per year.

**6-8** World Rugby Council meeting in Dublin. The International calendar for 2020–2032 is agreed. The June test window in the southern hemisphere is shifted to the first three weeks in July, which will remove the three-week break in Super Rugby; the year after a World Cup the SANZAAR unions will host only two tests; the northern hemisphere test window will move forward one week to the first three weeks in November; world cups to start one week earlier in the second week of September; a minimum 110 Tier One v Tier Two matches will take place (an increase of 39 per cent); Georgia and Romania will host matches against Six Nations unions in the July window; SANZAAR unions will host Tier Two nations in July; Six Nations unions to collectively host six Tier Two fixtures every November; the Pacific Islands, USA, Canada and Japan will host tours.

**8** The Mitre 10 Cup and Heartland Championship draws are released.

**9–10**  SANZAAR meeting in London. Agreement is reached on what the shape of Super Rugby should be for 2018, but it requires approval from each union's stakeholders and broadcasters. No announcement will be made in the meantime.

**10**  Auckland City Council commissions a feasibility study into a central city waterfront stadium. Potential sites would be considered for a rectangular 25,000–50,000-seat stadium. The cost could be up to $1 billion.

**11**  Competition club rugby starts with the Counties Manukau and East Coast unions.

**14**  Referees in all 14 Mitre 10 Cup unions, and three Heartland unions, will implement a blue card to a player they suspect of having concussion. This will apply in all adult matches (18 years and older). The player must leave the field and cannot return to play until completing an automatic minimum three-week stand-down. To return to play the player must receive a clearance from a qualified medical professional with expertise in neurology.

**15**  Tawera Kerr-Barlow announces he has signed a three-year deal with French club La Rochelle and will leave after the Mitre 10 Cup . . . Samoa and Fiji have been added to the Oceania Under-20 tournament to make it a four-team competition.

**17**  With 170,000 New Zealanders currently playing, coaching or refereeing in the country, NZR launches website www.headfirst.co.nz targeting mental health and wellbeing in the rugby community. One in five New Zealanders experiences mental illness each year and New Zealand's suicide rate per 1000 is one of the highest in the world.

**22**  Bay of Plenty records a profit of $369,000.

**23**  Steve Tew confirms: the All Blacks will play the UK Barbarians on their November tour; a midweek match (not a test) in France is being investigated; the Wellington Sevens made a financial loss for the first time this year and alternative venues are being looked at; the All Blacks will now play a match before the Lions series, against a yet-to-be-determined opponent . . . Christchurch City Council decides to demolish Lancaster Park, which has been closed since the 22 February 2011 earthquake. The Hadlee Stand had been demolished in 2012 because it had sustained significant damage. Last December it was deemed uneconomic to repair ($255–275 million) with insurance worth $143 million. No decision has been made on the future use of the site . . . The Tonga v Wales match set for Nuku'alofa on 17 June has been shifted to Auckland after concern raised by Wales about the stadium at Nuku'alofa. Last month World Rugby agreed with the concern, and the match will be played on 16 June.

**27**  Counties Manukau records a profit of $268,203 . . . Otago a profit of $161,106.

**29**  Taranaki records a profit of $342,169 . . . Northland $78,398 . . . Wellington $191,000 . . . North Harbour $145,165 . . . Waikato $402,000.

## APRIL

**3**  ACC figures show a record $78.2 million was paid out in rugby-related injuries last year, up from $76.5 million in 2015. However, the number of cases — 62,336 — was down on the 63,598 from 2015.

**8**  Kieran Read plays his first game of the year, due to wrist surgery, with 40 minutes for his club University. It is his first club appearance since 2008.

**9**  SANZAAR announces three teams will be cut from Super Rugby for 2018 — two from South Africa and one from Australia. The Australian and South African Unions will decide which of their teams will be cut. Across all markets television viewership and spectator attendance have dropped significantly and there have been lopsided results. The Super 15 will play in three conferences. The NZ conference will comprise the five NZ teams, the Australian conference will comprise four Australian teams and the Sunwolves, while the SA conference will comprise four SA teams and the Jaguares. Each team will play 16 matches and two byes. Each team will play every other team in their conference twice (home and away), and eight of the other 10 teams once. Eight teams will make the quarter-final playoffs — the conference winners and the fourth-placed team will host quarter-finals. The format will stay in place to the end of 2020 when the current broadcast deals will expire. The values of the current broadcast deals (2016–20) remain unchanged. A full round robin for the 15 teams was investigated but not implemented, being deemed a player-welfare issue with increased travel demands.

10     Tasman records a profit of $139,832.

12     Nineteen players are named for the NZ Barbarians team to play the British and Irish Lions. All 14 Mitre 10 Cup unions and Heartland champions Wanganui are represented. More players will be added.

16     To commemorate its 125th jubilee, NZR launches an interactive site at www. nzrugbyhistory.co.nz to celebrate the milestone.

22     Sky TV announces a reduction in the number of high school first XV matches to be screened this year, down to 26 matches from last year's 49.

26     Southland records a profit of $378,000.

27     NZRU AGM: record income of $161.7 million received. A loss of $7.5 million (budgeted loss was $9 million) is announced as a result of choosing to increase funding to provincial unions to $32 million, a 54 per cent increase on 2015. Andrew Golightly and Stewart Mitchell are re-elected to the Board unopposed, and Peter Kean is reappointed to the Board by the Appointments and Remuneration Committee for a further three years. Maurice Trapp is new President and Bill Osborne is new Vice-President after a vote with Blair Furlong.

28     James Broadhurst announces his retirement due to ongoing concussion issues.

## MAY

9     NZR announces the All Blacks will play Samoa at Eden Park on 16 June at no cost to Samoa. The curtain-raiser will be the Tonga v Wales match shifted from Nuku'alofa.

10     World Rugby Council meeting in Kyoto: the draw of pools is made for the 2019 World Cup. New Zealand is drawn in Pool B with South Africa, Italy and two qualifiers; residential qualification for a foreign-born player to represent a country is now to be 60 months' continuous residence prior to selection, and will be effective from 31 December 2020; anyone who has moved countries before 31 December 2017 will fall under the current 36 months' qualification; foreign-born players who have had 10 years' cumulative residency (not consecutive) can represent a country effective immediately; from 1 January 2018 a national under-20 team can no longer be classed as a country's 'next senior national representative team', meaning playing under-20 rugby for a country will not prevent a player from playing for a different country at test level; sevens players will only be captured by a country and unable to play for another if they are 20 years or older when representing a country's sevens team or they have reached the age of majority (can differ from country to country) when competing in an Olympics or Sevens World Cup.

14     The Black Ferns squad for the Four Nations test series next month includes two uncapped players: Rebecca Wood and Theresa Fitzpatrick.

17     A 19-year-old Wellington club colts grade player dies. He left the field before the end of Saturday's match displaying concussion symptoms and was rushed to hospital where he had brain surgery and was placed in an induced coma . . . The All Blacks will play a test against Japan in Japan on 3 November next year.

19     All Blacks defence coach Wayne Smith announces he will step down from the role after this year's Rugby Championship.

**22** NZR announces Hamilton will be the new host of the New Zealand legs of the IISBC World Rugby Sevens Series, for 2018 and 2019 . . . Vodafone signs a four-year deal with NZR as a new sponsor to be 'connectivity partner'. They will provide a new All Blacks app with features for inside and outside the stadium.

**23** All Blacks assistant coach Ian Foster and forwards coach Mike Cron sign new contracts taking them to the 2019 World Cup.

**24** The All Blacks win the 2017 Princess of Asturias Award for Sport. Inaugurated in 1981, the awards are a series of prizes awarded in Spain acknowledging notable achievements in arts, humanity, literature, sports, science, and culture. The All Blacks were nominated for the award by the Spanish Ambassador to New Zealand.

**25** A 22-year-old Waitohi club player dies five days after suffering a cardiac arrest during a match against Nelson club. He had been taken to Nelson Hospital from the ground and placed in an induced coma . . . Hika Elliot signs a two-year deal with French club US Oyonnax, commencing after Super 18.

**29** The All Blacks will wear a new jersey just for the series against the British and Irish Lions, with the key feature being a newly designed crest inspired by the one worn by the 1930 All Blacks, which will include the years 1904 at the top and 2017 at the bottom . . . At the East Coast RU AGM, the union officially adopts a name change to Ngati Porou East Coast RU.

**30** Leading Swiss watchmaker Tudor becomes a new sponsor to NZR. The All Blacks will become brand ambassadors for Tudor.

**31** adidas extends its role of Principal Partner of NZR and Principal Sponsor of the All Blacks as apparel, boots and equipment supplier to NZR's national teams from 2020 to 2023. A portion of the income will be tagged to the community game.

## JUNE

**2** A 52-year-old Hamilton Marist President's Grade player dies on the field during a game in Cambridge against Leamington.

**4** Jarrad Hoeata has returned from overseas and signed with North Harbour.

**5** Queen's Birthday Honours List: former All Black Michael Jones receives a knighthood; former Hawke's Bay/NZ Maori rep Heitia Hiha is an Officer of NZOM; former NZRU Council/Board member Tim Gresson a Member of NZOM; former Black Ferns manager Jackie Barron is a Member of NZOM; former North Otago rep David Finlay receives QSM; former Golden Bay Motueka rep Barry Pomeroy receives QSM.

**17** Highlanders assistant coach Scott McLeod is appointed to replace Wayne Smith as All Blacks defence coach.

**19** A 2.7-metre bronze statue of Sir Colin Meads is unveiled at Te Kuiti.

**29** NZ Secondary Schools Sports Council census records 27,261 pupils (23,800 boys, 3461 girls) playing rugby for the 2016 school year, second behind netball with 29,257 pupils. Since 2000, the peak year for rugby was 31,203 players in 2011, and the lowest 28,313 players in 2003. Since 2000, rugby has been the highest participatory sport in the years 2000, 2004–12 and second behind netball in the other years.

## JULY

**5** The Black Ferns squad for next month's World Cup is named. There are no new caps among the 28 players.

**7** South African Rugby Union announces the Cheetahs and the Southern Kings will be its two teams cut from Super Rugby.

**10** Wairarapa Bush announces the signing of Piri Weepu who has returned from overseas.

17    Chiefs arrive in South Africa for their quarter-final match v Stormers. At Johannesburg airport Alex Nankivell is sent back home as his visa had an expiration date of 31 June (sic). All the Chiefs players' passports had been sent to Wellington in April and visas had been updated with expiration date of 31 August, except for Nankivell's, which suffered the clerical error. Chase Tiatia is sent for as a replacement.

18    A fifth match is added to the All Blacks' end-of-year tour with a midweek match against a French XV at Lyon.

20    Mike Delany has returned from overseas and signed for Bay of Plenty . . . World Rugby Executive Committee has approved the following six law amendments which will be trialled in the northern hemisphere from 1 August and in the southern hemisphere from 1 January 2018, and will apply in the November 2017 tests in the northern hemisphere. They had been used in the recent World Under 20 championship in Georgia.

Law 15 Tackle: Ball Carrier Brought to Ground: the tackler must get up before playing the ball and then can only play from their own side of the tackle 'gate' (to make the tackle/ruck simpler for player and referees and more consistent with the rest of the law).

Law 16 Ruck: a ruck commences when at least one player is on their feet and over the ball which is on the ground (tackled player and tackler). At this point the offside lines are created. Players on their feet may use their hands to pick up the ball before an opposition player arrives. As soon as an opposition player arrives no hands can be used (to make the ruck simpler for players and referees). A player must not kick the ball out of a ruck; it can only be hooked in a backwards motion. Sanction, a penalty (to promote player welfare and make it consistent with scrum law).

Law 20 Scrum: no signal from referee for halfback to put the ball in the scrum. The halfback must throw the ball in straight but is allowed to align their left shoulder on the middle of the scrum allowing them to stand a shoulder width towards their own side of the middle of the scrum (to promote scrum stability, a fair contest for possession while also giving an advantage to the team throwing the ball in). The number eight shall be allowed to pick the ball from the feet of the second-row players (to promote continuity). Once the ball touches the ground in the tunnel, any front-row player may use either foot to win possession of the ball. One player from the team putting the ball in must strike for the ball. Sanction, a free kick (to promote a fair contest for possession).

21    Malakai Fekitoa has signed for French club Toulon and will leave after the Mitre 10 Cup . . . The Highlanders scheduled 5.30 pm flight to Christchurch, for tomorrow's Super Rugby quarter-final, is cancelled due to wet weather in Dunedin. Going by bus was ruled out as State Highway 1 being closed due to flooding.

22    The Highlanders arrive in Christchurch by plane at 12.40 pm, just under seven hours before kick-off.

25    NZ Secondary Schools Sports Council and Drug Free Sports NZ inform the 24 schools still in contention for the National Secondary Schools First Fifteen semi-finals this year that the players will be randomly selected for drug testing for the first time. Workshops have been available to schools since February, but only five of the 24 schools have attended . . . This year's Farah Palmer Cup will be increased to 11 teams, from last year's nine teams, with the addition of Tasman for the first time and the return of Hawke's Bay. As with the Mitre 10 Cup, there wil be a Premiership division and a Championship division.

**26** Ben Smith will take a contracted sabbatical for the rest of the year after the second Bledisloe Cup match on 26 August.

**27** Kolinio Tamanitoakula is sentenced to jail for three years, four months, two weeks (see 22 February) . . . World Rugby judicial committee rules that Sonny Bill Williams cannot play for NZ v Australia on 19 August. Sent off in the second test v B&I Lions (1 July), he was served a four-week suspension. This was originally thought to have him to miss the third test (8 July), Blues v Sunwolves (15 July), Counties Manukau v North Harbour (29 July), and Counties Manukau trial (5 August); however, World Rugby has ruled the Counties Manukau trial and the All Blacks game of Three Halves (11 August) are not meaningful matches and will not count in his suspension. Therefore, the Bledisloe Cup on 19 August will be the fourth match of his suspension. NZR have 48 hours to appeal.

**28** Colin Cooper stands down as NZ Maori coach, having been appointed Chiefs coach last December.

## AUGUST

**1** Aaron Mauger is appointed Highlanders coach on a three-year deal.

**2–3** Thirty-four players attend an All Blacks two-day wider training camp in Christchurch. Four of them are uncapped: Richard Buckman, Tom Franklin, Akira Ioane and Atu Moli. Notable omission is Malakai Fekitoa. Crusaders players are not included in the camp as they are in Johannesburg preparing for the Super 18 final.

**3** World Rugby's independent appeal committee rules Sonny Bill Williams can play against Australia on 19 August, with the All Blacks game of Three Halves encounter now to count as the fourth meaningful match in his suspension.

**4** World Rugby expresses surprise at the appeal committee's decision and accepts the committee's decision, but will refer the definition of a 'match' to the next meeting (September) of its regulations committee. World Rugby's current Regulation 1 definition of a match is 'a game in which two teams compete against each other'.

**7–8** In Sydney, first two days of hearing into the All Blacks bugging incident from last year (see 7 Feb). All Blacks manager Darren Shand gives evidence by videolink.

**7–14** Fairfax Media NZ (stuff.co.nz and its printed newspapers around New Zealand) imposes a ban on reporting rugby stories in repsonse to NZR's accreditation terms issued to media for the Rugby Championship. A clause allowed NZR to revoke accreditation if it felt a media outlet breached copyright by running brief video highlights packages of Sky TV's footage. Media had done this in the past under section 42 of the Copyright Act of 'fair dealing'. In May Sky TV went to the Auckland High Court to argue against Fairfax Media NZ, TVNZ, NZME, and Mediaworks being able to do exactly that.

**7** The 33-man squad for the Rugby Championship is announced. Notable omission is Julian Savea. There are no new caps, but Chiefs prop Atu Moli will train with the squad in an apprentice role during home tests.

**11** Australian RU announces the Force will be the team cut from Super Rugby . . . In the game of Three Halves at Pukekohe, Counties Manukau defeat Taranaki 28–7, the All Blacks defeat Taranaki 57–7 and then defeat Counties Manukau 49–0 . . . South African Rugby CEO Jurie Roux says the move of the Cheetahs and the Southern Kings into an expanded Pro-12 competition (Ireland, Italy, Scotland, Wales) will not change South Africa's relationship with SANZAAR.

**15** Fairfax Media NZ resumes reporting rugby stories.

**16** NZR announces the Duane Monkley Medal will be awarded to the Mitre 10 Cup player of the year, and the Fiao'o Fa'amausili Medal will be awarded to the Farah Palmer Cup player of the year. The match officials in each match will award 3-2-1 points to the three best players . . . With the All Blacks in Sydney preparing for the opening Bledisloe Cup match, the Daily Mail Australia resurrects last year's Aaron Smith story with new allegations made by the woman involved.

**17** NZR announces it has engaged an independent lawyer to investigate the Aaron Smith matter further.

**18** At the final day of hearing in the All Blacks bugging incident, Kieran Read gives evidence by phone. Adrian Gard, the head of the security firm, is found not guilty of public mischief (making up the claim he found the bugging device) but found guilty of carrying out a security operation without a licence.

**19** On the day of the Bledisloe Cup match in Sydney, Jerome Kaino returns to NZ following publication in the Sydney *Daily Telegraph* of an extra-marital affair. Kaino was not in the All Blacks match day squad.

**21** The day after Sir Colin Meads' death TVNZ rescreens the 1988 episode This Is Your Life —Colin Meads.

**24** All Mitre 10 Cup and Heartland Championship matches this week, and the test v Australia, will hold a minute's silence for Sir Colin Meads prior to the game.

**25** NZR announces the All Blacks six home tests next year will be held at Auckland (2), Wellington (2), Dunedin and, for the first time, Nelson.

**26** In honour of Meads, King Country takes the field for their Heartland match against West Coast without a number five jersey and in the club socks of Meads' club Waitete . . . The All Blacks take the field against Australia with Meads' All Black number 583 on their sleeves.

**28** Sir Colin Meads' funeral is screened live on TVNZ.

**30** The NZ Heartland Team will only play one fixture this year – the annual clash v NZ Marist.

## SEPTEMBER

**6** Hurricanes assistant coach Jason Holland will coach the NZ Secondary Schoolboys team this year . . . World Rugby confirms the 10-tournament schedule for the 2017–2018 Sevens Series. The NZ tournament, leg four, will be played 3–4 February. Hamilton instead of Wellington is the only venue change.

**7** NZR releases the report by the independent panel headed by Kathryn Beck (appointed September last year) to conduct an extensive review of New Zealand Rugby's issues with respect and responsibility. Thirty-six cases of misconduct were dealt with by NZR from 2013 to 2017. In more than half the situations alcohol played a key factor. The report also states that NZR is already engaged in several initiatives to address issues. Six areas are advised for NZR to focus on: (1) Inclusive Leadership, driven by charter of values, (2) Progressive, developing and engaging well-rounded people, (3) Integrity, nurturing wellbeing, developing life plans during and after rugby, (4) Empowering, gender equality in all rugby environments, (5) Respectful, proactive engagement to reflect diverse communities, (6) World Leading, plan, monitor and report on outcomes of the above with the aid of an independent complaints and resolution system and Advisory Panel. The report was approved and adopted by the NZR Board last month and the following actions will occur over the next 12–24 months: establish an Executive Governance group; create a cross-functional project team; appoint a Project Manager; develop a Project Plan; develop a charter that rugby is for all; and independent Advisory to provide, advise and receive regular reports.

**9** Black Fern Emma Jensen becomes the first woman to play 100 NPC matches when she plays for Auckland against Canterbury. It is her 76th match for Auckland after previously having played 24 matches for Waikato.

**11**   Bay of Plenty coach Clayton McMillan is announced as NZ Maori coach.

**16**   After five minutes in the Thames Valley v Buller match, Thames Valley prop Hayden Anderson suffers a broken tibia. The referee stops the game and Anderson is kept still on the ground as the ambulance is called for, and the players leave the field. After Anderson is carefully placed in the ambulance, the match resumes after a delay of around 90 minutes.

**21**   Next year's Super Rugby draw is released. New Zealand teams will start on the weekend of 23–24 February, but South African teams will start a week earlier. The final is set for 4 August . . . After last night's 0–57 loss to Bay of Plenty, Southland management and Board call the loss 'unacceptable' and apologise to all their stakeholders for performances so far in the Mitre 10 Cup. The statement outlines the challenges the union faces off the field. Their season record is 0–6 so far.

**25**   France, Ireland and South Africa make their bid presentations to the World Rugby Council for hosting the 2023 World Cup. The bids will be reviewed by the Rugby World Cup Board who will recommend their preference to the Council who will vote. France, Ireland and South Africa will not be involved in the voting.

**28**   Auckland advertises its head coaching position for 2018, with still three matches to play this year . . . Black Ferns victory parade in Auckland.

## OCTOBER

**4**   Black Ferns victory parade in Wellington.

**12**   With 41 international matches being played in November, the following New Zealanders gain refereeing appointments: Brendon Pickerill (2 ref, 1 ar), Jamie Nutbrown (1 ar), Aaron Paterson (1 tmo), Nick Briant (1 ref), Mike Fraser (1 ar), Ben Skeen (1 tmo), Paul Williams (1 ref, 1 ar), Ben O'Keeffe (2 ref), Glen Jackson (1 ref, 1 ar).

**17**   At its Board meeting, Waikato decides to implement an independent review to 're-evaluate the organisation's high performance rugby from the Board downwards' in the wake of Waikato's relegation from the Premiership to the Championship.

**18**   NZR Special General Meeting: a change to election of Board members is passed. Provincial unions will now elect only three of the nine members to the Board and nominate three candidates (including the Maori representative) to the Appointments and Remuneration Committee for consideration among the six positions to be appointed by the A+R Committee. From 2018 the A+R Committee must contain at least one female member. (The A+R Committee comprises three provincial union representatives — two from Mitre 10 Cup unions, one from the Heartland unions— two independent members appointed by NZR Board, and the NZR Chairman.) If the provincial unions do not select a woman among their three spots, then the NZR Board will select one from their two choices.

**20**   NZR and Sky TV will partner to livestream the All Blacks' upcoming matches against the Barbarians and French XV, and the Maori All Blacks' matches against Canada and French Barbarians, as pay-per-view events on AllBlacksTV.com.

**22**   Mid Canterbury shifts the hosting of the Lochore Cup final to Methven instead of its usual home venue of the Ashburton Showgrounds. The Showgrounds venue has been prior booked next weekend for the annual A&P show.

**23**   The All Blacks' 37-man squad for the end-of-year tour is announced. There are four new caps: Asafo Aumua, Matt Duffie, Jack Goodhue and Tim Perry. Five additional players — Dominic Bird, Mitchell Drummond, Dillon Hunt, Atunaisa Moli and Richie Mo'unga — will play for the Barbarians against the All Blacks and then join the All Blacks for the week in France. Six players — Kieran Read, Dane Coles, Wyatt Crockett, Sam Whitelock, Anton Lienert-Brown and Sonny Bill Williams — will leave a few days after the rest of the squad does and won't be involved in the opening match v the Barbarians

. . . The Maori All Blacks team is named for their end-of-year tour and contains nine new caps . . . Rieko Ioane is one of the finalists for World Rugby's Breakthrough Player of the Year award.

25 The Heartland team is named for its sole fixture of the year next month.

30 Michaela Blyde and Ruby Tui are finalists for World Rugby's Women's Sevens Player of the Year. There are no NZ finalists for Men's Sevens Player of the Year.

31 The Rugby World Cup Board releases the 220-page report made by its technical review committee into the three bids to host the 2023 World Cup. The report recommends South Africa be awarded the hosting rights. The World Rugby Council will vote next month on the decision.

## NOVEMBER

1 The full squads for the five Super Rugby squads next year are revealed. Of the 190 players named, 42 are new.

2 The match schedule for the 2019 World Cup is made, with the All Blacks to play South Africa in their first match.

3 NZR confirms it has issued Aaron Smith with a formal warning (see 16, 17 August).

5 NZR releases its player numbers for 2017 — a record 156,067, of which a record 24,295 are female. Small Blacks (5–12-year-olds) total 86,237 and aged 21 and over total 28,449, all being up on 2016. Teenagers (13–20-year-olds) total 41,381, coaches total 12,366 and referees total 1750, all being down on last year.

6 Jerome Kaino is invalided out of the All Blacks' tour and Luke Whitelock is his replacement. Wellington/Hurricanes Brad Shields was the first-choice replacement but declined due to his wife having recently given birth.

8 The Mitre 10 Cup unions make their crossover selections for the 2018 tournament.

11 Former Taranaki/Highlanders/Hurricanes rep Jayden Hayward makes his debut for Italy, having qualified through residence.

13 Beauden Barrett and Rieko Ioane are finalists for World Rugby's Men's Player of the Year award, and Kelly Brazier and Portia Woodman are finalists for Women's Player of the Year.

15 France is elected host of the 2023 World Cup after the World Rugby Council voted 24–15 in its favour against South Africa in the final ballot. Ireland was eliminated in the first ballot.

25 Former Bay of Plenty/Chiefs/Highlanders rep Phil Burleigh makes his debut for Scotland, having qualified through residence.

26 World Rugby Awards: Michaela Blyde is Women's Sevens Player of the Year; Rieko Ioane wins Breakthrough Player of the Year; Beauden Barrett is Men's Player of the Year; Portia Woodman is Women's Player of the Year; the Black Ferns win Team of the Year.

## DECEMBER

1 Super Rugby squads, minus the All Blacks and Maori All Blacks, begin training.

2 Former Manawatu/Auckland/Blues/Hurricanes rep Hadleigh Parkes makes his debut for Wales, having qualified through residency.

3 Sam Whitelock shaves off his hair and beard for the Chalky Charitable Trust, raising $15,000. He has had the beard for two years.

9 A New Zealand Herald story reveals Drug Free Sport NZ is investigating the transactions of a Christchurch man jailed earlier this year who supplied clenbuterol and anabolic

steroids through a website. Up to 80 New Zealand athletes have been implicated, with more than 40 per cent being rugby players. No All Blacks or Olympians are said to be involved.

**11**   Auckland announces a record profit of $2,702,000.

**12**   Tasman announces it is to change the wording of its Mitre 10 Cup team name and logos from Tasman Makos to Tasman Mako. The 's' is dropped to acknowledge the correct use of the Maori name.

**14**   New Zealand Rugby Awards: Sarah Goss is Women's Player of the Year; Sam Whitelock is Kelvin R. Tremain Memorial Men's Player of the Year; Black Ferns are Team of the Year; Steinlager Salver for outstanding contribution goes to Wayne Smith.

**21**   NZR announces the national provincial sevens tournament will shift from a January time slot to December, and shift the venue from Rotorua to Tauranga for three years starting December 2018. This will allow provincial unions to field stronger teams by having more access to players in their Mitre 10 Cup, Heartland Championship and Farah Palmer Cup competitions squads. It will also align with the All Black Sevens' and Black Fern Sevens' high-performance programmes.

**22**   Super Rugby squads disband for Christmas . . . George Moala has signed for French club Clermont and will leave after next year's Super Rugby competition.

**30**   New Year Honours List: former All Black Bryan Williams receives a knighthood; former Bay of Plenty/North Auckland/Manawatu/NZ Maori rep Fred Graham is an Officer of NZOM; former North Auckland rep/coach Russell Kemp is also an Officer of NZOM.

# INTERNATIONAL RESULTS 2017

| Feb 03 | Brazil | 17 | Chile | 3 | Sao Paulo | C Cativelli (*Uruguay*) |
|---|---|---|---|---|---|---|
| Feb 04 | United States | 29 | Uruguay | 23 | San Antonio | C Assmus (*Canada*) |
| Feb 11 | Germany | 41 | Romania | 38 | Offenbach | M Chalon (*France*) |
| Feb 11 | Spain | 16 | Russia | 6 | Madrid | D Phillips(*Ireland*) |
| Feb 11 | Canada | 36 | Chile | 15 | Langford | D Summers (*USA*) |
| Feb 11 | Georgia | 31 | Belgium | 6 | Brussels | B Whitehouse (*Wales*) |
| Feb 11 | United States | 51 | Brazil | 3 | Round Rock | P Deluca (*Argentina*) |
| Feb 18 | Russia | 25 | Belgium | 18 | Brussels | S Attalah (*France*) |
| Feb 18 | Romania | 13 | Spain | 3 | Bucharest | E Rizzo (*Italy*) |
| Feb 18 | Uruguay | 23 | Brazil | 12 | Punta Del Este | P Deluca (*Argentina*) |
| Feb 18 | United States | 51 | Canada | 34 | Burnaby | D Schneider (*Argentina*) |
| Feb 25 | Uruguay | 17 | Canada | 13 | Maldonado | D Summers (*USA*) |
| Feb 25 | United States | 57 | Chile | 9 | Santiago | R Sant'Anna (*Brazil*) |
| Mar 03 | Brazil | 24 | Canada | 23 | Sao Paulo | D Schneider (*Argentina*) |
| Mar 04 | Romania | 30 | Russia | 10 | Socchi | S Gallagher (*Ireland*) |
| Mar 04 | Germany | 34 | Belgium | 29 | Offenbach | I Atorrasagasti (*Spain*) |
| Mar 04 | Georgia | 20 | Spain | 10 | Madrid | C Evans (*Wales*) |
| Mar 04 | Uruguay | 45 | Chile | 14 | Montevideo | K Weaver (*USA*) |
| Mar 11 | Spain | 32 | Germany | 15 | Cologne | L Linton (*Scotland*) |
| Mar 11 | Romania | 33 | Belgium | 17 | Brussels | C Blessano (*Italy*) |
| Mar 12 | Georgia | 28 | Russia | 14 | Tbilisi | I Tempest (*England*) |
| Mar 18 | Spain | 30 | Belgium | 0 | Madrid | V Iordachescu (*Romania*) |
| Mar 19 | Romania | 8 | Georgia | 7 | Bucharest | L Pearce (*England*) |
| Mar 19 | Russia | 52 | Germany | 25 | Socchi | C Marchat (*France*) |
| Apr 22 | Japan | 47 | Korea | 29 | Incheon | S Copeman (*Hong Kong*) |
| Apr 29 | Japan | 80 | Korea | 10 | Tokyo | M Rodden (*Hong Kong*) |
| May 06 | Japan | 29 | Hong Kong | 17 | Tokyo | T Baker (*Hong Kong*) |
| May 13 | Japan | 16 | Hong Kong | 0 | Hong Kong | S Kubo (*Japan*) |
| May 27 | Hong Kong | 43 | Korea | 17 | Yesan | T Otsuki (*Japan*) |
| May 27 | Germany | 30 | Kenya | 29 | Nairobi | C Jadezweni (*SA*) |
| Jun 03 | Hong Kong | 39 | Korea | 3 | Hong Kong | A Aso (*Japan*) |
| Jun 10 | Ireland | 55 | United States | 19 | Newark | L Pearce (*England*) |
| Jun 10 | Scotland | 34 | Italy | 13 | Singapore | P Williams (*NZ*) |
| Jun 10 | Georgia | 13 | Canada | 0 | Calgary | A Brace (*Ireland*) |
| Jun 10 | England | 38 | Argentina | 34 | San Juan | N Owens (*Wales*) |
| Jun 10 | Spain | 15 | Namibia | 13 | Montevideo | J Montes (*Uruguay*) |
| Jun 10 | Brazil | 25 | Portugal | 21 | Sao Paulo | D Schneider (*Argentina*) |

| Jun 10 | Japan | 33 | Romania | 21 | Kumamoto | A Ruiz (*France*) |
|---|---|---|---|---|---|---|
| Jun 10 | Australia | 37 | Fiji | 14 | Melbourne | M Carley (*England*) |
| Jun 10 | South Africa | 37 | France | 14 | Pretoria | G Jackson (*NZ*) |
| Jun 14 | Uruguay | 32 | Russia | 29 | Montevideo | K Weaver (*USA*) |
| Jun 16 | Wales | 24 | Tonga | 6 | Auckland | N Briant (*NZ*) |
| Jun 16 | New Zealand | 78 | Samoa | 0 | Auckland | M Raynal (*France*) |
| Jun 17 | Ireland | 50 | Japan | 22 | Shizuoka | M Van der Westhuizen (*SA*) |
| Jun 17 | Russia | 31 | Namibia | 10 | Montevideo | K Weaver (*USA*) |
| Jun 17 | Romania | 25 | Canada | 9 | Edmonton | S Kubo (*Japan*) |
| Jun 17 | England | 35 | Argentina | 25 | Santa Fe | J Lacey (*Ireland*) |
| Jun 17 | Scotland | 24 | Australia | 19 | Sydney | W Barnes (*England*) |
| Jun 17 | Georgia | 21 | United States | 17 | Atlanta | F Anselmi (*Argentina*) |
| Jun 17 | Fiji | 22 | Italy | 19 | Suva | P Williams (*NZ*) |
| Jun 17 | Uruguay | 24 | Spain | 14 | Montevideo | V Iordachescu (*Romania*) |
| Jun 17 | South Africa | 37 | France | 15 | Durban | B O'Keeffe (*NZ*) |
| Jun 23 | Wales | 19 | Samoa | 17 | Apia | M Van der Westhuizen (*SA*) |
| Jun 24 | Romania | 56 | Brazil | 5 | Bucharest | D Jones (*Wales*) |
| Jun 24 | Ireland | 35 | Japan | 13 | Tokyo | J Doyle (*Ireland*) |
| Jun 24 | Fiji | 27 | Scotland | 22 | Suva | P Gauzere (*France*) |
| Jun 24 | Australia | 40 | Italy | 27 | Brisbane | M Carley (*England*) |
| Jun 24 | New Zealand | 30 | British And Irish Lions | 15 | Auckland | J Peyper (*SA*) |
| Jun 24 | Argentina | 45 | Georgia | 29 | San Salvador | L Pearce (*England*) |
| Jun 24 | South Africa | 35 | France | 12 | Johannesburg | A Gardner (*Australia*) |
| Jul 01 | British And Irish Lions | 24 | New Zealand | 21 | Wellington | J Garces (*France*) |
| Jul 08 | New Zealand | 15 | British And Irish Lions | 15 | Auckland | R Poite (*France*) |
| Aug 19 | New Zealand | 54 | Australia | 34 | Sydney | W Barnes (*England*) |
| Aug 19 | Kenya | 19 | Hong Kong | 19 | Nairobi | E Seconds (*SA*) |
| Aug 19 | South Africa | 37 | Argentina | 15 | Port Elizabeth | R Poite (*France*) |
| Aug 26 | South Africa | 41 | Argentina | 23 | Salta | P Gauzere (*France*) |
| Aug 26 | Hong Kong | 43 | Kenya | 34 | Nairobi | R Rasivhenge (*SA*) |
| Aug 26 | New Zealand | 35 | Australia | 29 | Dunedin | N Owens (*Wales*) |
| Sep 09 | Australia | 23 | South Africa | 23 | Perth | G Jackson (*NZ*) |
| Sep 09 | New Zealand | 39 | Argentina | 22 | New Plymouth | A Gardner (*Australia*) |
| Sep 16 | Australia | 45 | Argentina | 20 | Canberra | J Lacey (*Ireland*) |
| Sep 16 | New Zealand | 57 | South Africa | 0 | Albany | N Owens (*Wales*) |

| Sep 30 | New Zealand | 36 | Argentina | 10 | Buenos Aires | J Peyper (*SA*) |
|---|---|---|---|---|---|---|
| Sep 30 | South Africa | 27 | Australia | 27 | Bloemfontein | B O'Keeffe (*NZ*) |
| Oct 07 | Australia | 37 | Argentina | 20 | Mendoza | M Raynal (*France*) |
| Oct 07 | New Zealand | 25 | South Africa | 24 | Cape Town | J Garces (*France*) |
| Oct 21 | Australia | 23 | New Zealand | 18 | Brisbane | W Barnes (*England*) |
| Nov 04 | Australia | 63 | Japan | 30 | Yokohama | N Briant (*NZ*) |
| Nov 10 | Chile | 23 | Kenya | 3 | Hong Kong | M Burlet (*Belgium*) |
| Nov 10 | Russia | 16 | Hong Kong | 13 | Hong Kong | F Anselmi (*Argentina*) |
| Nov 11 | New Zealand | 38 | France | 18 | Paris | A Gardner (*Australia*) |
| Nov 11 | Australia | 29 | Wales | 21 | Cardiff | G Jackson (*NZ*) |
| Nov 11 | Scotland | 44 | Samoa | 38 | Edinburgh | N Berry (*Australia*) |
| Nov 11 | Italy | 19 | Fiji | 10 | Catania | J Lacey (*Ireland*) |
| Nov 11 | England | 21 | Argentina | 8 | London | M Van der Westhuizen (*SA*) |
| Nov 11 | Georgia | 54 | Canada | 22 | Tbilisi | B Whitehouse (*Wales*) |
| Nov 11 | Germany | 45 | Brazil | 12 | Leipzig | M Adamson (*Scotland*) |
| Nov 11 | Ireland | 38 | South Africa | 3 | Dublin | B O'Keeffe (*NZ*) |
| Nov 14 | Hong Kong | 13 | Chile | 6 | Hong Kong | M Burlet (*Belgium*) |
| Nov 14 | Russia | 31 | Kenya | 10 | Hong Kong | S Copeman (*Hong Kong*) |
| Nov 18 | United States | 46 | Germany | 17 | Wiesbaden | B Pickerill (*NZ*) |
| Nov 18 | Argentina | 31 | Italy | 15 | Florence | J Peyper (*SA*) |
| Nov 18 | Uruguay | 52 | Namibia | 36 | Windhoek | E Seconds (*SA*) |
| Nov 18 | Canada | 37 | Spain | 27 | Madrid | I Tempest (*England*) |
| Nov 18 | New Zealand | 22 | Scotland | 17 | Edinburgh | M Carley (*England*) |
| Nov 18 | Brazil | 23 | Belgium | 19 | Brussels | C Maxwell-Keys (*England*) |
| Nov 18 | South Africa | 18 | France | 17 | Paris | N Owens (*Wales*) |
| Nov 18 | Ireland | 23 | Fiji | 20 | Dublin | P Williams (*NZ*) |
| Nov 18 | Romania | 17 | Samoa | 13 | Bucharest | D Wilkinson (*Ireland*) |
| Nov 18 | Wales | 13 | Georgia | 6 | Cardiff | M Raynal (*France*) |
| Nov 18 | Hong Kong | 40 | Kenya | 30 | Hong Kong | F Anselmi (*Argentina*) |
| Nov 18 | England | 30 | Australia | 6 | London | B O'Keeffe (*NZ*) |
| Nov 18 | Russia | 42 | Chile | 11 | Hong Kong | S Copeman (*Hong Kong*) |
| Nov 18 | Japan | 39 | Tonga | 6 | Toulouse | A Brace (*Ireland*) |
| Nov 25 | South Africa | 35 | Italy | 6 | Padua | R Poite (*France*) |
| Nov 25 | Chile | 32 | Germany | 10 | Offenbach | D Jones (*Wales*) |
| Nov 25 | New Zealand | 33 | Wales | 18 | Cardiff | W Barnes (*England*) |
| Nov 25 | Tonga | 25 | Romania | 20 | Bucharest | T Foley (*England*) |

| Nov 25 | Uruguay | 39 | Namibia | 34 | Windhoek | R Rasivhenge (SA) |
| Nov 25 | France | 23 | Japan | 23 | Lille | L Pearce (England) |
| Nov 25 | Georgia | 21 | United States | 20 | Tbilisi | P Brousett (France) |
| Nov 25 | Ireland | 28 | Argentina | 19 | Dublin | M Raynal (France) |
| Nov 25 | Scotland | 53 | Australia | 24 | Edinburgh | P Gauzere (France) |
| Nov 25 | England | 48 | Samoa | 14 | London | A Brace (Ireland) |
| Nov 25 | Spain | 67 | Brazil | 28 | Alicante | S Gallagher (Ireland) |
| Nov 25 | Fiji | 57 | Canada | 17 | Narbonne | M Carley (England) |
| Dec 02 | Wales | 24 | South Africa | 22 | Cardiff | J Garces (France) |

## SIX-NATIONS CHAMPIONSHIP

| Feb 04 | England | 19 | France | 16 | London | A Gardner (Australia) |
| Feb 04 | Scotland | 27 | Ireland | 22 | Edinburgh | R Poite (France) |
| Feb 05 | Wales | 33 | Italy | 7 | Rome | JP Doyle (Ireland) |
| Feb 11 | England | 21 | Wales | 16 | Cardiff | J Garces (France) |
| Feb 11 | Ireland | 63 | Italy | 10 | Rome | G Jackson (NZ) |
| Feb 12 | France | 22 | Scotland | 16 | Paris | J Peyper (SA) |
| Feb 25 | Ireland | 19 | France | 9 | Dublin | N Owens (Wales) |
| Feb 25 | Scotland | 29 | Wales | 13 | Edinburgh | J Lacey (Ireland) |
| Feb 26 | England | 36 | Italy | 15 | London | R Poite (France) |
| Mar 10 | Wales | 22 | Ireland | 9 | Cardiff | W Barnes (England) |
| Mar 11 | France | 40 | Italy | 18 | Rome | B O'Keeffe (NZ) |
| Mar 11 | England | 61 | Scotland | 21 | London | M Raynal (France) |
| Mar 18 | France | 20 | Wales | 18 | Paris | W Barnes (England) |
| Mar 18 | Ireland | 13 | England | 9 | Dublin | J Garces (France) |
| Mar 18 | Scotland | 29 | Italy | 0 | Edinburgh | P Gauzere (France) |

## FINAL TABLE

|  | P | W | D | L | For | Against | Pts |
|---|---|---|---|---|---|---|---|
| England | 5 | 4 | 0 | 1 | 146 | 81 | 19 |
| Ireland | 5 | 3 | 0 | 2 | 126 | 77 | 14 |
| France | 5 | 3 | 0 | 2 | 107 | 90 | 14 |
| Scotland | 5 | 3 | 0 | 2 | 122 | 118 | 14 |
| Wales | 5 | 2 | 0 | 3 | 102 | 86 | 10 |
| Italy | 5 | 0 | 0 | 5 | 50 | 201 | 0 |

## RUGBY WORLD CUP QUALIFICATION MATCHES

| May 13 | Uruguay | 45 | Paraguay | 19 | Asuncion | P Deluca (*Argentina*) |
|---|---|---|---|---|---|---|
| May 13 | Chile | 15 | Brazil | 10 | Santiago | J Montes (*Uruguay*) |
| May 20 | Uruguay | 41 | Brazil | 27 | Montevideo | J Sylvestre (*Argentina*) |
| May 20 | Chile | 66 | Paraguay | 7 | Santiago | H Platais (*Brazil*) |
| May 27 | Uruguay | 27 | Chile | 11 | Montevideo | F Anselmi (*Argentina*) |
| May 27 | Brazil | 57 | Paraguay | 6 | Sao Paulo | D Schneider (*Argentina*) |
| Jun 24 | Canada | 28 | United States | 28 | Hamilton | B Whitehouse (*Wales*) |
| Jul 01 | Tonga | 30 | Samoa | 26 | Nuku'alofa | M Mitrea (*Romania*) |
| Jul 01 | United States | 52 | Canada | 16 | San Diego | A Brace (*Ireland*) |
| Jul 05 | Morocco | 57 | Madagascar | 33 | Casablanca | C Clave (*France*) |
| Jul 05 | Ivory Coast | 58 | Botswana | 25 | Casablanca | L Cayre (*France*) |
| Jul 08 | Madagascar | 47 | Botswana | 24 | Casablanca | C Clave (*France*) |
| Jul 08 | Morocco | 8 | Ivory Coast | 3 | Casablanca | L Cayre (*France*) |
| Jul 08 | Fiji | 14 | Tonga | 10 | Nuku'alofa | N Briant (*NZ*) |
| Jul 15 | Fiji | 38 | Samoa | 16 | Apia | P Williams (*NZ*) |
| Aug 04 | Tahiti | 13 | Cook Islands | 9 | Rarotonga | A Aiolupotea (*Samoa*) |

# THE FOREIGN LEGION
*by John Lea*

These New Zealand origin players were either contracted with professional overseas clubs for play in 2017/18, or commenced and completed an overseas contract during 2017 (denoted by *). Those no longer eligible for New Zealand have their country of allegiance shown in brackets.

## AUSTRALIA
*Super Rugby*

| | |
|---|---|
| ACT Brumbies: | Nigel Ah-Wong*, Jarrad Butler*, Wharenui Hawera, Christian Lealifano (Australia), Nick Mayhew, Jordan Smiler (Australia)*, Henry Speight (Australia) |
| Melbourne Rebels: | Jackson Garden-Bachop*, Pat Leafa (Samoa), Tyrell Lomax, Callum Retallick, Toby Smith (Australia), Jordan Uelese (Australia) |
| NSW Waratahs: | Sekope Kepu (Australia), Dean Mumm (Australia), Ira Simone, Will Skelton (Australia), Angus Ta'avao |
| Queensland Reds: | Quade Cooper (Australia), Leroy Houston (Australia), Karmichael Hunt (Australia), Adam Korczyk, Duncan Paia'aua (Australia), Hendrix Tui (Japan), Lukhan Tui (Australia), Taniela Tupou (Australia) |
| Western Force: | Jermaine Ainsley (Australia), Pek Cowan (Australia), Tetera Faulkner (Australia), Semisi Masirewa, Chance Peni-Ataera, Anaru Rangi, Curtis Rona (Australia), Michael Ruru |

*NRC*

| | |
|---|---|
| Brisbane City: | Quade Cooper (Australia), Karmichael Hunt (Australia), Adam Korczyk, Lukhan Tui (Australia) |
| Canberra Vikings: | Jordan Smiler (Australia), Henry Speight (Australia), Isaac Thompson |
| Melbourne Rising: | Pat Leafa (Samoa), Toby Smith (Australia), Sione Taufa, Jordan Uelese (Australia) |
| NSW Country Eagles: | Tayler Adams, Dean Mumm (Australia) |
| Perth Spirit: | Jermaine Ainsley (Australia), Pek Cowan (Australia), Manihera Eden, Semisi Masirewa, Ammon Matuauto, Hadleigh May, Anaru Rangi, Michael Ruru, Auega Seumanutafa |
| Queensland Country: | Duncan Paia'aua (Australia), Brad Thorn, Taniela Tupou (Australia) |
| Sydney Rays: | Jono Malo (Samoa), Ira Simone, Josh Turner |
| West Sydney Rams: | Albert Nikoro (Samoa), Tupou Sopoaga, Andrew Tuala, Jordan Tuapou, Filimone Tufui |

## ENGLAND
*Aviva Premiership*

| | |
|---|---|
| Bath: | Kahn Fotuali'i (Samoa), Peter Grant, Anthony Perenise (Samoa), Jack Wilson (England), James Wilson |
| Exeter Chiefs: | Tom Hendrickson, Thomas Waldrom (England), Nick White (Ireland) |
| Gloucester: | John Afoa, Willie Heinz, Josh Hohneck, Tom Marshall, Motu Matu'u (Samoa), Jeremy Thrush, Jason Woodward |

| | |
|---|---|
| Harlequins: | Elia Elia (Samoa), Jono Kitto*, Matt Luamanu, Mark Reddish*, Francis Saili, Winston Stanley (Samoa) |
| Leicester Tigers: | Mike FitzGerald, Valentino Mapapalangi (Tonga) Brendon O'Connor, Afa Pakalani (Tonga), Telusa Veianu (Tonga) |
| London Irish: | Mike Coman, Blair Cowan (Scotland), Ben Franks, William Lloyd, James Marshall, Filo Paulo (Samoa), Asaeli Tikoirotuma (Fiji) |
| London Wasps: | Jimmy Gopperth, Nathan Hughes (England), Brad Shields, Matt Symons |
| Newcastle Falcons: | Tevita Cavubati (Fiji), Mike Delaney*, Nili Latu (Tonga), Sinoti Sinoti (Samoa), Sonatane Takulua (Tonga) |
| Northampton Saints: | Piers Francis (England), Teimana Harrison (England), Dylan Hartley (England), Michael Paterson, Ken Pisi (Samoa), Apisoloma Ratuniyarawa (Fiji), Ahsee Tuala (Samoa), Nafi Tuitavake (Tonga) |
| Sale Sharks: | Halani Aulika (Tonga), Bryn Evans, TJ Ioane (Samoa), Johnny Leota (Samoa), Denny Solomona (England) |
| Saracens: | Sean Maitland (Scotland), Will Skelton (Australia), Mako Vunipola (England) |
| Worcester Warriors: | Bryce Heem, Ben Te'o (England), Jackson Willison |
| *RFU Championship* | |
| Bedford Blues: | Paul Tupai (Samoa) |
| Bristol: | Jack Lam (Samoa), Joe Latta, Alapati Leuia (Samoa), Steven Luatua, Alby Mathewson*, Tusi Pisi (Samoa), Charles Piutau, Mark Sorenson*, Soane Tonga'uiha (Tonga), Chris Vui (Samoa) |
| Cornish Pirates: | Don Koster, Marien Walker |
| Doncaster Knights: | Jack Ram (Tonga) |
| Ealing Trailfinders: | Mark Bright (England), Grayson Hart (Scotland), Daniel Temm |
| Jersey: | Samisoni Fisilau* (Tonga), Regan King, Uili Kolo'ofai (Tonga), Tom Quarrie |
| London Scottish: | Chris Walker |
| Richmond: | Rob Kirby, Jordan Simpson-Hefft |
| Rotherham Titans: | Tom Burns |
| Yorkshire Carnegie: | Mike Mayhew, Richard Mayhew, Jack Whetton |

## FRANCE
*Top 14*

| | |
|---|---|
| Agen: | Filipo Nakosi (Fiji), Paul Ngauamo (Tonga), George Tilsley, Ryan Tongia*, Sam Vaka |
| Bordeaux Begles: | Ole Avei (Samoa), Luke Braid, Hugh Chalmers, Ed Fidow (Samoa), Fa'asiu Fuatai, Simon Hickey, Leroy Houston (Australia), Iliesa Ratuva Tavuyara (Fiji), Jayden Spence, Ben Volavola (Fiji) |
| Brive: | James Johnston (Samoa), Poutasi Luafutu (Australia), Dominiko Waqaniburotu (Fiji) |
| Castres: | Eric Sione, David Smith (Samoa), Alex Tulou (Samoa), Ma'ama Vaipulu (Tonga) |

| | |
|---|---|
| Clermont: | Peter Betham, (Australia), Fritz Lee, Tim Nanai Williams (Samoa), Isaia, Toeava, Loni Uhila, John Ulugia |
| Grenoble. | Dayna Edwards, Leva Fifita (Tonga), Dylan Hayes, Nigel Hunt, Stephen Setephano (Cook Islands), Taiso Silifai-Leeana, Nuku Swerling, Latu Talakai (Tonga), Alisona Taumalolo (Tonga), Edgar Tuinukuafe, Lolagi Visinia |
| La Rochelle: | Uini Antonio (France), Jason Eaton, Hikairo Forbes, Tawera Kerr-Barlow, David Raikuna*, Rene Ranger, Victor Vito |
| Montpellier: | Aaron Cruden, Nemani Nadolo (Fiji), Joseph Tomane (Australia) |
| Oyonnax: | Ben Botica, Hika Elliot, Rory Grice, Roimata Hansell-Pune, Vili Ma'afu (Tonga), Quentin MacDonald, Hoani Tui |
| Pau: | Frank Halai, Chris King*, Jamie Mackintosh, Daniel Ramsey, Peter Saili, Colin Slade, Conrad Smith, Benson Stanley, Tom Taylor |
| Racing 92: | Dan Carter*, So'otala Fa'aso'o, Census Johnston (Samoa), Casey Laulala, Edwin Maka, Chris Masoe*, Ope Peleseuma (Samoa), Joe Rokocoko, Ben Tameifuna (Tonga), Anthony Tuitavake, Virimi Vakatawa (France), Albert Vulivuli (Fiji) |
| Stade Francais: | Paul Alo-Emile (Samoa), Tony Ensor, Brandon Nansen (Samoa), Zac Taulafo (Samoa), Paul Williams (Samoa) |
| Toulon: | Malakai Fekitoa, Alby Mathewson, Luke McAlister, Ma'a Nonu |
| Toulouse: | Carl Axtens, Piua Fa'asalele (Samoa), Charlie Faumuina, Paul Perez (Samoa), Joe Tekori (Samoa) |

*Second Division*

| | |
|---|---|
| Albi: | Daniel Kirkpatrick*, William Whetton |
| Aurillac: | Alex Luatua, Jack McPhee, Danny Tusitala (Samoa) |
| Bayonne: | Matt Graham, Baptiste Heguy, Tanerau Latimer, Manu Leiataua (Samoa), Kade Poki |
| Beziers: | Steve Fualau (Samoa), Lua Lokotui (Tonga), Lachie Munro, Elijah Niko, Jordan Puletua |
| Biarritz: | Elvis Levi, Felipe Manu, Sikeli Nabou (Fiji), Nemia Soqeta (Fiji) |
| Charente Angouleme: | Kimami Sitauti (Australia), Rome Taelega, Pingi Tala'apitaga |
| Colomiers: | Jonny Fa'amatuainu (Tonga), Daniel Faleafa (Tonga), Randall Kamea, Chris Tuatara-Morrison |
| Dax: | Asa Faitotoa, Aisea Koliavu, Billy Ropiha, Joe Tuineau (Tonga) |
| Lyon: | Toby Arnold, Josh Bekhuis, Michael Harris (Australia), Cameron Mapusua, Taiasina Tuifu'a (Samoa), Rudi Wulf |
| Massy: | Matt Talaese (Samoa), Sasa Tofilau, Jotham Wrampling |
| Montauban: | Richard Haddon, Aviata Silago, Taleta Tupuola |
| Narbonne: | Stephen Brett, Hosea Gear, Maselino Paulino (Samoa), Pelu Taele-Pavihi (Samoa), Neemia Tialata, Matt Wright* |
| Nevers: | Fa'atoina Autagavaia (Samoa), Auvasa Faleali'i (Samoa) |
| Perpignan: | Shahn Eru, Michael Faleafa (Tonga), Lifeimi Mafi, Genesis Mamea Lemalu (Samoa) |
| Stade Montois: | Matt James |
| Vannes: | Sione Anga'aelangi (Tonga), Phil Kite (Tonga), Pat Leafa (Samoa), Ash Moeke |

# IRELAND
*RaboDirect Pro 12*

| | |
|---|---|
| Connacht: | Pita Ahki, Bundee Aki (Ireland), Jarrad Butler, Naulia Dawai (Fiji), Tom McCartney, James Heenan, Stacey Ili, Dominic Robertson-McCoy |
| Leinster: | Michael Bent (Ireland), Jamison Gibson-Park, James Lowe, Isa Nacewa (Fiji) |
| Munster: | Tyler Bleyendaal, Rhys Marshall, Te Aihe Toma* |
| Ulster: | Rodney Ah You (Ireland), Christian Leali'ifano (Australia), Jared Payne (Ireland), Charles Piutau, Sean Reidy (Ireland) |

# ITALY
*RaboDirect Pro 12*

| | |
|---|---|
| Benetton Treviso: | Marty Banks, Dean Budd (Italy), Whetu Douglas, Sam Christie*, Hame Faiva, Monty Ioane, Jayden Hayward (Italy), Nasi Manu, Michael Tagicakibau (Fiji) |
| Zebre: | Kurt Baker*, James Tucker |

*Continental Shield*

| | |
|---|---|
| Calvisano: | Seko Kalou (Fiji), Ben Seymour, Jimmy Tuivaiti |
| Petrarca: | Jeremy Su'a (Samoa) |
| Rovigo: | Billy Ngawini, Josh Robertson-Weepu |
| Viadana: | Jacob Whittaker |

# JAPAN
*Super Rugby*

| | |
|---|---|
| Sunwolves | Aisea Ai Valu (Japan), Derek Carpenter (Japan), Hayden Cripps (Japan), Timothy Lafaele (Japan), Michael Leitch (Japan), Lomano Lemeki (Japan), Craig Miller, Liaki Moli*, Hayden Parker, Robbie Robinson, Jamie-Jerry Taulagi (Samoa) |

*Top League*

| | |
|---|---|
| Canon Eagles: | Kane Falconer |
| Coca Cola Red Sparks: | Mark Abbott, Dan Hollinshead, Solomon King, Timothy Lafaele (Japan), Daniel Peters, Joe Tupe, Will Tupou (Japan) |
| Kintetsu Liners: | Iopu Iopu-Aso, Mike Stolberg, Luke Thompson (Japan), Solomon T-Pole |
| Kobelco Steelers: | Nigel Ah Wong, Fraser Anderson (Tonga), Dan Carter, Nick Ealey, Andrew Ellis, Semisi Masirewa, Cody Rei, Toni Vaihu, Matt Vant Leven |
| Kubota Spears | Justin Ives (Japan), Patrick Osborne (Fiji), Nick Ross |
| Munakata Sanix Blues: | Siliva Ahio, Josh Gordon, Karne Hesketh (Japan), Bryce Robbins (Japan), Andre Taylor |
| NEC Green Rockets: | Maritino Nemani, Jordan Payne, George Risale, Amanaki Savieti, Sanaila Waqa |
| NTT Docomo: | Jeffrey Ierome |
| NTT Shining Arcs: | Brackin Karauria-Henry (Australia), Isaac Ross |

| | |
|---|---|
| Ricoh Black Rams: | Colin Bourke, Mike Broadhurst (Japan), Tamati Ellison, Josh Mau, Robbie Robinson, Alex Woonton (Cook Islands) |
| Panasonic Wild Knights: | Richard Buckman*, Digby Ioane (Australia), Craig Millar, Emerson Tamura-Paki, Tevita Tupou |
| Suntory Sun-Goliath: | Derek Carpenter (Japan), Kosei Ono (Japan), Jordan Smiler (Australia), Hendrix Tui (Japan), Joe Wheeler |
| Toshiba Brave Lupus: | Stephen Donald, Cory Jane, Richard Kahui, Michael Leitch (Japan), Liam Messam* |
| Toyota Shokki: | Scott Fuglistaller, Peni Iowane* |
| Toyota Verblitz: | Asaeli Ai Valu (Japan), Shneil Singh, Stephen Yates |
| Yamaha Jubilo: | Johan Bardoul, Rocky Havili (Tonga), Matt McGahan, Male Sa'u (Japan), Mose Tuiali'i |

*Top Challenge*

| | |
|---|---|
| Chubu Electric Power | Simon Munro |
| Hino: | Hayden Cripps (Japan), Joel Everson, Gillies Kaka, Liaki Moli |
| Honda Heat: | John Akauola, Lomano Lemeki (Japan), David Milo, Tomasi Soqeta (Fiji) |
| Kamaishi Seawaves: | Scott Manson, Seilala Mapusua (Samoa), Dallas Tatana (Japan), Michael Toloke |
| Mazda: | James Kamana (Cook Islands), Tevita Koloamatangi (Tonga), Isaac Thompson |
| Mitsubishi Dynaboars: | Albert Anae, Hamish Gard, Dan Hawkins, Tevita Lepolo, Fili Levave (Samoa), Ryan Nicholas (Japan) |

## ROMANIA
*Continental Shield*

| | |
|---|---|
| Timisoara Saracens: | Eddie Aholelei (Tonga), Sosene Anesi, Stefano Hunt, Paula Kinikinilau (Romania)*, Viliami Moala, Michael Stewart, Stephen Shennan (Romania), Jack Umaga (Romania) |

## RUSSIA
*Continental Shield*

| | |
|---|---|
| Krasny Yar: | Eddie Paea (Tonga)* |
| Yenisei: | Richard Kingi (Australia) |

## SCOTLAND
*RaboDirect Pro 12*

| | |
|---|---|
| Edinburgh: | Simon Berghan (Scotland), Phil Burleigh (Scotland), Robbie Fruean*, John Hardie (Scotland), Simon Hickey, Nick McLennan (Scotland)* |
| Glasgow: | Brian Alainu'uese, Hugh Blake (Scotland)*, Corey Flynn, Callum Gibbins, Nick Grigg (Scotland), Siosiua Halanukonuka (Tonga), Lelia Masaga, Hagen Schulte (Germany)*, Samu Vunisa (Italy) |

## SOUTH AFRICA
*Super Rugby*
Stormers:                    Shaun Treeby

## SPAIN
*Division de Honour*

| | |
|---|---|
| Alcobendas: | Brad Linklater (Spain), Hoani Matenga |
| El Salvador: | Chris Talanoa |
| Gernika: | Justin Harding, Tui Katoa, Lionel Skipwirth, Jamie Verran |
| Getxo Artea: | Pryor Collier |
| Independente Santander: | Joshua Fraser, Mark Jackman |
| Santboiana: | Harrison Fitzsimons, Afa Tauli (Spain), Sam Thomas, Brad Truesdale |
| Vigo: | Campbell Johnstone, Chris McLaren |
| VRAC Quesos: | Jody Allen, Chris Eaton, Casey Stone, Leigh Thompson |

## WALES
*RaboDirect Pro 12*

| | |
|---|---|
| Cardiff Blues: | Gareth Anscombe (Wales), Pele Cowley (Samoa)*, Tau Filise (Tonga), Willis Halaholo, Jarrad Hoeata*, Ray Lee-Lo (Samoa), Nick Williams |
| Dragons: | Sam Beard |
| Llanelli Scarlets: | Johnny McNicholl, Hadleigh Parkes (Wales) |
| Ospreys: | Ma'afu Fia, Kieran Fonotia (Samoa), Brendan Leonard |

# NEW ZEALAND ORIGIN AND FIRST-CLASS PLAYERS CAPPED OVERSEAS, 2017

*Compiled by John Lea*

Provincial Union and Year indicate most recent first-class play when applicable.

| Player | Country | Provincial Union | Year |
|---|---|---|---|
| Jermaine Ainsley | Australia XV | Otago | ... |
| Quade Cooper | Australia | Waikato | – |
| Tetera Faulkner | Australia | Bay of Plenty | – |
| Karmichael Hunt | Australia | Auckland | – |
| Sekope Kepu | Australia | Counties Manukau | 2007 |
| Duncan Paia'aua | Australia XV | Wellington | – |
| Matthew Philip | Australia | Southland | 2016 |
| Curtis Rona | Australia | Taranaki | – |
| Toby Smith | Australia | Waikato | 2013 |
| Henry Speight | Australia | Waikato | 2011 |
| Lukhan Tui | Australia | Auckland | – |
| Taniela Tupou | Australia | Auckland | – |
| Jordan Uelese | Australia | Wellington | – |
| Tyler Ardron | Canada | Bay of Plenty | 2017 |
| Hubert Buydens | Canada | Manawatu | 2014 |
| Jake Ilnicki | Canada | Manawatu | 2016 |
| Josh Larsen | Canada | Northland | 2017 |
| Djustice Sears-Duru | Canada | North Otago | 2014 |
| Ilai Arona | Cook Islands | Northland | ... |
| Tiano Arona | Cook Islands | Northland | – |
| Te-Ara Henderson | Cook Islands | Wellington | – |
| Reece Joyce | Cook Islands Sevens | Counties Manukau | – |
| Junior Kiria | Cook Islands Sevens | Auckland | – |
| Alex Matapo | Cook Islands | Auckland | – |
| Greg Mullany | Cook Islands | Wellington | – |
| Matt Mullany | Cook Islands | Wellington | – |
| Junior Napara | Cook Islands Sevens | Auckland | – |
| William Raea | Cook Islands Sevens | Auckland | – |
| O'Neal Rongo | Cook Islands | Auckland | – |
| Francis Smith | Cook Islands | Tasman | 2013 |
| Joshua Brajkovic | Croatia | Auckland | – |
| Nathan Earle | England | Canterbury | 2016 |

| Player | Country | Provincial Union | Year |
|---|---|---|---|
| Piers Francis | England | Blues | 2017 |
| Dylan Hartley | England | Bay of Plenty | – |
| James Haskell | England | Highlanders | 2012 |
| Nathan Hughes | England | Auckland | 2013 |
| Denny Solomona | England | Auckland | – |
| Ben Te'o | England | Auckland | – |
| Mako Vunipola | England | Auckland | – |
| Tom Wood | England | North Otago | 2006 |
| Tevita Cavubati | Fiji | Tasman | 2014 |
| Naulia Dawai | Fiji | Otago | 2016 |
| Sikeli Nabou | Fiji | Counties Manukau | 2015 |
| Nemani Nadolo | Fiji | Crusaders | 2014 |
| Nemani Nagusa | Fiji | Tasman | 2012 |
| Patrick Osborne | Fiji | Highlanders | 2017 |
| Akapusi Qera | Fiji | Wanganui | 2004 |
| Apisoloma Ratuniyarawa | Fiji | North Harbour | 2012 |
| Peni Ravai | Fiji | Southland | 2016 |
| Ropate Rinakama | Fiji | Northland | 2017 |
| John Stewart | Fiji | Poverty Bay | 2015 |
| Tuapati Talemaitoga | Fiji | Southland | 2014 |
| Asaeli Tikoirotuma | Fiji | Chiefs | 2014 |
| Ben Volavola | Fiji | North Harbour | 2017 |
| Albert Vulivuli | Fiji | Waikato | – |
| Dominiko Waqaniborotu | Fiji | Waikato | 2010 |
| Uini Atonio | France | Counties Manukau | 2011 |
| Virimi Vakatawa | France | Canterbury | – |
| Rob May | Germany | Horowhenua-Kapiti | 2005 |
| Hagen Schulte | Germany | Buller | 2015 |
| Nick Hewson | Hong Kong | Taranaki | – |
| Ryan Meacheam | Hong Kong Sevens | Waikato | – |
| Ben Rimene | Hong Kong | Waikato | – |
| Bundee Aki | Ireland | Counties Manukau | 2014 |
| Joey Carberry | Ireland | Auckland | – |
| Jared Payne | Ireland | Northland | 2011 |
| Sean Reidy | Ireland | Auckland | – |
| Dean Budd | Italy | Northland | 2011 |
| Josh Furno | Italy | Otago | 2017 |
| Kelly Haimona | Italy | Bay of Plenty | 2016 |

| Player | Country | Provincial Union | Year |
|---|---|---|---|
| Jayden Hayward | Italy | Taranaki | 2012 |
| Asaeli Ai Valu | Japan | Otago | – |
| Derek Carpenter | Japan | Northland | 2013 |
| Leon Ellison | Japan Sevens | Wellington | – |
| Shota Horie | Japan | Otago | 2012 |
| Timothy Lafaele | Japan | Auckland | – |
| Michael Leitch | Japan | Chiefs | 2017 |
| Lomano Lemeki | Japan | Auckland | – |
| Male Sa'u | Japan | Blues | 2016 |
| Kaito Shigeno | Japan | Auckland | 2015 |
| Fumiaki Tanaka | Japan | Highlanders | 2016 |
| Dallas Tatana | Japan Sevens | Canterbury | – |
| Luke Thompson | Japan | Canterbury | – |
| Hendrix Tui | Japan | Auckland | – |
| Will Tupou | Japan | Auckland | – |
| Willie Ambaka | Kenya Sevens | Manawatu | 2017 |
| Josh Gascoigne | Netherlands | Waikato | 2016 |
| Liam McBride | Netherlands | Taranaki | 2015 |
| Rob Verbakel | Netherlands | Otago | 2012 |
| Chance Bunce | Niue Sevens | Thames Valley | 2016 |
| Whakawhiti Ranana Rangi | Niue Sevens | Counties Manukau | – |
| David Robinson-Polkey | Philippines | Auckland | – |
| Paula Kinikinilau | Romania | Otago | 2010 |
| Steven Shennan | Romania | Auckland | – |
| Jack Umaga | Romania | Tasman | 2010 |
| Jake Ale | Samoa Sevens | Waikato | 2016 |
| Thomas Alosio | Samoa A | Wellington | 2015 |
| Paul Alo-Emile | Samoa | Waikato | 2013 |
| Donald Brighouse | Samoa | Otago | 2017 |
| Pele Cowley | Samoa | Waikato | 2017 |
| Elia Elia | Samoa | Canterbury | – |
| Piua Fa'asalele | Samoa | Wellington | – |
| Auvasa Faleali'i | Samoa | Auckland | 2013 |
| Ed Fidow | Samoa Sevens | Auckland | – |
| Neria Fomai | Samoa Sevens | Southland | 2017 |
| Kieron Fonotia | Samoa | Tasman | 2016 |
| Kahn Fotuali'i | Samoa | Hawke's Bay | 2011 |
| Bronson Fotuali'i Tauakipulu | Samoa | North Harbour | – |

| Player | Country | Provincial Union | Year |
|---|---|---|---|
| Daniel Hytongue | Samoa A | Buller | 2016 |
| TJ Ioane | Samoa | Otago | 2014 |
| Tom Iosefo | Samoa Sevens | Hawke's Bay | – |
| Census Johnston | Samoa | Taranaki | 2006 |
| Danny Kayes | Samoa Sevens | Bay of Plenty | – |
| Jack Lam | Samoa | Waikato | 2013 |
| James Lay | Samoa | Bay of Plenty | 2017 |
| Jordan Lay | Samoa | Bay of Plenty | 2017 |
| Nephi Leatigaga | Samoa | Auckland | – |
| Ray Lee-Lo | Samoa | Hurricanes | 2015 |
| Manu Leiataua | Samoa | North Harbour | 2013 |
| Alapati Leuia | Samoa | Wellington | 2014 |
| Fa'atiga Lemalu | Samoa | Auckland | – |
| Nu'uli Lene | Samoa A | Wellington | – |
| Jeff Lepa | Samoa A | Buller | 2017 |
| D'Angelo Leuila | Samoa | Southland | 2016 |
| Faifili Levave | Samoa | Hurricanes | 2014 |
| Motu Matu'u | Samoa | Hurricanes | 2015 |
| Tim Nanai-Willliams | Samoa | Chiefs | 2017 |
| Brandon Nansen | Samoa | North Harbour | 2017 |
| Albert Nikoro | Samoa | Counties Manukau | 2017 |
| Opetera Peleseuma | Samoa A | Wellington | 2014 |
| Paul Perez | Samoa | Taranaki | 2009 |
| Ken Pisi | Samoa | North Harbour | 2011 |
| Dwayne Polataivao | Samoa | Auckland | 2015 |
| Savelio Ropati | Samoa Sevens | Counties Manukau | 2016 |
| Hisa Sasagi | Samoa | Otago | 2017 |
| Fa'alemiga Selesele | Samoa | Hawke's Bay | 2017 |
| Matt Talaese | Samoa A | Northland | 2016 |
| Galu Taufale | Samoa | Wellington | 2017 |
| Jamie-Jerry Taulagi | Samoa | Auckland | – |
| Ahsee Tuala | Samoa | Counties Manukau | 2014 |
| Mathew Tuatagaloa | Samoa Sevens | Northland | – |
| Taiasina Tu'ifua | Samoa | Counties Manukau | 2011 |
| Danny Tusitala | Samoa Sevens | Auckland | – |
| Josh Tyrell | Samoa | North Harbour | 2017 |
| Chris Vui | Samoa | North Harbour | 2016 |
| Simon Berghan | Scotland | Canterbury | – |
| Hugh Blake | Scotland Sevens | Bay of Plenty | 2017 |

| Player | Country | Provincial Union | Year |
|---|---|---|---|
| Blair Cowan | Scotland | Wellington | – |
| Nick Grigg | Scotland | Wellington | – |
| John Hardie | Scotland | Highlanders | 2015 |
| Grayson Hart | Scotland Sevens | North Harbour | 2010 |
| Sean Maitland | Scotland | Canterbury | 2012 |
| Byron McGuigan | Scotland | Bay of Plenty | 2014 |
| Nick McLennan | Scotland Sevens | Hawke's Bay | 2012 |
| Brad Linklater | Spain | Auckland | – |
| Dan Snee | Spain | Otago | 2008 |
| Afa Tauli | Spain | Manawatu | – |
| Halani Aulika | Tonga | Otago | 2011 |
| Paea Fa'anunu | Tonga | Canterbury | 2013 |
| Daniel Faleafa | Tonga | Northland | 2012 |
| Michael Faleafa | Tonga | Northland | 2017 |
| Jethro Felemi | Tonga | North Harbour | 2016 |
| Leva Fifita | Tonga | Waikato | 2017 |
| Siegfried Fisi'ihoi | Tonga | Chiefs | 2017 |
| Latiume Fosita | Tonga | Auckland | 2017 |
| Leon Fukofuka | Tonga | Auckland | 2017 |
| Kali Hala | Tonga | Counties Manukau | 2017 |
| Siosiua Hananukonuka | Tonga | Tasman | 2017 |
| Phil Kite | Tonga | Northland | 2017 |
| Nili Latu | Tonga | Bay of Plenty | 2006 |
| Penikolo Latu | Tonga | Waikato | 2016 |
| Sione Lea | Tonga | Taranaki | 2017 |
| Fotu Lokotui | Tonga | Counties Manukau | 2017 |
| Valentino Mapapalangi | Tonga | Manawatu | 2016 |
| Paul Ngauamo | Tonga | Canterbury | 2011 |
| Atieli Pakalani | Tonga | Auckland | 2010 |
| Siale Piutau | Tonga | Highlanders | 2012 |
| Sila Puafisi | Tonga | Tasman | 2013 |
| Jack Ram | Tonga | Northland | 2017 |
| Viliami Tahitu'a | Tonga | Northland | 2014 |
| Kiti Taimani | Tonga | Auckland | – |
| Sonatane Takulua | Tonga | Northland | 2014 |
| Latu Talakai | Tonga | Waikato | 2017 |
| Ben Tameifuna | Tonga | Waikato | 2015 |
| Suliasi Taufalele | Tonga | Counties Manukau | 2016 |
| Tevita Taufui | Tonga | Waikato | 2017 |
| Nafi Tuitavake | Tonga | North Harbour | 2015 |
| Ma'ama Vaipulu | Tonga | Chiefs | 2016 |
| Cooper Vuna | Tonga | Auckland | – |

| Player | Country | Provincial Union | Year |
|---|---|---|---|
| Chris Baumann | United States | Wellington | 2016 |
| Todd Clever | United States | North Harbour | 2006 |
| Tony Lamborn | United States | Hawke's Bay | 2017 |
| Gareth Anscombe | Wales | Auckland | 2014 |
| Hadleigh Parkes | Wales | Auckland | 2014 |

# OVERSEAS PLAYERS IN NEW ZEALAND FIRST-CLASS RUGBY 2017

For previously capped players the most recent year and level of selection are shown. Some players have since, or soon will, also become eligible for New Zealand.

| Player | Country | Year | NZ Team in 2017 |
|---|---|---|---|
| Tyler Campbell | Australia Schools | 2015 | Waikato |
| Lalakai Foketi | Australia Under 20 | 2014 | Bay of Plenty |
| Matthew Garland | Australia Schools | 2009 | Bay of Plenty |
| Digby Ioane | Australia | 2013 | Crusaders |
| Tyrell Lomax | Australia Under 20 | 2016 | Tasman |
| Guy Millar | Australia Schools | 2010 | Southland |
| Nick Palmer | Australia | Uncapped | Hawke's Bay |
| Peter Samu | Australia | Uncapped | Tasman |
| Chris Collett | England | Uncapped | North Harbour |
| Tom Crozier | England Students | 2014 | Manawatu |
| Warwick Lahmert | England Sevens | 2015 | Taranaki |
| Dan Lewis | England | Uncapped | North Otago |
| Phil Mills | England | Uncapped | Mid Canterbury |
| Kaveni Dabonaise | Fiji Under 20 | 2015 | Wanganui |
| Ironi Dawai | Fiji | Uncapped | South Canterbury |
| Alex Hodgman | Fiji Under 20 | 2012 | Canterbury |
| Sekonaia Kalou | Fiji | 2012 | Wanganui |
| Jone Macilai-Tori | Fiji | Uncapped | Northland |
| Tevita Nabura | Fiji | Uncapped | Counties Manukau |
| Viliame Rarasea | Fiji Under 20 | 2014 | Counties Manukau |
| Iliesa Ratuva Tavuyara | Fiji | 2013 | Waikato |
| Asaeli Sorovaki | Fiji Under 20 | 2015 | Taranaki |
| Pita-Gus Sowakula | Fiji | Uncapped | Taranaki |
| Newton Tudreu | Fiji | Uncapped | Manawatu |
| Poasa Waqanibau | Fiji Under 20 | 2014 | Canterbury |
| Anthony Wise | Fiji | 2010 | King Country |
| Harrison Brewer | Ireland Under 20 | 2015 | Manawatu |
| Oliver Jager | Ireland Under 18 | 2013 | Canterbury |
| Rory Malony | Ireland Under 20 | 2015 | Thames Valley |
| Kelly Haimona | Italy | 2016 | Bay of Plenty |
| Tim Bond | Japan A | 2012 | Northland |
| Toni Pulu | Niue Sevens | 2012 | Chiefs |
| Jared Adams | Samoa Under 20 | 2015 | Counties Manukau |

| Player | Country | Year | NZ Team in 2017 |
|---|---|---|---|
| Michael Ala'alatoa | Samoa Under 20 | 2011 | Manawatu |
| Jamason Fa'anana-Schultz | Samoa Under 20 | 2015 | Auckland |
| Jonathan Fa'auli | Samoa Under 20 | 2015 | Taranaki |
| Mario Fepuleai | Samoa Under 20 | 2015 | Auckland |
| Josh Ioane | Samoa Under 20 | 2015 | Otago |
| Luteru Laulala | Samoa Under 20 | 2014 | Counties Manukau |
| Orbyn Leger | Samoa Under 20 | 2015 | Counties Manukau |
| Lio Lolo | Samoa | 2014 | North Otago |
| Steven Luatua | Samoa Under 20 | 2010 | Blues |
| Melani Nanai | Samoa Under 20 | 2012 | Auckland |
| Ti'i Paulo | Samoa | 2014 | Tasman |
| Emil Pittman | Samoa Under 20 | 2014 | Northland |
| James So'oialo | Samoa | 2011 | Horowhenua-Kapiti |
| Henry Stowers | Samoa Under 20 | 2014 | Bay of Plenty |
| William Talataina-Mu | Samoa Under 20 | 2014 | Southland |
| Jordan Taufua | Samoa Under 20 | 2011 | Tasman |
| Mike Tamoaieata | Samoa Under 20 | 2015 | North Harbour |
| Jonathan Taumateine | Samoa Under 20 | 2015 | Counties Manukau |
| Kane Thompson | Samoa | 2015 | Taranaki |
| Chase Tiatia | Samoa Under 20 | 2015 | Bay of Plenty |
| Murray Douglas | Scotland | Uncapped | Northland |
| Juan-Pierre Koen | South Africa | Uncapped | South Canterbury |
| Dylan Nel | South Africa | Uncapped | Canterbury |
| Pita Ahki | Tonga Under 21 | 2011 | Waikato |
| Tolu Fahamokioa | Tonga | Uncapped | Wellington |
| Malakai Fekitoa | Tonga Sevens | 2009 | Highlanders |
| Vaea Fifita | Tonga Under 18 | 2010 | Wellington |
| Shannon Frizzell | Tonga Under 20 | 2014 | Tasman |
| Billy Fukofuka | Tonga Under 20 | 2015 | Southland |
| Sosefo Ma'ake | Tonga | 2015 | North Otago |
| George Moala | Tonga Under 20 | 2010 | Auckland |
| Petelo Pouhila | Tonga Under 20 | 2015 | North Otago |
| Latu Vaeno | Tonga Under 19 | 2011 | Taranaki |
| Josateki Veikune | Tonga A | 2012 | South Canterbury |

# OFFSHORE NEW ZEALAND ORIGIN COACHES 2017

| Country | Team | Coach |
|---|---|---|
| Australia | Waratahs | Daryl Gibson |
| Canada | National | Mark Anscombe |
| Croatia | National | Milan Yelavich |
| England | Bath | Todd Blackadder |
| England | Bristol | Pat Lam |
| Fiji | National | John McKee |
| France | Montpellier | Vern Cotter |
| France | Pau | Simon Mannix |
| France | Stade Francais | Greg Cooper |
| Georgia | National | Milton Haig |
| Ireland | Connacht | Kieran Keane |
| Ireland | National | Joe Schmidt |
| Italy | Benetton Treviso | Kieran Crowley |
| Italy | Rovigo | Joe McDonnell |
| Japan | Coca Cola Red Sparks | Earl Va'a |
| Japan | NEC Green Rockets | Peter Russell |
| Japan | NTT Shining Arcs | Rob Penney |
| Japan | Pansonic Wild Knights | Robbie Deans |
| Japan | National and Sunwolves | Jamie Joseph |
| Laos | National | Ian Snook |
| Romania | Timisoara Saracens | Granger Heikell |
| Samoa | National | Alama Ieremia |
| Samoa | National Sevens | Sir Gordon Tietjens |
| Scotland | Glasgow | Dave Rennie |
| South Africa | Blue Bulls | John Mitchell |
| United States | National | Dave Hewett |
| Wales | National | Warren Gatland |
| Wales | Scarlets | Wayne Pivac |

# ALL BLACKS
# TEST MATCH RECORD

*to January 1, 2018*

| Opponents | Played | Won | Lost | Drawn | For | Against |
|---|---|---|---|---|---|---|
| Argentina | 26 | 25 | – | 1 | 1049 | 365 |
| Australia | 161 | 111 | 43 | 7 | 3375 | 2273 |
| British Isles | 41 | 30 | 7 | 4 | 700 | 399 |
| Canada | 5 | 5 | – | – | 313 | 54 |
| England | 40 | 32 | 7 | 1 | 969 | 560 |
| Fiji | 5 | 5 | – | – | 364 | 50 |
| France | 58 | 45 | 12 | 1 | 1469 | 763 |
| Georgia | 1 | 1 | – | – | 43 | 10 |
| Ireland | 30 | 28 | 1 | 1 | 862 | 359 |
| Italy | 13 | 13 | – | – | 754 | 128 |
| Japan | 3 | 3 | – | – | 282 | 30 |
| Namibia | 1 | 1 | – | – | 58 | 14 |
| Pacific Islands | 1 | 1 | – | – | 41 | 26 |
| Portugal | 1 | 1 | – | – | 108 | 13 |
| Romania | 2 | 2 | – | – | 99 | 14 |
| Samoa | 7 | 7 | – | – | 411 | 72 |
| Scotland | 31 | 29 | – | 2 | 922 | 349 |
| South Africa | 95 | 57 | 35 | 3 | 1945 | 1482 |
| Tonga | 5 | 5 | – | – | 326 | 35 |
| United States | 3 | 3 | – | – | 171 | 15 |
| Wales | 34 | 31 | 3 | – | 1070 | 374 |
| World XV | 3 | 2 | 1 | – | 94 | 69 |
| | **566** | **437** | **109** | **20** | **15,425** | **7,454** |

*The All Blacks have won 77.21 per cent of all test matches.*
*This figure has increased in 16 out of the last 17 years.*

## COMPARATIVE FIGURES FOR
## NEW ZEALAND'S MAJOR RIVALS TO 1/1/18

| | Played | Won | Win % |
|---|---|---|---|
| South Africa | 477 | 298 | 62.47 |
| France | 743 | 402 | 54.10 |
| England | 715 | 394 | 55.10 |
| Wales | 705 | 364 | 51.63 |
| Australia | 618 | 316 | 51.13 |
| Ireland | 678 | 298 | 43.95 |
| Scotland | 675 | 289 | 42.81 |

# ALL BLACK STATISTICS
*to January 1, 2018*

## LEADING ALL BLACK APPEARANCES IN ALL MATCHES

| | | | | | |
|---|---|---|---|---|---|
| R.H. McCaw | 149 | S.S. Wilson | 85 | B.J. Lochore | 68 |
| C.E. Meads | 133 | I.J. Clarke | 83 | B.A. Retallick | 68 |
| K.F. Mealamu | 133 | A.K. Hore | 83 | C.W. Dowd | 67 |
| S.B.T. Fitzpatrick | 128 | J. Kaino | 83 | C.R. Jack | 67 |
| T.D. Woodcock | 118 | S.C. McDowall | 81 | A.D. Oliver | 67 |
| A.M. Haden | 117 | J.F. Umaga | 79 | G.M. Somerville | 67 |
| I.A. Kirkpatrick | 113 | G.J. Fox | 78 | I.J.A. Dagg | 66 |
| B.G. Williams | 113 | R.W. Loe | 78 | G.A. Knight | 66 |
| D.W. Carter | 112 | A.J. Williams | 78 | B.R. Smith | 65 |
| K.J. Read | 110 | W.J. Whineray | 77 | A.J. Whetton | 65 |
| I.D. Jones | 105 | W.K. Little | 75 | A.R. Sutherland | 64 |
| M.A. Nonu | 104 | M.N. Jones | 74 | T.J. Wright | 64 |
| J.M. Muliaina | 102 | J.T. Lomu | 73 | B.J. Barrett | 63 |
| B.J. Robertson | 102 | P.A.T. Weepu | 73 | D.C. Howlett | 63 |
| G.W. Whetton | 101 | W.W.V. Crockett | 72 | K.L. Skinner | 63 |
| Z.V. Brooke | 100 | A.P. Mehrtens | 72 | R. So'oialo | 63 |
| J.J. Kirwan | 96 | M.G. Mexted | 72 | M.R. Brewer | 61 |
| S.L. Whitelock | 96 | A.L. Smith | 71 | M.J. Brownlie | 61 |
| O.T. Franks | 95 | J.W. Wilson | 71 | G.N.K. Mourie | 61 |
| C.G. Smith | 94 | R.M. Brooke | 69 | R.W. Norton | 61 |
| D.B. Clarke | 89 | O.M. Brown | 69 | T.C. Randell | 61 |
| J.W. Marshall | 88 | F.E. Bunce | 69 | D. Young | 61 |
| S.M. Going | 86 | J.T. Rokocoko | 69 | C.M. Cullen | 60 |
| K.R. Tremain | 86 | M.W. Shaw | 69 | B.C. Thorn | 60 |

## LEADING POINTS-SCORERS IN
## ALL MATCHES FOR NEW ZEALAND

| | | Matches | Points |
|---|---|---|---|
| D.W. Carter | 2003–15 | 112 | 1598 |
| G.J. Fox | 1985–93 | 78 | 1067 |
| A.P. Mehrtens | 1995–2004 | 72 | 994 |
| D.B. Clarke | 1956–64 | 89 | 781 |
| B.J. Barrett | 2012–17 | 63 | 471 |
| W.F. McCormick | 1965–71 | 44 | 453 |
| B.G. Williams | 1970–78 | 113 | 401[1] |
| C.J. Spencer | 1995–2004 | 44 | 383 |
| W.J. Wallace | 1903–08 | 51 | 379 |
| A.R. Hewson | 1979–84 | 34 | 357 |
| J.F. Karam | 1972–75 | 42 | 345 |
| A.W. Cruden | 2010–17 | 50 | 322 |
| K.J. Crowley | 1983–91 | 35 | 316 |
| J.W. Wilson | 1993–2001 | 71 | 299 |
| M.F. Nicholls | 1921–30 | 51 | 284 |
| J.J. Kirwan | 1984–94 | 96 | 275 |
| R.G. Wilson | 1976–80 | 25 | 272 |
| C.M. Cullen | 1996–2002 | 60 | 266 |
| R.M. Deans | 1983–85 | 19 | 252 |
| J.A. Gallagher | 1986–89 | 41 | 251 |

[1]*includes a penalty try*

## LEADING TRY-SCORERS IN ALL MATCHES

|  |  | Matches | Tries |
|---|---|---|---|
| J.J. Kirwan | 1984–94 | 96 | 67 |
| B.G. Williams | 1970–78 | 113 | 66ᵗ |
| C.M. Cullen | 1996–2002 | 60 | 52 |
| I.A. Kirkpatrick | 1967–77 | 113 | 50 |
| J.W. Wilson | 1993–2001 | 71 | 50 |
| S.S. Wilson | 1976–83 | 85 | 50 |
| D.C. Howlett | 2000–07 | 63 | 49 |
| T.J. Wright | 1986–92 | 64 | 49t |
| J. Hunter | 1905–08 | 36 | 48 |
| J.T. Rokocoko | 2003–10 | 69 | 47 |
| B.G. Fraser | 1979–84 | 55 | 46 |
| S.J. Savea | 2012–17 | 54 | 46 |
| G.B. Batty | 1972–77 | 56 | 45 |
| J.T. Lomu | 1994–2002 | 73 | 43 |
| Z.V. Brooke | 1987–97 | 100 | 42 |
| M.J. Dick | 1963–70 | 55 | 42 |

ᵗ*includes a penalty try*

## MOST APPEARANCES IN INTERNATIONALS

| | | | | | | |
|---|---|---|---|---|---|---|
| R.H. McCaw | 2001-15 | 148 | | J.J. Kirwan | 1984–94 | 63 |
| K.F. Mealamu | 2002–15 | 132 | | J.T. Lomu | 1994–2002 | 63 |
| T.D. Woodcock | 2002–15 | 118 | | B.J. Barrett | 2012–17 | 62 |
| D.W. Carter | 2003–15 | 112 | | R.M. Brooke | 1992–99 | 62 |
| K.J. Read | 2008–17 | 109 | | D.C. Howlett | 2000–07 | 62 |
| M.A. Nonu | 2003–15 | 103 | | R. So'oialo | 2002–09 | 62 |
| J.M. Muliaina | 2003–11 | 100 | | C.W. Dowd | 1993–2000 | 60 |
| S.L. Whitelock | 2010–17 | 96 | | J.W. Wilson | 1993–2001 | 60 |
| O.T. Franks | 2009–17 | 95 | | A.D. Oliver | 1997–2007 | 59 |
| C.G. Smith | 2004–15 | 94 | | B.C. Thorn | 2003–11 | 59 |
| S.B.T. Fitzpatrick | 1986–97 | 92 | | Z.V. Brooke | 1987–97 | 58 |
| A.K. Hore | 2002–13 | 83 | | G.W. Whetton | 1981–91 | 58 |
| J. Kaino | 2004–17 | 81 | | C.M. Cullen | 1996–2002 | 58 |
| J.W. Marshall | 1995–2005 | 81 | | B.T. Kelleher | 1999–2007 | 57 |
| I.D. Jones | 1990–99 | 79 | | O.M. Brown | 1992–98 | 56 |
| A.J. Williams | 2002–12 | 77 | | L.R. MacDonald | 2000–08 | 56 |
| J.F. Umaga | 1997–2005 | 74 | | F.E. Bunce | 1992–97 | 55 |
| W.W.V. Crockett | 2009–17 | 71 | | M.N. Jones | 1987–98 | 55 |
| A.L. Smith | 2012–17 | 71 | | C.E. Meads | 1957–71 | 55 |
| P.A.T. Weepu | 2004–13 | 71 | | J.A. Kronfeld | 1995–2000 | 54 |
| A.P. Mehrtens | 1995–2004 | 70 | | S.J. Savea | 2012–17 | 54 |
| B.A. Retallick | 2012–17 | 68 | | C.S. Jane | 2008–14 | 53 |
| J.T. Rokocoko | 2003–10 | 68 | | Q.J. Cowan | 2004–11 | 51 |
| C.R. Jack | 2001–07 | 67 | | T.C. Randell | 1997–2002 | 51 |
| I.J.A. Dagg | 2010–17 | 66 | | W.K. Little | 1990–98 | 50 |
| G.M. Somerville | 2000–08 | 66 | | R.D. Thorne | 1999-2007 | 50 |
| B.R. Smith | 2009–17 | 64 | | | | |

## MOST POINTS FOR NEW ZEALAND IN INTERNATIONALS

| | Matches | Tries | Con | PG | DG | Mark | Points |
|---|---|---|---|---|---|---|---|
| D.W. Carter | 112 | 29 | 293 | 281 | 8 | – | 1598 |
| A.P. Mehrtens | 70 | 7 | 169 | 188 | 10 | – | 967 |
| G.J. Fox | 46 | 1 | 118 | 128 | 7 | – | 645 |
| B.J. Barrett | 62 | 24 | 111 | 41 | – | – | 465 |
| A.W. Cruden | 50 | 5 | 63 | 56 | 1 | – | 322 |
| C.J. Spencer | 35 | 14 | 49 | 41 | – | – | 291 |
| D.C. Howlett | 62 | 49 | – | – | – | – | 245 |
| C.M. Cullen | 58 | 46 | 3 | – | – | – | 236 |
| J.W. Wilson | 60 | 44 | 1 | 3 | 1 | – | 234 |
| J.T. Rokocoko | 68 | 46 | – | – | – | – | 230 |
| S.J. Savea | 54 | 46 | – | – | – | – | 230 |
| D.B. Clarke | 31 | 2 | 33 | 38 | 5 | 2 | 207 |
| A.R. Hewson | 19 | 4 | 22 | 43 | 4 | – | 201 |
| J.T. Lomu | 63 | 37 | – | – | – | – | 185 |
| J.F. Umaga | 74 | 37t | – | – | – | – | 185 |
| T.E. Brown | 18 | 5 | 43 | 20 | – | – | 171 |
| J.M. Muliaina | 100 | 34 | – | – | – | – | 170 |
| M.A. Nonu | 103 | 31 | – | – | – | – | 155 |
| C.L. McAlister | 30 | 7 | 26 | 22 | – | – | 153 |
| L.R. MacDonald | 56 | 15t | 25 | 7 | – | – | 146 |
| S.W. Sivivatu | 45 | 29 | – | – | – | – | 145 |
| B.R. Smith | 64 | 29 | – | – | – | – | 145 |
| J.J. Kirwan | 63 | 35l | – | – | – | – | 143 |
| R.H. McCaw | 148 | 28t | – | – | – | – | 140 |
| I.J.A. Dagg | 66 | 26 | 1 | 2 | – | – | 138 |
| C.G. Smith | 94 | 26 | – | – | – | – | 130 |
| W.F. McCormick | 16 | – | 23 | 24 | 1 | – | 121 |
| J.W. Marshall | 81 | 24 | – | – | – | – | 120 |
| K.J. Read | 109 | 23 | – | – | – | – | 115 |
| S.D. Culhane | 6 | 1 | 32 | 15 | – | – | 114 |
| K.J. Crowley | 19 | 5 | 5 | 23 | 2 | – | 105 |
| N.J. Evans | 16 | 5 | 30 | 6 | – | – | 103 |
| P.A.T. Weepu | 71 | 7 | 10 | 16 | – | – | 103 |

*1 includes three tries at five points*
*t includes penalty try*

## MOST STARTS IN EACH POSITION
## FOR NEW ZEALAND IN INTERNATIONALS

| | | | | | | | | |
|---|---|---|---|---|---|---|---|---|
| Fullback | J.M. Muliaina | 2003–11 | 83 | No 8 | K.J. Read | 2009–17 | 100 |
| Wing | J.T. Rokocoko | 2003–10 | 66 | Flanker | R.H. McCaw | 2001–15 | 139 |
| Centre | C.G. Smith | 2004–15 | 90 | Lock | S.L. Whitelock | 2010–17 | 78 |
| 2nd five-eighth | M.A. Nonu | 2003–15 | 81 | Prop | T.D. Woodcock | 2002–15 | 105 |
| 1st five-eighth | D.W. Carter | 2004–15 | 94 | Hooker | S.B.T. Fitzpatrick | 1986–97 | 91 |
| Halfback | J.W. Marshall | 1995–05 | 74 | Substitute | K.F. Mealamu | 2002–15 | 55 |

*The player must have started the match in that position. Appearances as replacements are not included except in this case Mealamu.*

## MOST TRIES FOR NEW ZEALAND IN INTERNATIONALS

| | Matches | Tries | | Matches | Tries |
|---|---|---|---|---|---|
| D.C. Howlett | 62 | 49 | S.W. Sivivatu | 45 | 29 |
| C.M. Cullen | 58 | 46 | R.H. McCaw | 148 | 28t |
| J.T. Rokocoko | 68 | 46 | B.R. Smith | 64 | 29 |
| S.J. Savea | 54 | 46 | C.G. Smith | 94 | 26 |
| J.W. Wilson | 60 | 44 | I.J.A. Dagg | 66 | 26 |
| J.T. Lomu | 63 | 37 | B.J. Barrett | 62 | 24 |
| J.F. Umaga | 74 | 37ᵗ | J.W. Marshall | 81 | 24 |
| J.J. Kirwan | 63 | 35 | K.J. Read | 109 | 23 |
| J.M. Muliaina | 100 | 34 | F.E. Bunce | 55 | 20 |
| M.A. Nonu | 103 | 31 | | | |
| D.W. Carter | 112 | 29 | | | |

## MOST TRIES IN AN INTERNATIONAL

| | | | | | |
|---|---|---|---|---|---|
| M.C.G. Ellis | v Japan, 1995 | 6 | J.T. Lomu | v England, 1995 | 4 |
| J.W. Wilson | v Fiji, 1997 | 5 | C.M. Cullen | v Scotland, 1996 | 4 |
| D. McGregor | v England, 1905 | 4 | J.W. Wilson | v Samoa, 1999 | 4 |
| C.I. Green | v Fiji, 1987 | 4 | J.M. Muliaina | v Canada, 2003 | 4 |
| J.A. Gallagher | v Fiji, 1987 | 4 | S.W. Sivivatu | v Fiji, 2005 | 4 |
| J.J. Kirwan | v Wales, 1988 | 4 | Z.R. Guildford | v Canada, 2011 | 4 |

## MOST PENALTY GOALS IN AN INTERNATIONAL

| | | | | | |
|---|---|---|---|---|---|
| A.P. Mehrtens | v Australia, 1999 | 9 | D.W. Carter | v Australia, 2007 | 7 |
| A.P. Mehrtens | v France, 2000 | 9 | P.A.T. Weepu | v Argentina, 2011 | 7 |
| G.J. Fox | v W Samoa, 1993 | 7 | B.J. Barrett | v BI Lions, 2017 | 7 |
| A.P. Mehrtens | v South Africa, 1999 | 7 | | | |

## MOST CONVERSIONS IN AN INTERNATIONAL

| | | | | | |
|---|---|---|---|---|---|
| S.D. Culhane | v Japan, 1995 | 20 | C.J. Spencer | v Argentina, 1997 | 10 |
| N.J. Evans | v Portugal, 2007 | 14 | D.W. Carter | v Canada, 2003 | 9 |
| T.E. Brown | v Tonga, 2000 | 12 | C.R. Slade | v Japan, 2011 | 9 |
| L.R. MacDonald | v Tonga, 2003 | 12 | G.J. Fox | v Italy, 1987 | 8 |
| T.E. Brown | v Italy, 1999 | 11 | G.J. Fox | v Wales, 1988 | 8 |
| G.J. Fox | v Fiji, 1987 | 10 | A.P. Mehrtens | v Italy, 2002 | 8 |

## HIGHEST POINTS-SCORERS IN AN INTERNATIONAL

| | Opponent | Tries | Con | PG | DG | Points |
|---|---|---|---|---|---|---|
| S.D. Culhane | Japan, 1995[1] | 1 | 20 | – | – | 45 |
| T.E. Brown | Italy,1999 | 1 | 11 | 3 | – | 36 |
| D.W. Carter | Lions, 2005 | 2 | 4 | 5 | – | 33 |
| C.J. Spencer | Argentina, 1997[1] | 2 | 10 | 1 | – | 33 |
| A.P. Mehrtens | Ireland, 1997 | 1 | 5 | 6 | – | 33 |
| N.J. Evans | Portugal, 2007 | 1 | 14 | – | – | 33 |
| T.E. Brown | Tonga, 2000 | 1 | 12 | 1 | – | 32 |
| M.C.G. Ellis | Japan, 1995 | 6 | – | – | – | 30 |
| T.E. Brown | Samoa, 2001 | 3 | 3 | 3 | – | 30 |
| A.P. Mehrtens | Australia, 1999 | – | 1 | 9 | – | 29 |
| A.P. Mehrtens | France, 2000 | – | 1 | 9 | – | 29 |
| L.R. MacDonald | Tonga, 2003 | 1 | 12 | – | – | 29 |
| D.W. Carter | Canada, 2007 | 3 | 7 | – | – | 29 |
| A.P. Mehrtens | Canada, 1995[1] | 1 | 7 | 3 | – | 28 |
| D.W. Carter | Wales, 2010 | 2 | 4 | 3 | – | 27 |
| A.R. Hewson | Australia, 1982 | 1 | 2 | 5 | 1 | 26 |
| G.J. Fox | Fiji, 1987 | – | 10 | 2 | – | 26 |
| D.W. Carter | Wales, 2005 | 2 | 5 | 2 | – | 26 |
| D.W. Carter | England, 2006 | 1 | 3 | 5 | – | 26 |
| T.E. Brown | Samoa, 1999[1] | – | 7 | 4 | – | 26 |
| B.J. Barrett | Wales, 2016 | 2 | 5 | 2 | – | 26 |
| D.W. Carter | South Africa, 2006 | – | 2 | 7 | – | 25 |
| G.J. Fox | Western Samoa, 1993 | – | 2 | 7 | – | 25 |
| J.W. Wilson | Fiji, 1997 | 5 | – | – | – | 25 |
| C.J. Spencer | South Africa, 1997 | 1 | 4 | 4 | – | 25 |
| D.W. Carter | France, 2004 | 1 | 4 | 4 | – | 25 |
| W.F. McCormick | Wales, 1969 | – | 3 | 5 | 1 | 24 |
| B.J. Barrett | Samoa, 2017 | 2 | 7 | – | – | 24 |

[1] *international debut*

## NEW ZEALAND INTERNATIONAL CAPTAINS

| | | | | | | |
|---|---|---|---|---|---|---|
| R.H. McCaw | 2004–15 | 110 | R.R. King | 1937 | 3 |
| S.B.T. Fitzpatrick | 1992–97 | 51 | D.J. Graham | 1964 | 3 |
| K.J. Read | 2012–17 | 34 | D.S. Loveridge | 1980 | 3 |
| W.J. Whineray | 1958–65 | 30 | K.F. Mealamu | 2008–11 | 3 |
| R.D. Thorne | 2002–07 | 23 | J.M. Muliaina | 2009 | 3 |
| T.C. Randell | 1998–2002 | 22 | F.J. Oliver | 1978 | 3 |
| J.F. Umaga | 2004–05 | 21 | J. Richardson | 1924 | 3 |
| G.N.K. Mourie | 1977–82 | 19 | F. Roberts | 1910 | 3 |
| B.J. Lochore | 1966–70 | 18 | R.W. Roberts | 1914 | 3 |
| A.G. Dalton | 1981–85 | 17 | G.G. Aitken | 1921 | 2 |
| G.W. Whetton | 1990–91 | 15 | S.J. Cane | 2015–16 | 2 |
| W.T. Shelford | 1988–90 | 14 | R.H. Duff | 1956 | 2 |
| D.E. Kirk | 1986–87 | 11 | J.L. Griffiths | 1936 | 2 |
| T.J. Blackadder | 2000 | 10 | A. McDonald | 1913 | 2 |
| A.R. Leslie | 1974–76 | 10 | N.A. Mitchell | 1938 | 2 |
| A.D. Oliver | 2001 | 10 | M.J. O'Leary | 1913 | 2 |
| I.A. Kirkpatrick | 1972–73 | 9 | A.R. Reid | 1957 | 2 |
| C.G. Porter | 1925–30 | 7 | K.L. Skinner | 1952 | 2 |
| F.R. Allen | 1946–49 | 6 | J.B. Smith | 1949 | 2 |
| R.R. Elvidge | 1949–50 | 5 | P.B. Vincent | 1956 | 2 |
| R. So'oialo | 2008–09 | 5 | S.S. Wilson | 1983 | 2 |
| R.C. Stuart | 1953–54 | 5 | J. Duncan | 1903 | 1 |
| M.J. Brownlie | 1928 | 4 | P.W. Henderson | 1995 | 1 |
| D. Gallaher | 1905–06 | 4 | A.K. Hore | 2011 | 1 |
| M.J.B. Hobbs | 1985–86 | 4 | C.R. Laidlaw | 1968 | 1 |
| J. Hunter | 1907–08 | 4 | H.T. Lilburne | 1929 | 1 |
| P. Johnstone | 1950–51 | 4 | R.M. McKenzie | 1938 | 1 |
| F.D. Kilby | 1932–34 | 4 | J.R. Page | 1934 | 1 |
| J.E. Manchester | 1935–36 | 4 | E.J. Roberts | 1921 | 1 |
| J.W. Marshall | 1997 | 4 | B.R. Smith | 2017 | 1 |
| C.E. Meads | 1971 | 4 | J.C. Spencer | 1905 | 1 |
| R.W. Norton | 1977 | 4 | W.A. Strang | 1931 | 1 |
| J.W. Stead | 1904–08 | 4 | K.R. Tremain | 1968 | 1 |
| I.J. Clarke | 1955 | 3 | S.L. Whitelock | 2017 | 1 |
| J. Collins | 2006–07 | 3 | | | |

## MOST TEST MATCH WINS

| | | | | |
|---|---|---|---|---|
| R.H. McCaw | 131 | | A.L. Smith | 62 |
| K.F. Mealamu | 114 | | P.A.T. Weepu | 62 |
| T.D. Woodcock | 102 | | J.W. Marshall | 61 |
| D.W. Carter | 99 | | I.J.A. Dagg | 60 |
| K.J. Read | 94 | | I.D. Jones | 59 |
| M.A. Nonu | 91 | | J.F. Umaga | 59 |
| S.L. Whitelock | 85 | | B.R. Smith | 58 |
| J.M. Muliana | 84 | | C.R. Jack | 57 |
| C.G. Smith | 84 | | B.J. Barrett | 56 |
| O.T. Franks | 82 | | J.T. Rokocoko | 55 |
| S.B.T. Fitzpatrick | 74 | | G.M. Somerville | 55 |
| A.K. Hore | 70 | | R. So'oialo | 53 |
| J. Kaino | 68 | | D.C. Howlett | 51 |
| W.W.V. Crockett | 66 | | B.C. Thorn | 51 |
| A.J. Williams | 65 | | D.S. Coles | 50 |
| B.A. Retallick | 62 | | G.W. Whetton | 50 |

## HIGHEST SCORES IN TEST MATCHES

| Opponent | Home | | Away | | Opponent | Home | | Away | |
|----------|------|---|------|---|----------|------|---|------|---|
| Argentina | 93–8 | (1997) | 54–18 | (2012) | Namibia | – | – | 58–14 | (2015) |
| Australia | 51–20 | (2014) | 54–34 | (2017) | Pacific Islands | 41–26 | (2004) | – | |
| British Isles | 48–18 | (2005) | – | | Portugal | – | | 108–13 | (2007) |
| Canada | 79–15 | (2011) | 68–8 | (2003) | Romania | – | | 85–8 | (2007) |
| England | 64–22 | (1998) | 45–29 | (1995) | Samoa | 101–14 | (2008) | 25–16 | (2015) |
| Fiji | 91–0 | (2005) | – | | Scotland | 69–20 | (2000) | 51–15 | (1993) |
| | | | | | | | | 51–22 | (2012) |
| France | 61–10 | (2007) | 62–13 | (2015) | South Africa | 57–0 | (2017) | 57-15 | (2016) |
| Georgia | – | – | 43–10 | (2015) | Tonga | 102–0 | (2000) | 91–7 | (2003) |
| Ireland | 66–28 | (2010) | 63–15 | (1997) | USA | – | | 74–6 | (2014) |
| Italy | 70–6 | (1987) | 101–3 | (1999) | Wales | 55–3 | (2003) | 53–37 | (2003) |
| Japan | 83–7 | (2011) | 145–17 | (1995) | | | | | |

## MOST POINTS BY AN ALL BLACK AGAINST AN OPPONENT

| Opponent | In an International | | | In a Career | |
|----------|-----|------|------|-----|------|
| Argentina | 33 | C.J. Spencer | 1997 | 103 | G.J. Fox |
| Australia | 29 | A.P. Mehrtens | 1999 | 366 | D.W. Carter |
| British Isles | 33 | D.W. Carter | 2005 | 46 | A.R. Hewson |
| Canada | 29 | D.W. Carter | 2007 | 47 | D.W. Carter |
| England | 26 | D.W. Carter | 2006 | 178 | D.W. Carter |
| Fiji | 26 | G.J. Fox | 1987 | 29 | C.M. Cullen |
| France | 29 | A.P. Mehrtens | 2000 | 146 | D.W. Carter |
| Georgia | 15 | S.J. Savea | 2015 | 15 | S.J. Savea |
| Ireland | 33 | A.P. Mehrtens | 1997 | 81 | A.P. Mehrtens |
| Italy | 36 | T.E. Brown | 1999 | 53 | D.W. Carter |
| Japan | 45 | S.D. Culhane | 1995 | 45 | S.D. Culhane |
| Namibia | 18 | B.J. Barrett | 2015 | 18 | B.J. Barrett |
| Pacific Islands | 11 | D.W. Carter | 2004 | 11 | D.W. Carter |
| Portugal | 33 | N.J. Evans | 2007 | 33 | N.J. Evans |
| Romania | 17 | N.J. Evans | 2007 | 17 | N.J. Evans |
| Samoa | 30 | T.E. Brown | 2001 | 56 | T.E. Brown |
| Scotland | 23 | A.P. Mehrtens | 1995 | 108 | A.P. Mehrtens |
| South Africa | 25 | C.J. Spencer | 1997 | 255 | D.W. Carter |
| | 25 | D.W. Carter | 2006 | | |
| Tonga | 32 | T.E. Brown | 2000 | 32 | T.E. Brown |
| USA | 14 | J.P. Preston | 1991 | 14 | J.P. Preston |
| Wales | 27 | D.W. Carter | 2010 | 162 | D.W. Carter |

## WINNING PERCENTAGE
*Minimum 30 test appearances*

| | | | | | |
|---|---|---|---|---|---|
| W.W.V. Crockett | 66/71 | 93.0% | B.C. Thorn | 51/59 | 86.4 |
| B.J. Franks | 43/47 | 91.5 | T.D. Woodcock | 102/118 | 86.4 |
| S. Williams | 42/46 | 91.3 | Q.J. Cowan | 44/51 | 86.3 |
| B.A. Retallick | 62/68 | 91.2 | O.T. Franks | 82/95 | 86.3 |
| I.J.A. Dagg | 60/66 | 90.9 | K.J. Read | 94/109 | 86.2 |
| B.R. Smith | 58/64 | 90.6 | G.W. Whetton | 50/58 | 86.2 |
| B.J. Barrett | 56/62 | 90.3 | A.G. Dalton | 30/35 | 85.7 |
| L. Romano | 28/31 | 90.3 | L.R. MacDonald | 48/56 | 85.7 |
| C.G. Smith | 84/94 | 89.4 | R. So'oialo | 53/62 | 85.5 |
| D.S. Coles | 50/56 | 89.3 | C.R. Jack | 57/67 | 85.1 |
| S.J. Savea | 48/54 | 88.9 | C.S. Jane | 45/53 | 84.9 |
| S.J. Cane | 47/53 | 88.7 | A.J. Williams | 65/77 | 84.4 |
| R.S. Crotty | 31/35 | 88.6 | A.K. Hore | 70/83 | 84.3 |
| A.J. Whetton | 31/35 | 88.6 | J.M. Muliana | 84/100 | 84.0 |
| R.H. McCaw | 131/148 | 88.5 | R.D. Thorne | 42/50 | 84.0 |
| S.L. Whitelock | 85/96 | 88.5 | J. Kaino | 68/81 | 83.9 |
| D.W. Carter | 99/112 | 88.4 | J.P.T. Moody | 26/31 | 83.9 |
| L.J. Messam | 38/43 | 88.4 | G.M. Somerville | 55/66 | 83.3 |
| N.S. Tialata | 38/43 | 88.4 | I. Toeava | 30/36 | 83.3 |
| M.A. Nonu | 91/103 | 88.3 | G.J. Fox | 38/46 | 82.6 |
| T.T.R. Perenara | 37/42 | 88.1 | S.C. McDowall | 38/46 | 82.6 |
| A.W. Cruden | 44/50 | 88.0 | D.C. Howlett | 51/62 | 82.3 |
| C.C. Faumuina | 44/50 | 88.0 | S.W. Sivivatu | 37/45 | 82.2 |
| V.V.J. Vito | 29/33 | 87.9 | J.T. Rokocoko | 55/68 | 80.9 |
| J. Collins | 42/48 | 87.5 | B.T. Kelleher | 46/57 | 80.7 |
| A.J.D. Mauger | 39/45 | 87.3 | S.B.T. Fitzpatrick | 74/92 | 80.4 |
| A.L. Smith | 62/71 | 87.3 | C.W. Dowd | 48/60 | 80.0 |
| P.A.T. Weepu | 62/71 | 87.3 | C.J. Hayman | 36/45 | 80.0 |
| T.J. Wright | 26/30 | 86.7 | C.L. McAlister | 24/30 | 80.0 |
| K.F. Mealamu | 114/132 | 86.4 | | | |

# INTERNATIONAL COMPARISONS

## MOST TRIES IN TEST MATCHES

|              | Tries | Tests | Average |
|--------------|-------|-------|---------|
| **New Zealand** | **2010** | **566** | **3.55** |
| France       | 1714  | 743   | 2.31    |
| Australia    | 1624  | 618   | 2.63    |
| England      | 1592  | 715   | 2.23    |
| Wales        | 1522  | 705   | 2.16    |
| South Africa | 1339  | 477   | 2.81    |

## MOST POINTS IN TEST MATCHES

|              | Points | Tests | Average |
|--------------|--------|-------|---------|
| **New Zealand** | **15,425** | **566** | **27.25** |
| France       | 13,545 | 743   | 18.23   |
| Australia    | 13,025 | 618   | 21.07   |
| Wales        | 12,173 | 715   | 17.00   |
| England      | 11,985 | 705   | 17.03   |
| South Africa | 11,059 | 477   | 23.18   |

## POINTS DIFFERENTIAL IN TEST MATCHES

|              | For | Against | Differential |
|--------------|-----|---------|--------------|
| **New Zealand** | **15,425** | **7,454** | **7971** |
| South Africa | 11,059 | 7,664   | 3,395        |
| England      | 12,173 | 9,041   | 3,132        |
| France       | 13,545 | 11,240  | 2,305        |
| Australia    | 13,025 | 10,790  | 2,235        |
| Wales        | 11,985 | 1,0616  | 1,369        |

# PLAYING RECORDS
# OF NEW ZEALAND TEAMS
*1884–2017*

| | | Played | Won | Lost | Drawn | Points for | Points against |
|---|---|---|---|---|---|---|---|
| 1884 | in **New South Wales** and **New Zealand** | 9 | 9 | – | – | 176 | 17 |
| 1893 | in **New Zealand, New South Wales** and **Queensland** | 11 | 10 | 1 | – | 175 | 48 |
| 1894 | **New South Wales** in **New Zealand** | 1 | – | 1 | – | 6 | 8 |
| 1896 | **Queensland** in **New Zealand** | 1 | 1 | – | – | 9 | 0 |
| 1897 | in **New Zealand, New South Wales** and **Queensland** | 11 | 9 | 2 | – | 238 | 83 |
| 1901 | **New South Wales** in **New Zealand** | 2 | 2 | – | – | 44 | 8 |
| 1903 | in **Australia** and **New Zealand** | 11 | 10 | 1 | – | 281 | 27 |
| 1904 | **Great Britain** in **New Zealand** | 1 | 1 | – | – | 9 | 3 |
| 1905 | in **Australia** and **New Zealand** | 7 | 4 | 1 | 2 | 89 | 30 |
| | **Australia** in **New Zealand** | 1 | 1 | – | – | 14 | 3 |
| 1905/06 | in **the British Isles, France** and **North America** | 35 | 34 | 1 | – | 976 | 59 |
| 1907 | in **Australia** | 8 | 6 | 1 | 1 | 115 | 53 |
| 1908 | **Anglo-Welsh** in **New Zealand** | 3 | 2 | – | 1 | 64 | 8 |
| 1910 | in **Australia** and **New Zealand** | 8 | 7 | 1 | – | 138 | 78 |
| 1913 | **Australia** in **New Zealand** | 4 | 3 | 1 | – | 79 | 52 |
| | in **North America** | 16 | 16 | – | – | 610 | 6 |
| 1914 | in **Australia** and **New Zealand** | 11 | 10 | 1 | – | 260 | 69 |
| 1920 | in **Australia** and **New Zealand** | 10 | 9 | – | 1 | 352 | 91 |
| 1921 | **South Africa** and **New South Wales** in **New Zealand** | 4 | 1 | 2 | 1 | 18 | 31 |
| 1922 | in **Australia** and **New Zealand** | 8 | 6 | 2 | – | 198 | 102 |
| 1923 | **New South Wales** in **New Zealand** | 3 | 3 | – | – | 91 | 26 |
| 1924/25 | in **Australia, New Zealand, the British Isles, France** and **Canada** | 38 | 36 | 2 | – | 981 | 180 |
| 1925 | in **Australia** and **New Zealand** | 8 | 6 | 2 | – | 132 | 67 |
| | **New South Wales** in **New Zealand** | 1 | 1 | – | – | 36 | 10 |
| 1926 | in **Australia** and **New Zealand** | 8 | 6 | 2 | – | 187 | 109 |
| 1928 | in **South Africa** and **Australia** | 23 | 17 | 5 | 1 | 397 | 153 |
| | **New South Wales** in **New Zealand** | 4 | 3 | 1 | – | 79 | 40 |
| 1929 | in **Australia** | 10 | 6 | 3 | 1 | 186 | 80 |
| 1930 | **Great Britain** in **New Zealand** | 5 | 4 | 1 | – | 87 | 40 |
| 1931 | **Australia** in **New Zealand** | 1 | 1 | – | – | 20 | 13 |
| 1932 | in **Australia** and **New Zealand** | 11 | 9 | 2 | – | 331 | 135 |
| 1934 | in **Australia** and **New Zealand** | 9 | 7 | 1 | 1 | 201 | 107 |
| 1935/36 | in **the British Isles** and **Canada** | 30 | 26 | 3 | 1 | 490 | 183 |
| 1936 | **Australia** in **New Zealand** | 3 | 3 | – | – | 65 | 32 |
| 1937 | **South Africa** in **New Zealand** | 3 | 1 | 2 | – | 25 | 37 |
| 1938 | in **Australia** | 9 | 9 | – | – | 279 | 73 |
| 1946 | **Australia** in **New Zealand** | 2 | 2 | – | – | 45 | 18 |
| 1947 | in **Australia** and **New Zealand** | 10 | 8 | 2 | – | 263 | 113 |
| 1949 | in **South Africa** | 25 | 14 | 7 | 4 | 241 | 157 |
| | **Australia** in **New Zealand** | 2 | – | 2 | – | 15 | 27 |

| | | Played | Won | Lost | Drawn | Points for | Points against |
|---|---|---|---|---|---|---|---|
| 1950 | **British Isles** in **New Zealand** | 4 | 3 | – | 1 | 34 | 20 |
| 1951 | in **Australia** and **New Zealand** | 13 | 13 | – | – | 375 | 86 |
| 1952 | **Australia** in **New Zealand** | 2 | 1 | 1 | – | 24 | 22 |
| 1953/54 | in **the British Isles, France** and **North America** | 36 | 30 | 4 | 2 | 598 | 152 |
| 1955 | **Australia** in **New Zealand** | 3 | 2 | 1 | – | 27 | 16 |
| 1956 | **South Africa** in **New Zealand** | 4 | 3 | 1 | – | 41 | 29 |
| 1957 | in **Australia** and **New Zealand** | 14 | 13 | 1 | – | 472 | 94 |
| 1958 | **Australia** in **New Zealand** | 3 | 2 | 1 | – | 45 | 17 |
| 1959 | **British Isles** in **New Zealand** | 4 | 3 | 1 | – | 57 | 42 |
| 1960 | in **Australia** and **South Africa** | 32 | 26 | 4 | 2 | 645 | 187 |
| 1961 | **France** in **New Zealand** | 3 | 3 | – | – | 50 | 12 |
| 1962 | in **Australia** | 10 | 9 | 1 | – | 426 | 49 |
| | **Australia** in **New Zealand** | 3 | 2 | – | 1 | 28 | 17 |
| 1963 | **England** in **New Zealand** | 2 | 2 | – | – | 30 | 17 |
| 1963/64 | in **the British Isles, France** and **Canada** | 36 | 34 | 1 | 1 | 613 | 159 |
| 1964 | **Australia** in **New Zealand** | 3 | 2 | 1 | – | 37 | 32 |
| 1965 | **South Africa** in **New Zealand** | 4 | 3 | 1 | – | 55 | 25 |
| 1966 | **British Isles** in **New Zealand** | 4 | 4 | – | – | 79 | 32 |
| 1967 | **Australia** in **New Zealand** | 1 | 1 | – | – | 29 | 9 |
| | in **the British Isles, France** and **Canada** | 17 | 16 | – | 1 | 370 | 135 |
| 1968 | in **Australia** and **Fiji** | 12 | 12 | – | – | 460 | 66 |
| | **France** in **New Zealand** | 3 | 3 | – | – | 40 | 24 |
| 1969 | **Wales** in **New Zealand** | 2 | 2 | – | – | 52 | 12 |
| 1970 | in **Australia** and **South Africa** | 26 | 23 | 3 | – | 789 | 234 |
| 1971 | **British Isles** in **New Zealand** | 4 | 1 | 2 | 1 | 42 | 48 |
| 1972 | **Internal Tour** | 9 | 9 | – | – | 355 | 88 |
| | **Australia** in **New Zealand** | 3 | 3 | – | – | 97 | 26 |
| 1972/73 | in **the British Isles, France** and **North America** | 32 | 25 | 5 | 2 | 640 | 266 |
| 1973 | **Internal Tour** and **England** in **New Zealand** | 5 | 2 | 3 | – | 88 | 83 |
| 1974 | in **Australia** and **Fiji** | 13 | 12 | – | 1 | 446 | 73 |
| | in **Ireland, Wales** and **England** | 8 | 7 | – | 1 | 127 | 50 |
| 1975 | **Scotland** in **New Zealand** | 1 | 1 | – | – | 24 | – |
| 1976 | **Ireland** in **New Zealand** | 1 | 1 | – | – | 11 | 3 |
| | in **South Africa** | 24 | 18 | 6 | – | 610 | 291 |
| | in **Argentina** and **Uruguay** | 9 | 9 | – | – | 321 | 72 |
| 1977 | **British Isles** in **New Zealand** | 4 | 3 | 1 | – | 54 | 41 |
| | in **France** and **Italy** | 9 | 8 | 1 | – | 216 | 86 |
| 1978 | **Australia** in **New Zealand** | 3 | 2 | 1 | – | 51 | 48 |
| | in **the British Isles** | 18 | 17 | 1 | – | 364 | 147 |
| 1979 | **France** in **New Zealand** | 2 | 1 | 1 | – | 42 | 33 |
| | in **Australia** | 2 | 1 | 1 | – | 41 | 15 |
| | **Argentina** in **New Zealand** | 2 | 2 | – | – | 33 | 15 |
| 1979 | in **England** and **Scotland** | 11 | 10 | 1 | – | 192 | 95 |
| 1980 | in **Australia** and **Fiji** | 16 | 12 | 3 | 1 | 507 | 126 |

|  |  | Played | Won | Lost | Drawn | Points for | Points against |
|---|---|---|---|---|---|---|---|
|  | Fiji in New Zealand | 1 | 1 | – | – | 33 | – |
|  | in North America and Wales | 7 | 7 | – | – | 197 | 41 |
| 1981 | Scotland in New Zealand | 2 | 2 | – | – | 51 | 19 |
|  | South Africa in New Zealand | 3 | 2 | 1 | – | 51 | 55 |
|  | in Romania and France | 10 | 8 | 1 | 1 | 170 | 108 |
| 1982 | Australia in New Zealand | 3 | 2 | 1 | – | 72 | 53 |
| 1983 | British Isles in New Zealand | 4 | 4 | – | – | 78 | 26 |
|  | in Australia | 1 | 1 | – | – | 18 | 8 |
|  | in Scotland and England | 8 | 5 | 2 | 1 | 162 | 116 |
| 1984 | France in New Zealand | 2 | 2 | – | – | 41 | 27 |
|  | in Australia | 14 | 13 | 1 | – | 600 | 117 |
|  | in Fiji | 4 | 4 | – | – | 174 | 10 |
| 1985 | England in New Zealand | 2 | 2 | – | – | 60 | 28 |
|  | Australia in New Zealand | 1 | 1 | – | – | 10 | 9 |
|  | in Argentina | 7 | 6 | – | 1 | 263 | 87 |
| 1986 | France in New Zealand | 1 | 1 | – | – | 18 | 9 |
|  | Australia in New Zealand | 3 | 1 | 2 | – | 34 | 47 |
|  | in France | 8 | 7 | 1 | – | 218 | 87 |
| 1987 | World Cup | 6 | 6 | – | – | 298 | 52 |
|  | in Australia | 1 | 1 | – | – | 30 | 16 |
|  | in Japan | 5 | 5 | – | – | 408 | 16 |
| 1988 | Wales in New Zealand | 2 | 2 | – | – | 106 | 12 |
|  | in Australia | 13 | 12 | – | 1 | 476 | 96 |
| 1989 | France in New Zealand | 2 | 2 | – | – | 59 | 37 |
|  | Argentina in New Zealand | 2 | 2 | – | – | 109 | 21 |
|  | Australia in New Zealand | 1 | 1 | – | – | 24 | 12 |
|  | in Canada, Wales and Ireland | 14 | 14 | – | – | 454 | 122 |
| 1990 | Scotland in New Zealand | 2 | 2 | – | – | 52 | 34 |
|  | Australia in New Zealand | 3 | 2 | 1 | – | 57 | 44 |
|  | in France | 8 | 6 | 2 | – | 175 | 110 |
| 1991 | in Argentina | 9 | 9 | – | – | 358 | 80 |
|  | in Australia | 1 | – | 1 | – | 12 | 21 |
|  | Australia in New Zealand | 1 | 1 | – | – | 6 | 3 |
|  | World Cup | 6 | 5 | 1 | – | 143 | 74 |
| 1992 | Centenary matches in New Zealand | 3 | 2 | 1 | – | 94 | 69 |
|  | Ireland in New Zealand | 2 | 2 | – | – | 83 | 27 |
|  | in Australia and South Africa | 16 | 13 | 3 | – | 567 | 252 |
| 1993 | British Isles in New Zealand | 3 | 2 | 1 | – | 57 | 51 |
|  | Australia in New Zealand | 1 | 1 | – | – | 25 | 10 |
|  | Western Samoa in New Zealand | 1 | 1 | – | – | 35 | 13 |
|  | in England and Scotland | 13 | 12 | 1 | – | 386 | 156 |
| 1994 | France in New Zealand | 2 | – | 2 | – | 28 | 45 |
|  | South Africa in New Zealand | 3 | 2 | – | 1 | 53 | 41 |
|  | in Australia | 1 | – | 1 | – | 16 | 20 |
| 1995 | Canada in New Zealand | 1 | 1 | – | – | 73 | 7 |
|  | World Cup | 6 | 5 | 1 | – | 327 | 119 |
|  | Australia in New Zealand | 1 | 1 | – | – | 28 | 16 |

|      |                                                      | Played | Won | Lost | Drawn | Points for | Points against |
|------|------------------------------------------------------|--------|-----|------|-------|------------|----------------|
|      | in **Australia**                                     | 1      | 1   | –    | –     | 34         | 23             |
|      | in **Italy** and **France**                          | 8      | 7   | 1    | –     | 339        | 126            |
| 1996 | **Western Samoa, Scotland** in **NZ**                | 3      | 3   | –    | –     | 149        | 53             |
|      | **Tri Nations**                                      | 4      | 4   | –    | –     | 119        | 60             |
|      | in **South Africa1**                                 | 7      | 5   | 1    | 1     | 190        | 139            |
| 1997 | **Fiji, Argentina, Australia1** in **NZ**            | 4      | 4   | –    | –     | 256        | 36             |
|      | **Tri Nations**                                      | 4      | 4   | –    | –     | 159        | 109            |
|      | in **British Isles**                                 | 9      | 8   | –    | 1     | 395        | 119            |
| 1998 | **England** in **New Zealand**                       | 2      | 2   | –    | –     | 104        | 32             |
|      | **Tri Nations**                                      | 4      | –   | 4    | –     | 65         | 88             |
|      | in **Australia1**                                    | 1      | –   | 1    | –     | 14         | 19             |
| 1999 | **Internal, Samoa, France** in **NZ**                | 3      | 3   | –    | –     | 147        | 31             |
|      | **Tri Nations**                                      | 4      | 3   | 1    | –     | 103        | 61             |
|      | **World Cup**                                        | 6      | 4   | 2    | –     | 255        | 111            |
| 2000 | **Tonga, Scotland** in **New Zealand**               | 3      | 3   | –    | –     | 219        | 34             |
|      | **Tri Nations**                                      | 4      | 2   | 2    | –     | 127        | 117            |
|      | in **France** and **Italy**                          | 3      | 2   | 1    | –     | 128        | 87             |
| 2001 | **Samoa, Argentina, France** in **NZ**               | 3      | 3   | –    | –     | 154        | 37             |
|      | **Tri Nations**                                      | 4      | 2   | 2    | –     | 79         | 70             |
|      | in **Ireland, Scotland** and **Argentina**           | 5      | 5   | –    | –     | 179        | 98             |
| 2002 | **Italy, Ireland, Fiji** in **New Zealand**          | 4      | 4   | –    | –     | 187        | 42             |
|      | **Tri Nations**                                      | 4      | 3   | 1    | –     | 97         | 65             |
|      | in **England, France** and **Wales**                 | 3      | 1   | 1    | 1     | 91         | 68             |
| 2003 | **England, Wales, France** in **New Zealand**        | 3      | 2   | 1    | –     | 99         | 41             |
|      | **Tri Nations**                                      | 4      | 4   | –    | –     | 142        | 65             |
|      | **World Cup**                                        | 7      | 6   | 1    | –     | 361        | 101            |
| 2004 | **England, Argentina, Pacific Islands** in **New Zealand** | 4 | 4 | –    | –     | 154        | 48             |
|      | **Tri Nations**                                      | 4      | 2   | 2    | –     | 83         | 91             |
|      | in **Europe**                                        | 4      | 4   | –    | –     | 177        | 60             |
| 2005 | **Fiji, Lions** in **New Zealand**                   | 4      | 4   | –    | –     | 198        | 40             |
|      | **Tri Nations**                                      | 4      | 3   | 1    | –     | 111        | 86             |
|      | in **Europe**                                        | 4      | 4   | –    | –     | 138        | 39             |
| 2006 | **Ireland** in **New Zealand**                       |        |     |      |       |            |                |
|      | **New Zealand** in **Argentina**                     | 3      | 3   | –    | –     | 86         | 59             |
|      | **Tri Nations**                                      | 6      | 5   | 1    | –     | 179        | 112            |
|      | in **Europe**                                        | 4      | 4   | –    | –     | 156        | 44             |
| 2007 | **France, Canada** in **New Zealand**                | 3      | 3   | –    | –     | 167        | 34             |
|      | **Tri Nations**                                      | 4      | 3   | 1    | –     | 100        | 59             |
|      | **World Cup**                                        | 5      | 4   | 1    | –     | 327        | 55             |
| 2008 | **Ireland, England, Samoa** in **New Zealand**       | 4      | 4   | –    | –     | 203        | 57             |
|      | **Tri Nations**                                      | 6      | 4   | 2    | –     | 152        | 106            |
|      | in **Hong Kong, United Kingdom** and **Ireland**     | 6      | 6   | –    | –     | 152        | 54             |
| 2009 | **France, Italy** in **New Zealand**                 | 3      | 2   | 1    | –     | 63         | 43             |
|      | **Tri Nations**                                      | 6      | 3   | 3    | –     | 141        | 131            |
|      | in **Japan** and **Europe**                          | 6      | 5   | 1    | –     | 147        | 80             |

|  |  | Played | Won | Lost | Drawn | Points for | Points against |
|---|---|---|---|---|---|---|---|
| 2010 | **Ireland, Wales** in **New Zealand** | 3 | 3 | – | – | 137 | 47 |
|  | **Tri Nations** | 6 | 6 | – | – | 184 | 111 |
|  | in **Hong Kong, United Kingdom** and **Ireland** | 5 | 4 | 1 | – | 174 | 88 |
| 2011 | **Fiji** in **New Zealand** | 1 | 1 | – | – | 60 | 14 |
|  | **Tri Nations** | 4 | 2 | 2 | – | 95 | 64 |
|  | **World Cup** | 7 | 7 | – | – | 301 | 72 |
| 2012 | **Ireland** in **New Zealand** | 3 | 3 | – | – | 124 | 29 |
|  | **Rugby Championship** and **Bledisloe Cup** | 7 | 6 | – | 1 | 195 | 84 |
|  | In **Europe** | 4 | 3 | 1 | – | 147 | 80 |
| 2013 | **France** in **New Zealand** | 3 | 3 | – | – | 77 | 22 |
|  | **Rugby Championship** and **Bledisloe Cup** | 7 | 7 | – | – | 243 | 148 |
|  | In **Japan** and **Europe** | 4 | 4 | – | – | 134 | 69 |
| 2014 | **England** in **New Zealand** | 3 | 3 | – | – | 84 | 55 |
|  | **Rugby Championship** and **Bledisloe Cup** | 7 | 5 | 1 | 1 | 193 | 119 |
|  | In **USA** and **United Kingdom** | 4 | 4 | – | – | 156 | 59 |
| 2015 | In **Samoa, Rugby Championship** and **Bledisloe Cup** | 5 | 4 | 1 | – | 151 | 94 |
|  | **World Cup** | 7 | 7 | – | – | 290 | 97 |
| 2016 | **Wales** in **New Zealand** | 3 | 3 | - | - | 121 | 49 |
|  | **Rugby Championship** and **Bledisloe Cup** | 7 | 7 | - | - | 299 | 94 |
|  | In **USA, Italy, Ireland** and **France** | 4 | 3 | 1 | - | 142 | 78 |
| 2017 | **Samoa, Lions** in **New Zealand** | *4* | *2* | *1* | *1* | *144* | *54* |
|  | **Rugby Championship** and **Bledisloe Cup** | *7* | *6* | *1* | – | *264* | *142* |
|  | In **England, France, Scotland** and **Wales** | *5* | *5* | – | – | *152* | *98* |
|  | **TOTALS** | *1291* | *1090* | *162* | *39* | *35,221* | *12,654* |

<sup>1</sup>non Tri Nations

# SURVIVING NEW ZEALAND REPRESENTATIVES

*(over the age of 71 years as at 31 December, 2017)*

| | Born | Represented New Zealand |
|---|---|---|
| R.R. Elvidge | 2 March, 1923 | 1946-49-50 |
| R.A. Roper | 11 August, 1923 | 1949-50 |
| J.M. Tanner | 11 January, 1927 | 1950-51-53-54 |
| S.F. Hill | 9 April, 1927 | 1955-56-57-58-59 |
| W.A. McCaw | 26 August, 1927 | 1951-53-54 |
| C.P. Erccg | 28 November, 1928 | 1951-52 |
| M.S. Cockerill | 8 December, 1928 | 1951 |
| L.B. Steele | 19 January, 1929 | 1951 |
| K.F. Meates | 20 February 1930 | 1952 |
| D. Young | 1 April, 1930 | 1956-57-58-60-61-62-63-64 |
| K. Davis | 21 May, 1930 | 1952-53-54-55-58 |
| E.S. Diack | 22 July, 1930 | 1959 |
| S.G. Bremner | 2 August, 1930 | 1952-56-60 |
| W.R. Archer | 19 September, 1930 | 1955-56-57 |
| D.D. Wilson | 30 January, 1931 | 1953-54 |
| D.L. Ashby | 15 February, 1931 | 1958 |
| C.J. Loader | 10 March, 1931 | 1953-54 |
| D.N. McIntosh | 1 April, 1931 | 1956-57 |
| B.P.J. Molloy | 12 August, 1931 | 1957 |
| W.S.S. Freebairn | 12 January, 1932 | 1953-54 |
| L.J. Townsend | 3 March, 1934 | 1955 |
| I.N. MacEwan | 1 May, 1934 | 1956-57-58-59-60-61-62 |
| F.S. McAtamney | 15 May, 1934 | 1956-57 |
| W.D. Gillespie | 6 August, 1934 | 1957-58-60 |
| K.F. Laidlaw | 9 August, 1934 | 1960 |
| M.W. Irwin | 10 February, 1935 | 1955-56-58-59-60 |
| R.J. Boon | 23 February, 1935 | 1960 |
| R.J. Conway | 22 April, 1935 | 1959-60-65 |
| D.M. Connor | 9 September, 1935 | 1961-62-63-64 |
| J.R. Watt | 29 December, 1935 | 1957-58-60-61-62 |
| T.R. Lineen | 5 January, 1936 | 1957-58-59-60 |
| S.R. Nesbit | 13 February, 1936 | 1960 |
| J.F. McCullough | 8 August, 1936 | 1959 |
| A.J. Soper | 7 September, 1936 | 1957 |
| R.W. Caulton | 10 January, 1937 | 1959-60-61-63-64 |
| B.E. McPhail | 26 January, 1937 | 1959 |
| J.N. Creighton | 10 March, 1937 | 1962 |
| B.T. Thomas | 21 July, 1937 | 1962-64 |
| D.W. McKay | 7 August, 1937 | 1961-62-63 |
| A.H. Clarke | 23 February, 1938 | 1958-59-60 |
| S.T. Meads | 12 July, 1938 | 1961-62-63-64-65-66 |
| D.H. Cameron | 17 November, 1938 | 1960 |
| K.A. Nelson | 26 November, 1938 | 1962-63-64 |
| B.A. Watt | 12 March, 1939 | 1962-63-64 |
| W.F. McCormick | 24 April, 1939 | 1965-67-68-69-70-71 |
| N.W. Thimbleby | 19 June, 1939 | 1970 |
| W.M. Birtwistle | 4 July, 1939 | 1965-67 |

| | | |
|---|---|---|
| E.W. Kirton | 29 December, 1939 | 1963-64-67-68-69-70 |
| D.W. Clark | 22 February, 1940 | 1964 |
| A.G.T. Jennings | 15 June, 1940 | 1967 |
| W.J. Nathan | 8 July, 1940 | 1962-63-64-66-67 |
| J. Major | 8 August, 1940 | 1963-64-67 |
| B.J. Lochore | 3 September, 1940 | 1963-64-65-66-67-68-69-70-71 |
| A.J. Stewart | 11 October, 1940 | 1963-64 |
| M.J. Dick | 3 January, 1941 | 1963-64-65-66-67-69-70 |
| D.A. Arnold | 10 January, 1941 | 1963-64 |
| J.F. Burns | 17 February, 1941 | 1970 |
| R.A. Guy | 6 April, 1941 | 1971-72 |
| A.G. Steel | 31 July, 1941 | 1966-67-68 |
| M.C. Wills | 11 October, 1941 | 1967 |
| T.N. Wolfe | 20 October, 1941 | 1961-62-63-68 |
| T.J. Morris | 3 January, 1942 | 1972-73 |
| P.H. Clarke | 23 January, 1942 | 1967 |
| R.W. Norton | 30 March, 1942 | 1971-72-73-74-75-76-77 |
| B.L. Muller | 11 June, 1942 | 1967-68-69-70-71 |
| A.E. Smith | 10 December, 1942 | 1967-69-70 |
| W.L. Davis | 15 December, 1942 | 1963-64-67-68-69-70 |
| I.R. MacRae | 6 April, 1943 | 1963-64-66-67-68-69-70 |
| S.M. Going | 19 August, 1943 | 1967-68-69-70-71-72-73-74-75-76-77 |
| K. Murdoch | 9 September, 1943 | 1970-72 |
| C.R. Laidlaw | 16 November, 1943 | 1963-64-65-66-67-68-70 |
| A.R. Sutherland | 4 January, 1944 | 1968-70-71-72-73-76 |
| R.A. Urlich | 8 February, 1944 | 1970-72-73 |
| P.A. Johns | 16 March, 1944 | 1968 |
| L.A. Clark | 1 May, 1944 | 1972-73 |
| W.D.R. Currey | 2 June, 1944 | 1968 |
| A.J. Wyllie | 31 August, 1944 | 1970-71-72-73 |
| A.R. Leslie | 10 November, 1944 | 1974-75-76 |
| S.C. Strahan | 25 December, 1944 | 1967-68-70-72-73 |
| R.J. Barber | 14 January, 1945 | 1974 |
| G.C. Williams | 26 January, 1945 | 1967-68 |
| B.D.M. Furlong | 10 March, 1945 | 1970 |
| A.J. Kreft | 27 March, 1945 | 1968 |
| K.J. Tanner | 25 April, 1945 | 1974-75-76 |
| M.O. Knight | 20 May, 1945 | 1968 |
| I.M. Eliason | 6 June, 1945 | 1972-73 |
| G.F. Kember | 15 November, 1945 | 1967-70 |
| G.M. Crossman | 30 November, 1945 | 1974-76 |
| P.C. Harris | 11 January, 1946 | 1976 |
| L.W. Mains | 16 February, 1946 | 1971-76 |
| G.S. Thorne | 25 February, 1946 | 1967-68-69-70 |
| B. Holmes | 7 April, 1946 | 1970-72-73 |
| M.W. O'Callaghan | 27 April, 1946 | 1968 |
| I.A. Kirkpatrick | 24 May, 1946 | 1967-68-69-70-71-72-73-74-75-76-77 |
| G.J. Whiting | 4 June, 1946 | 1972-73 |
| S.E.G. Cron | 7 July, 1946 | 1976 |
| P.J. Whiting | 6 August, 1946 | 1971-72-73-74-76 |
| A.J. Gardiner | 10 December, 1946 | 1974 |

# NEW ZEALAND REPRESENTATIVES

*1881 2017*

Union affiliations are shown in parentheses, preceded by date of birth and, where applicable, date of death. A few of these dates have proved impossible to be traced and these are indicated with a question mark. War casualties are denoted by an asterisk. The numbers that follow each entry show the number of games played for New Zealand. These are followed in parentheses by the number of appearances in test matches, which are included in the total. Franchise team rather than Provincial teams have been used from 2013.

**Abbott H.L.** 1882–1971
(Taranaki) 1905–06 — 11 (1)
**Adkins G.T.A.** 1910–1976
(South Canterbury) 1935–36 — 10 (–)
**Afeaki B.T.P.** 1988–
(Chiefs) 2013 — 1 (1)
**Afoa I.F.** 1983–
(Auckland) 2005–06–08–09–10–11 — 38 (36)
**Aitken G.G.** 1898–1952
(Wellington) 1921 — 2 (2)
**Alatini P.F.** 1976–
(Otago) 1999–2001 — 20 (17)
**Algar B.** 1894–1989
(Wellington) 1920–21 — 6 (–)
**Allan J.** 1860–1934 (Otago) 1884 — 8 (–)
**Allen F.R.** 1920–2012
(Auckland) 1946–47–49 — 21 (6)
**Allen L.** 1870–1932
(Taranaki) 1896–97–1901 — 13 (–)
**Allen M.R.** 1967–
(Taranaki) 1993–95–96
(Manawatu) 1997 — 27 (8)
**Allen N.H.** 1958–1984
(Counties) 1980 — 9 (2)
**Alley G.T.** 1903–1986
(Southland) 1926
(Canterbury) 1928 — 19 (3)
**Anderson A.** 1961–
(Canterbury) 1983–84–85–87–88 — 25 (6)
**Anderson B.L.** 1960–
(Wairarapa Bush) 1986–87 — 3 (1)
**Anderson E.J.** 1931–2014
(Bay of Plenty) 1960 — 10 (–)
**Anesi S.R.** 1981–
(Waikato) 2005 — 1 (1)
**Archer J.A.** 1900–1979
(Southland) 1925 — 2 (–)
**Archer W.R.** 1930–
(Otago) 1955
(Southland) 1956–57 — 13 (4)
**Argus W.G.** 1921–2016
(Canterbury) 1946–47 — 10 (4)
**Armit A.M.** 1874–1899
(Otago) 1897 — 9 (–)
**Armstrong A.L.** 1878–1959
(Wairarapa) 1903 — 5 (–)
**Arnold D.A.** 1941–
(Canterbury) 1963–64 — 15 (4)
**Arnold K.D.** 1920–2006
(Waikato) 1947 — 8 (2)

**Ashby D.L.** 1931–
(Southland) 1958 — 1 (1)
**Asher A.A.** 1879–1965
(Auckland) 1903 — 11 (1)
**Ashworth B.G.** 1949–
(Auckland) 1978 — 7 (2)
**Ashworth J.C.** 1949–
(Canterbury) 1977–78–79–80–81
–82–83–84
(Hawke's Bay) 1985 — 52 (24)
**Atiga B.A.C.** 1983–
(Auckland) 2003 — 1 (1)
**Atkinson H.J.** 1888–1949
(West Coast) 1913 — 10 (1)
**Aumua A.J.** 1997–
(Wellington) 2017 — 2 (–)
**Avery H.E.** 1885–1961
(Wellington) 1910 — 6 (3)

**Bachop G.T.M.** 1967–
(Canterbury)
1987–88–89–90–91–92–94–95 — 54 (31)
**Bachop S.J.** 1966–
(Otago) 1992–93–94 — 18 (5)
**Badeley C.E.O.** 1896–1986
(Auckland) 1920–21–24 — 15 (2)
**Badeley V.I.R.** 1898–1971
(Auckland) 1922 — 5 (–)
**Bagley K.P.** 1931–1999
(Manawatu) 1953–54 — 20 (–)
**Baird D.L.** 1894–1943
(Southland) 1920 — 9 (–)
**Baird J.A.S.*** 1893–1917
(Otago) 1913 — 1 (1)
**Balch W.** 1871–1949
(Canterbury) 1894 — 1 (–)
**Ball N.** 1908–1986
(Wellington) 1931–32–35–36 — 22 (5)
**Barber R.J.** 1945–
(Southland) 1974 — 6 (–)
**Barrell C.K.** 1967–
(Canterbury) 1996–97 — 4 (–)
**Barrett B.J.** 1991–
(Taranaki) 2012
(Hurricanes) 2013–14–15–16–17 — 63 (62)
**Barrett J.** 1888–1971
(Auckland) 1913–14 — 3 (2)
**Barrett J.M.** 1997
(Hurricanes) 2017 — 2 (2)
**Barrett S.K.** 1993–
(Crusaders) 2016–17 — 18 (16)

**Barry E.F.** 1905–1993  
(Wellington) 1932–34    10   (1)  
**Barry K.E.** 1936–2014  
(Thames Valley) 1962–63–64    23   (–)  
**Barry L.J.** 1971–  
(North Harbour) 1993–95    10   (1)  
**Bates S.P.** 1980–  
(Waikato) 2004    2   (1)  
**Batty G.B.** 1951–  
(Wellington) 1972–73–74–75  
(Bay of Plenty) 1976–77    56   (15)  
**Batty W.** 1905–1979  
(Auckland) 1928–30–31    6   (4)  
**Bayly A.** 1866–1907  
(Taranaki) 1893–94–97    20   (–)  
**Bayly W.** 1869–1950  
(Taranaki) 1894    1   (–)  
**Beatty G.E.** 1925–2004  
(Taranaki) 1950    1   (1)  
**Bell J.R.** 1900–1963  
(Southland) 1923    1   (–)  
**Bell R.C.** 1893–1960  
(Otago) 1922    8   (–)  
**Bell R.H.** 1925–2016  
(Otago) 1951–52    9   (3)  
**Belliss E.A.** 1894–1974  
(Wanganui) 1920–21–22–23    20   (3)  
**Bennet R.** 1879–1962  
(Otago) 1905    1   (1)  
**Berghan T.** 1914–1998  
(Otago) 1938    6   (3)  
**Berry M.J.** 1966–  
(Wairarapa Bush) 1986  
(Wellington) 1993    10   (1)  
**Berryman N.R.** 1973–2015  
(Northland) 1998    1   (1)  
**Best J.J.** 1914–1994  
(Marlborough) 1935–36    6   (–)  
**Bevan V.D.** 1921–1996  
(Wellington) 1947–49–50–53–54    25   (6)  
**Bird D.J.** 1991–  
(Crusaders) 2013–14  
(Chiefs) 2017    3   (2)  
**Birtwistle W.M.** 1939–  
(Canterbury) 1965  
(Waikato) 1967    12   (7)  
**Black J.E.** 1951–  
(Canterbury) 1976–77–78–79–80    26   (3)  
**Black N.W.** 1925–2016  
(Auckland) 1949    11   (1)  
**Black R.S.**★ 1893–1916  
(Otago) 1914    6   (1)  
**Blackadder T.J.** 1971–  
(Canterbury) 1995–96–97–98–  
99–2000    25   (12)  
**Blair B.A.** 1979–  
(Canterbury) 2001–02    6   (4)  
**Blair J.A.** 1872–1911  
(Wanganui) 1897    9   (–)  
**Blake A.W.** 1922–2010  

(Wairarapa) 1949    1   (1)  
**Blake J.M.** 1902–1988  
(Hawke's Bay) 1925–26    13   (–)  
**Bligh S.** 1887–1955  
(West Coast) 1910    5   (–)  
**Blowers A.F.** 1975–  
(Auckland) 1996–97–99    18   (11)  
**Bloxham K.C.** 1954–2000  
(Otago) 1980    2   (–)  
**Boe J.W.** 1955–  
(Waikato) 1981    2   (–)  
**Boggs E.G.** 1922–2004  
(Auckland) 1946–49    9   (2)  
**Bond J.G.P.** 1920–1999  
(Canterbury) 1949    1   (1)  
**Boon R.J.** 1935–  
(Taranaki) 1960    6   (–)  
**Booth E.E.** 1876–1935  
(Otago) 1905–06–07    24   (3)  
**Boric A.F.** 1983–  
(North Harbour) 2008–09–10–11    25   (24)  
**Boroevich K.G.** 1960–  
(King Country) 1983–84  
(Wellington) 1986  
(North Harbour) 1988    26   (3)  
**Botica F.M.** 1963–  
(North Harbour) 1986–87–88–89    27   (7)  
**Botting I.J.** 1922–1980  
(Otago) 1949    9   (–)  
**Bowden N.J.G.** 1926–2009  
(Taranaki) 1952    1   (1)  
**Bowers R.G.** 1932–2000  
(Wellington) 1953–54    15   (2)  
**Bowman A.W.** 1915–1992  
(Hawke's Bay) 1938    6   (3)  
**Bradanovich N.M.** 1907–1961  
(Otago) 1928    2   (–)  
**Braddon H.Y.** 1863–1955  
(Otago) 1884    7   (–)  
**Braid D.J.** 1981–  
(Auckland) 2002–03–08–10    6   (6)  
**Braid G.J.** 1960–  
(Bay of Plenty) 1983–84    13   (2)  
**Brake L.J.** 1952–  
(Bay of Plenty) 1976    5   (–)  
**Bremner S.G.** 1930–  
(Auckland) 1952  
(Canterbury) 1956–60    18   (2)  
**Brewer M.R.** 1964–  
(Otago) 1986–87–88–89–90–91–92  
(Canterbury) 1993–94–95    61   (32)  
**Briscoe K.C.** 1936–2009  
(Taranaki) 1959–60–62–63–64    43   (9)  
**Broadhurst J.P.** 1987–  
(Hurricanes) 2015–    1   (1)  
**Brooke R.M.** 1966–  
(Auckland) 1992–93–94–95–96–97–98–99    69   (62)  
**Brooke Z.V.** 1965–  
(Auckland) 1987–88–89–90–91–92–93–94–95–96–97    100   (58)

| | | |
|---|---|---|
| **Brooke-Cowden M.** 1963 | | |
| (Auckland) 1986–87 | 6 | (3) |
| **Brooker F.J.** 1876–1939 | | |
| (Canterbury) 1897 | 4 | (–) |
| **Broomhall S.R.** 1976– | | |
| (Canterbury) 2002 | 4 | (4) |
| **Brown C.** 1887–1966 | | |
| (Taranaki) 1913–20 | 11 | (2) |
| **Brown H.M.** 1910–1965 | | |
| (Auckland) 1935–36 | 8 | (–) |
| **Brown H.W.** 1904–1973 | | |
| (Taranaki) 1924–25–26 | 20 | (–) |
| **Brown O.M.** 1967– | | |
| (Auckland) | | |
| 1990–92–93–94–95–96–97–98 | 69 | (56) |
| **Brown R.H.** 1934–2014 (Taranaki) | | |
| 1955–56–57–58–59–61–62 | 25 | (16) |
| **Brown T.E.** 1975– | | |
| (Otago) 1999–2000–01 | 19 | (18) |
| **Brownlie C.J.** 1895–1954 | | |
| (Hawke's Bay) 1924–25–26–28 | 31 | (3) |
| **Brownlie J.L.** 1899–1972 | | |
| (Hawke's Bay) 1921 | 1 | (–) |
| **Brownlie M.J.** 1896–1957 | | |
| (Hawke's Bay) 1922–23–24– | | |
| 25–26–28 | 61 | (8) |
| **Bruce J.A.** 1887–1970 | | |
| (Auckland) 1913–14 | 10 | (2) |
| **Bruce O.D.** 1947– | | |
| (Canterbury) 1974–76–77–78 | 41 | (14) |
| **Bryers R.F.** 1919–1987 | | |
| (King Country) 1949 | 1 | (1) |
| **Buchan J.A.S.** 1961– | | |
| (Canterbury) 1987 | 2 | (–) |
| **Budd A.** 1880–1962 | | |
| (South Canterbury) 1910 | 3 | (–) |
| **Budd T.A.** 1922–1989 | | |
| (Southland) 1946–49 | 2 | (2) |
| **Bullock-Douglas G.A.H.** 1911–1958 | | |
| (Wanganui) 1932–34 | 15 | (5) |
| **Bunce F.E.** 1962– | | |
| (North Harbour) 1992–93–94– | | |
| 95–96–97 | 69 | (55) |
| **Burgess G.A.J.** 1954– | | |
| (Auckland) 1980–81 | 2 | (1) |
| **Burgess G.F.** 1883–1961 | | |
| (Southland) 1905 | 1 | (1) |
| **Burgess R.E.** 1949– | | |
| (Manawatu) 1971–72–73 | 30 | (7) |
| **Burgoyne M.M.** 1951–2016 | | |
| (North Auckland) 1979 | 6 | (–) |
| **Burke P.S.** 1927–2017 | | |
| (Taranaki) 1951–55–57 | 12 | (3) |
| **Burns J.F.** 1941– | | |
| (Canterbury)1970 | 9 | (–) |
| **Burns P.J.** 1881–1943 | | |
| (Canterbury) 1908–10–13 | 9 | (5) |
| **Burrows J.T.** 1904–1991 | | |
| (Canterbury) 1928 | 9 | (–) |
| **Burry H.C.** 1930–2013 | | |
| (Canterbury) 1960 | 11 | (–) |
| **Burt J.R.** 1874 1933 | | |
| (Otago) 1901 | 1 | (–) |
| **Bush R.G.** 1909–96 | | |
| (Otago) 1931 | 1 | (1) |
| **Bush W.K. TeP.** 1949– | | |
| (Canterbury) 1974–75–76–77– | | |
| 78–79 | 37 | (12) |
| **Butland H.** 1872–1956 | | |
| (West Coast) 1893–94 | 9 | (–) |
| **Butler V.C.** 1907–1971 | | |
| (Auckland) 1928 | 1 | (–) |
| **Buxton J.B.** 1933–2007 | | |
| (Canterbury) 1955–56 | 2 | (2) |
| **Cabot P.S. deQ.** 1900–1998 | | |
| (Otago) 1921 | 1 | (–) |
| **Cain M.J.** 1885–1951 | | |
| (Taranaki) 1913–14 | 24 | (4) |
| **Calcinai U.P.** 1892–1963 | | |
| (Wellington) 1922 | 5 | (–) |
| **Callesen J.A.** 1950– | | |
| (Manawatu) 1974–75–76 | 18 | (4) |
| **Calnan J.J.** 1876–1947 | | |
| (Wellington) 1897 | 9 | (–) |
| **Cameron D.** 1887–1947 | | |
| (Taranaki) 1908 | 3 | (3) |
| **Cameron D.H.** 1938– | | |
| (Mid Canterbury) 1960 | 8 | (–) |
| **Cameron L.M.** 1959– | | |
| (Manawatu) 1979–80–81 | 17 | (5) |
| **Cane S.J.** 1992– | | |
| (Bay of Plenty) 2012 | | |
| (Chiefs) 2013–14–15–16–17 | 54 | (53) |
| **Carleton S.R.** 1904–1973 | | |
| (Canterbury) 1928–29 | 21 | (6) |
| **Carrington K.R.** 1950– | | |
| (Auckland) 1971–72 | 9 | (3) |
| **Carroll A.J.** 1895–1974 | | |
| (Manawatu) 1920–21 | 8 | (–) |
| **Carson W.N.\*** 1916–1944 | | |
| (Auckland) 1938 | 3 | (–) |
| **Carter D.W.** 1982– | | |
| (Canterbury) 2003–04–05–06– | | |
| 07–08–09–10–11–12 | | |
| (Crusaders) 2013–14–15 | 112 | (112) |
| **Carter G.** 1854–1922 | | |
| (Auckland) 1884 | 7 | (–) |
| **Carter M.P.** 1968– | | |
| (Auckland) 1991–97–98 | 10 | (7) |
| **Cartwright S.C.** 1954– | | |
| (Canterbury) 1976 | 7 | (–) |
| **Casey S.T.** 1882–1960 | | |
| (Otago) 1905–06–07–08 | 38 | (8) |
| **Cashmore A.R.** 1973 | | |
| (Auckland) 1996–97 | 2 | (2) |
| **Catley E.H.** 1915–1975 | | |
| (Waikato) 1946–47–49 | 21 | (7) |
| **Caughey T.H.C.** 1911–1993 | | |
| (Auckland) 1932–34–35–36–37 | 39 | (9) |
| **Caulton R.W.** 1937– | | |
| (Wellington) 1959–60–61–63–64 | 50 | (16) |

**Cherrington N.P.** 1924–1979
(North Auckland) 1950–51 — 7 (1)
**Christian D.L.** 1923–1977
(Auckland) 1949 — 11 (1)
**Clamp M.** 1961–
(Wellington) 1984–85 — 15 (2)
**Clark D.W.** 1940–
(Otago) 1964 — 2 (2)
**Clark F.I.** 1902–1972
(Canterbury) 1928 — 4 (–)
**Clark L.A.** 1944–
(Otago) 1972–73 — 7 (–)
**Clark W.H.** 1929–2010
(Wellington) 1953–54–55–56 — 24 (9)
**Clarke A.H.** 1938–
(Auckland) 1958–59–60 — 14 (3)
**Clarke D.B.** 1933–2002
(Waikato) 1956–57–58–59–60–
61–62–63–64 — 89 (31)
**Clarke E.** 1968–
(Auckland) 1992–93–98 — 24 (10)
**Clarke I.J.** 1931–1997
(Waikato) 1953–54–55–56–57–
58–59–60–61–62–63–64 — 83 (24)
**Clarke P.H.** 1942–
(Marlborough) 1967 — 4 (–)
**Clarke R.L.** 1909–1972
(Taranaki) 1932 — 9 (2)
**Cobden D.G.**★ 1914–1940
(Canterbury) 1937 — 1 (1)
**Cockerill M.S.** 1928–
(Taranaki) 1951 — 11 (3)
**Cockroft E.A.P.** 1890–1973
(South Canterbury) 1913–14 — 7 (3)
**Cockroft S.G.** 1864–1955
(Manawatu) 1893
(Hawke's Bay) 1894 — 12 (–)
**Codlin B.W.** 1956–
(Counties) 1980 — 13 (3)
**Coffin P.H.** 1964–
(King Country) 1996 — 3 (–)
**Coles D.S.** 1986–
(Wellington) 2012
(Hurricanes) 2013–14–15–16–17 — 56 (56)
**Colling G.L.** 1946–2003
(Otago) 1972–73 — 21 (–)
**Collins A.H.** 1906–1988
(Taranaki) 1932–34 — 15 (3)
**Collins J.** 1980–2015
(Wellington) 2001–03–04–
05–06–07 — 50 (48)
**Collins J.L.** 1939–2007
(Poverty Bay) 1964–65 — 3 (3)
**Collins W.R.** 1910–1993
(Hawke's Bay) 1935 — 7 (–)
**Colman J.T.H.** 1887–1965
(Taranaki) 1907–08 — 6 (4)
**Coltman L.J.** 1990–
(Highlanders) 2016 — 1 (1)
**Conn S.B.** 1953–
(Auckland) 1976–80 — 6 (–)

**Connolly L.S.** 1921–2005
(Southland) 1947 — 5 (–)
**Connor D.M.** 1935–
(Auckland) 1961–62–63–64 — 15 (12)
**Conrad W.J.M.** 1925–1972
(Waikato) 1949 — 10 (–)
**Conway R.J.** 1935–
(Otago) 1959–60
(Bay of Plenty) 1965 — 25 (10)
**Cooke A.E.** 1901–1977
(Auckland) 1924–25
(Hawke's Bay) 1926
(Wairarapa) 1928
(Wellington) 1930 — 44 (8)
**Cooke A.E.** 1870–1900
(Canterbury) 1894 — 1 (–)
**Cooke R.J.** 1880–1940
(Canterbury) 1903 — 10 (1)
**Cooksley M.S.B.** 1971–
(Counties) 1992–93
(Waikato) 1994–95–97–2001 — 23 (11)
**Cooper G.J.L.** 1965–
(Auckland) 1986
(Otago) 1992 — 7 (7)
**Cooper M.J.A.** 1966–
(Hawke's Bay) 1987
(Waikato) 1992–93–94–96 — 26 (8)
**Corbett J.** 1880–1945
(West Coast) 1905 — 16 (–)
**Corkill T.G.** 1901–1966
(Hawke's Bay) 1925 — 4 (–)
**Corner M.M.N.** 1908–1992
(Auckland) 1930–31–32–34–35–36 — 25 (6)
**Cossey R.R.** 1935–1986
(Counties) 1958 — 1 (1)
**Cottrell A.I.** 1907–1988
(Canterbury) 1929–30–31–32 — 22 (11)
**Cottrell W.D.** 1943–2013
(Canterbury) 1967–68–70–71 — 37 (9)
**Couch M.B.R.** 1925–1996
(Wairarapa) 1947–49 — 7 (3)
**Coughlan T.D.** 1934–2017
(South Canterbury) 1958 — 1 (1)
**Cowan Q.J.** 1982–
(Southland) 2004–05–06–08
–09–10–11 — 53 (51)
**Creighton J.N.** 1937–
(Canterbury) 1962 — 6 (1)
**Cribb R.T.** 1976–
(North Harbour) 2000–01 — 15 (15)
**Crichton S.** 1954–
(Wellington) 1983–84–85 — 7 (2)
**Crockett W.W.V.** 1983–
(Canterbury) 2009–11–12
(Crusaders) 2013–14–15–16–17 — 72 (71)
**Cron S.E.G.** 1946–
(Canterbury) 1976 — 6 (–)
**Cross T.** 1876–1930
(Canterbury) 1901
(Wellington) 1904–05 — 3 (2)

**Crossman G.M.** 1945–
(Bay of Plenty) 1974–76   19   (–)
**Crotty R.J.** 1988–
(Crusaders) 2013–14–15–16–17   35   (35)
**Crowley K.J.** 1961–
(Taranaki) 1983–84–85–86–
87–90–91   35   (19)
**Crowley P.J.B.** 1923–1981
(Auckland) 1949–50   21   (6)
**Cruden A.W.** 1989–
(Manawatu) 2010–11–12
(Chiefs) 2013–14–16–17   50   (50)
**Culhane S.D.** 1968–
(Southland) 1995–96   9   (6)
**Cullen C.M.** 1976–
(Manawatu) 1996–97
(Wellington) 1998–99–2000–01–02   60   (58)
**Cummings W.** 1889–1955
(Canterbury) 1913–21   3   (2)
**Cundy R.T.** 1901–1955
(Wairarapa) 1929   6   (1)
**Cunningham G.R.** 1955–
(Auckland) 1979–80   17   (5)
**Cunningham W.** 1874–1927
(Auckland) 1901–05–06–07–08   39   (9)
**Cupples L.F.** 1898–1972
(Bay of Plenty) 1922–23–24–25   29   (2)
**Currey W.D.R.** 1944–
(Taranaki) 1968   7   (–)
**Currie C.J.** 1955–
(Canterbury) 1978   4   (2)
**Cuthill J.E.** 1892–1970
(Otago) 1913   16   (2)

**Dagg I.J.A.** 1988–
(Hawke's Bay) 2010–11–12
(Crusaders) 2013–14–15–16–17   66   (66)
**Dalley W.C.** 1901–1989
(Canterbury) 1924–25–26–28–29   35   (5)
**Dalton A.G.** 1951–
(Counties) 1977–78–79–80–81–
82–83–84–85   58   (35)
**Dalton D.** 1913–1995
(Hawke's Bay) 1935–36–37–38   21   (9)
**Dalton R.A.** 1919–1997
(Wellington) 1947
(Otago) 1949   20   (2)
**Dalzell G.N.** 1921–1989
(Canterbury) 1953–54   22   (5)
**D'Arcy A.E.** 1870–1919
(Wairarapa) 1893–94   7   (–)
**Davie M.G.** 1955–
(Canterbury) 1983   5   (1)
**Davies W.A.** 1939–2008
(Auckland) 1960
(Otago) 1962   17   (3)
**Davis C.S.** 1975–
(Manawatu) 1996   2   (–)
**Davis K.** 1930–
(Auckland) 1952–53–54–55–58   25   (10)

**Davis L.J.** 1943–2008
(Canterbury) 1976–77   16   (3)
**Davis W.L.** 1942–
(Hawke's Bay) 1963–64–67–
68–69–70   53   (11)
**Davy E.** 1850–1935
(Wellington) 1884   3   (–)
**Deans I.B.** 1960–
(Canterbury) 1987–88–89   23   (10)
**Deans R.G.** 1884–1908
(Canterbury) 1905–06–08   24   (5)
**Deans R.M.** 1959–
(Canterbury) 1983–84–85   19   (5)
**Delamore G.W.** 1920–2008
(Wellington) 1949   9   (1)
**Delany M.P.** 1982–
(Bay of Plenty) 2009   2   (1)
**de Malmanche A.P.** 1984–
(Waikato) 2009–10   5   (5)
**Dermody C.** 1980–
(Southland) 2006   3   (3)
**Devine S.J.** 1976–
(Auckland) 2002–03   10   (10)
**Dewar H.*** 1883–1915
(Taranaki) 1913   16   (2)
**Diack E.S.** 1930–
(Otago) 1959   1   (1)
**Dick J.** 1912–2002
(Auckland) 1937–38   5   (3)
**Dick M.J.** 1941–
(Auckland) 1963–64–65–
66–67–69–70   55   (15)
**Dickinson G.R.** 1903–1978
(Otago) 1922   5   (–)
**Dickson D.McK.** 1900–1978
(Otago) 1925   7   (–)
**Dixon E.C.** 1989–
(Highlanders) 2016   3   (3)
**Dixon M.J.** 1929–2004
(Canterbury) 1953–54–56–57   28   (10)
**Dobson R.L.** 1923–1994
(Auckland) 1949   1   (1)
**Dodd E.H.*** 1880–1918
(Wellington) 1901–05   3   (1)
**Donald A.J.** 1957–
(Wanganui) 1981–83–84   20   (7)
**Donald J.G.** 1898–1981
(Wairarapa) 1920–21–22–25   22   (2)
**Donald Q.** 1900–1965
(Wairarapa) 1923–24–25   23   (4)
**Donald S.R.** 1983–
(Waikato) 2008–09–10–11   25   (23)
**Donaldson M.W.** 1955–
(Manawatu) 1977–78–79–80–81   35   (13)
**Donnelly T.J.S.** 1981–
(Otago) 2009–10   15   (15)
**Dougan J.P.** 1946–2006
(Wellington) 1972–73   12   (2)
**Douglas J.B.** 1890–1964
(Otago) 1913   9   (–)

**Dowd C.W.** 1969–
(Auckland) 1993–94–95–96–
97–98–99–2000    67 (60)
**Dowd G.W.** 1963–
(North Harbour) 1992    8 (1)
**Downing A.J.*** 1886–1915
(Auckland) 1913–14    26 (5)
**Drake J.A.** 1959–2008
(Auckland) 1985–86–87    12 (8)
**Drake W.A.** 1879–1941
(Canterbury) 1901    1 (–)
**Drummond M.D.** 1994–
(Crusaders) 2017–    1 (–)
**Duff R.H.** 1925–2006
(Canterbury) 1951–52–55–56    18 (11)
**Duffie M.D.** 1990
(Blues) 2017    2 (–)
**Duggan R.J.L.** 1972–
(Waikato) 1999    1 (1)
**Dumbell J.T.** 1859–1936
(Wellington) 1884    5 (–)
**Duncan J.** 1869–1953
(Otago) 1897–1901–03    10 (1)
**Duncan M.G.** 1947–
(Hawke's Bay) 1971    2 (2)
**Duncan W.D.** 1892–1961
(Otago) 1920–21    11 (3)
**Dunn E.J.** 1955–
(North Auckland) 1978–79–81    20 (2)
**Dunn I.T.W.** 1960–
(North Auckland) 1983–84    13 (3)
**Dunn J.M.** 1918–2003
(Auckland) 1946    1 (1)

**Earl A.T.** 1961–
(Canterbury)
1986–87–88–89–91–92    45 (14)
**Eastgate B.P.** 1927–2007
(Canterbury) 1952–53–54    17 (3)
**Eaton J.J.** 1982–
(Taranaki) 2005–06–08–09    17 (15)
**Eckhold A.G.** 1885–1931
(Otago) 1907    3 (–)
**Eliason I.M.** 1945–
(Taranaki) 1972–73    19 (–)
**Elliot H.T.P.** 1986–
(Hawke's Bay) 2008–10,12
(Chiefs) 2015    5 (4)
**Elliott K.G.** 1922–2006
(Wellington) 1946    2 (2)
**Ellis A.M.** 1984–
(Canterbury) 2006–07–08–
09–10–11
(Crusaders) 2015    28 (28)
**Ellis M.C.G.** 1971–
(Otago) 1992–93–95    21 (8)
**Ellison T.E.** 1983–
(Wellington) 2009
(Otago) 2012    5 (4)
**Ellison T.R.** 1867–1904
(Wellington) 1893    7 (–)

**Elsom A.E.G.** 1925–2010
(Canterbury) 1952–53–54–55    22 (6)
**Elvidge R.R.** 1923–
(Otago) 1946–49–50    19 (9)
**Elvy W.L.** 1901–1977
(Canterbury) 1925–26    12 (–)
**Erceg C.P.** 1928–
(Auckland) 1951–52    9 (4)
**Evans B.R.** 1984–
(Hawke's Bay) 2009    2 (2)
**Evans C.E.** 1896–1975
(Canterbury) 1921    1 (–)
**Evans D.A.** 1886–1940
(Hawke's Bay) 1910    4 (1)
**Evans N.J.** 1980–
(North Harbour) 2004
(Otago) 2005–06–07    16 (16)
**Eveleigh K.A.** 1947–
(Manawatu) 1974–76–77    30 (4)

**Fanning A.H.N.** 1890–1963
(Canterbury) 1913    1 (1)
**Fanning B.J.** 1874–1946
(Canterbury) 1903–04    9 (2)
**Farrell C.P.** 1956–
(Auckland) 1977    2 (2)
**Faumuina C.C.** 1986–
(Auckland) 2012
(Blues) 2013–14–15–16–17    50 (50)
**Fawcett C.L.** 1954–
(Auckland) 1976    13 (2)
**Fea W.R.** 1898–1988
(Otago) 1921    1 (1)
**Feek G.E.** 1975–
(Canterbury) 1999–2000–01    10 (10)
**Fekitoa M.F.** 1992–
(Highlanders) 2014–15–16–17    24 (24)
**Fifita V.T.L.** 1992–
(Hurricanes) 2017    6 (5)
**Filipo R.A.** 1979–
(Wellington) 2007–08    5 (4)
**Finlay B.E.L.** 1927–1982
(Manawatu) 1959    1 (1)
**Finlay J.** 1916–2001
(Manawatu) 1946    1 (1)
**Finlay M.C.** 1963–
(Manawatu) 1984    2 (–)
**Finlayson I.** 1899–1980
(North Auckland) 1925–26–
28–30    36 (6)
**Fisher T.** 1891–1968
(Buller) 1914    5 (–)
**Fitzgerald C.J.** 1899–1961
(Marlborough) 1922    5 (–)
**Fitzgerald J.T.** 1928–1993
(Wellington) 1952–53–54    17 (1)
**Fitzpatrick B.B.J.** 1931–2006
(Poverty Bay) 1951
(Wellington) 1953–54    22 (3)
**Fitzpatrick S.B.T.** 1963–
(Auckland) 1986–87–88–89–90
91–92–93–94–95–96–97    128 (92)

**Flavell T.V.** 1976–
(North Harbour) 2000–01
(Auckland) 2006–07 22 (22)
**Fleming J.K.** 1953–
(Wellington) 1978–79–80 35 (5)
**Fletcher C.J.C.** 1894–1973
(North Auckland) 1921 2 (1)
**Flynn C.R.** 1981–
(Canterbury) 2003–04–08–09–
10–11 17 (15)
**Fogarty R.** 1891–1980
(Taranaki) 1921 2 (2)
**Ford B.R.** 1951–
(Marlborough) 1977–78–79 20 (4)
**Ford W.A.** 1895–1959
(Canterbury) 1921–22–23 9 (–)
**Forster S.T.** 1969–
(Otago) 1993–94–95 12 (6)
**Fox G.J.** 1962–
(Auckland) 1984–85–86–87–
88–89–90–91–92–93 78 (46)
**Francis A.R.H.** 1882–1957
(Auckland) 1905–07–08–10 18 (10)
**Francis W.C.** 1894–1981
(Wellington) 1913–14 12 (5)
**Franks B.J.** 1984–
(Tasman) 2008–10–11–12
(Hurricanes) 2013–14–15 48 (47)
**Franks O.T.** 1987–
(Canterbury) 2009–10–11–12
(Crusaders) 2013–14–15–16–17 95 (95)
**Fraser B.G.** 1953–
(Wellington) 1979–80–81–82–83–84 55 (23)
**Frazer H.F.** 1915–2003
(Hawke's Bay) 1946–47–49 15 (5)
**Freebairn W.S.S.** 1932–
(Manawatu) 1953–54 14 (–)
**Freitas D.F.E.** 1901–1968
(West Coast) 1928 4 (–)
**Fromont R.T.** 1969–
(Auckland) 1993–95 10 (–)
**Frost H.** 1869–1954
(Canterbury) 1896 1 (–)
**Fryer F.C.** 1886–1958
(Canterbury) 1907–08 9 (4)
**Fuller W.B.** 1883–1957
(Canterbury) 1910 6 (2)
**Furlong B.D.M.** 1945–
(Hawke's Bay) 1970 11 (1)

**Gage D.R.** 1868–1916
(Wellington) 1893–96 8 (–)
**Gallagher J.A.** 1964–
(Wellington) 1986–87–88–89 41 (18)
**Gallaher D.** 1873–1917
(Auckland) 1903–04–05–06 36 (6)
**Gard P.C.** 1947–1990
(North Otago) 1971–72 7 (1)
**Gardiner A.J.** 1946–
(Taranaki) 1974 11 (1)

**Gardner J.H.** 1870–1909
(South Canterbury) 1893 4 (–)
**Gatland W.D.** 1963–
(Waikato) 1988–89–90–91 17 (–)
**Gear H.E.** 1984–
(Wellington) 2008–10–11–12 15 (14)
**Gear R.L.** 1978–
(North Harbour) 2004
(Nelson Bays) 2005
(Tasman) 2006
(Canterbury) 2007 20 (19)
**Geddes J.H.** 1907–1990
(Southland) 1929 6 (1)
**Geddes W.McK.** 1893–1950
(Auckland) 1913 1 (1)
**Gemmell B.McL.** 1950–
(Auckland) 1974 6 (2)
**Gemmell S.W.** 1896–1970
(Hawke's Bay) 1923 1 (–)
**George V.L.** 1908–1996
(Southland) 1938 7 (3)
**Gibbes J.B.** 1977–
(Waikato) 2004–05 8 (8)
**Gibson D.P.E.** 1975–
(Canterbury) 1999–2000–02 19 (19)
**Gilbert G.D.M.** 1911–2002
(West Coast) 1935–36 27 (4)
**Gillespie C.T.** 1883–1964
(Wellington) 1913 1 (1)
**Gillespie W.D.** 1934–
(Otago) 1957–58–60 23 (1)
**Gillett G.A.** 1877–1956
(Canterbury) 1905–06
(Auckland) 1907–08 38 (8)
**Gillies C.C.** 1912–1996
(Otago) 1936 2 (1)
**Gilray C.M.** 1885–1974
(Otago) 1905 1 (1)
**Given F.J.** 1876–1921
(Otago) 1903 9 (–)
**Glasgow F.T.** 1880–1939
(Taranaki) 1905–06
(Southland) 1908 35 (6)
**Glenn W.S.** 1877–1953
(Taranaki) 1904–05–06 19 (2)
**Glennie E.** 1870–1908
(Canterbury) 1897 6 (–)
**Goddard J.W.** 1920–1996
(South Canterbury) 1949 8 (–)
**Goddard M.P.** 1921–1974
(South Canterbury) 1946–47–49 20 (5)
**Going K.T.** 1942–2008
(North Auckland) 1974 3 (–)
**Going S.M.** 1943–
(North Auckland) 1967–68–69–70–
71–72–73–74–75–76–77 86 (29)
**Goldsmith J.A.** 1969–
(Waikato) 1988 8 (–)
**Good A.** 1867–1938
(Taranaki) 1893 4 (–)

**Good H.M.** 1871–1941
(Taranaki) 1894 — 1 (–)
**Goodhue B.J.** 1995–
(Crusaders) 2017 — 1 (–)
**Gordon S.B.** 1967–
(Waikato) 1989–90–91–93 — 19 (2)
**Gordon W.R.** 1965–
(Waikato) 1990 — 3 (–)
**Graham D.J.** 1935–2017
(Canterbury) 1958–60–61–62–
63–64 — 53 (22)
**Graham J.B.** 1884–1941
(Otago) 1913–14 — 19 (3)
**Graham M.G.** 1931–2015
(New South Wales) 1960 — 1 (–)
**Graham W.G.** 1957–
(Otago) 1978–79 — 8 (1)
**Granger K.W.** 1951–
(Manawatu) 1976 — 6 (–)
**Grant L.A.** 1923–2002
(South Canterbury) 1947–49–51 — 23 (4)
**Gray G.D.** 1880–1961
(Canterbury) 1908–13 — 14 (3)
**Gray K.F.** 1938–1992
(Wellington) 1963–64–65–66–
67–68–69 — 50 (24)
**Gray R.** 1870–1951
(Wairarapa) 1893 — 2 (–)
**Gray W.N.** 1932–1993
(Bay of Plenty) 1955–56–57 — 11 (6)
**Green C.I.** 1961–
(Canterbury) 1983–84–85–86–87 — 39 (20)
**Greene K.M.** 1949–
(Waikato) 1976–77 — 8 (–)
**Grenside B.A.** 1899–1989
(Hawke's Bay) 1928–29 — 21 (6)
**Griffiths J.L.** 1912–2001
(Wellington) 1934–35–36–38 — 30 (7)
**Gudsell K.E.** 1924–2007
(Wanganui) 1949 — 6 (–)
**Guildford Z.R.** 1989–
(Hawke's Bay) 2009–10–11–12 — 10 (10)
**Guy R.A.** 1941–
(North Auckland) 1971–72 — 9 (4)

**Haden A.M.** 1950–
(Auckland) 1972–73–76–77–78–
79–80–81–82–83–84–85 — 117 (41)
**Hadley S.** 1904–1970
(Auckland) 1928 — 11 (4)
**Hadley W.E.** 1910–1992
(Auckland) 1934–35–36 — 25 (8)
**Haig J.S.** 1924–1996
(Otago) 1946 — 2 (2)
**Haig L.S.** 1922–1992
(Otago) 1950–51–53–54 — 29 (9)
**Halai F.** 1988–
(Blues) 2013 — 1 (1)
**Hales D.A.** 1947–
(Canterbury) 1972–73 — 27 (4)
**Hames K.S.** 1988–
(Chiefs) 2016–17 — 10 (9)

**Hames K.S.** 1988–
(Chiefs) 2016 — 1 (1)
**Hamilton D.C.** 1883–1925
(Southland) 1908 — 1 (1)
**Hamilton S.E.** 1980–
(Canterbury) 2006 — 2 (2)
**Hammett M.G.** 1972–
(Canterbury) 1999–2000–01–
02–03 — 30 (29)
**Hammond I.A.** 1925–1998
(Marlborough) 1951–52 — 8 (1)
**Handcock R.A.** 1874–1956
(Auckland) 1897 — 8 (–)
**Hardcastle W.R.** 1874–1944
(Wellington) 1897 — 7 (–)
**Harding S.** 1980–
(Otago) 2002 — 1 (1)
**Harper E.T.**★ 1877–1918
(Canterbury) 1904–05–06 — 11 (2)
**Harper G.** 1867–1937
(Nelson) 1893 — 3 (–)
**Harris J.H.**★ 1903–1944
(Canterbury) 1925 — 8 (–)
**Harris N.P.** 1992–
(Chiefs) 2014–16–17 — 13 (11)
**Harris P.C.** 1946–
(Manawatu) 1976 — 4 (1)
**Harris W.A.** 1876–1950
(Otago) 1897 — 9 (–)
**Hart A.H.** 1897–1965
(Taranaki) 1924–25 — 17 (1)
**Hart G.F.**★ 1909–1944
(Canterbury) 1930–31–32–34–
35–36 — 35 (11)
**Harvey B.A.** 1959–
(Wairarapa Bush) 1986 — 1 (1)
**Harvey I.H.** 1903–1966
(Wairarapa) 1924–25–26–28 — 18 (1)
**Harvey L.R.** 1919–1993
(Otago) 1949–50 — 22 (8)
**Harvey P.** 1880–1949
(Canterbury) 1904 — 1 (1)
**Hasell E.W.** 1889–1966
(Canterbury) 1913–20 — 7 (2)
**Havili D.K.** 1994–
(Crusaders) 2017 — 5 (3)
**Hay-MacKenzie W.E.** 1874–1946
(Auckland) 1901 — 2 (–)
**Hayman C.J.** 1979–
(Otago) 2001–02–04–05–06–07 — 46 (45)
**Hayward H.O.** 1883–1970
(Auckland) 1908 — 1 (1)
**Hazlett E.J.** 1938–2014
(Southland) 1966–67 — 12 (6)
**Hazlett W.E.** 1905–1978
(Southland) 1926–28–30 — 26 (8)
**Heeps T.R.** 1938–2002
(Wellington) 1962 — 10 (5)
**Heke W.R.** (played as W. Rika)
1894–1989
(North Auckland) 1929 — 6 (3)

**Helmore G.H.N.** 1862–1922
(Canterbury) 1884 — 7 (–)
**Hemara B.S.** 1957–
(Manawatu) 1985 — 3 (–)
**Hemi R.C.** 1933–2000
(Waikato) 1953–54–55–56–57–
59–60 — 46 (16)
**Henderson P.** 1926–2014
(Wanganui) 1949–50 — 19 (7)
**Henderson P.W.** 1964–
(Otago) 1989–90–91
(Southland) 1992–93–95 — 25 (7)
**Hendrie J.M.** 1951–
(Western Australia) 1970 — 1 (–)
**Herewini M.A.** 1940–2014
(Auckland) 1962–63–64–65–66–67 — 32 (10)
**Herrold M.** 1869–1949
(Auckland) 1893 — 2 (–)
**Hewett D.N.** 1971–
(Canterbury) 2001–02–03 — 24 (22)
**Hewett J.A.** 1968–
(Auckland) 1991 — 1 (1)
**Hewitt N.J.** 1968–
(Hawke's Bay) 1993
(Southland) 1995–96–97–98 — 23 (9)
**Hewson A.R.** 1954–
(Wellington) 1979–81–82–83–84 — 34 (19)
**Hickey P.H.** 1899–1942
(Taranaki) 1922 — 2 (–)
**Higginson G.** 1954–
(Canterbury) 1980–81
(Hawke's Bay) 1982–83 — 20 (6)
**Hill D.W.** 1978–
(Waikato) 2001–06 — 3 (1)
**Hill S.F.** 1927–
(Canterbury) 1955–56–57–58–59 — 19 (11)
**Hines G.R.** 1960–
(Waikato) 1980 — 12 (1)
**Hobbs F.G.** 1920–1985
(Canterbury) 1947 — 6 (–)
**Hobbs M.J.B.** 1960–2012
(Canterbury) 1983–84–85–86 — 39 (21)
**Hoeata J.M.R.A.** 1982–
(Taranaki) 2011 — 3 (3)
**Hoeft C.H.** 1974–
(Otago) 1998–99–2000–01–03 — 31 (30)
**Hogan J.** 1881–1945
(Wanganui) 1907 — 2 (–)
**Holah M.R.** 1976–
(Waikato) 2001–02–03–04–05–06 — 39 (36)
**Holden A.W.** 1907–1970
(Otago) 1928 — 3 (–)
**Holder E.C.** 1908–1974
(Buller) 1932–34 — 10 (1)
**Holmes B.** 1946–
(North Auckland) 1970–72–73 — 31 (–)
**Hook L.S.** 1905–1979
(Auckland) 1928–29 — 12 (3)
**Hooper J.A.** 1913–1976
(Canterbury) 1937–38 — 7 (3)

**Hopa A.R.** 1971–1998
(Waikato) 1997 — 4 (–)
**Hopkinson A.E.** 1941–1999
(Canterbury) 1967–68–69–70 — 35 (9)
**Hore A.K.** 1978–
(Taranaki) 2002–04–05–06–07–08
–09–10–11–12
(Highlanders) 2013 — 83 (83)
**Hore J.** 1907–1979 (Otago)
1928–30–32–34–35–36 — 45 (10)
**Horsley R.H.** 1932–2007
(Wellington) 1960
(Manawatu) 1963 — 31 (3)
**Hotop J.** 1929–2015
(Canterbury) 1952–55 — 3 (3)
**Howarth S.P.** 1968–
(Auckland) 1993–94 — 10 (4)
**Howden J.** 1900–1978
(Southland) 1928 — 1 (–)
**Howlett D.C.** 1978–
(Auckland) 2000–01–02–03–04–
05–06–07 — 63 (62)
**Hughes A.M.** 1924–2005
(Auckland) 1947–49–50 — 7 (6)
**Hughes D.J.** 1869–1951
(Taranaki) 1894 — 1 (–)
**Hughes E.** 1881–1928
(Southland) 1907–08
(Wellington) 1921 — 9 (6)
**Hullena L.C.** 1965–
(Wellington) 1990–91 — 9 (–)
**Humphreys G.W.** 1870–1933
(Canterbury) 1894 — 1 (–)
**Humphries A.L.** 1874–1953
(Taranaki) 1897–1901–03 — 15 (–)
**Hunt D.** 1995–
(Highlanders) 2017 — 1 (–)
**Hunter B.A.** 1950–
(Otago) 1970–71 — 10 (3)
**Hunter J.** 1879–1962
(Taranaki) 1905–06–07–08 — 36 (11)
**Hurst I.A.** 1951–
(Canterbury) 1972–73–74 — 32 (5)

**Ieremia A.** 1970–
(Wellington) 1994–95–96–97–
99–2000 — 40 (30)
**Ifwersen K.D.** 1893–1967
(Auckland) 1921 — 1 (1)
**Innes C.R.** 1969–
(Auckland) 1989–90–91 — 30 (17)
**Innes G.D.** 1910–1992
(Canterbury) 1932 — 7 (1)
**Ioane A.L.** 1995–
(Blues) 2017 — 1 (–)
**Ioane R.E.** 1997–
(Blues) 2016–17 — 13 (13)
**Irvine I.B.** 1929–2013
(North Auckland) 1952 — 1 (1)
**Irvine J.G.** 1888–1939
(Otago) 1914 — 10 (3)

**Irvine W.R.** 1898–1952
(Hawke's Bay) 1923–24–25–26
(Wairarapa) 1930    41   (5)
**Irwin M.W.** 1935–
(Otago) 1955–56–58–59–60    25   (7)
**Ivimey F.E.B.** 1880–1961
(Otago) 1910    1   (–)

**Jack C.R.** 1978–
(Canterbury) 2001–02–03–04–05
(Tasman) 2006–07    68   (67)
**Jackson E.S.** 1914–1975
(Hawke's Bay) 1936–37–38    11   (6)
**Jacob H.** 1894–1955
(Horowhenua) 1920    8   (–)
**Jacob J.P. LeG.** 1877–1909
(Southland) 1901    2   (–)
**Jaffray J.L.** 1950–
(Otago) 1972–75–76–77–78
(South Canterbury) 1979    23   (7)
**Jaffray M.W.R.** 1949–
(Otago) 1976    4   (–)
**Jane C.S.** 1983–
(Wellington) 2008–09–10–11–12
(Hurricanes) 2013–14    55   (53)
**Jarden R.A.** 1929–1977
(Wellington) 1951–52–53–54–
55–56    37   (16)
**Jefferd A.C.R.** 1953–
(East Coast) 1980–81    5   (3)
**Jennings A.G.T.** 1940–
(Bay of Plenty) 1967    6   (–)
**Jervis F.M.** 1870–1952
(Auckland) 1893    10   (–)
**Jessep E.M.** 1904–1983
(Wellington) 1931–32    8   (2)
**Johns P.A.** 1944–
(Wanganui) 1968    6   (–)
**Johnson L.M.** 1897–1983
(Wellington) 1925–28–30    25   (4)
**Johnston D.** 1903–1938
(Taranaki) 1925    2   (–)
**Johnston W.** 1881–1951
(Otago) 1905–07    27   (3)
**Johnstone B.R.** 1950–
(Auckland) 1976–77–78–79–80    45   (13)
**Johnstone C.R.** 1980–
(Canterbury) 2005    3   (3)
**Johnstone P.** 1922–1997
(Otago) 1949–50–51    26   (9)
**Jones I.D.** 1967–
(North Auckland) 1989–90–91–92–93
(North Harbour) 1994–95–96–
97–98–99    105   (79)
**Jones M.G.** 1942–1975
(North Auckland) 1973    5   (1)
**Jones M.N.** 1965–
(Auckland) 1987–88–89–90–91–
92–93–94–95–96–97–98    74   (55)

**Jones P.F.H.** 1932–1994
(North Auckland) 1953–54–55–
56–58–59–60    37   (11)
**Joseph H.T.** 1949–
(Canterbury) 1971    2   (2)
**Joseph J.W.** 1969–
(Otago) 1992–93–94–95    30   (20)

**Kahui R.D.** 1985–
(Waikato) 2008–10–11    18   (17)
**Kaino J.** 1983–
(Auckland) 2004–06–08–09–10–11
(Blues) 2014–15–16–17    83   (81)
**Kane G.N.** 1952–
(Waikato) 1974    7   (–)
**Karam J.F.** 1951–
(Wellington) 1972–73–74
(Horowhenua) 1975    42   (10)
**Katene T.** 1929–1992
(Wellington) 1955    1   (1)
**Keane K.J.** 1953–
(Canterbury) 1979    6   (–)
**Kearney J.C.** 1920–1998
(Otago) 1947–49    22   (4)
**Kelleher B.T.** 1976–
(Otago) 1999–2000–01–02–03–04
(Waikato) 2004–05–06–07    58   (57)
**Kelly J.W.** 1926–2002
(Auckland) 1949–53–54    16   (2)
**Kember G.F.** 1945–
(Wellington) 1967–70    19   (1)
**Kenny D.J.** 1961–
(Otago) 1986    3   (–)
**Kerr A.** 1871–1936
(Canterbury) 1896    1   (–)
**Kerr-Barlow T.N.J.** 1990–
(Waikato) 2012
(Chiefs) 2013–14–15–16–17    29   (27)
**Ketels R.C.** 1954–
(Counties) 1979–80–81    16   (5)
**Kiernan H.A.D.** 1876–1947
(Auckland) 1903    8   (1)
**Kilby F.D.** 1906–1985
(Wellington) 1928–32–34    18   (4)
**Killeen B.A.** 1911–1993
(Auckland) 1936    2   (1)
**King R.M.** 1980–
(Waikato) 2002    1   (1)
**King R.R.** 1909–1988
(West Coast) 1934–35–36–37–38    42   (13)
**Kingstone C.N.** 1895–1960
(Taranaki) 1921    3   (3)
**Kirk D.E.** 1961–
(Otago) 1983–84
(Auckland) 1985–86–87    34   (17)
**Kirkpatrick A.** 1898–1971
(Hawke's Bay) 1925–26    12   (–)
**Kirkpatrick I.A.** 1946–
(Canterbury) 1967–68–69
(Poverty Bay) 1970–71–72–73–
74–75–76–77    113   (39)

**Kirton E.W.** 1939–
(Otago) 1963–64–67–68–69–70 49 (13)
**Kirwan J.J.** 1964–
(Auckland) 1984–85–86–87–88–
89–90–91–92–93–94 96 (63)
**Kivell A.L.** 1897–1988
(Taranaki) 1929 5 (2)
**Knight A.** 1906–1990
(Auckland) 1926–28–34 14 (1)
**Knight G.A.** 1951–
(Manawatu) 1977–78–79–80–81–
82–83–84–85–86 66 (36)
**Knight L.A.G.** 1901–1973
(Auckland) 1925 5 (–)
**Knight L.G.** 1949–
(Auckland) 1974
(Poverty Bay) 1976–77 35 (6)
**Knight M.O.** 1945–
(Counties) 1968 8 (–)
**Koteka T.T.** 1956–
(Waikato) 1981–82 6 (2)
**Kreft A.J.** 1945–
(Otago) 1968 4 (1)
**Kronfeld J.A.** 1971–
(Otago) 1995–96–97–98–99–2000 56 (54)
**Kururangi R.** 1957–
(Counties) 1978 8 (–)

**Laidlaw C.R.** 1943–
(Otago) 1963–64–65–66–67
(Canterbury) 1968 (Otago) 1970 57 (20)
**Laidlaw K.F.** 1934–
(Southland) 1960 17 (3)
**Lam P.R.** 1968–
(Auckland) 1992 1 (–)
**Lambert K.K.** 1952–
(Manawatu) 1972–73–74–76–77 40 (11)
**Lambie J.T.** 1870–1905
(Taranaki) 1893–94 12 (–)
**Lambourn A.** 1910–1999
(Wellington) 1934–35–36–37–38 40 (10)
**Larsen B.P.** 1969–
(North Harbour) 1992–93–
94–95–96 40 (17)
**Latimer T.D.** 1986–
(Bay of Plenty) 2009 6 (5)
**Laulala C.D.E.** 1982–
(Canterbury) 2004–06 3 (2)
**Laulala N.E.** 1991–
(Crusaders) 2015–17 13 (13)
**Laumape K.H.** 1993–
(Hurricanes) 2017 6 (4)
**Lauaki S.T.** 1981–2017
(Waikato) 2005–07–08 17 (17)
**Law A.D.** 1904–1961
(Manawatu) 1925 4 (–)
**Lawson G.P.** 1899–1985
(South Canterbury) 1925 2 (–)
**Lecky J.G.** 1863–1917
(Auckland) 1884 7 (–)

**Lee D.D.** 1976–
(Otago) 2002 2 (2)
**Leeson J.** 1909–1960
(Waikato) 1934 5 (–)
**LeLievre J.M.** 1933–2016
(Canterbury) 1962–63–64 25 (1)
**Lendrum R.N.** 1948–
(Counties) 1973 3 (1)
**Leonard B.G.** 1985–
(Waikato) 2007–09 14 (13)
**Leslie A.R.** 1944–
(Wellington) 1974–75–76 34 (10)
**Levien H.J.** 1935–2008
(Otago) 1957 8 (–)
**Leys E.T.** 1907–1989
(Wellington) 1929 5 (1)
**Lienert-Brown A.R.** 1995–
(Chiefs) 2016–17 23 (22)
**Lilburne H.T.** 1908–1976
(Canterbury) 1928–29–30
(Wellington) 1931–32–34 40 (10)
**Lindsay D.F.** 1906–1978
(Otago) 1928 14 (3)
**Lindsay W.G.** 1879–1965
(Southland) 1914 4 (–)
**Lineen T.R.** 1936–
(Auckland) 1957–58–59–60 35 (12)
**Lister T.N.** 1943–2017
(South Canterbury) 1968–69–
70–71 26 (8)
**Little P.F.** 1934–1993
(Auckland) 1961–62–63–64 29 (10)
**Little W.K.** 1969–
(North Harbour) 1989–90–91–92–
93–94–95–96–97–98 75 (50)
**Loader C.J.** 1931–
(Wellington) 1953–54 16 (4)
**Lochore B.J.** 1940–
(Wairarapa) 1963–64–65–66–67–
68–69–70
(Wairarapa Bush) 1971 68 (25)
**Lockington T.M.** 1913–2001
(Auckland) 1936 1 (–)
**Loe R.W.** 1960–
(Waikato) 1986–87–88–89–90–91–92
(Canterbury) 1994–95 78 (49)
**Lomas A.R.** 1894–1975
(Auckland) 1925–26 15 (–)
**Lomu J.T.** 1975–2015
(Counties Manukau) 1994–95–96–
97–98–99
(Wellington) 2000–01–02 73 (63)
**Long A.T.** 1879–1960
(Auckland) 1903 10 (1)
**Loveday J.K.** 1949–
(Manawatu) 1978 7 (–)
**Loveridge D.S.** 1952–
(Taranaki) 1978–79–80–81–82–
83–85 54 (24)
**Loveridge G.** 1890–1970
(Taranaki) 1913–14 11 (–)

**Lowen K.R.** 1976–
(Waikato) 2002    1   (1)
**Luatua D.S.** 1991
(Blues) 2013–14.16    15   (15)
**Lucas F.W.** 1902–1957
(Auckland) 1923–24–25–28–30    41   (7)
**Lunn W.A.** 1926–1996
(Otago) 1949    2   (2)
**Lynch T.W.** 1892–1950
(South Canterbury) 1913–14    23   (4)
**Lynch T.W.** 1927–2006
(Canterbury) 1951    10   (3)

**Maber G.** 1869–1894
(Wellington) 1894    1   (–)
**McAlister C.L.** 1983–
(North Harbour) 2005–06–
07–09    31   (30)
**McAtamney F.S.** 1934–
(Otago) 1956–57    9   (1)
**McCahill B.J.** 1964–
(Auckland) 1987–88–89–90–91    32   (10)
**McCarthy P.** 1893–1976
(Canterbury) 1923    1   (–)
**McCashin T.M.** 1944–2017
(Wellington) 1968    7   (–)
**McCaw R.H.** 1980–
(Canterbury) 2001–02–03–04–05–06–
07–08–09–10–11–12
(Crusaders) 2013–14–15    149 (148)
**McCaw W.A.** 1927–
(Southland) 1951–53–54    32   (5)
**McCleary B.V.** 1897–1978
(Canterbury) 1924–25    12   (–)
**McClymont W.G.** 1905–1970
(Otago) 1928    3   (–)
**McCool M.J.** 1951–
(Wairarapa Bush) 1979    2   (1)
**McCormick A.G.** 1899–1969
(Canterbury) 1925    1   (–)
**McCormick J.** 1923–2006
(Hawke's Bay) 1947    3   (–)
**McCormick W.F.** 1939–
(Canterbury) 1965–67–68–
69–70–71    44   (16)
**McCullough J.F.** 1936–
(Taranaki) 1959    3   (3)
**McDonald A.** 1883–1967
(Otago) 1905–06–07–08–13    41   (8)
**Macdonald A.J.** 1981–
(Auckland) 2005    2   (2)
**Macdonald H.H.** 1947–1
(Canterbury) 1972–73–74
(North Auckland) 1975–76    48   (12)
**MacDonald L.R.** 1977–
(Canterbury) 2000–01–02–03–
05–06–07–08    56   (56)
**McDonnell P.** 1874–1950
(Wanganui) 1896    1   (–)
**McDonnell J.M.** 1973–
(Otago) 2002    8   (8)

**McDowall S.C.** 1961–
(Auckland) 1985–86–87–88
(Bay of Plenty) 1989
(Auckland) 1989–90–91–92    81   (46)
**McEldowney J.T.** 1947–2012
(Taranaki) 1976–77    10   (2)
**MacEwan I.N.** 1934–
(Wellington) 1956–57–58–59–
60–61–62    52   (20)
**McGahan P.W.** 1964–
(North Harbour) 1990–91    6   (–)
**McGrattan B.** 1959–
(Wellington) 1983–84–85–86    23   (6)
**McGregor A.A.** 1953–
(Southland) 1978    3   (–)
**McGregor A.J.** 1889–1963
(Auckland) 1913    11   (2)
**McGregor D.** 1881–1947
(Canterbury) 1903
(Wellington) 1904–05–06    31   (4)
**McGregor N.P.** 1901–1973
(Canterbury) 1924–25–28    27   (2)
**McGregor R.W.** 1874–1925
(Auckland) 1901–03–04    10   (2)
**McHugh M.J.** 1917–2010
(Auckland) 1946–49    14   (3)
**MacIntosh C.N.** 1869–1918
(South Canterbury) 1893    4   (–)
**McIntosh D.N.** 1931–
(Wellington) 1956–57    13   (4)
**McKay D.W.** 1937–
(Auckland) 1961–62–63    12   (5)
**Mackay J.D.** 1905–1985
(Wellington) 1928    2   (–)
**McKechnie B.J.** 1953–
(Southland) 1977–78–79–81    26   (10)
**McKellar G.F.** 1884–1960
(Wellington) 1910    5   (3)
**McKenzie D.S.** 1995–
(Chiefs) 2016–17    12   (12)
**MacKenzie R.H.** 1869–1940
(Auckland) 1893    2   (–)
**MacKenzie R.H.C.** 1904–1993
(Wellington) 1928    2   (–)
**McKenzie R.J.** 1892–1968
(Wellington) 1913
(Auckland) 1914    20   (4)
**MacKenzie R.M.** 1909–2000
(Manawatu) 1934–35–36–37–38    35   (9)
**McKenzie W.** 1871–1943
(Wairarapa) 1893
(Wellington) 1894–96–97    20   (–)
**Mackintosh J.L.** 1985–
(Southland) 2008    2   (1)
**Mackrell W.H.C.** 1881–1917
(Auckland) 1905–06    7   (1)
**Macky J.V.** 1887–1951
(Auckland) 1913    1   (1)
**McLachlan J.S.** 1949–
(Auckland) 1974    8   (1)

**McLaren H.C.** 1926–1992
(Waikato) 1952 — 1 (1)
**McLean A.L.** 1898–1964
(Bay of Plenty) 1921–23 — 3 (2)
**McLean C.** 1892–1965
(Buller) 1920 — 5 (–)
**McLean H.F.** 1907–1997
(Wellington) 1930–32
(Auckland) 1934–35–36 — 29 (9)
**McLean J.K.** 1923–2005
(King Country) 1947
(Auckland) 1949 — 5 (2)
**McLean R.J.** 1960–
(Wairarapa Bush) 1987 — 2 (–)
**McLeod B.E.** 1940–1996
(Counties) 1964–65–66–67–68–
69–70 — 46 (24)
**McLeod S.J.** 1973–
(Waikato) 1996–97–98 — 17 (10)
**McMeeking D.T.M.** 1896–1976
(Otago) 1923 — 2 (–)
**McMinn A.F.** 1880–1919
(Wairarapa) 1903
(Manawatu) 1905 — 10 (2)
**McMinn F.A.** 1874–1947
(Manawatu) 1904 — 1 (1)
**McMullen R.F.** 1933–2004
(Auckland) 1957–58–59–60 — 29 (11)
**McNab J.A.** 1895–1979
(Hawke's Bay) 1925 — 1 (–)
**McNab J.R.** 1924–2009
(Otago) 1949–50 — 17 (6)
**McNaughton A.M.** 1947–
(Bay of Plenty) 1971–72 — 9 (3)
**McNeece J.*** 1885–1917
(Southland) 1913–14 — 11 (5)
**McNicol A.L.R.** 1944–2017
(Wanganui) 1973 — 5 (–)
**McPhail B.E.** 1937–
(Canterbury) 1959 — 2 (2)
**MacPherson D.G.** 1882–1956
(Otago) 1905 — 1 (1)
**Macpherson G.** 1962–
(Otago) 1986 — 1 (1)
**MacRae I.R.** 1943–
(Hawke's Bay) 1963–64–66–67–
68–69–70 — 45 (17)
**McRae J.A.** 1914–1977
(Southland) 1946 — 2 (2)
**McRobie N.** 1873–1929
(Southland) 1896 — 1 (–)
**McWilliams R.G.** 1901–1984
(Auckland) 1928–29–30 — 27 (10)
**Maguire J.R.** 1886–1966
(Auckland) 1910 — 6 (3)
**Mahoney A.** 1908–1979
(Bush) 1929–34–35–36 — 26 (4)
**Mains L.W.** 1946–
(Otago) 1971–76 — 15 (4)
**Major J.** 1940–
(Taranaki) 1963–64–67 — 24 (1)

**Maka I.** 1975–
(Otago) 1998 — 4 (4)
**Maling T.S.** 1975–
(Otago) 2001–02–04 — 13 (11)
**Manchester J.E.** 1908–1983
(Canterbury) 1932–34–35–36 — 36 (9)
**Mannix S.J.** 1971–
(Wellington) 1990–91–94 — 9 (1)
**Markham P.F.** 1891–1953
(Wellington) 1921 — 1 (–)
**Marshall J.W.** 1973–
(Canterbury) 1995–96–97–98–
99–2000–01–02–03–04–05 — 88 (81)
**Masaga L.T.C.** 1986–
(Counties Manukau) 2009 — 1 (1)
**Masoe M.C.** 1979–
(Taranaki) 2005
(Wellington) 2006–07 — 20 (20)
**Mason D.F.** 1923–1981
(Wellington) 1947 — 6 (1)
**Masters F.H.** 1893–1980
(Taranaki) 1922 — 4 (–)
**Masters R.R.** 1900–1967
(Canterbury) 1923–24–25 — 31 (4)
**Mataira H.K.** 1910–1979
(Hawke's Bay) 1934 — 5 (1)
**Matheson J.D.** 1948–
(Otago) 1972 — 13 (5)
**Mathewson A.S.** 1985–
(Wellington) 2008–10 — 5 (4)
**Mathieson R.G.** 1899–1966
(Otago) 1922 — 4 (–)
**Matson J.T.F.** 1973
(Canterbury) 1995–96 — 5 (–)
**Mattson H.A.** 1900–1980
(Auckland) 1925 — 6 (–)
**Mauger A.J.D.** 1980–
(Canterbury) 2001–02–03–04–
05–06–07 — 46 (45)
**Mauger N.K.** 1978–
(Canterbury) 2001 — 2 (–)
**Max D.S.** 1906–1972
(Nelson) 1931–32–34 — 8 (3)
**Maxwell N.M.C.** 1976–
(Canterbury) 1999–2000–01–
02–04 — 36 (36)
**Mayerhofler M.A.** 1972–
(Canterbury) 1998 — 6 (6)
**Meads C.E.** 1936–2017
(King Country) 1957–58–59–
60–61–62–63–64–65–66–67–
68–69–70–71 — 133 (55)
**Meads S.T.** 1938–
(King Country) 1961–62–63–64–
65–66 — 30 (15)
**Mealamu K.F.** 1979–
(Auckland) 2002–03–04–05–
06–07–08–09–10–11–12
(Blues) 2013–14–15 — 133 (132)
**Meates K.F.** 1930–
(Canterbury) 1952 — 2 (2)

**Meates W.A.** 1923–2003
(Otago) 1949–50    20   (7)
**Meeuws K.J.** 1974–
(Otago) 1998–99–2000–01–02–04
(Auckland) 2003    45   (42)
**Mehrtens A.P.** 1973–
(Canterbury) 1995–96–97–98–
99–2000–01–02–04    72   (70)
**Mehrtens G.M.** 1907–1954
(Canterbury) 1928    3   (–)
**Messam L.J.** 1984–
(Waikato) 2008–09–10–11–12
(Chiefs) 2013–14–15    45   (43)
**Metcalfe T.C.** 1909–1969
(Southland) 1931–32    7   (2)
**Mexted G.G.** 1927–2009
(Wellington) 1950–51    5   (1)
**Mexted M.G.** 1953–
(Wellington) 1979–80–81–82–
83–84–85    72   (34)
**Mika B.M.** 1981–
(Auckland) 2002    3   (3)
**Mika D.G.** 1972–
(Auckland) 1999    8   (7)
**Mill J.J.** 1899–1950
(Hawke's Bay) 1923–24–25–26
(Wairarapa) 1930    33   (4)
**Miller P.C.** 1975–
(Otago) 2001    2   (–)
**Miller T.J.** 1974–
(Waikato) 1997    4   (–)
**Milliken H.M.** 1914–1993
(Canterbury) 1938    7   (3)
**Mills H.P.** 1873–1905
(Taranaki) 1897    8   (–)
**Mills J.G.** 1960–
(Auckland) 1984    2   (–)
**Millton E.B.** 1861–1942
(Canterbury) 1884    7   (–)
**Millton W.V.** 1858–1887
(Canterbury) 1884    8   (–)
**Milner H.P.** 1946–1996
(Wanganui) 1970    16   (1)
**Milner-Skudder N.R.** 1990–
(Hurricanes) 2015,17    11   (11)
**Mitchell J.E.P.** 1964–
(Waikato) 1993    6   (–)
**Mitchell N.A.** 1913–1981
(Southland) 1935–36–37
(Otago) 1938    32   (8)
**Mitchell T.W.** 1950–
(Canterbury) 1974–76    17   (1)
**Mitchell W.J.** 1890–1959
(Canterbury) 1910    5   (2)
**Mitchinson F.E.** 1884–1978
(Wellington) 1907–08–10–13    31   (11)
**Moala G.** 1990
(Blues) 2015–16    4   (4)
**Moffitt J.E.** 1889–1964
(Wellington) 1920–21    12   (3)

**Moli A.** 1995–
(Chiefs) 2017    1   (–)
**Molloy B.P.J.** 1931–
(Canterbury) 1957    5   (–)
**Moody J.P.T.** 1988–
(Crusaders) 2014–15–16–17    31   (31)
**Moore G.J.T.** 1923–1991
(Otago) 1949    1   (1)
**Moreton R.C.** 1942–2016
(Canterbury) 1962–64–65    12   (7)
**Morgan H.D.** 1902–1969
(Otago) 1923    1   (–)
**Morgan J.E.** 1945–2002
(North Auckland) 1974–76    22   (5)
**Morris T.J.** 1942–
(Nelson Bays) 1972–73    23   (3)
**Morrison T.C.** 1913–1985
(South Canterbury) 1938    5   (3)
**Morrison T.G.** 1951–
(Otago) 1973    5   (1)
**Morrissey B.L.** 1952–
(Waikato) 1981    3   (–)
**Morrissey P.J.** 1939–2013
(Canterbury) 1962    3   (3)
**Mourie G.N.K.** 1952–
(Taranaki) 1976–77–78–79–80–
81–82    61   (21)
**Mo'unga R.** 1994–
(Crusaders) 2017    1   (–)
**Mowlem J.** 1870–1951
(Manawatu) 1893    4   (–)
**Muliaina J.M.** 1980–
(Auckland) 2003–04–05
(Waikato) 2006–07–08–09–10–11    102 (100)
**Muller B.L.** 1942–
(Taranaki) 1967–68–69–70–71    35   (14)
**Mumm W.J.** 1922–1993
(Buller) 1949    1   (1)
**Munro H.G.** 1896–1974
(Otago) 1924–25    9   (–)
**Murdoch K.** 1943–
(Otago) 1970–72    27   (3)
**Murdoch P.H.** 1941–1995
(Auckland) 1964–65    5   (5)
**Murray F.S.M.** 1871–1952
(Auckland) 1893–97    20   (–)
**Murray H.V.** 1888–1971
(Canterbury) 1913–14    22   (4)
**Murray P.C.** 1884–1968
(Wanganui) 1908    1   (1)
**Myers R.G.** 1950–
(Waikato) 1977–78    5   (1)
**Mynott H.J.** 1876–1924
(Taranaki) 1905–06–07–10    39   (8)

**Naholo W.R.** 1991
(Highlanders) 2015–16–17    19   (18)
**Nathan W.J.** 1940–
(Auckland) 1962–63–64–66–67    37   (14)
**Nelson K.A.** 1938–
(Otago) 1962–63–64    18   (2)

**Nepia G.** 1905–1986
(Hawke's Bay) 1924–25
(East Coast) 1929–30 ........ 46  (9)
**Nesbit S.R.** 1936–
(Auckland) 1960 ........ 13  (2)
**Neville W.R.** 1954–
(North Auckland) 1981 ........ 4  (–)
**Newby C.A.** 1979–
(North Harbour) 2004–06 ........ 3  (3)
**Newton F.** 1881–1955
(Canterbury) 1905–06 ........ 19  (3)
**Ngatai C.J.** 1990–
(Chiefs) 2015 ........ 1  (1)
**Nicholls H.E.** 1900–1978
(Wellington) 1921–22–23 ........ 7  (1)
**Nicholls H.G.** 1897–1977
(Wellington) 1923 ........ 1  (–)
**Nicholls M.F.** 1901–1972
(Wellington) 1921–22–24–25–26–
28–30 ........ 51  (10)
**Nicholson G.W.** 1878–1968
(Auckland) 1903–04–05–06–07 ........ 39  (4)
**Nonu M.A.** 1982–
(Wellington) 2003–04–05–06–07–08–
09–10–11–12
(Highlanders) 2013
(Blues) 2014
(Hurricanes) 2015 ........ 104 (103)
**Norton R.W.** 1942–
(Canterbury) 1971–72–73–74–
75–76–77 ........ 61  (27)

**O'Brien A.J.** 1897–1969
(Auckland) 1922 ........ 3  (–)
**O'Brien J.** 1871–1946
(Wellington) 1901 ........ 1  (–)
**O'Brien J.G.** 1889–1958
(Auckland) 1914–20 ........ 12  (1)
**O'Callaghan M.W.** 1946–
(Manawatu) 1968 ........ 3  (3)
**O'Callaghan T.R.** 1925–2004
(Wellington) 1949 ........ 1  (1)
**O'Connor T.B.** 1860–1936
(Auckland) 1884 ........ 7  (–)
**O'Dea R.J.** 1930–1986
(Thames Valley) 1953–54 ........ 5  (–)
**O'Donnell D.H.** 1921–1992
(Wellington) 1949 ........ 1  (1)
**O'Donnell J.M.** 1860–1942
(Otago) 1884 ........ 7  (–)
**O'Dowda B.C.** 1874–1954
(Taranaki) 1901 ........ 2  (–)
**O'Halloran J.D.** 1972–
(Wellington) 2000 ........ 1  (1)
**O'Leary M.J.** 1883–1963
(Auckland) 1910–13 ........ 8  (4)
**O'Neill K.J.** 1982–
(Waikato) 2008 ........ 1  (1)
**Old G.H.** 1956–
(Manawatu) 1980–81–82–83 ........ 17  (3)

**Oliphant R.** 1870–1956
(Wellington) 1893
(Auckland) 1896 ........ 3  (–)
**Oliver A.D.** 1975–
(Otago) 1996–97–98–99–2000
01–03–04–05–06–07 ........ 67 (59)
**Oliver C.J.** 1905–1977
(Canterbury) 1928–29–34–35–36 ........ 33  (7)
**Oliver D.J.** 1907–1990
(Wellington) 1930 ........ 3  (2)
**Oliver D.O.** 1930–1997
(Otago) 1953–54 ........ 20  (2)
**Oliver F.J.** 1948–2014
(Southland) 1976–77
(Otago) 1978–79
(Manawatu) 1980–81 ........ 43 (17)
**Orchard S.A.** 1875–1947
(Canterbury) 1896–97 ........ 8  (–)
**Ormond J.** 1891–1970
(Hawke's Bay) 1923 ........ 1  (–)
**Orr R.W.** 1923–2011
(Otago) 1949 ........ 1  (1)
**Osborne G.M.** 1971–
(North Harbour) 1995–96–
97–99 ........ 29 (19)
**Osborne W.M.** 1955–
(Wanganui) 1975–76–77–78–
80–82 ........ 48 (16)
**O'Sullivan J.M.** 1883–1960
(Taranaki) 1905–07 ........ 29  (5)
**O'Sullivan T.P.A.** 1936–1997
(Taranaki) 1960–61–62 ........ 16  (4)

**Paewai L.** 1906–1970
(Hawke's Bay) 1923–24 ........ 8  (–)
**Page J.R.** 1908–1985
(Wellington) 1931–32–34–35 ........ 18  (6)
**Page M.L.** 1902–1987
(Canterbury) 1928 ........ 1  (–)
**Palmer B.P.** 1901–1932
(Auckland) 1928–29–32 ........ 18  (3)
**Parker J.H.** 1897–1980
(Canterbury) 1924–25 ........ 21  (3)
**Parkhill A.A.** 1912–1986
(Otago) 1937–38 ........ 10  (6)
**Parkinson R.M.** 1948–2009
(Poverty Bay) 1972–73 ........ 20  (7)
**Parsons J.W.** 1986–
(Blues) 2014.16 ........ 2  (2)
**Paterson A.M.** 1885–1933
(Otago) 1908–10 ........ 9  (5)
**Paton H.** 1881–1964
(Otago) 1907–10 ........ 8  (2)
**Pauling T.G.** 1873–1927
(Wellington) 1896–97 ........ 9  (–)
**Pene A.R.B.** 1967–
(Otago) 1992–93–94 ........ 26 (15)
**Pepper C.S.★** 1911–1943
(Auckland) 1935–36 ........ 17  (–)
**Perenara T.T.R.** 1992–
(Hurricanes) 2014–15–16–17 ........ 43 (42)

**Perry A.** 1899–1977
(Otago) 1923     1   (–)
**Perry R.G.** 1953–
(Mid Canterbury) 1980     1   (–)
**Perry T.G.** 1988–
(Crusaders) 2017     2   (–)
**Petersen L.C.** 1897–1961
(Canterbury) 1921–22–23     8   (–)
**Phillips W.J.** 1914–1982
(King Country) 1937–38     7   (3)
**Philpott S.** 1965–
(Canterbury) 1988–90–91     14   (2)
**Pickering E.A.R.** 1936–2016
(Waikato) 1957–58–59–60     21   (3)
**Pierce M.J.** 1957–
(Wellington) 1984–85–86–87–
88–89–90     54   (26)
**Piutau S.T.** 1991–
(Blues) 2013–14–15     17   (17)
**Pokere S.T.** 1958–
(Southland) 1981–82–83
(Auckland) 1984–85     39   (18)
**Pollock H.R.** 1909–1984
(Wellington) 1932–36     8   (5)
**Porteous H.G.** 1875–1951
(Otago) 1903     3   (–)
**Porter C.G.** 1899–1976
(Wellington) 1923–24–25–26–
28–29–30     41   (7)
**Potaka W.P.** ca 1903–1967
(Wanganui) 1923     2   (–)
**Preston J.P.** 1967–
(Canterbury) 1991–92
(Wellington) 1993–96–97     27   (10)
**Pringle A.** 1899–1973
(Wellington) 1923     1   (–)
**Pringle W.P.** 1869–1945
(Wellington) 1893     5   (–)
**Procter A.C.** 1906–1989
(Otago) 1932     4   (1)
**Pulu A.W.** 1990–
(Chiefs) 2014     2   (2)
**Purdue C.A.** 1874–1941
(Southland) 1901–05     3   (1)
**Purdue E.** 1879–1939
(Southland) 1905     1   (1)
**Purdue G.B.** 1909–1981
(Southland) 1931–32     7   (4)
**Purvis G.H.** 1960–
(Waikato) 1989–90–91–92–93     28   (2)
**Purvis N.A.** 1953–2008
(Otago) 1976     12   (1)

**Quaid C.E.** 1908–1984
(Otago) 1938     4   (2)

**Ralph C.S.** 1977–
(Auckland) 1998
(Canterbury) 2001–02–03     16   (14)
**Ranby R.M.** 1977–
(Waikato) 2001     1   (1)

**Randell T.C.** 1974–
(Otago) 1995–96–97–98–99–
2000–01–02     61   (51)
**Randle R.Q.** 1974–
(Waikato) 2001     2   (–)
**Ranger R.M.N.** 1986–
(Northland) 2010
(Blues) 2013     6   (6)
**Rangi R.E.** 1941–1988
(Auckland) 1964–65–66     10   (10)
**Rankin J.G.** 1914–1989
(Canterbury) 1936–37     4   (3)
**Rawlinson G.P.** 1978–
(North Harbour) 2006–07     4   (4)
**Read K.J.** 1985–
(Canterbury) 2008–09–10–11–12
(Crusaders) 2013–14–15–16–17     110   (109)
**Reedy W.J.** 1880–1939
(Wellington) 1908     2   (2)
**Reid A.R.** 1929–1994
(Waikato) 1951–52–56–57     17   (5)
**Reid H.R.** 1958–
(Bay of Plenty) 1980–81–83–
84–85–86     40   (9)
**Reid K.H.** 1904–1972
(Wairarapa) 1929     5   (2)
**Reid S.T.** 1912–2003
(Hawke's Bay) 1935–36–37     27   (9)
**Reihana B.T.** 1976–
(Waikato) 2000     2   (2)
**Reside W.B.** 1905–1985
(Wairarapa) 1929     6   (1)
**Retallick B.A.** 1991–
(Hawke's Bay/Bay of Plenty) 2012
(Chiefs) 2013–14–15–16–17     68   (68)
**Rhind P.K.** 1915–1996
(Canterbury) 1946     2   (2)
**Richardson J.** 1899–1994
(Otago) 1921–22
(Southland) 1923–24–25     42   (7)
**Rickit H.A.** 1951–
(Waikato) 1981     2   (2)
**Ridge M.J.** 1969–
(Auckland) 1989     6   (–)
**Ridland A.J.*** 1882–1918
(Southland) 1910     6   (3)
**Riechelmann C.C.** 1972–
(Auckland) 1997     10   (6)
**Righton L.S.** 1898–1972
(Auckland) 1923–25     9   (–)
**Roberts E.J.** 1891–1972
(Wellington) 1913–14–20–21     26   (5)
**Roberts F.** 1882–1956
(Wellington) 1905–06–07–08–10     52   (12)
**Roberts H.** 1862–1949
(Wellington) 1884     7   (–)
**Roberts R.W.** 1889–1973
(Taranaki) 1913–14     23   (5)
**Roberts W.** 1871–1937
(Wellington) 1896–97     8   (–)

**Robertson B.J.** 1952–
(Counties) 1972–73–74–76–
77–78–79–80–81 · 102 (34)
**Robertson D.J.** 1947–
(Otago) 1974–75–76–77 · 30 (10)
**Robertson G.S.** 1859–1920
(Otago) 1884 · 8 (–)
**Robertson S.M.** 1974–
(Canterbury) 1998–99–
2000–01–02 · 23 (23)
**Robilliard A.C.C.** 1903–1990
(Canterbury) 1924–25–26–28 · 27 (4)
**Robins B.G.** 1958–
(Taranaki) 1985 · 4 (–)
**Robinson A.G.** 1956–
(North Auckland) 1983 · 4 (–)
**Robinson C.E.** 1927–1983
(Southland) 1951–52 · 11 (5)
**Robinson J.T.** 1906–1968
(Canterbury) 1928 · 3 (–)
**Robinson K.J.** 1976–
(Waikato) 2002–04–06–07 · 12 (12)
**Robinson M.D.** 1975–
(North Harbour) 1997–98–2001 · 8 (3)
**Robinson M.P.** 1974–
(Canterbury) 2000–02 · 9 (9)
**Rokocoko J.T.** 1983–
(Auckland) 2003–04–05–06–07–
08–09–10 · 69 (68)
**Rollerson D.L.** 1953–2017
(Manawatu) 1976–80–81 · 24 (8)
**Romano L.** 1986–
(Canterbury) 2012
(Crusaders) 2013–14–15–16–17 · 32 (31)
**Roper R.A.** 1923–
(Taranaki) 1949–50 · 5 (5)
**Ross I.B.** 1984–
(Canterbury) 2009 · 8 (8)
**Ross J.C.** 1949–
(Mid Canterbury) 1981 · 5 (–)
**Rowlands G.D.** 1947–
(Bay of Plenty) 1976 · 4 (–)
**Rowley H.C.B.** 1924–1956
(Wanganui) 1949 · 1 (1)
**Rush E.J.** 1965–
(North Harbour) 1992–93–95–96 · 29 (9)
**Rush X.J.** 1977–
(Auckland) 1998–2004 · 8 (8)
**Rushbrook C.A.** 1907–1987
(Wellington) 1928 · 10 (–)
**Rutledge L.M.** 1952–
(Southland) 1978–79–80 · 31 (13)
**Ryan E.** 1891–1965
(Wellington) 1921 · 1 (–)
**Ryan J.** 1887–1957
(Wellington) 1910–14 · 15 (4)
**Ryan J.A.C.** 1983–
(Otago) 2005–06 · 9 (9)
**Ryan P.J.** 1950–1985
(Hawke's Bay) 1976 · 5 (–)

**Ryan T.** 1863–1927
(Auckland) 1884 · 9 (–)
**Sadler B.S.** 1914–2007
(Wellington) 1935–36 · 19 (5)
**Saili F.** 1991–
(Blues) 2013 · 2 (2)
**Salmon J.L.B.** 1959–
(Wellington) 1980–81 · 7 (3)
**Sapsford H.P.** 1949–2009
(Otago) 1976 · 7 (–)
**Savage L.T.** 1928–2013
(Canterbury) 1949 · 12 (3)
**Savea A.S.** 1993–
(Hurricanes) 2016–17 · 24 (22)
**Savea S.J.** 1990–
(Wellington) 2012
(Hurricanes) 2013–14–15–16–17 · 54 (54)
**Saxton C.K.** 1913–2001
(South Canterbury) 1938 · 7 (3)
**Sayers M.** 1947–
(Wellington) 1972–73 · 15 (–)
**Schuler K.J.** 1967–
(Manawatu) 1989–90
(North Harbour) 1992–95 · 13 (4)
**Schuster N.J.** 1964–
(Wellington) 1987–88–89 · 26 (10)
**Schwalger J.E.** 1983–
(Wellington) 2007–08 · 2 (2)
**Scott R.W.H.** 1921–2012
(Auckland) 1946–47–49–50–
53–54 · 52 (17)
**Scott S.J.** 1955–1994
(Canterbury) 1980 · 4 (–)
**Scown A.I.** 1948–
(Taranaki) 1972–73 · 17 (5)
**Scrimshaw G.** 1902–1971
(Canterbury) 1928 · 11 (1)
**Secar G.A.** 1952–
(Otago) 1976–77–78–79 · 34 (12)
**Seeling C.E.** 1883–1956
(Auckland) 1904–05–06–07–08 · 39 (11)
**Sellars G.M.V.*** 1886–1917
(Auckland) 1913 · 15 (2)
**Senio K.** 1978–
(Bay of Plenty) 2005 · 1 (1)
**Seymour D.J.** 1967–
(Canterbury) 1992 · 3 (–)
**Shannon H.G.** 1869–1912
(Manawatu) 1893 · 6 (–)
**Shaw M.W.** 1956–
(Manawatu) 1980–81–82–83–84–85
(Hawke's Bay) 1986 · 69 (30)
**Shearer J.D.** 1896–1963
(Wellington) 1920 · 5 (–)
**Shearer S.D.** 1890–1973
(Wellington) 1921–22 · 8 (–)
**Sheen T.R.** 1905–1979
(Auckland) 1926–28 · 8 (–)

**Shelford F.N.K.**1955–
(Bay of Plenty) 1981–84–85
(Hawke's Bay) 1983    22   (4)
**Shelford W.T.** 1957–
(North Harbour) 1985–86–87–88–
89–90    48   (22)
**Sherlock K.** 1961–
(Auckland) 1985    3   (–)
**Siddells S.K.** 1897–1979
(Wellington) 1921    1   (1)
**Simon H.J.** 1911–1979
(Otago) 1937    3   (3)
**Simonsson P.L.J.** 1967–
(Wellington) 1987    2   (–)
**Simpson J.G.** 1922–2010
(Auckland) 1947–49–50    30   (9)
**Simpson V.L.J.** 1960–
(Canterbury) 1985    4   (2)
**Sims G.S.** 1951–
(Otago) 1972    1   (1)
**Sinclair R.G.B.** 1896–1932
(Otago) 1923    2   (–)
**Sivivatu S.W.** 1982–
(Waikato) 2005–06–07–08–09–11    46   (45)
**Skeen J.R.** 1928–2001
(Auckland) 1952    1   (1)
**Skinner K.L.** 1927–2014
(Otago) 1949–50–51–52–53–54
(Counties) 1956    63   (20)
**Skudder G.R.** 1948–
(Waikato) 1969–72–73    14   (1)
**Slade C.R.** 1987–
(Canterbury) 2010–11
(Highlanders) 2013–14
(Crusaders) 2014–15    21   (21)
**Slater G.L.** 1971–
(Taranaki) 1997–2000    6   (3)
**Sloane P.H.** 1948–
(North Auckland) 1973–76–79    16   (1)
**Smith A.E.** 1942–
(Taranaki) 1967–69–70    18   (3)
**Smith A.L.** 1998–
(Manawatu) 2012
(Highlanders) 2013–14–15–16–17    71   (71)
**Smith B.R.** 1986–
(Otago) 2009–11–12
(Highlanders) 2013–14–15–16–17    65   (64)
**Smith B.W.** 1959–
(Waikato) 1983–84    10   (3)
**Smith C.G.** 1981–
(Wellington) 2004–05–06–07–08–
09–10–11–12
(Hurricanes) 2013–14–15    94   (94)
**Smith C.H.** 1909–1976
(Otago) 1934    2   (–)
**Smith G.W.** 1874–1954
(Auckland) 1897–1901–05    39   (2)
**Smith I.S.T.** 1941–2017
(Otago) 1963–64
(North Otago) 1965–66    24   (9)

**Smith J.B.** 1922–1974
(North Auckland) 1946–47–49    9   (4)
**Smith P.** 1924–1954
(North Auckland) 1947    3   (–)
**Smith R.M.** 1929–2002
(Canterbury) 1955    1   (1)
**Smith W.E.** 1881–1945
(Nelson) 1905    1   (1)
**Smith W.R.** 1957–
(Canterbury) 1980–82–83–84–85    35   (17)
**Smyth B.F.** 1891–1972
(Canterbury) 1922    3   (–)
**Snodgrass W.F.** 1898–1976
(Nelson) 1923–28    3   (–)
**Snow E.M.** 1898–1974
(Nelson) 1928–29    16   (3)
**Solomon D.** 1913–1997
(Auckland) 1935–36    8   (–)
**Solomon F.** 1906–1991
(Auckland) 1931–32    9   (3)
**Somerville G.M.** 1977–
(Canterbury) 2000–01–02–03–
04–05–06–07–08    67   (66)
**Sonntag W.T.C.** 1894–1988
(Otago) 1929    8   (3)
**So'oialo, R.** 1979–
(Wellington) 2002–03–04–05–
06–07–08–09    63   (62)
**Soper A.J.** 1936–
(Southland) 1957    8   (–)
**Sopoaga L.Z.** 1991
(Highlanders) 2015–16–17    18   (16)
**Souter R.** 1905–1976
(Otago) 1929    4   (–)
**Speight C.R.B.** 1870–1935
(Auckland) 1893    7   (–)
**Speight M.W.** 1962–
(North Auckland) 1986    5   (1)
**Spencer C.J.** 1975–
(Auckland) 1995–96–97–
98–2000–02–03–04    44   (35)
**Spencer G.** 1878–1950
(Wellington) 1907    5   (–)
**Spencer J.C.** 1880–1936
(Wellington) 1903–05–07    6   (2)
**Spiers J.E.** 1947–
(Counties) 1976–79–80–81    28   (5)
**Spillane A.P.** 1888–1974
(South Canterbury) 1913    2   (2)
**Squire L.I.J.** 1991–
(Highlanders) 2016–17    16   (15)
**Stalker J.** 1881–1931
(Otago) 1903    6   (–)
**Stanley B.J.** 1984–
(Auckland) 2010    3   (3)
**Stanley J.C.** 1975–
(Auckland) 1997    3   (–)
**Stanley J.T.** 1957–
(Auckland) 1986–87–88–89–90–91    49   (27)
**Stapleton E.T.** 1930–2005
(New South Wales) 1960    1   (–)

Stead J.W. 1877–1958
(Southland) 1903–04–05–06–08   42   (7)
Steel A.G. 1941–
(Canterbury) 1966–67–68   23   (9)
Steel J. 1898–1941 (West Coast)
1920–21–22–23–24–25   38   (6)
Steele L.B. 1929–
(Wellington) 1951   9   (3)
Steere E.R.G. 1908–1967
(Hawke's Bay) 1928–29–30–31–32   21   (6)
Steinmetz P.C. 1977–
(Wellington) 2002   1   (1)
Stensness L. 1970–
(Auckland) 1993–97   14   (8)
Stephens O.G. 1947–
(Wellington) 1968   1   (1)
Stevens I.N. 1948–
(Wellington) 1972–73–74–76   33   (3)
Stevenson D.R.L. 1903–1962
(Otago) 1926   4   (–)
Stewart A.J. 1940–
(Canterbury) 1963
(South Canterbury) 1964   26   (8)
Stewart D.T. 1872–1931
(South Canterbury) 1894   1   (–)
Stewart E.B. 1901–1979
(Otago) 1923   1   (–)
Stewart J.D. 1889–1973
(Auckland) 1913   2   (2)
Stewart K.W. 1953–
(Southland) 1972–73–74–75–
76–79–81   55   (13)
Stewart R.T. 1904–1982
(South Canterbury) 1923–24–25–
26–28 (Canterbury) 1930   39   (5)
Stewart V.E. 1948–
(Canterbury) 1976–79   12   (–)
Stohr L. 1889–1973
(Taranaki) 1910–13   15   (3)
Stokes E.J.T. 1950–
(Bay of Plenty) 1976   5   (–)
Stone A.M. 1960–
(Waikato) 1981–83–84
(Bay of Plenty) 1986   23   (9)
Storey P.W. 1897–1975
(South Canterbury) 1920–21   12   (2)
Strachan A.D. 1966–
(Auckland) 1992
(North Harbour) 1993–95   17   (11)
Strahan S.C. 1944–
(Manawatu) 1967–68–70–72–73   45   (17)
Strang W.A. 1906–1989
(South Canterbury) 1928–30–31   17   (5)
Stringfellow J.C. 1905–1959
(Wairarapa) 1929   7   (2)
Stuart A.J. 1858–1923
(Wellington) 1893   7   (–)
Stuart K.C. 1928–2005
(Canterbury) 1955   1   (1)
Stuart R.C. 1920–2005
(Canterbury) 1949–53–54   27   (7)

Stuart R.L. 1948–
(Hawke's Bay) 1977   6   (1)
Sullivan J.L. 1915–1990
(Taranaki) 1936–37–38   9   (6)
Surman J.F. 1866–1925
(Auckland) 1896   1   (–)
Surridge S.D. 1970–
(Canterbury) 1997   3   (–)
Sutherland A.R. 1944–
(Marlborough)
1968–70–71–72–73–76   64   (10)
Svenson K.S. 1898–1955
(Buller) 1922
(Wellington) 1924–25–26   34   (4)
Swain J.P. 1902–1960
(Hawke's Bay) 1928   16   (4)
Swindley J.T. 1876–1918
(Wellington) 1894   1   (–)

Taiaroa J.G. 1862–1907
(Otago) 1884   9   (–)
Taituha P. 1901–1958
(Wanganui) 1923   2   (–)
Tamanivalu S. 1992–
(Chiefs) 2016–17   5   (3)
Tanner J.M. 1927–
(Auckland) 1950–51–53–54   24   (5)
Tanner K.J. 1945–
(Canterbury) 1974–75–76   27   (7)
Taumoepeau S. 1979–
(Auckland) 2004–05   4   (3)
Taylor C.J. 1989
(Crusaders) 2015–16–17   29   (29)
Taylor G.L. 1970–
(North Auckland) 1992–96   6   (1)
Taylor H.M. 1889–1955
(Canterbury) 1913–14   23   (5)
Taylor J.M. 1913–1979
(Otago) 1937–38   9   (6)
Taylor K.J. 1957–
(Hawke's Bay) 1980   1   (–)
Taylor M.B. 1956–
(Waikato) 1976–79–80   30   (7)
Taylor N.M. 1951–
(Bay of Plenty) 1976–77–78
(Hawke's Bay) 1982   27   (9)
Taylor R.★ 1889–1917
(Taranaki) 1913   2   (2)
Taylor T.J. 1989–
(Crusaders) 2013   3   (3)
Taylor W.T. 1960–
(Canterbury) 1983–84–85–86–
87–88   40   (24)
Tetzlaff P.L. 1920–2009
(Auckland) 1947   7   (2)
Thimbleby N.W. 1939–
(Hawke's Bay) 1970   13   (1)
Thomas B.T. 1937–2018
(Auckland) 1962
(Wellington) 1964   4   (4)
Thomas L.A. 1897–1971
(Wellington) 1925   3   (–)

**Thompson B.A.** 1947–2006
(Canterbury) 1979    8   (–)
**Thomson A.J.** 1982–
(Otago) 2008–09–10–11–12    31   (29)
**Thomson H.D.** 1881–1939
(Wanganui) 1905–06
(Wellington) 1908    15   (1)
**Thorn B.C.** 1975–
(Canterbury) 2003–09–10–11
(Tasman) 2008    60   (59)
**Thorne G.S.** 1946–
(Auckland) 1967–68–69–70    39   (10)
**Thorne R.D.** 1975–
(Canterbury) 1999–2000–01–02–03–
04–06–07    51   (50)
**Thornton N.H.** 1918–1998
(Auckland) 1947–49    19   (3)
**Thrush J.I.** 1985–
(Hurricanes) 2013–14–15    12   (12)
**Tialata N.S.** 1982–
(Wellington) 2005–06–07–08–
09–10    44   (43)
**Tiatia F.I.** 1971–
(Wellington) 2000    2   (2)
**Tilyard F.J.** 1896–1954
(Wellington) 1923    1   (–)
**Tilyard J.T.** 1889–1966
(Wellington) 1913–20    10   (1)
**Timu J.K.R.** 1969–
(Otago) 1989–90–91–92–93–94    50   (26)
**Tindill E.W.T.** 1910–2010
(Wellington) 1935–36–38    17   (1)
**Tiopira H.** 1871–1930
(Hawke's Bay) 1893    8   (–)
**Todd M.B.** 1988–
(Crusaders) 2013,15–16–17    13   (13)
**Toeava I.** 1986–
(Auckland) 2005–06–07–08–
09–10–11    37   (36)
**Tonu'u O.F.J.** 1970–
(Auckland) 1996–97–98    8   (5)
**To'omaga–Allen J.L.** 1990–
(Hurricanes) 2013–17    3   (1)
**Townsend L.J.** 1934–
(Otago) 1955    2   (2)
**Tregaskis C.D.** 1965–
(Wellington) 1991    4   (–)
**Tremain K.R.** 1938–1992
(Canterbury) 1959
(Auckland) 1960
(Canterbury) 1961
(Hawke's Bay) 1962–63–64–65–
66–67–68    86   (38)
**Trevathan D.** 1912–1986
(Otago) 1937    3   (3)
**Tuck J.M.** 1907–1967
(Waikato) 1929    6   (3)
**Tuiali'i M.M.** 1981–
(Auckland) 2004–05–06    10   (9)
**Tuigamala V.L.** 1969–
(Auckland) 1989–90–91–92–93    39   (19)

**Tuipulotu P.T.** 1993–
(Blues) 2014–16–17    18   (16)
**Tuitavake A.S.M.** 1982–
(North Harbour) 2008    7   (6)
**Tuitupou S.** 1982–
(Auckland) 2004–06    9   (9)
**Tunnicliff R.G.** 1894–1973
(Buller) 1923    1   (–)
**Turnbull J.S.** 1898–1947
(Otago) 1921    1   (–)
**Turner R.S.** 1968–
(North Harbour) 1992    2   (2)
**Turtill H.S.*** 1880–1918
(Canterbury) 1905    1   (1)
**Tu'ungafasi A.O.H.M.** 1992–
(Blues) 2016–17    16   (14)
**Twigden T.M.** 1952–
(Auckland) 1979–80    15   (2)
**Tyler G.A.** 1879–1942
(Auckland) 1903–04–05–06    36   (7)

**Udy D.K.** 1874–1935
(Wairarapa) 1901–03    9   (1)
**Udy H.** 1860–1933
(Wellington) 1884    8   (–)
**Umaga J.F.** 1973–
(Wellington) 1997–99–2000–01–
02–03–04–05    79   (74)
**Urbahn R.J.** 1934–1984
(Taranaki) 1959–60    15   (3)
**Urlich R.A.** 1944–
(Auckland) 1970–72–73    35   (2)
**Uttley I.N.** 1941–2015
(Wellington) 1963    2   (2)

**Valli G.T.** 1954–
(Southland) 1980    1   (–)
**Vanisi O.K.** 1972–
(Wellington) 1999    1   (–)
**Vidiri J.** 1973–
(Counties Manukau) 1998    2   (2)
**Vincent P.B.** 1926–1983
(Canterbury) 1956    2   (2)
**Vito V.V.J.** 1987–
(Wellington) 2010–11–12
(Hurricanes) 2013–14–15    33   (33)
**Vodanovich I.M.H.** 1930–1995
(Wellington) 1955    3   (3)
**Vorrath F.H.** 1908–1972
(Otago) 1935–36    12   (–)

**Waldrom S.L.** 1980–
(Taranaki) 2008    1   (–)
**Wallace W.J.** 1878–1972
(Wellington) 1903–04–05–06–
07–08    51   (11)
**Waller D.A.G.** 1974–
(Wellington) 2001    3   (1)
**Walsh P.T.** 1936–2007
(Counties) 1955–56–57–58–59–
63–64    27   (13)

**Walter J.** 1904–1966
(Taranaki) 1925 | 7 | (–)
**Warbrick J.A.** 1862–1903
(Auckland) 1884 | 7 | (–)
**Ward E.P.** 1899–1958
(Taranaki) 1928 | 10 | (–)
**Ward F.G.** 1900–1990
(Otago) 1921 | 1 | (–)
**Ward R.H.** 1915–2000
(Southland) 1936–37 | 4 | (3)
**Waterman A.C.** 1903–1997
(North Auckland) 1929 | 7 | (2)
**Watkins E.L.** 1880–1949
(Wellington) 1905 | 1 | (1)
**Watson J.D.** 1872–1958
(Taranaki) 1896 | 1 | (–)
**Watson W.D.** 1869–1953
(Wairarapa) 1893–96 | 3 | (–)
**Watt B.A.** 1939–
(Canterbury) 1962–63–64 | 29 | (8)
**Watt J.M.** 1914–1988
(Otago) 1936 | 2 | (2)
**Watt J.R.** 1935–
(Southland) 1957
(Wellington) 1958–60–61–62 | 42 | (9)
**Watts M.G.** 1955–
(Taranaki) 1979–80 | 13 | (5)
**Webb D.S.** 1934–1987
(North Auckland) 1959 | 1 | (1)
**Webb P.P.** 1854–1920
(Wellington) 1884 | 8 | (–)
**Weber B.M.** 1991
(Chiefs) 2015 | 1 | (1)
**Webster T.R.D.** 1920–1972
(Southland) 1947 | 4 | (–)
**Weepu P.A.T.** 1983–
(Wellington) 2004–05–06–07–08–
09–10–11–12
(Blues) 2013 | 73 | (71)
**Wells J.** 1908–1994
(Wellington) 1936 | 3 | (2)
**Wells W.J.G.** 1867–1911
(Taranaki) 1897 | 7 | (–)
**Wesney A.W.*** 1915–1941
(Southland) 1938 | 3 | (–)
**West A.H.** 1893–1934
(Taranaki) 1920–21–23–24–25 | 24 | (2)
**Weston L.H.** 1892–1963
(Auckland) 1914 | 1 | (–)
**Whetton A.J.** 1959–
(Auckland) 1984–85–86–87–88–
89–90–91 | 65 | (35)
**Whetton G.W.** 1959–
(Auckland) 1981–82–83–84–85–
86–87–88–89–90–91 | 101 | (58)
**Whineray W.J.** 1935–2012
(Canterbury) 1957
(Waikato) 1958
(Auckland) 1959–60–61–62–63–
64–65 | 77 | (32)

**White A.** 1894–1968
(Southland) 1921–22–23–24–25 | 38 | (4)
**White H.L.** 1929–2016
(Auckland) 1953–54–55 | 16 | (4)
**White R.A.** 1925–2012
(Poverty Bay) 1949–50–51–52–
53–54–55–56 | 55 | (23)
**White R.M.** 1917–1980
(Wellington) 1946–47 | 10 | (4)
**Whitelock G.B.** 1986–
(Canterbury) 2009 | 1 | (1)
**Whitelock L.C.** 1991–
(Crusaders) 2013–17 | 3 | (2)
**Whitelock S.L.** 1988–
(Canterbury) 2010–11–12
(Crusaders) 2013–14–15–16–17 | 96 | (96)
**Whiting G.J.** 1946–
(King Country) 1972–73 | 31 | (6)
**Whiting P.J.** 1946–
(Auckland) 1971–72–73–74–76 | 56 | (20)
**Wickes C.D.** 1962–
(Manawatu) 1980 | 1 | (–)
**Wightman D.R.** 1929–2012
(Auckland) 1951 | 4 | (–)
**Williams A.J.** 1981–
(Auckland) 2002–03–04–05–06–07–
08–11–12 | 78 | (77)
**Williams A.L.** 1898–1972
(Otago) 1922–23 | 9 | (–)
**Williams B.G.** 1950–
(Auckland) 1970–71–72–73–74–
75–76–77–78 | 113 | (38)
**Williams C.W.** 1916–1998
(Canterbury) 1938 | 4 | (–)
**Williams G.C.** 1945–
(Wellington) 1967–68 | 18 | (5)
**Williams P.** 1884–1976
(Otago) 1913 | 9 | (1)
**Williams R.N.** 1909–2001
(Hawke's Bay) 1932 | 1 | (–)
**Williams R.O.** 1963–
(North Harbour) 1988–89 | 10 | (–)
**Williams S.** 1985–
(Canterbury) 2010–1–12
(Chiefs) 2014–15 | 33 | (33)
(Blues) 2017 | 46 | (46)
**Williment M.** 1940–1994
(Wellington) 1964–65–66–67 | 9 | (9)
**Willis R.K.** 1975–
(Waikato) 1998–99–2002 | 12 | (12)
**Willis T.E.** 1979–
(Otago) 2001–02 | 7 | (5)
**Willocks C.** 1919–1991
(Otago) 1946–47–49 | 22 | (5)
**Willoughby S. de L.P.** 1904–1985
(Wairarapa) 1928 | 4 | (–)
**Wills M.C.** 1941–
(Taranaki) 1967 | 5 | (–)
**Wilson A.** 1874–1932
(Auckland) 1897 | 8 | (–)

**Wilson A.L.** 1927–2009
(Southland) 1951 — 7 (–)
**Wilson B.W.** 1956–
(Otago) 1977–78–79 — 12 (8)
**Wilson D.D.** 1931–
(Canterbury) 1953–54 — 14 (2)
**Wilson F.R.** ★ 1885–1916
(Auckland) 1910 — 2 (–)
**Wilson H.B.** 1957–
(Counties) 1983 — 3 (–)
**Wilson H.C.** 1868–1945
(Wellington) 1893 — 7 (–)
**Wilson H.W.** 1924–2004
(Otago) 1949–50–51 — 13 (5)
**Wilson J.W.** 1973–
(Otago) 1993–94–95–96–97–98–
99–2001 — 71 (60)
**Wilson N.A.** 1886–1953
(Wellington) 1908–10–13–14 — 21 (10)
**Wilson N.L.** 1922–2001
(Otago) 1949–51 — 20 (3)
**Wilson R.G.** 1953–
(Canterbury) 1976–78–79–80 — 25 (2)
**Wilson R.J.** 1861–1944
(Canterbury) 1884 — 6 (–)
**Wilson S.S.** 1954–
(Wellington)
1976–77–78–79–80–81–82–83 — 85 (34)
**Wilson V.W.** 1899–1978
(Auckland) 1920 — 7 (–)
**Wise G.D.** 1904–1971
(Otago) 1925 — 7 (–)
**Witcombe D.J.C.** 1978–
(Auckland) 2005 — 5 (5)
**Wolfe T.N.** 1941–
(Wellington) 1961–62
(Taranaki) 1963–68 — 14 (6)
**Wood M.E.** 1876–1956
(Wellington) 1901
(Canterbury) 1903
(Auckland) 1904 — 12 (2)
**Woodcock T.D.** 1981–
(North Harbour) 2002–04–05–06–
07–08–09–10–11–12
(Highlanders) 2013
(Blues) 2014–15 — 118 (118)

**Woodman F.A.** 1958–
(North Auckland) 1980–81 — 14 (3)
**Woodman T.B.K.** 1960–
(North Auckland) 1984 — 6 (–)
**Woods C.A.** 1929–
(Southland) 1953–54 — 14 (–)
**Wright A.H.** 1914–1990
(Wellington) 1938 — 4 (–)
**Wright D.H.** 1902–1966
(Auckland) 1925 — 7 (–)
**Wright T.J.** 1963–
(Auckland) 1986–87–88–89–90–
91–92 — 64 (30)
**Wright W.A.** 1905–1971
(Auckland) 1926 — 1 (–)
**Wrigley E.** 1886–1958
(Wairarapa) 1905 — 1 (1)
**Wulf R.N.** 1984–
(North Harbour) 2008 — 4 (4)
**Wylie J.T.** 1887–1956
(Auckland) 1913 — 12 (2)
**Wyllie A.J.** 1944–
(Canterbury) 1970–71–72–73 — 40 (11)
**Wyllie T.** 1954–
(Wellington) 1980 — 1 (–)
**Wynyard J.G.** ★ 1914–1942
(Waikato) 1935–36–38 — 13 (–)
**Wynyard W.T.** 1867–1938
(Wellington) 1893 — 7 (–)

**Yates V.M.** 1939–2008
(North Auckland) 1961–62 — 9 (3)
**Young D.** 1930–
(Canterbury) 1956–57–58–60–
61–62–63–64 — 61 (22)
**Young F.B.** 1874–1946
(Wellington) 1896 — 1 (–)

# NZR ANNUAL AWARDS

Since 1994 the NZRU has hosted, at the end of each year, an annual awards function to honour players, personalities and teams. With the exception of the Tom French Cup all trophies were new. The Tom French Cup had been presented in 1949 by Mr J. Morris of Sydney, following the New Zealand Maori tour of Australia, in honour of the team's coach Mr T.A. French. The trophy has been awarded to the outstanding Maori player each season.

## PLAYER OF THE YEAR
### Kelvin Tremain Memorial Trophy

| | |
|---|---|
| 1994 | Zinzan Brooke (*Auckland*) |
| 1995 | Jonah Lomu (*Counties*) |
| 1996 | Sean Fitzpatrick (*Auckland*) |
| 1997 | Jeff Wilson (*Otago*) |
| 1998 | Josh Kronfeld (*Otago*) |
| 1999 | Andrew Mehrtens (*Canterbury*) |
| 2000 | Tana Umaga (*Wellington*) |
| 2001 | Todd Blackadder (*Canterbury*) |
| 2002 | Chris Jack (*Canterbury*) |
| 2003 | Richard McCaw (*Canterbury*) |
| 2004 | Daniel Carter (*Canterbury*) |
| 2005 | Daniel Carter (*Canterbury*) |
| 2006 | Richard McCaw (*Canterbury*) |
| 2007 | Daniel Braid (*Auckland*) |
| 2008 | Andrew Hore (*Taranaki*) |
| 2009 | Richard McCaw (*Canterbury*) |
| 2010 | Kieran Read (*Canterbury*) |
| 2011 | Jerome Kaino (*Auckland*) |
| 2012 | Richie McCaw (*Canterbury*) |
| 2013 | Kieran Read (*Canterbury*) |
| 2014 | Brodie Retallick (*Waikato*) |
| 2015 | Ma'a Nonu (*Wellington*) |
| 2016 | Beauden Barrett (*Taranaki*) |
| 2017 | Samuel Whitelock (*Canterbury*) |

## SUPER RUGBY PLAYER OF THE YEAR

| | |
|---|---|
| 1996 | Joeli Vidiri (*Blues*) |
| 1997 | Christian Cullen (*Hurricanes*) |
| 1998 | Andrew Mehrtens (*Crusaders*) |
| 1999 | Byron Kelleher (*Highlanders*) |
| 2000 | Scott Robertson (*Crusaders*) |
| 2001 | Deon Muir (*Chiefs*) |
| 2002 | Chris Jack (*Crusaders*) |
| 2003 | Carlos Spencer (*Blues*) |
| 2004 | Daniel Carter (*Crusaders*) |
| 2005 | Rico Gear (*Crusaders*) |
| 2006 | Daniel Carter (*Crusaders*) |
| 2007 | James Cowan (*Highlanders*) |
| 2008 | Andrew Hore (*Hurricanes*) |
| 2009 | Mils Muliaina (*Chiefs*) |
| 2010 | Alby Mathewson (*Blues*) |
| 2011 | Wyatt Crockett (*Crusaders*) |
| 2012 | Conrad Smith (*Hurricanes*) |

| | |
|---|---|
| 2013 | Ben Smith (*Highlanders*) |
| 2014 | Jerome Kaino (*Blues*) |
| 2015 | Lima Sopoaga (*Highlanders*) |
| 2016 | Beauden Barrett (*Hurricanes*) |
| 2017 | Samuel Whitelock (*Crusaders*) |

## TEAM OF THE YEAR

| | |
|---|---|
| 2000 | New Zealand Under 21 |
| 2001 | Canterbury |
| 2002 | New Zealand Sevens |
| 2003 | All Blacks |
| 2004 | Canterbury |
| 2005 | All Blacks |
| 2006 | All Blacks |
| 2007 | Auckland |
| 2008 | All Blacks |
| 2009 | Canterbury |
| 2010 | Black Ferns |
| 2011 | All Blacks |
| 2012 | All Blacks |
| 2013 | All Blacks |
| 2014 | All Blacks |
| 2015 | All Blacks |
| 2016 | All Blacks |
| 2017 | Black Ferns |

## PREMIER DIVISION PLAYER OF THE YEAR
### Duane Monkley Medal
#### from 2017

| | |
|---|---|
| 2006 | Richard Kahui (*Waikato*) |
| 2007 | Isa Nacewa (*Auckland*) |
| 2008 | Jamie Mackintosh (*Southland*) |
| 2009 | Mike Delany (*Bay of Plenty*) |
| 2010 | Robbie Fruean (*Canterbury*) |
| 2011 | Aaron Cruden (*Manawatu*) |
| 2012 | Robbie Fruean (*Canterbury*) |
| 2013 | Andy Ellis (*Canterbury*) |
| 2014 | Seta Tamanivalu (*Taranaki*) |
| 2015 | George Moala (*Auckland*) |
| 2016 | Jordie Barrett (*Canterbury*) |
| 2017 | Jack Goodhue (*Northland*) |

## HEARTLAND CHAMPIONSHIP PLAYER OF THE YEAR

| | |
|---|---|
| 2006 | Scott Leighton (*Poverty Bay*) |
| 2007 | Ross Hay (*North Otago*) |
| 2008 | Cameron Crowley (*Wanganui*) |
| 2009 | Asaeli Tikoirotuma (*Wanganui*) |
| 2010 | Peter Rowe (*Wanganui*) |
| 2011 | Jon Smyth (*Wanganui*) |
| 2012 | Peter Rowe (*Wanganui*) |
| 2013 | Jon Dampney (*Mid Canterbury*) |
| 2014 | James Lash (*Buller*) |
| 2015 | Lindsay Horrocks (*Wanganui*) |
| 2016 | Te Rangatira Waitokia (*Wanganui*) |
| 2017 | Scott Cameron (*Horowhenua Kapiti*) |

## MAORI PLAYER OF THE YEAR
### Tom French Cup

| | |
|---|---|
| 1949 | Johnny Smith (*North Auckland*) |
| 1950 | Manahi Paewai (*North Auckland*) |
| 1951 | Percy Erceg (*Auckland*) |
| 1952 | Keith Davis (*Auckland*) |
| 1953 | Keith Davis (*Auckland*) |
| 1954 | Keith Davis (*Auckland*) |
| 1955 | Pat Walsh (*South Auckland*) |
| 1956 | Bill Gray (*Bay of Plenty*) |
| 1957 | Muru Walters (*North Auckland*) |
| 1958 | Pat Walsh (*Counties*) |
| 1959 | Bill Wordley (*King Country*) |
| 1960 | Mac Herewini (*Auckland*) |
| 1961 | Victor Yates (*North Auckland*) |
| 1962 | Waka Nathan (*Auckland*) |
| 1963 | Mac Herewini (*Auckland*) |
| 1964 | Ron Rangi (*Auckland*) |
| 1965 | Ron Rangi (*Auckland*) |
| 1966 | Waka Nathan (*Auckland*) |
| 1967 | Sid Going (*North Auckland*) |
| 1968 | Sid Going (*North Auckland*) |
| 1969 | Sid Going (*North Auckland*) |
| 1970 | Sid Going (*North Auckland*) |
| 1971 | Sid Going (*North Auckland*) |
| 1972 | Sid Going (*North Auckland*) |
| 1973 | Tane Norton (*Canterbury*) |
| 1974 | Tane Norton (*Canterbury*) |
| 1975 | Bill Bush (*Canterbury*) |
| 1976 | Kent Lambert (*Manawatu*) |
| 1977 | Bill Osborne (*Wanganui*) |
| 1978 | Eddie Dunn (*North Auckland*) |
| 1979 | Vance Stewart (*Canterbury*) |
| 1980 | Hika Reid (*Bay of Plenty*) |
| 1981 | Frank Shelford (*Bay of Plenty*) |
| 1982 | Steven Pokere (*Southland*) |
| 1983 | Hika Reid (*Bay of Plenty*) |
| 1984 | Michael Clamp (*Wellington*) |
| 1985 | Wayne Shelford (*North Harbour*) |
| 1986 | Frano Botica (*North Harbour*) |
| 1987 | Wayne Shelford (*North Harbour*) |
| 1988 | Wayne Shelford (*North Harbour*) |
| 1989 | Wayne Shelford (*North Harbour*) |
| 1990 | Steve McDowell (*Auckland*) |
| 1991 | John Timu (*Otago*) |
| 1992 | Zinzan Brooke (*Auckland*) |
| 1993 | Arran Pene (*Otago*) |
| 1994 | Zinzan Brooke (*Auckland*) |
| 1995 | Robin Brooke (*Auckland*) |
| 1996 | Errol Brain (*Counties Manukau*) |
| 1997 | Mark Mayerhofler (*Canterbury*) |
| 1998 | Tony Brown (*Otago*) |
| 1999 | Norman Maxwell (*Canterbury*) |
| 2000 | Daryl Gibson (*Canterbury*) |
| 2001 | Caleb Ralph (*Canterbury*) |
| 2002 | Carlos Spencer (*Auckland*) |
| 2003 | Carlos Spencer (*Auckland*) |
| 2004 | Carl Hayman (*Otago*) |
| 2005 | Rico Gear (*Nelson Bays*) |
| 2006 | Carl Hayman (*Otago*) |
| 2007 | Daniel Braid (*Auckland*) |
| 2008 | Piri Weepu (*Wellington*) |
| 2009 | Zac Guildford (*Hawke's Bay*) |
| 2010 | Hosea Gear (*Wellington*) |
| 2011 | Piri Weepu (*Wellington*) |
| 2012 | Liam Messam (*Waikato*) |
| 2013 | Liam Messam (*Waikato*) |
| 2014 | Aaron Smith (*Manawatu*) |
| 2015 | Nehe Milner-Skudder (*Manawatu*) |
| 2016 | Dane Coles (*Wellington*) |
| 2017 | Rieko Ioane (*Auckland*) |

## NZ RUGBY PLAYERS' ASSN KIRK AWARD

| | |
|---|---|
| 2016 | Justin Collins (*Northland*) |
| 2017 | DJ Forbes (*Counties Manukau*) |

## AGE GRADE PLAYER OF THE YEAR

| | |
|---|---|
| 1994 | Taine Randell (*Otago*) |
| 1995 | Anton Oliver (*Otago*) |
| 1996 | Andrew Blowers (*Auckland*) |
| 1997 | Norman Maxwell (*Northland*) |
| 1998 | Doug Howlett (*Auckland*) |
| 1999 | Samiu Vahafolau (*Auckland*) |
| 2000 | Ben Blair (*Canterbury*) |
| 2001 | *Under 21* |
| | Richard McCaw (*Canterbury*) |
| | *Under 19* |
| | Sam Tuitupou (*Auckland*) |
| 2002 | Luke McAlister (*North Harbour*) |

| | |
|---|---|
| 2003 | Ben Atiga (*Auckland*) |
| 2004 | Jerome Kaino (*Auckland*) |
| 2005 | Isaia Toeava (*Auckland*) |
| 2006 | Michael Paterson (*Canterbury*) |
| 2007 | Zac Guildford (*Hawke's Bay*) |
| 2008 | Zac Guildford (*Hawke's Bay*) |
| 2009 | Aaron Cruden (*Manawatu*) |
| 2010 | Liaki Moli (*Auckland*) |
| 2011 | Sam Cane (*Bay of Plenty*) |
| 2012 | Jason Emery (*Manawatu*) |
| 2013 | Ardie Savea (*Wellington*) |
| 2014 | Damian McKenzie (*Waikato*) |
| 2015 | Akira Ioane (*Auckland*) |
| 2016 | Jordie Barrett (*Canterbury*) |
| 2017 | Asafo Aumua (*Wellington*) |

## SEVENS
## PLAYER OF THE YEAR
**Richard Crawshaw Memorial Trophy
from 1998**

| | |
|---|---|
| 1994 | Eric Rush (*North Harbour*) |
| 1995 | Jonah Lomu (*Counties*) |
| 1996 | Christian Cullen (*Manawatu*) |
| 1997 | Caleb Ralph (*Bay of Plenty*) |
| 1998 | Rico Gear (*Auckland*) |
| 1999 | Orene Ai'i (*Auckland*) |
| 2000 | Karl Te Nana (*North Harbour*) |
| 2001 | Karl Te Nana (*North Harbour*) |
| 2002 | Chris Masoe (*Taranaki*) |
| 2003 | Eric Rush (*North Harbour*) |
| 2004 | Liam Messam (*Waikato*) |
| 2005 | Amasio Valence (*Hawke's Bay*) |
| 2006 | Tafai Ioasa (*Hawke's Bay*) |
| 2007 | D.J. Forbes (*Auckland*) |
| 2008 | D.J. Forbes (*Counties Manukau*) |
| 2009 | Zar Lawrence (*Bay of Plenty*) |
| 2010 | Kurt Baker (*Taranaki*) |
| 2011 | Tim Mikkelson (*Waikato*) |
| 2012 | Tomasi Cama (*Manawatu*) |
| 2013 | Kurt Baker (*Taranaki*) |
| 2014 | DJ Forbes (*Counties Manukau*) |
| 2015 | Scott Curry (*Bay of Plenty*) |
| 2016 | Rieko Ioane (*Auckland*) |
| 2017 | DJ Forbes (*Counties Manukau*) |

## WOMEN'S
## PLAYER OF THE YEAR

| | |
|---|---|
| 1994 | Anna Richards (*Auckland*) |
| 1995 | Rochelle Martin (*Wellington*) |
| 1996 | Vanessa Cootes (*Waikato*) |
| 1997 | Louisa Wall (*Auckland*) |
| 1998 | Farah Palmer (*Otago*) |
| 1999 | Suzanne Shortland (*Auckland*) |
| 2000 | Fiona King (*Otago*) |

| | |
|---|---|
| 2001 | Annaleah Rush (*Auckland*) |
| 2002 | Monique Hirovanaa (*Auckland*) |
| 2003 | Monalisa Codling (*Auckland*) |
| 2004 | Stephanie Mortimer (*Canterbury*) |
| 2005 | Melissa Ruscoe (*Canterbury*) |
| 2006 | Amiria Marsh (*Canterbury*) |
| 2007 | Victoria Heighway (*Auckland*) |
| 2008 | Victoria Grant (*Auckland*) |
| 2009 | Victoria Heighway (*Auckland*) |
| 2010 | Carla Hohepa (*Otago*) |
| 2011 | Fiao'o Faamausili (*Auckland*) |
| 2012 | Rawinia Everitt (*Auckland*) |
| 2013 | Kelly Brazier (*Otago*) |
| 2014 | Rawinia Everitt (*Counties Manukau*) |
| 2015 | Kendra Cocksedge (*Canterbury*) |
| 2016 | Selica Winiata (*Manawatu*) |
| 2017 | Sarah Goss (*Manawatu*) |

## FARAH PALMER CUP
## PLAYER OF THE YEAR
**Fiao'o Faamausili Medal**

| | |
|---|---|
| 2017 | Hazel Tubic (*Counties Manukau*) |

## WOMEN'S SEVENS PLAYER
## OF THE YEAR

| | |
|---|---|
| 2013 | Portia Woodman (*Auckland*) |
| 2014 | Sarah Goss (*Manawatu*) |
| 2015 | Tyla Nathan-Wong (*Auckland*) |
| 2016 | Sarah Goss (*Manawatu*) |
| 2017 | Ruby Tui (*Canterbury*) |

## COACH OF THE YEAR

| | |
|---|---|
| 1994 | Brad Meurant (*North Harbour*) |
| 1995 | Graham Henry (*Auckland*) |
| 1996 | John Hart (*All Blacks*) |
| 2001 | Colin Cooper (*New Zealand Under 21*) |
| 2002 | Robbie Deans (*Crusaders*) |
| 2003 | Wayne Pivac (*Auckland*) |
| 2004 | Vern Cotter (*Bay of Plenty*) |
| 2005 | Graham Henry (*All Blacks*) |
| 2006 | Graham Henry (*All Blacks*) |
| 2007 | Peter Russell (*Hawke's Bay*) |
| 2008 | Graham Henry (*All Blacks*) |
| 2009 | Dave Rennie (*New Zealand Under 20*) |
| 2010 | Gordon Tietjens (*New Zealand Sevens*) |
| 2011 | Graham Henry (*All Blacks*) |
| 2012 | Steve Hansen (*All Blacks*) |
| 2013 | Steve Hansen (*All Blacks*) |
| 2014 | Steve Hansen (*All Blacks*) |
| 2015 | Steve Hansen (*All Blacks*) |
| 2016 | Steve Hansen (*All Blacks*) |
| 2017 | Glenn Moore (*Black Ferns*) |

## REFEREE OF THE YEAR

| | |
|---|---|
| 1994 | Colin Hawke (*South Canterbury*) |
| 1995 | Paddy O'Brien (*Southland*) |
| 1996 | Paddy O'Brien (*Southland*) |
| 1997 | Steve Walsh jnr (*North Harbour*)* |
| 1998 | Paddy O'Brien (*Southland*) |
| 1999 | Colin Hawke (*South Canterbury*) |
| 2000 | Colin Hawke (*South Canterbury*) |
| 2001 | Kelvin Deaker (*Hawke's Bay*) |
| 2002 | Paddy O'Brien (*Southland*) |
| 2003 | Paddy O'Brien (*Southland*) |
| 2004 | Paddy O'Brien (*Southland*) |
| 2005 | Paul Honiss (*Waikato*) |
| 2006 | Paul Honiss (*Waikato*) |
| 2007 | Steve Walsh (*North Harbour*) |
| 2008 | Bryce Lawrence (*Bay of Plenty*) |
| 2009 | Bryce Lawrence (*Bay of Plenty*) |
| 2010 | Bryce Lawrence (*Bay of Plenty*) |
| 2011 | Bryce Lawrence (*Bay of Plenty*) |
| 2012 | Glen Jackson (*Bay of Plenty*) |
| 2013 | Chris Pollock (*Hawke's Bay*) |
| 2014 | Glen Jackson (*Bay of Plenty*) |
| 2015 | Glen Jackson (*Bay of Plenty*) |
| 2016 | Glen Jackson (*Bay of Plenty*) |
| 2017 | Ben O'Keeffe (*Wellington*) |

* for the Outstanding Referee Performance
(Canterbury v Auckland round robin match)

## STEINLAGER SALVER
### For outstanding service to rugby

| | |
|---|---|
| 1999 | Colin Meads |
| 2000 | Zinzan Brooke* |
| 2001 | Sir Terry McLean |
| 2002 | Fred Allen |
| 2003 | Sir Brian Lochore |
| 2004 | Peter Bush |
| 2005 | Richie Guy |
| 2006 | Stan Hill |
| 2007 | Ron Don |
| 2008 | Tane Norton |
| 2009 | John Graham |
| 2010 | Keith Quinn |
| 2011 | Jock Hobbs |
| 2012 | Ray Harper |
| 2013 | Graham Mourie |
| 2014 | Dick Littlejohn |
| 2015 | Mike Eagle |
| 2016 | Gavin Service |
| 2017 | Wayne Smith |

* celebrating 25 years of the NPC

## VOLUNTEER OF THE YEAR
### Charles Monro Memorial Trophy
### from 2009

| | |
|---|---|
| 2002 | John George (*Taranaki*) |
| 2003 | Ru Rangi (*Wellington*) |
| 2004 | Adelle Wakely (*Hawke's Bay*) |
| 2005 | Daphne Boden (*Hawke's Bay*) |
| 2006 | Jason Martin (*Otago*) |
| 2007 | Robbie Ball (*Northland*) |
| 2008 | Ken Swain (*Horowhenua Kapiti*) |
| 2009 | Blair Crawford (*Otago*) |
| 2010 | Hilton Williams (*Horowhenua Kapiti*) |
| 2011 | Andy MacDonald (*Canterbury*) |
| 2012 | Ray Watson (*Bay of Plenty*) |
| 2013 | Rob Jones (*Manawatu*) |
| 2014 | Dean File (*Horowhenua Kapiti*) |
| 2015 | Tania Karaitiana and |
| | Vio Ugone (*Wellington*) |
| 2016 | Gary Donovan (*Auckland*) |
| 2017 | Sid Tatana (*Wairarapa Bush*) |

## SKY FANS TRY OF THE YEAR

| | |
|---|---|
| 2013 | Selica Winiata (*Black Ferns*) |
| 2014 | Malakai Fekitoa (*Highlanders*) |
| 2015 | Samu Kubunavanua (*Wanganui*) |
| 2016 | Isaiah Punivai (*Christ's College*) |
| 2017 | Portia Woodman (*Black Ferns*) |

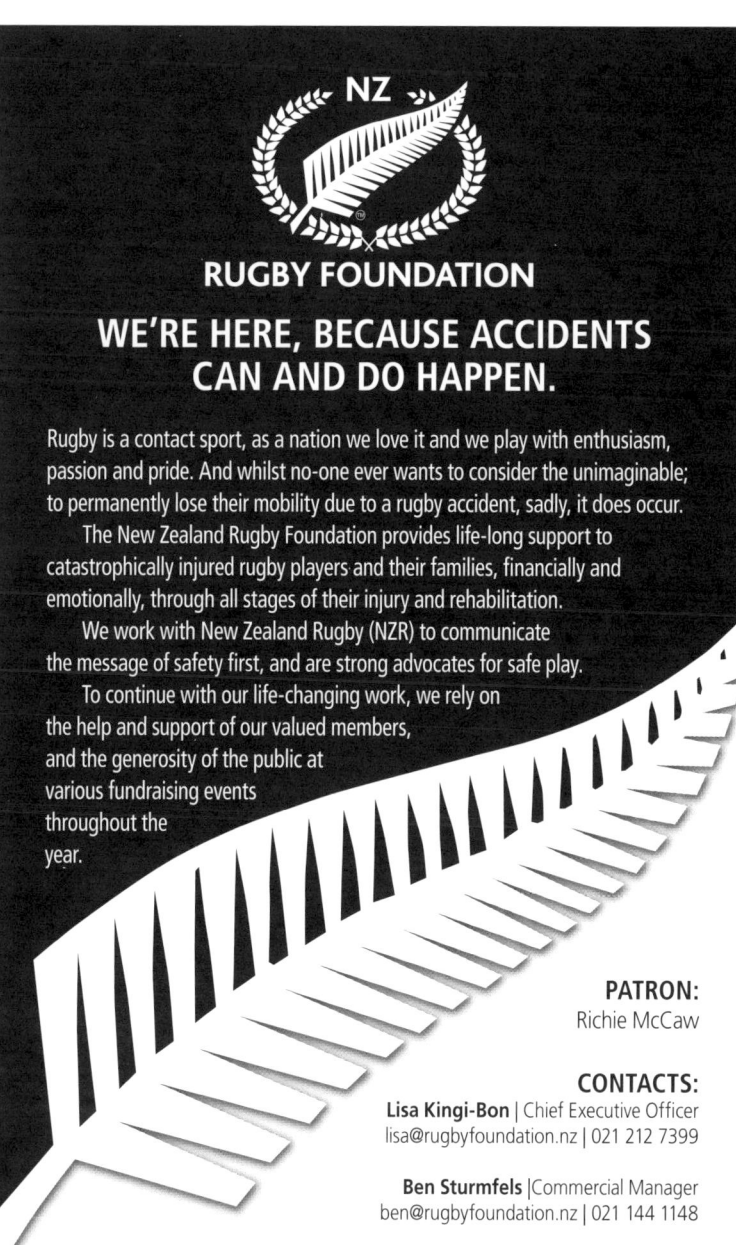

## RUGBY FOUNDATION

# WE'RE HERE, BECAUSE ACCIDENTS CAN AND DO HAPPEN.

Rugby is a contact sport, as a nation we love it and we play with enthusiasm, passion and pride. And whilst no-one ever wants to consider the unimaginable; to permanently lose their mobility due to a rugby accident, sadly, it does occur.

The New Zealand Rugby Foundation provides life-long support to catastrophically injured rugby players and their families, financially and emotionally, through all stages of their injury and rehabilitation.

We work with New Zealand Rugby (NZR) to communicate the message of safety first, and are strong advocates for safe play.

To continue with our life-changing work, we rely on the help and support of our valued members, and the generosity of the public at various fundraising events throughout the year.

**PATRON:**
Richie McCaw

**CONTACTS:**
**Lisa Kingi-Bon** | Chief Executive Officer
lisa@rugbyfoundation.nz | 021 212 7399

**Ben Sturmfels** |Commercial Manager
ben@rugbyfoundation.nz | 021 144 1148

## www.rugbyfoundation.nz

# OBITUARIES

## *NEW ZEALAND REPRESENTATIVES*

**Peter Standish Burke** *(Bay of Plenty and Taranaki)* toured Australia in 1951 but didn't receive a recall until 1955when he made his test debut in the third test against Australia at Wellington. Not required for the 1956 Springbok series, he returned in 1957 for his second tour across the Tasman where he played in both tests. His provincial career spanned 14 seasons and his omission from the 1953/54 tour to Britain was considered to be a surprise as he had performed well at lock during the trials including scoring four tries, one during the inter-island fixture. The *Almanack* noted, 'Burke appeared to be certain of New Zealand selection once more, and must surely be one of the unluckiest players in the country.'

Burke made his first-class debut in 1946 with an appearance for Bay of Plenty. The 18-year-old marked the occasion by kicking a conversion. After a season in Auckland where he represented the B team, Burke settled in Taranaki in 1948 and commenced his 117-game career with the union. On his form of 1950 the *Almanack* commented on him being 'a first-class prospect for the near future'. In May 1951 he appeared in the trials and was appointed captain of the North Island team that defeated South Island. He played as a flanker in that game and All Blacks selection followed, and in Australia all his games were at lock.

From 1954 through until retiring at the end of 1959, Burke was the regular Taranaki captain, the undoubted highlight being the winning of the Ranfurly Shield late in 1957 and retaining the trophy until 1959. His All Blacks career may well have been extended had he not made himself unavailable for international rugby in 1958. When Taranaki union celebrated its 125th anniversary, 1885–2010, a Dream Team was chosen from past representatives and Burke was selected as the number eight.

Having retired from active rugby in 1959 at the age of 32, Burke was immediately elected onto the union's three-man selection panel in 1960, a position he held for nine years and which included a second golden era of the Ranfurly Shield, 1963–65. In 1970 he was promoted to the North Island selection panel then the New Zealand panel in 1978 and he coached several national Colts and Juniors teams.

As All Blacks coach during 1981–82 his teams played 11 tests for nine wins and two losses. The series win during the controversial Springboks tour was followed by a tour to Romania and France late in the year. In 1982 the All Blacks won the three-test series against the visiting Wallabies.

Burke was a life member of Taranaki Rugby Union and president in 1989. He was president of NZRFU 1994 and made a life member in 2008 and served on the union's Appeal Council for several years. In 1997 he was made an Officer of the NZ Order of Merit (ONZM) for services to rugby.

Peter Burke's first-class record:

| For | Matches | Tries | Con | PG | Points |
|---|---|---|---|---|---|
| Bay of Plenty (Edgecumbe) 1946 | 1 | – | 1 | – | 2 |
| Taranaki (Stratford) 1948(7), 1949(7), 1950(7), 1951(9) (Tukapa) 1952(10), 1953(9), 1954(13) (Hawera) 1955(6), 1956(13), 1957(8), 1958(16), 1959(12) | 117 | 6 | 5 | 3 | 37 |
| Auckland B (Marist) 1947 | 2 | – | – | – | 0 |
| Barbarians Club 1953 | 1 | – | – | – | 0 |
| Centurions Club 1955, 1956, 1957, 1961 | 4 | – | – | – | 0 |
| Evergreens Club 1958 | 1 | – | – | – | 0 |

| | | | | | |
|---|---|---|---|---|---|
| P.S. Burke's XV 1959 | 1 | – | – | – | 0 |
| North Island XV 1956 | 1 | – | – | – | 0 |
| North Island 1951, 1952, 1953, 1954, 1957 | 5 | 1 | – | – | 3 |
| New Zealand Trials 1951, 1953(3), 1956, 1957(2) | 7 | 3 | – | – | 9 |
| White XV 1957 | 1 | – | – | 1 | 3 |
| Rest of New Zealand 1954, 1955 | 2 | – | – | – | 0 |
| New Zealand XV 1955, 1956 | 2 | – | – | – | 0 |
| NEW ZEALAND 1951(6), 1955, 1957(5) | 12 | 2 | – | – | 6 |
| **TOTALS** | **157** | **12** | **6** | **4** | **60** |

At New Plymouth, 2 October 2017, aged 90.

**Thomas Desmond Coughlan** *(South Canterbury and King Country)* was in his seventh year of provincial rugby when chosen for the first test against Australia, at Wellington, in 1958, yet he was aged only 24. New Zealand comfortably won 25–3, but the flanker was dropped to the reserves for the second test and never required again.

Born in Dunedin on 30 April 1934 and completing his education at St Kevin's College, Oamaru, Tom Coughlan entered the South Canterbury rep team in 1952 when aged 18. The following year the teenager took part in trials for selection for the All Blacks tour to Britain. Although his career commenced at lock, most of his games were as a flanker and through to 1960 it was rare for the South Canterbury team to take the field without Coughlan. He was also a regular member of combined teams when neighbouring unions Mid Canterbury and North Otago joined forces with South Canterbury for games against Australia (1955), South Africa (1956) and British Isles (1959). Coughlan captained the rep team on numerous occasions from 1958. In 1961 he moved north and partnered the Meads brothers in the King Country forward pack.

Although he played in numerous trials and inter-island fixtures, Coughlan could be considered unlucky not to have worn the black jersey more often. Perhaps his chances would have been higher had he been playing in a major union.

Tom Coughlan served as South Canterbury selector during 1973–74. Two sons also wore the New Zealand jersey. Tom representing NZ Colts and NZ Universities, and John was chosen for NZ Under 17 in 1982. John passed away unexpectedly in February 2017, aged 51.

Tom Coughlan's first-class record:

| For | Matches | Tries | Points |
|---|---|---|---|
| South Canterbury (Temuka) 1952(5), 1953(7), 1954(9), 1955(6), 1956(11), 1957(9), 1958(9), 1959(10), 1960(10) | 76 | 10 | 30 |
| King Country (Aria-Mokauiti) 1961 | 5 | – | 0 |
| Hanan Shield Unions 1955, 1956(3), 1959 | 5 | 1 | 3 |
| Hanan Shield Unions Trial 1957 | 1 | 1 | 3 |
| Cantabrians Club 1958 | 1 | – | 0 |
| South Island 1955, 1957, 1958, 1960 | 4 | – | 0 |

| New Zealand Trials 1953(3), 1956, 1957(2), 1958, 1959(3), 1960(3), 1961 | 14 | 5 | 15 |
|---|---|---|---|
| Rest of New Zealand 1960 | 1 | – | 0 |
| New Zealand XV 1955 | 1 | – | 0 |
| NEW ZEALAND 1958 | 1 | – | 0 |
| **TOTALS** | **109** | **17** | **51** |

At Christchurch, 9 November 2017, aged 83.

**David John Graham** KNZM, CBE, Ed *(Auckland and Canterbury)* was a distinguished All Black and three-test captain, but his contribution to New Zealand society had even more dimensions than that. He was one of the country's foremost educationists, an inspiring headmaster for 21 years of Auckland Boys' Grammar School and Chancellor of the University of Auckland.

Though justly proud of his rugby exploits, and with a lifelong devotion to the game, Graham's most enduring satisfactions were always with his educational achievements. Of considerable personal pride was the number of the young men who taught under him who became school principals. His 2011 knighthood was as much for his academic feats as his sporting. But while he became Sir John, he always preferred to be known as 'DJ' rather than his title. And while most of his life was spent in Auckland, he was essentially a New Zealander with significant ties to Waikato, Taranaki and Canterbury.

Born in Stratford on 1 January 1935, and raised on a Putaruru dairy farm, Graham came from a family with a deep rugby passion. His elder brother Jim, a prop, played in the powerful Waikato Ranfurly Shield teams of the 1950s and represented North Island in 1951–52–53–54. He, too, was knighted, for his services to the farming industry.

His younger brother Bob, though also missing All Black honours, was a fine loose forward who played more than 100 games for Auckland and was Auckland's captain for most of its 1960s Ranfurly Shield reign, often against John when he was leading Canterbury. All three boys boarded at New Plymouth Boys' High School where John in 1952 was head prefect and captain of the first XV. There he came under his first major rugby influence in a then member of the teaching staff, and first XV coach, JJ Stewart, another forthright, independent thinker.

In Auckland John Graham played in successful University club sides as a light, mobile loose forward. In 1955–57 he played in three winning Gallaher Shield teams and played 20 games for Auckland, as well as New Zealand Universities. Graduating with honours in history, he became a teacher at Christchurch Boys' High School and the bulk of his top rugby career was with Canterbury. He quickly made the Canterbury side and was in the All Blacks for the first two tests against the 1958 touring Wallabies. In the first test, Wilson Whineray's debut as captain, Graham scored a try.

He missed the 1959 series against the Lions, but helped Canterbury beat the tourists, forming a potent loose forward trio that season with Kel Tremain and Hugh Burry and winning a recall to the All Blacks for the 1960 tour of South Africa. He remained a constant selection for the All Blacks until 1964, finishing with 22 tests. In 1964, with Whineray unavailable, he captained the All Blacks in three tests against the touring Wallabies. His leadership qualities had been long obvious, and he was often captain in non-test matches on all his New Zealand tours and captained Canterbury from 1961 until retiring in 1965.

Graham returned to Auckland in 1972 to become the Grammar School's headmaster. Despite his high-profile educational role, he remained close to rugby, as he had been in Christchurch, through coaching and occasionally in the media.

In Auckland he was assistant coach to Eric Boggs in Auckland's 1974–76 shield reign, and he also helped John Hart when he coached the Waitemata club side. Then in 1992–93 he assisted another future All Black coach, his one-time pupil Graham Henry, with Auckland.

Never one to slavishly follow any set establishment line, Graham saw early the damage to rugby in trying to continue relations with apartheid South Africa and declined to attend matches on the 1981 Springbok tour. Yet he served in many administrative roles: on the Rugby Foundation, the secondary schools council, as Auckland union president in 1996–97 and New Zealand union president in 2005–06. He also managed the New Zealand cricket team in 1996–99.

Though firm in his views, he was a man of the utmost integrity and like his contemporary and friend, Whineray, Sir John Graham was an exceptional New Zealander. *(Obituary contributed by Lindsay Knight).*

John Graham's first-class record:

| For | Matches | Tries | Points |
| --- | --- | --- | --- |
| Auckland (Univ) 1956(13), 1957(7) | 20 | 9 | 27 |
| Canterbury (HSOB) 1958(13), 1959(11), 1960(2), 1961(12), 1962(12), 1963(11), 1964(9), 1965(8) | 78 | 13 | 39 |
| Auckland B 1955 | 1 | 1 | 3 |
| Barbarians Club 1955, 1964 | 2 | 1 | 3 |
| Evergreens Club 1962 | 1 | – | 0 |
| North Island Universities 1956, 1957 | 2 | – | 0 |
| New Zealand Universities 1957 | 1 | – | 0 |
| South Island 1958, 1961, 1962, 1963, 1964, 1965 | 6 | 1 | 3 |
| New Zealand Trials 1958, 1960(3), 1961(2), 1962(2), 1963(4), 1965 | 13 | 3 | 9 |
| White XV 1957 | 1 | 2 | 6 |
| Rest of New Zealand 1965 | 1 | – | 0 |
| New Zealand XV 1958 | 1 | 1 | 3 |
| NEW ZEALAND 1958(2), 1960(14), 1961(3), 1962(9), 1963(22), 1964(3) | 53 | 11 | 33 |
| *TOTALS* | *180* | *42* | *126* |

At Auckland, 2 August 2017, aged 82.

**Sione Tu'itupu Heimoana Lauaki** *(Auckland and Waikato)* was a big and powerful loose forward, playing in 17 tests, but he never commanded a regular place in the starting XV as 11 of his appearances were as a substitute. A powerful runner, he could use his 117 kg to devastating effect, but he lacked consistency in performance.

Born at Ha'apai, Tonga on 22 June 1981, at a young age Lauaki was brought to Auckland where he received all his education, finishing at Kelston Boys' High School where he was in the first XV, 1998–2000. After impressing at two World Under 21 tournaments (2001–02) he became a regular substitute with Auckland throughout the 2003 season and not having been picked up by the Blues franchise he joined the Chiefs for the 2004 Super 12. He played in the 2004 All Blacks trial in June then joined the Pacific Islands squad and was a flanker in each of the three tests, against the Wallabies, All Blacks and Springboks. Although on the losing side in each test, Lauaki scored a try in each game.

Good form during the 2005 Super 12 was followed by selection to the All Blacks squad. He made his debut off the bench against Fiji and was again a substitute during the first two tests against the touring Lions. He was given a start in the third test. On the end-of-year tour he played in the tests against Ireland and Scotland. Missing selection during 2006, Lauaki was recalled for the Rugby World Cup of 2007 and appeared in each of the four pool games. The year 2008 was to be his last in the All Blacks jersey, coming off the bench in six tests. The *Almanack* noted that 'It seems impossible to get 80 minutes of effort from Sione Lauaki otherwise he would be a world beater.'

Lauaki played with the Junior All Blacks in the Pacific Nations Cup in 2009 and had a final season with the Chiefs in 2010 then went to France and joined Clermont Auvergne club. In 2011 he moved to Bayonne club but was released the following year because of poor health. It was revealed that he was suffering renal failure and cardiovascular problems.

Sione Lauaki's first-class record:

| For | Matches | Tries | Points |
|---|---|---|---|
| Auckland (Waitemata) 2002(3), 2003(12), 2004(9) | 24 | 3 | 15 |
| Waikato (Te Awamutu Sports) 2005(3), 2006(10), 2007(2) (Morrinsville Sports) 2008(5), 2009 | 21 | 5 | 25 |
| New Zealand Under 21 2001(3), 2002(5) | 8 | 4 | 20 |
| Chiefs 2004(11), 2005(10), 2006(8), 2007(10), 2008(12), 2009(13), 2010(6) | 70 | 14 | 70 |
| New Zealand Trials 2004, 2005 | 2 | – | 0 |
| Junior All Blacks 2007(2), 2009(3) | 5 | 4 | 20 |
| NEW ZEALAND 2005(7), 2007(4), 2008(6) | 17 | 3 | 15 |
| **TOTALS** | **147** | **33** | **165** |

At Auckland, 12 February 2017, aged 35.

**Thomas Norman Lister** *(South Canterbury and Wellington)* died after a short battle with cancer. He was one of New Zealand's most outstanding loose forwards in the 1960s and 70s. A fast, aggressive flanker, Lister had a sporadic international career and managed just eight tests for the All Blacks in the 1968–71 seasons. But that was more a reflection of the high standard of back-row forwards in New Zealand rugby during his career. Among his contemporaries were other fine players like Kel Tremain, Brian Lochore, Waka Nathan, Ian Kirkpatrick, Graham Williams, Alan Sutherland and Alex Wyllie.

Lister had not been long out of Waitaki Boys' High School when aged 18 in 1962 he first played for South Canterbury, making such an impact that he was named among the *Rugby Almanack*'s five most promising players for that season. Further national honours came his way in 1964 when he toured Australia with a strong national under 23 side that was captained by Chris Laidlaw and included a number of others who were already All Blacks in Ian Smith, Bill Davis, Ian MacRae, Ray Moreton and Neil Wolfe.

In 1965 Lister transferred to Wellington and he and another of the 1964 under 23 side, hooker Terry McCashin, also a future All Black, joined the Athletic club, which that season under the captaincy of a fine All Black lock Nev MacEwan won the Jubilee Cup competition. Lister and McCashin also worked as rubbish collectors, a contrast to McCashin's later success as a brewery entrepreneur. However, it was an occupation of considerable benefit to their physical fitness.

In 1965–67 Lister played 40 games for Wellington, as part of a powerful pack that also included MacEwan and Ken Gray, and had an effective back-row trio in Lister, the equally promising Williams and Gary Hermansson. In 1965–66 the Bill Freeman-coached Wellington side achieved a notable double with wins over the Springboks and the Lions.

Lister was one of the unlucky omissions from the All Blacks who toured Britain and France in 1967, but was eventually rewarded with selection in the 1968 side that toured Australia. He played both tests on that tour and in the first against the touring French later that year. In 1969 he had another two tests against Wales, being preferred to Tremain, then in the twilight of his career, and in 1970 he toured South Africa, playing in the first and fourth tests. His final All Black appearance came in the 1971 fourth test against the British and Irish Lions when he scored his second test try.

Having dropped out of all rugby in 1972, Lister was never again an All Black. But he resumed playing for South Canterbury in 1973 and in 1974 helped his union to an upset Ranfurly Shield win over Marlborough. South Canterbury soon after lost the shield to Wellington but only after Lister had produced a stupendous performance that came close to snatching a draw. That performance earned Lister a recall to the South Island side for the inter-island match, but by then he was nearly 31 and that was to be his last major appearance.

Lister came from a distinguished sporting family, his younger brother John being a top professional golfer who won a major tournament on the United States circuit. *(Obituary contributed by Lindsay Knight)*.

Tom Lister's first-class record:

| For | Matches | Tries | Points |
|---|---|---|---|
| South Canterbury (HSOB) 1962(13), 1963(9), 1964(11), 1968(6), 1969(11), 1970(2), 1971(5), 1973(6), 1974(9) | 72 | 15 | 48 |
| Wellington (Athletic) 1965(14), 1966(14), 1967(12) | 40 | 7 | 21 |
| Hanan Shield Unions 1971 | 3 | – | 0 |
| Centurions Club 1964, 1970 | 2 | – | 0 |
| Wellington Invitation XV 1967 | 1 | – | 0 |
| New Zealand Colts Trial 1964 | 1 | – | 0 |
| New Zealand Colts 1964 | 4 | 1 | 3 |
| New Zealand Juniors 1965, 1966(2) | 3 | 1 | 3 |
| South Island 1968, 1969, 1971, 1974 | 4 | 1 | 3 |
| New Zealand Trials 1965(2), 1967(2), 1968, 1969, 1970(2), 1971(2) | 10 | 1 | 3 |
| NEW ZEALAND 1968(10), 1969(2), 1970(13), 1971 | 26 | 11 | 33 |
| *TOTALS* | *166* | *37* | *94* |

At Timaru, 23 July 2017, aged 73.

**Terence Michael McCashin** *(Horowhenua, Wellington, King Country and Marlborough)* was a rarity among All Blacks in that his celebrity status was due more to his achievements in the business world than for his exploits, worthy as they were, on the rugby field. After he had finished his playing career in the late 1970s, McCashin extended his involvement in the hotel industry to beer brewing and as such he was one of the early pioneers in establishing craft brewing in New Zealand. He thus helped revolutionise the drinking habits of New Zealanders, breaking some of the dominance of the two major breweries. Mac's Gold, at least in New Zealand, became as much a recognisable brand as Coca-Cola.

It was a remarkable rise for someone who in 1965 on moving to Wellington to further his rugby career had worked as a rubbish collector, along with another who became an All Black in Tom Lister and whose death preceded McCashin's by three months. The pair, who had been teammates on the 1964 tour of Australia with the New Zealand under 23 side, joined Athletic, which that season won the capital's premier club competition for the Jubilee Cup.

A product of Levin, McCashin made his first-class debut aged only 19 with Horowhenua in 1963, impressing so much that a season later he was chosen for an under 23 side that toured Australia and which included a number of players already All Blacks. After another representative season with Horowhenua, McCashin transferred to Wellington, but unlike Lister had difficulty breaking into a strong Wellington A side. His five first-class appearances in 1965 were limited to what was a competitive B selection, which won all its matches.

In 1966 he managed only one game for Wellington A, with another New Zealand Junior, Ken Grant, the preferred hooker. But he did appear for the national under 23s in their match against the touring Lions at Athletic Park and in 1967 became the first choice as well as having the first of his four All Black trials.

He won his All Black jersey on the 1968 tour of Australia and Fiji as the hooker understudy to Bruce McLeod. He made seven tour appearances. While he didn't win a cap, he was reserve in those days of stricter replacement rules to McLeod in the tests later that season against France and in 1969 against Wales. But soon after the tour of Australia the residential requirements then in force caused him to return to Horowhenua and perhaps playing a couple of seasons in a small union affected his international aspirations. In 1970, despite having been a test reserve in 1968–69, he was not even given a trial for the team to tour South Africa.

He was back with Wellington for a full 1970 representative season, but was never again a serious All Blacks contender. His work as a hotelier, which led to him becoming such a successful entrepreneur, took him to various New Zealand areas and reappearances in provincial rugby for King Country in 1972, including its match against the touring Wallabies, and Marlborough in 1977. *(Obituary contributed by Lindsay Knight).*

Terry McCashin's first-class record:

| For | Matches | Tries | Points |
|---|---|---|---|
| Horowhenua (Horowhenua COB) 1963(7), 1964(7), 1968(3), 1969(6) | 23 | 1 | 3 |
| Wellington (Athletic) 1966, 1967(14), 1970(20) | 35 | 4 | 12 |
| King Country (Piopio) 1972 | 11 | 1 | 4 |
| Marlborough (Waitohi) 1977 | 3 | – | 0 |
| Wellington B 1965 | 5 | – | 0 |
| Wellington Invitation XV 1967 | 1 | – | 0 |

| | | | |
|---|---|---|---|
| Centurions Club 1964 | 1 | – | 0 |
| New Zealand Colts Trial 1964 | 1 | – | 0 |
| New Zealand Colts 1964 | 3 | – | 0 |
| New Zealand Juniors 1966 | 2 | – | 0 |
| New Zealand Trials 1967(2), 1968, 1969 | 4 | 1 | 3 |
| NEW ZEALAND 1968 | 7 | 1 | 3 |
| **TOTALS** | **96** | **8** | **25** |

At Nelson, 31 October 2017, aged 73.

**Alasdair Lindsay Robert 'Sandy' McNicol** *(Wanganui)* was a 28-year-old prop who probably considered any chance of being an All Black had long gone. During the 1972/73 tour of Britain and France the All Blacks had lost Keith Murdoch who had been sent home and replaced by Lindsay Clark. Two weeks later, in mid-December, Jeff Matheson was badly injured in the test against Scotland. Tour management hesitated for a week, even considering the team could play the remaining 14 games with three props, before finally deciding that a second replacement prop was required. The call was made to the NZRFU on Christmas Eve for another prop. McNicol was about to sit down to Christmas dinner at his parents' home in Palmerston North when the union phoned him on Christmas Day. It is likely he is the only All Black to be informed of selection on Christmas Day.

Sandy McNicol was born at Lower Hutt on 15 June 1944 and received his secondary education at Onslow College (1958–60) and Whangarei Boys' High School 1961–62, playing at lock in the first XV both years. He was at Victoria University 1964–65, represented Wellington Colts and later, in 1968, Manawatu B. He returned to Whangarei and played for Waipu club before joining the army, where he was a teacher at Waiouru.

He made his first-class debut for Wanganui, coached by JJ Stewart, in 1970 and later in the year represented NZ Services, which included a four-match tour of Australia. In 1971 he was given a national trial at Palmerston North and another appearance for the Services team, having been promoted in rank from lieutenant to captain.

Selection in the North Island team came in 1972 and later he was in the first of the two final trial games for selection to tour Britain, but he considered any hope was dashed when he was forced to retire after 20 minutes with a knee injury. The Christmas Day present phone call was followed by a quick trip to Wellington to be outfitted then flying to London. He made his debut in the twenty-third tour game, against Newport on 10 January 1973. He became a regular midweek player for the remaining games with a game in Ireland and two in France where he played particularly well at the front of the lineout, scrummaging and in general play. His form impressed the French and he was invited to return and play in France.

Back home he informed the union that he was not prepared to play any games against the Springboks who were scheduled to tour during 1973. His decision did not please many rugby fans and he received many threatening letters. The tour was cancelled by the government and McNicol played a full season with Wanganui. He accepted the invitation to play in France and spent three seasons with Tarbes club and teaching English. One critic rated McNicol the best prop in French rugby, but he took a battering in the hard physical play that the French are renowned for. Sadly, it has been suggested that the rigours of rugby contributed towards the early development of dementia that gradually took a hold of him and which was influential in him taking his own life.

Sandy McNicol's first-class record:

| For | Matches | Tries | Points |
|---|---|---|---|
| Wanganui (Waiouru Army) 1970(5), 1971(7) (Wanganui & HSOB) 1972(11), 1973(11) | 34 | 3 | 12 |
| Wanganui-King Country 1971 | 1 | – | 0 |
| Centurions Club 1972 | 1 | – | 0 |
| I.A. Kirkpatrick's XV 1973 | 1 | – | 0 |
| New Zealand Services 1970(5), 1971 | 6 | 1 | 3 |
| North Island 1972 | 1 | 1 | 4 |
| New Zealand Trials 1971, 1972 | 2 | – | 0 |
| NEW ZEALAND 1973 | 5 | – | 0 |
| **TOTALS** | **51** | **5** | **19** |

At Noosa, Australia, 20 April 2017, aged 74.

**Colin Earl Meads** *(King Country)* As befitted his nickname, 'Pinetree', Colin Meads in his 14 years as an All Black from 1957 to 1971, and especially in the 1960s, was a towering figure in New Zealand rugby. A farming product of backblocks New Zealand, Meads was rugged and uncompromising and soon became a genuine folk hero. Adding to his legend was that he achieved his iconic status playing for his small King Country union.

Meads was about 1.92 m and 100 kg and would be too small to be a lock in today's rugby. But he always gave the impression of being a giant, complementing natural athleticism with a rare ferocity. His aggressive style meant he was involved in plenty of controversy. In 1967 he became the second All Black ordered off in a test when dispatched for dangerous play against Scotland at Murrayfield. He was vilified, too, by Australians because they believed his reckless action in trying to pull Ken Catchpole from a ruck prematurely ended the Wallaby halfback's career. There were other occasions when Meads erred with an indiscreet punch. Yet, while Meads would never be intimidated and was quick to take action if a teammate was suffering from an illegality, he was never deliberately dirty.

Meads emerged in 1955, when just 19, in the first of his 139 matches for King Country. He not only scored a try against Counties but, remarkably for a lock, dropped a goal. Later in 1955 he was the biggest player in the New Zealand under 21 side that toured Ceylon (now Sri Lanka), playing with another soon to become an All Black immortal in Wilson Whineray. Meads played all eight matches, and was recognised by the *Rugby Almanack* as one of that year's most promising players.

In 1956 Meads played in national trials and for the North Island. Though not risked in tests against the Springboks, his promotion to the All Blacks was now assured and in 1957 he toured Australia, playing 10 matches and both tests against the Wallabies. Most of his early tests were as a flanker or No. 8 and in his second test he scored the first of his seven international tries, deputising for an injured Frank McMullen on the wing.

Though mostly an automatic test selection, there were occasional interruptions. He missed the first test against the 1959 Lions and after a lacklustre performance against Australia in 1962 was replaced for the next test by his brother Stan. Meads had an outstanding tour of South Africa in 1960, scoring a try in the second test win. For the next decade he monopolised a locking position, often alongside Stan, but in 1964 he returned to No. 8, only for the All Blacks to be thrashed by the Wallabies and he was never tried there again.

On the 1963-64 tour of Britain and France, Meads excelled in a formidable pack. He and other champions like Ken Gray, Kel Tremain and Brian Lochore were then the basis of the side that had series wins in 1965 and 1966 against the Springboks and the Lions and on another successful tour of Britain and France in 1967.

Meads was vice-captain for the 1970 tour of South Africa, but broke an arm in an early match. He played the final two tests with an arm guard, but was not quite the force of old. In 1971 he led an inexperienced All Blacks team to a narrow series loss to the Lions and that ended his illustrious test career. Near the end of 1971 he injured his back in a road accident and though he recovered was never seriously considered for the All Blacks again.

Of his 361 first-class matches, 133, including 55 tests, were for the All Blacks. He was the first to reach 50 tests and in a time of limited programmes that was a colossal feat, easily the equivalent of 100 today.

In 1973 he appeared in two President's XV matches against the All Blacks, which were billed as his farewell to New Zealand rugby. In the first at Athletic Park the Meads-led invitation XV upset the All Blacks led by Ian Kirkpatrick. His 1974 biography by Alex Veysey, *Colin Meads All Black*, was a best-seller.

He then turned to administration and coaching, becoming chairman of the King Country union and after selecting and coaching North Island sides joined the national selection panel in 1986. But he chose to go on the unauthorised Cavaliers tour of South Africa as coach and was axed from the panel. He was soon forgiven, though, and in 1992 joined the NZRFU council and in 1994–95, including the World Cup tournament in South Africa, he was the All Blacks manager. When the council was replaced by a board in 1996 Meads left administration. But his legend continued to grow and as professionalism took over Meads was seen as a defender of the game's old values, becoming a popular after-dinner speaker.

Meads was also acclaimed for his community work, particularly for the intellectually handicapped. He was inducted into the International Hall of Fame and the New Zealand Sports Hall of Fame. In 1999 he was proclaimed the New Zealand Player of the Century. In 2001 he was made a New Zealand Companion of Merit and when knighthoods were restored in 2009 he became Sir Colin. And just as significant was the unveiling shortly before his death of a statue in the main street in Te Kuiti. *(Obituary contributed by Lindsay Knight).*

Colin Meads' first-class record:

| For | Matches | Tries | Con | DG | Points |
|---|---|---|---|---|---|
| King Country (Waitete) 1955(2), 1956(6), 1957(6), 1958(9), 1959(6), 1960, 1961(7), 1962(9), 1963(10), 1964(9), 1965(10), 1966(11), 1967(11), 1968(9), 1969(10), 1970, 1971(8), 1972(14) | 139 | 31 | – | 1 | 99 |
| Wanganui-King Country 1956(3), 1965, 1966(2), 1971 | 7 | 3 | – | – | 9 |
| King Country-Counties 1959 | 2 | – | – | – | 0 |
| Centurions Club 1956, 1957, 1958, 1961, 1970 | 5 | 3 | – | – | 9 |
| W.J. Whineray's XV 1959, 1966 | 2 | 1 | – | – | 3 |
| Barbarians Club 1973 | 2 | – | – | – | 0 |
| Harlequins Club 1974 | 1 | – | – | – | 0 |
| South African 75th Jubilee XV (in SA) 1964 | 3 | 2 | – | – | 6 |
| NZRFU President's XV 1973 (v NZ) | 1 | – | – | – | 0 |
| NZRFU Invitation XV 1973 (v NZ) | 1 | – | – | – | 0 |

| | | | | |
|---|---|---|---|---|
| President's Overseas XV (in England) 1971 | 3 | – | – | – | 0 |
| Tongan Invitation XV (in Tonga) 1973 | 2 | 2 | – | – | 8 |
| North Island Colts 1955 | 1 | – | – | – | 0 |
| New Zealand Colts 1955 | 8 | 3 | – | – | 9 |
| New Zealand Juniors Trial 1957 | 1 | – | – | – | 0 |
| New Zealand Juniors 1958 | 10 | 3 | – | – | 9 |
| Black XV 1957 | 1 | – | – | – | 0 |
| North Island XV 1956 | 1 | – | – | – | 0 |
| North Island 1956, 1957, 1958, 1959, 1962, 1963, 1965, 1966, 1967, 1968, 1969, 1971 | 12 | 1 | – | – | 3 |
| New Zealand Trials 1956, 1957(2), 1958, 1959, 1960(2), 1962, 1963(4), 1965, 1966, 1967(2), 1968, 1969, 1970(2), 1971(2) | 22 | 4 | – | – | 12 |
| Rest of New Zealand 1956 | 1 | – | – | – | 0 |
| New Zealand XV 1958, 1965, 1966 | 3 | – | – | – | 0 |
| NEW ZEALAND 1957(10), 1958(3), 1959(3), 1960(23), 1961(3), 1962(8), 1963(26), 1964(3), 1965(4), 1966(4), 1967(12), 1968(13), 1969(2), 1970(15), 1971(4) | 133 | 28 | 1 | – | 86 |
| **TOTALS** | **361** | **81** | **1** | **1** | **253** |

At Te Kuiti, 20 August 2017, aged 81.

**Douglas Leslie Rollerson** *(Manawatu)* was a very talented and competitive player who could play equally well at fullback as he could in either of the five-eighth positions. He toured Argentina in 1976 as a second five-eighth and appeared in both 'test' matches. Touring Wales in 1980, he was fullback and gained his first official test cap at Cardiff. The following year he was at first five-eighth in the second test against Scotland and in the three-test series with South Africa during which he opposed Naas Botha. Late in 1981 on the tour of Romania and France, he appeared in both tests as well as the test against Romania. He was not the recognised goal-kicker for the All Blacks, sharing the kicking duties with Allan Hewson during 1981.

Born at Papakura on 14 May 1953, Doug Rollerson was a versatile sportsman and played a considerable amount of soccer before concentrating on rugby when a member of the Wesley College first XV coached by Hiwi Tauroa. He was a Counties schoolboy representative at rugby, tennis, cricket and athletics.

In 1972 19-year-old Rollerson joined a very young but talented Massey University senior team, playing outside All Black first five-eighth Bob Burgess. Also in the team were future All Blacks Kent Lambert and Dick Myers. Rollerson was soon promoted to the Manawatu team and commenced an outstanding career of 91 games. He had three years in the NZ Juniors team, many as captain. He became a regular in the NZ Universities teams, the highlight being captain of the 1977 side that defeated the touring Lions.

1976 was a big year for Rollerson; he became the star in Manawatu's winning of the Ranfurly Shield at Eden Park, contributing 10 points (try, penalty and dropped goal) in the historic 12–10 victory. Late in the season he took on more of the goal-kicking duties. In October he gained All

Blacks selection for the tour to Argentina. Manawatu successfully defended the shield through 1977, but Rollerson's 1978 season was spoilt by the need to have a knee operation in June, after which he chose to go overseas, playing rugby in Los Angeles, Colorado and London.

Rollerson returned in 1980 and became a key player in Manawatu's winning of the first division championship title. The next season was to be his last, scoring 171 points for the Manawatu team that finished runners-up in the championship. In 1982 Rollerson signed with North Sydney league club where he spent two seasons, playing mainly in the reserve grade. From 1997 through to 2004 he was the chief executive of North Harbour union. During the recent seven years he had been suffering poor health due to cancer.

Doug Rollerson's first-class record:

| For | Matches | Tries | Con | PG | DG | Points |
|---|---|---|---|---|---|---|
| Manawatu (Univ) 1972(9), 1973(10), 1974(5), 1975(13), 1976(15), 1977(11), 1980(13), 1981(15) | 91 | 33 | 76 | 60 | 17 | 515 |
| Manawatu XV 1981 | 1 | – | 5 | – | 1 | 13 |
| Manawatu-Horowhenua 1977 | 1 | – | – | 3 | – | 9 |
| Nelson Bays Invitation XV 1975 | 1 | – | 1 | – | – | 2 |
| Barbarians Club 1977 | 2 | – | – | – | – | 0 |
| North Island Universities 1974, 1975 | 2 | – | – | – | – | 0 |
| New Zealand Universities 1973(2), 1974, 1976(3), 1977(3) | 9 | 4 | 4 | 4 | 1 | 39 |
| New Zealand Juniors 1974(3), 1975(5), 1976(4) | 12 | 4 | 4 | 2 | – | 30 |
| New Zealand Trials 1975, 1976, 1977 | 3 | – | – | – | – | 0 |
| NEW ZEALAND 1976(7), 1980(5), 1981(12) | 24 | 7 | 14 | 13 | 5 | 110 |
| **TOTALS** | **146** | **48** | **104** | **82** | **24** | **718** |

At Auckland, 3 May 2017, aged 63

**Ian Stanley Talbot 'Spooky' Smith** *(Otago, North Otago and Southland)* was a popular member of the 1963/64 touring team and although he didn't break into the test team he scored eight tries in his 15 appearances. Smith had played most of his provincial rugby at centre, but the selectors chose to place him on the wing for the final trial. The 22-year-old scored two tries and impressed the selectors sufficiently to include him in the touring squad. Nicknamed 'Spooky' and sometimes referred to as 'The Gimmerburn Ghost', he became a regular test wing during the home series over the next three years, against Australia in 1964, South Africa 1965 and the British Isles 1966. In his six tests he scored twice, both tries being in the fourth test against the Springboks.

Born at Dunedin on 20 August 1941, Ian Smith was educated at Milton and Dunedin, finishing at King's High School, 1955–59. Fifteen days before his twentieth birthday Smith made his Otago debut in 1961 and became the regular centre for three seasons and represented South Island in 1963. During the 1962 season he left Dunedin and returned to the country to join the small Gimmerburn club.

Following the long four-month All Blacks tour Smith, and several other tourists, had only a couple of months at home before heading away again. This time it was a seven-match tour of Australia with the NZ Colts team. During 1965–66 Smith played for North Otago, but by September 1966 he had moved again, to Southland where he remained until completing his first-class career in 1968. He was a Southland selector in 1971. He worked as a stock agent until later becoming a farmer. A son, Hamish, represented Marlborough in 2000.

Ian Smith's first-class record:

| For | Matches | Tries | Points |
|---|---|---|---|
| Otago (Pirate) 1961(8) (Pirate/Gimmerburn) 1962(11), (Gimmerburn) 1963(11), 1964(7) | 37 | 9 | 27 |
| North Otago (Oamaru Old Boys) 1965(7), 1966(5) | 12 | 7 | 21 |
| Southland (Wyndham) 1966(4), 1967(3) (Woodlands) 1968(11) | 18 | 3 | 9 |
| Hanan Shield Unions 1965, 1966 | 2 | – | 0 |
| New Zealand Colts Trial 1964 | 1 | 1 | 3 |
| New Zealand Colts 1964 | 5 | 4 | 12 |
| South Island 1963, 1964, 1965, 1966 | 4 | 1 | 3 |
| New Zealand Trials 1962, 1963(2), 1966, 1967(2) | 6 | 3 | 9 |
| Rest of New Zealand 1965, 1966 | 2 | – | 0 |
| NEW ZEALAND 1963(15), 1964(3), 1965(3), 1966(3) | 24 | 10 | 30 |
| **TOTALS** | **111** | **38** | **114** |

At Nelson, 29 September 2017, aged 76.

**Barry Trevor Thomas** *(Auckland and Wellington)* was an admirable tight forward for Auckland during the 1960s, especially in the grand Ranfurly Shield era of 1960–63, and as a prop might have enjoyed an equally illustrious international career had it not been for bad luck with injuries. These limited him to just four All Blacks appearances, the third test against the touring Wallabies at Eden Park in 1962 and all three tests when the Wallabies again toured New Zealand in 1964.

Though achieving test recognition as a prop, where his size and strength made him an effective scrummager, much of his early representative rugby was spent at lock. He then faced competition for a regular front row position from the likes of other All Blacks, Wilson Whineray and 'Snow' White. But despite being on the short side for a lock, his work ethic in the tight made him an invaluable member of the Auckland pack, for whom he became a regular selection in 1960.

After a successful test debut in 1962, Thomas looked set for a long All Black tenure, only to be struck down by injury early in the 1963 season, which ruled him out of the two home tests against England and for the 1963–64 tour of Britain and France. He also missed, after being selected, the 1963 inter-island match. His replacement in the North Island side was Ken Gray, who took his opportunity so successfully he gained the position that might have been Thomas's on the Britain and France tour and soon established himself as one of New Zealand's greatest props.

Thomas regained his All Blacks position in 1964 when, with Whineray unavailable, he was Gray's propping partner in the series against the Wallabies. But with Whineray's return as captain in 1965, and with Gray now seen as the premier prop, Thomas was overlooked for the series against the Springboks. But he continued to be an All Black trialist up until 1968, played for the

North Island in 1965 and in that year he was in the Auckland side that beat the Springboks and that beat Taranaki to win the Ranfurly Shield.

While the bulk of his provincial career was with Auckland, for whom he played 86 games, Thomas spent the 1964 season on temporary transfer to Wellington, and in nine games for that union helped form with the likes of Gray and former All Black Nev MacEwan one of Wellington's strongest ever packs.

An amiable man off-field, Thomas was known by the nickname 'Bear', in part because of his build but also because of his favourite tipple. He was a coach and administrator of Auckland's Manukau club and a keen worker for the Barbarians. Two sons, Greg and Kevin, appeared briefly at first-class level, as did a grandson, Sam. *(Obituary contributed by Lindsay Knight).*

Barry Thomas's first-class record:

| For | Matches | Tries | Points |
|---|---|---|---|
| Auckland (Manukau Rovers) 1958(2), 1960(15), 1961(14), 1962(14), 1963(4), 1965(15), 1966(8), 1967(14) | 86 | 1 | 3 |
| Wellington (Athletic) 1964 | 9 | – | 0 |
| Auckland B 1959 | 2 | – | 0 |
| North Island 1965 | 1 | – | 0 |
| New Zealand Trials 1963(3), 1965, 1966, 1967(2), 1968 | 8 | – | 0 |
| NEW ZEALAND 1962, 1964(3) | 4 | – | 0 |
| **TOTALS** | **110** | **1** | **3** |

At Auckland, 5 January 2018, aged 80.

## *PROVINCIAL REPRESENTATIVES*

**Patrick Vivian Bailey** *(Golden Bay-Motueka)* played 22 games, at prop, between 1955 and 1963. At Nelson, 27 December 2016.

**Ken Norman Bain** *(Ashburton County and Canterbury)* was a lock forward appearing twice for Ashburton County during army training in 1942. After serving in North Africa and Italy he returned and played eight games for Canterbury in 1946. At Christchurch, 15 September 2017, aged 96.

**Murray Hone Ball** *(Manawatu and Wellington)* appeared in All Blacks trial matches in 1959 and 1960 and represented NZ Juniors against the 1959 touring Lions. A talented midfield back, he played 37 games for Manawatu 1958–62 and made one appearance for Wellington in each of the 1958 and 1963 seasons. A cartoonist, he became a household name with the success of his *Footrot Flats* series. In 2002 he was made an Officer of the NZ Order of Merit (ONZM) for services as a cartoonist. At Gisborne, 12 March 2017, aged 78.

**Matiu 'Mattie' Blackburn** *(Wellington and Auckland)* played at first five-eighth in 52 games for Wellington 1966–70 and made one appearance for Auckland in 1971. A NZ Maori representative in 1969, he kicked 19 dropped goals in his 67 first-class games. He was a NZ Maori selector 1979–89 and a member of the NZRFU council 1990–95. At Wellington, 7 December 2017, aged 73.

**Paul William Broederlow** *(Manawatu and Taranaki)* was a reliable midfield back during Manawatu's Ranfurly Shield era 1976–78. He made 27 appearances during 1975–78 followed by three games for Taranaki in 1979. He was a NZ Under 21 representative in 1976. At Mount Maunganui, 16 May 2017, aged 60.

**Norman John Brown** *(Auckland)* appeared at five-eighth or fullback in 29 games 1955–60 and was also a NZ Universities representative 1957–60. At Auckland, 1 September 2017, aged 82.

**Lawrence John Burns** *(Thames Valley)* made three appearances on the wing in 1965. Later chairman of the union 1993–98, president 2002–06 and a life member from 2002. At Hamilton, 5 November 2017, aged 76.

**Wallace Buchan 'Wally' Cameron** *(Taranaki)* was a member of a well-known rugby family, three brothers also playing for Taranaki and a fourth being a first-class referee. A halfback, he played 30 games during 1946–53 and appeared in two NZ Trials in 1948. At Hamilton, 19 January 2017, aged 90.

**Walter Charles 'Wally' Candy** *(South Canterbury)* was a halfback, making two first-class appearances for Otago B in 1957 and one for Wellington B the following year. In 1961 he played six games for South Canterbury and a further six in 1963. He was a South Canterbury co-selector in 1969. At Timaru, 28 April 2017, aged 86.

**Raymond Cash** *(Hawke's Bay)* made one first-class appearance for his union's colts team in 1948, but it wasn't until 1954 that the wing made his solitary appearance for the senior team. At Hastings, 25 March 2017, aged 89.

**Thomas James Chestnut** *(Waikato)* played at hooker for the Te Awamutu Old Boys club in 27 games from 1963 to 1965. At Cambridge, 16 February 2017, aged 80.

**Leslie Alan Clark** *(Wellington and Otago)* was a loose forward playing 59 games for Wellington 1952–57 followed by one appearance for Otago in 1958. He appeared in NZ Trials in 1957. In first-class cricket he represented Wellington, Otago and Auckland. At Auckland, 21 September 2017, aged 86.

**Thomas Coyne** *(Buller)* made 20 appearances between 1940 and 1946. In his final year he was hooker in the combined Seddon Shield Unions side that played Australia. At Westport, 31 October 2017, aged 98.

**Stanley George Crawshaw** *(Wanganui)* was a fullback, playing 18 games during 1959–60 and kicked 70 points. At Whakatane, 11 May 2017, aged 82.

**Colin Richard Cunningham** *(North Auckland)* was a wing, playing 17 games during 1957–61. He appeared in the NZ Juniors trial in 1957 and one national trial the following year. At Whangarei, 12 March 2017.

**Bruce Francis Duncan** *(Otago)* toured Australia and Ceylon with the 1955 NZ Colts team but didn't debut for his province until 1958 when he commenced his 58-game career as a hooker until finishing in 1966. From the Matakanui club he represented South Island in 1965. At Alexandra, 22 May 2017, aged 79.

**Ian Campbell Ellery** *(Counties)* made two appearances for his union in 1957. He was a five-eighth from Waiuku club. At Auckland, 23 July 2017, aged 84.

**Ned Erceg** *(North Auckland)* played 45 games over a 12-year period 1953–64. Playing on the wing, he scored 18 tries. At Orewa, 24 June 2017, aged 84.

**Jack Ngahaki Samson Gardiner** *(Bay of Plenty and King Country)* played 11 games for Bay of Plenty in 1946, 1951 and 1953 and made one appearance for King Country in 1949. A five-eighth or fullback, he also represented NZ Maori in 1946. He served in the Maori Battalion during the Second World War and later with Jayforce in Japan. At Rotorua, 7 July 2017, aged 90.

**Kenneth Bruce Goodall** *(Golden Bay-Motueka)* was a forward, appearing in 11 games during 1957–58. At Riwaka, 28 May 2017.

**Clive William Gowler** *(Bush)* played 11 games on the wing for his union between 1966 and 1968. He was later a senior club referee in Manawatu. At Palmerston North, 4 December 2017, aged 75.

**Roland Leslie 'Roly' Green** *(South Canterbury)* was a halfback, playing 19 games for his union 1950–53 and was the last surviving member of the 1950 team that won the Ranfurly Shield. He had two national trials in 1951 and represented South Island Minor Unions in 1952. At Timaru, 29 October 2017, aged 90.

**John de Berri Graham Groome** *(Canterbury)* made one appearance for his union in 1946, against Buller, at Westport. The following month the flanker played for NZ Universities against Wellington. He then moved across the Tasman and represented ACT and NSW Country. At Christchurch, 4 February 2017, aged 91.

**Malcolm John Frederick Guy** *(Horowhenua)* played 11 games during 1960–64. Later mayor of Horowhenua District Council 1989–95. In 2004 he received the Queen's Service Medal for public service. His son Nathan, who also played for Horowhenua, is a current Member of Parliament. At Koputaroa, 20 May 2017, aged 80.

**Adam Robert Edmond 'Bert' Haig** *(Otago)* played 30 games between 1948 and 1953 and returned in 1956 for a further seven games. In 1951 the halfback appeared in two national trials fixtures. At Dunedin, 22 December 2016, aged 89.

**Kevin Douglas Harmon** *(Golden Bay-Motueka)* was a second five-eighth who appeared in all 10 of his union's games during 1960. At Christchurch, 13 November 2017, aged 80.

**Te Whiwhi Vivian Hata** *(Poverty Bay and Bay of Plenty)* made 15 appearances for Poverty Bay 1947–51 and one appearance for Bay of Plenty in 1948. During the 1950s he served in the navy and represented NZ Services in 1957. At Hamilton, 29 June 2017, aged 92.

**Allan Douglas Hunter** *(Hawke's Bay)* appeared twice for his union in 1949. During the war he played in army teams and in 1945 made three appearances for the NZ Services team in Britain. He was later a teacher in Napier, Wairarapa and Upper Hutt prior to being principal of Burnside High School in Christchurch. In 2005 became a Member of the NZ Order of Merit for services to education and the community. At Christchurch, 12 July 2017, aged 94.

**Kerry Patrick Hurley** *(Taranaki)* was a versatile back, representing his union for 13 seasons 1959–71 for a total of 121 games during which he scored 255 points including 26 tries. He appeared in two national trials, on the wing in 1966 and at fullback the next year. At Christchurch, 29 August 2017, aged 79.

**Roy Frederick Johnson** *(Hawke's Bay and Taranaki)* made one appearance for Hawke's Bay in 1953 then moved to Taranaki where he played nine games on the wing, scoring six tries, in

1956. Returning to Hawke's Bay, he made five further appearances for that union in 1958, At Auckland, 9 May 2017, aged 86.

**Alan Joseph Jury** *(Taranaki)* made 12 appearances for Taranaki, nine in 1960, one in 1962 and two in 1965. At New Plymouth, 24 November 2017, aged 83.

**George Thomas Kain** *(South Canterbury)* played four games, in the forwards, in 1939 before joining the army where he became a captain in the 26th Battalion. At Christchurch, 20 July 2017, aged 99.

**William Angus 'Bill' Kerby** *(Thames Valley)* was a five-eighth, appearing in 32 games from 1956 through to 1960. He had a national trial in 1959. At Brisbane, 25 July 2017, aged 80.

**Jamie Kerridge** *(Bush)* played 11 seasons for his union during 1952–62, totalling 92 games of which 61 were in succession between 1956 and 1962. A lock forward, he was in combined Wairarapa-Bush teams that met the 1955 Wallabies, 1956 Springboks and 1959 Lions. He appeared in national trial fixtures in 1953 and 1959. His first-class career totalled 100 games. At Palmerston North, 27 October 2017, aged 86.

**William Leonard 'Len' King** *(South Canterbury)* was a lock forward, playing 26 games between 1964 and 1968. In later years he was president of his union 2001–02 and made a life member in 2008. At Timaru, 28 August 2017, aged 73.

**David Walter Koni** *(King Country)* was a promising wing in 1969, scoring seven tries in nine games for his union, had a trial for NZ Juniors and represented NZ Maori but did not return until 1972 when he played a further 11 games for his union. At Auckland, 28 October 2017, aged 69.

**Barry Samuel Leader** *(Manawatu)* made two appearances in 1956 as a number eight. At Auckland, 28 October 2017, aged 83.

**Arthur George 'Bill' McCaa** *(Golden Bay-Motueka)* was a flanker, playing 10 games during 1955–56 seasons and a further two in 1960. He was a union selector in 1962. At Murchison, 12 February 2017, aged 85.

**John Archibald McCaskie** *(Manawatu)* made one appearance in 1961, at second five-eighth against Wairarapa, during which he kicked two conversions and two penalty goals. At Palmerston North, 23 July 2017, aged 80.

**John Alastair McKinnon** *(Hawke's Bay)* had two games in 1952 and five in 1955 before becoming a regular squad member from 1957 to 1961 when the flanker added a further 41 appearances. At Hastings, 1 June 2017, aged 85.

**John Aitken McLay** *(Mid Canterbury)* played 100 first-class games, 97 for his union during 1974–86, represented NZ Colts in 1974 and while at Lincoln College represented NZ Universities in 1975. He was an uncle of Richie McCaw. At Ashburton, 22 October 2017, aged 62.

**Manukapua Maniapoto** *(Bay of Plenty)* was a lock, playing 107 games for his union during 1960–69 and 13 games for NZ Maori 1960–66. His father Hema played for Tai Tokerau in 1928 and a son Richard appeared for the Bay in the late 1980s. Manu's brothers Huri and Jim also played for the Bay. At Rotorua, 24 January 2017, aged 81.

**Douglas Victor Manson** *(Golden Bay-Motueka)* was a lock, playing 15 games during 1950–54. He represented South Island Minor Unions in 1952 and the following year had a national trial. At Invercargill, 1 March 2017, aged 85.

**George Arthur 'Bull' Mellow** *(Bay of Plenty)* played 37 games, at hooker, for the Bay between 1957 and 1962. His son Wilson played for the Bay in 1995. At Tauranga, 5 November 2017, aged 82.

**Frank William Millington** *(Thames Valley)* was a flanker, appearing in 11 games during 1954–55 seasons. At Thames, 8 June 2017, aged 84.

**Colin Richard Moore** *(Otago and Southland)* played alongside his brother Graham (All Black in 1949) for Otago during 1949–50. After five appearances for Otago and having graduated as a dentist he moved to Invercargill and represented Southland in 17 games in 1952–53. A three-quarter, he represented NZ Universities and had two trials for selection of the 1953 All Blacks. He was a dentist in London 1953–56, Auckland 1956–61 and at Te Awamutu from 1961. At Hamilton, 30 September 2017, aged 89.

**Barry Sydney Bingham Muntz** *(Southland)* had eight games for Southland in 1960. A loose forward, he later played for Wellington B in 1963 and 1965. At Tairua, 12 January 2017.

**William Douglas Murcott** *(Southland and Nelson Bays)* was a strong prop, appearing in 34 games for Southland 1978–83 and, a decade later, for Nelson Bays in 16 games in 1994–95. He represented NZ Juniors 1979–80 and South Island in 1980. At Nelson, 25 July 2017, aged 59.

**John Ainslie Murray** *(Otago B)* made one first-class appearance for Otago B, against North Otago, in 1948. Later lived in Auckland where he was honoured with life membership of the North Shore club. At Auckland, 24 March 2017, aged 91.

**Robert Allan 'Robbie' Newlands** *(Poverty Bay)* had a long 14-year career for his union, playing 131 games between 1972 and 1985. He played at number eight and at prop and had three years in the NZ Juniors (Under-23) team during 1974–75–76. At Gisborne, 26 March 2017, aged 63.

**Mark Davies 'Dave' O'Connor** *(Nelson and Golden Bay-Motueka)* made one appearance for Nelson, at centre, in 1946. During 1949–50 he played four games for Golden Bay-Motueka, appearing at five-eighth and halfback. At Hamilton, 30 June 2017, aged 90.

**Patrick James O'Connor** *(Golden Bay-Motueka)* never represented his union but appeared in a trial game for selection of the combined Nelson, Marlborough and Golden Bay-Motueka to meet the 1950 touring Lions. He was a halfback from the Cobb Hydro club. At Whitianga, 19 June 2016, aged 88.

**Francis Derrick O'Grady** *(Ashburton County and Golden Bay-Motueka)* made one appearance for Ashburton County, at halfback, in 1951, also representing South Island Colts in the inter-island colts fixture. During 1953–54 he played five games for Golden Bay-Motueka. At Christchurch, 21 September 2017, aged 86.

**Arthur James 'Jim' Olsen** *(Bay of Plenty and Thames Valley)* was a hooker, playing three games for Bay of Plenty in 1953 and later 18 games for Thames Valley during 1955–57. At Auckland, 8 September 2017, aged 92.

**Arthur Francis Pauling** *(Golden Bay-Motueka and Wairarapa)* made one appearance for Golden Bay-Motueka in each of the 1958 and 1959 seasons before becoming a regular lock in 1960 with nine appearances. In 1961 he played eight games for Wairarapa. At Hastings, 5 May 2017, aged 86.

**Ronald Henry Trevor Pope** *(Hawke's Bay and Wairarapa)* played three games for Hawke's Bay in 1949 followed by nine games for Wairarapa 1951–52. At Masterton, 7 November 2017, aged 92.

**Raymond Lewis 'Pinto' Price** *(Hawke's Bay)* played 44 games for his union 1947–53, scoring 13 tries. He played at wing, centre and later at five-eighth. At Hastings, 22 December 2017, aged 89.

**John Reginald Read** *(Horowhenua)* was a lock from Foxton club, making 57 appearances for his union between 1962 and 1971. At Palmerston North, 14 January 2017, aged 72.

**Paul John Renton** *(Manawatu, Mid Canterbury and Hawke's Bay)* was a fine loose forward who had a first-class career totalling 90 games. While at Massey University he made one appearance for Manawatu in 1983. This was followed by 21 games for Mid Canterbury 1984–85 then 44 games for Hawke's Bay 1986–89. He represented NZ Colts 1983, NZ Juniors 1984, NZ Emerging Players 1986, North Island 1986, Central Zone 1988–89, NZ Divisional 1988–89, and national trial games 1987–88. At Mangatahi, Hawke's Bay, 2 August 2017, aged 54.

**Alexander 'Lucky' Roberts** *(Hawke's Bay, Wellington and Auckland)* made one appearance for Hawke's Bay in 1958 followed by seven games for Wellington 1960–62 and two for Auckland in 1965. He also represented Wellington at cricket. At Napier, 6 November 2017, aged 78.

**Michael James Rohrlach** *(Thames Valley)* played three games in the forwards during 1963. At Thames, 26 September 2017, aged 70.

**James Newton 'Jim' Rolfe** *(Bay of Plenty)* returned from war service to make three appearances for his union in 1948–49. While teaching in Perth during the 1950s he represented Western Australia. At Pakuranga, 28 August 2017, aged 95.

**Robert Philip Ryan** *(South Canterbury)* played 50 games for his union between 1961 and 1968. He was a forward from Temuka club. At Timaru, 26 May 2017, aged 78.

**Alan John Sayers** *(Waikato)* had competed in the 220 and 440 yards track events at the Empire Games in Sydney early in 1938 and in June made one appearance for Waikato, on the wing, against Auckland. He later changed to league before serving in the Pacific during the Second World War. He had a career as a journalist and photographer with the *Auckland Star* and *NZ Herald* and was a co-author of the Sir Fred Allen biography *Fred The Needle* published in 2011. In 1998 he was made a Member of the NZ Order of Merit (MNZM) for services to journalism and sport. At Auckland, 19 August 2017, aged 101.

**James Harington Wilmot 'Jim' Seton** *(Bay of Plenty and Waikato)* had seven games for Bay of Plenty in 1946–47 followed by seven for Waikato 1948–49. His brother David also played for both unions. At Auckland, 6 July 2017, aged 90.

**William Hope 'Bill' Simpson** *(Golden Bay-Motueka)* was a hooker, playing seven games during 1956. His brother Doug also played for the union. At Nelson, 20 December 2016, aged 82.

**John Arthur 'Jack' Skinner** *(Otago)* played three games for Otago in 1951. He was a brother of All Black Kevin Skinner. At Wellington, 13 January 2017, aged 93.

**Edward Neil 'Eddie' Vercoe** *(Northland)* made four appearances, all as a forward substitute, in 1996. At Whangarei, 11 September 2017, aged 51.

**Bernard James Walsh** *(Taranaki)* was halfback in 17 games during 1949–52, his nine games in 1949 attracting the attention of national selectors for the 1950 trials where he opposed Vince Bevan in the main trial. A selector, looking to improve the All Blacks team following the drawn first test with the Lions, watched Walsh during Taranaki's game against Wanganui, but Walsh was injured during the game and Bevan was retained for the second test. Walsh, however, went to Christchurch as a reserve. He is one of a group of players to appear in official All Blacks team photos but never to take the field. He was a Taranaki selector in 1962. At New Plymouth, 11 December 2017, aged 90.

**Eric Alexander Watson** *(Otago)* made one appearance in 1946, as a five-eighth, against Wairarapa. Otago rep selector 1962–71 and served on the union's management committee 1973–80. Coach of successful NZ Juniors teams during the 1970s, a highlight being the shock 14–10 defeat of the 1973 All Blacks. A national selector 1974–80, he coached the All Blacks during 1979–80. At Dunedin, 25 March 2017, aged 91.

**Charles Perry Webber** *(Bay of Plenty)* made three appearances on the wing in 1955. At Gisborne, 3 July 2017, aged 84.

**Hemi Te Kotuku Williams** *(Counties)* played 13 games on the wing during 1984. He also represented Northern Maori the same season. At Whakatane, 16 January 2017, aged 60.

**Cecil 'Ces' Wilson** *(South Canterbury)* played six games in 1957 and one in each of the following two seasons. A five-eighth, his final first-class game was for the combined Hanan Shield Unions against the touring Lions in 1959. He later moved to Auckland where he served on that union's management committee and was honoured with life membership in 1992. At Auckland, 5 October 2017, aged 81.

## DISTINGUISHED OPPONENTS

**Kenneth William Catchpole** *(Australia)* was one of the great halfbacks, playing in 27 tests during 1961–68 and opposing the All Blacks in 1962, 1964, 1967. In 1968 the Wallaby captain's career was terminated when Colin Meads attempted to extract him from a ruck, causing severe muscle injury. When aged 20 Catchpole captained New South Wales against the 1960 All Blacks. At Sydney, 21 December 2017, aged 78.

**Elie Cester** *(France)* toured New Zealand in 1968, appearing in six games including two tests. The lock also opposed New Zealand in the 1973 test at Paris. At Bourg-les-Valence, France, 3 January 2017, aged 74.

**William Patrick 'Willie' Duggan** *(Ireland and British Isles)* visited New Zealand with the 1976 Irish team and played in the test. The next year the loose forward returned with the 1977 Lions and played in all four tests. His last test against the All Blacks was at Dublin in 1978. He was capped 41 times for Ireland during 1975–84. At Dunmore, Kilkenny, Ireland, 28 August 2017, aged 67.

**Sir Ewen Fergusson** GCMG, GCVO *(Scotland)* played five tests for Scotland in 1954 including against the All Blacks. A lock, he also opposed the tourists while representing Oxford University.

At Vaison-la-Romaine, France, 20 April 2017, aged 84.

**Paul Labadie** *(France)* was capped 21 times during 1952–57 and was hooker in 1954 when France defeated the touring All Blacks at Paris. At Bayonne, 12 January 2017, aged 88.

**Dr Cecil Moss** *(South Africa)* was on the wing in all four tests against the touring All Blacks in 1949. He also captained Natal against the tourists. The doctor was the anaesthetist at the world's first heart transplant in 1967, performed by Chris Barnard. In 1979 he was also involved when Nelson Mandela, then a prisoner on Robben Island, received surgery. At Cape Town, 27 October 2017, aged 92.

**Stanislaus Josef Pilecki** *(Australia)* played 18 tests during 1978–83 including six against New Zealand. He was the first to play 100 games for Queensland, many being against New Zealand provincial teams. One of the characters of rugby, the prop first visited New Zealand with the 1970 Queensland team when aged 23, but it was many years later, when aged 31, before he gained his first test cap. At Brisbane, 20 December 2017, aged 70.

**Patrick Salas** *(France)* toured New Zealand in 1979, appearing in seven of the eight games including both tests, the second being a memorable 24–19 victory at Eden Park. He had seven tests during 1979–82, appearing at prop, lock and number eight. At Narbonne, 9 January 2017, aged 62.

**David Shedden** *(Scotland)* was on the wing against the touring All Blacks in 1972. It was the first of his 15 tests. At Linwood, 27 October 2017, aged 73.

**Frank Douglas Sykes** *(England)* visited with the 1963 England team. The 35-year-old wing appeared in the second test and in the test against Australia soon after. His other two caps for England had been eight years earlier, in 1955. He also toured South Africa with the 1955 Lions. At Seattle, USA, 12 May 2017, aged 89.

**Joost Heystek van der Westhuizen** *(South Africa)* was a tall halfback and respected opponent in Super and test rugby. He played a record 89 tests during 1993–2003, scoring a record 38 tries, and was one of the great Springbok halfbacks. In 2011 he was diagnosed with motor neurone disease and died at Johannesburg, 6 February 2017, aged 45.

**Karel Thomas 'Tom' van Vollenhoven** *(South Africa)* was the leading try scorer during the 1956 tour of New Zealand, scoring 13 tries in 15 games, but played only one test, at Christchurch, against the All Blacks. He made his test debut against the touring Lions in 1955. In 1957 he commenced a long and highly successful league career in England, playing 409 games for St Helens 1957–68, scoring 392 tries. At Bethlehem, 21 October 2017, aged 82.

**Daniel Joseph Vickerman** *(Australia)* was a familiar opponent of New Zealand teams, the tall lock appearing for the Brumbies and Waratahs and 63 tests between 2002 and 2011. At Sydney, 18 February 2017, aged 37.

**Lionel Geoffrey Wilson** *(South Africa)* was an outstanding fullback who played 27 tests, commencing in 1960 in the final two tests against the touring All Blacks. He toured New Zealand in 1965, appearing in all four tests and was chosen as one of the *Almanack*'s five players of the year. In later years he resided in Palmerston North and Auckland, back in Africa for a time then retiring to Hawke's Bay. At Napier, 17 September 2017, aged 84.

## FIRST-CLASS REFEREES

**John Miles Luckin** *(Taranaki)* controlled nine games between 1973 and 1979 with six being national championship fixtures. He was later Taranaki selector-coach 1991–93. At New Plymouth, 19 September 2017, aged 82.

**Nelson Burton Whittaker** *(Manawatu and Bay of Plenty)* had a career spanning 22 years with 26 games during 1965–78 when with the Manawatu association and a further 20 games 1978–86 when in Bay of Plenty. At Tauranga, 1 March 2017, aged 78.

**Maxwell Edward Wischnowsky** *(Manawatu)* had 23 first-class appointments during 1962–75, the majority being Manawatu home games. At Palmerston North, 24 August 2017, aged 84.

## ADMINISTRATOR

**Graham William John Atkin** was a member of the NZRFU council from 1986 to 1993. He served on Wellington's management committee 1972–93 during which time he was chairman for 16 years and made a life member in 1991. At Wellington, 21 October 2017, aged 86.

## JOURNALIST

**John Kennedy Brooks** was the gentlemanly rugby writer for The Press in Christchurch for about 30 years. No public announcement was made and a service was held for him at a small suburban café, at which one of the speakers was the former All Blacks captain and NZRU president, Tane Norton. John had had Alzheimer's disease for about six years. John Brooks wrote on a number of sports including swimming and golf and elegantly and with considerable wit on rugby. John was seconded to the New Zealand Press Association in 1972 to cover the tour of the UK, Ireland and France, during which he gained the nickname 'JC' from Terry McLean. John was actually JK Brooks but Terry gave him JC because of John's measured approach to life, including deadlines. Terry, whose frustration threshold was low, used to get agitated while waiting for John, whether it was departure time for a game or after a game when Terry was ready to move, but John far from it. Terry would utter, again and again, 'Jesus Christ Brooks . . .' John famously gave the All Blacks front row of the early 1980s the nickname of 'The Geriatrics'. It happened at the Burnham military camp south of Christchurch where the All Blacks trained for the first test against the 1983 Lions. During an otherwise unremarkable post-training interview with captain Andy Dalton, Brooks mentioned the advancing years of some of the players. 'What about their age?' bristled Dalton. 'Well,' said John, in that unhurried delivery of his, 'some are saying that some of you are getting a bit geriatric.' Dalton bristled a bit more but got so used to the idea that three years later, when Dalton, Gary Knight and John Ashworth combined for a book written by Lindsay Knight, it was called The Geriatrics. At Christchurch, 4 February 2017, aged 82. (Obituary contributed by Lindsay Knight)

# AMENDMENTS

*to 2017 edition*

| | |
|---|---|
| Page 64 | Ambrose Curtis (Manawatu) was omitted from the squad list. |
| Page 83 | score v Chiefs was 23–29. |
| Page 96 | score v Kings was 57–24; score v Jaguares was 32–15. |
| Page 103 | Lions v Cheetahs. Jantjies kicked 3 conversions, Combrinck 1 conversion. |
| Page 105 | Stormers v Sunwolves. Jantjies did not score, de Jongh was the try scorer. |
| Page 106 | Rebels v Cheetahs. Score was 36–14. Add Ellison (try) and Debreczeni 4 conversions. |
| | Sunwolves v Jaguares. Tatekawa scored a try, not Tamura. |
| Page 107 | Reds v Cheetahs. Game was played at Brisbane, not Bloemfontein. |
| Page 108 | Blues v Kings. Watts and Visser each kicked one penalty. |
| Page 109 | Bulls v Sharks. Should read Bulls v Stormers. |
| | Kings v Jaguares. N. Briant was the referee, not van der Westhuizen. |
| Page 110 | Cheetahs v Force. S. Kobo (Japan) was the referee, not Shuhei. |
| | Highlanders v Kings. Played on July 2. |
| | Chiefs v Reds. Played at Brisbane, not Melbourne. |
| Page 154 | P. Manuel was the try scorer v King Country. |
| Page 197 | Vasurakuta was with Mackenzie club, not Timaru OB. |
| Page 207 | v Hawke's Bay. Score was 55–28; v Wellington, score was 54–31. |
| Page 221 | v Counties Manukau. Score was 26–35. |
| Page 252 | Morrison has 4 N2 games, not 5. |
| Page 346 | J.D.L. Beard's career total should read 18 Sevens appointments and 49 total appointments. |
| Page 347 | Lee Jeffrey was TMO at the tests played between NZ and Australia at Auckland and Albany. |